JOHNSON COUNTY
The Heart of Eastern Kentucky

POUND GAP

On the Kentucky-Virginia State Border, through which the Early Settlers Passed on Their Way to Settle in the Big Sandy Valley

JOHNSON COUNTY KENTUCKY

A History of the County, and Genealogy of Its People Up to the Year 1927

BY

MITCHEL HALL

Genealogist, Historian, and Author
Member Kentucky State Historical Society

Volume I

Southern Historical Press, Inc.
Greenville, South Carolina

This volume was reproduced from
a personal copy located in the
Publisher's private library
Greenville, South Carolina

All rights reserved. No part of this publication may be reproduced, stored in a retieval system, Transmitted in any form, posted on to the web in any form or by any means without the prior permission of the publisher.

Please direct ALL correspondence and book orders to:
www.southernhistoricalpress.com
or
Southern Historical Press, Inc.
PO Box 1267
Greenville, SC 29602-1267
southernhistoricalpress@gmail.com

Originally published: Louisville, KY 1928
ISBN #978-1-63914-044-2
All Rights Reserved
Printed in the United States of America

Section I

Dedicated to
JOHNSON COUNTIANS
EVERYWHERE

IN SPITE OF ALL HER FAULTS

I hail from Old Kentucky,
   The State of Bluegrass fame,
I love her rolling meadows,
   Her quaint, historic name.

Along her winding byways
   No hostile steps resound;
Our fathers made it sacred,
   This dark and bloody ground.

I hail it as a treasure,
   The State that gave me birth;
It is beyond all measure,
   The fairest spot on earth.

And when my weary spirit
   Is wafted home to God;
I ask but that my body
   Rest 'neath its Bluegrass sod.

Then give me Old Kentucky,
   The State that I love best,
Yes, give me Old Kentucky,
   The world may have the rest.

PREFACE

This book is a history of Johnson County and Eastern Kentucky, from the period of first settlement up to and including the year 1927. From the table of contents, it will be seen that the history treats on matters, not only essential to Johnson County, but of interest to all Eastern Kentucky.

The history of Eastern Kentucky's valleys and mountains, its animals, trees, and flowers, its music and literature, and its men and women, "all weave into a story, in part epic, in part high romance, altogether thrilling, inspiring, and challenging." (Quoted from an editorial in the Louisville Times.)

Of late years there has been a lamentable tendency, noticeable in discourteous remarks from the "outside," toward belittling this section of Kentucky. Particularly has this been true from people misled through motion pictures like Johnny Hines in "Rainbow Riley," through the novels of John Fox Jr., and the works of Cora Wilson Stewart. Of course the settlement schools sponsored by Miss Stewart are doing a good work; and they could well afford to have them in many sections of other states, as well as in the "slums" of the larger cities. To obtain the necessary donations to carry on the schools from people living in cities of the East Miss Stewart has always had to paint the unpleasant side of conditions, and, in this way, has done an injustice to the mountain people of Kentucky. The scenes of John Fox Jr.'s books, which are good, could as well have been laid in the Catskill or Adirondacks; but naturally, being a resident of the section, he took the Cumberlands.

Realizing that it is time the inhabitants of the towns and cities of Eastern Kentucky awaken to the need of broadcasting the truth regarding their section, this book is written in an effort to give an up-to-date picture of the region and to inspire more advertisement on its behalf. If it should be instrumental in bringing about a better understanding from other regions toward this section, the book will have served its purpose well.

To each and every present and former resident of Paintsville, of Johnson County, of the Big Sandy Valley, and of Eastern Kentucky, I submit it.

MITCHEL HALL.

Frankfort—Paintsville, Kentucky.

HOMESICK FOR KENTUCKY

In a State they call Kentucky
  In the very eastern part,
There's a rugged mountain region
  That is very near my heart.

And I'm yearning for these mountains,
  'Cause I'm far from them, alone,
Wandering in these parks with fountains,
  When I fain would be at home.

I can see them tall and somber,
  Sentinels detailed to overlook
The sweet fresh streams that wander
  Through the meadows at their foot.

I can see the staunch old houses,
  And the smoke spirally arise
From the kitchen where the spouses
  Fix those things we all so prize.

When I see these swains a-driging,
  And merry-making with the dames,
Then, in my throat a lump's arising—
  A feeling I cannot name.

For I have a maiden in Kentucky—
  Memories pierce me like a knife—
And I resolve, I soon will be there
  If God only spares my life.

"Man," said a chance acquaintance,
  "Why do you, your home opine?
I live across these stately Rockies,
  And I never think of mine".

"Sir," said I, and with assurance,
  "I will elucidate to you:
Your home's not in Kentucky
  Or you'd be homesick, too."

          —*JOHN FRED WILLIAMS.*

CONTENTS

SECTION I

	Page
DEDICATION	7
IN SPITE OF ALL HER FAULTS (Poem)	8
PREFACE	9
HOMESICK FOR KENTUCKY (Poem)	10
CONTENTS	11
LIST OF ILLUSTRATIONS	13

CHAPTER I
INTRODUCTION..................................... 19

CHAPTER II
ANGLO-SAXONS..................................... 21

CHAPTER III
ENGLISH COLONISTS................................ 28

CHAPTER IV
PREHISTORIC INHABITANTS.......................... 33

CHAPTER V
EARLY SETTLEMENT................................. 40

CHAPTER VI
GOVERNMENT....................................... 60

CHAPTER VII
TIMES AND CUSTOMS................................ 129

CHAPTER VIII
GEOLOGY.. 157

Page

CHAPTER IX
EDUCATION.. 274

CHAPTER X
RELIGIOUS PROGRESS... 291

CHAPTER XI
INDUSTRIAL DEVELOPMENT.. 337

CHAPTER XII
HISTORIES AND PUBLICATIONS.. 431

CHAPTER XIII
SERVICE MEN... 443

CHAPTER XIV
APPENDIX
   1925 TAX LIST.. 456
   VOTING PRECINCTS... 481
   COUNTY OFFICIALS... 481
   LAND GRANTS AND ENTRIES...................................... 514

ILLUSTRATIONS

	Page
POUND GAP	*Frontispiece*
PIONEER TRAILS	30
ARTIST'S CONCEPTION OF BLOCKHOUSE BOTTOM	54
MAP OF KENTUCKY SHOWING ORIGINAL THREE COUNTIES	65
MAP OF KENTUCKY SHOWING ORIGINAL MASON COUNTY	69
MAP OF KENTUCKY SHOWING ORIGINAL FLOYD COUNTY	73
MAP OF KENTUCKY SHOWING LOCATION OF JOHNSON COUNTY	85
JOHNSON COUNTY'S CAPITOL—THE COURT HOUSE AT PAINTSVILLE	114
THE OLD-TIME LOG CABIN (INSERT)	128
A MODERN WEDDING IN JOHNSON COUNTY	133
STEAMBOATING UP "SANDY"	145
THE HOUSE THAT MAYO BUILT	160
MAP OF JOHNSON COUNTY (INSERT)	160
SURROUNDINGS OF FISH TRAP CHURCH	161
THE SCENIC BIG SANDY	165
THE FIRST HOUSE ERECTED IN PAINTSVILLE	175
BIRD'S-EYE VIEW OF PAINTSVILLE	179
SOUTH SIDE OF MAIN STREET, PAINTSVILLE	185
LOOKING EAST, MAIN STREET, PAINTSVILLE	189
A SECTION IN THE BUSINESS DISTRICT OF PAINTSVILLE	195
COURT STREET, PAINTSVILLE	201
A RESIDENTIAL DISTRICT IN MARGARET HEIGHTS DIVISION, PAINTSVILLE	207
LOOKING EAST ON THIRD STREET	211
A SECTION OF MODERN PAINTSVILLE	217
RESIDENCE OF JAMES W. TURNER	223
PAINTSVILLE HOSPITAL	228
DR. J. H. HOLBROOK	229

	Page
A Street in the Business Section of Paintsville	235
Dr. Ernest E. Archer	239
Paintsville and Vicinity	243
Some Paintsville Business Men	247
Dr. Paul B. Hall	251
A Group of Paintsville D. A. R.'s	256
Paintsville Women	259
Scenes at Van Lear, Kentucky	263
White House, Kentucky	267
Scene Near West Van Lear	271
J. Melvin Hall	277
Physical Education at J. C. C. Mayo College	281
Red Cross Training, Paintsville City Schools	284
Paintsville City School Buildings	285
John C. C. Mayo College	289
Mayo Memorial M. E. Church, South	292
Reverend Arthur Green	300
Richard C. Thomas	307
H. B. Conley	313
Dr. John P. Wells	320
H. G. Sowards	331
An Additional Group of Business Men	336
Wives of Leaders	339
Auxier, Kentucky	343
John C. C. Mayo	347
E. R. Price	351
A Mine of the Consolidation Coal Company at Van Lear, Kentucky	355
A Mine of the North-East Coal Company at Thealka, Kentucky	359
Henry LaViers	363
"Shooting" a Well in the Johnson-Magoffin Oil Field	365
Gasoline Plant of Oliver Jenkins	367

	Page
E. J. Evans	371
Rafting Logs at the Mouth of Big Paint Creek	375
A River Bottom along the Big Sandy	379
Along the C. & O. in Johnson County	383
C. & O. Railroad Yard at Paintsville	387
Along the C. & O. up Big Sandy	389
Bridge on the Miller's Creek Railroad	391
Map of the Modern Big Sandy Valley	397
Concrete Bridge on the Mayo Trail on Tom's Creek	401
The Mayo Trail Near Paintsville	401
Along the Garrett Highway in Johnson County	405
Three in One	409
Judge Beecher Stapleton	413
John E. Buckingham	419
James W. Turner	423
D. H. Dorton	427
Mitchel Hall	433
Chas. A. Kirk	439
American Legion Memorial	447
Herbert Ward	451

Section I

History of Johnson County Kentucky

JOHNSON COUNTY KENTUCKY

CHAPTER I

INTRODUCTION

History is the story of the recorded life of man. Although many books have been written of the different ages, there is too much human life for books to cover properly. We therefore cannot deal with all historic peoples, and must narrow the field accordingly. We care most to know of those peoples whose life has borne fruit for our own life. We shall endeavor to give here that part of the recorded past which explains our present.

We frequently hear the rather boastful remark of our pure Anglo-Saxon blood. It is said that the people of Johnson County and Eastern Kentucky come as near to being of the pure Anglo-Saxon stock, unmarred by any pollution of foreign blood, as any living in the United States. In backing this statement, an attempt will be made to show in detail the history of events from the origin of this race to the present.

Noah had three sons, Shem, Ham, and Japheth. From Shem descended the Twelve Tribes of Israel and to them was the law given by Moses. They, being God's chosen people, were blessed all down through the ages, being led by such inspired men as the rulers and prophets of Israel; and, with all this teaching—even the angels coming to earth and forewarning them of impending destruction as a race, and prophets telling of their coming destruction—they did not heed. Today they are scattered to the four winds of the earth and still blind as pertains to Christ.

The descendants of Ham, Noah's second son, are said to be the colored race, whose true home is Central and Southern Africa. Some differ concerning this, claiming that the negro was not a descendant of Ham, but was first in the land of Nod in the time of Cain and Abel. It is enough for our purpose to say that they were a separate race.

The descendants of Japheth, the third son, are known in the Scripture as Gentiles, and as Aryans by race. Both the Semites and Aryans are divisions of the white or caucasian race. By language the Aryans are divided into five classes: the Asiatics, who constitute the Hindus, Medes and Persians; the Classical peoples, comprising the Greeks and Romans; the Celts, comprising the Gauls, Britons, Scots or Irish, and Picts; Slavs, comprising the Russians, Poles, etc.; and the Teutons, comprising the Scandinavians, Germans, and English. It is the last, or Teutonic, that we are interested in.

According to history, our civilization began several thousand years ago in the fertile valleys of Egypt and Western Asia. Slowly war and trade spread it around the eastern coasts of the Mediterranean. About 600 B.C. the Greeks, in their many settlements, scattered along all the Mediterranean coasts and became the leaders in civilization. They made marvelous advance in art, literature, philosophy, and in some sciences. After about three hundred years, under Alexander the Great, they suddenly conquered the East, becoming the leading power of the world.[1]

Greece continued to rule the world till unseated by Rome, about 200 B.C. All the time that Greece had been in power, Rome had been fighting for existence, and she finally won world-dominion. The Roman Empire was formed, and until 146 A.D. it was the greatest power of early history. After that time, it began to lose its prestige. The boundaries of its empire had become so extended, that it could not protect them. Barbaric tribes were crowding in. Among these were two, the *Cimbri* and *Teutones* (Teutons-Germans), advancing on the northern frontier. These two peoples, migrating slowly from the north with families, flocks, and goods, in search of new homes, made their appearance about the year 113, thus introducing one of the great eras in history.[2] During the next five centuries, at frequent intervals, after that first invasion, they continued beating upon the frontiers, and were successful in sending great swarms of their numbers, as prisoners and as peaceful colonists to dwell within the Empire. It was not long till they were to be known as conquerors. It will never be known exactly where these people came from, but it is known that the Rhine and Danube rivers had long separated the barbaric world from the Roman world. Between the Danube and the Baltic, north and south, and between the Rhine and Vistula, east and west, roamed many tribes known to themselves by no one name, but all called Germans (Teutons) by the Romans.[3] The Franks and Saxons were among the more important of these groups. While the Franks were migrating into Gaul, or France, fierce Saxon pirates had been cruelly harassing the eastern coasts—swooping down in their swift barks to burn, slay, and plunder, and vanishing as quickly as they came. In 408, the Roman legions were withdrawn from Britain to protect Italy from these German marauders, leaving Britain to defend herself, which she was not able to do, so that in time she was forced to unite with the Teutons to expel the Celts beyond the northern wall.[4]

REFERENCES TO CHAPTER I

[1] Ancient World, Willis Mason West, page 297.
[2] Ibid, page 429.
[3] Ibid, page 570.
[4] Ibid, page 580.

CHAPTER II

ANGLO-SAXONS[1]

The Teutonic settlement in Britain must, in the general history of Europe, be looked on as part of the great movement which drove so many of the Teutonic nations westward and southward. It was part, in short, of the general wandering of the nations. But it had in many respects a character of its own, which distinguishes it in a marked way from the other western and southern settlements of the Teutonic conquerors. These settlers came from lands which had been altogether untouched by the Roman power, and where the arts, the language, and the religion of Rome were altogether unknown. They had never been Roman subjects, Roman soldiers, or even Roman allies. They had received no grants from Roman princes, nor had their chiefs been honored with Roman titles. They were, in short, altogether free from Roman influences. Coming by sea, they were disposed to act as destroyers in a way in which the Teutonic invaders elsewhere did not. They had to win the land bit by bit by hard fighting.

The English conquest was a complete physical extermination of all previous tribes, as nearly as is possible to take place. In the course of this conquest we may be sure that the alternative of death or flight was the ordinary rule; but we may be equally sure that the rule had its exceptions. The women could be largely spared; even men would sometimes be allowed to escape death at the price of slavery. In all these ways it follows that, physically and genealogically, there were other elements in the early English nation, even in the most strictly Teutonic parts of England. No nation is of perfectly pure blood, and the English nation was no exception to the rule. In the sense of the physiologist or genealogist, the English nation was not purely Teutonic; but in their sense, no nation is purely anything. The point is that the English people were as strictly Teutonic, as the High-Germans were Teutonic, or as the Britons were Celtic.

Among the Teutonic tribes from Germany, responsible for the English conquest, three stand out conspicuously in the history of that conquest, the Angles, the Saxons, and the Jutes. The Angles and Saxons are plain enough; there is a certain degree of mystery about the Jutes, their name, and their origin. They probably came from the Danish peninsular—Jutland. But it is enough for our purpose that they were a third Teutonic people, distinguishable from the Angles and Saxons. Each had its share in the work of conquest and settlement. The Jutes, in all likelihood, formed the first permanent settlement. The Saxons and the Angles settled later; but each of them occupied a far larger part of the island than the Jutes. And each of these last gave a name to the Teutonic settlements as a whole. As soon as they were far enough settled or united to bear a common name, the received name on their lips was *English;* on the lips of their Celtic neighbors and enemies the received name was *Saxon.* The reason for this difference in nomenclature is plain. The Angles occupied a greater share of the land than the Saxons; they therefore gave the national name to the united people.

In the British narrative, the single Roman entry of these events called the Teutonic invaders *Saxons.* In the *Chronicles*[2] they appear as *Angelcyn, Angel, Engle, Angles,* or *English.* They are so called, not merely in the historical summary of the ninth century editor, but in the entry (473) which has the earliest ring of all about it. But when Baeda, and after him the Chronicler, give a short ethnological account of the invaders, they describe the Teutonic conquerors of Kent neither as Saxons, nor as Angles, but as Jutes. As the Jutes then, in the very record of their conquest, are spoken of, on the one hand as Saxons, on the other hand as English, it seems to follow that, from the very beginning, the Celtic inhabitants of Britain called all Teutonic invaders Saxons, while the invaders themselves from the very beginning used Angle or English as their common name. The general use of the Saxon name by the Celts is only what we should have looked for; the wide use of the English name among the Teutons themselves is a fact to be noticed. It is at least certain that, while the English name is often applied to Saxons and Jutes, it would be hard to find any case where an Angle called himself, or is called in his own tongue a Saxon. We need not infer that the English name had become the common name of all the three tribes before they left Germany; it certainly became so within no long time after they settled in Britain.

It is enough that all the royal races of the several kingdoms of England belonged to the three stocks, Saxon, Anglian, and Jutish. It was then by Saxon, Anglian, and Jutish settlers, or at all events by settlers under their leaders, that the greater part of Britain was changed into England. In the end seven or eight chief kingdoms were founded. The Jutes, the first to settle, occupied the smallest part of the country. Their dominions took in only Kent, with perhaps for a while Surrey, and Wight with a small part of the neighboring mainland of Hampshire. They were hemmed in on all sides by the Saxon settlements, all of which bore the Saxon name. Suthsexe, Westsexe, and Eastsexe, have been softened in modern speech into Sussex, Wessex, and Essex; but the names are strictly not territorial, but tribal. Westsexe and the rest are all of them names, not of a land, but of a people. The whole of the Saxon settlement was made on the southern and southeastern coasts; and it was the West-Saxons only who at any time carried their conquests to any distance inland. The South-Saxon settlement came next after the Jutish settlement in Kent. The date given to it is 477. The most remarkable event in the process of conquest was the storming of Anderida, now Pevensey, in 491. The forsaken walls of the Roman city still bear witness to the day when Aelle and Cissa slew all that were within. But the South-Saxons found a natural frontier to the north in the great wood of Anderida. Their kingdom always remained little more than a long strip of coast, cut off to a great extent from the other kingdoms of Britain, and playing but a small part in their general history. It still keeps its name and boundary as the modern county of Sussex.

The kingdom of the Gewissas or West-Saxons founded to the west of the South-Saxons, was destined to hold quite another place in English and British history. Two Saxon *ealdermen*, Cerdic and Cynric, founded in 495 a settlement on what is now the coast of Hampshire. That settlement grew into the Kingdom of England. Twenty-four years after their first landing, the two Saxon *ealdermen* deemed their position strong enough, and their conquests strong enough, for them to assume the kingly title. Thus began the royal line of the West-Saxons, which became the royal line of England. The third Saxon settlement, that of the East-Saxons, has no such definite date given to its foundation; but it certainly began not later than the first half of the sixth century. Like Sussex, it never extended itself far inland; but it derived some importance from its containing two of the great cities of Roman Britain. One was Colchester; the other was London. But London grew, with its district of the Middle-Saxons and by virtue of its admirable position, to a greatness which gave it a separate being.

The settlements of the Angles, who in course of time occupied a much larger part of the land to which they gave their name than was occupied by the Saxons, have quite another history from the kingdoms already mentioned. In Kent, in Sussex, in Wessex, the chief who led the settlement was himself the founder of the kingdom. In the case of Kent and Sussex the kingdom never permanently outgrew the bounds of the earliest conquests. The boundaries of Wessex advanced and fell back again and advanced again; but they advanced by the process of bringing fresh conquests, newly won from Britain, under the rule of the already existing kingly house of Wessex. The Anglian kingdoms grew in another way. Names are known in some cases at least, of their first kings; but those first kings do not appear as the first leaders of settlers from beyond sea. It would rather seem as if a crowd of small settlements, of the date and circumstances, each doubtless ruled by its own ealderman or petty king, were gradually grouped together into several large kingdoms. It is perfectly possible, though there is no evidence for the belief, that some of these original settlements may have been of earlier date than the landing of Cerdic, of Aelle, or of Hengest. What is certain, is that these Anglian states did not appear as organized kingdoms till a later time than Kent, Sussex, and Wessex. The chief Anglian powers were four. The East-Angles occupied the land to the north of the East-Saxons, a land which the vast fen region to the west of it made in those times, if not insular, at least peninsular. North of the Humbar arose two kingdoms, Bernicia and Deira, whose union at a later time formed the mighty realm of Northumberland stretching from the Humber to the Forth. Ida, who in 547 gathered together a number of Anglian settlements into the Kingdom of Bernicia, is the one Anglian prince during the first stage of conquest who stands out with a personal being like that of the Saxon and Jutish founders. Of the founder of the Kingdom of Deira, to the south of Bernicia, there is no such clear mention, nor is it known when or by what means that kingdom won the possession which gave it its chief importance. This was the former capital of Roman Britain, known as York.

Another crowd of Anglian tribes, which kept more or less of separate existence till a very late time, were gradually brought under the dominion of a single Anglian power. This power, as growing up on the British frontier, took the name of *Merce*, the men of the mark or border, and the name of *Mercia* gradually spread over all central England. The date of the beginning of the Mercian kingdom is fixed as late as 584. But this does not mean a fresh settlement from beyond sea, but simply the gathering together of several small settlements so as to form one considerable power. The boundaries of the true Mercian kingdom may be traced by the boundaries of the old diocese of Litchfield; but it could not have reached to anything like this extent so early as 584.

Summing it all up, these early settlers had, among a crowd of smaller states, a few kingdoms, seven or eight in number, which stood out prominently, and fill a place in the history of Britain.

For the space of two hundred years, there was an almost perpetual strife for supremacy among the leading states. Finally, Egbert, King of Wessex (A.D. 802-839), brought all the other kingdoms to a subject or tributary condition, and became in reality, though he seems never, save on one occasion, to have actually assumed the title, the first king of England.[8]

In the English conquest, the Anglo-Saxons succeeded in driving the Britons or Celts, into the northern part of the Isles. The Irish of Ireland, the Scotch Highlanders of Scotland, and the Welch of Wales, are the present representatives of these ancient Celts. Having been subjected to Roman influence for so long before the Teutonic settlement, it can be seen why the Irish are strong followers of the Roman Church.

WELCH.[1] It is noted that from the beginning of the English conquest the Teutonic conquerors spoke of their British enemies as *Welch* or strangers. The name is familiar in that sense both in Britain and on the mainland, but it seems never to be applied to any strangers but those who were either of Roman or of Celtic speech. And it would seem to be applied only to those Celts who had come under the Roman dominion.

In the eyes of general history these native inhabitants must be looked on, as they were in the eyes of their English conquerors themselves, as Britons. They were Britons modified no doubt in every respect by their long subjection to Rome, but still essentially a British, that is, a Celtic people. And it is further clear that they were a people who had been less modified by Roman influences than the inhabitants of the other provinces of the empire. This is shown by the fact that the ancient British language survived the Roman conquest and still remains the language of a not inconsiderable part of the Isle of Britain. The mere fact of the existence of the Welch language shows that Roman influences could not have been strong enough to exterminate the native customs and traits.

DANES. Nothing of importance occurred in the history of the Anglo-Saxons till the Danes began to make descents upon the English coast toward the close of the eighth century. These people, who formed the northern or fourth branch of the Teutonic family, were called Danes because those making settlements in England came mostly from Denmark. Northmen, Norsemen, Normans, and Scandinavians are different names applied in a general way to the early inhabitants of Denmark, Norway and Sweden. Not much is known of them in their remote northern home before they began venturing along the coasts of Britain, Ireland, and France. They soon established settlements, and in time secured a strong foothold in the northeastern part of England. In their expeditions and colonizing enterprises, they were not content with plunder, but, being pagans, took special delight in burning the churches and monasteries of the now Christian Anglo-Saxons, or English. The most noteworthy characteristic of these Northmen was the readiness with which they laid aside their own manners, habits, ideas, and institutions, and adopted those of the country in which they settled. In France, they became Frenchmen, and in England, Englishmen.

In a short time fully one-half of England was in their hands. For the next century, they and the English were in a constant struggle for controlling power. In the end the Danes got the mastery, and Canute, King of Denmark, became King of England (1016). For eighteen years he reigned in a wise and parental way. Altogether, the Danes ruled in England about a quarter of a century, and then the old English line was restored in 1042, in the person of Edward the Confessor.[4]

NORMANS. In the year 1066 Edward the Confessor died, and Harold, Earl of Wessex, became his successor. This was not agreeable to William, Duke of Normandy, who immediately invaded England. The Norman army landed in the south of England, at which place the battle of Hastings was fought, and William was victorious. He then marched upon London, and at Westminster, on Christmas Day, 1066, was crowned King of England.[5]

The most important result of the Norman conquest was the establishment in England of a strong centralized government, which became a real kingdom.[6]

The history of the Normans was simply a continuation of the story of the Danes or Northmen. At first they were pagans;[7] now they had become Christians. They were rough, wild, merciless corsairs; but had now become the most cultured, polished, and chivalrous people in Europe. They thus made the fourth tribe of Teutons who constituted the Anglo-Saxons of England.

With the Anglo-Saxons now settled in England, their story must be regarded as English history, which has been covered by many books. Consequently, we shall drop their part in English history, and let it blend with the events leading up to and including their settlement in this country. (See page 28.)

ANGLO-SAXONS IN AMERICA.[8] The Declaration of Independence, the Constitution, and the Gettysburg Address are descendants of the Magna Charta—supreme symbols of Anglo-Saxon souls striving for freedom, justice, and humanity. Anglo-Saxons established this nation, wrote its code, and sent their sons into the wilderness to gather fresh stars for the flag.

Anglo-Saxon purpose covered the intervening wastes, discovered world granaries beneath the prairies, scaled the grim western hills and unmasked Eldorado, questioned sullen deserts until they answered with gardens, and finished on the Pacific the great adventure begun at Plymouth Rock.

Then, when the last taunting horizon had been met and vanquished, when ax and rifle had won an empire, when scattered settlements were beaded on threads of steel, and a safe highway through opportunity had been paved in their generous blood, the pioneers, the risk-takers, tossed their port-keys into the ocean and invited all creation to come at leisure and share a "sure thing."

The making of America is fundamentally an Anglo-Saxon achievement. Anglo-Saxon brains have guided the course of the republic. Our ideals are Anglo-Saxon, our social traditions, our standards of honor, our quality of imagination and our indomitability.

But Anglo-Saxon opinion is a fast-diminishing force in national determinations. A review of the past fifty years discloses the fact that each year brings a tide of immigrants to this country. Intermarriage with them is steadily diluting the foundation strain. Although it is very evident in cities of the East, there are a very few aliens in the Big Sandy Valley; and this is the reason the inhabitants of that section boast of their pure Anglo-Saxon stock.

REFERENCES TO CHAPTER II

[1] Encyclopedia Britannica—Ninth Edition, Vol. VIII, pages 242-245.

[2] The Anglo-Saxon Chronicle here alluded to was a minute and chronological record of events, probably begun in systematic form in Alfred the Great's reign and continued down to the year 1154. It was kept by the monks of different monasteries, and forms one of our most valuable sources of early English history. General History, Phillip Van Ness Myers, page 381. Grim & Co., Boston, Mass., 1906.

[3] General History, Phillip Van Ness Myers, pages 339-340, Grim & Co., Boston, Mass., 1906.

[4] Ibid, pages 379, 380, 381.

[5] Ibid, page 397.

[6] Ibid, page 400.

[7] Ibid, page 396.

[8] Scum of the Melting Pot, Herbert Kaufman, McClure's Magazine.

CHAPTER III

ENGLISH COLONISTS

The first English in America were John Cabot and his sons, who were sent by Henry VII, King of England, to seek their fortune in discovery, and take possession, in the king's name, of all lands which they could find. They saw the coast of Labrador fourteen months before Columbus touched South America in 1498. The next year they discovered Newfoundland, and sailed along the coast as far south as Chesapeake Bay.[1]

The English made no real effort to found homes in North America until eighty years after the discoveries by the Cabots. All expeditions so far were in search of gold and treasures. None came to stay; consequently, these early adventurers failed. Sir Humphrey Gilbert, seeing the failure that resulted from the search for gold, planned a colony for fisheries and regular trade. But his two expeditions failed, and he was lost at sea.[2] His half-brother, Sir Walter Raleigh, was the next to undertake the task of settlement in this country, which also was unsuccessful. In 1585, under the reign of Queen Elizabeth, he sent 108 colonists over. Some of them returned with such glowing accounts of the beauty and richness of the land visited and settled that, in honor of the virgin queen, it was named *Virginia*.

A second colony, including some women and children, arrived at Roanoke in 1587. At this time war broke out between England and Spain, and ships that were to bring fresh supplies for the colonists, went in pursuit of Spanish ships, and were themselves taken, thereby leaving the new settlers without supplies. When Englishmen revisited Virginia, three years later, none were to be found. Whether the settlers had perished, or had taken refuge elsewhere, has never been known.[3]

Queen Elizabeth died in 1603, and King James I (under whose reign the new Bible was translated, known as the King James' Version, and published in 1611) succeeded to the throne of England. In 1606, he gave charters to two English companies for planting and ruling two colonies in Virginia. They were the Plymouth and London companies. The latter, under the leadership of Captain John Smith, founded Jamestown (1607), so named in honor of the King, which proved to be the first permanent English settlement within the limits of the United States. One hundred and five men made up the first colony.[4] The following winter 120 men were added, and in 1608, seventy more, including two women. In June, 1609, 500 more colonists sailed for Jamestown from England. Among them were the wife and daughters of Lieutenant General Gates, who were for a time nearly the only white women in this country.[5] In 1619, besides nearly twelve

PIONEER TRAILS

hundred other settlers, ninety honest girls came from England and became wives of planters.⁶

By 1660, Virginia had about 30,000 inhabitants. Other settlements had sprung up, which included Richmond and Williamsburg.⁷ From this date up to the time of the Declaration of Independence in 1776, the story of the English settlers is a continuation of the history of the American Colonies, which is covered in almost every history of the United States. It is enough for our purpose to say that their settlements for this period were confined to Eastern Virginia and the Atlantic coast. It was not until after the Revolution that they began to migrate into the interior.

Those who did so migrate before that time were principally exploring parties or soldiers—mostly French and English—who were playing the Old World game of trying to win territory for their governments. After the War of Independence there was a lull in the tide of westward traveling and expansion, while the new nation was finding itself. But that restless, daring spirit that drove the first Anglo-Saxons forth in quest of adventure and booty still stirred in the breasts of their descendants. Eager for pilgrimages and crusades, the pressure of settlement, and the desire for new and cheaper lands soon sent a great tide of adventurous men and women out into the vaster and wilder territory.

Attention is called to the fact that the wandering of these people toward the setting sun is only conforming to the history of the adventures of people of all time, in that civilization has always moved westward.

This movement of the colonists, for the most part, went west from the Atlantic seaboard. The earliest way was by water and portage. Mountains were obstacles. The French used the lakes. They came into what is now Pennsylvania by way of Niagara, then to Erie (Presque Isle), down French Creek to Franklin (Venango), and down the Allegheny to Pittsburgh (Fort Duquesne). The English of New York tried to go west by the Hudson Valley to Albany and by the Mohawk Valley to the lakes. The hostile Iroquois made that difficult.

Farther south, in Pennsylvania, there was a trail from Philadelphia up the Susquehanna and Juniata, across the mountains by the Kittanning Gorge, and down to the Allegheny River. A trail known as Nemacolin's Path went from Pittsburgh to the Potomac. Washington, when he went as a Colonial soldier from Virginia into Western Pennsylvania, went by Cumberland, Maryland, then Wills Creek, and over Nemacolin's Path. Braddock went by it to his defeat.⁸

The Mohawk Valley way and the Susquehanna way were bad for a long time because of Indians. There had been a tide of Scotch-Irish and Germans coming in by the port of Philadelphia, and, finding Pennsylvania lands high, they went south through the

Shenandoah Valley. That was another great Indian warpath. Then a gap was found to the west—Cumberland Gap.

The settlement of the upper Big Sandy was in fact an overflow from the great stream of immigration from the seaboard towns in Pennsylvania, Virginia, and the Carolinas. Making their way through Virginia, these pioneers passed from the Shenandoah onto the headwaters of the New River, and thence to the Holston, the Clinch, and the Powell rivers.

From this point the principal trail led most of them through the Cumberland Gap into central Kentucky over the wilderness road, some of them later crossing on into Ohio and Illinois. Instead of coming on through Cumberland Gap, some remained in southeastern Virginia. Others, however, followed down the Clinch and Holston and made their way overland into central Tennessee; some continued even farther into the southwest. During the height of this great migration from 1785 to 1810, a few annually turned northward into the New River Valley, and others left the trail for the north at Fort Chiswell. These were principally Virginians and Carolinians who were attracted by the reports of the rich bottoms in the Big Sandy Valley. They made their way over the heads of the Tug and Levisa forks of the Big Sandy, and through Pound Gap.[9] Thus told chronologically, we have introduced the Anglo-Saxon or English people to the Big Sandy Valley.

The reader should bear in mind that it is not claimed that all those coming to the Big Sandy region were direct descendants of Anglo-Saxons of England. It has been, and will be shown herein, as the reader progresses, that most of them did migrate from Virginia and the Carolinas, while some Scotch-Irish and Germans also came by way of the Shenandoah Valley. In view of the fact that Virginia was settled strictly by the English, and that the greater part of those coming to the Big Sandy territory, were from Virginia, it is reasonable to say that they were, for the most part, Anglo-Saxons.

REFERENCES TO CHAPTER III

[1] New Electric History of the United States, M. E. Thalheimer, page 33.
[2] Ibid, page 41.
[3] Ibid, page 42.
[4] Ibid, page 42.
[5] Ibid, page 44.
[6] Ibid, page 45.
[7] Ibid, page 48.
[8] Editorial, Liberty Magazine, New York, February 20, 1926.
[9] Jillson, W. R., The Big Sandy Valley, pages 97-98, J. P. Morton Co., Louisville, Ky.

CHAPTER IV

PREHISTORIC INHABITANTS[1]

It is reasonable to say that within the memory of living men, three distinct primordial races have multiplied and flourished in Kentucky. They are the Red, the Black, and the White races. To the Red Man this wondrous central region, to which he gave the name *Kentuck-e*, was a land of darkness and blood; to the Black it has been a field of "involuntary servitude"; to the White it is the seat of an advanced civilization. But, defying all ordinary methods of historic research, there lies a mysterious past, embosoming a mighty civilization, which we can only see through misty traditions and enigmatical remains.

Patient and critical investigation has found numerous traces in the Mississippi Valley of a remarkable race of men, peculiar, compact, and powerful in their social organization, sagacious and enterprising in war. These were the prehistoric inhabitants of the Big Sandy Valley and Kentucky.

While there is nothing inherently trustworthy or conclusive in the traditional lore of the wigwam, there has come down through the generations certain Indian traditions which, viewed in connection with the testimony of the mounds and antique remains, seem to cast a faint gleam of light into the gloom and mystery of those prehistoric days. There is an old tradition, for example, that the prehistoric inhabitants of Kentucky were at some indeterminate period overwhelmed by a tide of savage invasion from the North—a point upon which Indian tradition, as far as it goes, is positive and explicit. It is related, in a posthumous fragment on Western Antiquities, by Rev. John P. Campbell, M. D., which was published in the early part of the eighteenth century, that Colonel James Moore of Kentucky was told by an old Indian "that the primitive inhabitants of this State had perished in a war of extermination waged against them by the Indians; that the last great battle was fought at the Falls of the Ohio; that the Indians succeeded in driving the Aborigines into a small island below the Rapids, and that the whole of them were cut to pieces." The Indian further said this was an undoubted fact handed down by tradition, and that the Colonel would have proof of it under his eyes as soon as the waters of the Ohio became low. When the waters of the river had fallen, an examination of Sandy Island was made, and, "a multitude of human bones were discovered."

There is similar confirmation of this tradition in the statement of General George Rogers Clark that there was a great burying ground on the northern side of the river but a short distance below the Falls. According to a tradition imparted to Colonel Moore by the Indian chief, Tobacco, the battle of Sandy Island decided finally the fall of Kentucky, with its ancient inhabitants. When Colonel McKee commanded on the Kanawha (says Dr. Campbell), he was told by the Indian chief, Cornstalk, with whom he had frequent conversations, that Ohio and Kentucky had once been settled by a white people who were familiar with arts of which the Indians knew nothing; that these whites, after a series of bloody contests with the Indians, had been exterminated; that the old burial places were the graves of an unknown people, and that the old forts had not been built by the Indians, but had come down from a "very long ago" people, who were of a white complexion. There are also accounts of a tribe east of the Mississippi, known as Lenni-Lenape, having great conflicts with another set (Alligewi) in the west. (See page 36.)

In addition to this traditional testimony, various and striking traces of a deadly conflict have been found all along the Ohio border. To say nothing of the vast system of fortifications, coverings exposed, and important points, there are significant traces of former conflicts, clearly indicating a protracted and desolating struggle for the possession of this border-land. And doubtless the familiar appellation of *"The Dark and Bloody Ground"* originated in the gloom and horror with which the Indian imagination naturally invested the traditional scenes and events of that strange and troubled period. General Clark said (*vide* Dr. Campbell) that Kentuck-*e* in the language of the Indians, signified "the river of blood."

Such are some of the pointings of tradition regarding the shadowy beings who peopled this lurid past, now known only by their works. They are simply the *Mound-Builders*.

THE MOUND-BUILDERS

That there was a race of people inhabiting both South and Central America previous to, and far surpassing in civilization, that of the American Indian, or Red Man, is borne out in a large measure in the remains of the civilization of the Incas of the Andes, and by the recent excavations uncovering buried cities in Mexico and Central America. The remains of tools of stone and flint, implements of war and the chase, and drawings all denote a higher civilization. In the Andes there exist ruins of temples and cities, of the construction, history, or builders of which the people found there by European explorers could tell nothing. Hills were scientifically terraced for irrigation and cultivation long before the Christian era. The buried cities equaled in magnificence the ancient cities of the Old World.

In addition to the uncovering of buried cities in Mexico, many discoveries have been made which would establish the fact that the whole of North America might have been inhabited by a prehistoric race. A mummy was found in Mammoth Cave in 1813, while another was taken from a cavern near Glasgow, Kentucky, in 1815, and placed on exhibition for some time in the city of New York.[2] An image of Buddha was unearthed recently in the State of Jalisco, Mexico, and in January, 1926, more than 500 poems in three volumes belonging to the "lost literature of the Aztecs" were discovered near Mexico City. The poems are surprisingly perfect. Their poetical form is largely trochaic, or the meter of "Hiawatha," and the Finnish national epic, "Kalevala." One volume contains forty-seven metrical stories in Aztec, which Aztec pupils learned in schools or heathen temples before the white man set foot in America. Another volume contains 230 songs in Aztec, under the title "Cantares Mexicanos," or Mexican Songs. They comprise florid, imaginative, poetic songs, drum songs, and dance choruses, in which hundreds of persons joined.

The preceding references are given as an explanation of the possible migration of the Aborigines who were first in South America, next in Central America, then in Mexico, and eventually in the United States. This is in conformity with the conjectures of several historians that man first came to this country by means of a strip of land, or a continuous group of islands, extending from the shores of Africa to America; and that these immigrants established themselves on this continent, and that many years passed before seismic disturbances caused the land connection between the two continents to sink so that only scattered islands remain above the waters, while soundings have disclosed comparatively shallow water covering the remaining portion of this continent-to-continent connection.

While we have mentioned only the remains found in distant places, there are many evidences, even close to Paintsville, of the existence of prehistoric man. Unquestionably the first men of whose occupation we have any evidence to occupy the land now inhabited by the people of Johnson County were the Mound-Builders, and whether they were of Indian extraction or a people never seen by the white man will forever remain a mystery. Certain it is, however, that they lived in and near Paintsville. They left far better evidences and more permanent structures than the Indians. With their extinction, mound-building ceased, and if the builders were Indians no other Indian tribe was ever known to construct a mound. Near the mouth of Paint Creek and extending in a straight line south and parallel with the Big Sandy River, there were once visible four of these mounds, two of which remain today in distinctive shape. They are located in a level bottom, and are the shape of a huge sweet potato hill. There are no evidences there of the dirt having been taken from the bottom to make these mounds as no depressions in the land are noted, and evidently the dirt to form them was carried from a distance. These mounds diminished in size to the south and were about

200 yards apart. The first was located about 100 yards from Paint Creek and about the same distance from the river. The third and fourth mounds have corroded until there is no longer any evidence of them. The first and larger mound is now about fifteen feet in height and about 100 feet in circumference at the base. Excavations have been made in these mounds and many relics and trinkets have been removed therefrom. The arrow heads taken from them resemble those used by the American Indians but some of the implements found were distinct to those of Mound-Builders and resembled none found near old Indian camp sites. Another evidence in favor of the Mound-Builder, as against that of the Indian, is that the so-called "Indian graves," or burying places of the dead are usually found, in this territory, at the end of some high point or spur of a ridge.

There are other mounds to be found in the county, which have not been excavated for investigation, but those described are by far the most important.

Another evidence of prehistoric man in Eastern Kentucky was the finding of an inscribed stone by persons digging a cellar near the confluence of the Ohio and Big Sandy rivers on the Kentucky shore.

While these facts are indicative, any attempt to prove at this late period that these are the works of the American Indian or the Mound-Builder, as a prehistoric race, would be a matter of opinion on imperfect evidence.

THE INDIAN

The idea that the Indians came across the Bering Strait from Asia into Alaska is borne out by the resemblance between the Indians and some of the Asiatic races and the further fact that all migration of Indians have been from that direction. The first large migration of Indians, known to man, was that of the Iroquoian stock, which began at the headwaters of the Mississippi and Missouri rivers and extended to and through what is now known as Ohio. At this time there resided in Kentucky that race of sturdy, vigorous, and brave people, whose name and race will forever remain a mystery, who was very likely the Mound-Builder described in the preceding pages. The Iroquois attempted but could not dislodge them from their habitat and for this reason never maintained a tribal home in Kentucky.

Following this Iroquoian invasion came another tribe, called Lenni or Lenapes, who in turn were followed by the Mengwe. Each of these was also stopped at the Mississippi or at the Ohio. Finally, after many generations of warfare, as a last resort these tribes united to force their way eastward. The last stand of this mound-building race, called Alligewi, was made on Sandy Island, near Louisville, Kentucky, which is described on page 34. The Indians were successful in wiping this race out to the last man. Never in all history has there been a more desperate stand made by a race of people and never battle more terrible and bloody than this.

With the extinction of the Alligewi, human occupation of the eastern part of Kentucky ceased for several hundred years, as no Indian dared set foot on Kentucky soil with the idea of establishing a tribal home, so long as the memory and horror of that terrible conflict remained within the Indian mind. The Big Sandy territory was used by them as their favorite hunting ground while they had their villages to the north—mostly in the state of Ohio, and to the south in the state of Tennessee. By the time of the first explorations by the English, the Indians had established many a well-defined trail, suitable for their mode of travel, which took them over the lowest passes in the mountains, the most suitable fords, and usually following the ridges in preference to the river bottoms, to avoid the river, on their many hunting excursions through the valley.[3]

Although they at first only used the Big Sandy Valley as a hunting ground, they later came into the region and situated themselves in more or less permanent camps for varying periods while engaged in their hunting, and by this time for warring expeditions, which had begun against the white explorers and settlers.

The first record we have of Indian occupation of any part of Johnson County, is of the Toteros in 1699.[4] Pownall in his map of North America, in 1776, gives the Totteroy (Big Sandy) River. This Totero tribe was of the Siouian linguistic stock. The first Totero habitat in the county was at Hager Hill.

Other tribes that visited this section, many of whom unquestionably resided and had tribal homes here for a while at least, were the Miami, the Delawares, the Shawnees, the Cherokees, the Iroquois, Mingos, and Wyandots. Roving bands of these tribes were in this section and in Johnson County as late as 1860.

Evidences of Indian occupation of Paintsville and its vicinity are still found in the many Indian graves along the top of the highest ridges. Several of these can now be found along the ridge extending west and south from the "Hanging Rock," on Mill Branch, which is just a short distance southwest of the city. These burying places of the dead consist of huge piles of stones, usually of equal size and about the size a man could carry. Some of these piles of stone are made in places where the absence of stones is very evident, indicating that the stones had been carried great distances—probably up the mountain side.

In the vicinity of main Paint Creek early settlers found many of the large trees skinned of their bark with drawings of birds and animals done in red and black on the smooth undertrunk of the tree.[5] One of these, a giant elm, that once stood in what is now known as the Huff Cemetery near Bridgeford Addition, had been peeled of its bark for some twenty feet from the ground, and on it was painted, in black, a huge snake. These paintings were to be found up and down the creek, which caused it to be named Paint Creek.

At the old Flat Rock Ford, near Huff's Cemetery, and where now the bridge leading to the C. & O. railroad station spans Paint Creek, was once a large rockhouse said to have been frequently used by the Indians.[6]

About midway up the hill facing the river, some eight or nine hundred feet north of the Concord Baptist Church, is an Indian rock home, which no doubt was used by the red man for protection, replacing the wigwam in time of danger. It is completely enclosed by a natural rock formation and has had an opening cut in the rock, in the shape of a circle, and about two feet in diameter, for an entrance. In recent years school boys, playing Indian games of warfare and using the original home as a barricade, have notched one or two places in this entrance with their hatchets. Other than that mentioned, this point of interest remains intact as evidence of occupation before the settlement of Johnson County by the whites.

From the mouth of Mud Lick Creek, which is about four miles west of Paintsville, up to its junction with Little Mud Lick Creek, was the site of an old Indian village, which was probably that of the Shawnees. Early settlers found many Indian relics on this town site, and in the bottom lands near by. Although all evidences have become obliterated through natural weathering conditions, it is claimed by several now living that there were once visible on the sandstone cliffs along the creek at this site, and those below the present post office of Volga, numerous figures of buffalo, deer, and other primitive decorations, that had been painted in red and black colors.

The Indian, as well as the early Big Sandy explorer, generally located his camps near the natural salt licks, in order that game might be taken more easily, as buffalo, deer, and other animals, came to these licks at regular intervals. This probably accounts for the Shawnee encampment, mentioned in the preceding paragraph, as there once existed an old salt lick a short distance above it, on Mud Lick, which gave the creek its name.

Definite evidence of Indian occupation of Johnson County has been shown in detail, and, with this given, the remainder of the Indian story will be merged with the history of the first settlers, and the capture of Jennie Wiley.

SUMMARY

At the beginning it was pointed out that, according to history, civilization began in Egypt and Babylonia or Western Asia. It then spread along the coasts of the Mediterranean and into Eurasia. Gradually moving westward, we next learn of it in Greece, then Rome, then Gaul or France, and Germany, Norway, Sweden, Denmark, and next in England.

From England civilization spread to many countries. One of which was to America with the settlement of the colonies. The next movement in America was into the interior states.

These explanations of the movement of civilization present a possible solution of the migration of the ancestors of the present inhabitants of Johnson County.

As for the Indian, the predecessor of the whites in the county, it is not beyond reason to say that he is a descendant of some of those original tribes of Eurasia, later migrating into Alaska by way of Bering Strait, then south through Canada, and down the Mississippi into the Central United States.

Most every one is aware of the fact that the negro, or colored race, was imported into America by the English, beginning with the slaves shipped to Jamestown in 1619. They were brought directly from Africa, which after all reverts back to Egypt or the beginning of civilization. Johnson is one of the few counties of Kentucky that has never attracted the negro, and hence there is a very small number residing within its boundary.

The supposition that the Mould-Builder or prehistoric inhabitant of the county first came to this country by way of South America, as described on page 34, is in line with the statement that all races began in Egypt and scattered westwardly to the different parts of the globe.

While a reasonable solution has been given for the migration of the four primordial races that are said to have occupied Johnson County at some time, any attempt to prove this, after the passing of so many centuries, would be a matter of conjecture.

REFERENCES TO CHAPTER IV

[1] Thos. E. Pickett, M.D., Vol. 1, Collins, pages 381-4. (Written September 1871.)
[2] Vol. 1, page 388, Collins History of Kentucky, 1882.
[3] Jillson, W. R., The Big Sandy Valley, page 31, J. P. Morton Co., Louisville, Ky., 1923.
[4] Seventh Annual Report of the U. S. Bureau of Ethnology, page 116.
[5] Connelley, Wm. E., Harman's Station, 1910, pages 53, 54.
[6] Wells, J. K., Article in the Paintsville Herald.

CHAPTER V
EARLY SETTLEMENT
INDIAN HOSTILITIES

In migrating from Virginia into the Big Sandy Valley and Central Kentucky, the Cumberland Mountains formed a barrier to those pioneer settlers, which was incomparable though to the outrages of the resentful Indians. The Cherokees had been dispossessed and shoved westward, which was also a warning to those tribes living on the Scioto in Ohio. They recognized the advancing English settlers as land thieves and resisted their encroachments on their favorite hunting grounds and the burial places of their fathers. The French claimed by right of discovery that region lying north of the Ohio River, and the Mississippi Valley. A chain of forts and trading posts gave reality to their claim. By trading with them the French made friends with the Indians, and in this manner united their forces against the invaders, for the purpose of keeping the English out of so-called French territory. The Indian was easily persuaded, since the English were cutting down their forests and driving them away. The advance of the early settlers into the Big Sandy Valley was constantly crippled and checked by Indian massacres.

The French and their Indian friends sought in vain to dam this flood of immigration, but their combined efforts are known in our histories as the French and Indian War, which began in earnest in 1754. War parties of savages from the Ohio River villages made their way over the war trails leading through the Big Sandy Valley to attack the outlying settlers of southwestern Virginia. They burned the log cabins, scalped the helpless women and children, and carried the men away into captivity. Those who had established homes in the remote districts, were without protection from the ravages of bloodthirsty savages. The horror and the hopelessness of the times were wide spread. English scalps were paid for with French blankets, knives, hatchets, and guns. They were more desired, less useful, and brought a higher price than the skins of fur-bearing animals.

This carnage continued until February, 1763, when the Treaty of Paris was signed, whereby France gave up her claim to all territory in the Ohio and Mississippi valleys.

The Indians were not content with the transfer of their lands to the English by this treaty, and kept up the slaughter until the autumn of 1765 when two treaties were signed, one at Muskingum and the other at Niagara. The one at Muskingum was negotiated with the Delawares and Shawnees.[1]

Up to this date, few white men were hardy enough to enter the Big Sandy, much less to make any attempt to settle here. Con-

EARLY SETTLEMENT 41

ditions had become somewhat reconciled in the central part of Kentucky; the first settlers in Kentucky thus gave the valley a wide berth in favor of what was to be the Bluegrass.

The Indians still fought to keep their hunting ground and war trail through the valley open as a secure route for attack against the settlers of southwestern Virginia. Then, the records were few, but judging from the events recorded, it seems as if they were content for a while to use the valley for hunting; but that did not last long for again in 1774 many scalping parties took place all through southwestern Virginia by those Indians of the Ohio Valley, who would slip in by way of the Big Sandy trail and be upon the settlers with their tomahawks before the whites realized that a red man was in the neighborhood. These Indian reprisals did not cease, and Lord Dunmore decided to engage the Indians in battle and if possible bring about a lasting peace with them. Under the direction of Lord Dunmore and Colonel Lewis and composed mostly of the backwoods militia of southwestern Virginia an expedition was begun. The Indians were encountered at Point Pleasant at the confluence of the Ohio and Kanawha rivers, and the battle began Monday, October 10, 1774.[2] For a while it appeared as though the Indians, who were led by Chief Cornstalk, would be victorious; but due to a skillful flank attack executed by the then Lieutenant Isaac Shelby, later Kentucky's first Governor, the Indians fled in defeat. Chief Cornstalk realized that any further effort to keep the white settlers east of the Cumberland Mountains would be futile and a treaty was concluded with Lord Dunmore.

The effects of the treaty had hardly begun to be felt, however, when the Revolutionary War began in 1776. The English government sought in every way to cripple the colonies and therefore solicited the help of the Indians, who joined in with them, hoping to prevent more settlers moving in to occupy their lands, and with the hope of regaining their ancient hunting grounds. The British became the chief supporters of the Indians, supplying them with arms, ammunition and other supplies, and therefore many a marauding party of savages passed up the Big Sandy to attack, burn and pillage, on the Clinch and Holston. This warfare was kept up for years. No one in this day of leisure can fully understand the horror that the pioneer settler experienced. A typical example of the times was the massacre at Draper's Meadows in what is now Montgomery County, Virginia, in 1775, when Mrs. Mary Ingles, her two little boys, and her sister, Mrs. Draper, were taken prisoners by the Shawnee Indians. The captives were taken to the Indian Village at the mouth of the Scioto River, where they were subjected to great cruelties, including running the gauntlet. Later, Mrs. Ingles escaped while making salt at Big Boone Lick. An elderly Dutch woman, who had also been held prisoner for a long time, escaped with her. They made their way up the Ohio River to the Big Sandy and alone penetrated the primeval forests of the valley, which harbored the wily savage, deer, bear, and buffalo, spending many a lonely night in concealment from wild men and wild animals, in their successful attempt to regain their friends in Virginia. Although this distance could be made in a few hours now in automobile or airplane, it required months for them, during which time they lived on wild berries and such roots as they could find, as the small amount of Indian corn they carried was soon exhausted. Finally, in a most desperate plight, they reached friends in the upper Kanawha. William Ingles, her husband, started out at once with a searching party but one of the boys died before he could be reached, and the other was not found and returned until fifteen years after the massacre.[3]

These women were, no doubt, the first white women to set foot on the shores of the beautiful Big Sandy. The Kentucky Legislature, in 1924, honored Mrs. Ingles by naming the state highway, leading up the Ohio from Cincinnati to Ashland, after her.

With the surrender of Cornwallis at Yorktown in October, 1781, the conflict with the British ended. All troops had been withdrawn by the latter part of 1782, and the final treaty of peace was signed September 3, 1783,[4] by which the independence of the United States was acknowledged and their boundaries settled. The violence of the Indians did not cease with this treaty. Although organized invasions of central Kentucky were discontinued, small predatory bands were still hostile to the oncoming settlers. One of the first acts of the United States as an independent power was to bring about a reconciliation with the Indians. Treaties were signed with the more important tribes, granting them their land claims until they chose to sell them, which helped to bring about the discontinuing of organized invasions. The small bands that continued their depredations were those who were either urged on by British sympathizers, or were not satisfied with the outcome of the war, and struggled to keep back the advancing settler by numerous massacres of the whites.

Daring English hunters penetrating into the headwaters of the Big Sandy in the autumn of 1785 saw everywhere signs of warring and scalping parties, who still made their raids into southwestern Virginia.

In 1787 Jenny Wiley, wife of an outlying settler, Thomas Wiley, in Abb's Valley, was captured by a mixed band of Cherokees and Shawnees. While her family was being massacred, she was dragged away, her captors leading her into the Big Sandy Valley and almost to the mouth of the Scioto on the Ohio, near what is now Portsmouth, before they turned back to a temporary encampment near the mouth of Mud Lick Creek in Johnson County. From this camp, after many hardships and privations, she escaped in the night to the recently erected Harman's Station, just below the mouth of John's Creek in the Blockhouse Bottom. From this point Mrs. Wiley made her way back in safety to her husband; and years later both returned to the Big Sandy, where they took up their residence and started life anew near the mouth of Tom's Creek.[5]

Many a similar attack took place for several years after the Wiley massacre.

It was not until the treaty of peace was signed at Greenville, Ohio, with the Northwest Indians on August 20, 1795, that the Big Sandy Valley, the last warring stronghold of the red men in Eastern Kentucky, was thrown open to settlement. This treaty was brought about by General Anthony Wayne's decisive victory at Fallen Timbers, near Toledo, on August 3, which marked the passing of Indian warfare in Kentucky.[6]

Following this treaty, began the settlement of the Big Sandy Valley, from Pound Gap and the Breaks to the mouth, by pure Anglo-Saxon blood.

FIRST WHITE SETTLERS

Many explorations were led and discoveries made west of the Allegheny Mountains before any white man set foot on Johnson County soil. Hernando de Soto discovered the lower Mississippi in 1541; LaSalle explored in and around the Great Lakes in 1669; James Marquette, with his companion Louis Joliet, made his way to the upper waters of the Mississippi in 1673, and descended it in boats as far as the mouth of the Arkansas.[7] In the year 1671, Captain Thomas Batts and Robert Fallam had pushed their way over the great Appalachian divide and had discovered the middle waters of the Kanawha River in West Virginia.[8] On the return to the East of Batts and Fallam, came James Needham and Gabriel Arthur, on a mission for General Abraham Wood, who penetrated to the headwaters of the Tennessee River in 1673. Needham was killed by the Occaneechi Indians and Arthur remained with the Cherokees. The following year he accompanied them on a warring expedition, which led them into West Virginia and on down the Ohio, crossing the Big Sandy River near the mouth, on their way to battle the Shawnee Tribes located on either side of the Ohio near the mouth of the Scioto River in the vicinity of Fullerton, Kentucky, and Portsmouth, Ohio. During the ensuing attack, which was repulsed, Arthur was wounded and taken captive, but on learning that he was no Cherokee, was permitted to return to the Tennessee village as soon as his wounds had healed, from which place he soon left for Fort Henry, Virginia.

It has been indicated that on his release from the Shawnees on the Ohio, that Arthur ascended the Big Sandy and the Tug Fork to its head and then by way of Cumberland Gap reached the Cherokees. Whether or not he passed up the Big Sandy, it is evident that he certainly was on Kentucky soil and therefore the first representative of our race on record to visit what is now Kentucky. Three-quarters of a century later, John Peter Sally accompanied by John and Josiah Howard journeyed down the Kanawha and the Ohio in a canoe and was the first white man to see the mouth of the Big Sandy from a boat, which was in 1742.

Although there is no official record as to whether the Big Sandy had been penetrated heretofore by white men, it will be noted that it was thus early circumscribed. None of those already mentioned were at any time close to the present boundary of Johnson County, except possibly Arthur, taking the route up Big Sandy, as already indicated, on his return to Tennessee.

The first white man, on record, to see, what was later to be Johnson County was Dr. Thomas Walker. Mr. Walker, who was an able, ingenious and observing engineer, as well as a physician, had been employed by the Loyal Land Company of Virginia to go to the westward to discover and prepare a place for settlement. He, with his party, entered Kentucky through Cumberland Gap, and, passing over the waters of the Cumberland, Kentucky, and Licking rivers, came down and crossed the middle waters of the west fork of the Big Sandy, spending the period from June 6 to June 19, 1750, in exploring the valley. His route, which was an Indian trail, led him down Big Paint Creek, across the Big Sandy, and over the divide to the waters of the Tug Fork, which he followed to its source. He was the man who named the main or west fork of the Big Sandy the Louisa River, this occurring, according to his journal, on Thursday, June 7, 1750.[9] When Mr. Walker passed over the waters of Big Paint and Big Sandy he was unconsciously making history for Johnson County, since he was the first man of our race recorded to set foot on its soil.

Mr. Walker's exploration, however, was only the first of many yet to follow. Christopher Gist passed over the headwaters of Big Sandy on Elkhorn Creek, near the present site of Jenkins, on his route through Payne and Pound gaps, from the Ohio to the New River in Virginia, on his mission for the Ohio Land Company in 1851. Colonel Andrew Lewis and Colonel William Preston marched down the Tug Fork to near the mouth of Rockcastle Creek in their unsuccessful military movement against the Shawnees and their allies in 1756, which later became known as the "Sandy Creek Expedition."

SWIFT'S SILVER MINES

The next movement on the Big Sandy was that of John Swift, about 1760, which carries with it the tradition of Swift's Silver Mines.

The Swift legend has its basis in historical fact, and there are not many "Old-timers" in Johnson or Pike counties who cannot sit down and spin the story of John Swift and his silver mine. It appears that Mr. Swift, an English gentleman of education and means, traveled into this section of the State every year from 1760 to 1769, for the purpose of operating silver mines. Accompanied by a company of Englishmen, Frenchmen, and Shawnee Indians, he would journey from Alexandria, a Virginia seaport, into the forests of the Big Sandy, where he built furnaces, and burned charcoal, and presumably met with success, returning to the coast with large pack trains to meet the vessels from the Spanish seas. It seems that he had business connections in Virginia with a gentleman by the name of Montgomery, who owned and operated sailing vessels to the Spanish seas and was further engaged in the work of engraving and cutting dies for the coinage of silver and gold, he being an expert in this trade, having formerly worked in the Royal Mint in the Tower of London.[10]

A reorganization of the company was effected, which enlarged the enterprise. Additional ships were added to provide shipping facilities for the growing organization. Each succeeding year saw a return of Swift and his associates up to and including 1769 when it was determined to discontinue all operations.

The enterprise in which they were engaged, although well known to Swift's contemporaries, was carefully guarded at the time, and has remained a secret to the present. Swift was said to have kept a journal of his activities from which many transcripts have been made, but none ever proved correct. Of all these, one copy, which belonged to a Robert Alley, a native of east Tennessee, but a resident of Johnson County from 1859 till his death—about 1890, had the appearance of the original Swift document.[11] The exact location of these traditional silver mines of Swift's has been accredited to Johnson County, Floyd County, and Pike County, with Johnson County receiving most of the credit for its location, due to the finding of earthenware vessels in some caves, as well as the remains of old furnaces. Many years of ceaseless labor have been devoted and much money spent by parties attempting to find the location of these purported silver mines. This was especially true a generation ago; however, with the finding of any prehistoric article, new life is breathed into this romantic tale. One of the more recent episodes was in 1921 when a rumor started that it had been found on the farm where C. C. Meade now resides on Jenny's Creek about two miles from Paintsville. Still another was published in April, 1926, confining the location to Johnson County, after some silver coins and pottery vessels had been found in the local hills. The rumor was again revived in Floyd County in 1927 with the death of a certain Theo Robinson, a native of Quicksand Creek, Knott County, near the Floyd County line, who was supposed to hold a secret clue to the location of the lost mine. It is known that he took solitary trips into the forest-clad hills about his home, telling none whither he went, or for what reason, save that he had a silver mine. Any opinion on this man's long-kept secret would be on imperfect evidence, for he passed away, the mystery of his "mine" still veiled. Other fabulous tales have been reported. William Huff, of the same section as Mr. Robinson, has had similar experiences in seeking the hidden treasure, but his "mystery" has the appearance of a ghost story.

Dr. Willard Rouse Jillson, Kentucky State Geologist, in his "History of the Big Sandy," expresses the idea that these stories were really invented by Swift, to cover his operations while he and his counterfeiters were engaged in the spurious minting of silver and gold bullion into English currency which their constituents had obtained by their piratical sailing adventures on the Spanish seas. He bases his opinion on the fact that, with the exception of finding of an occasional bar of silver or lead, no actual mines have ever been discovered in any part of the Appalachian coal field, even though coal has been mined in that section for many years.

If the latter interpretation be correct, it is possible that a part of this treasure is still stored in some cave yet to be found.

Summing up all the facts, there are two theories as to the character of John Swift: that he was a pirate, not unlike Captain Kidd, operating from about 1760 till 1769, bringing silver from the Spanish Main to the Virginia coast, thence to the Kentucky hills, where he cached it, as Dr. Jillson surmises; or that he was an Englishman who found silver in this section and carried it secretly by pack train to the coast, whence it was shipped to England.

GEORGE WASHINGTON

Many individuals and organizations have tried to establish the fact that George Washington made the first surveys in the Big Sandy Valley, which were supposed to have been made from the years 1767 to 1770, at the junction of the Levisa and Tug forks, including the present site of Louisa.

In view of the fact that he was engaged in exploring west of the great divide about this time, and judging by his knowledge of the mountainous country of western Virginia, gained in surveying, it is reasonable to say that he did do so; however, that remains to be definitely proven.

EARLY SETTLEMENT 47

DANIEL BOONE

Daniel Boone, the patron saint of explorers, was certainly on the Big Sandy and in Johnson County. Until recently it has been assumed that his explorations were confined to the Kentucky River and Bluegrass regions, and many books have been written connecting him with its settlement. Only one publication—that of Dr. W. R. Jillson, "The Big Sandy Valley"—deals at length with his being in the valley at all, and that confines him to the upper waters of the Big Sandy. Boone, in company with William Hill, spent the winter of 1767 and 1768 exploring, hunting, and camping on the upper waters of the Big Sandy. These men started from the Yadkin country in the fall of 1767, perhaps accompanied by Squire Boone, and having crossed the Blue Ridge and Allegheny mountains, and the Holston and Clinch rivers near their sources, they fell upon the headwaters of the West Fork of Big Sandy. Boone and his companion, concluding from its course that this stream must flow into the Ohio, pursued their journey along its banks, until, as they thought, they had traveled near a hundred miles, and had penetrated considerably to the westward of the Cumberland Mountains; when probably striking a buffalo path, and pursuing it, they came to the Salt Spring, which some twenty-eight years afterwards was known as Young's Salt Works. This well is situated on the farm of Ben Hale at the mouth of Salt Lick Fork of the left fork of Middle Creek near Goodloe post office, which is about ten miles west of Prestonsburg, in Floyd County.

Here they were caught in a severe snowstorm, which compelled them to camp, and they at length concluded to remain all winter. As the salt lick attracted great numbers of wild animals, it afforded an easy way for Boone and Hill to keep an abundant supply of food. It was here that Boone saw his first buffaloes.

As the country thus far had been forbidding, quite hilly, and much over-run with laurel, they became discouraged; and as winter passed away, they abandoned all hope of finding anything by this route, and made the best of their way back to Carolina, unaware of the rich fertile bottoms they so nearly reached. Nor did Boone know, until several years afterwards, the name of the stream near which he had wintered."[a]

After his return to the Yadkin, he took part in the well-known explorations led by Findley through Cumberland Gap into the Bluegrass region in 1769, in which colonies were established at Boonesborough, Harrodsburg, and Bryant's Station. He spent several years in this part of the State, continuing his explorations, later moving to Limestone in Mason County, where he kept merchandise and a tavern.

In 1788, Boone moved from Limestone, now Maysville, to the Kanawha Valley, near Point Pleasant, situated at the junction of the Great Kanawha and Ohio rivers, in what was then the northwestern part of Virginia, but now within the limits of Mason County, West Virginia. With the exception of his being appointed a Lieutenant Colonel in the first military organization of Kanawha County, October 6, 1789, and elected as representative from Kanawha County in 1791, there is no record of Boone's life at Point Pleasant during the years immediately succeeding this, more than a number of surveys of land in that county, made by him in 1791, 1795, and 1798.[13] The last survey recorded, in which Boone took part, was made September 8, 1798.

The date 1798 would be in error if the following were correct, regarding his leaving for the upper part of Louisiana, now Missouri. The exact date of his departure is not known, but on Page 562, Volume II, Collier's *History of Kentucky*, is a paragraph stating that depositions show that he was in Northern Kentucky in 1795; and Reverend Thomas S. Hinde saw him in October, 1797, on pack horses, take up his journey for Missouri. It would appear that the statement of the surveys would be the more logical, in view of the fact that the county court order books of Mason County, Kentucky, show that he was appointed a deputy surveyor on August 23, 1796.

In a letter to Governor Isaac Shelby, in February, 1796, asking that he be appointed to supervise the building of a road through the wilderness, he gave his address as being on Hinkston Creek, which was in Bourbon County, Kentucky.[14]

It was about this time, while he was either living at Point Pleasant or in Bourbon County, and, either continuing his hunting and exploring expeditions or the surveying, that Boone, presumably, visited in Johnson County. The Auxiers state, in their family history, that he spent the winter of 1796-7 at the Blockhouse (Harman's Station), joining on many hunting trips. Nathaniel Auxier is said to have gone with Boone and the older members on several occasions to hunt bear, deer, wolf, etc., on Greasy Creek, when he was just sixteen years of age. They killed so much fat game that, carrying sacks full of the meat on horses, it greased the timber along the way, and they in turn called it Greasy, which creek still bears the name. They built a camp on that stream, still known as Boone's Camp. A post office, bearing the name, is located at the camp. Nat's Creek, just below Greasy Creek, was named after "Nat" or the Nathaniel Auxier mentioned above, because of his success in hunting on the serpentine stream.

M. L. K. Wells, in an article in the Paintsville Herald, December, 1922, writes that when he was a mere youth, there was an old hunter by name of Young, who lived in their neighborhood on Greasy Creek that told him of hunting with the Auxiers and others, how and where they made their powder. The hunter described a cave on the Wells farm, and how to find it. Mr. Wells found it as described. It was forty feet up in a cliff, and only one way to climb to it. The cave formed a bench, with the earth extending under a ledge of rock. On examination, he found the bones of a man buried there. Mr. Young further explained that the hunters gathered dirt and the saltpeter that spewed forth from the rocks, putting it in gums sawed from hollow trees, and when combined with water, that lye was drained therefrom, which was boiled down to make the powder.

Any of the older members of the Auxiers can point with pride to the spot in Blockhouse Bottom where once stood the stump of a large poplar tree which, on the completion of his stay there, Boone cut down to make the canoe in which he made his departure down the Big Sandy, with the furs and hides obtained on his visit and hunt. On leaving he gave "Nat" a powder horn and his mother, Sarah Brown Auxier, a buffalo hide, which she first used, by cutting notches in it, forming a kind of basket, to put the babies in and hang up to the ceiling; later using it on a corded bed—that is putting it next to the cords. This hide, Mrs. Auxier gave to her son Enoch, and he in turn passed it down through that branch of the family, to Joseph D., who in turn passed it on. It is now in the hands of Down Auxier who resides on Davis Branch, about two miles east of Paintsville.

Some of Wash Rice's people in Magoffin County have the horn that was given to Nathaniel.

In connection with this hunting excursion of Boone on the Big Sandy, there is a paragraph in the manuscript library of the late Dr. Lyman C. Draper in the archives of the Wisconsin State Historical Society at Madison, Wisconsin, as follows: "M. S. (Manuscript) Statement and notes of conversations with Col. Nathan Boone, who visiting Young's Salt Works in the winter of 1796-97, while on a hunt with his father in that region, received these facts from his father's own lips: At the Salt Spring called Young's Salt Works, settled by James Young, in early times, some sixty years ago the pioneers made salt; since then a well has been sunk at the same spot where some salt is yet made. It is now known as the Middle Creek Salt Works, and is situated in a wild mountainous country, the settlements in its immediate neighborhood being sparse. M. S. (Manuscript) letters of Edwin Trimble, Esq., of Prestonsburg, and John Howes, Esq., of Paintsville, Kentucky, March, 1853."

Another instance, substantiating the fact that Boone was in that section of the State at different intervals, was the finding of a large rock recently by Russell Scott on the farm of Robert Scott near Greenup, Kentucky, bearing the inscription: "D. Boone, 1784." The rock, which is about a foot in diameter, is the hard river boulder type—almost as hard as flint. The inscription is in crude lettering but is still very legible, and has been inspected by many residents of the vicinity. It was dug up near the Scott home on East Fork after having been buried in a gully for an unknown number of years. It is believed the stone was on the crest of East Fork hill when Boone cut his name and date upon it. It was dislodged during the following years, being covered up when rains washed dirt into the gully. The stone is valued highly by its owner, coming as a direct memento from the famous settler and fighter.

Judge Jesse Bryan Boone, a son of Daniel and Rebecca Boone, lived for some time in Greenup County, Kentucky, where he was inspector of salt-works for West Virginia and Justice of the Kentucky County Court for Greenup.[15]

Daniel Boone, the pioneer, was the patron saint of the steady movement of the western frontier. His place was beyond the frontier, outside of civilization, where he could hunt and fish and trap, where he could fight with primitive peoples, where he could live the life of freedom in the wilderness. He always moved on when the tide of population flowed into his place of abode. Hence, his leaving the Yadkin for the Bluegrass, then to Maysville, to West Virginia, back to Eastern Kentucky, and finally to Missouri, where he spent his last days. His remains are buried in the Frankfort, Kentucky, cemetery, at a point overlooking the Kentucky River, where a beautiful monument marks his last resting place.

The trail through Cumberland Gap to the Bluegrass, over which he passed in his explorations and now a National Highway, is named in his honor. In 1926, he was elected to the Hall of Fame in the National Pantheon, where he now is memorialized for his part in the winning of the West.

HARMAN'S STATION

Until 1787 no permanent settlement had been attempted on the Big Sandy. Numerous hunting excursions were noted, as well as the movements of the border militia. Chief of these hunting parties, was that of a party composed of William Thornton, James Fowler, and William Pittman, who, crossing over the headwaters of the Clinch River onto the Big Sandy by way of Pound and Shelby gaps, came as far down as Salt Lick Creek, where they discovered the old salt springs in 1775. Fowler, who was evidently a successful hunter, called the main stream of this region Beaver Creek, and it has held the name since. In 1773 Enoch Smith, Richard Spur, John Wilkerson and William.................... were pioneering on John's Creek.[16]

Although the Big Sandy Valley was much overrun at this time by small bands of vicious Indians, it was occasionally used of necessity by the militia. On June 12, 1775, Captain William

Russell, stationed at Point Pleasant at the mouth of the Kanawha, dispatched a letter to Colonel William Fleming, in which, among other things, he said: "I am this morning preparing to start off our cattle up Sandy, and expect that the command will leave this Wednesday, or Thursday, at farthest, and shall decamp myself with a convoy to the other stores next Monday, and expect to overtake the stock at the Big Painted Lick (near Paintsville) about sixty miles up Sandy." [17]

The first English settlement on the Big Sandy was that of Harman's Station near East Point in 1787. Next was that of the Vancouver's Station (also known as "Balchlutha") at Louisa in 1789, then Preston's Station at Prestonsburg, 1791; subsequently, Licking Station near Salyersville, and several others later. Although all were more or less important to each other in that trying time, the first is of major consequence to the history of Johnson County, and more detail is included herewith regarding its settlement.

Matthias Harman was born in or near Strasburg, Virginia, about the year 1732. His father, Heinrich Herrmann, came from Prussia to Pennsylvania, it is said, and from thence to the vicinity of Strasburg. Matthias Harman, and his brothers, of whom he had several, early became hunters and ranged the woods far and near. They joined every expedition into the wilderness made up in their community, and it is said that their father also joined, whether for hunting, exploration, or for war. The Harmans bore the Indian a bitter hatred and believed in his extermination. There came to America two brothers of Heinrich Herrmann, Adam and Jacob, but they came at a later date. These three brothers and their families were among the first settlers at Draper's Meadows in 1748. Michael Steiner, or Stoner, was a cousin to Matthias Harman, and was also an early settler at Draper's Meadows. These men were called Dutchmen by the early settlers. They were all explorers of the wilderness, and hunting became a passion with them. Matthias Harman became infatuated with the life of the woodsman and the dangers of the frontier. In woodcraft and Indian warfare it is doubtful if he ever had a superior. He was one of the men employed to guide the Sandy Creek Voyage, and tradition says that if General Lewis had been governed by his judgment the expedition would not have failed of its purpose.

These Germans, and explorers with whom they were associated, became familiar with every part of the Big Sandy Valley soon after settling at Draper's Meadows. They built a hunter's cabin on the Louisa (Levisa) River just below the mouth of John's Creek about the year 1755, and they went there to hunt the deer, elk, buffalo, bear, beaver, and other game, every year. It was through these expeditions that Harman gained his first knowledge of the Big Sandy.

Captain Harman lived on Walker's Creek in Virginia. At the time he was familiar with all the country along the frontier, acquired by hunting and fighting Indians, and this brought his services into demand by persons seeking new lands suitable for settlement. In 1777, he led a number of settlers from **Strasburg, Virginia,** to **Abb's Valley.** He made a number of such settlements in the country west of the New River. It had been, for many years, his intention to make a settlement at the mouth of John's Creek on the Louisa River when the attitude of the Indians would permit him to do so in safety. Harman was infatuated with the Louisa River country because game was more abundant there than in any other region of which he knew. For this colony, Harman had enlisted a number of old-time associates and companions in wilderness exploration. In 1787 he believed it safe to establish this settlement, and it was agreed that it should be made in the winter of 1787-88.

Harman's father was still living. He always went with the other pioneers to hunt in the Louisa Valley. Except for a few years during the Revolution this hunt had been made annually for many years. As the hunters would not return when they went out this time (1787), and as Harman, senior, was now too old to go with the colony and was desirous of making a hunt with his sons this year, it was arranged that a party would go out for a few weeks prior to the departure to build the fort on the Louisa. Where the hunters made their camp is not known, but it probably was on the headwaters of both the Tug and Louisa rivers. It is said that about twenty hunters went out in this party. Henry Harman and his sons, Henry and James Skaggs, Robert Hawes, some of the Damrons, and a man named Draper, are known to have been in the party that went on this preliminary hunt.[18]

One day the camp was surprised and attacked by a roving band of Indians, in which the hunters were victorious. Henry Harman and Robert Hawes were wounded, but in the meantime a young Cherokee, son of the chief and leader, was killed, which aided materially in the retreat of the Indians.

When the Indians disappeared Matthias Harman determined to return home at once. He was certain that the Cherokee would fall upon the settlements and inflict what damage and murder he could as a revenge for the murder of his son. Because of the condition of their wounded, the hunters made no attempt to pursue the Indians, but made preparations to get them home. The surmise of Harman concerning the intention of the Cherokee chief proved correct. He had gone as directly to Walker's Creek as he could from the battlefield; thinking that they were attacking the home of the Harmans, he and his band committed the Wiley Massacre. (See page 42.)

AN ARTIST'S CONCEPTION OF BLOCKHOUSE BOTTOM (HARMAN'S STATION) AS IT WOULD APPEAR TODAY
(East Point Is in the Lower Right)

EARLY SETTLEMENT

In the afternoon of the day after the attack upon the Wileys, Harman and his long hunters returned to the settlement. The swollen streams, and the heavy loads carried by their horses had delayed them twenty-four hours; but for these impediments they would have arrived in time to have prevented the murders committed by the Indians. The confidence of the hunters that they would arrive in the settlement before the Indians, had caused them to neglect to send a runner to warn the settlers of their danger.

Immediately upon his return Matthias Harman went to the house of Wiley where he found many of the settlers. After making a minute examination around the house and finding evidence of the route taken by the Indians with their captives, he was confident that he could overtake them and recover the prisoners. His purpose to follow them was determined upon at once. Harman believed this raid was made more by accident than design and that it indicated no uprising of the Indians nor any purpose to harass the settlements. It was not regarded as of sufficient importance to delay the settlement to be made at the mouth of John's Creek. He assembled those interested in that enterprise and gave them instructions as to what they should carry with them, when to set out, what to do in case they should arrive before he could return there from pursuit of the Indians, and the most favorable route for them to take on the journey. There were about twenty-five men in this colony, but the exact number is not known, and their names are lost to us. We do know that among them were Matthias Harman, Absalom Lusk, Henry Skaggs and James Skaggs (brothers), Robert Hawes, Daniel Harman, Adam Harman and Henry Harman. It is believed that a man named Horn and also one named Leek were with the colonists. Harman selected ten of the most experienced Indian fighters to go with him in pursuit of the Indians having Mrs. Wiley and her child in captivity. Thomas Wiley was not a member of the colony and did not go with them. His son always stated that he had not returned from the pursuit of the Indian captors, which he made down New River. He also said that his father was unnerved by the destruction of his family, and that he was at the time unfit for the warpath.

Harman and his company of hunters made an unsuccessful pursuit of the Indians. Following them for several days, they came upon the camps already abandoned, found the slain child of Mrs. Wiley and buried it. The Indians were aware of the fact that their pursuers were on horseback and for this reason abandoned the old warpath and took to the small streams which made it difficult for those following. They also swam the larger streams which were flooding, and crossed over stony ridges which mainly caused Harman and his companions to abandon, with regret, the pursuit at a point where the Indians had last crossed the Louisa River.

From this point the hunters ascended the river to the mouth of John's Creek, where they went into camp, and awaited the arrival of the other colonists, who were several days getting there after they made camp. There they erected the famous blockhouse and effected the settling of Harman's Station in the winter of 1787-88.[19]

The Indians attacked the blockhouse several times during the summer of 1788. The settlers surrounded it with a stockade. The Indians maintained something of a siege which lasted for about three weeks. On account of their constant presence no crops could be raised that summer. Some of the settlers became discouraged, and as soon as cold weather enabled them to do so they returned to the Virginia settlements. Thus weakened, it was not believed that the fort could be defended another year. The settlers all returned to Virginia during the winter of 1788-89. The Indians immediately destroyed the blockhouse. It was burned, together with other cabins which the settlers had erected in the vicinity.

In the winter of 1789-90 some of the settlers returned to the blockhouse site. They were accompanied by other settlers, a majority of whom were from Lee and Scott counties, Virginia. They erected a second blockhouse where the first one had stood and although it was not as substantial as the first, it was never again to be given up to the Indians. The settlement was troubled much by them for several years, but never enough to break it up.[20]

PERMANENT ESTABLISHMENT

Following the second establishment of the blockhouse and discontinuation of trouble by the Indians in 1790, many homeseekers came, and by 1791 this section was being settled very rapidly. About this time came the Auxiers, Borders, Browns, Damrons, Grahams, Hagers, Hammonds, Justices, Laynes, Lackeys, Leslies, Marrs, Marcums, Mayos, Morgans, Prestons, Pinsons, Walkers, Weddingtons, Williamsons, and others, who followed closely in their trail to the Big Sandy.[21] While these pioneer families were migrating to the Big Sandy, the Adamses, Campbells, Mays, Finleys, Martins, Hays, Blackburns, Andersons, Salyers, Days, Smiths, Taylors, Combs, Stallards, Lewises, Collinses, Webbs, Wrights, Kelleys, Caudills, Crafts, and Hammonds were settling on the headwaters of the Cumberland and Kentucky rivers. Many of these families also came to the Big Sandy.

Naturally the upper part of the valley was settled before scarcely anything had been done lower down, as most of the settlers came in at the head from Virginia, Maryland, and North

EARLY SETTLEMENT 57

Carolina. Following closely on those as above mentioned, came the Clarks, Belchers, Brewers, Bevins, Dixons, Cecils, Goffs, Garrards, Hatchers, Meades, Maguires, McDowells, Millards, Fulkersons, Hatfields, Porters, Runyons, Friends, Ratcliffs, Osborns, Staffords, Strattons, Robinsons, and Stumps.[22]

By 1800 many of these old families, whose descendants now mainly inhabit this section, had taken up their abode in the valley. An idea of how fast this section was being settled can be had from the number of taxpayers above the age of twenty-one listed as resident settlers of that section, then known as District No. 2 of Mason County, for the year of 1793, which was only three years after the second settling of Harman's Station.

There is some question as to which district of Mason County actually covered the Big Sandy Valley. Dr. W. R. Jillson gives a list for district one in his "History of the Big Sandy Valley," while the September, 1927, edition of the Registrar, which is the official publication of the Kentucky State Historical Society, lists district three.

By referring to the description of the division of these districts on page 68, the map of Mason County on page 69, and to some of the names in the list which are similar to those of many of the early settlers of the Big Sandy, it would appear that district two of Mason County would be the one covering the Big Sandy Valley. Below are given the names of that list.[23]

Original spelling has been retained in most instances.

A LIST OF TAXPAYERS WITHIN THE DISTRICT OF WM. LAMB, NO. 2, COMMISSIONER IN THE COUNTY OF MASON FOR THE YEAR 1793

Aldridge, Christopher
Aldridge, Henry
Allen, Jeremiah
Arms, William
Armstrong, James
Arrowsmith, Sam
Atkins, John
Bailey, Jane
Balding, John
Balla, George
Baltimore, Phillip
Bane, Richard
Banfield, Theodore
Barr, John
Bearley, Charles
Beck, Jeremiah
Beckley, William
Bennett, Joel
Bennett, Moses
Bennett, Robert
Bennett, William
Berry, George Jr.

Berry, George Sr.
Berry, Reuben
Berry, William
Blanchard, David
Boone, Jacob
Boyard, Jacob
Bradley, Moses
Bradrock, David
Brannon, Patrick
Branton, Thomas
Brion, John
Briont, Benjamin
Brooks, James
Brooks, Thomas
Brooks, William
Bulger, James
Bullock, Lewis
Burk, Thomas
Burkhorn, Zephaniah
Byron, Peter
Byron, William
Cain, John

Calvin, William
Campbell, James
Campbell, Mathew
Campbell, Squire
Campbell, William
Camron, Samuel
Cannon, Isaac
Carewine, Richard
Carrol, Daniel
Casherwood, Sam
Chandler, Nathaniel
Chaney, Edward
Cockran, Henry
Colgin, William
Collins, Edward
Collins, Thomas
Conaway, Richard
Conway, Miles
Connor, Peter
Consaules, James
Consoles, John
Cooper, John

HISTORY OF JOHNSON COUNTY

Cord, Jacob
Cornick, Thomas
Cox, Joseph
Craig, John
Crawford, John
Criswell, James
Cunningham, Thomas
Curtis, Isaiah
Dale, Lawrence
Dauson, Joseph
David, Zebaniah
Davis, Beeson
Davis, David
Davis, Phillip
Davis, Samuel
Davis, Sarah
Davy, John
Delap, William
Derrill, Richard
Dey, John
Dobyns, Edward
Dobyns, James
Dobyns, Thomas
Dougharty, Michael
Doughty, Benjamin
Dragoo, Bell
Drugan, Abraham
Druzan, Peter
Dunavan, Daniel
Duncan, Daniel
Dunleavy, Anthony
Dunn, Henry
Evans, Daniel
Evans, Francis
Evans, W. Richard
Ferguson, Isaac
Flaugher, Adam
Flin, Pethias
Fowler, Jonas
Fowler, Moses
Fox, Arthur
Frazer, Moses
Frazer, Samuel
Giffard, Elisha
Graham, John
Grey, Robert
Grimes, David
Grymes, Noble
Guthridge, James
Guthridge, John
Hall, Andrew
Hall, Benjamin
Hall, Edward
Hall, Elijah
Hall, Thomas
Hancock, Joseph
Haner, James
Hanna, James
Hanna, John
Hanum, Jonathan

Harris, Edward
Hatfield, Thomas
Haugham, Moses
Haughton, Aaron
Hempleman, Adam
Henry, James
Henson, John
Honsucker, Abraham
Honsucker, Joseph
Hopkins, Joseph
Hurst, Henry
Hurst, Michael
Hutton, Charles
Hutton, George
John, Thomas
Jones, Ignas
Judd, Joshua
Judd, William
Justus, John
Karr, Paul
Kenton, Simeon
Kilgease, George
Killin, John
Killin, Patrick
Kirk, Thomas
Knary, Charles
Ladwick, John
Lashbrook, John
Leak, Harmon
Lee, Anne
Lee, Henry
Lee, Lewis
Leming, Joseph
Lewis, George
Lewis, James
Lewis, John
Lindy, Hezekiah
Lock, Andrew
Lucian, John
Lucust, Thomas
Mackey, William
Mageveny, James
Mahan, Jawbin
Marney, Jonathan
Marshall, Thomas
Martin, Davis
Martin, Harry
Massey, Nathaniel
Master, William
Matslerr, Elizabeth
Mavhall, Timothy
McBride, John
McCannon, John
McCash, David
McClure, Francis
McCracken, John
McDonald, William
McKay, James
McKenny, Daniel
McKenny, John

Medola, John
Mefford, George
Mesner, Coonrad
Metcalfe, John
Middleton, Thomas
Mitchell, George
Mitchell, Ignas
Mitchell, John
Mizner, Henry
Moore, Hosea
Moore, Samuel
Moore, Thomas
Moore, William
Morgan, Abel
Neeley, Thomas
Nickels, John
Norris, Abraham
Orr, D. Alexander
Oursler, Charles
Owen, Amasa
Owens, Aaron
Owens, Bethall
Owens, John
Ozburn, Abraham
Pangburn, Sam
Parker, Richard
Parker, Winslow
Parkison, William
Parks, Robert
Parrimore, Ellis
Parrimore, Gideon
Patterson, James
Patton, Eleanor
Patton, James
Patton, Thomas
Pelham, Charles
Pelham, John
Perry, Anne
Philips, Ann
Philips, Gable
Philips, John
Philips, Moses
Pollard, Benjamin
Preston, Bernard
Price, William
Prickett, Isaac
Reed, Enoch
Reed, Isaac
Regin, Thomas
Rich, Thomas
Riggs, John
Riley, James
Ritter, John
Ritter, Richard
Roberts, Thomas
Roe, William
Roebuck, Ben
Rogers, James
Rogers, John
Rubert, Isaac

EARLY SETTLEMENT 59

Rubert, Samuel
Rust, Matthew
Sharp, Solomon
Shelby, Joshua
Shepherd, George
Shepherd, John Jr.
Shepherd, John Sr.
Shepherd, John W.
Shepherd, Solomon
Shepherd, William
Shields, William
Shilock, John
Sibbett, James
Simpson, Allen
Sites, Henry
Skimer, Jesse
Slack, John
Smart, Elizabeth
Smith, Ben
Smith, Christian
Smith, Moses
Southard, Hezekiah
Soward, Richard
Stafford, Sterling
Stansbury, Silas
Stansil, Henry
Staton, Joseph
Stevenson, James
Steward, William
Sticklet, Peter
Stout, Thomas
Strickland, David
Strode, Samuel
Stuart, Robert
Sutton, Benjamin
Swim, Jesse
Symonds, Henry
Talbert, Thomas
Taylor, Francis
Taylor, John
Templiss, James
Tevis, Peter
Thatcher, James
Thomas, David
Thomas, Ephriam
Thomas, John
Thomas, Levi
Thomas, Phineas
Thompson, George
Thompson, James
Thompson, John
Thompson, Zachariah
Thompson, William
Todd, Robert
Trebalds, Clem
Tups, Henry
Underwood, Isa
Utter, James Jr.
Utter, James Sr.
Walker, Alex Sr.
Walker, Robert
Waller, Edmond
Walsh, James
Wamsley, Isaac
Ward, James
Ward, Joseph
Ward, William
Waring, Thomas
Warringford, Ben
Watkins, William
Watson, Aaron
Watson, Michael
Wauldrom, David
Welch, George
Welch, James
Welch, John
Wells, Aaron
Wells, James Jr.
Wells, Joseph Sr.
Westbrook, Joseph
White, George
White, John
Williams, Charles
Williams, David
Williams, Francis
Williams, Jonathan
Williams, Pleasant
Willson, James
Willson, John
Wood, Moses
Wood, Nicholas
York, Joshua
Young, William

REFERENCES TO CHAPTER V

[1] New Electric History of the United States, M. E. Thalheimer, 1904, page 194.
[2] The Big Sandy Valley, Jillson, W. R., page 65, J. P. Morton Co., Louisville, Ky., 1923. Also the Paintsville Herald, 12-20-23.
[3] Jillson, W. R., The Big Sandy Valley, pages 59-60, J. P. Morton Co., Louisville, Ky., 1923. Also History of Kentucky, Collins, Vol. II, page 53, 1875. Also the Paintsville Herald, 12-20-23.
[4] New Electric History of the United States, M. E. Thalheimer, 1904, page 184.
[5] For full particulars of Mrs. Wiley's capture and escape, see account under sketch of the Wiley family, Section Two. Also Jillson, W. R., The Big Sandy Valley, pages 66-67, J. P. Morton Co., Louisville, Ky., 1923.
[6] Jillson, W. R., The Big Sandy Valley, page 68, J. P. Morton Co., Louisville, Ky., 1923. Also Ky., a part of Va., Duke, in The South in the Building of the Nation, Vol. I, page 263.
[7] New Electric History of the United States, M. E. Thalheimer, 1904, pages 34 and 98.
[8] Jillson, W. R., The Big Sandy Valley, page 38, J. P. Morton Co., Louisville, Ky., 1923.
[9] Ibid, page 40.
[10] Ibid, page 48.
[11] History of Kentucky, Kerr—assisted by Wm. E. Connelley, Vol. I, page 130.
[12] Jillson, W. R., The Big Sandy Valley, page 57, J. P. Morton Co., Louisville, Ky., 1923.
[13] The Boone Family, Spraker, 1922, page 576.
[14] Ibid.
[15] Ibid, page 125.
[16] Jillson, W. R., The Big Sandy Valley, pages 55 and 76, J. P. Morton Co., Louisville, Ky., 1923.
[17] Ibid, page 77.
[18] Connelley, Wm. E., Harman's Station, 1910, pages 27-28.
[19] Ibid, pages 64-68.
[20] Ibid, page 77.
[21] Ely, Wm., The Big Sandy Valley, page 11, Central Methodist Press, Catlettsburg, Ky., 1886.
[22] Ibid, page 20.
[23] (Original) Tax List for District No. 2, of Mason County, Kentucky (1793), Archives Kentucky State Historical Society.

CHAPTER VI
GOVERNMENT

Virginia was settled in 1607 by the London Company. The Council of Burgesses, which met at Jamestown in July, 1619, was the first law-making body in America which was chosen by the people. It was composed of the Governor and council, with two burgesses from each plantation, or town, elected by the people. By 1779, Virginia was the most extensive and powerful of the colonies. All the land north of the Ohio River, south of the Great Lakes, and east of the Mississippi was within her chartered limits. In 1778, General George Rogers Clark led a successful expedition from Virginia against outlying posts of British and savages north of the Ohio, and every soldier in the expedition in turn was given two hundred acres of the land which was organized and later became the county and now state of Illinois. Due to the great extent of Virginia's territory and the inconveniences caused the inhabitants of these settlements, several counties had heretofore been formed.

As the State of Kentucky covers a portion of the original territory which constituted different counties of Virginia, a copy of each county organized with its boundaries that indirectly effected the present location of Johnson County, is given herewith. The first county organized in Virginia, under the colonial system, which included what is now Kentucky, was Augusta.

AUGUSTA COUNTY

The county of Augusta was formed in 1738, in the twelfth year of George II, by an act of the colonial legislature, then held at the capitol in Williamsburg, as follows:

"*Be it enacted by the Lieutenant Governor, Council, and Burgesses, of this General Assembly, and it is hereby enacted, by the authority of same,* That all that territory and tract of land, at present deemed to be part of the county of Orange, on the rivers of Sherrando, Cohongoruton, and Opekon, and the branches thereof, on the northwest side of the Blue Ridge of mountains, and lying on the northwest side of the top of the said mountains, extending from thence northerly, westerly, and southerly, beyond the said mountains, to the utmost limits of Virginia, be separated from the rest of said county, and erected into two distinct counties and parishes; to be divided by a line to be run from the head spring of Hedgman River, to the head spring on the river Potowmack; and that all that part of the said territory, lying to the northeast of the said line, beyond the top of the said Blue Ridge, shall be one distinct county and parish; to be called by the name of the county of Frederick, and parish of Frederick;

and that the rest of said territory, lying on the other side of the said line, beyond the top of the said Blue Ridge, shall be one other distinct county, and parish; to be called by the name of the county of Augusta, and parish of Augusta." [1]

BOTETOURT COUNTY

In 1769, in the tenth year of George III, the county of Augusta was divided, and the county of Botetourt carved from part of it. [2]

"Whereas many inconveniences attend the inhabitants of the county and parish of Augusta, by reason of the great extent thereof, and the said inhabitants have petitioned this general assembly that the said county and parish be divided:

"*Be it therefore enacted, by the Governor, Council, and Burgesses, of this present General Assembly, and it is hereby enacted, by the authority of same,* That from and after the thirty-first day of January next ensuing, the said county and parish of Augusta be divided into two counties and parishes, by a line beginning at the Blue Ridge, running north fifty-five degrees west to the confluence of Mary's Creek, or the south river, with the north branch of James River, thence up the same to the mouth of Carr's Creek, thence up the said creek to the mountain, thence north fifty-five degrees west, as far as the courts of the two counties shall extend it; and that all that part of the said county and parish, which lies on the south side of the said line shall be one distinct county and parish and called and known by the name of Botetourt." [3]

"*Be it further enacted,* Whereas the people situated on the waters of the Mississippi in the said county of Botetourt, will be very remote from their court house, and must necessarily become a separate county, as soon as their numbers are sufficient which will probably happen in a short time: That the inhabitants of that part of the said county of Botetourt, which lies on the said waters, shall be exempted from the payment of any levies, to be laid by the said county court for the purpose of building a court house and prison, for the said county."

FINCASTLE COUNTY

In 1772, in the twelfth year of George III, the county of Botetourt was divided and the county of Fincastle made from part of same.

"*Be it therefore enacted, by the Governor, Council, and Burgesses, of this present General Assembly, and it is hereby enacted, by the authority of the same,* That from and after the first day of December next, the said county of Botetourt shall be divided into two distinct counties, that is to say, all that part of the said county, within a line, to run up the east side of New River to the mouth of Culbersons Creek, thence a direct line to the Catawba road, where it crosses the dividing ridge, between the north fork of Roanoke and the waters of New River, thence with the top of the ridge to the bend where it turns eastwardly, thence a south course, crossing Little River, to the top of the Blue Ridge of mountains shall be established as one distinct county, and called and known by the name of Fincastle." [4]

KENTUCKY COUNTY

"BY ACT of October, 1776, Chapter 44, the county of Fincastle was divided into Kentucky, Washington, and Montgomery and the name of Fincastle became extinct.

"*Be it enacted by the Lieutenant Governor, Council, and Burgesses, of this General Assembly, and it is hereby enacted, by the authority of same,* That all that part (of Fincastle County) which lies to the south and westward of a line beginning on the Ohio, at the mouth of the Great Sandy Creek and running up the same and the main or northeasterly branch thereof to the Great Laurel Ridge or Cumberland Mountain, thence southwesterly along the said mountain to the line of North Carolina, shall be one distinct county, and called and known by the name of Kentucky." [5] (For the complete description of the boundary of the State of Kentucky, see pages 216 to 218, "The Kentucky Statutes" by Barbour and Carroll, 1894.)

Anyone familiar with the two main forks of the Big Sandy will note that the above description of the boundary line was very indefinite. This in turn caused border arguments, which later came before the legislatures of the two states.

The Kentucky Legislature in 1795 passed an act authorizing the Governor to take up this matter with the Governor of Virginia. This was done and in due course, each state appointed three commissioners clothed with authority to interpret the existing laws by settling the growing controversy by definitely locating the line. Difficulties of a large nature arose in the course of the deliberations of the joint commission which served to delay the final decision for several years.[6] At last a joint meeting was held at the forks of the Big Sandy in October, 1799, and the following agreement was reached:

"AN ACT establishing the boundary line between the State of Virginia and this Commonwealth.[7] Approved December 12, 1799.

"Whereas, commissioners appointed by the State of Virginia and this commonwealth, did, in order to ascertain and establish the boundary line between the said states, on the fourteenth day of October, last, enter into a written agreement under their hands and seals, which is in the following words, to-wit:

"The commissioners for ascertaining and adjudging the boundary line between the states of Virginia and Kentucky, appointed pursuant to the act of separation between the two states, to-wit: Archibald Stuart, General Joseph Martin, and Creed Taylor, Esquires, on the former, and John Coburn, Robert Johnson, and Buckner Thurston, Esquires, on the part of the latter, having at this day met at the forks of the Great Sandy River, according to appointment, and taken into consideration the said act of separation, have, and by these presents do unanimously agree and declare, that the boundary line between the said states, is and shall be and remain as followeth, to-wit: To begin at the point where the Carolina, now Tennessee, line crosses the top of the Cumberland Mountain, near Cumberland Gap; thence northeastwardly along the top, or highest part of the said Cumberland Mountain, keeping between the headwaters of the Cumberland and Kentucky rivers, on the west side thereof, and the headwaters of Powell's and Guest's rivers, and the Pond (Pound) Fork of Sandy, on the east side thereof, continuing along the said top, or highest point of said mountain, crossing the road leading over the same at the Little Paint Gap, where by some it is called the Hollow Mountain, and where it terminates at the west fork of Sandy, commonly called Russell's Fork; thence with a line to be run north forty-five degrees east till it intersects the other great principal branch of Sandy, commonly called the northeastwardly branch; thence down the said northeastwardly branch to its junction with the main west branch, and down main Sandy to its confluence with the Ohio. *And whereas,* doubts have heretofore prevailed which of the main branches of Sandy the act for dividing the county of Fincastle (which is the act referred to for the line between the two states), meant and intended that the line should run up, and locaters have been led into errors in entering their land warrants; it is therefore unanimously further agreed between the said commissioners, that no land claims founded on entries within the forks of Sandy, or east of Cumberland Mountains on the waters of Sandy, previous to the first day of October, one thousand, seven hundred and ninety-nine, on either side of the beforementioned line to be run from the end of the said Cumberland Mountain to intersect the said main northeastwardly branch of Sandy, ought to be in any wise affected by said doubts which have existed respecting the said line; but that the said claims ought to remain valid and secure as if no such doubts had existed, or as if the said territory had been within the acknowledged limits of either state, that is to say, that all entries of land made in the office of either state, which by this adjustment of line falls into the other, shall be as valid as if made in the offices of that state in which the land lies; and that it be recommended to the said states to pass mutual laws for the ratification of the said claims pursuant to the meaning and intent of this agreement between us; and that until such laws shall be passed, this instrument shall not be in force, but shall take full effect immediately after the passage of such laws.

"And whereas, this commonwealth does approve and is willing to ratify and confirm the said agreement on its part,

"*Be it therefore enacted by the General Assembly,* That the boundary line as ascertained and described in the said agreement, is hereby ratified and confirmed; and all entries of lands made in the offices in the State of Virginia, previous to the first day of October, 1799, lying in the forks of Sandy or east of the Cumberland Mountains on the waters of Sandy, which by the establishment of the boundary line as aforesaid, do fall within the limits of this state, shall be as good and valid as if they had been made in the proper offices of this commonwealth.

"This act shall commence and be in force so soon as the State of Virginia shall, in conformity to the aforesaid agreement, on its part, pass a similar law."

There is an interesting tradition concerning the manner in which the Tug Fork was selected. It is said that the commissioners arrived at the point where Louisa now stands late in the day. Autumnal rains had been falling in the valley and both forks of the Big Sandy were rising. During the course of the evening it was decided that the boundary line should follow the largest fork of the Big Sandy. Throughout the night, the Tug Fork rose steadily and in the morning it appeared to be a much larger stream than the Levisa Fork. The commissioners decided that the Kentucky-Virginia boundary should lie in the waters of the Tug Fork. It is known that the commissioners departed before the slow rising tide of the longer stream, Levisa Fork, reached the forks, and all too plainly told which was the largest fork of the Big Sandy River. Widespread good humor resulted when it was learned that the smaller of the two was chosen as the Virginia boundary.'

DELEGATES TO VIRGINIA. On April 18, 1777, Colonel Richard Callaway and Colonel John Todd were elected to represent the people in the General Assembly of Virginia. Subsequently, Colonel John Miller, General Green Clay, Squire Boone, and Colonel Wm. Irvine, living in what is now Madison County, were members of the Virginia Legislature.

KENTUCKY COUNTY DIVIDED

In July, 1780, the county of Kentucky was subdivided into three counties. Jefferson, with John Floyd colonel, Wm. Pope lieutenant colonel, and George May surveyor; Lincoln, with Benjamin Logan colonel, Stephen Trigg lieutenant colonel, and James Thompson surveyor; and Fayette, with John Todd colonel, Daniel Boone lieutenant colonel, and Colonel Thomas Marshall (father of the great Chief Justice of the United States) surveyor.

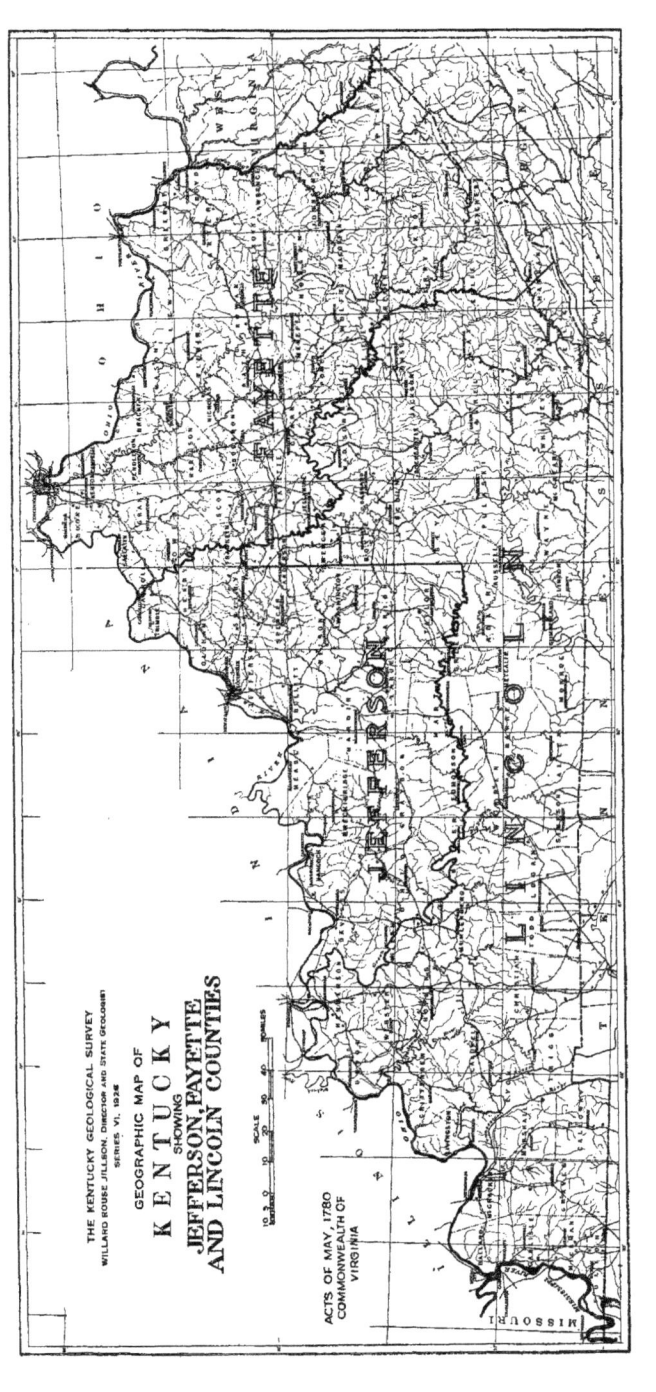

MAP OF KENTUCKY CONTAINING THE THREE ORIGINAL COUNTIES OF JEFFERSON, FAYETTE AND LINCOLN

GOVERNMENT

Fayette County received its name as a testimonial of gratitude to General Gilbert Motier de La Fayette, the gallant and generous Frenchman who volunteered as the champion of liberty on this side of the Atlantic, and proved to the world that although a nobleman by descent, he was a republican in principle, and was more ennobled by nature than by all the titles of hereditary rank.[9] His world-famous visit to Kentucky about this time probably accounts for the county receiving the honor.

"*Be it further enacted,* That all that part of the said county of Kentucky which lieth north of the line beginning at the mouth of the Kentucky River and up the same and its middle fork to the head, and thence southeast to the Washington line shall be another distinct county and called by the name of Fayette. May 1780."[10]

BOURBON COUNTY FORMED

The next county formed which later affected Eastern Kentucky was Bourbon. It was formed in the year of 1785, and is one of the nine organized by the Virginia Legislature before Kentucky became an independent state. It was named in compliment to the Bourbon family of France, a prince of that family, then upon the throne, having rendered the American colonies important aid, in men and money, in the struggle for independence.[11] The boundary of Bourbon County was defined in the following act:

AN ACT for dividing the county of Fayette.

"*Be it enacted by the General Assembly (of Virginia),* That from and after the first day of May, one thousand seven hundred and eighty-six the county of Fayette, shall be divided into two distinct counties, that is to say so much of the said county within the following lines: Beginning at the mouth of upper Howard's Creek, on Kentucky River, running up the main fork thereof to the head; thence with the dividing ridge between Kentucky and Licking Creek, until it comes opposite the head of Eagle Creek, from thence a direct line to the nearest part of Raven Creek, a branch of Licking, down Raven Creek to the mouth thereof; thence with Licking to the Ohio; thence with the Ohio to the mouth of Sandy Creek, up Sandy Creek, to the Cumberland Mountain, thence with the said mountain to the line of Lincoln County; thence with that line and down Kentucky River, to the beginning; shall be one distinct county, and called and known by the name of Bourbon, and the residue of the said county shall retain the name of Fayette."[12]

MASON COUNTY FORMED

Mason County—established in 1788 by the Legislature of Virginia, and named after George Mason, one of her most eminent lawyers and statesmen—was the eighth formed, of the nine which existed in 1792, when Kentucky was separated from the mother state and admitted into the Union. It was formed out of all that part of the then county of Bourbon which lay to the northeast of Licking River, from its mouth to the source; thence, by a direct line to the nearest point on the Virginia State line and county of Russell; thence along said line to Big Sandy River, down that river to the Ohio, and down the Ohio to the mouth of Licking—embracing all the territory out of which have been formed the following counties: Part of Campbell in 1794, Bracken in 1796, Fleming and part of Pendleton in 1798, part of Floyd and part of Nicholas in 1799, Greenup in 1803, Lewis in 1806, Lawrence and part of Pike in 1821, part of Morgan in 1822, Carter in 1838, Johnson in 1843, Rowan in 1856, Boyd and Magoffin in 1860, Robertson in 1867, Elliott in 1869, and Martin in 1870—nineteen in all.[13]

The town of Washington was the first county seat of Mason County. It was several years before any public buildings were erected, and consequently the county court was held at the home of individuals.

Limestone, Charlestown, and Kenton's Station (now extinct) were among the first towns of Mason County. Washington, Mayslick, Maysville, and Blue Lick have many places of historical interest. Some tombstones in the cemetery at Mayslick bear dates 128 years old.

DIVIDED INTO DISTRICTS

At a court held in the town of Washington, August 26, 1789: "Ordered that this county be laid off in three districts as follows, to-wit: District No. 1 to begin at and include Charles Town; thence along the way proposed for a road through Washington so as to include all the westward of the main street; thence along the main road to the North Fork; thence down the same to the river. No. 2 to begin at Charles Town and run the same lines as No. 1 to the North Fork, so as to include all the inhabitants east of said division. No. 3 to contain all south of the North Fork to the county line, and Miles W. Conway is appointed Commissioner of District No. 1, Arthur Fox of No. 2, and George Stockton of District No. 3."[14]

At a later date a fourth district was added, but it embraced the western section of the county and had no significance with the Big Sandy territory. In 1800 Floyd County was formed out of Mason County (see page 72), since which date no attempt has been made to give the records. Anyone desiring to go more into detail for the period from 1788 to 1800 while the present Johnson County was a part of Mason County, will find that the records, unlike those of Johnson, have been well preserved by Mason County officials.

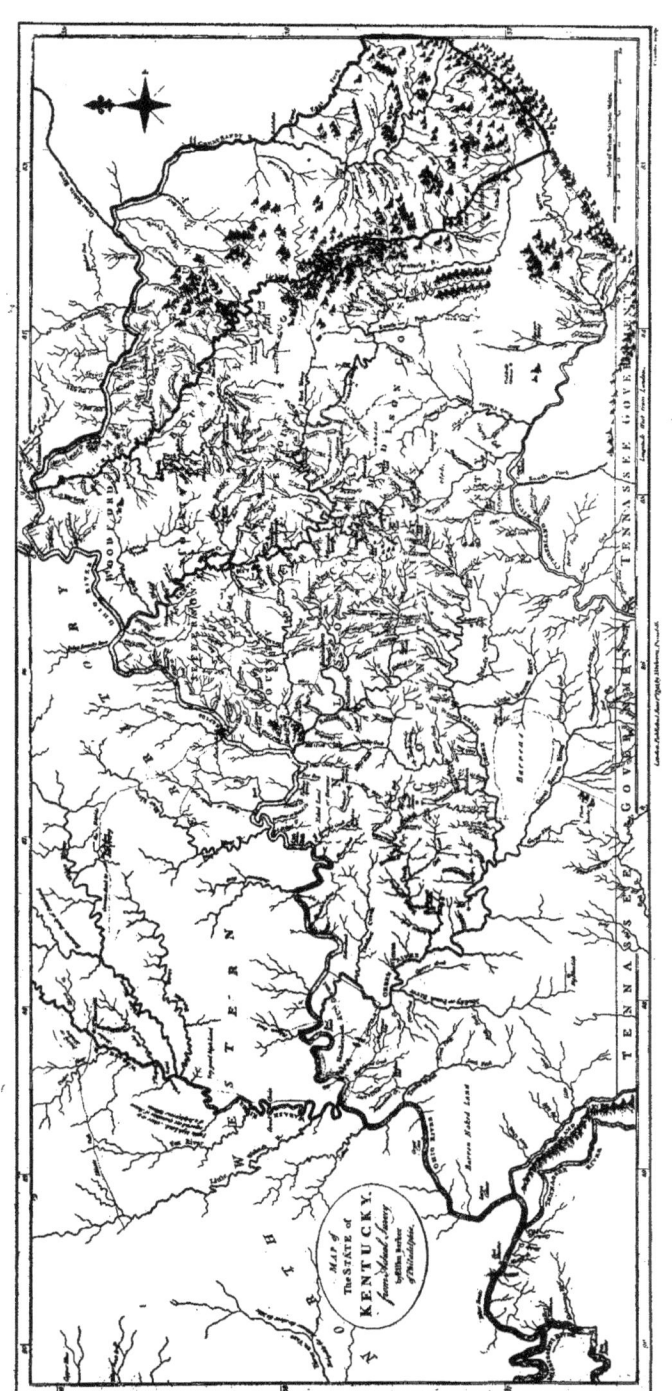

MAP OF KENTUCKY SHOWING THE ORIGINAL MASON COUNTY
Note the Names of the Present Big Sandy River, Big Paint Creek, etc.

Courtesy of the Kentucky State Historical Society

GOVERNMENT

It may be of interest to add that the first court in Mason County was held at the home of Robert Rankins in the town of Washington, May 25, 1789, and that Simeon Kenton, Alexander Hamilton, Thomas Boone, John Kenton, Daniel and Jacob Boone, and others are discussed all along through the court order books at this time, most of them being in land suits.

The place of holding court was next changed to the home of Wm. Parkinson on October 28, 1789, also in the town of Washington, next to the home of Daniel Peck in the same town, August 28, 1791, and finally to the town of Maysville. In going through early Mason County records, the following items were noted: Mason County residents, namely, Henry Lee, Miles W. Conway, Thos. Marshall, Simeon Kenton, and Meredith Helms, acknowledged a bond of $10,000 to Isaac Shelby, December 25, 1792.

That instead of Taverns or Saloons, they kept "Ordinary" houses then.

That the term of Lbs. was used for money values then, and that dollars were not mentioned in the records till May 22, 1791.

Those were the times when 159 shillings were paid for 33 wolf heads, 1/0 for a warm dinner, 1/3 for a cold dinner, 1/0 for breakfast, 1/3 for a supper, 0/0 for pasture of a horse over night, 2/0 for West India rum per pt., 10/0 for Claret, Port, or Lisbon wine per bottle, 1/3 per pt. for brandy, 0/9 per pt. for whiskey, 0/90 per qt. for cyder or beer, and 0/6 for lodging over night.

Virginia adopted the Constitution of the United States (then the thirteen original colonies or states) on June 26, 1788. An act concerning the erection of the district of Kentucky, which now included nine counties, into an independent state was passed the 18th of December, 1789, by the commonwealth of Virginia.[15] The first state admitted into the Union, after the adoption of the Federal Constitution, was Vermont, on March 4, 1791. The next was Kentucky, on June 1, 1792."[16]

MONTGOMERY COUNTY FORMED

AN ACT for the division of Clark County. Approved December 14, 1796.

"Be it enacted by the General Assembly, That from and after the first day of March, next, all that part of the county of Clark lying northwardly and eastwardly of the following bounds, to-wit: beginning on the Bourbon line at a red oak tree marked C. L. on the side of the road leading from Mt. Sterling to Paris, thence a straight line to strike the dividing ridge between Hingston's and Stoner's waters, where the road leading from Winchester to Mt. Sterling crosses said ridge; thence the same course continued, crossing Red River, until it strikes the Kentucky River, shall be

one distinct county, and called and known by the name of Montgomery."

FLEMING COUNTY FORMED

AN ACT for the division of Mason County. Approved February 10, 1798.

"Be it enacted by the General Assembly, That from and after the first day of March next, all that part of the County of Mason included within the following bounds, to-wit: run a line south from the courthouse of Mason County to the North Fork of Licking, thence up the North Fork nine miles, when reduced to a straight line; at this point make the beginning; thence a straight line to the mouth of the Flat Fork of Johnston; thence to the mouth of Fleming a straight line, unless it strike Fleming, in that case, down Fleming to the mouth, and up Licking to the head thereof, and with the line of Montgomery County to the Virginia line; thence with the said line to that branch of Sandy which divides this state from the state of Virginia; thence down the said branch till it intersects a line drawn from the beginning as follows, to-wit: from the beginning up the North Fork to the head of the South Fork thereof; thence with the dividing ridge between the waters of Licking and the Ohio, until it strikes the waters of Sandy, thence down such branch, east, to Sandy; to be called and known by the name of Fleming."

FLOYD COUNTY FORMED

AN ACT forming a new county out of the counties of Fleming, Mason and Montgomery. Approved December 13, 1799.

"Be it enacted by the General Assembly, That from and after the first day of June, 1800, all that part of the county of Fleming, Montgomery and Mason, included in the following boundary, to-wit: Beginning at the mouth of Beaver Creek, near the Narrows of Licking; thence north 30 degrees east to the Mason line; thence with said line to a point opposite the head of Little Sandy; thence along the division line between this state and the state of Virginia to the headwaters of the main branch of Kentucky; thence down the same to the mouth of Quicksand; thence a straight line to the fifty mile tree on the state road; thence along said road in a direction to Mt. Sterling, to Blackwater; thence down the same to the mouth thereof; thence down Licking to the beginning, shall be one distinct county, and called and known by the name of Floyd. But the said county of Floyd shall not be entitled to a separate representation, until the number of free male inhabitants therein contained, above the age of twenty-one years, shall entitle them to one representative, agreeable to the ratio that shall hereafter be established by law.

MAP OF KENTUCKY SHOWING THE ORIGINAL FLOYD COUNTY

Courtesy of the Kentucky State Historical Society

"A court for the said county shall be held by the justices thereof, on the first Monday in every month, except the months in which the courts of quarter sessions are held, after the said division shall take place, in like manner as is provided by law in respect to other counties, and as shall by their commissions directed.

"The justices to be named in the commission of peace for the said county of Floyd, shall meet at the house of James Brown, in the said county, on the first court day after the said division shall take place, and having taken the oaths prescribed by law, and a sheriff being legally qualified to act, the justices shall immediately proceed and qualify a clerk, and fix on a place for holding courts in said county; then the court shall proceed to erect the public buildings in such place; and until such buildings are completed, shall appoint such place for holding courts as they may think proper. *Provided always*, that the appointment of a clerk, and a place for erecting the public buildings, shall not be made, unless a majority of the justices of the court of said county concur therein; but such appointment shall be postponed until some court day when a majority can be had; but the said court may appoint a clerk pro tempore." (Another paragraph refers to the officers of Fleming, Montgomery and Mason counties.)

"The court of quarter sessions for the said county shall be held, annually, in the months of March, June, September and December, on the first Monday in each.

"This act shall commence and be in force from and after the first day of June next."

Floyd County received its name in honor of Colonel John Floyd, famous surveyor and Indian fighter.

The county's court house burned in 1807 or 1808, and it seems that all records were burned with it covering the period from 1800 to 1808. The first court records now on file in the county seat at Prestonsburg, were those for the court held on Monday, the 16th of May, 1808. The books were kept in a "hap-hazard" way until the plan of the circuit court respecting indexing of the orders was adopted in October, 1808, after which they were indexed and are in very good condition. Some of the order books just previous to the Civil War have been misplaced, but as this was after Johnson County was formed it did not affect getting a complete record of the affairs pertaining to Johnson County while it was a part of Floyd. The period from 1800 to 1808 could not be found, however, because of a fire which destroyed the court house.

Floyd County evidently was to the front in educational matters at a very early date, as the Prestonsburg Academy was in full operation in August, 1821. (See Page 50, Order Book No. 4.)

HISTORY OF JOHNSON COUNTY

The county was laid off into school districts in May, 1822. (Page 92, Order Book No. 4.)

The county long maintained the 98th Regiment of the Kentucky Militia, and many other things of historical interest, but only those things affecting what was later to be a part of Johnson County are included herein.

A tax list for the year 1837 is given in the following pages which will show who was in the county at that time. The reader will please remember that this list would also include the boundaries of the present Floyd County, besides those of Johnson and other counties which have been formed out of Floyd.

FLOYD COUNTY TAX LIST AS OF OCTOBER 4, 1837

Adams, Daniel
Adams, Gilbert
Adams, Lot
Adams, Stephen
Adams, William
Akers, Blackburn
Akers, Edward
Akers, David
Akers, James
Akers, Jonathan
Akers, Rodes
Akers, Solomon
Akers, Talbott
Allen, Adam
Allen, David
Allen, Felix
Allen, George
Allen, William
Arms, John
Arms, Moses
Arms, Saxon
Arnett, David
Arnett, Reuben
Arnett, Stephen
Ausburn (Osborn), Albert
Ausburn, Edmund
Ausburn, Edward L.
Ausburn, Jeremiah
Ausburn, Jesse
Ausburn, John
Ausburn, John P.
Ausburn, Levisa
Ausburn, Stephen
Ausburn, Thomas
Ausburn, William
Auxier, Daniel
Auxier, Enoch
Auxier, John
Auxier, Nathaniel
Auxier, Nathaniel Jr.
Auxier, Samuel

Bailey, Benjamin
Bailey, Hugh
Bailey, Joseph Jr.
Bailey, Joseph Sr.
Bailey, Prior
Bailey, Wallace Jr.
Bailey, Wallace Sr.
Balden, Joel G.
Baldridge, Andy
Baldridge, Arnett
Baldridge, John
Baldridge, Polley
Banks, David Jr.
Banks, David Sr.
Barnett, James
Barnett, John
Barnett, Motley
Barnett, Nelson
Barnett, William
Barnett, William
Barnett, Wilson
Baty, David
Bays, Daniel
Bays, Elijah
Bays, Pleasant
Berry, Isaac
Berry, John
Berry, William
Blair, George
Blair, Levy
Blair, Noble
Blair, William
Blanton, George Sr.
Blanton, William
Blevins, Daniel
Blevins, David
Blevins, Hiram
Blevins, James
Boin, Alfred
Bowlin, William
Boyd, David
Boyd, John

Boyd, Joseph
Boyd, Thomas
Boyd, William Jr.
Boyd, William Sr.
Bradley, Elias
Bradley, William
Branham, Benjamin
Branham, Elisha
Branham, Harrison
Branham, Isham
Branham, Turner
Brown, Aaron
Brown, Berry
Brown, Daniel G.
Brown, Fleming H.
Brown, Francis A.
Brown, James
Brown, John
Brown, Kalum
Brown, Samuel
Brown, Thomas
Brown, Thomas C.
Brown, William
Brown, William Abbott
Bryant, David
Bryant, James O.
Bryant, Stephen
Burchett, Armstead
Burchett, Druery
Burchett, Thomas
Burgess, Elizabeth
Burks, Charles
Burks, Richard
Burks, William
Burnett (?Barnett), Adam
Burnett, John B.
Burnett, William
Butler, David K.
Butler, George
Butler, Samuel
Canady, Andrew
Canady, Elijah

GOVERNMENT

Canard, Elias
Cantrill, Elijah
Cantrill, Henry
Cantrill, John
Carpenter, William
Carter, Frederick
Carter, Joseph
Casebolt, Jonathan
Cassaday, Thomas Sr.
Cassady, Thomas
Castle, Baswell
Castle, Benjamin
Castle, Inman
Castle, James
Castle, Jiles
Castle, John
Castle, Lindsey
Castle, Nathan
Castle, Zachariah
Caudle, Abner
Caudle, Bige
Caudle, Stephen
Caudle, Thomas
Cecil, James M.
Cecil, Thomas
Cecil, William
Chandler, Abraham
Clark, Alexander
Clark, Lorenzo
Clark, John
Clark, Samuel
Clay, Matheu
Clay, Peter
Clay, Robert
Clay, Solomon
Click, David
Click, James
Cobern, David
Cobern, Jacob
Cobern, Jeremiah Jr.
Cobern, Jeremiah Sr.
Cobern, John
Cobern, Samuel
Cobern, Samuel Jr.
Cockraham, Harden
Cole, James
Cole, John
Colee, William
Colins, Christopher
Colins, John
Collins, David
Collins, Isaac
Collins, Joshua
Collinsworth, David
Collinsworth, Mason
Collinsworth, Thomas
Colvin, Abiude
Colvin, John Jr.
Colvin, John Sr.
Colyer, Caleb

Conley, Constantine
Conley, David
Conley, David Jr.
Conley, David H.
Conley, David M.
Conley, Edmund
Conley, Edmund Jr.
Conley, Edmund Sr.
Conley, Henry Jr.
Conley, Henry Sr.
Conley, John
Conley, Joseph
Conley, Samp
Conley, Susannah
Conley, Thomas
Conley, Thomas Jr.
Corder, James
Crank, Nathaniel
Crider, John
Crisp, David
Crisp, Joel
Crum, Henry Jr.
Crum, Henry Sr.
Crum, John
Crum, John Jr.
Crum, Jonathan
Crum, Michael
Crump, Abner
Dale, Reuben
Daniels, Andy
Daniels, James
Daniels, Joseph
Daniels, Salley
Daniels, Thomas
Davidson, Samuel P.
Davis, Alfred
Davis, Elias
Davis, James
Davis, John
Davis, Thomas
Dawson, William
Dawson, Winston
Dearing, Richard
Dearing, Sarah
Delong, George
Derosit, James
Dickerson, Griffith
Dickerson, Silas
Dikes, Isham
Dillard, James
Dillion, James
Dixon, Andrew T.
Dixon, Henry
Dixon, Martin
Dixon, William
Dorton, Edward
Dunlap, William
Dunnahoo, James T.
Dutton, James
Dyer, Harvey

Earls, Jesse
Eastep, Samuel
Edwards, Joseph
Elington, John
Elliott, John
Elswick, Bradley
Evans, Harrison
Fairchiles, Enoch
Farechilds, Abiud
Farechilds, Asa
Farechilds, Lowery
Fitzpatrick, James
Fitzpatrick, Jeremiah
Fitzpatrick, John
Fitzpatrick, John F.
Fitzpatrick, John Sr.
Fitzpatrick, Jonathan
Fitzpatrick, Sally
Fitzpatrick, Thomas Jr.
Fitzpatrick, Thomas Sr.
Flanery, Isaac
Flanery, John
Fleming, John
Fleming, Robert
Fletcher, Elizabeth
Fletcher, George
Flint, John
Ford, John
Foster, Charles
Foster, Isaac
Foster, John
Fraley, James
Fraley, Jesse
Fraley, John
Fraley, Stephen
Franklin, Abraham
Franklin, James
Franklin, John
Franklin, Martin
Frasure, John
Frasure, William
Frazure, Robert
French, Banfill & Co.
Friend, Catherine
Friend, Charles W.
Friend, George
Friend, Isaac B.
Friend, John
Friend, Samuel K.
Garett, Barton
Garett, Gabriel
Garett, Harden
Garett, Jane
Garett, Salley
Garrell, James
Gearhart, Adam
Gearhart, Chrisley
Gearhart, John Jr.
Gearhart, John Sr.
Gearhart, Joseph

HISTORY OF JOHNSON COUNTY

Gearhart, Valentine
Gearhart, William
Genkins, Gilbert
Genkins, Robert
George, Alexander
George, John
George, Robert M.
Gilbert, Joseph
Gilbert, Thomas
Gillum, Chesley
Gipson, Hiram
Gipson, Isam
Gipson, Joel
Gipson, Leonard
Gobble, Isaac
Goodman, Enoch
Goodman, Pleasant
Graham, Rebecca
Gray, Samuel
Grim, Charles
Grim, Frederick
Gullett, Christopher
Hackworth, Abner
Hackworth, George
Hackworth, Jeremiah
Hackworth, John
Hackworth, Nicholas
Hager, Daniel
Hager, James
Halbert, John
Hale, Birce
Hale, Franklin
Hale, James
Hale, John
Hale, Sally
Hale, Smith
Hale, William
Hall, David
Hall, Elijah
Hall, Jarsey
Hall, Jesse
Hall, Mesias
Hall, Riley
Hall, Rodden
Hall, Squire
Hall, William
Hamilton, David
Hamilton, James
Hamilton, Jesse
Hamilton, Samuel
Hamilton, Stephen
Hamilton, Stephen Jr.
Hamilton, Thomas
Hammons, Joseph
Hammons, William
Handy, Beverage
Handy, William
Hannah, John
  (Mudlick)
Hannah, Samuel

Hanshow, Andrew
Hanshow, Harrison
Harkins, Hugh
Harmon, Adam
Harmon, Aquilla
Harmon, Elizabeth
Harmon, Henry C.
Harmon, James
Harmon, Rachael
Harrell, James
Harrell, Robert
Harris, Benjamin
Harris, David
Harris, Elizabeth
Harris, Henry C.
Harris, James
Harris, James P.
Harris, John B.
Harris, Joseph S.
Harris, Kilsey N.
Harris, Nancy
Harris, Samuel
Harris, William
Harris, William Jr.
Harvey, J. J.
Hatcher, James G.
Hatcher, John G.
Hatcher, John Sr.
Hatfield, Robert
Hatfield, Samuel
Haw, John W.
Hays, John Jr.
Hays, John Sr.
Haywood, John H.
Haywood, Lewis
Healms, Jacob
Henderson, William
Heriford, James H.
Heron, James
Hicks, George
Hicks, Hiram
Hicks, Reuben
Hicks, Sulse
Hill, Ephram E.
Hill, Spencer
Hill, William
Hitchcock, John
Holebrook, Randolph
Horn, John
Horn, Thomas
Hoskins, Moses
Howard, Benjamin Jr.
Howard, Benjamin Sr.
Howard, William
Howchim, James
Howe, Elexious
Howel, Clinton
Howel, David
Howel, Henderson
Howel, Joel

Howel, John
Hows, Elkijah
Hows, John
Hubbard, Salley
Hubbard, Solomon
Huff, Jeremiah W.
Huff, John
Huttan, James G.
Hylton, Benjamin
Hylton, Nathan P.
Hylton, Robertson H.
Isaacs, Godfrey
Isaacs, Isea
Isaacs, James
Isaacs, Samuel
Isaacs, William
Ivans, Jonathan
Ivens, Samuel
James, Abner
James, Panina
Jarrel, Ambrose
Jarrel, Carrell F.
Jarrel, Parks
Jarrel, Ruel
Jarrel, William
John, Bishuel
Johnes, John
Johnson, David
Johnson, Edward
Johnson, Elizabeth
Johnson, Harvey
Johnson, John
Johnson, Joseph
Johnson, Lemiel
Johnson, Lewis
Johnson, Patrick
Jones, Charles
Jones, Claibaren
Jones, David D.
Jones, Griffeth
Jones, John
Jones, Lindsey
Jones, Nathaniel
Justice, Allison
Justice, Amos
Justice, Caleb
Justice, Edmund
Justice, Israel
Justice, John
Justice, Jonathan
Justice, Peyton
Justice, Right
Kelley, Joseph
Kelley, Samuel
Kelley, William
Kestner, William
Kinderick, William
Krantz, Thomas
Lackey, Alexander
Lackey, Greenville

GOVERNMENT

Lackey, James M.
Lawson, James
Layne, James S.
Layne, John
Layne, John N.
Layne, Lewis
Layne, Lindsey
Layne, Samuel P.
Layne, Tandy M.
Layne, William H.
Leak, Thompson
Leek, Shelton
Lemasters, Eleazor
Lemasters, Francis
Lemasters, James
Lemasters, James T.
Lemasters, John Jr.
Lemasters, John Sr.
Lemasters, John V.
Lemasters, Lewis
Lemasters, Richard
Lewis, Benjamin
Lewis, George
Lewis, John
Lewis, Squire
Lewis, Thomas Sr.
Litteral, Daniel
Litteral, George
Litteral, Harston
Litteral, John B.
Litteral, John Sr.
Mann, Moses
Mann, Samuel
Marshall, George
Marshall, James
Marshall, John
Marshall, Johnson
Marshall, Reuben
Martin, Andrew
Martin, David
Martin, Elemander
Martin, George
Martin, James
Martin, James
Martin, James
Martin, Job
Martin, Joel
Martin, John
Martin, John P.
Martin, William
May, Blair
May, David
May, Reuben
May, Samuel
May, Thomas
Mayo, H. B. W.
Mayo, Jacob
Mayo, James J.
Mayo, Lewis
Mayo, Mial

Mayo, Wilson
Mayo, Winston
McBee, Pleasant
McBrayer, Ichabod
McBride, Robert
McGinnie, Hiram
McGuire, Harry S.
McGuire, Isaac
McGuire, Samuel
McGuire, William
McKenney, Daniel
McKinsey, James
Meade, Daniel
Meade, Moses
Meade, Robert
Meade, Robert Jr.
Meade, Rodes
Meade, William
Meeks, Isaac
Meeks, William
Meeks, William Sr.
Merrix, Charles Jr.
Merrix, Charles Sr.
Merrix, John
Milam, Edmund
Miller, Benjamin
Mills, George
Mills, Thomas
Mills, William
Montgomery, John
Moore, Andrew
Moore, Edwin
Moore, John
Moore, Obadiah
Morgan, David
Morgan, Morgan
Morgan, Wiley
Morgan, Wiley
Morris, Daniel P.
Morris, Ezekiel
Morris, John Jr.
Morris, John Sr.
Morris, William
Moseley, Jacob
Moseley, Thomas
Mosiley, William
Mullins, Ambrose
Mullins, Andy
Mullins, Isaac
Mullins, Reuben
Mullins, William Sr.
Newland, Stephen
Newson, Federick
Nix, Elisha
Not, Arbuth A.
Nowlan, Jeremiah
Oney, Allen
Oney, William
Orr, Joseph
Owens, Elias

Pack, William
Parks, John
Paterick, Henry
Paterick, Hiram
Paterick, Hugh
Paterick, Jeremiah
Paterick, John
Paterick, Meredith
Paterick, Richard
Paterick, Robert Jr.
Paterick, William
Patrick, Hugh
Patrick, Jesse
Patrick, Robert Sr.
Patton, Christopher
Patton, David
Patton, Frasure
Patton, Granvill
Patton, Henry Jr.
Patton, James
Patton, John
Patton, Samuel
Peery, Lou B.
Pelfrey, Alexander
Pelfrey, James
Pelfrey, Lydia
Pelfrey, William
Pendleton, James
Penix, Henry
Pennington, Joshua
Perkins, Joshua
Perkins, Lewis
Pew, George
Pew, William
Philips, Sarah
Pigg, James
Pitts, Mexico
Poe, Edward
Poe, James Jr.
Poe, James Sr.
Porter, John
Porter, Samuel
Porter, William B.
Powel, Halloway
Powel, John
Powel, John W.
Powel, Lewis
Prater, Adams
Prater, Elijah Jr.
Prater, Elijah Sr.
Prater, John
Prater, John
Prater, Jonathan
Prater, Joseph
Prater, Nancy
Prater, Thomas
Prater, William
Prater, William Jr.
Prater, William Sr.
Preston, Eliphas

Preston, Isaac
Preston, James
Preston, Jeffrey
Preston, Moses
Preston, Shaderick
Preston, Thomas
Pridemore, John
Priest, William
P'Simer, David
P'Simer, John
P'Simer, Nathaniel
P'Simer, Samuel
P'Simer, Thomas
Puckett, Caleb
Puckett, Isaac
Puckett, Morgan
Ramey, Alexander
Ramey, Charles
Ramey, Daniel
Ramey, Ephriam
Ramey, James Jr.
Ramey, James Sr.
Ramey, John
Ramey, William P.
Ramey, William Sr.
Randolph, Henry H.
Ratliff, Jas.
Ratliff, Silas
Ratliffe, Lewis
Ray, Jesse
Reed, Asa
Reed, Hannah
Reed, John
Reed, Thomas
Reffit, Daniel
Reynolds, Hamilton
Reynolds, Reuben
Reynolds, Thomas
Reynolds, Thomas K.
Rice, John
Rice, Martin
Rice, Martin F.
Rice, Samuel Jr.
Rice, Samuel Sr.
Richardson, Daniel
Richardson, Daniel
Risener, Elie
Risener, James
Risener, William
Robinson, Elizabeth
Robinson, Jesse
Robinson, John Sr.
Robinson, Samuel
Robinson, William
Robinson, William
Rowland, Armstrong
Rowland, Daniel
Rowland, John
Rule, Andrew
Rule, Andrew M.

Rule, Harrison B.
Salmons, Carter
Salmons, Fanny
Salmons, Neek
Salmons, Thomas
Salsbury, Elijah
Salsbury, William
Salyers, Abner
Salyers, Benjamin
Salyers, Fielding
Salyers, Henry
Salyers, Jacob
Salyers, John
Salyers, Joseph
Salyers, Levi
Salyers, Samuel
Scutchfield, Farmer
Sellards, John
Sellards, John W.
Sellards, Thomas
Senters, Solomon
Setser, Alfred
Shepherd, Abel
Shepherd, David
Shepherd, Jacob
Shepherd, John
Sizemore, George
Sizemore, John
Sizemore, William
Slone, Harden
Slone, Hiram
Slone, Isham
Slone, James
Slone, Reuben
Slone, Shaderick
Slone, William
Slusher, Philip
Smith, John
Smith, William
Smith, William M.
Spears, Enoch (Spars)
Spears, Spencer
Spears, Thomas
Spence, Hammon
Spradlin, Abraham
Spradlin, Benjamin
Spradlin, James
Spradlin, Jesse
Spradlin, John
Spradlin, John
Spradlin, Josiah
Spradlin, Nehemiah
Spradlin, Robert
Spry, Nancy
Spurlock, Francis
Spurlock, Martha
Stacey, Simon
Stafford, John
Stafford, William
Stambaugh, Frederick

Stambaugh, John
Stambaugh, Jonathan
Stambaugh, Philip
Stambaugh, Samuel
Stapleton, Bazwell
Stapleton, Jacob
Stapleton, Joshua
Stapleton, Zedekiah
Stephenson, William
Stiz, John
Stone, Cutbeth
Stone, Cutbeth Jr.
Stone, James
Stone, John
Stone, John
Stone, John S.
Stone, William
Stratton, Charles
Stratton, Harry
Stratton, John S.
Stratton, Polley
Stratton, Solomon
Stratton, Solomon C.
Stratton, Solomon H.
Sturgeon, Elias
Sturgeon, Elijah
Sturgeon, John W.
Sturgeon, William
Sutton, John
Sweatman, Zephaniah
Syllivan, David
Tackett, John
Tackett, Lewis
Tackett, Phillip
Tackett, Robert
Tackett, Thomas
Tackett, William
Tate, David
Taylor, Minrod
Terry, Leonard
Thomas, Owen
Thomas, William
Thomsbury, Edwin
Thomsbury, Isaac
Thomsbury, John
Thomsbury, Walter
Tirey, Daniel
Todd, Lewis
Tolley, Eleano
Trant, Daniel
Trimble, Edwin
Triplett, Daniel
Triplett, Lee
Tunmire, Isaac
Turner, Adam
Turner, James W.
Turner, John
Turner, Sudduth D.
VanHoose, James
VanHoose, Jesse

GOVERNMENT 81

VanHoose, John Jr.
VanHoose, John Sr.
VanHoose, Thomas
VanHoose, Valentine
VanHoose, William
Vaughn, Ayers Jr.
Vaughn, Ayers Sr.
Vaughn, Burwell
Vaughn, John P.
Vaughn, Leroy
Vaughn, Paterick
Wadkins, James
Wadkins, Mull
Wadkins, Thomas
Wadkins, Thomas Jr.
Wadkins, Thomas Sr.
Waldeck, John
Waldeck, Nicholas
Walker, Christopher
Walker, Dellaware
Walker, James T.
Walker, Jesse
Walker, John
Walker, John W.

Walker, Lucy
Wallace, Thomas
Waller, Jacob
Walters, Calvan
Ward, Hiram
Ward, Jonathan
Ward, Kiah
Ward, Shaderick Jr.
Ward, Solomon
Ward, S. R.
Watson, Jonathan
Webb, Jonathan
Webb, William B.
Webb, William Jr.
Webb, William Sr.
Wells, George
Wells, John
Wells, Moses
Wells, Peter
Wells, Richard
Wells, William
Wheeler, Catherine
Wheeler, Jesse
Wheeler, John

Wheeler, John Jr.
Whit, John B.
Whitaker, Francis
Whitaker, James
Whitaker, Johnson
White, James
Wierman, Abraham
Wierman, Jacob
Wierman, John
Wiley, Vardaman
Wiley, William
Williams, Elijah
Williams, John
Williams, Joseph
Witten, Thomas
Witten, William
Wood, Aaron
Wood, Nathaniel
Yates, John
Yates, William
Young, Charles
Young, Charles W.
Young, William

Chapter CCLXXLV, Page 332, Acts 1821.

LAWRENCE COUNTY FORMED

"*Be it enacted by the General Assembly of the Commonwealth of Kentucky,* That from and after the second Monday of February next, all that part of the counties of Greenup and Floyd, contained in the following boundaries, to-wit: Beginning at the mouth of Whites Creek; thence up the same to the head of that fork which Lockwood's road runs out at, and with that road to the dividing ridge between the east fork of Little Sandy River and Williams Creek; thence a straight line to the mouth of Straights Creek; thence a straight line to the mouth of the Dry Fork of Little Sandy River; thence up main Sandy to the mouth of Newcombs Fork; thence up the said fork to the head thereof, and to the top of the ridge dividing the waters of Licking and Little Sandy rivers; thence with the said ridge to a point between Rockhouse Creek and Big Blane; thence with the dividing ridge between Big Blane and Big Paint, to the head of Tom's Creek; thence with the dividing ridge between Tom's Creek and George's Creek, to the head of the first branch above the widow Border's, and down the said branch to its mouth, to the Levice Fork of Big Sandy River; thence a straight line to the first point above Adam Bowen's; thence with the ridge between the waters of Greasy Creek and Rockcastle, thence with the dividing ridge between Rockcastle and John's Creek, to the head of Wolf Creek, and down the same to the forks thereof; thence down the same so as to include the inhabitants that are on the east side of said creek from the forks downwards, who live in the bottoms thereof, to its mouth; thence down the Tug Fork of Big Sandy to the forks thereof, and down main Sandy to the beginning, shall be one distinct county, called and known by the name of Lawrence, in honor of Captain James Lawrence, late of the United States Navy."

Approved December 14, 1821.

Chapter CCCCLX, Page 145, Acts 1822.

Approved December 7, 1822.

MORGAN COUNTY FORMED

"Be it enacted by the General Assembly of the Commonwealth of Kentucky, That from and after the second Monday in March next, all that part of the counties of Floyd and Bath, contained in the following boundary, to-wit: Beginning opposite the mouth of the North Fork of Licking River; thence with the dividing ridge between Beaver and Blackwater creeks, to the Indian Valley; thence with the Montgomery County line to the Estill County line, to the Perry County line; thence with the Perry County line to a point so as to run a straight line to include Reuben Patricks farm and strike Licking River at the ford between Mason Williams and James Prathers, where the state road crosses, thence down Licking River to the mouth of the State Road Fork, thence up the State Road Fork to a large left hand branch, known by the name of the Twenty-two Mile Branch, thence up said branch to the dividing ridge between the waters of Licking and Sandy rivers; thence with said ridge to the Lawrence County line; thence with the Lawrence County line to the Greenup County line; thence with the Greenup County line to the Fleming County line; thence with the Fleming County line to the Licking River; thence up Licking River to the beginning, shall be one distinct county and known by the name of Morgan."

JOHNSON COUNTY FORMED

The formation and boundaries of the previously mentioned counties have been included herein and arranged in the order of their organization to show how the formation of Johnson County was brought about. All of them affected to some extent the government and boundaries of what was later to be one of the most important counties of Eastern Kentucky.

Johnson County was formed from the territory included in the counties of Floyd, Lawrence, and Morgan, by legislative action February 24, 1843, and effective from April 1, 1844. All acts pertaining thereto are given in the following pages.

GOVERNMENT 83

Chapter 167, Page 27, Acts 1843.

SECTION 1. *Be it enacted by the General Assembly of the Commonwealth of Kentucky,* That from and after the first day of April next, all the parts of Floyd, Lawrence, and Morgan counties within the following boundary: Beginning at the mouth of Little Paint Creek, in the county of Floyd, where it discharges itself into the Big Sandy River; thence up Sandy River to opposite the mouth of John's Creek; thence crossing Sandy River and up John's Creek, with its several meanders, to the first ridge above the mouth of Daniel's Creek; thence with that ridge including the waters of Daniel's Creek to the dividing ridge between Daniel's Creek and Rockcastle Creek; thence with the dividing ridge in an easterly direction, between John's Creek and the waters of Rockcastle Creek to the head of Wolf Creek; thence with the dividing ridge between the waters of Wolf and Rockcastle creeks to the head of Turkey Creek; thence in a straight line to James Ward's on Rockcastle Creek, so as to include said Ward's house; thence a straight line to the Chestnut shoal on Big Sandy River; thence a straight line to John Borders on George's Creek, including said Border's house; thence a straight line to Richard Kezee's on Hood's Fork of Blaine Creek, including said Kezee's house; thence a straight line to Samuel Sagrave's mill; thence a straight line to the mouth of Keeton's Fork of Blaine Creek; thence with the dividing ridge between Keeton's Fork and main Blaine Creek to the Morgan County line; thence with said line to the road leading from Paintsville to John Hammond's; thence a straight line to Edmond Conley's on the head of the State Road Fork of Licking River, including Edmond Conley's house, and with the dividing ridge between Paint Creek and the State Road Fork of Licking River to the dividing ridge between the Burning Spring Fork of Licking River and Jenny's Creek, to the narrows at the head of Jenny's Creek; thence a straight line to Robert Jenkins, including his house; thence a straight line to the beginning, shall be, and the same is hereby, erected into a separate and distinct county, to be called and known by the name of Johnson.

SECTION 2. The county of Johnson shall have eleven Justices of the Peace, who being qualified, shall convene at the house of James Franklin in Paintsville, and qualify their sheriff and appoint a clerk, if a majority of all the Justices in commission can agree to such appointment, and if they cannot agree they may appoint a clerk pro tem., until such majority can agree.

SECTION 3. That the officers of Floyd, Lawrence, and Morgan counties shall have power to collect all judgment and fee bills and taxes within said counties as if this act had not passed.

SECTION 4. That Elisha Smith, of Rockcastle County; William Waters, of Lawrence; Mason Williams, of Morgan; Meredith Patrick and J. V. L. McKee, of Laurel County, be, and they are hereby, appointed commissioners, who shall convene at Paintsville on the first Monday in April next, or so soon thereafter as convenient, who, or any three of them, having first taken an oath faithfully and without partiality, to locate the seat of justice for said county, shall purchase or receive as donation, a site for said seat of justice for said county, and locate the same thereon, and shall report their proceedings to the County Court, who shall cause the same to be entered of record; and the County Court shall provide suitable buildings to hold the courts, until public buildings are erected; and they shall cause suitable public buildings to be erected on the site selected; they shall appoint five Constables, and lay off the county into suitable Constables districts.

SECTION 5. That the surveyor of Pike County, shall run and mark the lines of Johnson County; that the commissioners to locate the seat of justice, shall be allowed two dollars, each, per day, the surveyor two dollars and fifty cents per day, and the surveyor's assistants one dollar per day, each, to be paid out of the county tax of 1843; that the sheriffs of Floyd, Lawrence, and Morgan shall pay to the sheriff of Johnson County, the county levy collected by them for 1843, of the citizens within Johnson County.

SECTION 6. That the citizens of Johnson County shall vote at all elections, as heretofore, and the sheriff of Johnson County shall compare the polls of elections as prescribed by law.

SECTION 7. That Johnson County shall be attached to the ....Judicial district, and the circuit court for said county shall be held on the...................., and the County Court shall be held on the..........................

Approved February 24, 1843.

Chapter 299, Page 68, Acts 1844.

BOUNDARY LINE CHANGED

"*Be it enacted by the General Assembly of the Commonwealth of Kentucky,* That the boundary line between the counties of Floyd and Johnson, be, and is hereby, established as follows: Beginning at a point where the Johnson line divides the waters of Rockcastle and Wolf creeks; thence running to the mouth of the Beech Branch on Wolf Creek."

Chapter 272, Page 55, Acts 1843.

SECTION 1. *Be it enacted by the General Assembly of the Commonwealth of Kentucky,* That the county of Johnson be, and the same is hereby, added to the eleventh judicial district, and the

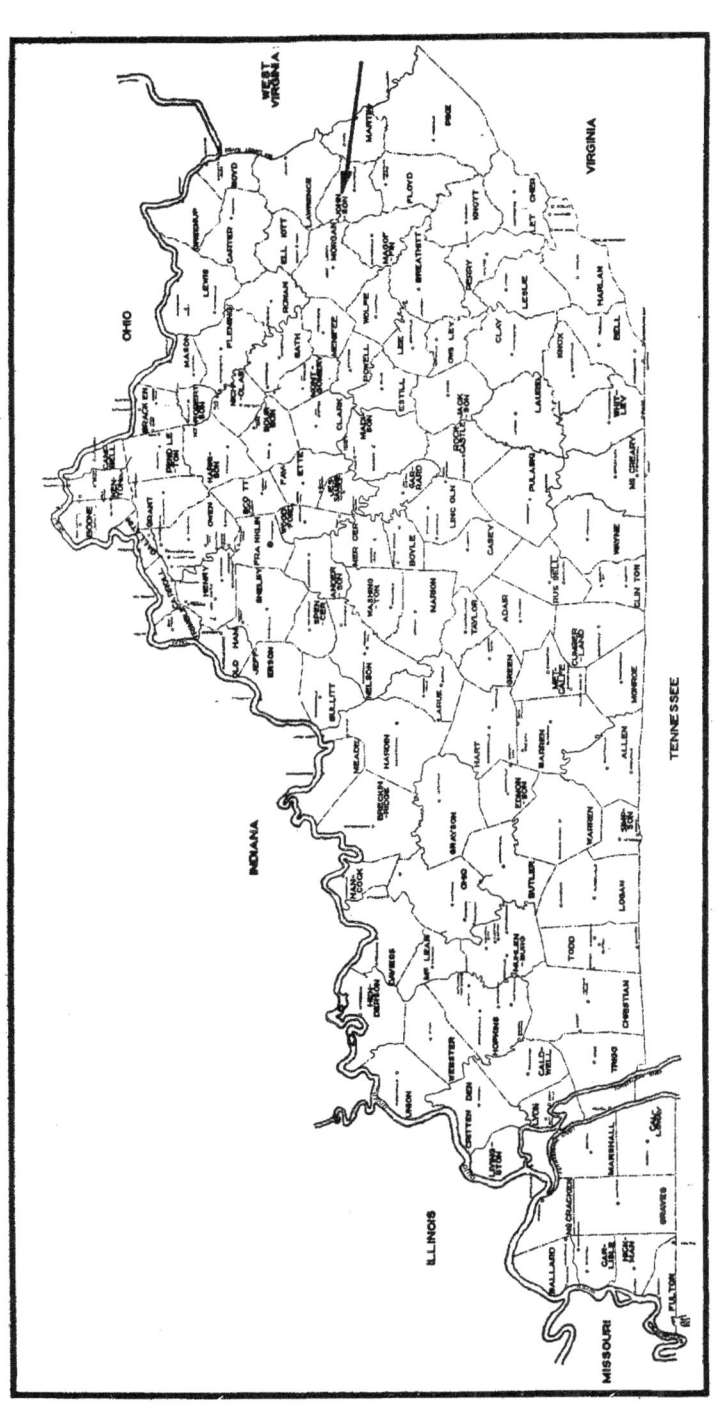

MAP SHOWING THE LOCATION OF JOHNSON COUNTY WITH RELATION TO ITS GEOGRAPHIC POSITION IN THE STATE OF KENTUCKY
(Arrow Points to Johnson County)

GOVERNMENT

circuit court shall be held on the fourth Mondays in May, August, and November, and shall sit for four judicial days, if the business thereof shall require it; and the County Courts shall be held on the first Mondays in each month, except such months as the circuit courts are held.

SECTION 2. *Be it further enacted,* That from and after the passage of this act, there shall be but two terms of the circuit courts in this Commonwealth, one to be held in the spring and the other in the fall, in the months that they are now held; and the summer terms of said courts are hereby abolished: *Provided,* That the special terms of the several courts for the trial of chancery causes, shall be holden and continue as heretofore.

Approved March 9, 1843.

Unfortunately, all the earlier tax lists of Johnson County have been destroyed or misplaced, probably by the soldiers during the Civil War (see Acts elsewhere herein); and a list of names, as found in the first court order books in the Clerk's office at Paintsville, has been prepared to aid those interested in knowing who resided here when the county was formed. They are as follows:

A LIST OF PERSONS RESIDING IN JOHNSON COUNTY WHEN IT WAS FORMED—COVERING THE PERIOD FROM 1844 TO 1848

Auxier, Christopher
Auxier, Daniel
Auxier, John B.
Auxier, Joseph
Auxier, Nathaniel Jr.
Auxier, Samuel
Auxier, Willis
Baker, Ira
Baker, Nathaniel
Bailey, Daniel
Baldridge, Andrew
Bannister, Pleasant
Barter, Ben
Bayes, Elijah
Bayes, George W.
Bayes, Samuel E.
Bennett, Wellman
Benny, James
Berny, James
Berry, Wm.
Blair, Briton
Blair, George
Blair, John
Blair, Levi
Blair, Noble
Blair, William
Blevins, Elisha

Blevins, James
Blevins, Levi
Blevins, Rhoda
Blevins, Samos
Blevins, Samuel
Blevins, Thomas A.
Borders, David
Borders, Franklin
Bowen, Henry
Brown, Daniel
Brown, Daniel G.
Brown, Francis A.
Brown, John
Burchett, Benjamin
Burchett, James R.
Burkett, Rowland
Burks, John
Burks, Richard
Burnett, John M.
Burton, Andrew
Butcher, Arty
Butcher, William
Butler, George
Butler, Jacob
Butler, Samuel
Cantrell, Henry

Carier (Cary's), Benjamin
Castle, Bazwell
Castle, Benjamin
Castle, Harvey
Castle, Henderson
Castle, Henry
Castle, Inman
Castle, Ira
Castle, Israel
Castle, Lindsey
Castle, Nathan
Castle, Zachariah
Castle, Zephaniah
Caudill, William
Cecil, K. B.
Chandler, Abraham
Chandler, James
Chandler, James L.
Clay, James
Clay, Jordan
Clay, Martin G.
Clay, Maston G.
Clay, Mathew
Clay, Peter
Coleman, Peter
Colinsworth, Reuben

88   HISTORY OF JOHNSON COUNTY

Collins, Hiram
Collins, Isaac
Collins, Joshua
Collins, Lindsey
Colvin, Abiud
Colvin, Allen
Colvin, John
Conley, Constantine
Conley, David
Conley, Edmond
Conley, Henry
Conley, Isiah
Conley, John
Conley, William W.
Craft, Gilman
Craft, Tilman
Craft, Wiley
Dale, Reuben
Daniel, Andrew
Daniel, David
Daniel, Isham
Daniel, James
Daniel, John
Daniel, Joseph
Daniel, Thomas
Davis, Elias
Davis, John
Davis, Michael
Davis, Richard
Davis, Thomas
Deboard, Joseph
Delarry, James
Delong, George
Delong, James
Delong, Samuel
Discon, A. J.
Discon, William
Dixon, A. J.
Dixon, J. C.
Dixon, William
Dorton, Edward
Elliot, John M.
Fairchild, Abiud
Fairchild, Asa
Fairchild, Asa J.
Fairchild, Enoch
Fairchild, Isiah
Fairchild, Jeremiah
Fairchild, Joseph
Fairchild, Moses
Fitzpatrick, Jeremiah
Fitzpatrick, John
Fleming, William P.
Fortune, James
Franklin, James
Franklin, John
Franklin, Joseph
Franklin, Martin
Friend, Samuel K.
Fuller, Francis L.

Gamble, Martin
Gartune, James
Godsey, James H.
Green, Giles
Grim, Charles J.
Grim, Charles W.
Gullett, Wiley
Hackworth, Nicholas
Hager, Daniel
Hager, John
Hager, John B.
Hager, John J.
Hager, William J.
Hamilton, Benjamin
Hamilton, Samuel
Hamilton, Stephen
Hanna, Ebenezer
Hanna, Samuel
Hannah, John
Harkins, Hugh
Harris, Harvey C.
Harris, John B.
Harris, Lawrence
Harris, Littleton
Harris, L. T.
Harris, William
Hayden, James
Herald, Robert
Hicks, Isaac
Hill, Edward P.
Hill, E. J.
Hill, Spencer
Hill, Wesley
Hitchcock, John
Hite, Inlius
Holbrook, James
Holbrook, Pleasant
Home, Thomas
Hound, Ebenezer
Hound, Samuel
House, E. K.
Howes, Elescious
Howes, Elijah
Howes, James M.
Howes, John
Huff, German W. (Jerman)
Huff, Inman W.
Hurt, Garland
Hutcheson, John N.
Hyden, Aran
Hyden, Milum
Hyden, William
Hylton, Aran
Hylton, Benjamin
Hylton, Eliphus P.
Hylton, Nathan P.
Hylton, Nathaniel F.
Hylton, William
Jackson, James

James, Ephriam
Jayne, Daniel
Jayne, Henry
Johnson, Andrew
Justice, Abriam
Kelly, Joseph J.
Kelly, Mathias
Kelly, Pleasant
Kelly, Samuel
Kelze, Richard
Kendal, Francis
Kezee, Charles
Kezee, Richard
Kimbler, A. B.
King, Marcus L.
Larkins, Presly
Law, Stephen
Law, William
Lemaster, Eleazor
Lemaster, Elisha
Lemaster, Francis
Lemaster, James
Lemaster, John P.
Lemaster, Lewis
Lemaster, William
Littrell, Daniel
Littrell, George
Littrell, Hamilton
Littrell, Houstin
Littrell, John
Livingston, A. B.
Livingston, B. J.
Livingston, Henry A.
Lyon, David
Marshall, Reuben
Martan, William A.
Martin, James
Matney, John
May, Caleb
Mayo, George W.
Mayo, Winston
McCarten, John
McGinnis, Hiram
McKenzie, David
McKenzie, James
Meek, Isaac
Meek, William
Melvin, George
Milam, Henderson
Miller, Phillip
Mollett, James
Mullett, Elias
Murray, George W.
Murray, Rhoderick H.
Nott, Arbuth A.
O'Bryan, James
O'Bryan, Valentine
Osborn, Jesse
Pelphry (Pelfry), A.
Pelphry, Alexander

GOVERNMENT

Pelphry, James
Pelphry, Stephen
Pelphry, William
Penix, Allen
Picklesimer, John
P'Simer, David
P'Simer, Nathaniel
Porter, Joseph
Porter, Samuel
Porter, Samuel W.
Pratt, James
Prest, Alexander
Prest, James
Preston, Burgess
Preston, Eliphus
Preston, Greenville
Preston, I.
Preston, James
Preston, James W.
Preston, Jeffry
Preston, Maper
Preston, Moses
Preston, Nathan
Preston, Retherford
Preston, Shadrach
Preston, Thassius
Price, George W.
Price, Jackson
Price, Jefferson
Price, Jesse
Price, Thomas
Price, Thomas F. (lawyer)
Priet, Alexander
Ramey (Remy), James
Ramey (Remy), William
Randall, Michael
Randall, Peeras
Rape, William
Rapp, Robert
Ratliff, Silas
Reed, A.
Reed, Asa J.
Reed, W.
Reed, William
Rice, A.
Rice, Jackson
Rice, John
Rice, Martin M.
Rice, Samuel
Rice, William
Right (Wright), Balis
Right (Wright), James
Robinson, Harrison H.
Rose, Thomas
Rose, William
Rowland, Armstrong
Rowland, Daniel
Rowland, John
Rule, Andrew

Rule, A. W.
Rule, Harrison B.
Sagraves, Samuel
Salyer, Benjamin J.
Salyer, David
Salyer, Jacob
Salyer, James
Salyer, John
Salyer, Levy (Levi)
Selson, George
Selson, Mathias
Setser (Setster), Abner
Setser, Alfred
Sherman, Henry
Short, Thomas
Sians, John
Smith, William W.
Sparks, Mathew
Sparks, Thomas
Spears, Enoch
Spears, Samuel
Spears, Spencer
Spears, Thomas
Spencer, Jake
Spradlin, Benjamin
Spradlin, James Jr.
Spradlin, James Sr.
Spradlin, Ivan
Spradlin, Josiah
Stafford, James
Stafford, John
Stambaugh, John
Stambaugh, Samuel
Stapleton, Basel
Stapleton, Joshua
Stapleton, Zephaniah
Steel, Daniel
Stepp, James
Stepp, Joseph
Stepp, Robert
Sturgeon, Elijah
Sturgill, John W.
Sublett, Mathew
Sutton, James
Swetman, Zephaniah
Tackett, John
Tackett, Levi
Tackett, Thomas
Tackett, William
Thompson, Russell
Thorp, Robert
Todd, Lewis
Trimble, James
Trimble, Randall
Turner, George W.
Turner, James
Turner, James W.
Vanhoose, Brackenridge

Vanhoose, James
Vanhoose, Jesse
Vanhoose, Levi
Vanhoose, Valentine
Vaughan, John
Vaughan, Stephen
Waldeck, Nicholas C.
Wales, Caleb G.
Walker, Delaner
Waller, Jacob
Ward, George J.
Ward, Hezekiah
Ward, James Sr.
Ward, James Jr.
Ward, Jesse
Ward, Shadrach
Ward, Solomon
Ward, William (Kiah's son)
Ward, William Jefferson
Webb, Edward R.
Webb, George W.
Webb, Jonathan
Welch, Ebby
Welch, James
Wells, G. W.
Wells, Isaac
Wells, John
Wells, Maper
Wells, Moses
Wells, William
Wells, William G.
Wheeler, Daniel
Wheeler, Jesse
Wheeler, John
Wheeler, William
Wheeler, William R.
White, Francis J.
White, Jackson
Wiley, Adam P.
Wiley, A. J.
Wiley, Richard
Wiley, William
Williams, H. H.
Williams, James
Williams, John M.
Williams, Joseph
Williams, Lucas F.
Williams, Robert
Wright (Right), Balis
Wright (Right), James
Young, Charles
Young, Charles W.
Young, John

RICHARD M. JOHNSON

As the county was named in honor of Colonel Richard M. Johnson, the noble fighter and statesman, many times a member of the State Legislature, of Congress, and vice-president of the United States, it is with pride, that an account of his life is included herewith, most of which is taken from one of Kentucky's best histories—Collins, Pages 400-404, Vol. II.

Richard Mentor Johnson, the third son of Colonel Robert Johnson of Scott County, was born at Bryant's Station, in Kentucky, on the 17th day of October, 1781.

As the literary institutions of Kentucky were then in their infancy, and the facilities for thorough education exceedingly limited, Richard remained with his father until the age of fifteen, receiving only such instructions as the circumstances allowed. At this age he left his father's house, intent upon advantages superior to those afforded in that vicinity, and entered a country school, where he acquired a knowledge of grammar, and the rudiments of the Latin language. Afterwards, he entered Transylvania University, where, by unremitted industry, he made rapid progress in acquiring an education.

Upon quitting the university, he entered upon the study of law under the guidance and instruction of that celebrated jurist and statesman, Colonel George Nicholas. On the death of this gentleman, which took place in a few weeks after his young student had entered his office, the subject of this biography placed himself under the instruction of the Honorable James Brown, late a Senator in Congress from Louisiana, and subsequently a minister from the United States to the Court of France, but then a distinguished member of the Kentucky bar. With this eminent citizen he finished his preparatory studies at the early age of nineteen, and entered upon the arduous duties of his profession.

In his vocation as a lawyer he was successful, and displayed the same active energy of mind and kindness of heart which have since distinguished him in higher and more responsible stations. He despised injustice and oppression, and never omitted an occasion to render his services, without prospect of reward, where honest poverty, or injured innocence was found struggling against the oppressions of wealth. The inability of a client to pay a fee never deterred him from attending sedulously to his cause, no matter how intricate and laborious were these services. By these means, even at so early an age, he secured to himself the just reward of his virtues, and the approbation and esteem of the public.

Scarcely had he been installed in the duties of his profession, before an opportunity was afforded for public service which has since identified him with some of the noblest feats of American valor. In 1802, the port of New Orleans in violation of an existing treaty, was closed against the United States by the Spanish intendant. The occurrence gave rise to immense excitement throughout America, especially in the Ohio and Mississippi valleys, and a rupture between Spain and the United States, likely to end in war, was the consequence. Richard M. Johnson, then only in his twentieth year, with many other young men of his neighborhood, promptly volunteered his services to pass down the western waters and make a descent on New Orleans, in the event of war. In a few days, chiefly through his exertions, a large company was enrolled, and he was chosen to the command. The speedy adjustment of the dispute with Spain deprived him and the brave youths under his command of the opportunity of signalizing themselves and the State upon the field of battle.

Before he had attained the age of twenty-one, at which period the Constitution of Kentucky fixes the eligibility of the citizen to a seat in the Legislature, the citizens of Scott County elected him by acclamation to a seat in that body. As a member of the Legislature he acquitted himself with credit, and to the entire satisfaction of his constituents. Having served two years in that body, at the age of twenty-four he was elected a Representative in the Congress of the United States; and in October, 1807, being then just twenty-five, took a seat in that body.

He entered upon the theater of national politics at a period when party excitement ran high, and attached himself to the Republican Party, more from a uniform and fixed devotion to the principles of democracy than from any selfish policy. He was immediately placed upon some of the more important committees, and at the second session of the term for which he was elected, was appointed chairman of the committee of claims, at that time among the most important House committees. His zealous and faithful devotion to business, and the distinction which he had acquired in Congress and throughout the Union, as a genuine friend of the liberty and happiness of his country, increased his popularity at home, and insured his re-election by his constituents, who from that time, never failed to manifest their devoted attachment to him whenever he was a candidate for office, either under the State or national government.

In 1811, our relations with Great Britain were such as, in the opinion of many, to render an appeal to arms inevitable. Richard M. Johnson was among those who were convinced that no other alternative remained to the people of the United States; and accordingly, after supporting with great energy all the preparatory measures which the crisis demanded, in June, 1812, gave his vote for the declaration of war. This important measure was shortly afterwards followed by an adjournment of Congress, when he hastened home, raised the standard of his country, and called around him many of the best citizens of his neighborhood, some of whom, schooled in the stormy period of the early settlement of the State, were veteran warriors, well suited for the service for which they were intended. With this battalion, composed of three companies, he hastened to the frontier, and when they arrived at St. Mary's on the 13th of September, his force, by general orders, was augmented by a battalion of mounted volunteers, and he elected to the command of the regiment thus formed. Only a portion of the regiment during that season had an opportunity of engagement; and this was a party of the mounted battalion under Major Suggett, which, in communicating with Fort Wayne, besieged by a superior force, encountered an equal number of the enemy whom it routed, killing an Indian chief of some distinction. After an active campaign of about ten months, Colonel Johnson returned home for the purpose of proceeding to Washington to re-enter Congress, having added to his reputation as a statesman that of an energetic and patriotic soldier.

In the winter following, while in attendance upon Congress, he rendered material aid to the president in arranging the plan of campaign for the ensuing summer. His views, being adopted, were subsequently carried out, and contributed to the successes which followed on the frontier. Colonel Johnson was authorized by the Secretary of War to raise, organize, and hold in readiness a regiment of mounted volunteers to consist of one thousand men. Accordingly upon the adjournment of Congress in March, he hastened home, and in a few weeks secured from the patriotic citizens of the State the full complement of volunteers; to the organization and discipline of whom he gave his sedulous attention. In this important part of his military duty, he had the aid of his skillful and intrepid brother, Lieutenant Colonel James Johnson, whose military talents have entitled him to a full share of the glory acquired by the regiment. Colonel Johnson, with his accustomed energy, lost no time in going with his command to the frontier of Ohio, which was the center of operations. His regiment soon acquired a name that attracted the admiration of the country. In making inroads upon the enemy, and in various skirmishes their success was always complete.

In October, 1813, the decisive crisis in the operations of the northwestern army arrived—the battle of the Thames, which led to the termination of hostilities in that quarter, was fought and won. The distinguished services of Colonel Johnson and his brave regiment in that bloody engagement have scarcely a parallel in the heroic annals of our country. The British and Indians, the former under the command of General Proctor, and the latter under that of Tecumseh, the celebrated Indian warrior, had taken an advantageous position, the British in line between the River

Thames and a narrow swamp, and the Indians in ambush on their right, and west of the swamp, ready to fall upon the rear of Colonel Johnson, should he force a retreat of the British. Colonel Johnson, under the orders of the commander-in-chief, divided his regiment into two battalions, one under the command of his brother, James, and the other to be led by himself. Colonel Johnson with his battalion passed the swamp and attacked the Indians, at the same moment that his brother, James, fell upon and routed the British regulars. The most interesting feature of the battle of the River Thames, and one of greatest importance to the people of the frontiers—because of the death of the great Tecumseh, the only Indian chief who could always rouse and concentrate against the whites the deadliest hate and revenge of the red men—was the fight in the Indian quarter. The scene of the battle was a beech forest over two miles long without any clearing and near to the bank of the river. At from 200 to 300 yards from the river, and parallel to it, a swamp extended throughout the whole distance. The ground between the river and the swamp was dry, and in many places clear of underbrush, although the trees were fairly thick. The British troops, over 840 strong, were drawn up across this strip, their left resting on the river and supported by artillery in the wagon road, their right in the swamp, covered by the whole force of over 1,500 Indians. A small swamp, and back of it a narrow piece of dry land, extended in front of the Indians, and at right angles to the main strip of land above. General Harrison, after learning from Colonel Richard M. Johnson and his brother, Lieutenant Colonel James Johnson, that in drilling their corps of Kentuckians they had occasionally on their march practiced charging on horseback, determined to take advantage of a singular position of the British General Proctor, and thus attack him. The first battalion, under Lieutenant Colonel James Johnson, was placed in front of the British lines; and, when the order was given, moved steadily forward, supported by several brigades of infantry. They had gone but a short distance when the British opened fire along their whole line, followed quickly by another fire. The horses recoiled at first, but under the order to charge, the column soon got in motion, and went dashing forward with irresistible force upon an astounded and bewildered enemy, broke through their ranks, and wheeled and poured in upon it a destructive fire. The British officers saw no hope for their disordered ranks, and immediately surrendered over 600 troops; their commander, General Proctor—who feared to trust himself in the hands of soldiers against whose people he had incited the cruelties of Indian warfare—with 204 of his troops effected his escape.

On the left the scene was different. Colonel Richard M. Johnson, after reconnoitering, was determined upon a prompt hand-to-hand fight with the Indians, and marched his second battalion through the first or small swamp, right in their faces—forming in two columns on horseback, with a company on foot in front, himself leading the right column, and Major Thompson the left. The contest for a while was obstinate and bloody, the slaughter great, but success complete. The gallant Colonel was in the very midst and thickest of the fight, and though perforated with bullets, his bridle arm shattered and bleeding profusely, he continued to fight until he encountered and slew an Indian chief, who formed the rallying point of the savages. This chief was supposed to be the famous Tecumseh himself, upon whose fall the Indians raised a yell and retreated. Some differ as to who killed the great Tecumseh, claiming that David King, a soldier of the company of Captain James Davidson (afterwards treasurer of Kentucky), killed him, while others believe that he fell by the hand of the old Indian fighter, Colonel Wm. Whitley." (See pages 404 to 410, Volume II, Collins' "History of Kentucky," for full particulars.) Below is Colonel Johnson's own account of this part of the battle, and of the death of the chief he afterwards supposed to be Tecumseh—given in a speech in Indiana:

"Colonel Johnson said that at his age it was wrong to put on any false modesty; and as he had been called upon to relate that portion of the fight which took place with the Indians, he would endeavor to do so. The Indians were 1,400 strong, commanded by Tecumseh, one of the bravest warriors that ever drew breath. He was a sort of Washington among the Indians—that is, they looked upon him as we look upon Washington. The Indians were in ambush, on the other side of what we were informed was an impassable swamp; but just before the battle came on, a narrow passage across this swamp was discovered.

"'Knowing well the Indian character, I determined to push forward with about twenty men, in order to draw forth the Indian fire, so that the remainder of the regiment might rush upon them while their rifles were empty. Having promised the wives, mothers, and sisters of my men, before I left Kentucky, that I would place their husbands, sons, and brothers in no hazard which I was unwilling to share myself, I put myself at the head of these twenty men, and we advanced upon the covert in which I knew the Indians were concealed. The moment we came in view, we received the whole Indian fire. Nineteen of my twenty men dropped in the field. I felt that I was myself severely wounded. The mare I rode staggered and fell to her knees; she had fifteen bullets in her, as was afterwards ascertained; but the noble animal recovered her feet by a touch of the rein. I waited but a few moments, when the remainder of the troops came up and we pushed forward on the Indians, who instantly retreated. I noticed an Indian chief among them who succeeded in rallying them three different times. This I thought I would endeavor to prevent;

because it was at this time known to the Indians that their allies, the British, had surrendered. I advanced singly upon him, keeping my right arm close by my side, and covered by the swamp; he took a tree and from thence deliberately fired upon me. Although I previously had four bullets in me, this last wound was more acutely painful than all of them. His bullet struck me on the knuckle of the left hand, passed through my hand, and came out just above the wrist. I ran my left hand through my bridle rein, for my hand instantly swelled and became useless. The Indian supposed he had mortally wounded me, and came out from behind the tree and advanced upon me with uplifted tomahawk. When he had come within my mare's length of me, I drew my pistol and instantly fired, having a dead aim upon him. He fell, and the Indians shortly after either surrendered or fled. My pistol had one ball and three buckshot in it; and the body of the Indian was found to have a ball through his body, and three buckshot in different parts of his breast and head.' Colonel Johnson said he did not know that it was Tecumseh at the time."

Of the forlorn hope, spoken of by Colonel Johnson, the names of ten of the band were ascertained, and given on Page 410, Volume II, Collins' "History of Kentucky," as follows: Lieutenant Logan; a young printer named Mansfield; Joseph Taylor; Benj. Chambers, a member of the Kentucky Legislature; Dr. Samuel Theobald, of Lexington, Kentucky, and the only one left on horseback besides Colonel Johnson, after a few minutes; Robert Payne; Wm. Webb; Garrett Wall, foragemaster; and Eli Short, assistant deputy quartermaster. The five last named, and Colonel Johnson, survived the terrible ordeal; most, if not all, of the other fifteen were killed in the charge or died of wounds.

After the advance of this Spartan band, the Colonel ordered the whole battalion dismounted. They then fought on foot for nearly half an hour, until the Indians lost their leader, Tecumseh, whose voice was silent in death, and no longer urged them to fight. The heroic Colonel, covered with wounds, twenty-five balls having been shot into him, his clothes, and his horse, was borne from the battle ground, faint from exertion and loss of blood, and almost lifeless. Never was victory so complete. Fifteen hundred Indians were engaged against the battalion of Colonel Johnson, and eight hundred British regulars against that of his brother. Both forces were completely routed, and an effectual end put to the war upon the northern frontier, distinguished as it had been by so many murderous cruelties upon the part of the savage allies of the British.

The war in that quarter being now ended, in a short time the army took up its march homeward; but Colonel Johnson, being unable to continue with his regiment, was carried to Detroit, from whence after a short confinement he departed for home. After a distressing journey, during which he endured the most painful suffering, he reached his home in Kentucky early in November. In February, 1814, still unable to walk, he reached Washington City, and resumed his seat in Congress. Everywhere upon the route, and at the capitol, he was met with the most enthusiastic and cordial greeting of a grateful people. Even his political opponents, deeply sensible of his sincerity, his patriotism, and his valor, cordially united in doing honor to the man who had, at so much sacrifice, rendered such glorious service to the country. Congress by joint resolution made appropriate acknowledgment of his gallant deeds, and directed him to be presented with a suitable testimonial of his services.

He continued to serve his constituents in Congress until the year 1819, when he voluntarily retired, carrying with him the esteem of the whole nation. But his native State, of which he was justly the idol, would not suffer him to remain in retirement. The people of Scott County immediately returned him to the State Legislature, and that body elected him to the United States Senate. An honor so exalted, from a source so honored, he could not resist; and accordingly in December, 1819, he took his seat in the United States Senate, and after serving his term was unanimously re-elected, a circumstance which serves to show how well he preserved the confidence of the people of his native State, and how deeply he was enshrined in their affections.

His career as a legislator was scarcely less brilliant and useful than that in which he distinguished himself as a warrior. His speeches and reports are monuments of his wisdom and liberality as a statesman. No man labored more in behalf of private claimants than did Colonel Johnson; and so faithful was he in the discharge of his duty toward all who applied for his services that he never failed while in Congress to attend to a single application that was made to him.

In 1836 he was made vice-president of the United States, and presided over the Senate with great dignity for the term of four years, at the expiration of which, he retired to his farm, in Scott County, Kentucky. The remainder of his life, with the exception of two terms in the State Legislature, was devoted to improving his private fortunes, somewhat impaired by a too liberal hospitality and constant attention to the public affairs. He was a member of the Legislature at the time of his death, which occurred in Frankfort, the 19th day of November, 1850.

He was buried in the Frankfort cemetery, where a beautiful monument marks his last resting place. On one side is an engraving of him, on another is one of him killing Tecumseh, while another includes the following:

"To the memory of Colonel Richard M. Johnson, a faithful public servant for nearly half a century as a member of the Kentucky Legislature, and Representative and Senator in Congress, author of the Sundry mail report, and of the laws abolishing imprisonment for debt in Kentucky and the United States; distinguished by his valor as Colonel of Kentucky regiment in the battle of the Thames, for four years vice-president of the United States, Kentucky his native state, to mark the sense of his eminent services in the cabinet and in the field, has erected this monument in the resting place of her illustrious dead."

Colonel Johnson once taught in the old Choctaw Indian Academy at Great Crossings. Clifton, the colonial home of the Johnsons, is located only seven miles from what is now Georgetown, Kentucky, on the State road leading to Owenton. The old house, set far back on a large lawn covered with great trees, contains a small museum of relics of the pioneer days of America. On the walls of the great lofty-ceilinged rooms hang oil portraits of people whose names are prominent among the early Kentuckians. Probably the most interesting of the portraits is that of the Colonel himself. Besides these hang souvenirs of practically every war that America has been engaged in. In one room hang relics of the Indians and of the Revolutionary War. Among these is a pouch of the softest leather imaginable, beautifully decorated in colors—an Indian product which a chief gave to Colonel Johnson. There are several other interesting Indian relics, including weapons that were used in the wars with the Indians, in addition to many things of historical value, in the way of guns and antique furniture.

Although the Johnsons, at one time, owned the land for miles around this colonial mansion, scores of slaves, and thousands of acres of land further south, only a fragment of the old plantation remains in the hands of their descendants.[18]

LEGISLATIVE ACTS AND COUNTY COURT ORDERS

The first official business of Johnson County was transacted at the house of James Franklin, at Paintsville, the present county seat, in April, 1844, in which eleven justices of the peace were appointed (see first list of Magistrates with County Officials). The site for the public buildings was purchased by five commissioners, whose names appear in the original act (see page 83).

The act provided that the county line was to be run by William Cecil, county surveyor of Pike County, but was amended next year to provide for a Johnson County man to do so. John B. Auxier was chosen. His assistants were Joseph Auxier, John Brown, John Davis, John Stafford, Peter Coleman, Abner Setzer, Houstin Littrell, Wiley Gullett, Francis Lemaster, and Randall

Trimble. Much could be said regarding the difficulties they encountered in running this line, the number of times required to establish their points and so on, but this part of the story is still fresh in the minds of some of the descendants of these early engineers, and, therefore, not necessary to repeat here.

The line, as originally run, was amended by Legislative Act in 1844 (see page 84) between Johnson and Floyd counties; also in 1860 when Magoffin County was formed (see page 106) from parts of Johnson, Floyd and Morgan counties; and again in 1870 when Martin County was formed (see page 109) from parts of Johnson, Lawrence, and Pike counties.

The first court house in the county was built by John B. and Henry C. Harris. It was begun in 1844 and completed in November, 1846. It was sufficiently complete to permit the first court to be held in it on March 3, 1845. The house of K. N. Harris was used for the first jail up to November, 1844.

In 1844, the county's number of white males over twenty-one years of age was 506; while 523 were paying taxes in 1845, 683 in 1847, and 852 in 1850. The total population for the latter date was 3,873, of which 3,843 were white and 30 were slaves. Each year witnessed an average increase. One thousand and six were paying taxes in 1851.

In 1846, land in the county was valued at $1.84 per acre. The total taxable property in the county at that time amounted to $266,074. In his tax returns on June 28, 1847, John B. Harris listed his property as follows: Three thousand, three hundred and fifty acres of land for $2,500, two lots in Paintsville $250, one slave over 16, one under for $550, and three horses for $120.

Chapter 98, Page 132, Acts 1844.

AN ACT to establish three election precincts.

"Be it enacted by the General Assembly of the Commonwealth of Kentucky, That there shall be established, in the county of Johnson, three election precincts, one of which shall be held at the house of Nathaniel Baker, another at the house of John Stafford, and another at the house of Henry Janes; and the taking of votes at said precincts, shall in all respects, be regulated by the laws now in force on the subject of elections."

Approved January 29, 1844.

Chapter 26, Page 11, Acts 1844.

"Be it enacted by the General Assembly of the Commonwealth of Kentucky, That, hereafter, all moneys arising from the appropriation of the vacant lands, lying within the county of Johnson, shall be applied to the erection of the public buildings in said

county, and the treasurer in said county is hereby directed to pay over to the County Court, or to their agent, duly authorized by said court to receive the same, all moneys that may come to his hands, arising from the appropriation of the vacant lands in said county."

Approved January 12, 1844.

Chapter 9, Page 95, Acts 1845.

AN ACT allowing an additional justice of the peace and constable.

"Be it enacted by the General Assembly of the Commonwealth of Kentucky, That the county of Johnson be allowed one additional justice of the peace, and one constable, who may reside in the neighborhood of the mouth of Daniels Creek."

Chapter 13, Page 98, Acts 1845.

AN ACT allowing another justice of the peace.

"Be it enacted by the General Assembly of the Commonwealth of Kentucky, That an additional justice of the peace be, and is hereby, allowed to the county of Johnson; *provided,* that, in such appointment, due regard be paid to the neighborhood on Rockcastle Creek, in said county."

Approved January 11, 1845.

The act creating the county specified that the first County Court should appoint five constables, and lay off the county into suitable constable's districts. Just how these districts were laid off is not known, as a thorough search failed to bring to light the whereabouts of the original description of these boundaries, which were probably lost during raids on the clerk's office in the Civil War, or dumped by a certain county clerk several years ago while getting rid of many of the old books which he termed "in the way." The act evidently was carried out in bounding the districts, as the following order will show:

At a court held in Paintsville on December 1, 1845, it was ordered that the third constable's district be changed, as follows: Beginning where the road leads from Paintsville to Carter court house strikes the near fork of Lower Creek; thence down same to its mouth; thence up Tom's Creek to the first point above the mouth of Sycamore on Tom's Creek; thence with said point to the dividing ridge between Lower Creek and George's Creek; thence with said ridge to the head of the Rockhouse Fork of Blain; thence with the ridge between the said Rockhouse Fork and the Brushy Fork of Blain to the county line; thence with the said line to the Richard Kelze farm on the Hoods Fork of Blain.

AN ORDER to divide the county into two tax-commissioner districts.

At a court held in Paintsville on the fifth day of January, 1846, "Ordered that the county be divided into two districts for the purpose of appointing two commissioners of tax, viz.: Beginning on Sandy River at the county line; thence up the river and its meanders to the mouth of Paint Creek; thence up Paint to the mouth of Jenny's Creek; thence with the dividing ridge between Jenny's Creek and Paint Creek to the county line."

Chapter 1, Page 1, Acts 1847.

AN ACT changing the time of holding court.

"Be it enacted by the General Assembly of the Commonwealth of Kentucky, That hereafter, the County Court of Johnson County, shall be held on the fourth Monday in each month, instead of the second Monday as heretofore."

Approved January 9, 1847.

Sixth constable's district made.

At a court held in Paintsville on May 24, 1847, "Ordered that an additional constable's district be created, to be known as constable's district No. 6, and bounded as follows: From the mouth of Buffalo Creek, including the waters of Buffalo, to the dividing ridge between Rockcastle and the waters of Big Sandy; thence with said ridge to the county line near the head of Daniels Creek; thence with the county line to the mouth of Johns Creek, and down Sandy to the beginning."

AN ORDER pertaining to vacant land.

At a court held in Paintsville on August 23, 1847, "Ordered that all vacant land be sold for $4.00 per hundred acres, instead of $5.00."

This price was again reduced to $2.50 per hundred acres, per court order of August 26, 1850. All transactions regarding vacant lands, permits, charters or grants, were handled by the county treasurer at that time.

Chapter 146, Page 149, Acts 1848.

AN ACT allowing an additional constable.

"Be it enacted by the General Assembly of the Commonwealth of Kentucky, That an additional constable be allowed to the county of Johnson, who may reside in the Flat Gap neighborhood."

Approved January 28, 1848.

Seventh constable's district made.

At a court held in Paintsville on the 27th day of March, 1848, "Ordered that an additional constable's district be created, to be known as constable's district No. 7, and bounded as follows: Beginning at the county line on Hoods Fork of Blaine; thence up same to the mouth of Puncheon Camp Branch; thence with the said branch to the head thereof; thence straight across to Paint Creek; thence up Paint to the county line; thence with the county line to the beginning."

Chapter 513, Page 357, Acts 1859.

AN ACT empowering the County Court to sell a part of the public square.

"*Be it enacted by the General Assembly of the Commonwealth of Kentucky,* That the Johnson County Court is hereby empowered to sell at public auction that part of the public square, in the town of Paintsville, in said county, situated on the northeast side of the said public square, and also a small portion of the said square on the south side thereof, and on the payment of said purchase money, by the purchaser or purchasers, said court shall cause to be conveyed, in fee simple, the parts of said public square, so sold, by a commissioner, appointed by said court for that purpose; which conveyance, when made, shall be recorded in the Johnson County Court Clerk's Office, as in other cases. The money arising from said sale shall be appropriated by the said court, to county purposes; said sale to be made upon such credit as the court may deem best."

Approved February 26, 1849.

CONSTITUTION CHANGED

On the 11th of June, 1850, the State of Kentucky adopted a new constitution. A glance at the county officials (see page 481), beginning their terms in 1851, will make this clear. Previous to this time, the county government was in the hands of the justices of the peace and constables. Although these offices were retained under the new constitution, most of their judicial power was taken from them, and placed in the hands of the newly created office of County Judge. All the districts were redivided, and cut to six in number. Their boundaries are given below.

Chapter 39, Page 4, Acts 1850.

AN ACT appointing commissioners to divide the counties of the State into districts, for the election of justices of the peace and constables.

"*Be it enacted by the General Assembly of the Commonwealth of Kentucky,* That the following persons be, and they are hereby, appointed commissioners in the several counties in this state—a majority of whom shall be competent to act—to lay off their respective counties into districts, of convenient size, for the election of justices of the peace and constables; and said commissioners shall receive for their services a reasonable compensation, to be allowed by the County Court of each county, at their court of claims in 1851.

"2. The following commissioners are hereby appointed for the county of Johnson: Daniel Hager, John Auxier, German W. Huff, Martin Franklin, and James Mullett, who shall divide said county into six districts.

"3. The term of office for the justices of the peace and constables, so elected, shall begin on the first of June in the year of their election."

Approved December 12, 1850.

Pursuant to the act of the General Assembly of December 12, 1850, the county was divided into magisterial districts on January 23, 1851, by Commissioners Daniel Hager, Martin Franklin, John B. Auxier, and German W. Huff, as follows:

DISTRICT No. 1

Beginning at the mouth of the Rockhouse Fork of Paint Creek and running with the dividing ridge between Rockhouse Creek and Jenny's Creek to the forks of Jenny's Creek below William Rices; thence running with the left hand fork of said creek of Jenny's Creek to the ford above John J. Myers house; thence with the dividing ridge to the mouth of the Limestone Branch on Sandy River; thence running down said river with its meanders to the upper end of the narrows at the lower end of Samuel Porters farm, including the house where Spencer Gibson now lives; thence running with the dividing ridge between the branch of Millers Creek and Buffalo Creek and the school house branches to the mouth of Buffalo Creek on Sandy River; thence down said river with its meanders to the mouth of Rockhouse; thence running up said branch to the head thereof; thence following the dividing ridge between the Muddy Branch on Tom's Creek to the head of the Meade Colvin Branch; thence down the ridge below the Meade Colvin Branch, crossing Tom's Creek and up the ridge above the mouth of the Lick Branch; thence running with the dividing ridge to the head of Little Mudlick; thence with the dividing ridge between Little and Big Mudlick creeks to the mouth of the Little Mudlick Fork; thence down Big Mudlick to the mouth; thence down Big Paint Creek with its meanders to the beginning. Place of voting, at court house, Paintsville.

DISTRICT No. 2

Beginning at the mouth of Buffalo Creek on Sandy River; thence running so as to include the house where Redeford Preston now lives and with the dividing ridge between Buffalo and Greasy creeks to the head of the Rockhouse Fork of Rockcastle Creek; thence running with the dividing ridge between Greasy Creek and Rockcastle Creek to the head of Lick Creek; thence running the ridge between the waters of Rockcastle Creek and Sandy River to the Johnson County line; thence with the county line to John Borders on George's Creek; thence running with the same to the top of the ridge between the Green Fork of George's Creek and the Brushy Fork of Blaine; thence with the dividing ridge between the waters of George's Creek and Blaine; thence with the ridge between George's Creek and Tom's Creek to the head of the Sycamore Fork of Tom's Creek; thence down the ridge on the west of the Sycamore Fork to the mouth of the same; thence crossing Tom's Creek and running with the dividing ridge between Tom's Creek and Nathan's Fork to the head of the Lick Branch and line of No. 1; thence with the line of No. 1 to the beginning. Place of voting, at mouth of Tom's Creek.

DISTRICT No. 3

Beginning at the mouth of Mudlick Creek; thence running with the line of No. 1 to the head of Little Mudlick and line of No. 2; thence running with the line of No. 2 to the Johnson County line; thence running with the county line to the mouth of the Mine Fork of Paint Creek; thence running with the dividing ridge between Big Paint and Colvin Branch to the head of the Gullett Branch; thence down the ridge below the Gullett Branch to Big Paint Creek; thence down Paint Creek to the beginning. Place of voting, at the house of Henry Jaynes.

DISTRICT No. 4

Beginning at the mouth of Big Mudlick Creek; thence running up Paint Creek with the line of No. 3 to the Jefferson County line; thence with the same to the top of the ridge between main Jenny's Creek and the Lick Fork; thence with the dividing ridge between the Lick Fork and Middle Fork of Jenny's Creek, to the ford of Jenny's Creek near John J. Hagers and corner of No. 1; thence with the line of No. 1 to the beginning. Place of voting, at house of William Caudill's near the forks of Barnett's Creek.

DISTRICT No. 5

Beginning at the mouth of Limestone Branch on Sandy River and corner of No. 1; thence running with the line of the same to the ford of Jenny's Creek near John J. Hagers; thence with the line of No. 4 to the county line at the head of the Lick Fork; thence with the county line to the head of Daniel's Creek; thence with the dividing ridge between Daniel's Creek and Rockcastle Creek to the head of Greasy Creek; thence with the dividing ridge between Greasy Creek and Buffalo Creek to the mouth of Buffalo; thence with the line of No. 1 to the beginning. Place of voting, Lewis Mills on John's Creek.

DISTRICT No. 6

Beginning at the Johnson County line at the head of Daniel's Creek; thence with the county line to the head of Turkey Creek; thence with the county line to James Ward's house; thence with the same to the head of Gnat's Creek; thence with the dividing ridge including all the waters of Rockcastle Creek in said county to the beginning at the head of Daniel's Creek. Place of voting, house of Ira Baker.

Section 7, Chapter 294, Page 216, Acts 1851.

AN ACT for the benefit of School No. 13.

"Be it enacted by the General Assembly of the Commonwealth of Kentucky, That the superintendent of public instruction be, and he is hereby, directed to issue his warrant on the second auditor in favor of the common school commissioners of Johnson County for the sum of twenty-four dollars and sixty cents, the amount district No. 13, in Johnson County, would be entitled to, had the trustees of said district reported in time for the year of 1849; the money to be paid over to the trustees of said district for the use of said school."

Chapter 167, Page 493, Acts 1851.

James H. Godsey, former sheriff in 1848-49, received an extension of time to collect his taxes, by legislative act on December 27, 1851. A copy of the act which was only of benefit to the sheriff is not included, due to its length. Several similar acts were passed for the different sheriffs at that time, probably for the reason of lack of means of travel to get around to collect the revenue.

Joseph Daniel, sheriff in 1853, received a similar extension by act of March 1, 1854. (Chapter 399, Page 28, Acts 1854.)

Chapter 199, Page 512, Acts 1852.

Time changed for holding County Court.

"Be it enacted by the General Assembly of the Commonwealth of Kentucky, That hereafter, the County Court of Johnson County,

shall be held on the first Monday in each month, instead of the fourth Monday as heretofore."

Approved January 1, 1852.

Chapter 199, Page 512, Acts 1852.

Time changed for holding quarterly court.

"Be it enacted by the General Assembly of the Commonwealth of Kentucky, That hereafter, the quarterly terms of the Johnson circuit court, shall be held on the first Monday in January, April, July, and October."

Approved January 1, 1852.

Chapter 369, Page 356, Acts 1852.

Time changed for holding circuit court.

"Be it enacted by the General Assembly of the Commonwealth of Kentucky, That, hereafter, the circuit court for Johnson County, shall be held on the fourth Monday in May and October."

Approved January 7, 1852.

Chapter 752, Page 336, Acts 1854.

Voting place in District No. 3 changed.

"Be it enacted by the General Assembly of the Commonwealth of Kentucky, That the voting place in district No. 3, in Johnson County, be, and the same is hereby changed from the house of Henry Jones to the school house, in school district No. 25, in said county."

Approved March 9, 1854.

Boundary of District No. 1 changed.

"At a court held in Paintsville on June 5, 1854, Ordered that the boundary line of magisterial district No. 3 be changed as follows: Beginning at the Limestone cleft; thence a straight line to the gap at the head of the Mile Branch; thence with the county line to the top of the ridge between main Jenny's Creek and the Mudlick Fork; thence with the top of said ridge to the mouth of the Middle Fork of Jenny's Creek near William Rice's."

Boundary of District No. 4 changed.

"At a court held in Paintsville on March 2, 1857, Ordered that the boundary line of magisterial district No. 4 be changed as follows: Beginning at the county line at the Narrows of Jenny's Creek; thence with the dividing ridge between said creek and Paint Creek to the head of Barnett's Creek, running so as to include John Marshall's, and James Spradlin Sr.; thence from said Spradlin's to the line near William Rice's; thence with the

dividing ridge between the Middle Fork of Jenny's Creek and the main fork of said creek to the beginning."

Chapter 437, Acts 1860, Page 44.

AN ACT to establish the county of Magoffin.

"Be it enacted by the General Assembly of the Commonwealth of Kentucky, That from and after the 25th day of April, 1860, so much of the counties of Morgan, Johnson and Floyd, as is included in the following boundary, is hereby erected into and established a separate and distinct county, viz.: Beginning on the dividing ridge between Licking River waters and Quicksand Creek at the Breathitt County line; thence with the Breathitt and Floyd counties line to the head of Johnson's Fork of Licking River so as to include all the citizens on the left hand fork of Johnson's Fork; thence a straight line to the head of White Oak Creek of Licking River; thence to the fork ridge, and down the same to a point opposite James Oney's; thence a straight line to the head of the McCormick Branch to where the county road crosses the ridge, so as to include said Oney on the left hand fork of White Oak Creek; thence a straight line to David Kennards, on the Rockhouse Fork of Licking River so as to include said Kennard; thence a straight line to the top of the ridge between the Rockhouse and Lacey's Creek; thence with said ridge to the waters of the Elk Fork of the Licking River; thence with the dividing ridge between the Elk Fork and Rockhouse Fork of Licking River, to the head of Brown's Fork of the Lacey Fork of Paint Creek on the waters of Sandy River; thence down Brown's Fork to its mouth including all the waters of same; thence down Lacey's Fork to its mouth, to the Johnson County line; thence a straight line to the head of the lower Little Mine Fork, or Tic-Lick Fork; thence keeping the dividing ridge between Luttrell's Fork, and others north of the same, to the head of said Luttrell's Fork; thence a straight line to John Luttrell's, on Paint Creek, so as not to include said Luttrell's dwelling house; thence a straight line to the upper end of the Narrows of Jenny's Creek, to the Floyd County line; thence with the Floyd County line to the beginning shall be one distinct county, called and known by the name of Magoffin."

Chapter 474, Page 82, Acts 1858.

AN ACT passed and approved February 13, 1858, granting Daniel Hager, late sheriff of Johnson County two years extension of time to collect levies. One passed also for A. W. Nicholl, March 1, 1860, as sheriff. (Chapter 882, Page 535.)

GOVERNMENT

Chapter 193, Page 26, Acts 1860.

That Johnson circuit court shall begin the Monday ensuing the close of the Lawrence circuit court, and continue six judicial days.

Approved February 11, 1860.

Another fixes it succeeding the Floyd circuit court. (Chapter 422, Page 82, Acts 1864.)

Approved February 19, 1864.

Chapter 654, Page 307, Acts 1862.

AN ACT passed and approved August 31, 1862, that it shall be lawful for James A. Ward, late sheriff of Johnson County, to present to the County Court of said county any claims that he may have upon the treasury of the State of Kentucky. Section 3 of this act includes any citizens of the county, who may or may hereafter have claims, when no circuit court is held as required by law. (Note that no courts had been held since May 1, 1861, by reason of the rebellion. The statutes were suspended by legislative action February 20, 1864, until law and order were restored.) (Chapter 507, Page 108, Acts 1864.)

Chapter 800, Page 462, Acts 1863.

AN ACT for the benefit of John Howes.

Whereas, John Howes was, at the August election, 1862, elected clerk of the county and circuit court of Johnson County, and has been discharging the duties of said office since his election, without qualifying and giving bonds as such, and has been unable to do so owing to the presence of rebel forces—therefore,

"Be it enacted by the General Assembly of the Commonwealth of Kentucky, That all the acts of said Howes, as clerk of said courts, be and the same are hereby legalized. This act shall take effect as of the first of April, 1863."

Approved February 6, 1863.

Chapter 465, Page 450, Acts 1864.

AN ACT passed and approved February 20, 1864, granting W. E. Hill, sheriff, an extension of time till June 1, 1864, to pay revenue due the State.

Chapter 1240, Page 141, Acts 1865.

AN ACT passed allowing two years further time for James Ramey to list and collect his uncollected fee bills.

Approved March 1, 1865.

Chapter 377, Page 304, Acts 1866.

AN ACT legalizing the collection of Militia fines, by Henry S. Vaughan, late sheriff, in 1864, who should have collected them in 1863.

Approved February 5, 1866.

Chapter 1306, Page 300, Acts 1867.

AN ACT to divide district No. 3, and to establish district No. 7.

"Be it enacted by the General Assembly of the Commonwealth of Kentucky, That justice's and constable's district No. 3, in Johnson County, be, and the same is hereby divided so that the following boundary shall hereafter constitute a new district, to be called district No. 7, viz.: Beginning at Sam Sagraves Mill, county line of Johnson, on lower Laurel of Blain; thence up the creek to the forks of same; thence with the dividing ridge between the two forks of said creek to the public road on Big Mudlick Creek; thence with the road to the Big Mudlick on said creek; thence crossing the creek, and with the ridge below Joseph Salyer's Jr. Branch to Big Paint Creek, crossing Big Paint Creek, and with the ridge below Ira Gullett's Branch, to the present line of district No. 3, and with said line to the county line, and with the county line to the beginning.

"2. Until changed in accordance with existing laws, the voting place in the district hereby established shall be at the house of Jackson Webb, and the voting place in district No. 3, shall be at the house of B. F. Salyer.

"3. The justices and constable now holding office in district No. 3 shall have jurisdiction over the whole of the present boundary thereof until the next regular election for such officers, when two justices and a constable shall be elected for said district No. 7."

Approved February 11, 1867.

This act was repealed March 5, 1868, and officers holding office in the original district No. 3, or "Old Flat Gap" restored to jurisdiction. (Chapter 766, Page 211, Acts 1868.)

Chapter 2131, Page 437, Acts 1869.

AN ACT passed for the benefit of Edward R. Webb, allowing him money ($48.40) for teaching in district No. 51.

Approved March 15, 1869.

Chapter 2152, Page 456, Acts 1869.

AN ACT passed directing the Secretary of State to purchase and furnish the clerks offices of Johnson County with necessary books, replacing those destroyed by armed soldiers in the late war.

Approved March 15, 1869.

Chapter 1824, Page 68, Acts 1869.

AN ACT for the benefit of the Johnson County Court.

"*Be it enacted by the General Assembly of the Commonwealth of Kentucky,* That the presiding judge of Johnson County is hereby authorized to cause to be summoned the justices of the peace for said county to attend and constitute a court; and a majority thereof shall have power to increase the county levy for the years of 1869-1870.

"2. That said court shall have the further power to levy and collect an ad valorem tax, not exceeding twenty cents upon each one hundred dollars worth of property subject to taxation in said county, for the purpose of building fireproof safes for clerks offices, and discharging the indebtedness of said county.

"3. This act shall take effect from its passage."

Approved March 9, 1869.

Chapter 554, Page 35, Acts 1870.

MARTIN COUNTY FORMED

"*Be it enacted by the General Assembly of the Commonwealth of Kentucky,* That from and after the first day of September, A.D. 1870, so much of the counties of Pike, Johnson, Floyd, and Lawrence as is included within the following boundary, is hereby erected into and established as a separate and distinct county, to be called the county of Martin, viz.: Beginning at the mouth of Big Creek in Pike County where it empties into the Tug Fork of the Big Sandy River, and to run from thence west to the dividing ridge between the dividing waters of Big Creek and Wolf Creek; thence by said dividing ridge until it strikes the dividing ridge between the waters of John's Creek and Wolf Creek; thence by the dividing ridge between the waters of John's Creek and Wolf Creek; thence by said dividing ridge so as to include all the land, waters, and tributaries of Wolf Creek and all the land, waters, and tributaries of Rockcastle Creek, to a point in said dividing ridge due north of the forks of Rockcastle Creek, at Henry Fanning's; thence by a straight line to the said forks of Rockcastle Creek; thence by a straight line to the mouth of Lick Branch, where it empties into the Tug Fork of the Big Sandy; thence with the meanders of the said Tug Fork to the place of beginning shall be one distinct county, called and known by the name of Martin."

Notwithstanding the fact that parts of Magoffin and Martin counties had now been formed out of a portion of Johnson County, there was a gradual increase in the population. In 1870, there were 1,163 white males over 21 years of age, with a total population of 7,494. Of the latter number 7,373 were white, while 37 were free colored, with 2,453 white, and 63 colored children between the ages of 6 and 20.

The value of land had increased from $1.84 per acre in 1846 to $2.81, in 1870, with a total valuation of $684,049. For the same year the county raised 5,355 pounds of tobacco, 479 tons of hay, 241,174 bushels of corn, and 8,098 bushels of wheat. The tax list for that year shows 1,225 horses, 42 mules, 4,713 cattle, and 5,042 hogs listed.

Chapter 1584, Page 110, Acts 1871.

AN ACT for the benefit of the county court clerk.

"*Whereas,* many of the papers of the Johnson circuit court are in a state of disarrangement, caused by the soldiery during the late war; *therefore, Be it enacted by the General Assembly of the Commonwealth of Kentucky,* That the clerk of the Johnson circuit court be, and he is hereby, directed to procure the necessary well bound books and indexes, and record such judgments and orders, and make such indexes as are necessary to enable litigants to more readily find their papers; and he is also directed to re-arrange, place in the proper bundle, and label such papers as may be necessary in his office: *provided* the fees of said clerk for such services, shall not exceed one hundred and fifty dollars. The County Court of Johnson County, a majority of all the justices, concurring therein, shall make said clerk a reasonable compensation for his services, in performing the work herein required of him, not, however, exceeding one hundred and fifty dollars.

"2. This act shall take effect from and after its passage."

Approved March 15, 1871.

Chapter 646, Page 121, Acts 1872.

AN ACT creating an additional justice's and constable's district.

"*Be it enacted by the General Assembly of the Commonwealth of Kentucky,* That there is hereby created and established in the county of Johnson an additional justice's and constable's district, bounded as following, viz.: Beginning on the line between the counties of Lawrence and Johnson, on the east side of Big Sandy River; thence running up said river to the mouth of Buffalo Creek; thence to the top of the dividing ridge between the waters of said Buffalo Creek and Millers Creek; thence with the dividing ridge (east) to their source; thence with the top of same ridge, being the divide between the waters of Greasy and Daniels Creek, to the Martin County line; thence with said Martin County line to the Lawrence County line; thence with the Lawrence County line to the beginning.

"The said district shall be entitled to two justices of the peace and one constable, who shall be elected on the first Saturday in May, 1872, and shall hold their offices until the next May election for justices and constables. The justices shall be commissioned as other justices, and they shall have the same power as other justices. The said district shall be called No. 8, and the voting place shall be at the school house at the mouth of Two Mile on Greasy Creek."

Chapter 859, Page 313, Acts 1872.

AN ACT to require the clerk to index certain order books and other records in his office.

"Be it enacted by the General Assembly of the Commonwealth of Kentucky, That the county court clerk of Johnson County be, and he is hereby, directed to index such order books and other records in his office, as may be directed by the judge of Johnson County Court; and when such work is completed and approved by the court, said clerk shall be entitled to a reasonable compensation for his services, to be allowed and paid out of the county levy of said county, not exceeding seventy-five dollars.

"This act shall take effect from its passage."

Approved March 27, 1872.

Chapter 973, Page 723, Acts 1876.

AN ACT for the benefit of James A. Ward, sheriff of Johnson County for the years of 1859-60-61, was passed and approved March 20, 1876, giving him two years from the latter date to collect taxes, which he had accounted and paid for personally, but had not collected.

Chapter 931, Page 434, Acts 1873.

AN ACT for the benefit of the bondsmen for Alexander W. Nickell.

"Whereas, there was a judgment in the Franklin circuit court, in favor of the Commonwealth of Kentucky, and against Alexander W. Nickell, sheriff of Johnson County for the year of 1867, and B. F. Salyer, James C. Castle, Phillip Stambaugh, Fred Stambaugh, and Benjamin Stambaugh, his securities, for the revenue of said county for the year of 1867; and

"*Whereas,* there was issued on the 16th day of July, 1869, an execution on said judgment which execution was placed in the hands of J. W. Helton, sheriff of Johnson County, who proceeded to levy the same, on the lands of the securities of said Nickell, said sheriff proceeded to sell said land levied upon, and at said sale, the Commonwealth, by her agent and attorney, John Harkins, Esq., became the purchaser, sums sufficient to satisfy said judgment and execution; and *Whereas,* it is represented that the said securities desire to redeem their said lands; for remedy whereof,

"*Be it enacted by the General Assembly of the Commonwealth of Kentucky,* That when the said B. F. Salyer shall pay into the treasury of the Commonwealth one-fifth of the amount of said judgment, interest, costs, and attorney fees, exclusive of damages, that his land sold on said execution shall stand redeemed."

2. (Is the same as above, only for James C. Cartle [Castle].)

3. (Is the same as above, only for Phillip Stambaugh.)

4. (Is the same as above, only for the benefit of Fred Stambaugh.)

5. (Is the same as above, only for the benefit of Benjamin Stambaugh.)

6. This act shall be in force from and after its passage.

Approved April 21, 1873.

Chapter 847, Page 201, Acts 1882.

AN ACT for the benefit of Green Meek.

"*Whereas,* it appears that Green Meek, deputy sheriff, in Johnson County did, in January, 1882, pursue and capture one Joseph Ward, charged in the county of Johnson with murder, and bring him to justice; and it appearing that said Ward was convicted of said charge, and is now confined in the penitentiary for life; and it appearing further that the court failed to allow said Meeks claim, because there had been no affidavit filed before the justice issuing the warrant for Ward's arrest; *Therefore, be it enacted by the General Assembly of the Commonwealth of Kentucky,* That the auditor of public accounts be, and he is hereby, directed to draw his warrant on the treasurer in favor of Green Meek for the sum of ninety-eight dollars, to be paid out of any funds in the treasury not otherwise appropriated.

"2. This act to take effect from and after its passage."

Approved April 7, 1882.

Chapter 1606, Page 1448, Acts 1884.

AN ACT passed and approved May 8, 1884, authorizing the court of claims to levy and collect an ad valorem tax, not to exceed twenty-five cents on the hundred dollars worth of taxable property.

Chapter 1628, Page 1472, Acts 1884.

AN ACT was passed for the benefit of Frank Preston, a pauper idiot, committee of George W. Hill, directing the auditor to issue warrant on the treasurer for the sum of thirty-seven dollars and fifty cents, covering the amount of Hill's claim due him. This act became a law without the signature of the Governor.

A similar act was passed for the benefit of Daniel Sparks, for keeping said Frank Preston, February 29, 1888. It also was without the approval of the Governor.

Chapter 469, Page 27, Acts 1888, is AN ACT to incorporate Chestnut Grove Church in Johnson County, with G. W. Butler, W. J. McKenzie, and W. B. Rice as trustees.

Chapter 1266, Page 495, Acts 1888.

AN ACT passed and approved April 25, 1888, to provide for the holding of primary elections in the county, and regulating the conditions under which they were held, making it unlawful for anyone to bet or falsely certify to any fact, or to offer to influence the vote of another by the use of money.

Chapter 1334, Page 109, Acts 1888.

AN ACT to change the holding of criminal court.

"Be it enacted by the General Assembly of the Commonwealth of Kentucky:

"That the Johnson Criminal Court shall begin on the Monday succeeding the termination of the Floyd Criminal Court and continue six judicial days.

"2. That all acts touching the holding of said court inconsistent with this act are hereby repealed.

"3. This act shall take effect from and after July 1, 1888."

Approved April 30, 1888.

Chapter 932, Page 1056, Acts 1890.

A rather lengthy act was passed and approved April 19, 1890, authorizing the County Court of Levy and Claims to issue and sell bonds, and provide payment of same, for the purpose of building a court house, jail and clerk's office; and for the appointment of a county treasurer. It specified that the amount was not to exceed thirty-five thousand dollars, in denominations of not less than one hundred nor more than one thousand dollars, payable in not less than five or more than twenty years; required that a commissioner and receiver be appointed to collect the tax, which was not to exceed twenty-five cents on the hundred dollars, to receive the money obtained by the sale of the bonds, and to restrict their preparation.

This act also provided for the appointment of a county treasurer, beginning with October, 1890, and every four years thereafter, whose duty it was to receive all money ordered into his hands belonging to the county; said treasurer to file bond in excess of all money that is likely to come into his hands.

Pursuant to the above act, the county court house was built in 1892, during the administration of J. K. Dixon who was county

JOHNSON COUNTY'S CAPITOL—THE COURT HOUSE AT PAINTSVILLE

judge at that time, and under the supervision of Frank P. Milburn, famous architect. The building was considered one of the best, and the last word in architecture in its day, and has stood the test of time. The brick used in the building was manufactured on the ground, as the work progressed, and the stone was taken from local quarries and cut by hand. It stands today as an example of the durability of the local building material.

As the State constitution again changed in 1891, shifting most of the official duties to the county courts, no legislative acts, in general, are included after that date.

Another tax list for the year 1890 is shown in the following pages to give the reader an idea who was in our county a generation ago. The original spelling has been retained in most cases.

GOVERNMENT

TAX LIST FOR THE YEAR OF 1890

Ackerman, Samuel
Ackerman, Samuel Jr.
Adams, David B.
Adams, Douglas
Adams, Green F.
Adams, Haden
Adams, Hardin
Adams, Harmon
Adams, H. N.
Adams, James
Adams, James H.
Adams, Joel
Adams, Joseph D.
Adams, Thomas
Adams, William
Adkins, Levi
Adkins, Thomas J.
Akers, George
Akers, James E.
Akers, James H.
Akers, John
Akers, John C.
Akers, John R.
Akers, Mack
Akers, M. L.
Akers, Nancy
Akers, Reuben B.
Akers, Samuel K.
Akers, Thomas G.
Akers, Walter S.
Akers, William R.
Allen, G. J.
Alley, Rebecca
Amos, James
Anderson, William W.
Armantrout, John
Armantrout, Leander
Armes, Elias
Arms, A. C.
Arms, Elijah B.
Arms, Henry
Arms, Samiel R.
Arms, Wallis B.
Arms, William M.
Arrowood, Garrett
Arrowood, George W.
Arrowood, James M.
Arrowood, John
Arrowood, John J.
Astrop, Albert
Astrop, Sidney
Atkenson, William T.
Auxier, Agnes
Auxier, Alvin E.
Auxier, George W.
Auxier, Henry J.
Auxier, J. C. B.
Auxier, John B.
Auxier, J. K. P.
Auxier, Joseph S.
Auxier, Nathaniel L.
Auxier, Samiel R.
Auxier, Thomas J.
Auxier, William L.
Bailey, Andrew H.
Bailey, David B.
Bailey, Jefferson D.
Bailey, John R.
Bailey, N. H.
Bailey, Thomas
Bailey, Thomas M.
Bailey, Thomas W.
Bailey, Wales W.
Bailey, W. H.
Baldridge, Andrew J.
Baldridge, Henry B.
Baldridge, Lilburn
Baldridge, Thomas
Baldridge, William
Baldwin, William A. Jr.
Baldwin, William A. Sr.
Ball, Enoch
Banfield, Allen
Barker, John C.
Barker, John D.
Barker, J. Smith
Barnes, James E.
Bayes, David S.
Bayes, Eligo
Bayes, Eliphur D.
Bayes, Filmore
Bayes, Francis Marion
Bayes, George A.
Bayes, James J.
Bayes, John W.
Bayes, J. W.
Bayes, Leander
Bayes, Nathaniel L.
Bayes, Samuel
Bayes, Samuel B.
Bayes, William
Belcher, Alexander
Bevins, John
Bickford, George R.
Bishop, Claybourn W.
Blair, Alamander
Blair, Amos B.
Blair, Andrew J.
Blair, Britton J.
Blair, Eda
Blair, Edward
Blair, Frank
Blair, George
Blair, Harrison
Blair, Harry P.
Blair, Jackson
Blair, James
Blair, James F.
Blair, James G.
Blair, James Henry C.
Blair, Jesse
Blair, J. H.
Blair, John
Blair, John F.
Blair, John M.
Blair, John P.
Blair, Lavis G.
Blair, Leander
Blair, Levy
Blair, Lewis
Blair, Samuel
Blair, Sarah Ann
Blair, Wallace B.
Blair, William P. J.
Blair, William S.
Bland, John W.
Blanton, George W.
Blanton, Gilbert
Blanton, Henry
Blanton, Jack
Blanton, James H.
Blanton, James M.
Blanton, James P.
Blanton, Jesse
Blanton, John A.
Blanton, John E.
Blanton, John M.
Blanton, Mastin
Blanton, Santford
Blanton, William
Blanton, William A.
Blessing, Thomas J.
Blevins, Alvis
Blevins, Andrew J.
Blevins, Elisha
Blevins, James
Blevins, John
Blevins, J. T.
Blevins, Luke
Blevins, Robert
Blevins, Samuel
Blevins, Solomon
Blevins, W. B.
Blevins, William
Blevins, William B.
Boggs, James M.
Boggs, William G.
Bolling, Jeff. Davis
Bolling, Seymour
Bond, Stephen P.
Booth, George W.
Booth, Luke L.
Booth, Marion

Booth, Valentine
Booth, William
Borders, Henry Allen
Borders, John
Borders, Joseph
Borders, Wallis
Borders, William
Bow, Andrew J.
Bow, James A.
Bowens, Andrew
Bowens, Daniel
Bowens, Elijah
Bowens, George W.
Bowens, James
Bowens, John W.
Bowlen, Columbus
Bowlen, William
Boyd, George W.
Boyd, Jackson
Boyd, John
Boyd, Monterville
Boyd, Reuben
Boyd, William D.
Bradley, Millard F.
Brafford, Minta E.
Branham, Andrew J.
Briant (O'Briant), Wm. P.
Brint (Briant), James F.
Brint, Valentine
Brint, William H.
Brooks, George
Brown, Annie
Brown, Arch
Brown, Beauregard
Brown, Canada
Brown, David K.
Brown, Elijah
Brown, Elizabeth
Brown, F. A.
Brown, George W.
Brown, George W.
Brown, Gideonroark
Brown, Henry C.
Brown, James
Brown, James B.
Brown, Jerry
Brown, J. H.
Brown, John
Brown, John C.
Brown, John M.
Brown, John P.
Brown, Joseph
Brown, Larkin
Brown, Lewis W.
Brown, Thomas
Brown, Thomas C.
Brown, Wallis M.
Brown, W. W.

Brummett, Calvin W.
Brummett, Nathan
Buniard, John T.
Burchett, Andrew
Burchett, David
Burchett, E. E.
Burchett, Henry
Burchett, James M.
Burchett, Landrum
Burchett, Leonard
Burchett, Thomas
Burchett, Thomas J.
Burchett, William J.
Burchett, William W.
Burgess, James E.
Burke (Burks), Isaac
Burke (Burks), John
Burke (Burks), Owen
Burton, James
Burton, Ora F.
Burton, Thomas
Bush, Charley
Butcher, Allen
Butcher, Francis M.
Butcher, George W.
Butcher, Henderson H.
Butcher, Henry
Butcher, James W.
Butcher, Louise
Butcher, Marcus L.
Butcher, Richard E.
Butcher, Simon
Butcher, William
Butler, Colfax
Butler, Eda E.
Butler, Garfield
Butler, George W.
Butler, John
Butler, John P.
Butler, Minta
Butler, Robert P.
Calwell, Crud
Calwell, William L.
Cantrell, Benjamin
Cantrell, Henry
Cantrell, James
Cantrell, John R.
Cantrell, Noah
Cantrell, William
Carlisle, John G.
Carpenter, James
Castle, Allen
Castle, Amos
Castle, Anderson
Castle, Andrew
Castle, Andy
Castle, Benjamin F.
Castle, Beverly L.
Castle, Charles
Castle, Charles J.

Castle, Daniel
Castle, Drewery P.
Castle, Edward
Castle, Eli
Castle, Emery
Castle, Francis M.
Castle, George F.
Castle, Grandville
Castle, Harrison C.
Castle, Henderson S.
Castle, Hezekiah
Castle, Israel
Castle, Jackson
Castle, Jacob
Castle, James (Dist. No. 1)
Castle, James
Castle, James
Castle, James A. (Dist. No. 10)
Castle, James G.
Castle, James M.
Castle, Jefferson
Castle, John
Castle, John S.
Castle, John W.
Castle, Joseph M.
Castle, J. W.
Castle, Lafe
Castle, Lewis M.
Castle, Lonzo
Castel, Lucy
Castle, Malinda
Castle, Mantford
Castle, Marcum
Castle, Marion (Dist. No. 5)
Castle, Marion
Castle, Martin
Castle, Matilda
Castle, Miles H.
Castle, Moses
Castle, Noah
Castle, Roscoe
Castle, Thomas
Castle, Thomas
Castle, Ward
Castle, William
Castle, William
Castle, William (I. S.'s Son)
Castle, William S.
Castle, Willis
Castle, Zachariah
Caudill, Amos H.
Caudill, Athol
Caudill, Ben F.
Caudill, C. E.
Caudill, Daniel
Caudill, Edmond

GOVERNMENT 117

Caudill, Elizabeth
Caudill, Harmon D.
Caudill, Henry
Caudill, Jessie
Caudill, John
Caudill, Mary Ann
Caudill, Mathew
Caudill, Mathew J.
Caudill, Wesley
Caudill, William
Caudill, Wm. (Dist. No. 1)
Caudill, Winston
Caverns, George W.
Cazee, John
Chandler, Catherine
Chandler, George
Chandler, George W.
Chandler, Henry
Chandler, Isaac
Chandler, James
Chandler, John
Chandler, Lafayette
Chandler, Susan
Chapman, John
Chatman, Greenville
Cheek, Edward C.
Cheek, James W.
Childers, Albert
Childers, Perry (Tip)
Christian, Lewis
Clark, Calwell
Clark, Henry
Clark, James H.
Clark, Manuel R.
Clark, Rulford
Clark, Samuel
Clark, Wesley M.
Clark, William
Clay, Daniel P.
Clay, John M.
Coakley, Harkles
Cochran, James L. Sr.
Coldiron, William
Collier, Nelson
Collins, Andrew B.
Collins, Andrew J.
Collins, Charles N.
Collins, David
Collins, Enoch
Collins, Garfield
Collins, George A.
Collins, Isaac N.
Collins, James M.
Collins, James R.
Collins, Peter
Collins, Peter (Dist. No. 5)
Collins, Samuel J.
Collins, Wallas N.
Collins, William
Collins, William P.
Collins, Wiley M.
Collinsworth, Wm. A.
Columbus, George
Columbus, John
Columbus, Rhoda
Columbus, Ulyssus
Colvin, Isaac
Colvin, Jackson
Colvin, Jefferson B.
Colvin, Montford
Colvin, Riley
Colvin, William
Combs, Calvin
Combs, Elbert S.
Combs, William
Conley, Benjamin F.
Conley, B. H.
Conley, Burns
Conley, C. C.
Conley, David J.
Conley, Edmund
Conley, Francis M.
Conley, Frank P.
Conley, George W.
Conley, German W.
Conley, H. B.
Conley, Henry C.
Conley, Henry J.
Conley, H. F.
Conley, Hiram
Conley, James L.
Conley, James M.
Conley, James R.
Conley, John (Dist. No. 1)
Conley, John
Conley, John A.
Conley, John C. N.
Conley, John E.
Conley, John M.
Conley, John W.
Conley, Linsey
Conley, Marion Francis
Conley, Martin V.
Conley, Mason
Conley, Millard
Conley, Morris L.
Conley, Mosy A.
Conley, Sidney
Conley, Stephen M.
Conley, Thomas
Conley, Thomas J.
Conley, Thomas M.
Conley, William
Conley, William J.
Conley, William M.
Conley, W. T. S.
Cook, James
Cooper, Cashius M.
Cooper, Thomas
Cornmel, John
Cox, A. S.
Cox, Harmon
Cox, Moses F.
Crace, Peter
Crace, William
Craft, Benjamin
Craft, Henderson
Craiger, Thomas
Crider, Alfred
Crislip, Abraham R.
Crislip, Edward E.
Crislip, George
Crumb, James B.
Crumb, John W.
Crumb, William
Cumbo, Calvin
Cumpton, James H.
Cunningham, George
Cunningham, Samuel P.
Dale, Daniel B.
Damson, Alexander
Daniels, Albert
Daniels, Alfonzo
Daniels, Basil
Daniels, Dave
Daniels, David
Daniels, David
Daniels, David J.
Daniels, David K.
Daniels, Edward
Daniels, Emeline
Daniels, Flem C.
Daniels, Fred
Daniels, George (Dist. No. 1)
Daniels, George
Daniels, George W.
Daniels, George W. (Dist. No. 5)
Daniels, Greenville
Daniels, Harry A.
Daniels, Henry
Daniels, Isom (Dist. No. 2)
Daniels, Isom
Daniels, Isom Jr.
Daniels, Isom P.
Daniels, James
Daniels, James (Dist. No. 7)
Daniels, James H.
Daniels, James M.
Daniels, Jesse
Daniels, Jesse H.
Daniels, John H.
Daniels, John R.

Daniels, John V.
Daniels, John W.
Daniels, Joseph
Daniels, Joseph (Dist. No. 5)
Daniels, Josh
Daniels, Mary J.
Daniels, Milroy
Daniels, Peter
Daniels, Pitman
Daniels, Solomon
Daniels, Thomas P.
Daniels, Ulysses G.
Daniels, Valentine
Daniels, Wayne
Daniels, Wiley
Daniels, William (Dist. No. 1)
Daniels, William (Dist. No. 3)
Daniels, Winfield
Daniels, Winston
Daniels, Wyatt
Davidson, Isaac
Davis, Bracken L.
Davis, Charley
Davis, Dan
Davis, Eleckish P. (Leck)
Davis, Enoch
Davis, George W. (Wash)
Davis, Harvey C.
Davis, Henry
Davis, Henry (Dist. No. 4)
Davis, Isaac
Davis, James
Davis, James M.
Davis, John D.
Davis, John W.
Davis, Joseph
Davis, Lee
Davis, Lewis B.
Davis, Mary C.
Davis, R. L.
Davis, Roscoe
Davis, Telitha
Davis, William
Davis, William J.
Davis, William L.
Davis, William P.
Dawson, William
Day, William T.
Dials, John
Dickerson, Thomas
Dills, Emmet
Dills, George W.
Dills, James Jr.
Dills, James M.
Dills, Noah
Dills, William
Dixon, Alonzo
Dixon, Andrew F.
Dixon, Henry F.
Dixon, Isaac
Dixon, Joseph K.
Dixon, Thomas P.
Dollarhide, Harry
Dollarhide, Winfield
Dorton, William H.
Duncan, John M.
Duncan, Maston T.
Dutton, George
Dutton, James
Dutton, William
Duty, David
Duty, Noah B.
Dye, J. F.
Dyles, Nancy
Dyles, William D.
Edgarton, James
Edgarton, Lee
Edwards, John W.
Elliott, Abram M.
Elliott, James
Elliott, Nancy J.
Elliott, Peter G.
Elric, Bradley
Ellwood, Robert
Ely, David A.
Ely, Elizabeth
Ely, Samuel J.
Ely, Scott
Ely, William
Epling, John B.
Estep, A. J.
Estep, Alamander
Estep, C. H.
Estep, Eliga
Estep, Francis
Estep, George
Estep, Harry
Estep, Hiram
Estep, James (Dist. No. 2)
Estep, James
Estep, John
Estep, Joseph
Estep, Lilburn
Estep, Lucinda
Estep, Martin
Estep, Richard
Estep, Samuel
Estep, S. J.
Estep, William H.
Estep, William W.
Evans, Mairda H.
Evans, Marion
Evens, Ellousy
Evins, Mary A.
Evins, Warren
Fairchild, Abner
Fairchild, Andrew J.
Fairchild, Asa
Fairchild, Benjamin C.
Fairchild, Charley
Fairchild, David A.
Fairchild, D. J.
Fairchild, Eli W.
Fairchild, Grant
Fairchild, James
Fairchild, James H.
Fairchild, Jessie
Fairchild, John
Fairchild, John M.
Fairchild, John R.
Fairchild, Joseph
Fairchild, Levi
Fairchild, Lewis G.
Fairchild, L. G.
Fairchild, M. S.
Fairchild, R. A.
Fairchild, Sarah
Fairchild, Shadrack
Fairchild, Susan
Fairchild, Thomas
Fairchild, Thomas A.
Fairchild, William
Fairchild, William F.
Fannin, Cullen
Fannin, John
Fannin, Nancie Hattie
Fannin, Samuel
Farmer, John W.
Ferguson, David H.
Ferguson, James P.
Ferguson, L. P.
Ferguson, T. M.
Fields, Elijah
Fife, A. J.
Fife, Felix
Fife, James H.
Fife, M. F.
Fife, S. H.
Fife, William H. H.
Fifer, ———
Fillips, William
Fitch, Henry
Fitch, Isaac H.
Fitch, James M.
Fitch, Louisa J.
Fitch, Mandy
Fitchpatrick, Abraham
Fitchpatrick, Albert
Fitchpatrick, Charles
Fitchpatrick, Charles P.
Fitchpatrick, Charley
Fitchpatrick, James
Fitchpatrick, Jeremiah

GOVERNMENT

Fitchpatrick, John
Fitchpatrick, John C.
Fitchpatrick, John M.
Fitchpatrick, Mary
Fitchpatrick, Saviler
Fletcher, Walter
Fletcher, Winston
Ford, Martin Luther
Fox, Andrew J.
Fraley, George W.
Fraley, John W.
Fraley, Joseph L.
Franklin, Abe
Franklin, A. W.
Franklin, James L.
Frazier, Dollie A.
Frazier, Haden
Frazier, James
Frazier, John
Frazier, S. V.
Frazier, William J.
Freeman, James
Freeman, William
Freziel, Martin L.
Gambill, Alafax
Gambill, John
Gambill, Nathan H.
Gamble, C. J.
Gamble, Elijah H.
Gardner, William
Garter, Richard
George, Cornelius
George, Robert M.
Gibbs, Abraham
Gibbs, Sheridan
Gilbum, Isaac
Gilmore, John
Gilson, Frank
Glizzee, Nathaniel
Gobble, Christopher
Gobble, George
Gobble, J. M.
Goble, William A.
Golden, David
Green, Andrew J.
Green, George
Green, George (Dist. No. 1)
Green, G. W.
Green, Henry G.
Green, James M.
Green, Jemima
Green, John
Green, John W.
Green, Martin
Green, Martin L.
Green, Tilman
Green, Walin
Green, William
Green, Winfield S.

Greer, James F.
Greer, Moses H.
Greer, William W.
Grim, Benjamin H.
Grim, Benjamin Jr.
Grim, Charles J.
Grim, Charles J. Jr.
Grim, Francis
Grim, Harrison
Grim, John
Grim, John B.
Grim, John F.
Grim, John F. (Dist. No. 3)
Grim, Marion
Grim, Martha
Grim, Samuel
Grim, William W.
Gullett, David A.
Gullett, Ezekiel
Gullett, Ira
Gullett, James
Gullett, Jane
Gullett, J. M. E.
Gullett, Josephus
Hackworth, Samuel
Hackworth, William
Hager, B. F.
Hager, Dan M.
Hager, David
Hager, D. Mart
Hager, Edward D.
Hager, George
Hager, James
Hager, James H.
Hager, John L.
Hager, S. P.
Hall, Adam
Hall, Andrew
Hall, Calloway
Hall, Charley
Hall, David B.
Hall, Grant
Hall, Green W.
Hall, Jackson
Hall, James F.
Hall, James L.
Hall, James P.
Hall, Jason
Hall, Jesse
Hall, John H.
Hall, John M.
Hall, Lon
Hall, Nann
Hall, Tobbert
Hall, Willis
Hall, Wilson
Hamilton, Ben R.
Hamilton, David H.
Hamilton, Frank P.

Hamilton, Henry
Hamilton, H. H.
Hamilton, John
Hamilton, M. M.
Hamilton, Zepheniah
Hampton, Jesse
Hampton, John
Hampton, William H.
Hannah, Andy
Hannah, Ebenezer
Hannah, George W.
Hannah, Harmon
Hannah, Mantford
Hannah, Samuel
Hannah, William R.
Harmon, Ad
Harmon, Adam
Harmon, Henry J.
Harmon, Mathias
Harold, Elizabeth
Harris, B. H.
Harris, David G.
Harris, Elbert
Harris, James A.
Harris, John W.
Harrison, John
Hay, Lottie
Helton, George C.
Helton, J. B.
Herndon, Henry Clay
Hill, Andrew J.
Hill, John P.
Hill, Lafayette
Hiram, Reed
Hitchcock, Benjamin
Hitchcock, Daniel
Hitchcock, Elijah
Hitchcock, Garfield
Hitchcock, George W.
Hitchcock, General
Hitchcock, James M.
Hitchcock, J. B.
Hitchcock, Jeff
Hitchcock, J. R.
Hitchcock, Nimrod
Hite, Sherman
Hoge, Albert
Holbrook, Cammel
Holbrook, David
Holbrook, George
Holbrook, H. D.
Holbrook, James H.
Holbrook, John
Holbrook, John D.
Holbrook, J. R.
Holbrook, Larkin
Holbrook, Loronzo D.
Honeycut, Andrew P.
Honeycut, Esom

Honeycut, John R.
Honeycut, Mary
Honeycut, Nathan
Honeycut, William
Hopkins, Allice G.
Hopson, F. W.
Hopson, John D.
Horn, James L.
Horn, John W.
Horn, Thomas
Howe, James Henry
Howes, E. F.
Howes, George W.
Howes, Henry J.
Howes, Henry S.
Howes, Millard
Howes, Turner
Howes, William H.
Huff, Albert F.
Huff, German W.
Huff, Paulina
Hughes, James P.
Hughes, John A.
Hughes, John M.
Hughes, Mathias
Hunt, Elijah
Hurley, Mary
Hurt, James
Hurt, Joseph
Hurt, William H.
Hyatt, Robert
Hyden, Henry
Hyden, Samuel
Hyden, William
Isaac, Jemima C.
Isaac, John
Isbel, Jasper
Ivans, James H.
Jackson, Elisha
Jackson, Gabiel
Jackson, Hamilton H.
Jackson, Henderson
Jackson, James T.
Jackson, William
Jayne, David
Jayne, Henry
Jayne, Julia
Jayne, William
Jenkins, James P.
Jenkins, Juda
Johnson, C. C.
Johnson, Enoch
Johnson, Eperson
Johnson, George W.
Johnson, James
Johnson, Joe D.
Johnson, John
Johnson, Levi
Johnson, Richard
Johnson, Robert
Johnson, Sampson J.
Johnson, Thomas
Johnson, William
Johnson, William H.
Jones, Brownlow
Jones, L. B.
Jones, Lemuel
Jones, William
Jones, William P.
Justice, Andrew
Justice, Clifton
Justice, E. B.
Justice, Samuel
Justice, Scott
Justice, Sherman
Justice, William
Kazee, Elias L.
Kazee, Harrison
Keeze, George W.
Keeze, Sarahan
Kelly, George
Kelly, George W.
Kelly, Henry
Kelly, John
Kelly, John C.
Kelly, John S.
Kelly, Mathias J.
Kelly, Peter
Kelly, S. L.
Kelly, Wales
Kelly, William H.
Kertis (Curtis), James
Kimble, George W. H.
Kimbler, Francis
Kimbler, John W.
Kimbler, Silas
Kimbleton, Preston H.
King, Samuel P.
King, Thomas
King, William
King, Wm. (Dist. No. 5)
Kirk, Thomas L.
Kirtner, Louisa
Lambert, James
Lavender, Elijah
Lavender, John
Layne, B. H.
Lee, David F.
Lemaster, Annie
Lemaster, B. L.
Lemaster, Daniel
Lemaster, Daniel P.
Lemaster Darcus
Lemaster, D. B.
Lemaster, E. G.
Lemaster, Elijah G.
Lemaster, Ellen
Lemaster, Elnor J.
Lemaster, E. W.
Lemaster, Francis
Lemaster, Frank
Lemaster, Franklin N.
Lemaster, George O.
Lemaster, Henry J.
Lemaster, Henry R.
Lemaster, Isaac
Lemaster, James
Lemaster, James B.
Lemaster, James C.
Lemaster, James H.
Lemaster, James L.
Lemaster, James M.
Lemaster, James W.
Lemaster, Jessie
Lemaster, J. L.
Lemaster, John
Lemaster, John M.
Lemaster, John R.
Lemaster, John W.
Lemaster, Lafe
Lemaster, Lewis
Lemaster, Marion
Lemaster, Mary
Lemaster, Nancy E.
Lemaster, Rebecca
Lemaster, R. M.
Lemaster, Samson
Lemaster, Thomas
Lemaster, William
Lemaster, William D.
Lemaster, William F.
Lemaster, William H.
Lemaster, William J.
Lemaster, William L.
Lemaster, William R.
Lemaster, William R. F.
Leslie, Amanda
Leslie, Amos S.
Lewis, John
Litteral (Littrell), Daniel
Litteral (Littrell), Fleming M.
Litteral (Littrell), Francis M.
Litteral (Littrell), Harry
Litteral (Littrell), Harry B.
Litteral (Littrell), Henry H.
Litteral (Littrell), James H.
Litteral (Littrell), Lindsey
Litteral (Littrell), Minyard

Litteral (Littrell), Riley
Litteral (Littrell), Samuel
Litteral (Littrell), William E.
Long, Abraham
Long, Joel D.
Long, John R.
Long, Joseph
Long, Milton
Long, Rebecca
Long, Samuel M.
Long, W. W.
Low, Amos
Lucas, R. C.
Lucas, Robert
Luster, Jefferson
Lyons, Amous
Lyons, David L.
Lyons, Edward
Lyons, George
Lyons, Haden
Lyons, Henry
Lyons, James
Lyons, Jessie
Lyons, John
Lyons, Santford
Mahan, Amanda
Mahan, Gines
Mahan, Henry
Mahan, Joseph H.
Mahan, Mace M.
Mahan, William
Mahan, William R.
Marrs, William A.
Marshall, George
Marshall, James
May, Grant
May, Henry C.
May, Samuel D.
May, Samuel E.
May, Thomas G.
May, Thomas H.
May, William W.
Mayo, John C. C.
Mayo, John W.
Mayo, William
McCarty, D. J.
McCarty, James H.
McCarty, John C. B.
McCarty, Nelson
McCarty, Wiley
McCarty, William W.
McCloud, George
McCloud, John
McClure, Millard F.
McCurry, Lewis C.
McDowel, James
McDowel, Milton
McFaddin, Isaac
McFarland, William
McGuire, John A.
McKay, Harrison
McKenzie, Aaran
McKenzie, Andrew J.
McKenzie, B. H.
McKenzie, E. H.
McKenzie, Elisha M.
McKenzie, Elizabeth
McKenzie, Elzy
McKenzie, George N.
McKenzie, George W.
McKenzie, Henry
McKenzie, Jackson
McKenzie, J. D.
McKenzie, Jessie
McKenzie, John
McKenzie, John H.
McKenzie, John P.
McKenzie, Johnson
McKenzie, Joseph
McKenzie, Julia D.
McKenzie, Lafayette
McKenzie, Lamuel M.
McKenzie, Linsey
McKenzie, Marion
McKenzie, Martin B.
McKenzie, Martin L.
McKenzie, Martin M.
McKenzie, Nancy J.
McKenzie, Olive B.
McKenzie, Reuben
McKenzie, Samuel G.
McKenzie, Samuel M.
McKenzie, Samuel P.
McKenzie, Sherman
McKenzie, Sorrena
McKenzie, Thomas F.
McKenzie, Thomas J.
McKenzie, Wallace
McKenzie, William
McKenzie, William B.
McKenzie, William H.
McKenzie, William J.
McKenzie, William W.
Meade, Henry P.
Meade, Levi
Meade, R. G.
Meade, Robert
Meadows, Simeon
Meadows, William
Meddaugh (Middaugh), Elisha
Meddaugh (Middaugh), G. C. (Craig)
Meddaugh (Middaugh), John
Medley, William
Meek, Aaron
Meek, Cornelius
Meek, Elias
Meek, Green
Meek, H. J.
Meek, James
Meek, Jasper
Meek, Jessie
Meek, John
Meek, Nathan
Meek, William B.
Meek, Winfield S.
Meek, Zephaniah
Melvin, Andy
Melvin, George
Melvin, John
Melvin, William
Middaugh (Meddaugh), Elisha
Middaugh (Meddaugh), G. C.
Middaugh (Meddaugh), John
Milem, Henry J.
Milem, James H.
Milem, James Jr.
Milem, John
Milem, Samuel
Milem, Samuel (Dist. No. 1)
Miller, Leander
Miller, Reese M.
Moles, Francis M.
Mollett, Benjamin
Mollett, David
Mollett, Elias B.
Mollett, George W.
Mollett, John B.
Mollett, John C.
Mollett, John R.
Mollett, Levi
Mollett, Margaret C.
Mollett, Shadrach W.
Mollett, William E.
Mollett, William T.
Moore, Elzy
Moore, George
Moore, George K.
Moore, Henry C.
Moore, John
Moore, John F.
Mullins, John
Mullins, William
Murchant, Kistner
Murphy, Henry
Murphy, James
Murphy, J. C.
Murphy, John
Murphy, Marion F.
Murphy, Robert A.

Murphy, William J.
Murray, Catherine
Murray, Dicy
Murray, Fred
Murray, George W.
Murray, Henry
Murray, Jane
Murray, Jessie
Murray, John
Murray, Jonathan
Murray, Kenos
Murray, Lewis W.
Murray, R. H.
Murray, Rhoderich H.
Murray, Rhoderich Jr.
Murray, Samuel Sr.
Murray, Samuel
Murray, Samuel R.
Murray, Samuel S.
Murray, Wash. L.
Murray, William R.
Music, Abra'm
Music, Charley H.
Music, David E.
Music, James
Music, John
Music, John A.
Music, John W.
Music, Michael F.
Music, Milton
Music, Newton
Music, William
Myers, John
Neibert, James N.
Newsom, Hart
Newsom, Jackson
Newsom, James
Nickell, George J.
Nickell, John M.
Nickell, Millard F.
Nickell, Nancy J.
Nickell, Stanton P.
Nickell, Valentine
O'Bryan, Henry
O'Bryan, James
O'Bryan, James H.
O'Bryan, John
O'Bryan, John H.
O'Bryan, Mantford C.
Osborn, Alfred
Osborn, C. A.
Osborn, Calvin
Osborn, David
Osborn, James
Osborn, John L.
Osborn, Marion
Osborn, Thomas
Osborn, Thomas R.
Oston (Austin), Isom
Owens, Will

Pack, Aaran
Pack, Allen
Pack, Bartley
Pack, Charles
Pack, Dorcas
Pack, Ephriam
Pack, Garfield
Pack, George W.
Pack, Harrison
Pack, John
Pack, Julina
Pack, Marion
Pack, Sherman
Pack, Stanley
Pack, William
Paine, George W.
Painly, Thomas J.
Patrick, Charles N.
Patrick, Herrod
Patrick, James M.
Patrick, J. P.
Patrick, Leander
Patrick, Reuben
Patrick, Samuel
Patrick, Samuel H.
Patrick, Merida
Patrick, Noah
Pay, Gabandee
Pelphry, Clarke
Pelphry, Daniel
Pelphry, Eliphus D.
Pelphry, James W.
Pelphry, Jefferson
Pelphry, John
Pelphry, Mathew
Pelphry, Samuel H.
Pelphry, William R.
Pendleton, Armintie
Pendleton, Charles M.
Pendleton, Ira W.
Pendleton, Samuel
Penix, Allen
Penix, John
Penix, Lafe G.
Penix, Lee
Pennington, George
Pennington, George W.
Pennington, James
Pennington, Jessie
Pennington, John
Pennington, Josh
Pennington, Levi
Penny, Andy
Penny, Sherman
Penson (Pinson), Elinden
Penson (Pinson), Harkness
Perkey (Purkey), Franklin

Perkey (Purkey), George C.
Perkey (Purkey), Robert
Perkins, George
Perry, George C.
Perry, George H.
Perry, George W.
Perry, Haden
Perry, John
Perry Mitchel
Perry, T. M.
Perry, William
Perry, William E.
Phelps, A. L.
Phelps, Thomas
Phillips, William
Picklesimer, B. F.
Picklesimer, Francis M.
Picklesimer, Hamilton
Picklesimer, I. J.
Picklesimer, John H.
Picklesimer, Nathaniel
Picklesimer, Phillip
Picklesimer, Samuel
Picklesimer, Thomas
Picklesimer, William
Porter, Canada L.
Porter, William E.
Powers, George
Powers, William
Pratt, Benjamin F.
Preston, Anderson B.
Preston, Angeline
Preston, Charley
Preston, C. M.
Preston, Cyrus M.
Preston, Daniel E.
Preston, Daniel L.
Preston, Edgar
Preston, Eliphus
Preston, Eliphus E.
Preston, Emanuel E.
Preston, Etchison
Preston, Francis M.
Preston, Frank
Preston, Frank H.
Preston, George
Preston, George W.
Preston, G. L.
Preston, Henry
Preston, Hereford
Preston, Isaac
Preston, James B.
Preston, James C.
Preston, James F.
Preston, James H.
Preston, James M.
Preston, Jemima
Preston, Jessie

GOVERNMENT

Preston, John
Preston, John D.
Preston, Jonathan
Preston, Lafayette
Preston, Lewis
Preston, L. T.
Preston, Lucinda
Preston, Martin
Preston, McClellan
Preston, M. G.
Preston, Monterville
Preston, Nathaniel
Preston, Patrick
Preston, Roscoe
Preston, Samuel
Preston, Samuel M.
Preston, Samuel S.
Preston, Santford
Preston, Sarah E.
Preston Shadrach
Preston, Steven G.
Preston, Thomas J.
Preston, Vina
Preston, William
Preston Wm. (Dist. No. 3)
Preston, William A.
Preston, Winfield
Preston, W. W.
Preston, Zina
Price, Bishop
Price, Fairway
Price, Frank
Price, Hamilton
Price, James M.
Price, M. L.
Price, N. K.
P'Simer, David
P'Simer, John M.
Puckett, James
Puckett, Wm. Ira
Purkey (Perkey), Franklin
Purkey (Perkey), George C.
Purkey, Robert
Ramey, Charley
Ramey, Ely
Ramey, George
Ramey, Henry C.
Ramey, James M.
Ramey, Joseph F.
Ramey, Sherman
Ramey, Thomas
Randolph, B. P.
Randolph, John B.
Randolph, William N.
Ratcliff, Ely
Ratcliff, Henry
Ratcliff, John
Ratcliff, William
Ratliff, Allen
Ratliff, Andrew
Ratliff, Harvey
Ratliff, James H.
Ratliff, William H.
Reed, A. J. N.
Reed, Andrew
Reed, Asa J.
Reed, Ben F.
Reed, Daniel B.
Reed, Daniel N.
Reed, George W.
Reed, John E.
Reed, Lydia
Reed, Sarah M.
Reed, William
Reed, William H.
Reffet, James G.
Reffet, Robert
Rice, A. J.
Rice, Alexander L.
Rice, Andrew J.
Rice, Andrew W.
Rice, Armstrong
Rice, Benjamin F.
Rice, Charles L.
Rice, Charley
Rice, Clint
Rice, Daniel
Rice, Daniel J.
Rice, Elizabeth
Rice, E. M.
Rice, George
Rice, George (4th Dist.)
Rice, George B.
Rice, George W.
Rice, George Win
Rice, German W.
Rice, Gilson P.
Rice, Grant
Rice, Green V.
Rice, Greenville
Rice, Hamilton
Rice, Harrison
Rice, Harvey B.
Rice, Henry H.
Rice, Henry M.
Rice, Isaac
Rice, Isaac (Dist. No. 1)
Rice, Isaac B.
Rice, James
Rice, James A.
Rice, James F.
Rice, James H.
Rice, James W.
Rice, Jessie
Rice, John
Rice, John J.
Rice, John R.
Rice, J. P.
Rice, Martin N.
Rice, Martin R.
Rice, Nancy
Rice, Nancy J.
Rice, Nathaniel J.
Rice, Patrick G.
Rice, Samuel
Rice, Samuel G.
Rice, Samuel J.
Rice, Samuel M.
Rice, Samuel R.
Rice, Sherman
Rice, Smith
Rice, Thomas J.
Rice, Wallis B.
Rice, Wiley
Rice, W. J.
Rice, William M. (Dist. No. 1)
Rice, William M. (Dist. No. 4)
Richardson, George S.
Richmond, James
Richmond, John
Richmond, Samuel
Riggley, John
Riggley, Thomas
Riggsby, John
Riggsby, John W.
Riggsby, Lewis M.
Riggsby, Squire
Riggsby, William F.
Rittenhouse, J. S.
Rivers, Andy M.
Rivers, George H.
Roberts, Bell
Roberts, Dan H.
Roberts, George
Roberts, Horace
Roberts, John W.
Roberts, Samuel
Roberts, Thomas P.
Robinson, Enoch W.
Robinson, Garfield
Robinson, James H.
Robinson, Jerome
Robinson, John C.
Robinson, John M.
Robinson, Martin L.
Robinson, Robert E.
Robinson, T. J.
Robinson, Walter M.
Robinson, William F.
Rose, T. C.
Rose, Thomas E.
Roseberry, Samuel
Ross, Angeline

Ross, B. F.
Ross, David
Ross, David M.
Ross, Eliphus
Ross, Jasper
Ross, Paulina A.
Ross, Rhoda
Ross, Stephen
Ross, William H.
Rowland, Armstrong
Rowland, Isaac
Rule, C. J.
Rule, Jerry C.
Rule, John N.
Ryland, W. E.
Sadler, James W. T.
Sagraves, J. H.
Sagraves, John O.
Sagraves, Silvester
Sagraves, William
Sagraves, Winson
Salmon, David M.
Salmon, Thomas S.
Salyer, A. L.
Salyer, Alexander
Salyer, Ben
Salyer, Ben F.
Salyer, Benjamin
Salyer B. F.
Salyer, B. H.
Salyer, C. C.
Salyer, David J.
Salyer, Elizabeth
Salyer, Ephriam
Salyer, Francis
Salyer, Franklin
Salyer, Gardner
Salyer, Green C.
Salyer, Greenville P.
Salyer, Hardin H.
Salyer, Henderson
Salyer, Henry
Salyer, Henry C.
Salyer, Hiram
Salyer, J. A.
Salyer, Jackson
Salyer, Jacob
Salyer, James (Dist. No. 2)
Salyer, James (Dist. No. 4)
Salyer, James (Dist. No. 5)
Salyer, James B.
Salyer, James H.
Salyer, James M.
Salyer, Jeff
Salyer, Jefferson G.
Salyer, John

Salyer, John (Dist. No. 2)
Salyer, John A.
Salyer, John B.
Salyer, John M.
Salyer, Joseph
Salyer, Levi
Salyer, Lewis
Salyer, Logan
Salyer, Lum
Salyer, Mantford
Salyer, Martha
Salyer, Martin L.
Salyer, Milton
Salyer, Robert
Salyer, Samuel P.
Salyer, S. B.
Salyer, Shanklin
Salyer, Thomas
Salyer, Thomas J.
Salyer, William
Salyer, William (Dist. No. 4)
Salyer, William (Dist. No. 2)
Salyer, William E.
Salyer, William H.
Sammons, Joseph
Sammons, William G.
Scarberry, Frederick
Scarberry, Henry
Scarberry, Robert
Scott, Alonzo
Segraves, E. G.
Segraves, Green V.
Segraves, Jessie
Segraves, William
Selvige, James
Selvige, John
Sescoe, Osterfit Allen
Setser, C. W.
Shavers, Rance
Sherman, Burgess G.
Sherman, H. B.
Sherman, Henry R.
Sherman, John
Sherman, L. C.
Short, Fred
Short, Isaac A.
Short, Isaac H.
Short, Silas J.
Simer, William P.
Simon, Taylor
Simpkins, N. S. Jr.
Skaggs, Allen
Skaggs, David W. F.
Skaggs, F. F.
Skaggs, George
Skaggs, Jerry

Skaggs, John
Skaggs, John C.
Skaggs, Louise
Skaggs, Mose B.
Skaggs, Peter J.
Skaggs, Sarah M.
Skaggs, W. F.
Skaggs, William F.
Skaggs, William M.
Sloan, Andy
Sloan, James W.
Sloan, John
Sloan, Manuel F.
Sloan, Martha
Sloan, William H.
Slone, Ira T.
Slur, Jessie
Small, Lee
Smith, Benjamin
Smith, David
Smith, David J.
Smith, Elijah
Smith, Henderson
Smith, Keath C.
Smith, Leonard
Smith, Martin
Smith, Samuel
Smith, Thomas S.
Smith, William C.
Sneed, William B.
Sparks, Allen
Sparks, Benjamin F.
Sparks, David
Sparks, Elisha
Sparks, James
Sparks, Martha
Sparks, Nicholas
Sparks, Robert
Sparks, Thomas T.
Sparks, William
Sparks, William H.
Sparks, William R.
Sparks, Wilson
Spears, Elias M.
Spears, Enoch
Spears, F. M.
Spears, Hamilton S.
Spears, James A.
Spears, John W.
Spears, Martin
Spears, Matilda
Spears, Samuel
Spears, William M.
Spears, William R.
Spencer, Andrew J.
Spencer, Benjamin
Spencer, C. C.
Spencer, John G.
Spencer, John M.
Spencer, Jordan

GOVERNMENT 125

Spencer, Wesley
Spokes, William G.
Spokes, William J.
Spradlin, Alonzo
Spradlin, Ben
Spradlin, Benjamin
Spradlin, Benjamin F.
Spradlin, Benjamin L.
Spradlin, Britton
Spradlin, Dan
Spradlin, David A.
Spradlin, Ellen M.
Spradlin, Elliot
Spradlin, George
Spradlin, Hamilton S.
Spradlin, Ivan
Spradlin, James
Spradlin, James H.
Spradlin, James S.
Spradlin, James T.
Spradlin, John
Spradlin, John (Dist. No. 5)
Spradlin, John W.
Spradlin, Josephine
Spradlin, Mantford
Spradlin, Reuben
Spradlin, Solomon
Spradlin, William
Spriggs, Henry
Spriggs, Lindsey
Stafford, Charley C.
Stafford, Francis M.
Stafford, George W.
Stafford, Henry M.
Stafford, James
Stafford, Jessie
Stafford, John
Stafford, John E.
Stafford, John F.
Stafford, Robert
Stafford, Thomas R.
Stafford, William
Stafford, W. W.
Staggs, Joseph
Stambough, Frank
Stambough, Fred
Stambaugh, Garfield
Stambaugh, Isaac W.
Stambaugh, James A.
Stambaugh, James B.
Stambaugh, James H.
Stambaugh, James M.
Stambaugh, Jeff
Stambaugh, John
Stambaugh, John A.
Stambaugh, John T.
Stambaugh, Jonothan
Stambaugh, Phillips

Stambaugh, Phillips (Dist. No. 5)
Stambaugh, Robert J.
Stambaugh, Samuel
Stambaugh, Samuel (Dist. No. 5)
Stambaugh, Samuel J.
Stambaugh, Thomas J.
Stambaugh, Troy
Stambaugh, William G. H.
Stambaugh, Winfield
Staniford, Andrew
Staniford, Zacharias
Stanley, Harvey
Stanley, Linton
Stapleton, Alden
Stapleton, Alford
Stapleton, Alie
Stapleton, B. F.
Stapleton, Charles D.
Stapleton, Edmond
Stapleton, Edward
Stapleton, Eli
Stapleton, Elizabeth
Stapleton, George
Stapleton, George B.
Stapleton, George W.
Stapleton, Greenville F.
Stapleton, Henry
Stapleton, Isaac
Stapleton, James
Stapleton, James H.
Stapleton, Jeff
Stapleton, John H.
Stapleton, Joseph
Stapleton, R. M.
Stapleton, Roscoe
Stapleton, Rosecrous
Stapleton, Samuel
Stapleton, Samuel (Dist. No. 3)
Stapleton, Sanford
Stapleton, Ulysus G.
Stapleton, William
Stapleton, William H.
Stapleton, William P.
Step, Joseph
Stephens, Buck
Stephenson, Zachariah
Stevens, John B.
Stewart, J. F.
Stinson, James
Stone, Samuel S.
Stricklen, Henry
Strutton, Thomas J.
Sturgeon, James
Sturgeon, William
Sturgill, Jefferson
Sturgill, Miles

Sublett, Allen
Sublett, James
Sublett, Mathew
Sumpter, Thomas
Swift, W. L.
Swiney, Silvener
Tackett, Andrew J.
Tackett, Elijah G.
Tackett, Hiram C.
Tackett, Isaac
Tackett, Levi
Tackett, Lewis
Tackett, Moses
Tackett, Sarah
Tackett, William
Taylor, Ambrose
Taylor, Emma
Taylor, G. W.
Taylor, Henry
Taylor, John P.
Taylor, Mary
Terry, Isaac
Thomas, Columbus
Thomas, E. S.
Thompson, John
Toliver, Drury S.
Toliver, John S.
Travis, Marion
Trimble, Clark
Trimble, Cynthia
Trimble, D. N.
Trimble, Green
Trimble, James
Trimble, John M.
Trimble, Ulyses G.
Trimble, William
Trimble, William H.
Trimble, William J.
Trimble, William M.
Trimble, Win J.
Turner, Edwin S.
Turner, Isaac R.
Turner, John W.
Turner, Samuel P.
Turvey, Dan
Vanhoose, Andrew
Vanhoose, Eliphus
Vanhoose, Eliphus (Dist. No. 5)
Vanhoose, Frank
Vanhoose, George
Vanhoose, Harry
Vanhoose, Henry
Vanhoose, Henry J.
Vanhoose, Hosea
Vanhoose, James
Vanhoose, James B.
Vanhoose, James H.
Vanhoose, James M.
Vanhoose, Jeff

126 HISTORY OF JOHNSON COUNTY

Vanhoose, Jessie
Vanhoose, Jessie
  (Dist. No. 5)
Vanhoose, John B.
Vanhoose, John Jr.
Vanhoose, Lafe
Vanhoose, Levi Jr.
Vanhoose, Levi Sr.
Vanhoose, Lucinda
Vanhoose, Major V.
Vanhoose, Mantford
Vanhoose, Marion
Vanhoose, Nathan P.
Vanhoose, Noah
Vanhoose, Pricy
Vanhoose, Robert
Vanhoose, Samuel
Vanhoose, Scott
Vanhoose, Thomas
Vanhoose, William R.
Vaughan, Andrew J.
Vaughan, Creed N.
Vaughan, Eliza J.
Vaughan, George
  Bascom
Vaughan, H. S.
Vaughan, John L.
Vaughan, Oney
Vaughan, Sarah Bell
Vaughan, Steven E. H.
Vaughan, W. H.
Vaughan, William
Vaughan, William J.
Vaughan, William W.
Waddle, James C.
Wadkins, Henry
Wadkins, John M.
Wadkins, R. D.
Wadkins, Serreny
Walker, Bernard
Walker, E. H.
Walker, George R.
Walker, James C.
Walker, John F.
Walker, John L.
Walker, John W.
Walker, Lon J.
Walker, Thomas P.
Walker, William
Walker, William F.
Wallen, C. F.
Wallen, Conley
Wallen, E. T.
Wallen, Haney T.
Waller, Green
Walters, George N.
Walters, Henry C.
Walters, James
Walters, James P.
Walters, John C.

Walters, John M.
Walters, Shadrach
Walters, Shadrach W.
  (Shade)
Walters, Ulyses S.
Walters, William
Walters, William J.
Walters, Winifred H.
Walton (Mitchel)
Walton (William F.)
Ward, Alfred
Ward, Andrew J.
Ward, Asberry
Ward, Ashley
Ward, Charles D.
Ward, Colby
Ward, Daniel A.
Ward, David
Ward, David
Ward, Elizabeth
Ward, Elzy
Ward, Francis M.
Ward, George W.
Ward, Green V.
Ward, Greenville
Ward, Harmon
Ward, Hezekiah Jr.
Ward, Hezekiah Sr.
Ward, Isaac
Ward, James
Ward, James H.
Ward, James M.
Ward, James W.
Ward, Jasper
Ward, Jessie
Ward, Jessie
  Carbon
Ward, John
Ward, John
Ward, John
Ward, John M.
Ward, John T.
Ward, John V.
Ward, John W.
Ward, Jonothan
Ward, J. R.
Ward, King
Ward, Lewis
Ward, Manuel
Ward, Martin A.
Ward, Martin V.
Ward, Marvin
Ward, Mary J.
Ward, Milton
Ward, Nancy
Ward, Phillip
Ward, Ransom
Ward, Sampson
Ward, Shadrach

Ward, Solomon
Ward, Steven
Ward, Thompson
Ward, Ulyses G.
Ward, Washington
Ward, William
Ward, William
Ward, William A.
Ward, William B.
Ward, William J.
Ward, William S.
Ward, Zollie C.
Watson, Alexander
Watson, Willis
Webb, Alsom
Webb, Ballard
Webb, Charles J.
Webb, Crate
Webb, George W.
Webb, Harmon G.
Webb, Ira
Webb, Isiah
Webb, Jacob
Webb, James
Webb, James (Dist.
  No. 4)
Webb, James A.
Webb, John
Webb, John N.
Webb, John W.
Webb, Julia
Webb, Mary H.
Webb, Nelson
Webb, Riley
Webb, Scott
Webb, Tommy
Webb, William
Webb, William
Webb, William
Webb, William T.
Welch, John C.
Welch, Peter S.
Welch, Sherman
Welch, Thomas J.
Welch, William
Wells, Aaron
Wells, Alexander
Wells, David C.
Wells, F. M.
Wells, General
Wells, Green
Wells, Henry C.
Wells, Henry L.
Wells, I. S.
Wells, Jacob G.
Wells, John
Wells, John K.
Wells, John P.
Wells, Lewis
Wells, M. L. K.

Wells, Moses
Wells, Nancy
Wells, Richard M.
Wells, R. M.
Wells, Sam B.
Wells, William A.
Wells, William G.
Wheatley, John B.
Wheeler, Annie
Wheeler, Benjamin R.
Wheeler, Columbus B.
Wheeler, Daniel
Wheeler, Edgar
Wheeler, Elizabeth
Wheeler, Franklin P.
Wheeler, George B.
Wheeler, Greenville P.
Wheeler, James B.
Wheeler, John B.
Wheeler, John J.
Wheeler, Joseph M.
Wheeler, Judyon
Wheeler, Martha
Wheeler, Martin V.
Wheeler, Samuel G.
Wheeler, S. S.
Wheeler, William B.
Wheeler, William H.
Wheeler, William P.
Wilcox, Annanias
Wilcox, George W.
Wilcox, Henry C.
Wilcox, John W.
Wilcox, Mary A.
Wilcox, Robert A.
Wiley, Amanda
Wiley, Andrew J.
Wiley, Bethlehem
Wiley, Chess
Wiley, John
Wiley, John M.
Wiley, Moses
Wiley, Rank
Wiley, William E.
Williams, Amanda
Williams, Amous
Williams, Andrew J.
Williams, Benjamin
Williams, C. H.
Williams, C. W.
Williams, Daniel B.
Williams, David
Williams, Eli H.
Williams, Elijah C.
Williams, Eliphus T.
Williams, Eliott E.
Williams, E. S.
Williams, E. V.
Williams, G. A.
Williams, G. P.
Williams, H. A.
Williams, Haden
Williams, Henry W.
Williams, Isaac
Williams, Isaac M.
Williams, James F.
Williams, James K.
Williams, James M.
Williams, James W.
Williams, J. M.
Williams, J. N.
Williams, John H.
Williams, John M.
Williams, John R.
Williams, John S.
Williams, John W.
Williams, Joseph
Williams, Joseph C.
Williams, Josie
Williams, L. C.
Williams, Lewis
Williams, Lewis G.
Williams, L. P.
Williams, Malissa
Williams, Margaret
Williams, Minerva
Williams, Moses
Williams, Napolian
Williams, N. K.
Williams, Noah
Williams, Noah N.
Williams, Powell J.
Williams, Preston C.
Williams, Robert W.
Williams, Sam
Williams, Samuel P.
Williams, Santford J.
Williams, Thomas
Williams, Thomas G.
Williams, Thomas N.
Williams, Thomas S.
Williams, William
Williams, William A.
Williams, William R.
William, Willie J.
Wilson, Elias
Wilson, Elijah
Wilson, William
Wireman, Abraham
Wireman, Martha
Witten, Francis M.
Witten, George H.
Witten, George W.
Witten, Isaac L.
Witten, James F.
Witten, John W.
Witten, Mary
Witten, Thomas F.
Witten, Wilk
Witten, William
Witten, William J.
Witten, William N.
Woods, Benjamin F.
Woods, George
Woods, James H.
Woods, John W.
Woods, Lucina
Workman, Al
Wright, David
Wright, Henry
Wright, Isabell
Wyatt, Thomas M.
Yates, A. L.
Yates, J. M.
Yates, John
Yates, John E.
Yates, Lee
Young, Charley
Young, George G.
Young, Mount
Young, William

REFERENCES TO CHAPTER VI

[1] Hening's Statutes at Large of Virginia. Page 79, Vol. V.

[2] Digest of the Statute Laws of Kentucky by Morehead and Brown, Albert G. Hodges, 1834, Page 45, Vol. I.

[3] Hening's Statutes at Large of Virginia. Page 395, Vol. VIII.

[4] Ibid. Page 600, Vol. VIII.

[5] Ibid. Page 257, Vol. IX.

[6] Jillson, W. R., The Big Sandy Valley, pages 115-116. J. P. Morton Co., Louisville, Ky., 1923.

[7] Acts of the Kentucky Legislature, Archives Kentucky State Library.

[8] Jillson, W. R., The Big Sandy Valley, pages 116-117. J. P. Morton Co., Louisville, Ky., 1923.

[9] Collins. History of Kentucky. Collins & Co., Covington, Ky., 1882.

[10] Hening's Statutes at Large of Virginia. Vol. X, Page 315, 1822.

[11] Collins. History of Kentucky. Collins & Co., Covington, Ky., 1874.

[12] Hening's Statutes at Large of Virginia. Vol. X, Page 315, 1822.

[13] Collins. History of Kentucky. Collins & Co., Covington, Ky., 1882.

[14] County Court Records of Mason County, Maysville, Ky.

[15] Digest of the Statute Laws of Kentucky, Morehead and Brown, Albert G. Hodges, 1834, Page 45, Vol. I.

[16] Collins. History of Kentucky. Collins & Co., Covington, Ky., 1882, Vol. I, Page 401.

[17] Archives of the Kentucky State Historical Society.

[18] "Georgetonian," Georgetown College, October 6, 1926.

ONE OF THE OLD-TIME LOG CABINS

CHAPTER VII

TIMES AND CUSTOMS
IN THE DAYS OF OLD

(Note: Not many of these conditions now exist and have no connection with modern methods, but they are included herein for their historical value.)

In the days of early pioneering in Eastern Kentucky, living conditions were splendid in the light of what the people were accustomed to. Not a church-house was to be found in the Big Sandy Valley for many years; even a calico dress was a curiosity. Mortars to pound the corn into meal, and the slow grinding hand mill were generally in use with only here and there a horse mill, which was later replaced by the water, or grist mill. Bear's grease or oil was used for shortening, and deer skins to make breeches for the men and moccasins for the women.

The pioneers lived in log houses—some merely poles daubed with mud. Most of them were built of logs which were hewn or faced with an ax called a broadax. These logs were put together in the form of a pen, or house, by the assistance of many neighbors, as the logs were too heavy for even two or four men to handle. After the walls were erected, came the covering of the roof, which was made of boards riven by hand. The upper floor frequently consisted of boards, the ground floor of large heavy slabs or puncheons split from large trees and hewed with the broadax; the doors were of boards fastened with a lock which consisted of a hole in a log with a round wood pin or peg which fastened the door. The hinges consisted of a hickory withe fastened at each end into a log at the top of the door. If the settler used any plank or lumber in the building of his house he had to secure this by hand, as follows: First, a good poplar tree was selected and cut, sawed into logs, then split, and hewed with the broadax, then lined with a line soaked in pokeberry juice or fire coals. They lined both on top and bottom, which served to indicate the thickness of the planks to be sawed, which were cut by means of the whipsaw.[1]

Two men could saw from two to three hundred feet of lumber per day. After the rough lumber dried, or seasoned, it was dressed by hand planes. It was then ready for use, after much work which required strength and patience.

These log houses usually had one wide open fireplace, into which logs of any size could be rolled. About all the cooking for the large families of that time was done on these open fireplaces. The mother would fill a kettle with fresh meat, or anything she wanted to cook; swing it over the open fire by means of a swing crane which was stationed at the side of the fireplace, and proceed with her spinning, weaving, or other work. Plenty of bear meat, venison, pheasant, and wild turkey, accompanied with maple molasses, wild honey in the comb, and spicewood or other teas, formed a home fare good enough to tempt the appetite of a modern. They did not use salt in their bread. The nearest place then to get salt was at King's Salt Works in "Old" Virginia, at the old salt works on Middle Creek, Warfield, or Maysville, which had to be carried on horseback, as their only way to move or transport anything was on horseback or on foot.

There were lots of wild animals, such as bears, wolves, and panthers, which afforded much sport for the hunters and plenty of game for the taking. A man could step out before breakfast and kill a dozen grey squirrels; and it was customary for some one in the neighborhood to take their hounds out before dawn and start a deer, and by ten o'clock, the dogs might usually be heard running the deer a short distance away, all the neighbors then joining in the chase.[2]

When the first settlers wanted to go somewhere through the woods, they would take a hand ax and cut the bark off one side of trees so they could find their way back. They called this blazing a route. They would travel the path until it became a plain beaten path, and then cut the timber from either side so as to make it wide enough to ride horseback. This was called a bridle-path.[3]

The man's time was occupied by hunting, clearing ground, cutting timber, building log houses for the new settlers, fencing, ditching meadow land, digging wells, building boats and canoes, schools, and roads. Where any large amount of work was to be done, all the neighbors were invited to join in the task, which included log-rollings, house-raisings, and corn-huskings. These gatherings produced the amusements for the time. Although there was no legal compulsion to the performance, every one was expected to do his duty. A person who did not do so, felt his punishment in their refusal to attend when his turn came for similar aid, and he was pointed out as a shirker.

These log-rollings, housewarming parties, husking-bees, dances, and political gatherings were always the occasion for the coming together of all the nearby settlers and the starting of many a courtship as most of them were participated in by the beaus and lasses. The inhabitants generally married young. There was no distinction of rank, a very little of fortune. The first impression of love generally resulted in marriage, and a family establishment cost but a little labor and nothing else.

When the youth had begun to "make some speed" with one of the damsels, she was supposed to give her time and attention to him, and to him alone; and vice versa. Calls were made at will, without any previous engagement or understanding. But the usual time for such functions was Saturday or Sunday, or both. It was no breach of etiquette whatever for the young man to pass the night at the house of his sweetheart's parents, and he often did this, staying over both Saturday and Sunday nights. While the youth was enjoying his call, it was a matter of small import if the hands of the clock incidentally pointed to 10:00 p. m. He may have prolonged his call indefinitely through the night. When a pioneer youth was seen calling on a girl, nine times out of ten, he meant business, for not much time was wasted on frivolous matters like love in those days. And the same per cent of weddings was "slipped." When the wedding came off, usually during the morning, the big dinner took place the same day, at the home of the bride. The night of the same day was given over to the gay festivities of the square dance, or the "shindig," and old games. The next day at noon, the "infair," or dinner came off at the home of the groom. One of these weddings in early times was a picturesque affair, and was an event which excited the attention of the whole community in which it occurred Below is given an account of one of them:

In the morning of the wedding day, the groom and his attendants assembled at the house of his father, for the purpose of proceeding to the mansion of his bride, which it is desirable to reach by noon, the usual time of celebrating the nuptials, which ceremony must at all events take place before dinner. Let the reader imagine an assemblage of people, without a store, tailor, or mantuamaker within twenty miles; an assemblage of horses without a blacksmith or saddler within like distance. The gentlemen dressed in shoe packs, moccasins, leather breeches, leggins, linsey hunting shirts, and all homemade. The ladies in linsey petticoats and linsey or linen bedgowns, coarse shoes, stockings, handkerchiefs, and buckskin gloves. If there were any buckles, rings, buttons, or ruffles, they were relics of old times. The horses were caparisoned with old saddles and bridles or halters, and pack saddles, with a bag or blanket thrown over them; a rope or string as often constituted the girth as a piece of leather.

The march, in double file, was often interrupted by the narrowness or obstructions of the horse-path, for roads there were none; and these difficulties were often increased by the jocularity, and sometimes the malice of the neighbors by felling trees and tying grapevines across the pathway. Sometimes an ambuscade was formed by the wayside, and an unexpected discharge of several guns took place, so as to cover the wedding company with smoke. One can imagine the scene which followed this discharge; the sudden spring of the horses, the shrieks of the girls, and the chivalric bustle of their partners to save them from falling. Sometimes, in spite of all that could be done to prevent it, some were thrown to the ground. If a wrist, elbow, or ankle happened to be sprained, it was tied with a handkerchief, and little more was thought or said about it. Another ceremony took place before the party reached the house of the bride, after whiskey was introduced, which was at an early period. When the party arrived within a mile of the house, two young men would single out to run for the bottle. The worse the path the better, as obstacles afforded an opportunity for the greater display of intrepidity and horsemanship. The start was announced by an Indian yell; logs, brush, muddy hollows, hills and glens were speedily passed by the rival ponies. The bottle was always filled for the occasion, and the first who reached the door was presented with the prize, with which he returned in triumph to the company.

The ceremony of the marriage preceded the dinner, which was a substantial backwoods feast of beef, pork, fowls, and sometimes venison and bear meat roasted and boiled, with plenty of potatoes, cabbage, and other vegetables. After dinner the dancing commenced, and generally lasted till next morning. The figures of the dances were three- and four-handed reels, or square set and jigs.

About nine or ten o'clock, a deputation of young ladies stole off the bride and put her to bed. This done, a deputation of young men in a like manner stole off the groom and placed him snugly by the side of his bride. The dance still continued, and if seats happened to be scarce, every young man, when not engaged in the dance, was obliged to offer his lap as a seat for one of the girls, and the offer was sure to be accepted. In the midst of this hilarity, the bride and groom were not forgotten. Pretty late in the night, some one would remind the company that the new couple must stand in need of some refreshments; "black betty," which was the name of the bottle, was called for and sent upstairs, but often "black betty" did not go alone. Sometimes as much bread, beef, pork, and cabbage were sent along with her, as would afford a good meal for half a dozen hungry men. The young couple were compelled to eat more or less of whatever was offered them.

The marriage being over, the next thing in order was to "settle" the young couple. A spot was selected on a piece of land of one of the parents for their habitation. A day was appointed shortly after their marriage, to commence the work of building the cabin. The fatigue party consisted of choppers, whose business it was to fell the trees and cut them off at the proper length; a man with a team for hauling them to the place and arranging them properly assorted at the sides and ends of the building; a carpenter, if such he might be called, whose business it was to search the woods for the proper tree for making clapboards for the roof. The tree for this purpose must be straight grained and from three to four feet in diameter. The boards were split four feet long with a large froe, and as wide as the timber would allow. They were used without planing or shaving. Another division was employed in getting puncheons for the floor of the cabin; this

A MODERN WEDDING IN JOHNSON COUNTY

was done by splitting trees about eighteen inches in diameter, and hewing the face of them with a broadax. They were half the length of the floor they intended to make. The materials being prepared, the neighbors collected for the raising. The roof and sometimes the floor were finished on the same day the house was raised. A third day was commonly spent by the carpenters in leveling the floor and making a clapboard door and table. This last was made of a split slab and supported by four round legs set in auger holes. Some three-legged stools were made in the same manner. Pins stuck in the logs at the back of the house supported clapboards which served as shelves for the table furniture. A single fork placed with its lower end in a hole in the floor and the upper end fastened to a joist, served for a bedstead, by placing a pole in the fork with one through a crack in the logs of the wall, with cord to lay the bed and quilts on, or from the front pole through a crack between the logs at the end of the house, the boards were placed to form the bottom of the bed. A few pegs around the wall for a display of the coats of the women and the hunting shirts of the men, and two small forks, or bucks' horns, to a joist for the rifle and shot pouch, completed the carpenters work.

The cabin being finished, the ceremony of housewarming took place before the young couple was permitted to move into it. This was a dance of a whole night's continuance, made of relations of the bride and groom and their neighbors. On the day following, the young people took possession of their new mansion.

Such were the weddings in those days. To prevent the reader's getting a bad impression of weddings in this section now, a picture of a modern church wedding is shown, which, it will be observed, is in direct contrast to the one just described, and comparable to those in "The Little Church around the Corner" at East 29th Street, New York City.

The wants of the hearty pioneer were few and simple. Clothing was altogether homemade from flax, cotton and wood. Flax was grown especially for linen; the mothers made their bed sheets, towels, and tablecloths from it, and often clothing was made of it, as well as shirts and trousers. The simple but hazardous way in which cloth was made is as follows: After the flax was pulled it was spread on the ground to lie for weeks in order that the pith or inner part of the stalk might rot, leaving only the fiber or outside of the stalk; then the stalks were gathered and tied into bundles or sheaves; the bundles were broken to pieces in a flax-breaker, leaving only the fiber mixed slightly with the pith; each broken bunch was then taken to a board driven in the ground and by means of a singling knife, the principal part of the pith was separated from the lint; but what was left was taken out completely by means of a hackle. This was a board about three inches thick and eight inches wide by fourteen inches long, with steel points driven through to the length of about six inches, and about one-half inch apart. These points were very sharp. The lint bunches were pulled through the teeth of the hackle till all appearances of the pith had disappeared; then these bunches of nice yellow lint were twisted like tobacco and taken to a small wheel and spun into threads on a broach of sufficient size to fit the hollow shuttle for the old-fashioned weaving loom; then the cloth was made. It was very rough but after washing several times it became soft and very white. As to cotton, nearly every housewife planted a small crop. After several cultivations, at which time the cotton bolls began to open, the picking began, very slowly as the bolls opened very irregularly. When all the cotton was gathered, the separation of the seed from the lint began. This was done by picking each little seed by hand or separation by means of a rude little hand cotton-gin made of wood. Cloth was made by nearly the same process as the flax, except the breaking and hackling. When the good, patient women wished to color their cloth this was done as follows: First, by gathering the bark of a white walnut or maple, steeping or boiling the bark till all the coloring matter was extracted, then adding sufficient copperas to make the desired shade or color. Then they dipped the cloth into this solution several times, each time permitting the cloth to air, so as to set the dye.

Wool has ever been an asset to the people, but not so much now as it was then. The clipping of the wool was done by means of hand shears. After clipping the wool, which was always full of burrs of various kinds because the sheep ran at large or in weed pastures, came the separation of the burrs from the wool, a very tedious and tiresome job, as it was done by hand. After picking the burrs, the wool was washed and dried and then carded by hand into small rolls; then spun into threads by means of a hand wheel into broaches; and, finally, twisted firm and close by means of a smaller wheel into broaches for the shuttle to be used in the hand loom. The coloring process was the same as in flax or cotton. Clothing made in this way was very durable and constituted the raiment of all classes. The making of all this homemade cloth was done by handsewing; no such thing existed as a sewing machine. Buttons were made of wood covered with cloth or cut from the shell of a gourd. Ladies used thorns obtained from a thorny shrub for pins. Washing was done by means of a large trough and battling stick. They had no washboards and it was just a matter of washing with their hands and beating their clothing clean with the paddle and a bench, usually done by the side of a nearby branch or creek. The soap used was strictly homemade by using commercial lye and meat cracklings, or drain from wood ashes.

There were no steam or gasoline mills. Corn meal was made by means of a hand mill. This consisted of two stones, one bedded firmly in a gum or box, the top stone being turned by hand by means of a shaft extended from the stone to a cross-bar above; this stone had a hole in the center extending down to the head stone to admit the corn while turning. Another way was to erect a spring pole and attach a perpendicular shaft to it so as to admit handles. This shaft (commonly known as a sweep mill), by means of the spring pole, crushed the grain which usually was placed in a large trough.

The overshot mill was used to some extent. This consisted of a large wheel some twenty or thirty feet in diameter with buckets attached to the rim about three feet apart; this wheel was placed near a fall or precipice and the water pouring over struck the buckets, thereby turning the wheel, which was assembled with smaller wheels, connecting the whole machinery so as to turn the grist mill attached to it. This process was very slow and could only be used in time of much rain or high waters.

Another very economical way was the grater. This consisted of a piece of tin punched with a nail, the punctures being very close together. After preparing the tin in this way, a board about three feet long was dressed and a hole just a bit smaller than the tin was made in the board; then the tin was attached to the board, and in this way soft corn could be converted into meal. Some have been known to parch or heat the corn until very brittle, then grind it into meal by means of a coffee-mill.

After making the meal by various processes, came the baking of the bread, which was done in open skillets or ovens which were heated over the fire, as previously mentioned. Another way of baking or cooking bread, known as the ash cake, was as follows: The dough was shaped into round or globular forms, without salt or soda, and placed in hot ashes, and covered well with hot coals. This remained sufficiently long for complete baking; then the ashes were removed and the bread was ready to serve.

Still another form of bread known as the johnny-cake, was baked as follows: A board was dressed very smoothly, and soaked thoroughly with oil or grease. When the dough was prepared it was placed on the johnny-board near enough to the fire to admit slow baking. When one side was sufficiently done it was reversed and the other side prepared in the same way, after which the johnny-cake was ready to serve.

Maple sugar was a luxury. This was made by tapping a sugar maple and draining the juice into pails with drains made from elders. The juice obtained was then boiled down and the residue, which was hardly ten per cent of the original liquid, formed the sugar.

Most every householder raised some sorghum cane in order that he might have molasses for his table. The way in which the juice was extracted from the cane was as follows: The farmer made his own mill, which consisted of two rollers of wood shaped by hand. These rollers contained cogs at the top, all of which were fastened between two boards or slabs sufficiently strong to bear the pressure needed. Soap of tallow was used for lubricating purposes; but frequently after all the friction was removed one could hear this mill in action some two or three miles away. It was necessary to run the cane through the mill at least three times to extract the juice. The juice was poured into kettles and boiled till the desired sweetness was reached. The farmer made his own barrels or jugs to hold the syrup.

Enough wheat was sown to supply the family with wheat bread, or brown biscuits. It was cut or harvested with a reap hook or cradle by hand, and threshed with sticks or flails, and cleaned or fanned with homemade blankets. Two men could thresh and clean some six or eight bushels a day. It was milled in the same manner as meal, already mentioned. After grinding in the hand mill, the crude flour was sifted through a fine cloth by hand to separate the bran from the finer flour, or else taken to a water mill and ground into flour; then the bran was separated from the flour by means of a bolt or chest. While this grade of flour was not so white, it certainly was nutritious, clean, and healthy, because it was pure wheat flour.

The women of that day were as busy as the men and saw to the carding and spinning of their wool and cotton into yarns, as well as going to the woods for barks to color the yarn and make their cloth in handsome stripes. They wove it and then cut and made their cloth by hand, as already described. Some of the cloth was bleached to a spotless white at the spring or branch. The women also helped to make the crops during the spring and summer, and then made their cloth and did their sewing during the winter.

A woman's social standing was regulated more by the quality of the products of her household than by anything else. They planted orchards, they dried their pumpkins and beans, and when they began to raise fruit, they gathered and cured both wild and cultivated fruits for the winter, as that was their only way of putting up food.

However, the pioneer did not lack for plenty to eat, and that of the best. His bill of fare was a very good one. A more tempting one could not be served today. What could be more appetizing than bear-meat boiled, or roasted before the fire, or on wooden bars over a furnace made for the purpose? Venison broiled on the coals, or boiled and eaten cold? Pheasants hung up before the fire and roasted to a fine brown? Johnny-cake made of corn meal beaten in mortars or ground on hand mills, shortened with bear-fat, with some stewed dried pumpkin put in the dough?

TIMES AND CUSTOMS 139

Wild honey in the comb, or strained; maple molasses in abundance in its season, and plenty of maple sugar to sweeten their spice or other domestic tea? Huckleberries, services, and other wild fruit as relishes? The epicure of today would delight in such a meal.

Every house had a spinning wheel, a reel, and a loom, and the wholesome damsels of that day knew how to use them; while the mother spun the flax and wool into thread, the grandmother knitted the hosiery and gloves for the family, and the little girls filled the quills. Those were busy days. An eight-hour day then would have been like a holiday, as their work was from sunrise to sunset, with very little time for rest. A prosperous farmer once had about fifteen men helping him work out his corn, and when they had hoed to the end of the rows, some of them took it upon themselves to take a little time out before starting the next row. The farmer noticed that a windstorm had blown down his rail fence and remarked, "Boys, let's carry these rails back up the hill while we're resting." All fences were made of rails, which necessitated much "rail splitting." A man's physique was judged by the number of rails that he could split in a day.

While they worked hard through the week, the week-end was taken off. No one worked on Sunday, while Saturday night was the time for amusements, which were adequate to their wants. It was very fashionable to have dances—what the people termed the "Old Virginia Hoedown." While many drinkers to excess were found in that day, as most every man partook of the beverage, a drunken man was rarely seen at one of these dances. In case someone took too much, they would "ship him." They would not stand for any disturbance. Some of his friends would take him away and keep him away. The women were not afraid of drunken men. The reason for this was that they knew the men would not allow any lady molested, or allow any bad conduct. The very best people took part in these sports, and it was not necessary to call the sheriff. The good men simply took the law into their hands and would not allow drunken men to disturb their plays. In 1844 whiskey could be obtained at any of the taverns at the following prices:[6]

One-half pint of whiskey for 6¼ cents; 1 pint, 10 cents; 1 quart, 18¾ cents; ½ gallon, 31¼ cents; 1 drink, 5 cents; 1 drink wine or brandy, 10 cents.

One would think that with whiskey, which was pure, so reasonable and accessible, that it would affect the morals of the people; but it did not. The men were brave, and the women virtuous. When men fell out, they generally very coolly fought it out with their fists, and ended the matter by shaking hands.

The only weapon of defense carried by the pioneer was the trusty old flintlock rifle with which he could bring down his target. A hatchet and hunting knife completed his means of protection as well as aiding him in securing his game for food.

In outlining the customs of these early settlers, mention should be made of what it is almost impossible for the present generation to imagine—their traditions and superstitions. Most of the older people believed in witches. If anything got wrong with a horse or cow, their first thought was that it was bewitched. If the cow failed to "give down" milk, she was bewitched. On the other hand, the cows of a supposed witch, who usually was an old person, always gave plenty of milk. There were many who professed to be able to expel the witch charm, and to do so disguised themselves in the form of a black cat, or other traditional unlucky thing.

Some of the superstitious beliefs were as follows: Never turn back, it is unlucky; don't let a black cat cross your path; Friday is unlucky; put a stone in the fireplace and the hawks will not catch the chickens; if a bird flies into the house someone in the family will die soon; killing toads will make the cows give bloody milk; thirteen is an unlucky number; if a person counts a hundred stars before looking down, he will drop dead; it is bad luck to sing at the table; if a ghost follows you, stop in the middle of a stream and cross your fingers; someone has just died when roosters crow in the night; it is bad luck for a hen to crow, to carry farming tools through the house, to take a cat with you when you move; if you go to bed singing, you will die that night; if a baby's finger nails are trimmed, it will be guilty of stealing before it is a year old; carry a rabbit's foot for good luck; put a horseshoe over the door for good luck; walk under mistletoe for love, or take the paddle of a goose's foot and boil it, then give the water to the girl to make her love you; throw love vine over your left shoulder, naming some girl without looking at the vine, and if it grows she loves you; and if you walk over a grave in a cemetery, you will be the next person to be buried there. These were the conditions under which they were reared, and it took many years to outlive these superstitions.

Although matches, lamps, gas, or electricity were unknown then, the question of lighting the house was very simple. About the first method used was to saturate a string in lard; place it in a metal holder, and refill as needed. Another method was that of burning plain old pine knots. The knots, however, were soon replaced by tallow candles, and little lamps made of lard and cotton wicks. Later on they used brass lamps, which later were discarded for glass lamps with glass globes.

Fires were started with flint and punk—that is rubbing a piece of steel with the flint, which was an oily stone, the sparks igniting with the soft dry wood, and with the addition of some fine pine kindling, a good fire was soon burning. Anyone knows who has

TIMES AND CUSTOMS 141

tried the above, that it is no easy matter, and for this reason, the fire was seldom let go out in the winter. They would bank or cover the fire with the ashes at night and still have fire the next morning.

Little can be said in favor of the means of communication of those days. The mails were so uncertain and slow that few people gave them much consideration. Sometimes a letter would lie in the post office for three months before the addressee would find it out. For many years there was only one post office in the county, which was at Paintsville. This condition existed for a long time, as the offices were few and far apart. The first mail route was from Catlettsburg to Pikeville. It was carried on horseback. Two trips were made a week—if it did not rain too much and swell the streams. After the railroad was built to Richardson, the mails were brought on to Paintsville by two mail hacks, such as were seen in some of the remote sections of the county a few years ago. A few routes are still covered by horseback. Money was never sent through the mails previous to the Civil War, but the owner took it up or down the river, or if it was going to Cincinnati, sent it by the Honshell line of steamers.[7]

Slaves were numerous then, but those who were able to own them were not "stuck up." For many years after the settlement of the county, more slaves in proportion to the population were to be found in that section of the State than in the Bluegrass. Few counties in the State now, however, have fewer colored people than Johnson.

Mention was made in a preceding paragraph of the transferring of money. There was very little of it in circulation, and as a matter of fact very few people had any currency. The skins of the bear, the deer, buffalo, and other fur-bearing animals, combined with the sale of ginseng and yellow-root, with a little added from wolf-scalps at $5.00 each, afforded about the only source of revenue. The bear-hides were sold to fur-traders for a price which varied from $1.00 to $3.00. The different hides were held by the local dealers, who numbered only about two, until the through trader bought and flatboated them down the Big Sandy to the Ohio,[8] where they were steamboated to market. The money received from these sources usually went to buy what little they got from the general store. Accounts were very commonly figured in English money as late as 1815, when one American dollar was worth six English shillings. While money was scarce, goods and eats were plentiful, such as they were. The thrifty housewife provided most everything for the table, and it was not necessary to buy much. They lived very cheaply. All people had to do was to have plenty of milch cows. The cows practically wintered in the woods on ferns and sprouts.

Those were the days when they had no taxes to pay, and every one was free to do almost as he pleased, instead of doing to please the policeman. Land titles were unsettled and it mattered not where one wandered. The old hunters just meant to camp and kill game, and that was all they cared for or worried about.

These old people as a rule were unlearned and ignorant of the ways of the world, but with all their rudeness, they were hospitable, and freely divided their rough fare with a neighbor or stranger, and would have been offended at the offer of pay. Some of them laid as much away for company as they did for themselves. They lived, they worked, they fought and feasted or suffered together in cordial harmony, and stood for the good principles which inspired and influenced the later generations to reach an average hard to equal by any in the country.

NOT SO LONG AGO

Although many advancements had been made by 1890-1900, the people of the county, as a whole, were still in a pioneering era. They had few books, inadequate schools, few amusements, and very few good newspapers, as well as slow means of transportation, to keep them in touch with the outside world. At that time the citizens were going to Richardson, a distance of eighteen miles, to get to the train. Paintsville had no paved streets, no waterworks, no electric lights, no telephone or telegraph facilities, no automobiles, no natural gas.

Those were the days when one could buy real beer for five cents a glass and the lunch was free. Eggs were three dozen for a quarter and milk five cents a quart. The butcher gave liver for the cat and treated the children to bologna. The grocer used a potato (now worth 10 cents) as a stopper for the lamp oil can and threw in the vegetables with a five-cent soup bone. The hired girl was satisfied with two dollars a week, and she did the washing. Women did not powder or paint, smoke, play poker, bridge, or the ponies. Stores were open every night until ten o'clock and twelve on Saturdays. The men wore boots and whiskers, chewed tobacco, worked eleven hours a day, and if one smoked cigarettes he was called a dude. A kerosene lamp and a stereopticon in the parlor were luxuries. Every home possessed an organ, and a marble-top parlor table, holding an album and a Bible. The largest washtub was put to family use every Saturday, when it was too cold to go to the creek or river. No one was operated on for appendicitis or tonsillitis, and the folks lived to a good old age just the same.[9]

It was a time when everybody knew Tom, Dick, or Harry, in addition to everything that went on throughout the county. They did not forget it either. Today, someone may get lost,

TIMES AND CUSTOMS 143

drowned, or killed, and tomorrow it is forgotten. Such was not the case then. Most any one of the older generation now living can tell all about how Uncle "Tip" Childer's child disappeared, as well as many other mysteries that were never solved.

In that day folks were buying *gold bricks* and aiding the *Spanish Prisoner* with their saw-log money. About the only sources of revenue were saw-logging, push-boating, school teaching, holding a political office, or farming. The word farming as applied here meant only the raising of corn, wheat, potatoes and sorghum, and not stock raising. Cattle were generally turned loose to roam where they could, which mainly was along the roads. Hogs were raised in the forest and their principal food was mast, very abundant each year. Some went wild. Hunting the wild hog then furnished something of the thrill of the old days when the early settlers pursued the panther and bear. In like manner hog-meat and beef had taken the place of bear-meat and venison. Coffee had come into use, but it was received green and had to be dried and roasted in the oven. Corn bread was served three times a day in most of the homes. The old water mill was still a familiar sight along all the larger streams of the county. It was a weekly occurrence for the father to put one of the boys on an old lazy mule with a two-bushel "turn" and send him to the mill to have his "turn" made into meal by the good-natured miller.

In addition to the hunting of wild hogs, coon hunting and fox chasing were the great sports at that time. A good coon dog or a pair of fox hounds were highly prized by the owner. Coons were numerous then, but now they are practically extinct, and their passing is regretted by the old hunters. A very few foxes are still to be found but not many, as in the nineties when anyone could sit on his porch and hear the hounds running a fox on a nearby ridge. This was sweeter music to many then than the voice of a cultured soprano on the radio today.

The music of the "Sourwood Mountain" fiddler, and the "jigs" of the three-fingered man with a banjo across his knee appealed more to the people than anything now heard in a modern vaudeville show. Of course all these compositions were played by ear and not by note, either to pass away time or at some entertainment, but they touched the heart when no other form of music would. This old-time music predominates to the present time in many of the homes. Songs such as "Sourwood Mountain," "Arkansaw Traveler," "Turkey in the Straw," "Billy in the Low Ground," "Fisher's Horn Pipe," "Pop, Goes the Weasel," "Little Brown Jug," and "The Forked Horn Deer," were usually preferred, but it was no uncommon thing for someone to break forth on his violin, singing:

"I'll tune up my fiddle, I'll rosin my bow,
I'll make myself welcome wherever I go."

Or, the banjo picker with:

"Gi' me the hook and gi' me the line,
Gi' me the gal ye call Car'line."

Or,

"Beefsteak when I'm hungry, corn liker when I'm dry,
Pretty little girl when I'm lonesome, sweet heaven when I die."

Or,

"There's salt in the ocean, there's fish in the sea,
The girl I love has gone back on me."

Another form of amusement was the annual pie social held in almost every schoolhouse to obtain funds to buy something necessary for the schoolroom. The ladies brought pies or cakes and sometimes a basket of eatables for the boy-friends to bid on. The highest bidder ate his purchase with the girl who prepared it, and, of course, took her home after the entertainment.

There were no big days except election day on the first Monday in August, and a big religious meeting in August. There were no shows or movies for the young people to go to see.

About this time many feuds existed among the people of several counties in Eastern Kentucky. Johnson County has always been free of these, as there is not one on record. Although much bitterness existed at times between individuals, it never got to the point where revenge was taken by wholesale murder in the families of those connected with these private controversies. Up to 1890, only four murders had been recorded within the county. Perry, Pike, Rowan, Breathitt, Knott, and Letcher counties, and the Kentucky-West Virginia state line were scenes of many of these dreadful feuds, in which many lives were lost.

If one were to approach some of the older men of the county, who, by the way, are not very willing to admit that they are advanced in years, and ask them to relate some of the fond memories of the days when they were young, they very likely would mention the days when they "push-boated" on "Sandy." There are not many of them who have not done this. The river was navigable only about two-thirds of the year to steamboats, and push-boating was resorted to the rest of the time for the transportation of goods. It was very hard work but it brought several men together, and they enjoyed it. Jokes and stories of push-boat occurrences are only excelled by those of the modern salesman.

The steamboat was to the people then what the railroad and highway bus are today. They were the only modes of travel up

STEAMBOATING UP "SANDY"
The Above Picture of *The Argand* Was One of the Familiar Scenes before the Advent of the Railroad

Big Sandy until twenty-five years ago. Many people, now living, made their first trip out of the valley via the steamboat. Not only were these boats convenient for travelers, but also for the transportation of freight. Shipments were received at Catlettsburg, and regular trips were made by such old boats as the Cando, Argand, Fannie Freese, Beulah Brown, Donkey, Sip Bayes, Thealka, and many others, to Pikeville. The shrill blast of their whistles never failed to bring a thrill as they headed Buffalo shoal or rounded the Muddy Branch bend. For the last few years before the coming of the railroad, the traffic was very heavy on the river. They had their competition then, as well as accidents, just the same as the automobiles and trains do now. A little incident between the Donkey and Argand is given. The Donkey was a small boat and very speedy. The Argand was large and could not get along so fast. In its effort to cut the traveling time on its trips, the Donkey would run around the larger boats. The Argand management tired of this and whenever or wherever it met the Donkey, it would turn crosswise in the river and, being so long, prevented the Donkey from passing, holding it up for an hour or more on several occasions. A person viewing the river now, with so many snags and stumps, or rocks blown from the hillside by contractors building the highways, or farmers felling the trees into it to cultivate the river banks, might wonder how such large boats navigated the river. Every year a boat commonly known as the stump-puller rid the stream of these obstacles, and the shoals were wing-dammed. Today the sight of a steamboat would be unusual.

Many citizens of the county, who read this, will recall to memory the time when:

Uncle "Conse" Conley ran the tan shop near where James Meek now lives.

Ladies rode on side-saddles instead of in limousines.

Alex Blevins ran the butcher shop.

It took half an hour to shine shoes with Mason's old-time blacking.

Men went to the oil fields on Paint with ox-teams instead of by airplanes.

Uncle Dan Hager, Frank Preston, John P. Wells and that bunch played checkers.

Men played mumble-the-peg, instead of poker and the ponies.

Doctors worked their patients, instead of the patients working them. That was when Doctors Turner, Atkinson, and Bayes were making the circuits.

Neighbors asked about your family and meant every word of it.

"Dick" Stafford ran the store on the corner near where Uncle Jesse now resides.

Ladies' dresses reached from the neck to the heels, always.

Professors Tom Mayo, Wheeler, and Randolph were the schoolmasters, the latter of whom engaged in some arguments. One was with Wiley Williams who had made some remark about Mr. Randolph's family, whereupon the latter replied: "How dare you, sir, you street scavenger, insult a man through whose veins flows the royal blood of John B. Randolph, of Roanoke, Virginia!"

Neighbors all got fresh meat at hog-killing time, maybe sausage, too.

Old Mace Mahan told his yarns at the livery stable.

A tin cup of red liquor for a nickel, and worth it.

Buck Price had the first barber shop.

Folks used goose-quill toothpicks, made at home, that lasted for a month.

John "Dunk" Preston, Cyrus Preston, and others played croquet.

Henry Mahan drove his hacks.

Farmers would have been offended at the offer of pay for a meal.

"Big Brother" William Vaughan sang bass at the Northern Methodist Church, and Captain John W. Castle sang soprano at the Methodist Episcopal Church, South.

Left-over noon victuals were finished at supper time, instead of being made into hash the next day.

Uncle John Hornett Blevins and his feeble-minded son peddled daily from house to house in Paintsville.

Only crooks on record were "lightning-rod" and "fruit-tree" agents.

William Fairchilds had the only blacksmith shop in town.

Quinine was taken in coffee, jelly, or molasses, and no frowns.

Captain Green Meeks had his boats all up and down "Sandy."

Folks boiled coffee, settled with an egg, and 'twas good.

Tom Akers ran the first jewelry shop in Paintsville.

Vermilion was used for hearth paint, instead of face coloring.

The Italian or Jewish peddler made his regular trip through with about three trunks strapped across his back.

The ladies took "Larkin" orders to receive a set of dishes as the premium.

TIMES AND CUSTOMS 149

Dialogues and recitations were the main entertainments in the schools.

Everyone in a community gathered with their seines and had fish fries; or with the old fox horn, stood on a ridge directing, and listening to, the music of a fox chase.

Transients used buckboards instead of Fords.

C. M. Cooper opened the first drug store in Paintsville.

Girls were safe from insults by the roughest class of men—whereas now a fellow has to get pretty rough to hold his ground with a flapper.

They didn't marry in haste and divorce with pleasure, and men kept the same wife for a lifetime.

Wild pigeons could be killed with clubs while coming through low gaps to roost at dusk.

The old-time spinning wheel was to be seen in every home, instead of in the antique shop.

The first automobile was built on lines of buggy design, and the driver, wearing goggles and a linen duster, was accompanied by ladies whose hats were tied securely on with flowing automobile veils. They talked of "cabby" instead of chauffeur.

The men wore cravats.

The blacksmith shop gave way to the garage.

There were no street lights, and the streets were mud lanes.

The girls talked of "rats" and puffs. No lipsticks, but plenty of "straight fronts."

No one-piece bathing suits disturbed the vision; but every pack of *sweet caps* had a picture of a burlesque queen in tights.

There were advertisements of hairpins and horseshoes, but none of permanent waves and balloon tires. The fire poker was used by the lassies for making "permanent waves."

Women did not vote or serve on juries.

Brick was made by means of an old mud mill with a long sweep drawn by a horse.

Following are given two brief histories—one of which was by the county's financial wizard, the late John C. C. Mayo, in 1891, of Johnson County, as prepared for reports of the Department of Agriculture of the State of Kentucky, which gives a fairly accurate account of the conditions at that time.

JOHNSON COUNTY—BRIEF HISTORY
By J. C. C. Mayo, 1891

Johnson County was organized in 1843, and took its name from Colonel Richard M. Johnson, vice-president of the United States from 1837-1841, during Van Buren's presidency. Colonel Johnson's is one of the brightest names contributed by Kentucky to the immortal muster roll of the nation's heroes and statesmen, being, preeminently, the hero of the decisive victory won over Indians and British, October, 1813, at the battle of the Thames, as well as distinguished for splendid abilities, as a state and national legislator.

The soil of Johnson County, which is of a sandy nature in most parts underlaid with a clay subsoil, is generally very productive. The principal grades of timber found in large quantities and merchantable, are poplar, ash, pine, oak, beech, hickory, locust, chestnut, and sycamore.

Iron ore is found in some localities, while coal is inexhaustible. Bituminous coal veins, ranging from two and one-half feet to eight feet in thickness are found throughout the country. A cannel coal mine has been opened four miles south of Paintsville, on Sandy River—which measures as follows: Solid roof bituminous coal three inches, cannel coal forty-nine inches, bituminous coal eight inches, base of vein. Cannel coal is also found on the eastern side of Sandy River, in veins ranging from thirty to forty inches.

Good church buildings are found in almost every locality, and schoolhouses have improved one hundred per cent within four years.

Paintsville, the county seat, a town of five hundred inhabitants, will erect during the summer graded school buildings, costing eight thousand dollars. There are no saloons in town, and a "local option" which prohibits, exists in every voting precinct in the county. Four murders only have been committed in this county since its formation, forty-six years ago. The population is now about twelve thousand.

Railroads

There are about four miles of railroad completed and in operation in the county. The same is a part of the Ohio, Kentucky, and Virginia which is known as the ten-mile extension of the Chattaroy Road, running to Mt. Carbon, Johnson County, Kentucky.

There are no railroads in course of completion. Several surveys, however, have passed through the county up the Big Sandy River—the surveys being those of the East Kentucky, Chattaroy, and Chicago, Cincinnati and Charleston railroads. There is considerable talk in regard to the early completion of the C. C. & C. but as yet nothing has been developed.

County Roads

During the winter season, the county roads are in bad condition, but are being traveled, not only on horseback, but by buggies, stages, etc. Our people are generally ready and willing to make and keep in repair the county roads. Our road law being a special act is regarded as a good and efficient one.

Turnpikes

Johnson has no turnpikes.

Streams

Paint, Tom's, and John's creeks furnish considerable waterpower for propelling machinery. Barnett's, Jenny's, Little Paint, Mud Lick, Greasy and other creeks are from ten to fifteen miles in length. Big Sandy River, flowing through the county, is navigable for steamboats and large rafts, perhaps two-thirds of the year.

Timber

Hickory, ash, locust, chestnut, oak, beech, pine, walnut, poplar, and other grades of timber are found in this county. The finest poplars and walnuts have been marketed. Other grades are found in enormous quantities, especially oak, hickory, ash, and beech. Our people depend on timber for our revenue.

Agricultural Products

Corn, wheat, potatoes, and sorghum are produced in large quantities, yet nearly all is consumed in the county, except sorghum.

Grasses

Herd's grass, timothy, orchard grass and clover seem best adapted to our soil. Bluegrass is being grown in some localities. It has, however, not been in the county long enough to test its adaptability to our soil.

Methods of Agriculture

To some extent, Johnson County may be said to be improving its methods of agriculture. A better class of farming implements is being introduced and used to an advantage over former methods.

Soil

The soil of our farming lands is noticeably improving. This results from the fact that the farmers are generally raising more grass instead of large crops of corn and sorghum as heretofore.

Immigration

There has been during the last two years no noteworthy immigration into our county, except in instances requiring miners for the cannel coal mines at Whitehouse in this county.

Population

The population of the county has probably increased five per cent—possibly more—within the past two years.

Mills and Manufactures

There has been, during the same period, no addition to the mills and manufacturing industries of the county, except to the large number of portable sawmills now in operation.

Preservation of Forests

Perhaps about forty per cent of our county's territory is still covered with timber; but no effort has, as yet, been made to prevent the destruction of forests.

Improved Field and Garden Seeds

Within the last few years quite a disposition has been manifested by the farmers of Johnson County to obtain and use improved field and garden seeds.

General Statistics

Farm laborers are plentiful in this county.

The average price paid to a laborer without family, board and lodging furnished by the employer, is $11.80 per month. Average price paid where he furnishes his own lodging and board, is $16.80 per month. The average price paid a laborer with family, the employer furnishing board and lodging for all, is $9.00 per month. Average price paid a laborer with family, the laborer furnishing his own and his family's board and lodging, is $14.75 per month.

The county has 36 churches, 1 parsonage, and 62 schoolhouses.

The average assessed value of land in the county, according to the assessors returns for 1890, is $4.73 per acre—164,525 acres.

Johnson County has two mines of cannel coal, employing 130 men, and a total output for the year ending June 30, 1891, was 21,847 tons.

(Written for the ninth biennial report of the Bureau of Agriculture, of the State of Kentucky, 1891.)

JOHNSON COUNTY
December 30, 1899

Johnson County is situated in central Eastern Kentucky, and was formed in 1843, and named in honor of a distinguished son of Kentucky, Colonel Richard M. Johnson, who was vice-president of the United States during the presidency of Martin Van Buren. The county is bounded on the north by Morgan and Lawrence, on the east by Martin, on the south by Floyd, and on the west by Magoffin. The county is well watered and well drained. The Big Sandy River flows through the eastern part of the county, and Paint Creek flows in a southeasterly direction through the central part of the county, and empties into the Big Sandy. Paint, Tom's, and John's creeks are the principal creeks in the county, though there are numerous others. The soil of Johnson County is probably as good as, if not better than, that of any county in Eastern Kentucky. It is of a sandy character and underlaid with a splendid clay subsoil, and is very strong and productive. The bottom lands along the numerous streams are very productive and as fertile land can be found along them as anywhere.

The timber supply of Johnson is still very great, though large quantities of valuable timber have been cut and marketed. Portable sawmills are found all over the county in the great timber belts, but fifty per cent of the fine timber of this county still remains. Poplar, ash, hickory, beech, oak, pine, locust, chestnut and sycamore can be found in large tracts and may be had at very cheap prices per acre.

Diversified farming is not engaged in, though fruit grows well here. Timber is the principal product of the county. The county is well underlaid with coal, both cannel and bituminous, and the supply is practically inexhaustible. Veins of bituminous coal eight feet in thickness are found. A most magnificent cannel coal mine is in operation about four miles south of Paintsville, the county seat, on the Sandy River. Iron ore of a superior quality is also found in some portions of the county. This county is rich in mineral and timber.

The Big Sandy River is navigable for steamers for about two-thirds of the year. There are no turnpike roads in the county, and our county roads, which are the common dirt roads of the country, are kept in reasonably good repair under a local road law we have for the county, and are traveled by buggies, even in the winter time, and by stage coaches. There are only about four miles of completed railroad in the county, which is an extension of the O. & B. S. railroad to Myrtle, in Johnson, and is located in the eastern part of the county. There have been other surveys made and roads talked of, but none now in the course of construction. Railroad facilities are what we need to develop the coal and minerals of this county, and to carry our timber after it is converted into lumber.

Corn, wheat, oats, potatoes, tobacco and sorghum are all raised, but only in quantities sufficient for home consumption, excepting tobacco and sorghum, and especially is the latter raised in large quantities for market elsewhere. The labor of the county is performed mostly by native whites, farm hands being paid from $10.00 to $15.00 per month with board, while hands for timbering receive from $18.00 to $20.00.

Good churches are found throughout the county everywhere, and our common schools are in good condition. All the districts have good and comfortable schoolhouses in them and the convenient modern appliances for teaching have been furnished each school, and good teachers have been supplied, and the schools are under an exceptionally good management. The population of Johnson County, according to the eleventh census of the United States, is 11,027, but a small and steady increase has since doubtless raised it to a much higher figure by this time. The county is in the Tenth Congressional, Seventh Appellate, Twenty-fourth Judicial, Thirty-third Senatorial, and Ninety-sixth Legislative District.

Paintsville is the county seat, and is situated on Paint Creek, just a little southeast of the center of the county. Its population in 1890 was 506, but is now estimated at about double that number. It is a flourishing village with enterprising merchants, good church buildings, and live congregations; have good graded schools and good new school buildings, with ample accommodations for all who see fit to attend. Hotel accommodations are good, and the citizens are quiet and law-abiding and hospitable to strangers.

POST OFFICES:—Asa, Barnetts Creek, Boons Camp, Coal, Denver, Eastpoint, Eliza, Flanery, Flatgap, Fuget, Galen, Kerz, Lowmansville, Manila, Mingo, Myrtle, Odds, Oil Springs, Paintsville, Red Bush, Riceville, River, Saintmaur, Sampson, Sip, Soto, Staffordsville, Toms and Winifred.

MODERN PROGRESS

The times and customs described in "The Days of Old" and "Not So Long Ago" were those of the county in a pioneer state. While real changes were in evidence in the nineties a great deal of the old-time atmosphere was retained in business and social and domestic life. Then came what is called modern progress. Things become new to persons who had lived in the preceding eras. The changed conditions now are almost unbelievable to those who were accustomed to living conditions of the nineties. Comparatively young people can remember when men achieved the goal of dreamers by making flight a reality. Then came the radio and the movie. The vision of a novelist was made actuality by the submarine. The world is moving faster and faster. Everything is speeding up, and the people of Johnson County are fast falling into line.

One big difference is apparent to all. In the older days men thought they could send their imaginations beyond what men could accomplish. Now the imagination hardly can keep up with what is being, and has been, achieved. It would be a daring, and perhaps a foolhardy, brain that would undertake to say what is beyond the present horizon in any line of human endeavor.

Today, nearly everybody rides in automobiles or airships, plays poker, shoots craps, plays the piano with their feet, and go to movies.

The youth calls on a girl who may be engaged to half a dozen boys at the time to take her to a vaudeville show, or escort her to a "Charleston" or "Black Bottom" dance that begins near midnight, and, when formal, the ladies wear beautiful evening gowns, and the gents tucks tailored to measure. The automobile has replaced the home for the spooning and midnight kisses, and the girl who goes with new friends in the car takes a chance of having to walk back. The engagement is announced at an aristocratic social affair, at which gorgeous gowns—what little there is of them—are displayed. The wedding is held in the church, followed by the honeymoon and by the shower, sometimes six months later, by some of the friends in which useful presents are given. The young couple then start their home in a furnished flat or apartment—pay in advance.

Instead of "black betty," it is the hip-pocket flask. Medicinal whiskey $6.00 a pint, and white the same if one should want to take chances on the contents. The moonshiner uses high-powered rifles and machine-guns in his defense. Women do their Christmas shopping before Thanksgiving, and wear their spring hats in winter; spend their time and money in the beauty parlor getting the boyish bob, marcel, or permanent wave; making their social calendar; serving on juries, mixing with men in politics, and organizing the different women's clubs and lodges.

Men play checkers in their place of business, play pool, tennis, baseball, football, basketball, for amusement, and even croquet by electric lights. They cannot hunt though, as there is no wild game left, unless they go to foreign territory; and then, except for forty-five days in the year, they run the risk of being fined.

Both men and women smoke cigarettes, and drink synthetic liquors that sell for $20.00 a quart. They seldom go to bed the same day they get up, and think they are having a wonderful time. This is the age of woman's rights, profiteers, radio bugs, and excess taxes, but who wants to go back to the "nineties"?

No one—more than a possible few of the very oldest who would like to live over their childhood days.

Not that the present age is superior. Folks now buy wildcat stock and undersea lots, read about bathtub parties, nude women, pajama dances on sleepers, and murders unequaled by those of any feud, and do acrobatic dancing with damage suits attached. But there is a difference.

It is very evident that most of the conditions have changed for the better—with improved county, State, and federal highways replacing the blazed routes or bridle-paths; telephone and telegraphic connections everywhere; trains every fifteen minutes, busses every hour with routes in every direction; mail delivered to the door within an hour or so after arriving at the post office; paved streets and alleys; sewers; good water systems; an all-time health unit; local Rotary, Kiwanis, D. A. R., and Eastern Star clubs, all striving for the best; modern homes and business houses of stucco, tile, and brick, all heated by gas, coal, hot water, steam, or hot air, and lighted with gas or electricity; the radio replacing the spinning wheel in these homes; modern methods of cooking with electric toasters, coffee pots; and other things too numerous to mention.

There are very few modern conveniences that are not enjoyed by the people of Johnson County. Indeed, these people possess high qualities, fine intellects, honesty, hospitality, and a general average much higher than some "outsiders" not familiar with the progress they have made, are willing to concede the mountain people.

More information on their "Modern Progress" may be had by referring to the chapters on Education, and Industrial Development.

REFERENCES TO CHAPTER VII

[1] Thomas, W. R., Life among the Hills and Mountains of Kentucky, pages 156-157. The Standard Printing Co., Louisville, Ky., 1924.
[2] Wells, M. L. K., Article in the Paintsville Herald, December 20, 1923.
[3] Walker, Mrs. Lizzie Auxier, Article in the Paintsville Herald, January 21, 1924.
[4] Thomas, W. R., Life among the Hills and Mountains of Kentucky, pages 165-167. The Standard Printing Co., Louisville, Ky., 1924.
[5] Ibid, pages 149 and 160.
[6] Johnson County Court Order Book No. 1.
[7] Ely, Wm., The Big Sandy Valley, page 415. Central Methodist Press, Catlettsburg, Ky., 1886.
[8] Jillson, W. R., The Big Sandy Valley, page 124. J. P. Morton Co., Louisville, Ky., 1923.
[9] The Paintsville Herald, 1926.

CHAPTER VIII
GEOLOGY
MAJOR DRAINAGE MODIFICATIONS OF BIG SANDY RIVER

BY DR. WILLARD ROUSE JILLSON, FRANKFORT, KENTUCKY

The Big Sandy River of southwestern Virginia, West Virginia, and Eastern Kentucky is only the upper middle portion of a former much larger stream. Recent discoveries of many erratic, streamworn, quartzite boulders, some of which carry pronounced wormborings have been made on the upper waters of the Licking River and the middle waters of the Big Sandy River. These boulders, ranging in weight from two to one hundred pounds, indicate that the ancient Big Sandy River had its headwaters in the Roan Mountain region of western North Carolina and southwestern Virginia. It is in this section of the Southern Appalachians, from Wytheville, Virginia, to Greenville, Tennessee, that the parent ledges of Middle Cambric quartzite (Hesse and Erwin formations) occur, from which these old stream-boulders were derived. This inference is further substantiated by many specimens of erratic vein-and-milky-quartz found at the same levels and in the same region as the quartzite boulders. Both are apparently identified with the old Cretacic peneplain, the present summit levels of this part of Eastern Kentucky.

Headwater piracy of the Clinch and the Bluestone rivers operating advantageously along northeast and southwest lines of favorable structure, beheaded, probably during Mid Tertic times, the upper one-fifth of the original Big Sandy River. The occurrence of so many of these quartzite boulders close to levels of the old Cretacic peneplain on the upper waters of the Licking River, as well as adjacent drainage courses, indicates that the Big Sandy River was through-flowing over the Licking to the northwest as late as the Cretacic period. The probability is that it had occupied this course since the uplift which marked the close of the Paleozoic era. Subsequent structural elevation along the nearly north and south axis of the Paint Creek uplift, in Johnson County, has operated to bisect the waters of the original Big Sandy, and shunted the upper waters to the northeast to join the Tug Fork, the course occupied today.

At the time the Big Sandy River flowed in the course of the Licking River, it did not, however, join the Ohio River in the vicinity of the present town site of Cincinnati, for during the Cretacic period there was no Ohio River, this stream being one of the direct products of Pleistocene glaciation. The original Big Sandy River, therefore, probably flowed on to the northwest in the region of southwestern Ohio and southeastern Indiana until it met major drainage and was turned to the southwest to the Gulf of Mexico, then heading at Cairo, Illinois, or what is more likely to have been the case, to the Great Lakes basin, by way of Lake Erie.

The old Big Sandy basin has thus been cut transversely three times: Firstly, about 75 miles below its headwaters by the Clinch and Bluestone rivers; secondly, 150 miles below its headwaters by the Paint Creek uplift; and thirdly, 300 miles below its headwaters by the newly formed glacial Ohio River. That all of these modifications occurred at the same time is highly improbable, but that they are all of post-Cretacic dates is quite certain. Various indications point to the Early and Mid Tertic periods, and Early Quaternic time.

[From the above, it will be observed that Dr. Jillson advances the idea that, at one time, the Big Sandy River connected with the Licking by way of Paint Creek. This, however, remains a matter of conjecture and is a subject for the geologists to discuss. It is included here to give the reader something to think about regarding the ancient formation of our section.]

JOHNSON COUNTY

Johnson County is located in the heart of the coal, oil and gas fields of east-central Kentucky, and is bounded on the north by Lawrence, on the east by Martin, on the south by Floyd, and on the west by Magoffin and Morgan counties.

Johnson is one of a group of counties said to be in the "Mountains," but in reality it is in a maturely dissected region known as the Cumberland Plateau which stretches from the Cumberland Mountains of the Southern Appalachians to the northward to the lowlands of the Ohio River. The people of this section do not regard themselves as living in the mountains at all.

The average elevation over the county is under 700 feet above sea level, which is very little above that of the Bluegrass section, while only a hundred miles up the valley it is a thousand feet higher. The lowest elevation, which is along the river, is 597 feet above sea level while the highest point is in the western part of the county on Salyers Fork of Little Paint Creek near Oil Springs. This elevation is 1,450 feet.

The soil is regarded as the best in Eastern Kentucky. It is of a sandy nature underlaid with an excellent quality of clay subsoil, and is especially adapted to the cultivation of vegetables and fruits which yield abundantly along the streams and bottom lands. The bottom and cove lands produce heavy crops of grain and meadow grasses, while the hillside lands do as well in grass, grain, and fruit, as other counties of the State. Some of these bottom lands were worn pretty thin by the one-time farmer who plowed them with water following in the furrow, and cultivated the hillsides till they washed, but the farmers are fast awakening to the danger and are now fertilizing the lowlands and using the hillsides for grazing purposes, or for orchards.

Blackberries and raspberries grow wild and need no cultivation. Some of the finest apples in the whole country are grown in the county, as is evidenced by first prizes awarded yearly to some of the local fruit growers at the annual State Fair.

CLIMATE

The productiveness of the soil is advanced by a very temperate climate, as this region is not a snow country. The winters, with a few exceptions, are as mild as northern Alabama or South Carolina. The summers do not show the excessive heat of the South or the uncomfortable humidity of the North. The summer nights are always cool. The average temperature in winter is from 24 to 40 degrees, and in summer from 60 to 80. On a few occasions, when cold was general over the United States, it has gone below zero, reaching 23 below in 1918, and as high as 101 in mid-summer. The canebrakes along the streams indicate a climate approximating that of the South.

STONE

There is one good building stone quarry, of the sandstone type, located on the "Bud" Stafford farm, south of Paint Creek, near Paintsville. The large columns in "The House That Mayo Built" are made of rock obtained from this site. Massive sandstones also occur in other localities. About a dozen quarries have already been tested and found suitable for masonry and base courses in road and street construction; one situated one-fourth mile south of the Chesapeake and Ohio railroad station at Paintsville, one near mouth of Paint Creek, one about a mile up Paint Creek from Paintsville, another on the Mayo Trail between Tay's Branch and Turner's Branch, one near the mouth of Turner's Branch, one one-half mile up Turner's Branch, another three or four miles north of the last one, another on the Mayo Trail on George's Creek, another at East Point, and one on the Garrett Highway at the mouth of Davis Branch two miles east of Paintsville. The following is what Charles H. Richardson has to say about them in his book, *The Road Materials of Kentucky:* "In some instances sandstones have sufficient binding material between the individual sand grains to hold the mass firmly together in such a manner as to render them fair road material. In a calcitic sandstone or quartzite like the one found on the Mayo Trail in Johnson County with a coefficient of wear of only 2.0, the lime should furnish binding material as rapidly as the stone is worn to dust. This sandstone will stand up under a roller."

By using 20 to 50 per cent extra cement over a 1-2-4 mix, good concrete can be made from this sandstone, by using the sandstone for coarse aggregate and sandstone screenings for fine aggregate. Screenings should be free of dust, and 95 per cent pass a one-quarter inch sieve.

Although smaller in size, there are numerous sandstone caverns in the county, similar to those of the limestone regions of the State. One of the largest is Peter Cave. It is about two miles

THE HOUSE THAT MAYO BUILT

east of Paintsville, on Davis Branch, and in what is known as the River Hill. Like Mammoth Cave, it drops in elevation at the entrance, rising and falling thereafter, with narrow passageways, leading to larger rooms. Although this cave has been explored by different parties, it has never been investigated from a geological standpoint. A few persons are said to have explored it for some distance several years back, but very few have gone farther than two hundred feet recently, for the reason that in the last few years, a large rock has fallen in the passageway at that distance which makes it difficult to go beyond. It should be removed in order to make a thorough investigation. This can be done at very little cost or trouble, on account of the position of the rock.

Other places of geological interest in the county in addition to those mentioned in the chapter on Prehistoric Inhabitants, are:

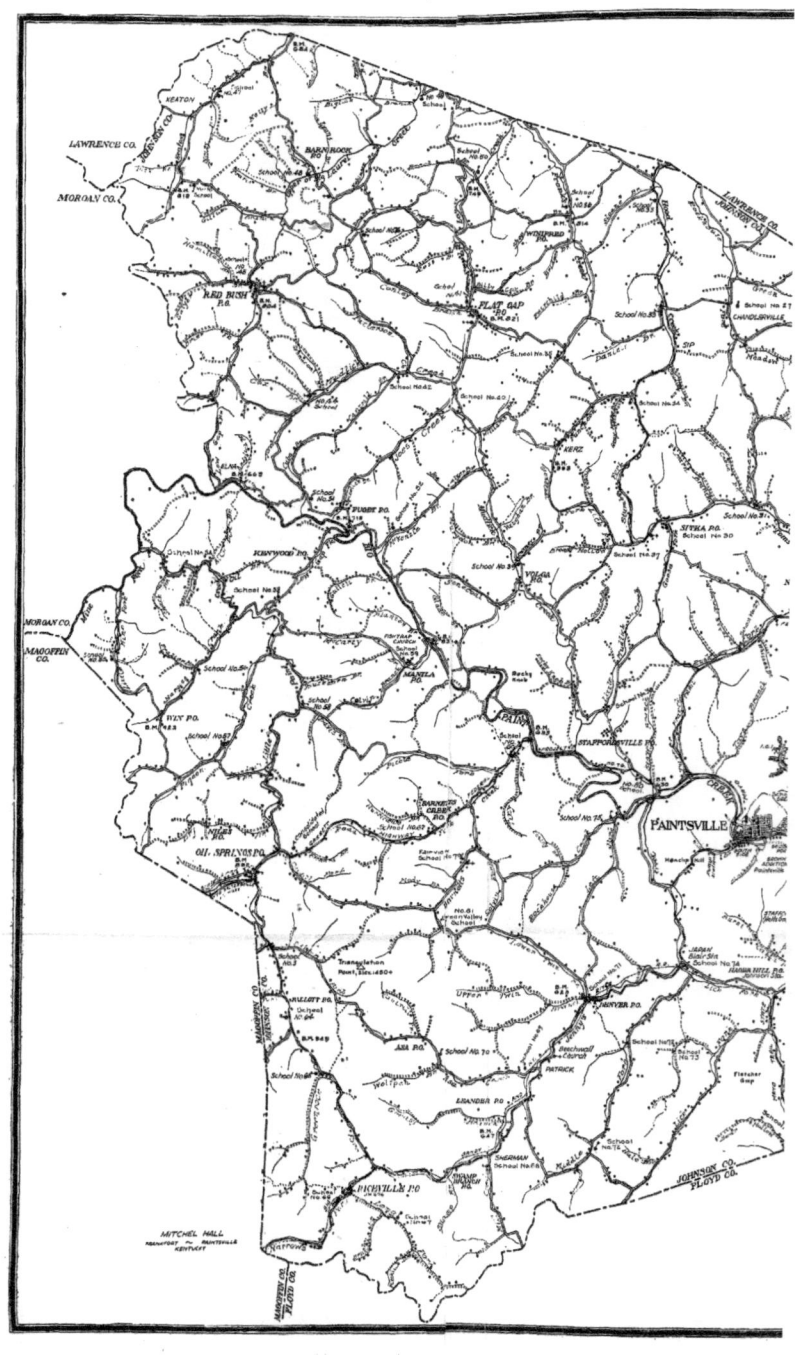

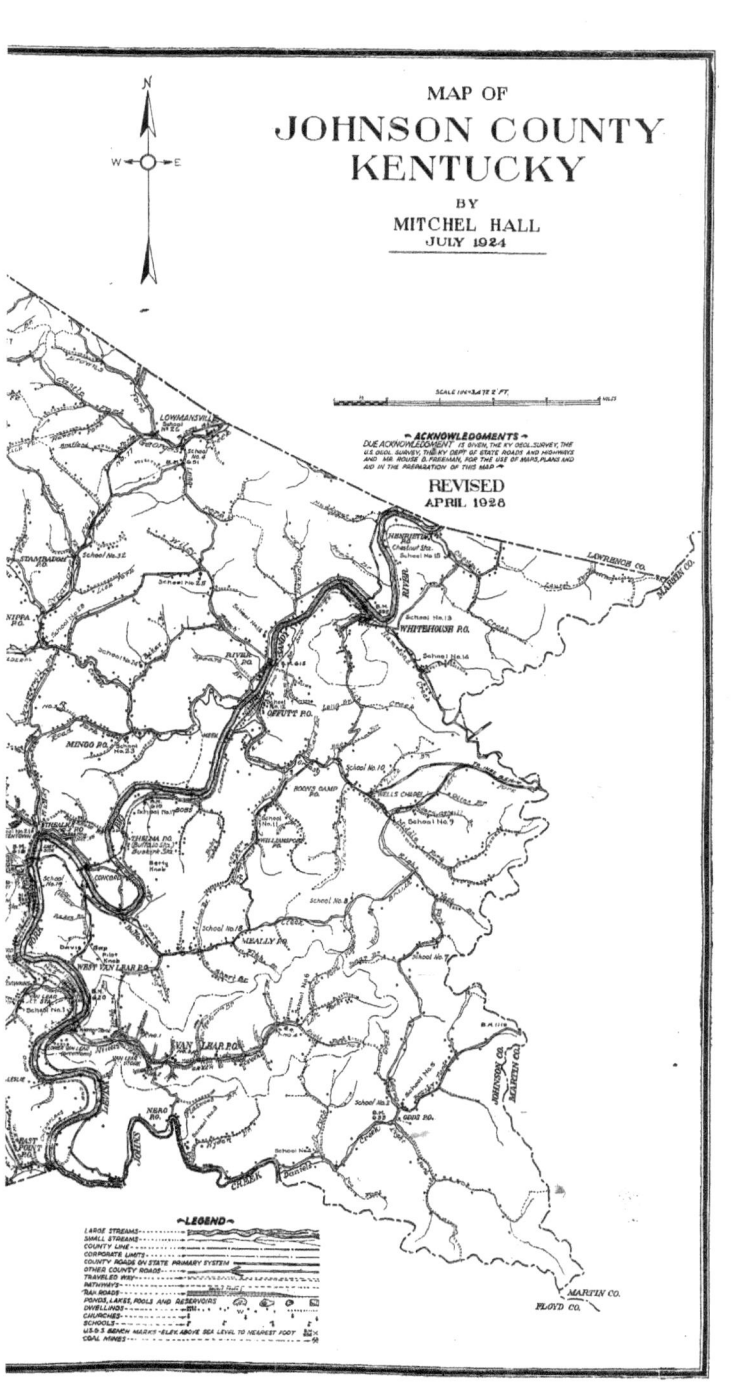

SOME OF THE BEAUTIFUL SURROUNDINGS OF FISH TRAP CHURCH ON BIG PAINT CREEK

GEOLOGY 163

Stafford Springs, near Staffordsville; the salt and sulphur well in Paintsville, now used for swimming pool purposes; Falls of Little Mud Lick; Hanging Rock; the artesian well on Teass Branch; and the rock cliffs on Big Paint near Fish Trap Church. Some of the most beautiful scenery in all Kentucky can be found at the last-named place.

The old artesian well on the Teass farm, which is just a few miles out of Paintsville, was the picnic ground and the gathering place of the youngsters at one time—they are now the mothers and fathers of Paintsville. This well is still running but it does not have the same appearance as formerly. The march of progress has caused the loss of the old box which forced the water up and out and provided many a cool and refreshing drink. The Falls of Little Mud Lick has also furnished the site of many an enjoyable picnic.

In the county are many broad and level creek and river bottoms, some being a mile wide, but the surface of the county is generally rolling and hilly. Some of the hills rise abruptly and to the person who is not accustomed to being surrounded by them, or to one returning after a long absence, they form a scene very beautiful; and to an "old-timer" bring back fond memories. Pilot Knob, Betty Knob, and Rocky Knob are some of the higher hills with elevation sufficient to warrant a name.

Far below the surface of these bottoms, and under the hills, lies the wonderful natural wealth of the county which makes it famous for its oil and coal, which it has in quantities which will require generations to exploit.

"When all these vast mineral resources have been exhausted; when the coal is gone and the oil has been taken away; when the industries have ceased to move, the Kentucky Mountains will still be the grandest place in the United States; the people will be the happiest; the roads will be hard-surfaced and the citizens better prepared for the building of character—the thing uppermost in the lives of those who pioneered the settlement of this beautiful country, and without which all institutions and industries must crumble to dust."[1]

STREAMS

The principal streams flowing in and through the county are: The Levisa Fork of the Big Sandy River, Big Paint Creek, John's Creek, Wiley Branch, Tom's Creek, Muddy Branch, Jenny's Creek, Little Paint Creek, Big and Little Mud Lick creeks, Millers Creek, Buffalo Creek, Greasy Creek, Lick Creek, Hammond Creek, and Keaton's, Upper and Lower Laurel, Frank's, Rockcastle, and Hood Forks of Blaine. The branches of these creeks are numerous and have chiseled the plateau into a network of low hills and valleys, and the various communities in the county are designated by their names.

The Levisa Fork of the Big Sandy River is the major stream of that section of the State. It meanders across the east central section of the county in a northerly direction, all of it being navigable two-thirds of the year. Much history is connected with the name of this river. The Indians knew it as the Totera, or Toteras, or Toteroy, as some of the Totero tribe had dwelt on it for a time. This tribe was also called the Shatteras. Sometimes the Indians pronounced the name so that it came to be Tateroy, Chateroi, or Chatarrawha. The name signified "river of sand bars." It was known officially in New York and Canada as early as 1699 as the Big Sandy River of Virginia. Hence in time, even though Dr. Thomas Walker, when he discovered it shortly after June 6, 1750, called it the Louisa River, it became known as the Big Sandy River. The early maps name the river variously. The Nuremburg Map of 1756 names it "Gt. Sandy." Evans in 1755 marked it "Tottery or Big Sandy C." Later in 1776 Pownall on his map of North America called it the "Totteroy" River, which, of course, meant "Big Sandy." But those tribes living at more remote points had quite a different name for the Big Sandy. The Miamis called it the "Wepepocone-cepewe," and the Delawares knew it as the "Sikea-cepe," meaning Salt Creek. The Shawnees knew the river by two names, "Mich-e-cho-be-ka-sepe," meaning the Mystery River; and "Me-tho-t-sepe," or the River of Many Buffalo. The Wyandot Indians called the Big Sandy "Sees-ta-ye-an-da-wa," the Fire River, from the natural gas springs which burned along its course.[2] During the early days of exploration and settlement, and indeed as late as 1835, the west fork or that one which flows through Johnson County went by the name of Louisa River, the name given it by Dr. Walker in 1750; but shortly thereafter it became corrupted into Levisa, which is now the official designation on maps and the like, though occasionally, it is called the Louisa River at the present time. It is said that Levisa is a colloquialization of the two French words *Le Visa*, meaning the picture or design. Tradition has it that an early French trader, whose own name has long since been forgotten, was prompted to name the Big Sandy River "Le Visa" because of the numerous Indian paintings of birds and beasts which he found on trees and rocks throughout the valley from Paint Creek to the headwaters.[3]

Dr. W. R. Jillson in his history of the Big Sandy Valley specifically states that "Levisa" is now the accepted name of the principal fork of the Big Sandy River, however it came about. It might be added that this is correct insofar as the "outside world" is concerned; but, if one were to ask the majority of those living on this principal fork of the river, the reply would be that they lived on Big Sandy River. Those residing on the other or

THE SCENIC BIG SANDY

Tug Fork say they live on "Tug," while those on the first named seldom refer to Levisa Fork at all, and have unanimously accepted the name "Big Sandy River." This last would appear to be correct as, at their junction the Tug Fork is 240 feet wide, while the other is 372 feet in width. In view of the fact that the Kentucky-West Virginia state line runs with the waters of Tug Fork (see pages 62 f.) it has been misleading to many in making maps, and they show that fork as the principal one, which is not the case. Practically all the official county records of Floyd County, dating back to 1808, refer to this stream as the "Sandy River." The Louisa Fork is referred to a very few times.

There is also an interesting story connected with the naming of the Tug Fork of the Big Sandy River. A little band of soldiers were sent out in the fall of 1757 by Governor Dinwiddie to seek revenge on a party of Shawnees who had destroyed the Roanoke settlement, and to establish a fort at the mouth of the "Great Sandy." Officers of this little army are said to have cut two buffalo hides, which had been left hanging by them some time before on a tree at the "Great Burning Spring," near the present town of Kermit, into tugs and given them to their soldiers to prevent starvation after their provisions had been exhausted and the proximity of Indians restrained them from firing a gun or kindling a fire. Thus the Tug River is said to have received its name.[4]

Both these rivers rise in southwest Virginia, twenty miles or less apart, both flowing almost directly north on approximately parallel lines from twenty-five to forty miles apart, until near their junction at Louisa, where they unite and flow on to the Ohio. The Big Sandy River (Levisa) is known as the Pound River in Virginia until it passes through the breaks of the Cumberlands. It is regarded by the Government as being navigable to the mouth of Shelby Creek, a distance of approximately one hundred and twenty miles, of which about forty miles is under lock and dam.

This valley, like all others, has had its floods. Of the more important was the one of 1862, when all that section of Paintsville next to the hill in the vicinity of the Mayo College is said to have been under water; the washout of July, 1875, in midsummer when all other streams were at low tide; the one of 1893; the 1918 ice flood caused by several days of continuous downpour of rain on an immense pact of snow and ice formed during one of the severest winters ever experienced in the section. This last tide reached its height at forty-six feet. A more recent high water just before Christmas, 1926, came within three feet of the 1918 deluge.

TO BIG SANDY RIVER

Dear River of Big Sandy!
  Dost thou know thy worth?
To the noblest sons and daughters,
  Thou hast given birth!

Thy hills, thy vales, and streamlets,
  All have issued forth
And added to the big world
  Things of endless worth.

Thy "Johns" alone, Dear River,
  Will stand a mighty test
For having given to the world
  The things that life holds best.

There was "John," the giant dreamer,
  Who from thy crusted hills,
Brought forth tons of black diamonds
  That the world's great coffer fills.

And there is "John," the banker,
  Who can shame his worth?
He fights for right, always,
  And his banks never burst.

We could write of "Johns" forever
  But it isn't fair
For the "Sams," "Bills," and others
  Must too, have a share.

There are statesmen, doctors, lawyers,
  Preachers and editors by the score,
Who from thy towns and hamlets
  A constant outcome pour.

Thy lovely, virtuous daughters
  Have added to the store
Of wondrous good and knowledge,
  That passes out thy door.

Many of thy noblest
  Are sleeping 'neath the sod—
But we know their souls are happy
  In the land of God.

> May thy trembling waters,
>   Ere their mournful dirges sing,
> As around their silent homes,
>   Thy surges ever cling.
>
> 'Tis not volumes of water
>   That makes a river great;
> 'Tis her loving souls and true ones,
>   And the way they deal with fate.
>
> —*DORIS ROBINSON HOLT,*
> Wilsonburg, W. Va.

Following are some legislative acts pertaining to this stream, and of historical value to the county.

Chapter 85, Page 173, Acts 1858.

"Be it enacted by the General Assembly of the Commonwealth of Kentucky, That Eliphus Preston, of Johnson County, be and he is hereby permitted to build a chute in Sandy River, in Johnson County, at the place where he proposes to build a mill, on one side of said river, so the same does not impair or obstruct the free navigation of said Sandy River. This act shall take effect from its passage."

Approved January 14, 1858.

Chapter 1225, Page 94, Acts 1888.

AN ACT to amend an act regarding fish.

"Be it enacted by the General Assembly of the Commonwealth of Kentucky, That the act entitled 'An act for the propagation and protection of food fishes in the waters of the state of Kentucky,' approved March 20, 1876, be, and the same is hereby, so amended as to provide that it shall be lawful for any one to catch fish with a seine or net in that part of the Big Sandy River and its tributaries, lying in Floyd and Johnson counties; *Provided,* That all fish so caught except those to be used for food, shall be returned to the water.

"2. This act shall take effect from its passage and apply to the counties of Floyd and Johnson only."

Became a law without approval of the Governor, April 25, 1888.

Chapter 730, Page 548, Acts 1888.

AN ACT for the benefit of Frank Preston and others.

"Be it enacted by the General Assembly of the Commonwealth of Kentucky, That it shall be lawful for said Frank Preston, Mont

Preston and G. B. Preston, their lessees, assignees and grantees to charge and collect a reasonable wharfage upon all shipment of goods or merchandise of any kind placed on said wharfboat while in course of shipment, said wharfage not to exceed the usual rates charged along said river upon similar articles. They shall also have a right to charge a fee, of not exceeding one dollar per day, for any boat or craft anchored, or tied at said wharfboat; *Provided,* That said fees shall not be charged of any boat or craft for landing merely to put off or take on freight. They shall have a lien for said wharfage upon all such goods or merchandise placed upon said wharfboat; said lien to be enforced as other liens for wharfage are enforced; and they may proceed against any boat or craft, by suit in any court of competent jurisdiction, for the fee herein provided for.

"2. This act shall take effect from and after its passage."

Became a law without approval of the Governor, March 27, 1888.

BIG PAINT CREEK heads in Morgan County, runs thirty miles east through the west central part of Johnson, and empties its turbid waters into the Big Sandy River at Paintsville. It is a short but very broad stream, deep enough to afford water to float out great rafts of logs from very near its head, for which it has been noted.

It drains about one-half of the area of the county. Its main tributaries are Mine Fork, Little Paint, Barnetts Creek, Big and Little Mud Licks, and Jenny's Creek.

It is said to have received its name from the numerous Indian paintings of birds and beasts found painted on rocks and trees from its mouth to the headwaters. (See page 37.)

The creek is declared navigable to the Morgan County line by legislative act.

Chapter 822, Page 223, Acts 1886.

AN ACT to re-enact an act to authorize Martin Preston and Company to keep a boom across the mouth of Paint Creek.

"Be it enacted by the General Assembly of the Commonwealth of Kentucky, That an act entitled an act to authorize Martin Preston and Company to keep a boom across the mouth of Paint Creek, in Johnson County, March 8, 1884, be, and the same is hereby re-enacted, and the same shall remain in full force and effect for the period of two years, from the passage of this act.

"2. That this act shall take effect and be in force from and after its passage."

Approved April 26, 1886.

JOHN'S CREEK is a stream long enough to be called a river (ninety-nine miles); heads up near the sources of the Big Sandy and Tug, between the two, and runs nearly parallel with them till it empties into the Big Sandy eight miles above the mouth of Paint Creek on the Johnson-Floyd County line. Although much longer, it is not so broad a stream as Big Paint Creek, probably because the latter has a larger drainage area per mile. Very little territory within the county is drained by this creek, as it merely borders on the county line. One of its main feeders, Daniel's Creek, however, is all within the county.

Chapter 300, Page 554, Acts 1882.

AN ACT authorizing W. H. Davis, J. S. Kelly and J. C. B. Auxier to erect and keep a boom at the mouth of John's Creek.

"*Be it enacted by the General Assembly of the Commonwealth of Kentucky,* That W. H. Davis, J. S. Kelly, and J. C. B. Auxier, and their assigns, heirs, and survivors, are authorized to erect and keep a boom in and across the mouth of John's Creek, in Floyd County, for the purpose of catching and securing such loose sawlogs as may come against it and they are authorized to charge the owners of the logs ten cents per log for catching and holding the same, and shall have a lien on the said logs for the charges; and when it becomes necessary to open said boom, if any of the owners of the logs should not be present and able to take care of their logs, then the owners of the boom are authorized to raft said logs and charge a reasonable compensation therefor, and have a like lien on the logs for the rafting as is given herein for catching; *Provided,* The keepers of said boom shall use a reasonable diligence in holding said boom; but shall not be responsible for unavoidable accidents.

"2. This act shall take effect from its passage."

Approved February 27, 1882.

Chapter 812, Page 216, Acts 1886.

AN ACT authorizing Henry C. Wells to erect a milldam across Daniel's Creek.

"*Be it enacted by the General Assembly of the Commonwealth of Kentucky,* That Henry C. Wells, be, and he is hereby, authorized to erect a milldam in and across Daniel's Creek, Johnson County. Said dam shall be so constructed as not to interfere nor obstruct the navigation of said creek for the purpose of drifting and floating logs and staves out of said creek.

"2. This act shall take effect from its passage."

Approved April 26, 1886.

TOM'S CREEK is a stream about twelve miles in length draining the northern part of the county on the west side of the river. Heading up against Mud Lick Creek and the headwaters of Blaine, it flows in an easterly direction and empties into the Big Sandy opposite Offutt. Its main tributaries are Road Fork, Bakers Branch, Whipperwill, Rush Fork, Sycamore Fork, Frogonery, and Lick Fork. One of the most disastrous storms and cloudbursts ever known in the county hit heaviest on this creek on May 30, 1927, causing great damage, enormous property loss, and the death of three persons.

Chapter 345, Page 17, Acts 1849.

AN ACT declaring Tom's and Paint creeks navigable.

"Be it enacted by the General Assembly of the Commonwealth of Kentucky, That Tom's Creek in Johnson County, be, and it is hereby, declared a navigable stream from its mouth to Charles Grim's.

"2. *Be it further enacted,* That Big Paint Creek in the said county, be, and it is hereby, declared navigable from Rule's Mill to the Morgan County line."

Chapter 432, Page 50, Acts 1850.

AN ACT extending navigation on Tom's Creek.

"Be it enacted by the General Assembly of the Commonwealth of Kentucky, That navigation on Tom's Creek in Johnson County, be, and is hereby, extended up to James Ramy's, Esq."

Approved March 6, 1850.

JENNY'S CREEK is a stream about fifteen miles in length draining the southwestern part of the county. Heading in Magoffin County, it flows in an easterly direction toward the Big Sandy till within three miles of the river, where it abandons what appears to have been in time the natural course through the Hager Hill Gap, and flows northerly to empty into Big Paint Creek. Its main feeders are Lick Fork, Middle Fork, Upper and Lower Twin branches, Asa Creek, Mill Creek, Greasy Branch, Greenrock, Long and Narrows forks.

This creek is named for the brave Jenny Wiley who traveled up it and its Lick Fork in her escape from the Indians. (See the Wiley family in section two.)

Chapter 37, Page 384, Acts 1851.

Jenny's Creek declared navigable.

"Be it enacted by the General Assembly of the Commonwealth of Kentucky, That Jenny's Creek in Johnson County be, and it is hereby, declared navigable, as far up as Martin R. Rice's place."

GEOLOGY

MUD LICK CREEK, LITTLE PAINT, and MINE FORK, all tributaries of Big Paint, have also been factors in the timber business in the county. Mud Lick was the site of an old Shawnee Indian village. Keaton's, Upper and Lower Laurel, Frank's, Rockcastle, and Hood forks of Big Blaine drain the northwestern or oil section of the county. The Castle and Brown's forks of George's Creek drain that portion of the section between the last-named creeks and the headwaters of Tom's Creek and Wiley's Branch.

Few counties in the State have such a network of streams as Johnson. Although they are not of such value now, except for drainage and water purposes, they were of inestimable worth in the day of timbering and the water mill.

Large tracts of timbers are still to be found on these creeks. Poplar, walnut, oak, ash, hickory, sycamore, linden, and pine are the principal timbers.

GREASY CREEK is one of the smaller creeks of the county, being about six and one-half miles long. It heads at the Martin County line and drains the northeastern section of the county. Its branches are Two Mile Creek, Buzzard's Roost, Hurricane, Pigeonroost, Left, Middle, and Right forks.

This creek, famous for its wild game, received its name from the hunting expeditions of Daniel Boone, Nat Auxier, and others, who are said to have carried their game in sacks on horseback. The sacks and skins rubbing against the trees along the paths left the trees greasy, and hence the title. (See page 48.)

Chapter 187, Page 507, Acts 1852.

Greasy Creek declared navigable.

"Be it enacted by the General Assembly of the Commonwealth of Kentucky, That Greasy Creek, in Johnson County be, and it is hereby, declared a navigable stream.

"This act shall take effect from its passage."

Approved January 1, 1852.

WILEY'S BRANCH is a small stream of only a few miles in length, hardly long enough to be called a creek but designated as such by the Government maps, that empties into the Big Sandy River just below the mouth of Tom's Creek. After the successful return of Jenny Wiley to her family in Virginia, they came back to the valley and settled near the mouth of this creek, and today its name is a monument to the memory of this heroic family.

Chapter 652, Page 61, Acts 1880.

AN ACT declaring Wiley's Branch a navigable stream.

"Be it enacted by the General Assembly of the Commonwealth of Kentucky, That Wylies [Wiley's] Branch, in Johnson County be, and it is hereby, declared navigable up to David K. Brown's."

There are several creeks in the county, larger and longer than the last named that have never been designated as navigable by legislative action, but which have long been used for floating and drifting saw-logs, ties, and staves to market. They are:

BUFFALO CREEK, which drains the central eastern part of the county, and named after the many bison said to have grazed along its waters.

MILLERS CREEK, a "twin sister" to Buffalo, of about equal length, running in the same direction and almost parallel, empties into the river at West Van Lear. It is the site of the mine operations of the Consolidation Coal Company, and is now a continuous town from the mouth to its head.

The same is true of MUDDY BRANCH, and LICK CREEK, where the Northeast Coal Company operates.

TOWNS

The towns of Johnson County are Paintsville, Van Lear, Thealka (Muddy Branch), White House, West Van Lear, East Point, Offutt, Oil Springs, Flat Gap, Denver, Riceville, and Red Bush. There are other villages, not large enough to be classed as towns, but better known by post offices as follows: Asa, Ballott, Swamp Branch, Hager Hill, Barnetts Creek, Niles, Win, Manila, Kenwood, Fuget, Barn Rock, Volga, Winifred, Staffordsville, Sitka, Nippa, Stambaugh, Mingo, River, Henrietta, Boons Camp, Williamsport, Meally, Nero, Thelma, Colista, Odds, and Lindbergh.

Community centers are Well's Chapel, Lomansville, Chandlerville, Concord, Japan, Kerz, Keaton, Elna, Fish Trap, Beech Wall, Dawkins, Patrick, Sherman, and Leslie.

Accounts are given in the following paragraphs of the different towns.

PAINTSVILLE—"THE HUB OF THE BIG SANDY"

Paintsville is the county seat and by far the most important town within its territory. It was originally an old trading post, called Paint Lick Station, known to have been in existence as early as the Revolution, as it is mentioned by Captain William Russell, in a letter to Colonel William Fleming, June 12, 1775.[5]

Not much history is recorded of the station for the next half century, in view of the fact that it was overshadowed by Har-

THE FIRST HOUSE TO BE ERECTED IN PAINTSVILLE, KY.

man's Station in Blockhouse Bottom and some of the others that grew faster then. The first record of importance was in 1826 when it is frequently mentioned in the records of Floyd County. It is mentioned as a post office and called Paintsville in the following letter. (See Page 340, Order Book No. 4, Floyd County.)

Paintsville, January the 23rd, 1826.

W. Jacob Mayo,

Dear Sir: This will inform you of my determination to resign my commission as Justice of the Peace. You will please act accordingly—inform the Court that I have never received the dockets of Thomas C. Brown and George Daniel to enable them to dispose of their papers together with the papers of my office.

Yours respectfully,

CHARLES RUMSEY.

It is also mentioned in the road orders on February 27, 1826. (See Page 347, Book 4, Floyd County.)

The next official record noted was the act establishing Paintsville as a town in 1834, as follows:

Chapter 554, Page 787, Acts 1834.

"Section 7. That the town of Paintsville in Floyd County, be, and the same is hereby, established, upon the plan laid out by Henry Dickson; a plat of the same is hereby directed to be recorded in the Floyd County Court Clerk's Office, which said plan is ratified and established by virtue of this act; and John Auxier, James Franklin, Thomas Wallace, James Harris, and John B. Laughhorn, be, and they are hereby, appointed trustees of said town, who as well as their successors, shall have the same power and authority, and shall perform the same duties as are given and empowered by the general laws of this Commonwealth in relation to trustees of towns.

"Section 8. That the trustees and citizens of said town shall in every respect be governed by the third, fourth, fifth, and sixth sections of this act."

Approved February 24, 1834.

The above plat could not be located in the clerk's office.

The sections mentioned and referred to in Section 8 were passed for the then town of Portland in the county of Jefferson, in connection with the establishment of said town, and by Section 8 included in the establishing of Paintsville. They are as follows:

"Section 3. *Be it further enacted*, That the said trustees shall remain in office until the first Monday in March, 1835, on which day, and on the first Monday in March in each succeeding year, the free male inhabitants of said town, of the age of twenty-one and upwards, shall meet at such place as may be designated by the trustees in said town, and choose by vote, viva voce, five fit persons for trustees, to serve for one year, and until their successors are duly elected.

"Section 4. *Be it further enacted,* That the said trustees shall appoint a town clerk, who shall continue in office, until the election succeeding his appointment; and in like manner each new board of trustees shall appoint a clerk to serve for the same term, whose duty it shall be to keep a fair record of the proceedings of the trustees, and to give public notice, by the advertisement in said town, at least ten days previous to any election for trustees; and he shall, together with any two of the trustees, conduct all elections and declare the persons elected, and make record of the same.

"Section 5. *Be it further enacted,* That if the citizens of said town shall at any time hereafter fail to have an election, on the day appointed in this act, that then and in that case, the clerk or any trustee, may upon giving ten days of previous notice have an election held for trustees, which shall be as legal as though it had taken place on the day herein appointed.

"Section 6. *Be it further enacted,* That the trustees herein appointed, and their successors in office, a majority of them concurring therein, shall have full power to pass all laws which they may from time to time think advisable for the government of said town; *Provided,* They be not contrary to the laws and constitution of this state."

Floyd County court order, March 9, 1835.

"ORDERED that the constables district or bounds be extended at Paintsville one-half mile each way from the public square."

When the county was formed in 1844, with Paintsville as the county seat, the corporate limits were extended, and the trustees given additional powers, as follows:

Chapter 300, Page 219, Acts 1844.

(Secs. 1 to 4 of this act are with reference to Columbus, a town in Hickman County.)

"Section 5. *Be it further enacted,* That the corporation limits of the town of Paintsville be, and the same are hereby, extended in manner as follows, to-wit: so as to include the lot of six acres belonging to B. F. Gardner, which embraces a portion of the public square; also, the orchard, lot and land of John Franklin; thence running up the creek to the upper lot in said town; thence from James Franklin's mill, including said mill, to low-water mark; thence from the end of Main Cross Street, near Jones'

BIRD'S-EYE VIEW OF PAINTSVILLE, KY.
(Taken from South Side Looking Down Big Paint Creek)

tan-yard, thirty poles north; thence a westwardly direction, so as to include Henry Dickson; thence southwardly to J. H. Huff's.

"Section 6. That Nicholas C. Waldeck, John Hows, Joseph T. Kelly, James Franklin and Winston Mayo, and their successors, be, and are hereby, created trustees of said town, and as such, shall, in addition to the powers heretofore granted in the act incorporating said town, have power, by ordinance, to grade, pave, repair, and improve any street, alley, market space, public landing, or common, upon the petition of not less than the owners of two-thirds of the property of any section, square or part of a square of said town, binding on such street, alley, market space, public landing, or common, so to be graded, paved or repaired, and to levy and collect a special tax, to defray the cost or expenses of the same; and the said trustees shall have power to provide, by ordinance, for the collection of the special tax herein authorized to be levied, by sale of the property binding on any street, alley, market space, public landing, or common, proposed to be graded, paved or repaired, in such manner as they may deem most expedient, and conducive to the safe, certain and speedy collection thereof; that the special tax levied for the purposes herein prescribed, shall be a lien upon the real estate upon which it may be assessed from the time of filing such petition, until it shall be paid and satisfied.

"Section 7. That all fines and forfeitures, accruing from any violation of the laws and ordinances of said town, shall be and the same are hereby appropriated to the use and benefit of said town."

Approved March 1, 1844.

Chapter 1266, Page 822, Acts 1860.

AN ACT enlarging the corporate limits of Paintsville.

"Be it enacted by the General Assembly of the Commonwealth of Kentucky, That the corporate lines of the town of Paintsville, in Johnson County, be so enlarged as to include within the corporate limits of said town the house and lot purchased by Jo Mahan from John Stafford.

"This act to take effect from and after its passage."

Approved March 3, 1860.

March 25, 1872.

AN ACT to incorporate the town of Paintsville.

"Be it enacted by the General Assembly of the Commonwealth of Kentucky:

"1. That the boundary of the town of Paintsville, in Johnson County, shall be as follows, viz.:

"Beginning at the mouth of the first ravine on the north side of Paint Creek, below the mill, including the bridge over it, and running thence to a rock at the point of the hill below town; thence with the foot of the hill, including the house of John W. How, to the ford of Paint Creek, known as the Spradlin Ford; thence down the creek including it to the highwater mark on the south side to a point opposite the beginning point; thence across the creek to the beginning.

"2. The suburban limits of said town shall be as follows:

"Beginning on Sandy River, at the head of Buffalo Shoal; thence by the top of the ridge to the head of A. W. Rule's Branch including all of it; thence to the branch opposite the mouth of Jennie's Creek, so far up as to include the house of A. J. Fox; thence south to Paint Creek, so as to include all the houses opposite the mouth of Jennie's Creek; from thence, including the house of Allen Collins, to the head of Hencliff, and from thence to Sandy River at Hell's Gate Shoal, including all the houses on the premises of F. M. Stafford; and from said shoal to the beginning, so as to include all the houses at the mouth of Buffalo.

"3. The municipal concerns of said town, with the government and control thereof, shall be vested in a board of three trustees and a police judge. The trustees and police judge shall be elected biennially on the first Saturday of May, beginning with 1872, by the qualified voters of the town proper. The police judge, by virtue of his office, shall be chairman of the board of trustees, and he and the three trustees shall each, in addition to the oath prescribed by the Constitution, take an oath of affirmation, to be administered by any person authorized to administer same, that they will faithfully and impartially discharge all the duties of their respective offices, a certificate of the officer administering same, to that fact shall be filed with the papers of the town. If any officer provided for in this act shall, for twenty days after his election, fail or refuse to qualify, he shall thereby vacate his office and the trustees who have qualified, if a majority shall so qualify, shall fill the vacancy or vacancies by appointment. If a majority fail to qualify, or if no election is held, the judge of the Johnson County Court, at its first regular term, after such failure to qualify, or to hold election, shall appoint the three trustees, who shall, after qualifying, proceed to appoint a chairman from their number or other person of the town, and the persons so appointed shall hold their respective offices until the next regular election for such offices.

"4. If the chairman of the board of trustees shall, at any time, resign his office, or a vacancy shall in any other manner occur, the trustees shall proceed to elect as provided for above in case of their being appointed by the county judge; and the person so appointed shall immediately be recommended by the trustees to the Governor of the State for commission, and when so commissioned shall proceed with all the powers of police judge as if regularly elected, and hold his office until next regular election for judge; and the police judge appointed or elected, as herein provided, shall be fully authorized, upon qualifying as trustee, to sit and act as chairman of the board of trustees, previous to the receipt of his commission as police judge.

"5. The chairman and a majority of the trustees shall constitute a quorum for transaction of business, and they may regulate, by ordinance, the time and place of their meetings. The chairman shall preside over the meetings of the trustees, which, in all cases must be public; shall vote only in cases of a tie; he may enforce good order at such meetings, and the attendance of the trustees by fine, not exceeding five dollars; and in his absence from town, the trustees may elect one of their own number to act as chairman for the time being, who shall in addition to his vote as trustee, exercise the powers of the chairman, but not of police judge. The chairman shall have the power to appoint committees among the trustees, and compel them to serve on the same, and perform their duties by fines, not exceeding ten dollars.

"6. The board of trustees shall have power to make by-laws and ordinances to maintain the peace, good order and government of the town, to regulate the trade, commerce, and manufacture thereof, not repugnant to the Constitution and laws of the state; they shall have no power to pass any such by-laws or ordinances inflicting a heavier penalty than fifty dollars, but may make such as will enable the judge of police court (to) carry into effect the objects, offices and vested powers of this act, not exceeding fines of fifty dollars.

"7. The said trustees shall also have power, in addition to the other powers granted by this charter:

"*First.* To provide for establishing and maintaining free schools.

"*Second.* Appoint biennially a clerk to record and keep their proceedings, who shall take oath as provided herein for trustees; he shall attend all meetings of said board of trustees, and make a full and fair record of their proceedings in a book to be furnished him; he shall be the custodian of the records and documents of the town. If said clerk fails for ten days to qualify, his office shall be declared vacant. The trustees may provide for paying said clerk for his services.

"*Third.* To appoint annually a competent person as treasurer, who shall receive and safely keep all moneys belonging to the town, and pay out the same under appropriations made by the board of trustees; but he shall only pay out money on warrants drawn by the clerk, and indorsed by the chairman; he shall keep a fair and accurate account of all his disbursements and receipts, when, from, and to whom, and for what purpose such moneys were received or paid, and shall exhibit the same, and furnish a certified copy of same, when required by the board so to do. He shall, before entering on the duties of his office, and shall execute a bond to said town, before said board of trustees, with one or more approved sureties, covenanting that he will account for, and pay over to the person entitled to receive the same, according to law, any and all moneys that may come into his hands as trustee of said town; that he settle his accounts whenever called on by the board of trustees so to do, and pay any balance in his hands to the person they may designate, and faithfully discharge all the duties of his office. Any person aggrieved may institute suit or motion on the bond given by the treasurer as aforesaid in the police court of Paintsville, or in Johnson Circuit Court against the treasurer and his sureties; and said bond shall not be satisfied or void till every person aggrieved is satisfied. The board of trustees may, at any time, require a new bond of the treasurer, or additional security; and a failure to comply satisfactorily with the notice, or to give bond on his appointment, for ten days, shall vacate his office. Nothing herein shall prevent one of the trustees from receiving the appointment of treasurer of the town.

"8. The trustees shall have power to assess, levy, and collect an ad valorem tax on all real and personal estate, and choses in action, as may be within the limits of the town; but said assessment shall be uniform, and on every description of property, and shall not, in any one year, exceed twenty cents on each one hundred dollars worth of property. They shall also have power to levy and collect a head tax, not to exceed two dollars on every male person over twenty-one years of age who has resided in said town three months.

"9. They shall also have power, in addition to the above ad valorem tax, to levy and collect a special tax, not exceeding twenty dollars per annum, upon all merchants, grocers, peddlers, brokers, bankers, tavern keepers, victualers, confectioners and auctioneers doing business in said town. They shall also have power to tax the sellers of spirituous or malt liquors within the town, or its suburban limits, in any sum not exceeding two hundred dollars per year, and enforce its collection. They shall also have power to tax all hacks, carriages, coaches, carts, drays, wagons, or other vehicles hauling for hire in said town, in any sum not exceeding ten dollars. Said board shall also have the power to license and tax, in any sum not exceeding ten dollars, all theatrical and other exhibitions, shows, amusements, circuses, menageries, lectures and musical entertainments.

"10. The said board shall have power, by ordinance, to provide to whom, when, and the manner in which all special taxes

SOUTH SIDE OF MAIN STREET, PAINTSVILLE, KY.

or licenses shall be paid, and the manner of enforcing the collection of the same, and to punish by fine all breaches of ordinances concerning them.

Police Court

"11. There shall be established in said town a court, to be styled the 'Police Court of Paintsville,' which shall be held by the judge, who shall be called the 'Police Judge of Paintsville.' He shall, before entering on the duties of his office, take the oath prescribed by section four of this act.

"12. For any violation of the by-laws or ordinances of said town and in felonies and misdemeanors, the jurisdiction of said court shall be as prescribed by the criminal code of practice. In civil cases, the jurisdiction of said court shall be concurrent, within the limits of said town, with the jurisdiction of a justice of the peace; and the fees of said judge shall be the same as fees of a justice of the peace for similar services, and collected in the same way.

"13. Whenever from any cause, the judge of said court fails to attend the court, or attend and cannot properly preside in a case or cases before it, the presiding judge of the Johnson County Court may preside in his place; and if, for cause, the county judge cannot preside in any such case, any justice of the peace of said county may preside; and the person so presiding shall, during the period he acts, have all the powers and be liable to all the responsibilities of the police judge, and shall receive all fees accruing for said period. If no court is held on the day and summons or warrants are made returnable, the cause shall be considered as, and by operation of law, continued from day to day.

"14. Appeals from the judgment of said court may be taken as now provided from the judgments of justices of the peace for similar amounts, and shall be regulated by the laws governing appeals from the courts of justices of the peace.

"15. Said police judge shall be his own clerk; but it shall be lawful for him to appoint a deputy as clerk, who may perform all the duties of clerk of said court. Said clerk shall be called the deputy clerk of the police court of Paintsville, and shall possess the same qualifications, and take the same oaths, before he enters on the duties of his office, as are required by law of a deputy clerk of a circuit court.

"16. All fines and forfeitures for a violation of any of the by-laws or ordinances of said town shall be paid into the treasury of said town.

"17. Said court shall be a court of record, and all copies of papers or records on file with the judge shall, when duly attested by him, or the deputy clerk, be received as evidence in all cases where the originals would be evidence; but nothing herein shall prevent any court from having the original record produced, and brought to court by proper process.

"18. Said trustees shall have power to employ an attorney for said town, prescribe his duties, and make him such compensation, and to be paid in such manner, as they may deem proper.

"19. Said board shall have power to appoint annually, a competent person as assessor of the town, prescribing his duties, who shall, within ten (10) days, qualify faithfully to perform his duties.

"20. It shall be the duty of the assessor to take a list of all the taxable property within said town, whether in good stock, manufactories, or other properties that may be designated by said board, giving the cash value of the same, the name of the owner thereof, making such division of said property in separate columns, as the board may direct; he shall also list all male persons over twenty-one (21) years of age, giving the occupation or profession of each; also a list of the public houses, stores, etc.; he shall file with the clerk of the board his books containing the above-mentioned lists, on or before the 8th day of July, 1872, and on or before the first of April each following year.

"21. He shall call on persons from whom taxes are collectable for a list of their taxable property, and administer the oath as county assessors do; and if any person fails or refuses to list his or her property, the assessor may list the same from the best of his information.

"22. Any person failing or refusing to give a list of his or her taxable property, when called upon so to do by the assessor, or giving a false or fraudulent return, shall be adjudged a delinquent, and fined a sum not exceeding twenty dollars ($20.00) and the assessor shall file a list of such delinquents with the clerk at the time he files his books, and state on same in what the fraud and falsehood consists, and the police court shall have jurisdiction over the case as of breach of town ordinances.

"23. The board of trustees shall annually appoint three discreet men, citizens of the town, and housekeepers, as a board of supervisors, who shall meet at the office of town clerk as soon as convenient after the assessor files his books, not exceeding fifteen days, and examine with care, and correct any errors therein, both of fact and valuation; that shall advertise by written posters for five days, the time and place of their sitting, at three public places in the town; they shall certify the books, when corrected, to the town clerk, and give every person a right to appear before them by attorney or in person, and introduce evidence concerning their property; they shall, so far as applicable, be governed by the general statutes with regard to tax supervisors.

LOOKING EAST, MAIN STREET, PAINTSVILLE, KY.

"24. That the trustees of said town shall have power, by ordinance to accept, receive, any alley or street or the extension of any such; and may make and declare them to be streets or alleys of the town of Paintsville, they shall also have power to keep open all streets and alleys, and remove any obstructions at the cost of person obstructing them, with such additional penalties as the board may, by ordinance, determine; they shall also have power, by ordinance, to cause any sidewalk of said town now established, or that may be hereafter established, or any part or portion thereof, to be graded, curbed, paved with stone, brick or plank, or otherwise improved as they may determine. at the cost and expense of the lot owners fronting on his or her own side of the street where said work is done, and to be paid by owners of lots in the proportion to the number of feet front of each lot or part of lot where such work is done; and a lien is hereby given to said town on all the lots and parts of lots fronting on such work to secure the payment of the costs of same.

"25. The town of Paintsville shall have a lien on all property on which taxes have been assessed, which shall not be defeated by sale or alienation; and may by ordinance, add ten per cent to all taxes not paid by the tenth of November in the year in which they are assessed; they may also, by ordinance, provide that taxpayers shall receive credit for the amount of the usual collectors commission for collecting taxes upon the payment of their taxes by a day fixed by said ordinance.

"26. The cost and expense of the improvements mentioned in the last section, either on a street or sidewalk, may be collected by the town marshal as other taxes are collected, who shall have power to sell; and when any lot or part of lot is sold for said improvement of tax, the owner shall have two years to redeem the name by paying the tax, cost of collection and ten per cent per annum interest on the same, with all the taxes and levies that may have subsequently accrued, with ten per cent per annum interest on them; provided, that infants shall two years after disability is removed to comply with the above.

"27. All intersections of streets and crossing of the walks from one side to the other, and the sidewalks and streets in front or side of schoolhouse and church property, shall be graded, guttered, macadamized, layed or stepping stones placed at the expense of the town.

"28. Where any street is improved as heretofore set forth, in accordance with instructions and requirements of the board, by the owner of any lot, which every owner shall have the right to do, the same shall be kept in repair by the town, and if any has heretofore had the street and sidewalk improved to the center, in accordance with the requirements of the board, he shall have credit for the same. The board of trustees may by ordinance, provide for the protection of the streets from injurious means of hauling or dragging over them, and for prohibiting persons from driving, riding, or hitching on the sidewalks.

Marshal

"29. A marshal shall be elected at the same time of the police judge, and hold his office for same term, and shall be called the marshal of Paintsville. He shall enter on the discharge of his duties at the same time the police judge enters on his; he shall, however, before so doing, execute a bond before said board of trustees, with one or more sureties, which shall be approved by said board, as follows: We.., marshal of town of Paintsville, and ...., his sureties, jointly and severally bind ourselves to the Commonwealth of Kentucky, the said ...., marshal shall well and truly execute, and in due return make note of all process to him directed and delivered from the police judge of the town, or any court of judicial officers, and will pay and satisfy all sums of money by him received upon any process, note, account, fee bill, taxes, fines, or other claims placed in his hands for collection, to the person entitled thereto, and shall, in all other things faithfully discharge all the duties of said office during his continuance therein. He shall also, before entering on (the) duties of his office, in addition to the oath prescribed by the Constitution, take an oath before said board that he will do right as well to the poor as the rich, in all things belonging to his office; that he will do no wrong to any man for any gift or reward, nor for favor or hatred, and in all cases he will execute the duties of his office according to the best of his knowledge and power. The same shall be filed with the papers of the town, and also, noted of record by the clerk thereof.

"30. He and his sureties shall be liable on said bond, and in the same manner as sheriffs and constables are; and the board of trustees may, at any time, notify said marshal to give additional security in his bond. Notice may be served as other notices are served under the civil code; and a failure for five days to comply, shall authorize the trustees to declare his office vacant.

"31. He shall be a peace officer, and shall possess all the power to arrest persons charged with offenses, and to execute within Johnson County, in criminal and penal cases, all writs, process, warrants, and orders to take bail, which is now or may be given to sheriffs or other peace officers; and he shall be entitled for his services to the same fees that other officers are entitled to for the same. He shall have power to levy and execute all process from said court which may issue on any judgment for violation of ordinances of town, or for any penal case, and collect the same as sheriffs do. He shall attend all meetings of the board of trustees and all sittings of the police court, and preserve order and act as crier of same. He shall have power to collect fee bills, and claims of all kind, and executions, from any inferior courts in civil cases, the same as constables have. He shall execute all ordinances of said board passed in pursuance of the powers herein granted them, whenever acts of his duties are specifically presented for him to perform; and he shall report to the police judge all infractions of the ordinances of said town, and all misdemeanors or felonies committed in this said town or its suburban limits, of which he may receive information. He shall be collector of the town, and shall be responsible on his bond for the collection and proper disposition of all tax of said town.

"32. He shall be entitled to the same fees that sheriffs and constables are, respectively, when he performs services similar to them, except that the trustees may regulate the percentage to be paid him for collecting taxes of the town.

"33. The judge of Johnson County Court shall, by order, appoint the officers to hold the first election under this act; and each second year thereafter, they shall be appointed by the police judge of the town; they and the trustees and all officers provided for in this act, shall be citizens of the town. The officers at the election held under this act shall open a poll for license and against license; and for that purpose all the qualified voters within the limits and suburban limits of the town may vote; and if a majority of votes cast, are against license, the judge of the County Court of Johnson County, nor the trustees, shall either grant license to any one to retail ardent spirits or fermented liquors of any kind, within the limits or suburban limits of said town.

"34. The board of trustees shall have power to prescribe penalties for the breach of all town ordinances passed by them in pursuance to this power herein granted, not exceeding fifty ($50.00) dollars. They also shall have power to erect a place of confinement for all parties violating the ordinances of the town, when the penalties prescribe imprisonment, and power to work all convicted prisoners on the improvements of streets of the town at any time. Said house or place shall be in the custody of the marshal of the town.

"35. The officers of the town election, the board of trustees, and the town clerk and the police court, shall all have the privilege of holding their elections, meetings, terms, sitting, and offices in the court house of Johnson County; but shall not do so when the Circuit, County or Quarterly Court of said county is in session.

"36. This act shall take effect from and after its passage; and all acts heretofore passed with reference to the town of Paintsville, if any such there are, are hereby repealed."

Approved March 25, 1872.

Chapter 820, Page 627-658, Acts 1890.

AN ACT to amend the acts incorporating the town of Paintsville.

"*Be it enacted by the General Assembly of the Commonwealth of Kentucky*:

BOUNDARY

"1. That the boundary of the town of Paintsville, in Johnson County, shall be the same as now prescribed by law.

TRUSTEES

"2. The fiscal, prudential and municipal concerns of said town, with the government and control thereof, shall be vested in one principal officer, to be styled the Chairman of the Board of Trustees of Paintsville; and five trustees, all of whom shall be elected annually, in the manner herein provided, for a term of one year, and shall continue in office until their successors are duly qualified.

OATH, VACANCIES

"3. That the chairman and trustees shall, before entering upon the discharge of their duties, take and subscribe an oath (in addition to the oath or affirmation prescribed by the Constitution) before a justice of the peace or some person authorized to administer oaths, that they will faithfully and impartially discharge all the duties of their respective offices, which oath, with the certificate of the justice, shall be filed with the papers of the town. If the chairman or any trustee shall fail or refuse to qualify within twenty days from his election, he shall thereby vacate his office; and the trustees who have qualified shall declare his office vacant, and proceed to appoint some other person in his place; but if not more than two of the persons elected trustees have qualified within the time prescribed above, then the former board of trustees shall fill, by appointment, the vacancies occurring by such failure. If there is a vacancy in said office by reason of anything other than above mentioned, it shall be filled by the then acting trustees; and any person appointed under this section shall hold his office until the next annual election, and until his successors be duly qualified, and shall have and exercise the same rights and powers as if he had been elected at the regular election.

QUORUM, CHAIRMAN, VOTE, DUTIES

"4. The chairman and the majority of the trustees shall constitute a quorum for the transaction of business, and they may regulate by ordinances and by-laws the times and places of their meetings. The chairman shall preside over the meetings of the

A SECTION IN THE BUSINESS DISTRICT OF PAINTSVILLE, KY.

trustees (which in all cases must be public), and shall give the casting vote when there shall be a tie; he may enforce good order at such meetings, and the attendance of the trustees by fine not exceeding five dollars, and during his absence the trustees may elect one of their own number to act as chairman *pro tempore,* who shall, in addition to his vote as trustee, have all the powers for the time that are herein granted to the chairman. The chairman may appoint all necessary committees among the trustees, and compel them to serve on the same, and perform their duties by fine not exceeding five dollars.

TRUSTEES MAKE BY-LAWS

"5. The said board of trustees shall have power to make such rules, regulations, by-laws and ordinances, for the purpose of maintaining the peace, good order, and government of the town, and the trade, commerce and manufactures thereof, as the board may deem expedient, not repugnant to the Constitution of the state and laws made in pursuance thereof; and to enforce the observance thereof by fine not exceeding one hundred dollars for any one offense, except as herein provided; and to make all ordinances which shall be necessary and proper for carrying into effect the powers vested by this act in the corporation, the town government, or any department of office thereof.

POWERS OF TRUSTEES

"6. The board of trustees shall have power within the limits of the town, in addition to the other powers granted by this charter:

"*First.* To appropriate money, and provide for the payments of the debts and expenses of the town.

"*Second.* To make regulations to prevent the introduction or spreading of contagious or infectious diseases in the town; to pass quarantine laws for that purpose, and to enforce the same in the town and within a half mile of the outside limits of the town.

"*Third.* To establish hospitals and pesthouses, and make regulations for the government of the same.

"*Fourth.* To make regulations to secure general health of the inhabitants of the town.

"*Fifth.* To provide the town with water, to erect hydrants, fire-plug cisterns, wells and pumps in the streets within the limits of the town for the convenience of the town and its environs.

"*Sixth.* To establish, erect and keep in repair, bridges, culverts, and sewers, and regulate the use of the same.

"*Seventh.* To establish, regulate, and support policemen, night-watchmen, patrols, and prescribe their duties and compensation.

"*Eighth.* To provide for the erection and repair of all needful public buildings for the town, and to provide for the enclosing and improving of all public grounds belonging to the town.

"*Ninth.* To suppress gaming, drunkenness, gambling houses, and disorderly houses of all kinds.

"*Tenth.* To provide for appointment of all officers, servants, or agents of the town, not otherwise provided for and fix compensation and fees for their services and the duration of the terms of their offices.

"*Eleventh.* To fix the compensation of all town officers, and provide for and regulate pay and fees of jurors, witnesses and others for services rendered under this act, or any ordinance of the town; to erect a workhouse, poorhouse and the house of correction, and provide for the regulation and government thereof, and to otherwise provide for the poor of the town.

"*Twelfth.* To prevent or restrain any riot, rout, and noise, disturbance or disorderly or unlawful assembly, in any street or other place in said town, or any breach of the peace therein, and to provide for the arrest and confinement, trial and punishment of the parties engaged or taking part in the same.

"*Thirteenth.* To prevent and remove any and all encroachments into or upon or over any street, alley, sidewalk, lane, avenue, or public square heretofore existing or established under the charter or by ordinance, and to exercise complete and perfect control over all public squares or commons belonging to the town, and over all property, real or personal, belonging to the town, lying within or beyond the limits of the town.

"*Fourteenth.* To appoint and remove at pleasure and to prescribe the duties, compensation and fees of the following officers, agents and servants of the town: warden or keeper of the workhouse and house of correction, keeper of the poorhouse, keeper of the pesthouse, superintendent of the hospital, town physician, market master, inspector, gaugers, sextons, weighers, and measurers.

"*Fifteenth.* To provide for the prevention of training or breaking horses or exhibiting stallions in the public streets and places of the town, or standing them within the limits of the same.

"*Sixteenth.* To provide for the removal from the limits of the town, or killing of mischievous, vicious and diseased animals, and for the punishment by suitable fine or penalty of the owner, or keeper of such animals for allowing them to go at large.

"*Seventeenth.* To tax all dogs kept within the limits of the town in any sum not exceeding ten dollars per annum, and pass ordinances to provide for the killing of all such dogs upon which the taxes are not paid, or for fining the owners thereof.

"Eighteenth. They shall have the right to prevent or abate and remove nuisances, at cost and expense of the owners or occupiers, or of the parties upon whose ground they exist; *Provided, however,* That if the thing complained of as the nuisance, be in the nature of a permanent improvement, or structure of the value of more than twenty dollars, or if the actual damage accruing to the owner from such abatement or removal, or cost or expense attended on, the abatement or removal, exceeds said sum, the person in actual possession of the property, if a resident of Johnson County, shall be notified in writing, that a motion will be made at a meeting of the said board of trustees to declare the thing complained of a nuisance, which notice shall state the time and place of the meeting, describe the thing proposed to be declared a nuisance; shall be signed by the chairman or one of the trustees, and may be served as notices are served under provision of the civil code; and if the thing complained of be declared a nuisance at the meeting mentioned in the notice, or at any meeting adjourned therefrom, and if the same is not abated or removed by the owner or occupier of the land within twenty-four hours therefrom, the chairman and board of trustees may cause such nuisance to be removed or abated at the cost and expense of the owner or occupier, or both, of the land; but if the person actually in possession of the land be not a resident of the county, the board of trustees of the town of Paintsville may proceed to remove or abate the nuisance without any such notice, at the cost and expense of any such parties. Said board shall have the power to define and declare by ordinance of anything already existing, or what shall be a nuisance, within the limits of the town, and to punish by fine any person for keeping, causing, erecting, or committing nuisance in any sum not exceeding two hundred and fifty dollars.

PURCHASE LANDS

"7. The board of trustees shall have power to purchase lands for and locate cemeteries in Johnson County, either within the town limits or elsewhere; sell the lots within the same, and appropriate the money arising from said sales to the benefit of the cemeteries or of the town; and they shall exercise full and complete control over any cemeteries that the town may now have or may hereafter purchase, and have power to erect and keep in repair public vaults at the expense of the town.

VULGAR LANGUAGES

"8. They shall have power to prevent by ordinance, any obscene, vulgar, or bawdy language, and any indecent practices, exposure or act in any public place within the limits of the town, and may punish, by suitable fines or penalties, any person so offending.

Paupers

"9. They shall have the power to prevent the introduction of the town, or within one mile of the limits of any person who is a pauper, or who is likely to become a charge upon the town, or county from disease, old age, or any other cause, and punished by fines in any sum not exceeding one hundred dollars, any person so offending, and return the pauper or person likely to become a charge upon the town at the cost and expense of the person or persons so offending.

Schools

"10. They shall have power to establish free schools in said town, and furnish rooms for the same, and make appropriations and receive donations for such purposes, and govern the same under such rules and regulations as they may make. The board of trustees are hereby authorized to have erected, at the expense of the town, a prison house for the confinement of persons convicted in the police court of said town, and for that purpose may levy and collect taxes upon property and persons residing in said town. They are empowered to make rules and regulations for the government of the same; and if no prison house is erected the town shall have the privilege of using the jail of Johnson County by paying the jailor the same fees that is paid by the county. The jailor shall be the custodian and keeper of the same, and subject to the order of the police judge.

Police Court

"11. There shall be established in said town a court to be styled a police court of Paintsville, which shall be held by the judge, who shall be called the police judge of Paintsville and shall be elected by the qualified voters on the first Saturday in July, one thousand, eight hundred and ninety (note that this date was changed by the new State Constitution), and holds his office for a term of two years, and until his successor is elected and qualified; and shall possess the same qualifications as county judges. He shall before entering upon the discharge of his duties, in addition to the oaths prescribed by the Constitution, take the oath prescribed for circuit judges; and on failure for twenty days so to do, his office shall be declared vacant by the board of trustees.

"12. Said court shall have exclusive jurisdiction in all prosecutions for all violations of the ordinances of said town, and original concurrent jurisdiction of all pleas of the Commonwealth arising within the limits of said town, or within one mile of the corporate limits thereof, except cases of felony. It shall have power to take recognizances from persons charged with offenses, cognizable before to appear and answer the same as circuit courts

COURT STREET, PAINTSVILLE, KY.

have, and like power to forfeit the same, and shall proceed in the same way thereon that circuit courts are directed to proceed. It may commit persons to jail or workhouse in default of bail; and shall have all the powers for all the arrest, trial, conviction and punishment of persons for all the offenses over which it has jurisdiction that are given the several courts of this State having jurisdiction over like offense; and may proceed in the same way for trial of such offenses, and may inflict a fine and punishment, and enforcement of the collection of same, as such courts are authorized by law to do.

"13. Said police court shall have original and concurrent jurisdiction of all cases of riot, routs, unlawful assemblies, assaults, batteries, affrays or other breaches of the peace committed within the limits of said town, or within one mile of the corporate limits thereof; it shall also have original and concurrent jurisdiction over all cases of larceny of goods, chattels, or other things of less value than ten dollars committed within the limits of said town; and over all cases of vagrancy therein or within one mile of the corporate limits thereof.

"14. It shall have concurrent and original jurisdiction with the quarterly court judges of this State in all civil cases and proceedings.

"15. There shall be a monthly term of said court, to begin on the second Monday of each month in the year, and hold as many days as the business of the court may require; but said court may be held at any time for the trial of criminal cases and cases for breaches of town ordinances; and the provisions of the criminal code except where inconsistent with this act shall apply to proceedings in all such cases; where a person is brought before said court charged with an offense over which it has jurisdiction but which requires an indictment, the court may either order a grand jury to be summoned at once, and, if they return an indictment, proceed with the trial as soon as may be at that term of the court, or it may sit as an examining court; and if the defendant or defendants are held for further trial, it may hold him to bail for his appearance before the court upon some subsequent day, which day shall not be beyond the first day of the succeeding term.

"16. Said court may issue *capias pro fine* on all its judgments for breach of the ordinances of said town, and on all judgments rendered in said court for a violation of any law, and in such cases shall enter a judgment specifying that the persons convicted shall be required to labor in the workhouse or forced to work on the streets or other places that the board of trustees may designate, until the fine assessed against him and the cost of the prosecution are both discharged, at the rate of one dollar per day, but in no wise to be required to labor more than ten hours per day at labor. The board of trustees shall have power to provide, by any means they may deem proper, to keep persons under confinement while at labor: *Provided, however,* That the person arrested and confined shall, by paying or replevying the full amount of the fine assessed and cost, be discharged from custody.

"17. The said police judge shall be commissioned by the Governor, and be a conservator of the peace; and he may order arrest for all offenses against the laws of the State or ordinances of the town of Paintsville; and for those committed in his presence he may order arrest without a warrant, the person offending to be dealt with according to laws of the State or ordinances of the town. He may administer oaths, take depositions in all cases, issue and try writ of *habeas corpus,* and grant injunctions and in the same restrictions, and in the same cases that county judges are now authorized to grant them, and shall have the same civil jurisdiction, in all cases as is conferred on quarterly court judges.

"18. Said judge shall be his own clerk; but it shall be lawful for him to appoint a deputy as clerk, who may perform all his duties as clerk of said court; said clerk shall be called the deputy clerk of the police court of Paintsville, and shall possess the qualification, and take the same oath before he enters upon the duties of his office, as is required by law of a deputy clerk of a court.

"19. Whenever, from any cause, the judge of said court fails to attend the court, or if in attendance, cannot properly preside, in a case or cases pending in said court, the presiding judge of the Johnson County Court, or any justice of the peace of Johnson County shall preside in his place; and the person so presiding shall, during the period that he acts, have all the powers and be liable to all the responsibilities for the police judge, and shall receive all fees accruing during said period; and any of said officers at any time issue a summons, warrant of arrest, or subpoena, and make the same returnable before said court; which said summons, warrant and subpoena shall be executed and returned in the same way, and have the same force and effect, and the person upon whom they are expected be dealt with the same as if they had been issued by the court, while regularly sitting. If no court is held on this day any summons or warrant are made returnable, and the same is not during regular term, the case shall be considered, and be by operation of law continued until the next regular term.

"20. Appeals from judgments of said police court shall lie in all civil cases, unless otherwise provided for, to the Johnson Quarterly Court, to which shall also lie all appeals from its judgments for breaches of ordinances of said town, when the penalties or forfeitures set forth in the ordinance exceeds fifteen and does not exceed fifty dollars; and in all pleas of the Commonwealth except in cases of vagrancy and larceny, where the full penalty imposed by law does not exceed fifty dollars and imprisonment for fifteen days, and said appeals and proceedings therein, except as herein provided, shall be governed by the general laws regulating appeals from justice courts to quarterly courts. In all other cases, except for breaches of ordinances where the fine is more than fifteen dollars, an appeal from the police court shall lie to the Johnson Circuit Court, and said appeal and proceedings thereon shall be governed by the general laws, except as herein provided, regulating appeals from inferior courts to circuit courts. If the judgment appealed from to either of said courts, be in a case of vagrancy or larceny or in a case where the judgment may specify that the defendant may or shall be imprisonment, there shall be executed in addition to the bond now required by law before the clerk of the court appealed to, in a penal bond, in a sum fixed by the clerk of the court appealed to, and with sureties approved by him, conditioned by the defendant will, at all times render himself amenable to the orders of and process of the court appealed to in the prosecution of the charge; and, if convicted, will render himself in execution thereof. Upon the execution of such bond, the defendant in custody, shall be discharged therefrom.

"21. The board of trustees shall elect annually an attorney for the time, prescribe his duties and fix his compensation; and upon their failure so to do it shall be the duty of the county attorney of Johnson County to prosecute all pleas of the Commonwealth in said court, or prosecution in the name of the town of Paintsville; and he shall receive the same fees in such cases, and the same percentage of the fines, penalties and forfeitures, imposed in the same, as are given by law to county attorneys, or to an attorney for the Commonwealth for similar services.

"22. Said court shall be a court of record; and all copies of papers or records on file with the judges shall, when duly attested by him or his deputy, be received as evidence in all cases where the original would be evidence; but nothing herein shall prevent any court from having the original record produced and brought to court by the proper process.

"23. The fees of said judge, whether acting as judge, clerk or otherwise, shall be the same in all cases, as are now or may hereafter be, given by law to officers performing like services; the fees and cost shall be taxed in cases in said court to the same extent and the same way and under the same regulations as in courts having the same jurisdiction.

Marshal

"24. A marshal shall be elected by the qualified voters of the said town on the first Saturday of July, one thousand eight hundred and ninety, to hold his office for a term of two years, and until his successor is elected and qualified, which marshal shall be called the marshal of Paintsville, and he shall enter on the discharge of his duties on the third Saturday in July next after his election; he shall, however, before so doing, execute a bond before said board of trustees with one or more sureties, which shall be approved by the board of trustees, in substance as follows: We, ..., marshal of the town of Paintsville, and........................, his sureties, jointly and severally, bind and obligate ourselves to the Commonwealth of Kentucky that the said........................, as marshal of the town of Paintsville, shall well and truly execute and in due return make all process and precepts to him directed and to him delivered, and all notice and orders of justice or other tribunals given him to execute, and will pay and satisfy all the sums of money by him received upon any process or precept or any note, account, fee bill, taxes of the town of Paintsville, fines or other claims placed in his hands for collection, to the person entitled thereto, and in all other things shall faithfully discharge all the duties of said office during his continuance therein. He shall also previous to entering upon his said duties, besides the oath prescribed by the Constitution, take an oath before the said board that he will do right, as well to the poor as the rich, in all things belonging to his said office; that he will do no wrong to any man for any gift or reward, nor for favor or hatred, and in all cases that he will truly and faithfully execute the duties of his office according to the best of his knowledge and power. It shall be noted on the records of the town that such bond and oath has been taken, and shall be filed with the papers of the town.

"25. Any person injured by a breach of the said bond may, in any court having jurisdiction, prosecute, on motion thereon, in their own name, and at their own cost, against the marshal and his sureties, in the manner now prescribed by law for proceedings against sheriffs or constables in cases of delinquence of breach of official duty.

"26. The board of trustees may, at any time, notify said marshal to give additional security on his bond, which notice shall be served as notices are directed to be served under civil code; and they may, upon his failure so to do within five days after such notice, declare his office vacant. If the marshal shall fail to execute bond or take said oath for twenty days after he, by this act, enters upon the discharge of his duties, the board of trustees may declare his office vacant.

"27. Said marshal shall be a peace officer, and shall possess all the power to arrest persons charged with offenses, and to execute within Johnson County in criminal cases all writs, process, warrants, and orders to take bail, which is now or may hereafter be given to sheriffs or other peace officers; and he shall be en-

A RESIDENTIAL DISTRICT IN MARGARET HEIGHTS DIVISION, PAINTSVILLE, KY.

titled for his services to the same fees which such officers are respectively entitled. He shall attend all meetings of the board of trustees, and all sittings of the said police court, preserve order, and act as crier at the same. He shall have power to levy and execute all process, executions or judgments, civil or criminal, which issue out of said court; and shall have the same powers to collect claims, fee bills, et cetera, and to act in all civil cases, and to execute all process and executions in said county, as is now or may hereafter be given by law to sheriffs; and he and his sureties shall be responsible for the proper execution of all process and collection of all claims put into his hands, and for his official acts in the same way and to the same extent that sheriffs and constables are now responsible. It shall be his duty to execute all orders of the said board passed in pursuance of the power herein granted them, whenever acts or duties are specifically presented for him to perform; and shall report to the police judge all infractions of the ordinances of said town, and all misdemeanors and felonies committed within town, of which he may receive information.

"28. The marshal shall be collector for said town, and have the power and shall collect all the taxes due said town, and he and his sureties shall be responsible on his bond for the collection and the disposition of all taxes due said town, and he may proceed in the same way for their collection as the collector by this act is empowered to proceed.

"29. The marshal shall be entitled to the same fees as the sheriff and constable are, respectively, whenever he performs services similar to those of sheriffs and constables.

"30. It shall be the duty of the clerk of the board of trustees to appoint annually a competent person to fill the office of clerk of the board of trustees; said clerk shall, before entering upon the discharge of his duties, take an oath to faithfully discharge all his duties under this act; and he shall hold his office, unless removed, until the first of August following his appointment, and until his successor be duly qualified. It shall be the duty of the clerk to attend all meetings of the board of trustees, and to make a full and fair record of their proceedings and transactions in a book furnished him by them; he shall keep all the papers and references and documents of said town, and perform whatever other duties may be prescribed for him by said board of trustees, not inconsistent with this act. If said clerk fails to qualify within ten days after his appointment, his office shall be declared vacant.

"31. It shall be the duty of the board of trustees to appoint annually a competent person to fill the office of treasurer of said town, which treasurer shall hold his office until the third Monday in July next, after his appointment or election, and until his successor be duly qualified. He shall before entering upon the discharge of his duties, and shall execute a bond to said town before said board, with one or more approved sureties, covenanting that he will account for and pay over to the person entitled to receive the same according to law, any and all moneys that may come to his hands as treasurer of said town; that he will at any and all times, whenever called upon by the board of trustees, settle his accounts as treasurer aforesaid, and pay over any moneys due the town from him to any person that said board may designate, and faithfully discharge all the duties of said office.

"32. It shall be the duty of the treasurer to receive and safely keep all moneys belonging to the town, and to pay out the same under appropriation made by the board of trustees; but shall only pay out money upon warrants drawn by the clerk and endorsed by the chairman. He shall keep a fair and accurate account of all his receipts and disbursements, when, from and to whom and for what purpose, and what account such moneys were received and paid; and shall exhibit the same and furnish a copy thereof whenever called upon by the board of trustees so to do. He shall perform such other duties as may be required of him by ordinance not inconsistent with this act, and shall receive such compensation for his services, as the said board may provide. The said board may require the treasurer to pay any rate of interest not to exceed eight per cent per annum, on the amount of such money received by him from the time of its reception, credited by his lawful disbursements from the time they are paid out; but no interest shall be required of the treasurer unless the same was imposed by ordinance previous to his qualification. Any person aggrieved may institute or motion on the bond given by the treasurer as aforesaid in the police court of Paintsville, or in the Johnson Circuit Court, against the treasurer and his sureties, and the bond shall not be void or satisfied, until every person aggrieved has been recompensed.

"34. If the treasurer fails to execute his said bond for twenty days after his appointment, the office shall by order of the board of trustees, be declared vacant, and the vacancy filled by the board of trustees.

"35. The board may, at any time, require and notify the treasurer to execute a new bond, or give additional security, and upon failure within five days after such notice to execute new bond, or give additional security, the office may by order of the board of trustees, be declared vacant, and filled by the board of trustees.

Taxation, Et Cetera, Et Cetera

"36. The board of trustees shall have power to assess, levy and collect ad valorem taxes on such real and personal estate and

LOOKING EAST ON THIRD STREET, PAINTSVILLE, KY.

choses in action, within the limits of said town, as the board may direct and designate; but such taxation shall be uniform on every description of property, and shall not exceed twenty cents on each one hundred dollars worth of property. They shall have power to levy and collect annually a head or personal tax, not exceeding two dollars on any male person over twenty years of age, who shall have resided in said town for three months. They shall also have power to collect and levy a tax of not more than fifty cents on each share of stock in all banks or other named corporations doing business in said town, and may also levy a tax of not more than one dollar on every one hundred dollars invested in brokers' establishments and private banks in said town.

"37. Said board may have power to appoint annually a competent person to fill the office of assessor, which assessor shall be qualified within ten days after his appointment to faithfully discharge his duties, and shall execute a bond before said board with one or more approved securities, covenanting with said town that he will faithfully discharge all the duties of his office, and upon his failure so to do the board may remove him.

"38. It shall be the duty of the assessor to take a list of all the taxable property within said town, whether in goods or stock, manufactories, or other property, that may be designated for the taxation by the board, together with the cash value of said property, and the name of the owner or owners thereof; and he shall make division of the different species of said property in separate columns in his book as the board may direct. The assessor shall list also all male persons over twenty-one years old who are subject to said personal or head tax and shall also list and report separately a list of all the houses, stores, taverns, and persons and things upon which a specific tax is levied by ordinance of said town, together with the names of owners or agents of such house, store, tavern and things; he shall file with the clerk of the board his books containing the above-mentioned list on or before the first day of April of each year.

"39. He shall call on persons from whom taxes are collectable for a list of their taxable property, and shall administer to them such an oath of affirmation as is administered by county assessors except to property owned the first of February; and if any person shall refuse to take such oath, or to give in his or her list of taxable property the assessor may assess the same from the best of his information.

"40. If any person shall fail or refuse to give a list of his or her personal property when legally called on so to do by the assessor, or give in a false or fraudulent list, he or she shall be adjudged a delinquent, and fined in any sum not to exceed one hundred dollars; and the assessor at the time he files his book with the clerk, or before directed, shall return a list of all delinquents, state in what the falsehood or fraud consists, whereupon a summons shall be issued from the police court, summoning the delinquent to appear before said court on some other day therein named to answer for his delinquency, and said court snall proceed in the trial of said case, and may enter same judgment, and issue same writ and process, and enforce the same as in causes of breach of town ordinances.

"41. The board of trustees shall appoint annually three direct men who are citizens and housekeepers of said town, as a board of supervisors of tax, who, or any two of them, shall meet as soon as convenient after the assessor's books shall have been filed with the clerk and examine with care the said books, and correct any errors of the assessor, whether in fact or in relation to the valuation of the estate listed; and, in cases where they shall be of the opinion that the estate has been incorrectly valued, to fix the same at its proper value; they shall have the power to add any list omitted by the assessor; and said board may adjourn from time to time until their business is complete; and they shall keep a full record of all their proceedings; *Provided, however,* That said board of supervisors shall, at least five days before the time of meeting, in three or more public places in said town, post up printed or written notices, stating the time and place of said meeting; *Provided further,* That all persons listed by the assessor may have the right to appear before them, by attorneys and in person, and introduce evidence concerning their property.

"42. All estate taxed accordingly to value as of the first of February preceding, and the person owning or possessing the same on that day, shall list it with the assessor, and remain bound for the taxes notwithstanding he may have sold or parted with the same.

"43. The taxes levied by this act shall be due and payable in the same year in which the estate is assessed, and the town of Paintsville shall have a lien for such taxes on the estate of such person assessed for taxation which shall not be defeated by sale or alienation.

"44. The board of trustees shall have power to provide by ordinance, that taxpayers shall receive a credit for the amount of the usual collectors commission, for conflicting taxes, upon the payment of their taxes by a day to be fixed by ordinance. They may also provide, by ordinance, that ten per cent may be added on all taxes not paid before the first day of August of each year, which percentage shall be accounted for by the collector.

"45. Said board of trustees shall have power to levy a specific tax, not exceeding one hundred dollars per year upon merchants, grocers, peddlers, brokers, bankers, pawnbrokers, private banks, money exchangers, confectioners, victualers, tavern keepers, and auctioneers doing business in said town; *Provided,* That no provision of this act shall be construed to authorize the authorities of the town of Paintsville to levy any tax upon the capital stock of any incorporated bank now exempted from such taxation by law. It shall have power to license and tax all coffee housekeepers, keepers of eating houses, retailers of spirituous liquors, and sellers and dealers in the same in any quantity, in any sum not exceeding one hundred and fifty dollars per year, and shall have full power to regulate the same; it shall have power to license and tax, in any sum not exceeding ten dollars per year, and regulate all hacks, carriages, coaches, carts, drays, wagons, or other vehicles plowing or hauling for hire in said town; it shall have power to tax all livery stables, insurance companies and insurance agencies, express companies, and agencies for the same doing business in said town, in a sum not exceeding fifty dollars per year; it shall have to license and tax, in any sum, not exceeding twenty-five dollars per year, billiard houses, bowling saloons and tenpin alleys within the limits of said town; and license and tax within said town, all theatrical and other exhibition shows, and amusements, circuses, menageries, lecturers, musical entertainments; but such tax shall not exceed twenty-five dollars for each exhibition.

"46. The imposition and collection of any specific taxes on the granting of license by the board shall not prevent the levying and collecting of the ad valorem taxes provided for by this act on the stock, goods, wares of merchandise, in any store or house, or on the value of any thing or implement upon which such specific tax is levied, or to keep which a license is granted.

"47. The said board may provide by ordinance when, to whom, and the manner in which such specific tax may be paid, and the manner, time, and conditions under which all licenses shall be granted, and to enforce the payment of such taxes and license and punish by fine all breaches of the ordinance passed concerning the same.

"48. The said trustees, if they deem it best, may select and appoint some competent person for collector, who shall be called the collector of the town of Paintsville, and shall hold his office until the first.................................next succeeding his appointment. It shall be his duty to collect all taxes assessed under the provisions under this charter, and all sums of money due the town of Paintsville from any person whatever; but before entering upon the discharge of the duties of his office before the board of trustees of said town, give bond, with approved sureties, which bond may be as follows, viz.: We, ..., collector of the town of Paintsville, and........................., his sureties, covenant, with the Commonwealth of Kentucky, that the said ...., collector of the town of Paintsville for the year ...., shall, during the present year, account for and pay to the treasurer of the town of Paintsville, at such times and in such manner prescribed by law, all fines or other claims due or owing to the town of Paintsville that may be put into my hand for collection for the year ....; and that the said.............................. shall, in all things, well demean himself, and faithfully discharge all the duties of said office of collector. Witness my hand this..........................day of ....

"49. Said collector shall also take and subscribe to an oath that he will faithfully discharge all the duties of his office, which oath and bond shall be filed with the papers of the town. Said board may notify the collector to give a new bond or additional sureties at any time; and upon his failure to do so within five days, or upon failure to qualify within ten days from his appointment, the said board may vacate his office.

"50. The town collector shall account for and pay into the town treasury all taxes and other public moneys for which he is bound, at such times and under such regulations as may be prescribed by ordinance of the board of trustees.

"51. The town collector shall, after the day he received the tax books each year, proceed to collect the taxes due the town, and upon failure by the person bound therefor to pay the same, may distrain the personal property owned by the persons from whom the taxes are due, notwithstanding the existence of any lien upon the same, and may proceed to sell the title of any such person in so much thereof as will pay the tax due and all cost and expenses of said sale; they must be for cash, and be made at the door of the court house, on some county or circuit court days; the time, place and term of sale shall be advertised as sheriffs are required to advertise in similar cases. If the town collector make an illegal or irresponsible seizure and distress for taxes, he shall be liable in damages to the parties aggrieved.

"52. If there be no personal estate which the town collector can distrain for taxes due on real estate, or the personal estate be insufficient to pay the whole of such tax, and the owner of the land or lot shall fail to pay the same by the first of October in each year in which the tax is due, the town collector shall, on the first day of some county or circuit court, at the door of the court house in the town of Paintsville, and thence from day to day until completed, proceed to sell the land and town lots, or so much thereof as may be necessary to pay the tax thereon, together with ten per cent penalty above specified, and the cost and expense of sale, to the highest bidder for cash; the time, place and terms of sale, together with a statement of the owners, occupants, number of, description of the lot, and the amount of tax and penalty due thereon, shall be published by the insertions in some weekly news-

A SECTION OF MODERN PAINTSVILLE, KY.

paper published in Johnson County, or and by notice posted at three or more public places in the town of Paintsville at least ten days before the date of sale.

"53. The town shall, as soon as practicable after making the sale of any real property for taxes make a full report of his proceedings to the board of trustees, include in said report a list of the property sold, and of the names of the owners or occupants of the property, names of the purchasers, amounts for which the property sold, and a description of the property; and he shall also hand in with the report the newspaper containing the advertisement of the sale, with the certificate of the printer or publisher; which certificate shall be sworn to before some justice of the peace; and the town collector shall also make oath before some justice of the peace that he has complied with all the requirements of this charter and the ordinance of the town with relation to the sale of the property for the taxes; which affidavit shall form part of the town collector's report.

"54. The board of trustees may designate an officer of the town to attend all sales of property sold for taxes due the town, who shall, if no other person will bid an amount sufficient to pay the taxes and all fees, costs and penalties accrued, bid in the property, or any part thereof, for the town.

"55. All lands and town lots sold by the town collector for taxes may be redeemed by the owner or his representative, at any time within two years from the day of sale, by paying to the purchaser his money, and interest thereon at the rate of ten per cent per annum from the day of sale until redeemed; the person thus redeeming shall take the receipt of the purchaser for the redemption money, and lodge the same with the clerk of the town, to be filed with the collector's report of the sale. If the purchaser, or his agent or representative, do not reside in the county of Johnson, or cannot be found therein, the owner of the property, or his representative, may make oath of the fact by affidavit, and pay the amount of the purchase money, with interest aforesaid, to the treasurer of the town therefrom; those whose tax could have been collected by the town collector by reasonable diligence, and from the balance of tax on such list, the said collector shall be entitled to credit to his settlement with the town; and all laws not in conflict with this act to remain in full force and effect.

"56. If, from any reason, there be no collector of the town of Paintsville, the said marshal shall exercise, by virtue of his office, all the duties, have all the powers, be subject to the obligations and penalties, and be, together with the sureties on his bond, liable in the same way and to same extent as the said collector.

"57. Any person aggrieved may institute suit, in the Johnson Circuit Court, on the bond of the collector, against him and his sureties; and the same shall not be considered void until all persons aggrieved are satisfied; and if he shall fail at any time to settle his accounts, when called upon by said board so to do, or shall fail to pay, according to the directions of said board, the amount of money belonging to said town in his hands, to the treasurer, or other person appointed by the board to receive the same, he and his sureties shall be liable for the amount in his hands, with interest at the rate of ten per centum, per annum, and ten per centum of said amount added thereon as damages, all of which may be recovered by motion in the Johnson County Court, or by suit or motion in the Johnson Circuit Court.

"58. Nothing contained herein shall be taken to interfere with or prevent the collection of any state or county taxes within the limits of said town.

Streets and Alleys

"59. The board of trustees of said town shall have power, by ordinance, to receive and accept any street or alley, or extension of any street or alley, laid out by any person or persons within the town limits, and make and declare the same an established street or alley of the town of Paintsville.

"60. The locality of all public streets and alleys in said town shall not be changed from their present location without the actual consent of the claimants of the ground affected by such change or alteration; *Provided, however,* The board of trustees may, by ordinance, by two-thirds of the number selected, and the yeas and nays being taken and recorded thereon in the journal of proceedings, whenever the public necessity shall require it, cause any new street or alley to be opened, or an old street or alley extended or widened, or establish any market place, and to procure the condemnation of any estate for such purposes, as follows: *Provided,* That in no case shall private property for any such purpose, without the written consent of the claimant or a just and full compensation therefor, be first paid in money to said claimants; if the amount of such compensation cannot be fixed by agreement, the board of trustees shall cause to be filed in the Johnson County Court, stating the street or alley opened or widened or extended, and the name of the owners, if known, of the lots and lands through which they desire to have said streets or alleys opened, widened or extended, and the width thereof; and thereupon said court shall order a summons to issue for such owner or owners to appear on some day of that, or some subsequent term of said court, to show why such street or alley should not be opened, widened or extended, which summons shall be executed on such owner or owners, if in the county of Johnson; if not, on his or their agents, if one is known; and on return of the summons executed, or the return of no inhabitant or known agent, and no one appearing, the said court may order the said street or alley to be opened, widened or extended, the town being liable, however, to pay the owners of the ground so taken; and if any one or more of such owners of lots appear and demand it, they shall award a writ of *ad quod damnum* to be directed to the proper county officers, to be executed and returned, as provided by law for writs of that nature for opening public roads; and the jury summoned under said writ shall, in addition to the verdict required by law, state whether, in their opinion, the public necessity requires the street or alley to be opened, widened or extended, as prayed for in the petition; and on the return of the writ duly executed, the court shall, if the jury report favorable to the prayer of the petition, order the board to pay the damages assessed to the party or parties entitled thereto, and shall order the street, or alley, to be opened, widened or extended, upon the payment of the said damages.

"61. The board shall have power, at any time before the final decree or order, to dismiss their petition, which shall not prevent them again instituting proceedings for opening, widening or extending such street or alley at any time after one year from said dismission.

"62. Appeals may be taken to the circuit court and Court of Appeals as is now provided in cases of open public roads.

"63. The board shall have full power to open and keep open all streets or alleys that belong to the town and other public place, and free from all obstructions, by the infliction of such suitable fines and penalties as may be prescribed by ordinance. The board shall have power, by ordinance, to cause any and all the streets and alleys in said town now established, or any portion thereof, to be graded, paved, macadamized, curbed and guttered in such manner as they may direct at the cost and expense of the lot owner fronting on each side of said street or alley. When such work is done, the cost and expense of such work, when completed, shall be apportioned between the owners of lots in each square fronting each street when the work is done in proportion to the number of feet owned by each person, and a lien is hereby given to the said town on all lots and parts of lots fronting on such work to secure the payment of the cost of such work; *Provided,* That in no case shall the total assessment of cost of improvement against any person or ground exceed in amount one-fourth the actual value of the ground owned by such person and subject to said assessment. The balance of the cost of the work shall be paid by the town out of the treasury.

"64. The board shall have full power, by ordinance, to cause and procure any or all of the sidewalks of said town now established, or hereafter to be established, to be graded and paved or improved in such manner as they may direct, at the cost and expense of the lot owner fronting such streets or alleys where the work is done; the cost and expense, when the work is complete, shall be apportioned between the owners of the lots fronting on the streets or alleys where the work is done in proportion to the number of front feet owned by such person; and a lien is hereby given to said town on all lots and parts of lots fronting such work to secure the payment of the cost of the work. If any lot owner refuse to have such work done, after he shall have been so ordered, and a copy of said order shall have been served upon him, or if he or they shall be non-residents, then to be served upon the occupant or agent of said person, of said lot or lots, for thirty days, it shall be the duty of said board to order its improvement committee to let the said work out, after advertising same ten days, to the lowest bidder, which shall be the amount due for said work.

"65. The cost and expense of the work, either for grading, paving, macadamizing, curbing or guttering, and for grading or paving sidewalks mentioned in the two preceding sections, together with the cost for collecting the same, may be collected as other taxes by the town collector, who shall have power to sell the lots or parts of lots sold for such work; those who have not consented in writing for said work to be done, shall have two years from the day of the sale to redeem the property sold on paying the purchase money, with ten per cent per annum interest thereon, with all the taxes and levies that may have subsequently accrued, and ten per centum thereon; and those who have consented in writing may redeem their property at any time within one year from the day of sale by paying the purchase money and interest at ten per centum thereon, and subsequent taxes and levies and ten per centum thereon; *And provided, also,* That infants shall have the privilege of redeeming on like terms at any time within one year after the disability is removed.

"66. All intersections of streets shall be paved, guttered, and stepping stones placed across walks made at the expense of the town, and the board may, if they deem it expedient, have all or any street, alley, or sidewalk guttered or macadamized at the cost of the town.

"67. When the guttering, grading and macadamizing of the streets and alleys mentioned above shall have been done at the expense of the owners of the lots fronting such street or alleys, under and according to the direction of the board, such street or alley shall be kept macadamized and graded at the expense of the town.

"68. When any person has had a street in front of his or her lot graded or guttered and paved to the center, and the sidewalk

RESIDENCE OF JAMES W. TURNER
One of the Many Beautiful Modern Homes of Paintsville. Compare This with the Picture of the First House Erected in Paintsville and Shown on Page 175

paved in accordance with the general plan of the work of the town, he shall be free from any assessment for such work done on the balance of the square on which he has had the work thus done; and any person hereafter desiring to do such work shall notify the board of the fact, and shall have the grades given by the board, and do the work according to its direction, or he shall not be exempted as aforesaid.

"69. The board shall have the power, for any of the work done on the streets as directed in the foregoing sections, to advance the money, and may, for that purpose, borrow the same and advance it to the contractors; *Provided, however,* That the lien shall always continue upon said lot until the entire cost of the work, and all expense of such work as aforesaid, are fully paid off and discharged.

"70. No person or persons shall lay out or extend any street or alley within the limits of the town without the consent of a majority of the board; and when any person or persons have with such consent laid out, or shall hereafter lay out or extend, any street or alley within the limits of the town, and shall have sold, or intend to sell, lots bounding thereon, the board shall declare the same to be established as a public street or alley, and exercise all the powers, jurisdiction and authority over the same that they have by this charter over other established streets or alleys, and may cause them to be improved as herein provided; but no street shall be laid out or accepted within the town limits which is less than forty feet wide, including the sidewalks or pavements, and the streets not to be more than sixty feet wide. It shall be the duty of the board of trustees to open all streets and alleys belonging to said town according to the original town plat, and keep them open for the use of the town.

"71. The election for the said chairman and trustees, and for all other officers of said town who are to be elected, and for the election of whom no provision is made by law, shall be held on the first Saturday in July, one thousand eight hundred and ninety, and on the same day each year thereafter.

"72. The board of trustees shall, before such election, appoint as officers thereof two persons, one as judge and the other as clerk, and the marshal of the town shall act as sheriff. If, from any reason, the appointees do not act, it shall be the duty of the marshal to appoint other persons in their stead; and if the marshal fails or refuses to act, the police judge may fill the vacancies by appointment of competent persons. The officers of town elections shall perform similar services, be entitled to like pay, and liable to the penalties and governed in all matters not inconsistent with this charter, in the same way as officers of State elections, which shall be paid by the town.

"73. Every male citizen of the age of twenty-one years, who has resided in this State two years, or in the said town one year next preceding the election, and who has paid his head and poll tax for the preceding year, shall be entitled to vote at said election; but such voters shall at the time of the election be a resident of said town, and have resided therein for sixty days preceding the same.

"74. The person acting as sheriff of said election shall, within one day after the same, deposit the poll book with the clerk of the Johnson County Court, who shall file said book in his office. Said county clerk, the judge of the police court of Paintsville, and the person acting as sheriff of the election, shall constitute a board for examining the poll book and giving certificates of election; any two of whom may constitute a board, which shall, within two days after the poll book is filed as aforesaid, and shall compare the poll and ascertain the correctness of the summing up of the votes for the offices for which the election was held, one of which certificate shall be given to the person elected and the other to the clerk of the board of trustees, who shall file the same with the papers of the town.

"75. Whenever any two or more persons shall receive the highest and equal number of votes for the office, such election shall be determined by lot, in such manner as the board of examiners may direct. The elections provided for in this act may be contested before the same board and the same proceedings had as when elections for county offices are contested under Chapter 32 of the Revised Statutes of Kentucky.

"76. Whenever any vacancies shall occur in the office of police judge or marshal, the board of trustees shall appoint some competent person to fill out the vacancy, who shall hold his office until the next succeeding July election, and until his successor is elected and qualified; and the said board of trustees shall issue a writ of election to fill the remaining vacancy, which writ shall be delivered to the sheriff of Johnson County, and on which he shall act as on writs issued from the elections of county officers under the provisions of Revised Statutes, Article 6, Chapter 32.

"All vacancies in the offices in said town, not otherwise provided for, shall temporarily be filled by the board of trustees by appointment until the next succeeding election in July, and until their successors be duly qualified; and the person appointed under this section shall exercise all the powers, perform the same duties, and be under the same responsibilities and restrictions as if they had been regularly elected.

"77. All resignations of the officers of said town of Paintsville shall be tendered to the board of trustees in writing, and shall be noted on the records of said town.

THE PAINTSVILLE HOSPITAL

Established November 1, 1920. Fully Equipped with the Latest Appliances and Ably Managed. It Is Meeting the Demands of This Section, and Is One of the Progressive Institutions That Is Rendering a Valuable Service to the Section It Serves

DR. J. H. HOLBROOK
Prominent Business Man, Physician, and Surgeon. He Is Connected with the Paintsville Hospital, and Was One of the Organizers of This Serviceable Institution

"78. The present police judge of the town of Paintsville shall remain in office and exercise all the powers conferred herein on the police judge of Paintsville, until the July election, one thousand eight hundred and ninety, and until his successor be duly qualified.

"79. The present acting town marshal of said town shall remain in office and exercise all the duties, and have all the powers conferred by this act on the marshal of the town of Paintsville until the July election, one thousand eight hundred and ninety, and until his successor be duly elected or appointed and qualified; all other officers of said town now in office shall hold the same and exercise all the powers given them by this act until their successors be duly elected or appointed or qualified.

"80. No bond for cost or other bond shall be required of the town of Paintsville in any suit, prosecution or legal proceedings, unless the same be lawfully required under similar circumstances of a resident citizen of this State.

"81. All ordinances of the town of Paintsville now in force not in conflict with this charter, shall continue in force until repealed by the board, and all laws vesting rights in or imposing duties, upon the town of Paintsville, not therein suspended or repealed by the General Assembly of the Commonwealth of Kentucky.

"82. The recognized records of the trustees of the town of Paintsville, and all bonds and contracts executed to said town shall remain in full force; and, remaining in the proper office or keeper thereof, shall be evidence in all courts to the same extent that the original would be on due proof; and the keepers of said records may be entitled to fees for copies of same, to be prescribed by ordinance.

"83. The said board of trustees shall have power to prescribe penalties for the breach of all ordinances passed by them, in pursuance of the powers herein granted; and whenever the penalties have not been prescribed by this act, said penalties may be in any sum not exceeding one hundred dollars.

"84. It shall be the duty of the board of trustees to provide for the use of said police court a suitable docket, judgment book, execution book, well bound, and provide for paying for same; and it shall be the duty of said board to make allowance to any officer for any cost worked out by any person on the streets or other place designated by said board.

"85. All laws or parts of laws in conflict with this act are hereby repealed.

"86. This act to take effect from and after its passage; and all laws not in conflict with the provisions of this act to remain in full force and effect."

Became a law April 17, 1890, without the approval of the Governor.

SOME ORDINANCES THAT ARE STILL IN FORCE

ORDINANCE CREATING OFFICE OF TOWN ENGINEER AND BUILDING ORDINANCE

"Section 1. That there shall be and is hereby created the office of town engineer, whose duty and compensation shall be prescribed by ordinance which be hereinafter enacted. The said engineer shall hold the office two years from the date of his appointment and may be removed at the pleasure of the board of trustees.

"Section 2. That no wall, structure, building, part or parts thereof, shall be built, constructed, altered or repaired in the town of Paintsville, except in conformity with the requirements of this ordinance.

"Section 3. That before the issual of any permit for the erection, construction or alteration of any building in the town of Paintsville, the owner, agent, architect or builder thereof shall submit to the town engineer the full plans and specifications of the proposed work and no wall structure, building, part or parts thereof shall be constructed, altered, or repaired without a permit from the town engineer, *Provided,* That where only slight repairs are to be made, or where no radical change or improvement is proposed, the same may be made without such permit. The town engineer shall issue no permits unless he approves of the location, plans and specifications of the proposed building or alteration.

"Section 4. Any person violating any provision of this ordinance shall be fined in any sum not exceeding $20.00 and cost for each offense.

"Section 5. The said engineer shall receive as his compensation for his labor performed hereunder, 50 cents for each building permit that may be issued by him which is to be paid by the party receiving such permit."

Approved February 19, 1906.

TO REQUIRE LOCATION OF LINES BEFORE BUILDING

"That it shall be the duty of all persons, or corporations, desiring or commencing to build on any lot within the town of Paintsville, to have the dividing line on the lot where the building is proposed and the adjoining lot to be located and defined by the town engineer before the foundations for such buildings are laid. It shall be the duty of the town engineer, upon the application of any person desiring to build on a lot, to locate the boundary line of such lot within a reasonable time after said applications.

TOWN ENGINEER SHALL BE INSPECTOR OF BUILDINGS

"Section 1. The town engineer shall be the inspector of roofs on all dwelling houses, outhouses and public houses within the town of Paintsville, Kentucky, and it shall be his duty when, in his opinion, or on the information or request of any trustworthy citizen that any roof or covering on any house or outbuilding shall be dangerous, after giving two days notice of his intention to the owner or person in charge thereof, to proceed at once for any supposed dangerous roof, or covering on any house, shall summon two discreet citizens, who, with him, shall at once examine said roof or covering, and if a majority of them, after such examination and hearing of evidence, if any offered by the owner or person in charge of the same, find such roof or covering to be dangerous, they shall condemn it; that upon such condemnation the town engineer shall serve a written notice upon the owner, agent or person in charge of the property, who, within twenty-four hours thereafter, shall be required to repair, or commence to repair, or disuse the same under a penalty of not more than ten dollars and cost for each successive twenty-four hours said repairs be omitted, after the expiration of the time allowed in said notice.

"Section 2. It shall hereafter be unlawful for any person, firm or corporation to put up on any building located on Main Street, Second Street, East Street, College Street, Court Street, or Church Street in the town of Paintsville, Kentucky, any board, shingle, or to cover any building with any covering of combustible nature, and it shall be the duty of the town engineer to make examination of any roof which he deems unsafe, or upon notice from any citizen that the same is not up to the requirements of this ordinance, to condemn the same as provided herein.

"Any person violating this provision shall be fined not to exceed five dollars for each offense.

"Section 3. This ordinance shall be in full force and effect after its passage and adoption as required by law."

Adopted May 27, 1907.

MARSHAL'S DUTIES

"The board of trustees of the town of Paintsville, Kentucky, do ordain as follows:

"Section 1. The marshal, by virtue of his office, shall be collector of all town taxes, unless the payment thereof is by law specially directed to be made by some other officer.

"Section 2. The marshal shall keep his office at the place wherein police court of the town shall sit in a room to be provided for that purpose by the board of trustees. He shall keep an accurate account of all money received by him, showing the amount thereof, the time when, and from whom received and on what account, also of all disbursements made by him, the amount thereof, to whom paid, the time of payment and on what account, and he shall so arrange and keep his books that the amounts received and paid on account of separate and distinct or specific appropriations will be exhibited in separate and distinct accounts. He shall balance his books on the first day of each month, so as to show the correct amount on hand belonging to each fund on the day the balance is made.

"Section 3. The marshal shall keep his office open for the collection of moneys which he may be entitled to receive at all reasonable times, except on Sunday and legal holidays, and when any money is paid to him, he shall immediately enter the same upon his books and give to the person paying it a receipt therefor, specifying therein the amount and on what account the same was paid, and when paying any money he shall take a similar receipt. He shall retain the amount of tax and other public dues against any person or corporation out of any claim allowed by the board of trustees.

"Section 4. All taxes shall be due and payable on and after the first day of March, after the assessment, and the marshal shall account for and pay all taxes for which he is bound into the town treasury by the first day of December in each year, and upon his failure to do so he and his sureties shall be liable therefor, and shall be proceeded against in a manner provided by law.

"Any person failing to pay their taxes by the first day of October in the year following the assessment for such taxes, shall pay six per cent additional on the tax so due and unpaid. The marshal shall be required by the town treasurer to pay a penalty of six per centum on all taxes due and unpayable unpaid by him on the first day of January in each year.

"Section 5. It shall be unlawful for the marshal to apply or use any money received by him for any purpose than for which such money shall have been paid or collected; every such misapplication shall be deemed a misdemeanor, and, on conviction he shall be fined not less than twenty-five dollars nor more than fifty dollars for each offense.

"Section 6. The marshal shall when required by the board of trustees, settle his accounts for town tax collected; and at the regular October meeting of the board of trustees, each year, shall appoint some competent person to settle the account of the marshal of the money due the town.

"Section 7. The marshal from and after the first day of March in each year shall collect the taxes due in the town, and

A STREET IN THE BUSINESS SECTION OF PAINTSVILLE, KY.
(No Parking Is Permitted on This Street Which Accounts for the Vacant Appearance)

upon the failure of the persons bound therefor to pay the same, may distrain the goods and chattels owned by or in the rightful possession of the person from whom the taxes are due, notwithstanding the existence of any lien upon the same; and may proceed to sell the title of such person in so much thereof as will pay the tax due, and all cost in the mode prescribed by law.

"Section 8. The marshal before he makes a levy for taxes shall demand the same from the persons from whom the taxes are due if a resident of and in the county, and tender a receipt therefor, if it be required, in which he shall specify the taxable estate with which such persons are charged, the value and amount thereof and the tax due.

"Section 9. The marshal shall, after having advertised at the court house door the time and place of sale for at least ten days, sell at public auction for money, so much of the property levied on for taxes as will pay the tax and cost.

"Section 10. If there be no personal property that the marshal can distrain for taxes due and the same shall not be paid by the first of July, the marshal shall sell for cash any real estate belonging to or listed by such delinquent taxpayer or as much thereof as will pay the taxes due and his commission in the manner that lands are sold under execution, except that the land shall not be valued or levied on and shall be advertised by posting for fifteen days before the sale, a written or printed notice at the court house door and by publication once a week for four weeks prior to the day of sale in a newspaper published in the town of Paintsville, and he shall, not less than fifteen days before the day of sale, mail to the delinquent a postal card, addressed to his place of business, if such can be ascertained, notifying him of the time and place of sale; and in order to cover the cost of such advertising and notification, the marshal shall have two dollars for each person whose property is advertised, to be paid by the delinquent, but in no event to be paid by the town.

"If the marshal shall sell any land for taxes as herein provided, he shall carry out in detail the provisions of Section 4152, and Sections 4153 and 4154 of the Kentucky Statutes, and Sections 4156, 4158, 4159, 4160, 4161, 4162, 4163, and 4164 of the said statute, are hereby made a part of this ordinance the same and to all intents and purposes as if said sections and each of them were copied at length herein.

"Section 11. All ordinances and parts of ordinances in conflict with any of the aforesaid ordinance of any section thereof is hereby repealed.

"Section 12. This ordinance shall be in full force and effect from and after its passage and posting as required by law."

Passed and approved 16th day of December, 1907.

DISTURBING A CONGREGATION

"If any person shall within the corporate limits of the town of Paintsville, wilfully disturb or interrupt a congregation assembled for or engaged in the worship of God, or shall wilfully interrupt or disturb any school, seminary or college, while the students of the same are engaged in their studies or undergoing a public examination, or any assemblage of people met for and engaged in a lawful purpose, he shall be fined not less than twenty dollars nor more than fifty dollars, or imprisoned not more than twenty days or both in the discretion of the jury."

Adopted September 18, 1894.

THROWING BALL, ETC., ON STREETS

"Whoever shall be guilty of throwing a ball, stone, or other missile on, over, or across any of the streets of said town, shall be guilty of a misdemeanor, and on conviction shall be fined not less than one nor more than ten dollars for each offense."

Adopted September 7, 1895.

ASSESSOR

"Section 1. That from and after this date, the assessor of the town of Paintsville shall be appointed by the board of trustees of said town.

"Section 2. That said assessor shall be appointed for any length of time within the discretion of the said board of trustees, so that the term for which said assessor is appointed, shall not exceed two years. Said assessor shall hold his office until his successor is appointed and qualified. The said assessor may, at any time, for good cause shown, be removed by the board of trustees.

"Section 3. This ordinance shall be in full force and effect from and after its passage and posting as required by law."

CORPORATE LIMITS

"The board of trustees of the town of Paintsville, do ordain as follows:

"Section 1. That pursuant to an ordinance entitled, 'An ordinance to correctly define the boundary of, and proposing to annex certain adjacent territory to the town of Paintsville, Kentucky,' enacted by the board of trustees of the town of Paintsville, on August 7, 1913, and pursuant to judgment of the Johnson Circuit Court, in an action wherein George W. Preston, et al., were plaintiffs, and the town of Paintsville was defendant, which judgment was certified to this board by the clerk of the Johnson

DR. ERNEST E. ARCHER
Mayor of Paintsville, Ky.
Connected with the Paintsville Hospital. One of the Leading Surgeons in All Eastern Kentucky, and Enjoys a Large Practice in His Profession, But Finds Time to Render Service to His City and the People

Circuit Court, and which certified judgment is recorded in Minute Book 3, Page ...., of the records of the town of Paintsville. The territory described in the second section thereof is hereby annexed to and made part of the town of Paintsville, Kentucky, and its corporate limits are hereby extended so as to embrace and include all the hereinafter set out lands, territories, lots and parts of lots; and the said annexed territory is hereby made and shall remain subject to the jurisdiction and control of the said town, to all its laws, orders, ordinances, rules and regulations now in force or that may hereafter be adopted for the government of said town.

"Section 2. The lands, territories, lots and parts of lots referred to in Section 1 and which are hereby annexed to the town of Paintsville, are included in the following description, to-wit:

"Beginning on the east bank of Paint Creek, where the Spradlin Ford crosses the same; thence running a northeasterly direction to the top of the point, about fifty feet south of the west end of the lower wall of the Mayo Cemetery; thence running a straight line, about two hundred feet to the southwest gate of the said cemetery; thence with the west wall of same, to and with the top of the point, to the gap near Alice Mayo Hall; thence up and along the top of the ridge; with the following courses and distances: N. 74-45 E. 421 feet; N. 25-20 E. 561 feet; N. 40-45 E. 413 feet; N. 74-10 E. 233 feet; N. 60-15 E. 194 feet; N. 99-45 E. 335 feet; N. 89-30 E. 420 feet; N. 89-50 E. 180 feet; thence with the center of the ridge to the northwest corner of the tract of land owned by the Frank Preston heirs; thence a straight line in a southeasterly direction to an elm standing about two hundred feet east of where Cross Street intersects with the county road, at the Preston Cemetery; thence a straight line in a southerly direction to the center of the Salt Well Branch, where it intersects with the county road leading off of the macadam; thence with the center of said branch and down the same to its mouth; thence up Paint Creek, with the low water mark of the same, to the present corporation line of the town of Paintsville, near the property owned by Dan M. Hager; thence with the east line of the present corporate limits, a northerly and westerly direction around the foot of the hill, as said line is now located, to the point of beginning.

"Section 3. This ordinance shall be in full force and effect from and after its passage as required by law."

CITY ORDINANCE TO ANNEX TERRITORY
ORDINANCE DEFINING TERRITORY AND LAND PROPOSED TO BE ANNEXED TO THE CITY OF PAINTSVILLE

"*The City Council of the city of Paintsville do ordain as follows*:

"That it is hereby declared to be desirable to annex to the city of Paintsville, Johnson County, Kentucky, the following defined and described boundary of land and territory to-wit:

"Beginning at the mouth of Salt Well Branch of Big Paint Creek; thence crossing Big Paint Creek to low water line of same; thence down said creek with its low water line to Big Sandy River; thence up along west low water line of said river 4,370 feet to a point on the bank of said river (at its low water line) 520 feet above the mouth of the first branch leading into said river, just below the Lafe VanHoose residence; thence up the hill crossing Chesapeake and Ohio Railway at or near point of upper switch to the Chesapeake and Ohio yards, due west 1,000 feet to an 'X' cut in a rock ledge near a cluster of chestnuts on top of spur ridge between Sandy River and Flat Rock Branch of Big Paint Creek being at the junction of the first point leading to said ridge above the hollow or branch, leading to the river just below the Lafe VanHoose house; thence N. 35, W. 2135 feet to a stake at the south intersection angle of a 30 foot roadway leading out of Flat Rock Branch and Lincoln Avenue as shown upon a revised map of the Stafford Addition to the city of Paintsville, recorded in Miscellaneous Instrument Book ...., Page .... Johnson County Court Records; thence with the south line of Lincoln Avenue to its junction with the west line of Seventh Street to a set stone at south edge of the Mill Branch Road thence up along with the Mill Branch Road to the Stafford-Fairchilds property line; thence with said property line a north course crossing said creek to the present corporation line of the city of Paintsville; thence to the beginning."

Adopted by the City Council September 13, 1927.

Approved by the mayor September 14, 1927.

Below is what William Ely has to say about Paintsville, in his *History of the Big Sandy* which was published in 1887.

"The county town of Johnson County was laid out in 1842 (1834), on the lands of the Dixons, one-half mile from the Sandy River, on Paint Creek. It has an old-time court house, built of brick, and of sufficient capacity to answer the purposes for which it was built at the formation of the county. The people year by year grow in morality; and four days, and often less, is sufficient time to keep the criminal court and grand jury in session; and three or four days finishes the docket of the circuit court. The

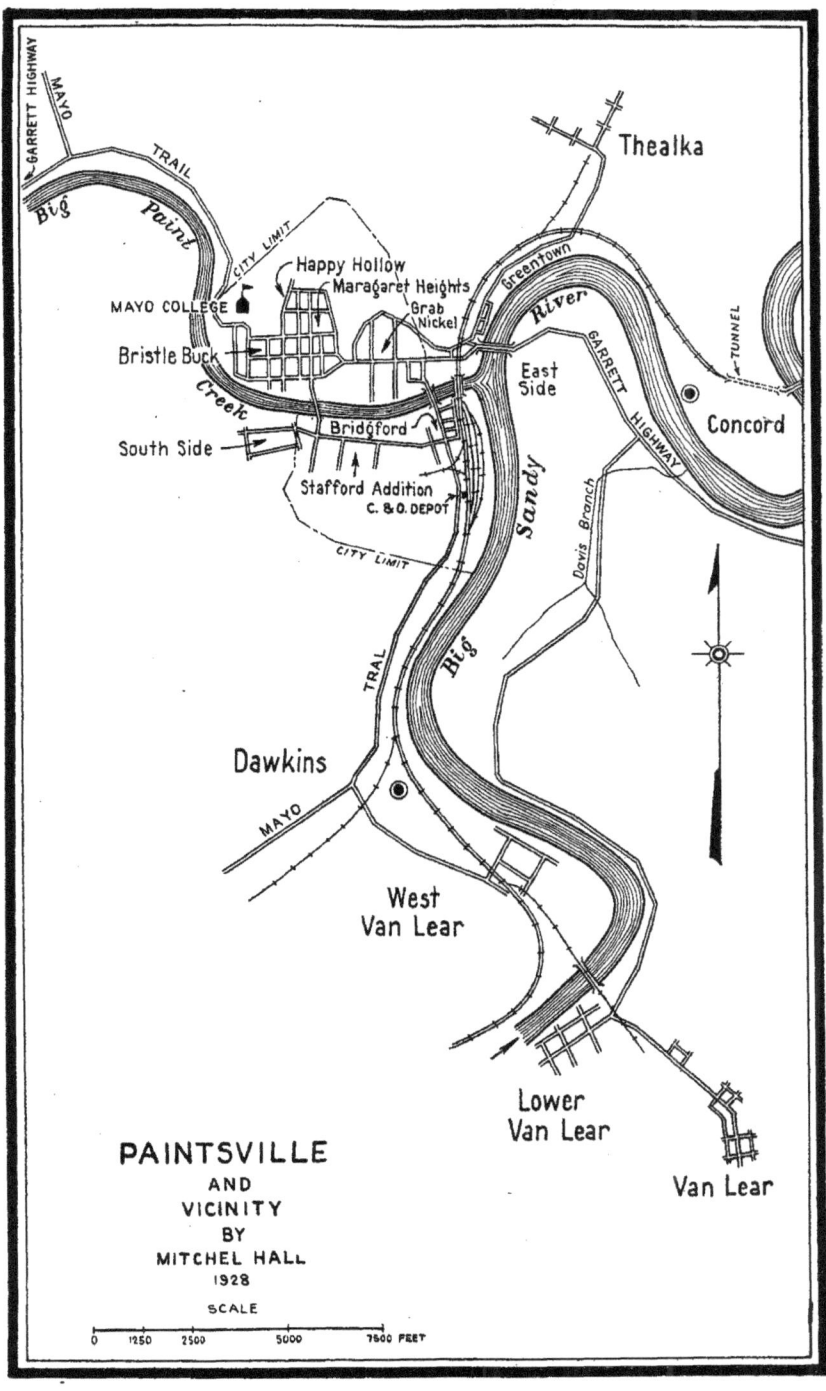

people are, perhaps, the most law-abiding of any county in the State, and all seem to pay their debts and settle their disputes without recourse to law.

"Paintsville and Johnson County have good schools and churches dotting the whole county. Paintsville has two frame schoolhouses and three church buildings. The first, built in 1866, the Methodist Episcopal, is a frame; the next, built in about 1880, the Methodist Episcopal Church, South, is a beautiful brick; and the last, a neat brick structure, belongs to the Christian or Reform Church." (The latter church is still standing and in use.)

Paintsville was a sixth-class city until 1922, when it was made a city of the fifth class by legislative act. (See Page 282, Chapter 108, Acts 1922.)

Under Kentucky's State Constitution, cities of the sixth class are governed by a board of trustees. When the town was made a fifth class, it practically changed the form of government. A mayor and council took the place of the trustees, and under their leadership, the town took on more of a city air, and has grown so in proportion that the 1926 General Assembly made it a fourth-class city, which includes those having a population of from 3,000 to 8,000 inhabitants.

The growth of Paintsville has not been a sensational one, but slow and substantial. Many improvements have taken place in the last decade. Within this period Paintsville has emerged from a small county seat town to a model little city with all modern conveniences. With reference to the latter, special mention should be made of the fact that it has more good paved streets in proportion to its size than any town in this section of the State; and the people enjoy the privilege of good water, gas, and electric light systems, and regular train, bus, mail, telephone and telegraph facilities. There has been a time when it was necessary to visit other cities to purchase some necessities, but this is no longer the case, as prospective buyers may now find right in Paintsville practically everything to be found in the stores of large cities.

Paintsville occupies a broad and level creek bottom one mile up from the mouth of Big Paint Creek. The overflow population out of the corporation limits extends to the Greentown section toward Thealka, across the creek to Southside and Stafford additions, and to the extensive Chesapeake and Ohio Railroad yards in Bridgeport and Brown additions. Travelers make their way from the station to town by bus or taxi on a broad concrete road and they are invariably delighted at the end of the trip to find a beautiful little city, for numerous shade trees line the paved streets and add to the attractiveness of the spacious lawns and well-spaced modern homes. As the town is in the center of the coal, oil, and gas fields, fuel to heat these homes is very convenient.

In 1870 Paintsville had a population of 247. The 1920 United States census gave the population as 1,383. This was just previous to the last boom in oil development in the county, which brought with it many inhabitants to settle there. An unofficial census taken of Paintsville in 1923 showed it as having a population of 2,210, not including the suburbs with a population of approximately 1,500. The suburbs are Bridgeford, Brown Addition, Southside, Stafford Addition, East Side, Hen Clip, and Greentown. The local divisions or districts of Paintsville, named from continuous use are known to the older settlers as Bristlebuck, which is the west section of the town within the corporate limits; Grabnickel, which is the lower, or east section; Happy Hollow, which is the north section; and Margaret Heights, the northeast section.

The county is located in the tenth congressional, seventh appellate, twenty-fourth judicial, thirty-fifth senatorial, and ninety-first legislative districts.

It lies within latitude 37° 53' and longitude 5° 48'. Has an area of 204,169 acres, 268 square miles, an assessed valuation of $8,082,944 (1923), and a population of 19,622 by the 1920 census, including the town of Paintsville, which had at the same time a population of 1,383. Paintsville had grown to a population of 2,210 by April, 1924, not including suburbs with approximately 1,500.

This does not include the new addition of Bridgeford, which was added to the corporation (see page 242) in 1927, making a total population for the town in 1927 of approximately 4,500 inhabitants.

TIME

Until the building of railroads in the county, "sun" time was used, which was one-half hour faster than what is now central time. Next railroad or central time was generally adopted and remained in use until the World War in 1917 when Daylight Saving Time, one hour faster, was used during the summer months. After the War, Central Standard Time was used throughout the year until April 3, 1927, the Big Sandy section of the State of Kentucky was transferred by the Interstate Commerce Commission to the Eastern zone, by request of the Cincinnati Chamber of Commerce, since the Daylight Saving Time had proved an advantage to that section.

The professions are well represented by men and women trained in the best American colleges. Those interested in public organizations should feel at home in Paintsville for they are. welcomed by Masons, Odd Fellows, Knights of Pythias, Red Men, Eastern Stars, Rebekahs, Daughters of the Revolution, Delphian, Rotary and Kiwanis clubs, in addition to the numerous church

SOME PAINTSVILLE BUSINESS MEN
DAN WHEELER L. J. PARRIGAN DUD HUFFMAN
RUSSELL HAGER J. K. BUTCHER EUGENE WARD
DR. GIRVEN STAFFORD FRED ATKINSON

societies. One thing lacking in this respect, which would be for the betterment of the town, is a live chamber of commerce to go after new industrial plants by offering proper inducements to outside capital to locate factories in the city. Paintsville is strategetically located in the center of the Big Sandy Valley with cheap power and fuel and other inducements which make it a good site for the location of almost any kind of industrial plant. Aside from the general everyday business in the average town, its main source of revenue is from the mining towns and oil fields near by. It has not sufficient industrial works to keep the laboring class of people constantly employed, and to invite outside employment.

Below are given some of the industries:

Hotels	3
Banks (National)	2
Hospitals	2
Wholesale establishments	4
Department stores	5
Dry goods stores	4
Furniture stores	2
Undertaking establishments	1
Hardware stores	2
Drug stores	3
Jewelry stores	1
Shoe stores	2
Grocery stores	10
Meat markets	2
Grist mills	1
Saw or planing mills	1
Lumber yards	2
Automobile dealers and garages	8
Ice plants	2
Dairies	1
Plumbing and lighting establishments	3
Supply companies	1
Machine shops	2
Restaurants	6
Bakeries	1

Among the towns that have gained prominence through advertising is Paintsville, often referred to as the "capital" or "hub" of the Big Sandy, for it is regarded as being one of the most influential and enterprising towns along the banks of this river.

There is not a town in the State that has shown greater development in the past few years than has Paintsville. It is ideally located for a picturesque highland town. Its business is diversified, there being practically every mercantile enterprise represented. The town is building rapidly, and the business houses and residences are of a high class, and add materially to the general appearance of the place.

It is the shipping point for all oil and gas well machinery and supplies to the Johnson-Magoffin oil field, and this distinction alone gives no little prominence, besides adding to the business of the town. Every sidewalk, street, and alley in the town is paved, and many of them are beautiful. It is a delightful place in which to live and engage in business, and every encouragement is given those who would like to better their condition in life by moving to a live, wide-awake town.

Paintsville is situated at the intersection of the Mayo Trail and Garrett Highway, and is located on broad creek and river bottoms that will provide room for the expansion of a town to many thousands. The new residential sections have already begun to expand toward the East Side, South Side and Stafford additions.

The growth and prosperity of any city are due in a great measure to the efficiency and public spirit of its officials and inhabitants. Due to that persistent "ever keeping at it" disposition of those of the present, as well as those in the past, Paintsville has taken her place as one of the best towns in Kentucky with a happy, contented people, and her prospects of future greatness are flattering.

There has been a healthy, steady, wonderful growth and advancement here for the past ten years. True there has been no stream of prospectors, except for the oil boom in 1920, added to the normal growth to cause the population to increase as rapidly as has been the case in many other cities of this size.

The growth in wealth and health has been phenomenal. The advancement in civic improvements, its streets, churches, schools, residences, coal mines, surrounded by oil and gas fields, is such that there is just cause for pride. There have been and are now as great opportunities for success here as there are in those new or proposed towns. The opportunity to grow up with the place, to get in on the ground floor holds as good in Paintsville as other places. Paintsville is going to continue to grow and develop. It has prospered. Real estate has steadily increased and will continue to increase as the years go by.

DR. PAUL B. HALL
President Paintsville-Van Lear Rotary Club
Prominent Physician and Surgeon, Connected with the Paintsville Hospital,
Head of the Local Post of the American Legion, and a Director
of the Paintsville National Bank

GEOLOGY

DIRECTORY

CIVIC ORGANIZATIONS

ROTARY CLUB

President—PAUL B. HALL
Vice-President—HARRY LaVIERS

DIRECTORS
Warrick Bailey
Chas. Feutter
H. C. Taylor
Paul B. Hall
Dudley Spencer
Harry LaViers

MEMBERS
Ernest Archer
James Auxier
Warrick Bailey
Claude Buckingham
Frank Conley
Green Daniel
Dave Dorton
Everette Evans
Chas. Feutter
Paul Hall
Fred Hefner
Jas. Holbrook
Fred Howes
Bob Jammison
Hatler Johnson
Chas. Kirk
Ked Kirk
Harry LaViers
Henry LaViers
John Lyons
Garland Rice
Ben Roberts
Tobe Rule
Bill Slone
Archie Smith
(Honorary)
Henry Sowards
Dudley Spencer
Bob Splane
Girven Stafford
Henry C. Taylor
Dick Thomas
Jim Turner
Arnold Webb
Zip Wells
Dan Wheeler
Oscar Wilson

KIWANIS CLUB

President—T. B. ASHLEY
Vice-President—J. E. FISHER
District Trustee—ARVILLE WHEELER
Secretary—O. W. CAIN
Treasurer—FRANK CHANDLER
Sheriff—ROY STAFFORD
Past-President—M. O. WHEELER

MEMBERS
Dr. Lloyd G. Meade
O. N. Evans
Dr. R. M. Wilhite
Howard Frail
Harry Conley
Eugene Ward
Warren L. Preston
Oliver Jenkins
John Jones
Douglas Turner
Dr. C. F. Holtegel
Dud Huffman
Jno. W. Wheeler
John B. Wells
Harrison Wheeler
Darwin Long
Beecher Stapleton
Rev. J. A. Parker
Lymon Parrigin
J. N. Woollum

LODGES

I. O. O. F.

Paintsville Lodge No. 288
Noble Grand—Jas. Mitchell
Vice-Grand—E. L. Daniel
Secretary—Mitchell Daniel

Pleasant Valley Rebekah No. 116
Noble Grand—Mrs. R. A. Belt
Vice-Grand—Mrs. B. H. Conley
Secretary—Miss Lurlie Pugh

Encampment No. 31
Chief Patriarch—B. F. Roberts
High Priest—Paul C. Hager
Senior Warden—J. F. Pelphrey
Junior Warden—Gus. Preston
Secretary—R. A. Belt
Treasurer—Don C. VanHoose

F. & A. M.

Master—G. C. Wells
Senior Warden—James Hammond
Junior Warden—Rudolph Oppenheimer
Secretary—Fred Atkinson
Treasurer—D. H. Dorton

Royal Arch Chapter No. 131
High Priest—J. K. Butcher
King—William R. Preston
Scribe—Frank Chandler
Secretary—Ray Turner

EASTERN STAR

Worthy Matron—Mrs. Fannie Archer
Worthy Patron—Paul C. Hager
Associate Matron—Miss Geraldine Pugh
Conductress—Miss Lurlie Pugh
Associate Conductress—Miss Elva Perry

A GROUP OF PAINTSVILLE D. A. R.'S
Celebrating Washington's Birthday with a Silver Tea

W. O. W.

Paintsville Camp No. 457

Consul Commander— Advisor Lieutenant—
J. C. WILLIAMS   MILTON LEMASTER
Clerk—GEORGE E. CLARK

O. R. M.

Eskabaga Tribe No. 462

Sachem—G. W. CARTER
Chief of Records—
    C. J. WILLIAMS
Prophet—MONROE SLONE
Senior Sagamore—S. J. VANHOOSE
Junior Sagamore—
    CECIL GOLLIHUE

D. A. R.

The Paintsville Chapter of the Daughters of the American Revolution was organized October, 1925, by Mrs. Eugene H. Ray, of Louisville, Kentucky, then State Regent, now Vice-President General, National Society Daughters of the American Revolution. This patriotic society aims to keep alive the principles of those who fought for American Independence. The Paintsville Chapter has promoted many patriotic and historic activities. Among them are: Co-operation with the American Legion in Fourth of July celebrations, Washington Birthday celebrations, one of the most interesting of which was a silver tea, at which there was a large display of antiques gathered from the old families of the town and county; and flag-raising ceremony at the monument for service men killed in the World War, in the court house square, at which time a large flag was presented by the D. A. R. The D. A. R. was also instrumental in getting all the business houses in Paintsville to buy large flags to be placed in front of their places of business on patriotic occasions.

The following graves of Revolutionary soldiers buried in Johnson County have been located and bronze markers have been placed at two of them:

Samuel Auxier—Blockhouse Bottom. Marked.
John Hager—Blockhouse Bottom.
Richard Wells—Blockhouse Bottom. Marked.
Simon Auxier—Burchett's Farm, near Blockhouse Bottom.
Joseph Davis—Near Chestnut.
Samuel Murray—Near Buffalo Station.

The charter members are:

Mrs. G. H. Rice (Mabel Auxier Rice), Regent.
Miss May Stafford, Vice-Regent.
Miss Stella Atkinson, Secretary, Treasurer.
Mrs. V. D. Splane (Geneva Wells Splane).
Mrs. O. C. Geiger (Virginia Hager Geiger), Registrar.
Mrs. Harry LaViers (Maxie Auxier LaViers), Corresponding Secretary.
Mrs. Pauline Robinson (Pauline Wells Robinson), Historian.

Miss Gertrude Patrick, Chaplain.
Mrs. Dan Wheeler (Beulah Patrick Wheeler). (Deceased.)
Mrs. E. E. Archer (Fannie Auxier Archer), Librarian.
Mrs. Lloyd Clay (Grace VanHoose Clay).
Mrs. F. F. Smith (Edna Stafford Smith).
Mrs. V. S. Taylor (Virginia Wells Taylor).

Additional members:

Mrs. Warrick B. Bailey (Sue Dixon Bailey).
Mrs. E. M. Clay (Carrie Vaughan Clay).
Mrs. G. M. Stafford (Lula Hager Stafford).
Mrs. J. G. Newman (Leona Auxier Newman).

Miss Victoria Trimble.
Mrs. W. J. Vaughan (Martha Auxier Vaughan).
Miss May Williams.
Miss Lula Leslie.
Mrs. Herbert Wheeler (Willa May Preston Wheeler).

The chapter has two honorary members: Mrs. Holmes Kirk and Mrs. W. J. Dempster.

THE DELPHIAN SOCIETY

The Paintsville Chapter of the Delphian Society was organized in June, 1925. It is a chapter of the National Delphian Society, which has its head office in Chicago, Illinois, and which has organized chapters in most of the large cities and towns of the United States. It is a society for study, culture and personal improvement. It has a six-years course, a year of study being given to each of the following: Ancient History and Literature, Drama, Art, Modern Literature, Poetry, Music.

The charter members are:

Mrs. E. J. Evans, President.
Mrs. W. L. Preston, Vice-President.
Mrs. Z. Wells, Secretary-Treasurer.
Miss May F. Stafford, Membership Secretary.
Mrs. G. H. Rice ⎫
Mrs. J. W. Turner ⎬ Advisory Board.
Miss Lucile Rice ⎭

Mrs. H. LaViers
Mrs. Paul B. Hall
Mrs. R. C. Thomas
Mrs. O. F. Patrick
Mrs. Lloyd Clay
Mrs. Will Davis
Mrs. Hobart Meade
Mrs. Jesse Stafford, Jr.

Additional members:

Mrs. Dan Wheeler (Deceased)
Mrs. Harry Davis
Mrs. Bacon R. Moore
Mrs. Frank Conley

Mrs. J. K. Butcher
Mrs. R. C. Quinn
Mrs. W. J. Dempster
Mrs. Lloyd Meade

PAINTSVILLE WOMEN WHO TAKE AN ACTIVE INTEREST IN SOCIAL
AND PUBLIC AFFAIRS
LORAINE CLAY MAY F. STAFFORD MRS. STANLEY TEMPLE
LILLIAN HOWES ELIZABETH BUCKINGHAM MRS. J. G. NEWMAN
MRS. ORION WHEELER ELIZABETH WELLS

CHURCHES

M. E. CHURCH

Pastor—W. B. Foley
Supt. of Sunday School—
  D. H. Dorton

Church services each Sunday morning and evening. Prayer meeting Thursday evening.

MAYO MEMORIAL CHURCH

Pastor—H. G. Sowards
Supt. of Sunday School—
  M. C. Kirk

Preaching Sunday morning and evening. Prayer meeting Wednesday evening.

CHRISTIAN CHURCH

Superintendent—J. H. Cooper
Sunday school each Sunday morning.

MISSIONARY BAPTIST CHURCH

Pastor—A. H. Webb
Supt. of Sunday School—
  H. LaViers

Morning and evening services each Sunday. Prayer service Wednesday evening each week.

UNITED BAPTIST CHURCH

Moderator—Lafe Walters
Assistant Moderator—
  Elder Guy Preston
Clerk—Sherman Wheeler

Church services fourth Saturday in each month.

FREE-WILL BAPTIST CHURCH

Pastor—Millard VanHoose
Services second Saturday and Sunday. Prayer meeting Thursday night. New church located on Third Street.

CITY OF PAINTSVILLE

Mayor—E. E. Archer
Police Judge—Fred Atkinson
City Clerk—J. G. Newman
City Treasurer—D. H. Dorton
City Attorney—F. P. Blair
Chief of Police—Wm. Preston

Members City Council—

Warren L. Preston
H. Cox
Harrison Wheeler

Roy Melvin
Clark Walters
Oliver Jenkins

Police Court is held fourth Monday in each month for the regular civil term.

A list of all city officials has not been included. An effort was made to obtain these, but one of the ordinance books has been lost, making it impossible to get all of them. For this reason only the names of those run across in copying other data, are included. They are as follows:

MAYORS

Mayor	Date
Dr. Sparks	1918-1920
R. C. Thomas	1920-1922
J. N. Meek	1922-1926
E. E. Archer	1926-1930

POLICE JUDGES

Police Judge	Date
William N. Randolph	1-5-1879
Henry Jane	6-7-1892
C. B. Wheeler	7-13-1892
M. F. Howes	1898-1902
Claude Buckingham	1910-1914
H. C. H. Conley	1914-1918
Charles A. Atkinson	1918-1922
R. G. Howes	1922-1926
Fred Atkinson	1926-1930

CLERKS

Clerk	Date
J. G. Newman	1926-1930

TREASURER

Treasurer	Date
D. H. Dorton	1926-1930

CITY ATTORNEYS

Attorney	Date
Z. Wells	1922-1926
Z. Wells	1926-1927
F. P. Blair	1928-

CHIEF OF POLICE

Chief of Police	Date
Frank Caudill	1922-1924
W. A. Ward	1924-1926
William Preston	1926-1930

TRUSTEES

Trustee	Date
Lewis Todd	3-2-1852
George Salmon	3-2-1852
Winston Mayo	3-2-1852
Henry Stephen Vaughan	3-2-1852
Hiram F. Strange	3-2-1852
Isaac R. Turner	10-4-1871
John W. Castle	10-4-1871
Thomas Brown	10-4-1871
John Preston	10-4-1871
James R. Burkett	10-4-1871

COUNCIL

Warren L. Preston (chn.)	1926-1930
Guy Preston	1926-1928
B. H. Cox	1926-1930
Clark Walters	1926-1930
John B. Wells	1926-1928
Oliver Jenkins	1926-1930

VAN LEAR, which is one of the larger coal-mining towns of Eastern Kentucky, is the site of operations of the Consolidation Coal Company. Although comparatively a new town, started in 1909 and 1910, it has grown to a population of over four thousand people. It started like a whirlwind. Timber was cleared, roads graded, homes constructed, and mines opened. Soon thousands of tons of the county's black diamonds were whirling to foreign markets.

Unlike the conditions of many of the smaller mining camps, Van Lear is a modern little town. Being controlled by one of the largest coal corporations in the United States, built and maintained by trained and technical men, from the time of its creation, it has developed into a type of town, where living conditions are such as to be inviting to anyone, with good houses, good streets and roads, water system, schools, churches, hotels, clubhouse, picture show, baseball park, and recreation grounds.

Previous to 1910, the narrow bottoms, and branches of Miller's Creek were occupied by farms and milldams. Today, there is a large community occupying it from head to mouth. The hotels, churches, schools, commissaries, postoffice, welfare and other buildings of similar character are well built, attractive, well

SCENES AT VAN LEAR, KY.
Note the Neat Appearance of the Yard in the Lower Picture, Which Is Maintained by the Coal Company

painted, electrically lighted, and provided with running water and sanitary toilets. Yards are of fair size, and the architecture of the house is sufficiently varied to make the place attractive. Green lawns and flowers are common in the yards of the lower section, and add to the appearance of the community.

It has an excellent school system. Teachers in these schools find good accommodations at the company clubhouse.

While a good portion of the population is of the foreign element, such a magnitude of mining compelling them to bring in outside labor, it is a peaceable town. Law and order are maintained at all times.

Two large playgrounds for the children are furnished and maintained by the mining company. Bathhouses for the miners are located at each mine. The town has four churches of different denominations and three school buildings. High school courses are given at the Central School Building. A large recreation building is located in the center of the town. This building contains a moving picture theater, soda fountain, and ice cream parlor, pool room, and office.

Van Lear is one of the best producers of coal in the State, employing hundreds of men, and adding to the wealth of the county.

THEALKA and WHITE HOUSE are both coal-mining towns of the Northeast Coal Company. Both are run in like manner and have conditions similar to the town of Van Lear, except that neither is as large. This is due in part to the fact that local labor is given preference to outside help, and as a consequence many of the part-time farmers are given employment, who never live within the mining camps. Thealka mines afford work for many who maintain their homes in Paintsville.

The population of these two towns is made up solely of white English-speaking American citizens. Colored and foreign-speaking people are not to be found in the camps.

Thealka is a mile and a half below Paintsville on Muddy Branch. It is one of the earliest of the mining centers of the county. It has little for amusement, but is close enough to Paintsville for the people to enjoy its privileges. Too much cannot be said of the officials in charge of the operations there. They promote the educational and religious development of the community, and will not permit people to remain in their employ, who do not further this spirit. As a consequence, Thealka is above the average mining town. It has one of the most modern consolidated school buildings in the Big Sandy Valley.

White House, so called because all the houses were originally painted white, is one of the oldest, if not the oldest mining operation in the county. There was a time when living conditions were very unsatisfactory here. The small amount of level land along the river bank and on Lick Creek made it difficult to have roads, and made it necessary to set the houses very close together, which always leads to unsanitary conditions. Pigs, cows, and chickens roamed at large, leaving their filth. The railroad track was practically the front yard, and the noise and smoke from trains added to the unfavorable conditions.

In the last few years, since the Northeast Coal Company took over the mine operations there, wonderful improvements have been made, and this situation is practically remedied. Many new and modern miners' homes have been built on up Lick Creek, to provide for the house shortage, and the surroundings have been improved in a manner that has brought this camp up to the average of modern mining camps. A few of the original "white houses" are still standing and occupied by some of the miners who own their own homes and have gardens. There are several private stores run there, in competition with the company's commissary. At one time the trains only came to White House, and the mails and passengers were brought on to Paintsville by hack. White House then enjoyed its greatest increase and prosperity. Living in White House now is much better than in the rural sections because of the opportunity afforded to supplement the income from work in the mines with the products of the small farms near by, operated during "lay-offs."

FLAT GAP received its popularity from its schools. The Reverend William Jayne, an educated Baptist preacher and teacher, did much to help along the education of school teachers in the county in his "Enterprise Academy," located at this place. (See page 275.)

Flat Gap is located in the divide between Mud Lick Creek and the Lower Laurel Fork of Blaine Creek in the northwestern section of the county. It has always been handicapped by the lack of improved roads in that section, and is off of any railroad. Being in a good grazing and farm section, it will no doubt grow fast as soon as the State Highway is constructed through that portion of the county.

OFFUTT has a history similar to that of White House. It was started by, and named in honor of, the president and general manager of the Rockcastle Lumber Company, who marketed vast tracts of timber on the heads of Greasy and Rockcastle creeks, with Offutt as the central shipping point. A narrow gauge road connected his mills with the railroad at this town. The town was also the destination of a narrow gauge road from the cannel coal mines on Two-Mile Creek, and afforded homes for the laborers on these works.

A SECTION OF WHITE HOUSE, KY.

The timber and cannel coal mines have now been abandoned, but there are still bituminous coal mines at this place run by the Royal Collieries Coal Company. The town has not grown any in the past ten years, and is fast losing its best citizens who are moving to the more modern places in the county.

EAST POINT is probably the oldest town in the county, excepting Paintsville, having been settled by the Auxiers and Greers soon after the abandonment of Harman's Station in Blockhouse Bottom, which is just across the river. It is a picturesque little place nestled on the banks of Little Paint and Big Sandy, with the old water mill still standing, about five and one-half miles south of Paintsville on the Floyd-Johnson county line. The town has always been small and ceased to grow soon after the railroad passed through. The houses are of the old-time design, with their lightning rods and gabled roofs, and are all of frame structure.

The town has always been noted for the good schools held there, many of its more important educators receiving their training in its combined grade and high school, which was abandoned many years. It was the site of the Masonic Hall and all members in the county received their initiation at the East Point lodge. It had several large stores doing business then, and at one time was the shipping point for many dealers in crossties.

Many of the old-time houses are now being torn down to make way for the Mayo Trail which passes through the place. East Point is not expected to grow much more in population as it has had its day, and there is very little employment there for inducement. It nevertheless is a place of historical interest.

Chapter 938, Page 1081, Acts 1890.

AN ACT to incorporate and define the corporate limits of the town of East Point.

"Section 1. *Be it enacted by the General Assembly of the Commonwealth of Kentucky*:

"That the town of East Point, in Johnson County, be, and the same is hereby, created a body-corporate and politic, with powers to sue and be sued, contract and be contracted with, under the name and style of the town of East Point; and the boundary line and corporate limits of said town shall be as follows, to-wit: Beginning at the mouth of Little Paint Creek, and running with same to the mouth of Bear Hollow Fork; thence up said fork to a point opposite the East Point schoolhouse; thence a straight line to said schoolhouse, and including the same and the grounds enclosed around it; thence east with the State road to a corner named in a deed from W. J. Conley to John Harrison; thence with their line to the top of the point; thence along the top of the point toward the river to a corner between W. J. Conley and J. K. P. Auxier; thence a straight line to the river, and up same to the beginning."

The remainder of the act, Sections 2 to 36 are similar to the act amending the act incorporating the town of Paintsville. (See page 241.)

Approved April 19, 1890.

The above charter has since been repealed.

WEST VAN LEAR (VAN LEAR JUNCTION) is one of the new towns fast coming to the front. It was laid out about twelve years ago on the broad and level river bottoms just below the mouth of Miller's Creek, and on the opposite side of the river, on what was once the Duncan farm, which can easily accommodate a population many times the present population of about five hundred. It is noted for the many stores, which mainly receive their trade from Van Lear; for the local citizens who do not hesitate to give their time for the promotion and advancement of their little city; and for the women who have built a modern church in their town through the effort of the "Ladies' Aid Society." It is a promising town, and will grow with time.

RED BUSH is a small but substantial little town, located on Upper (or Big) Laurel Creek in the farthermost part of the northwestern section of the county. It is in a section rich in lands, minerals, and timber, yet undeveloped to any extent because of the lack of transportation facilities. The 1926 State Legislature passed an act (see page 406) authorizing a State highway through this town, which when built, will be the beginning of a new era for Red Bush and that section. It is near the oil fields and is now enjoying prosperity brought about by their development.

Red Bush is by no means a new town, and with Flat Gap has long been the center of population of that district.

OIL SPRINGS is a small town on Little Paint Creek, and on the recently constructed Garrett Highway. Although more of a community gathering place than a town, it has grown recently to warrant the name. The people have devoted more of their time to county and public affairs than in developing the place into a town, or to indulging in extensive farming. The Litterals and others of that territory have long been associated with the public offices at the county's capital. The surroundings have never been suitable for farming and the settlers have had to look elsewhere for industries, first to timber, teaching, and growing of fruits, and now to road work and the oil and gas employ.

The building of the Garrett Highway has started a tide of prosperity there, which no doubt will continue until all the old decayed buildings, erected by the first settlers give way to modern structures like a few already constructed, such as the new consolidated school.

SCENE NEAR WEST VAN LEAR
A Part of the Town Can Be Seen in the Distance

DENVER, like East Point, is one of the older towns of the county, with its old-time dwellings, churches, and schools, but a town fast dropping out of sight, soon to be overshadowed by numerous little mining towns, recently started along the B. S. & K. R. Railroad.

It is just a small country town, located on Jenny's Creek and the B. S. & K. R. Railroad, with its one doctor, one church, one school, one individual whom the rest look up to, and two or three stores run in connection with the post office. These merchants probably do more "out of town" business than local, by exchanging groceries and goods for produce and the like, which they send to market.

Although the place may not grow, it at least will not be deserted by many of the Patricks, Pelphreys and Rices, who have made it what it is today.

RICEVILLE is a comparatively new town, which began when the B. S. & K. R. Railroad built its line up Jenny's Creek with the town as the terminal. Although the railroad has been extended into Magoffin and Breathitt counties, it still maintains its offices at Riceville. This section is noted for the Greenrock timber, which was primarily the reason for building the railroad into the territory.

It is located at the intersection of the Narrows Fork, Long Fork, and Greenrock Fork of Jenny's Creek, and has a large territory to draw trade from. It evidently is the coming town of the Jenny's Creek, or southwestern, section of the county.

REFERENCES TO CHAPTER VIII

[1] Edgar B. Hager, in an address to the Paintsville Kiwanis Club.

[2] Jillson, W. R., The Big Sandy Valley. Pages 29-30. J. P. Morton & Co., Louisville, Ky., 1923.

[3] Ibid. Page 42.

[4] The Big Sandy News, Louisa, Ky.

[5] Jillson, W. R., The Big Sandy Valley, Page 77. J. P. Morton & Co., Louisville, Ky., 1923.

CHAPTER IX
EDUCATION

During the early days, or period of pioneer settlement, education was in its infancy; teachers were permitted to teach by securing license and the only qualifications required of the teacher were spelling, reading, writing, and a little arithmetic. Schools were few and far apart; pupils would be compelled to attend very often six or seven miles away from their homes, walking to and from school, instead of going by bus. Schoolhouses were made of logs, with only one door, and a hole sufficing for a window. These schools have been the subject of many modern speakers before young audiences, which they urge to appreciate present facilities, considering what they (the lecturers) had to be contented with when they attended school in these mud-daubed one-room houses, and had rails for seats and a little two-by-four slab colored with maple bark and copperas for blackboards. The house was heated or warmed by a large chimney made out of loose rocks, sticks and clay. The fuel used in the large fireplace was wood, gathered in the nearby woods by a dozen of the larger boys designated weekly by the teacher.

The school term was seldom more than three months, but subscription or "winter" schools were gotten up by some of the teachers, and frequently held in private homes, which prolonged the time a couple of months. While the conditions may not have been very inviting, many made the best of them, and several future "Schoolmasters" received fair education from the old blue-backed speller and Ray's arithmetic, to the tune of a hickory stick.

Considering the part taken in advancing the cause of education in the county, no one will question the great work done by the following teachers who were leaders in their day:

Professor Wm. N. Randolph began teaching in the days when bears and wolves were molesting the inhabitants, and kept at it till the "nineties."

Charles Grim was an old-time teacher for many years, and being a very small man, always had to surrender to the boys on Christmas, according to the custom of those pioneer days. The rule then was, "Treat or be ducked," the treat consisting of not less than a bushel of apples or a dozen packages of stick candy.'

Lewis Mayo, Esq., was a teacher of ability. He commenced teaching in 1837, and held schools of high grade for twenty-five years. He died near the close of the Civil War.[2]

Professor John B. Wheatley taught many years in the city schools of Paintsville, and was instructor of numerous teachers' institutes. He made a name for himself that is still in the minds of the parents.

As much may be said of Professor Tom Mayo, who was a mathematician out of the ordinary.

Reverend William Jayne, an educated Baptist preacher, did much to help in the education of school teachers in his "Enterprise Academy," then located at Flat Gap. Below is given a general reference to an act regarding this school, and others.

Chapter 287, Page 516, Acts 1884.

AN ACT to incorporate the High School at Flat Gap.

A lengthy act was passed and approved March 3, 1884, appointing Henry Daniel, Dock Woods, William Jayne, Hiram E. Conley, Alexander Rice, Ranson Lyon and Wallace Bailey as board of directors and incorporating the Flat Gap High School Company.

Many sections are included in this act regarding capital stock, election of trustees, the treasurer, secretary, laws and by-laws.

After serving the purpose for which it was created for many years the Flat Gap school gradually lost prestige, especially after the death of Professor Jayne, until the enrollment and courses offered were no more than those of the other schools of that section. In the last year or so, the high school at that place has been re-established and hopes to soon become an educational center.

Chapter 685, Page 6, Acts 1886.

An act was passed and approved April 19, 1886, incorporating the East Point Graded School. This act is similar to the one for Flat Gap, only even lengthier.

Chapter 772, Page 633, Acts 1888.

A similar act was passed and approved March 29, 1888, for the "Ward City Graded Free School District."

Chapter 586, Page 275, Acts 1888.

Still another was passed and approved March 19, 1888, for school district No. 7, with Isaac Rice, James S. Spradlin, and Edward Blair as the board of directors.

AN ACT for the benefit of all schools.

Chapter 504, Page 59, Acts 1873.

"Be it enacted by the General Assembly of the Commonwealth of Kentucky:

"That the superintendent of public instruction is hereby directed and authorized to purchase a full set of charts, maps, globes, tellurian, orrery, cube root blocks, and such other apparatus as he may deem needful or useful in a teachers institute, not exceeding in cost however, the sum of three hundred dollars, and to draw his draft on the auditor for same, who is hereby authorized to cause the same to be paid out of the Johnson County school bond.

"2. The same, when purchased, shall be the property of the Johnson County Teachers Institute, and shall be transmitted to, and be in the care of the Johnson County school commissioner, who shall be responsible, on his official bond, for the same.

"3. This act shall take effect from its passage."

Approved March 22, 1873.

It can truthfully be said and with a bit of pride, that advances have been made for the cause of education in proportion to the progress attained in all other activities, and today there is an excellent school system in the county. Eighty conveniently distributed buildings provide for the education of the children in every community, governed by ninety-three teachers, outside of John C. C. Mayo College and the city schools at Van Lear and Paintsville. The county has 5,915 pupils in rural schools and 1,632 in the grades. There is one colored school in the county, located at Van Lear. Several consolidated and community schools are included in the above number, with a few giving two years of high school.

Of the more recent educators responsible for the intellectual development in the county, some of the outstanding ones are included herein, all of whom were well-trained and experienced instructors.

Professor W. C. Brandenburg, for many years superintendent of the Paintsville city schools, brought this school system up to class A rating by the State Department of Education, through his expert guidance. He holds an M.A. degree.

Professor George W. Butcher of Offutt has long been known for his ability as a normal instructor, and is at present connected with the J. C. C. Mayo College.

Milt McDowell of Manila taught for a number of years, and served as superintendent of schools of the county.

Calloway Hall was a familiar figure in all school activities, and at the time that teachers' examinations were held and graded within the county, he seldom failed to be one of the examiners. He was one of a very few good-natured schoolmasters, liked by all.

Professor J. Melvin Hall has spent some thirty years in educational work, having taught in every grade and most of the cen-

J. MELVIN HALL

trally located rural schools, as well as the Paintsville public schools, Mayo College, West Van Lear consolidated, and H. S. Howes community school, and served as school supervisor for the county. He began teaching at a time when discipline was very essential in the school, a factor which he notably maintained. Some of the fathers of today, who at some time or other attended his schools, often credit him for their education, and, as an example of how strict he was, jokingly recall the times when he, apparently reading a newspaper but looking through a hole made for the purpose, caught them sending love notes or throwing paper wads, which invariably called for a rebuke. Although well informed on most school problems and capable of teaching and superintending any grade or school in the county, he probably is best at instructing would-be teachers in normal, and preparing them for tests of the State Board.

John C. C. Mayo began his successful career teaching in the schools of Johnson County and was noted as one of the best mathematicians of his day.

Professor Ben. F. Conley of Drakes Fork is an old teacher in the county, and still active.

Fred Meade has been connected with the schools of the county for twenty-eight years and during sixteen years of that time was county superintendent. Quoting officials of the State Department of Education, he had the reputation of being one of the best superintendents in the State, in that he knew the needs of his county and what they could afford to finance. He always planned ahead and had his own way of working out his plans which resulted in a smooth and working organization. Not one time in these sixteen years in office did he exceed his budget. Mr. Meade did not believe in plunging his county into debt, but advocated the pay-as-you-go plan.

M. L. Robinson was both teacher and attorney, serving many years with the rod, which he believed in strongly. He taught several winter schools, and excelled in the post-season occupation. He abandoned the occupation during the last years of his life to take up the practice of law in Paintsville.

Don C. VanHoose taught enough to receive honorable mention as a teacher before entering politics. The field lost a capable instructor when he gave up the practice.

Professor W. B. Ward, probably the best-read man in the Big Sandy Valley today, is another who put his whole thought, time, and efforts in the work. Coming from Martin County, where he first taught a number of years, he took charge of what was then the Sandy Valley Seminary, later to become head of the Paintsville city schools which he supervised until recently. He next taught at Offutt and is now tutoring at Elkhorn City. He spent a fortune in collecting an individual library, of which he is master, and very likely today would not exchange it for the best farm in the county.

John C. Ward has always been familiar to the student-going public in the rural districts. He, however, has been contented to confine his work to the Offutt section.

Professor Willie Webb, known throughout the county in his time for his strict enforcement of the rule in the schoolroom, was a first-class instructor in the schools for many years. When some school got beyond the control of the teacher, and had received a name generally for its bad discipline, Professor Webb was hired and his presence in the room was sufficient to quell all disorders. He was very efficient in developing backward students. Many of the younger generation will tell you that he started them on the road to learning.

George M. Johnson, twice county superintendent, held high standards for teachers.

Below is given a list of those now guiding the intellectual development of the children of both city and rural schools of the county.

JOHNSON COUNTY TEACHERS—1926-1927

Adams, George
Allen, S. Y.
Arnett, Gladys
Arrowood, Samantha
Auxier, Garnett H.
Auxier, Margaret
Bailey, Ena
Baldridge, F. M.
Baldridge, Robert
Blair, Hester
Blankenship, Gracie
Blanton, Elizabeth
Borders, Kathryn
Brandenburg, W. C.
Branham, Iva B.
Brown, Sylvia
Burchett, Harry
Burchwell, Essa
Butcher, C. M.
Butcher, George W.
Butler, Claudia
Butler, Eva Lee
Castle, Effie Lee
Caudill, Carroll
Caudill, C. W.
Caudill, Kelly A.
Caudill, Oza
Caudill, Sarah
  (Auxier)
Chandler, H. G.

Clay, Loraine
Collins, Powell
Colvin, Lexie
Combs, Lexie Olive
Conley, Ben F.
Conley, John J.
Conley, Ray
Conley, Raymond
Conley, Virgie
Craft, Martha J.
Daniel, Edna
Daniel, Flora
Daniel, Jennie
Daniel, Kathryn
Daniel, Mitchel
Daniel, Mona
Daniel, Ora
Daniel, Sandless
Daniel, Sarah
Davis, James, Mrs.
Dingus, A. G.
Fairchilds, Alice
Ferguson, J. P. Jr.
Fitzpatrick, Earl
Ford, Lou
Frazier, Cova
Frazier, Ella C.
Fyffe, Normal K.
Geiger, Marion
Gibbs, Grace

Green, Faye
Green, J. J.
Griffith, Ada E.
Griffith, J. J.
Hager, Loretta
Hall, J. Melvin
Hall, Lenore
Hall, Wiley
Hamilton, Orville
Haney, Christine
Harris, Augusta E.
Harris, Nettie
Harris, Ruie
Hayes, Orville
Hitchcock, E. J.
Hitchcock, E. V.
Hitchcock, Fannie, Mrs.
Horne, Vern
Howes, Christine
Hughes, Fanny
Jones, Mary
Kelly, Beulah
Kennard, Bessie
Lemaster, Atha May
Lemaster, Flora
Lemaster, Herbert
Lemaster, Ruby
Lemaster, Terra A.
Lester, Mary
Litteral, Joy

PHYSICAL EDUCATION AT JOHN C. C. MAYO COLLEGE

EDUCATION 283

Lyon, Olga
Mahan, Dora
May, ——— Mrs.
McKenzie, Della
McKenzie, Edna E.
McKenzie, Harrison
McKenzie, Joyce
McKenzie, M. O.
Meade, Mabel E.
Meade, May
Meade, Ruth
Meek, Ruth
Mollett, Amanda
Napier, Garnett
Osborn, Susie, Mrs.
Pack, Golda
Patrick, Joe
Perry, Elva
Pickle, Robert
Picklesimer, Chas.
Picklesimer, Edna
Picklesimer, Hester R., Mrs.
Picklesimer, Robert
Preston, Mitchel
Preston, Ora (Music)
Ramey, George
Rice, Bernice E.
Rice, Gladys
Rice, Haden
Rice, Harvalee
Rice, Hilda Mae
Rice, June Meade, Mrs.
Rice, Mildred
Salyer, Afton S.
Salyer, Alpha
Setser, Pearl
Sloan, Kanawho
Sowards, H. G.
Sparks, Inis
Sparks, W. H.
Spears, Fanny
Stambaugh, Nellie
Stapleton, Dow
Stapleton, Erie
Stone, Golda
Stone, Eva
Stone, L. A.
Sturgill, John I.
Sturgill, V. I.
Sublett, Lionel
Tackett, Mayme
Temple, Stanley, Mrs.
Thomas, Vera
Travis, Hazel
Trimble, Victoria
VanHoose, C. B.
VanHoose, Claude
VanHoose, Dennis
VanHoose, Dewey, Mrs.
VanHoose, Eva
VanHoose, Mary, Mrs.
VanHoose, Walter
Vanhorne, G. D.
Vaughan, Maude
Vaughan, Nolan
Vaughan, Walter
Ward, Angie L.
Ward, Ena
Ward, Felix
Ward, Hannah
Ward, J. C.
Ward, Nellie
Ward, Pauline
Ward, Roma G.
Ward, Sally
Ward, Vera
Ward, Veva
Ward, Wiley
Webb, Gertrude Gladys
Webb, Iuka
Webb, Margaret
Welch, Fannie
Wells, Ellen
Wells, Hazel C.
Wells, Iuka
Wells, Margaret
Wheeler, Orville
Wheeler, Sophie
Wheeler, Velma
Whitt, Curtis
Whitt, Ellis
Williams, Chas. M.
Williams, Ethel
Williams, Julia
Williams, John Fred
Williams, Loretta
Williams, Marvin L.
Williams, May
Williams, Mervin
Williams, Neva Lee
Williams, Sankey
Witton, Orlando
Wyatt, Ruby

The number and name of the schools in which the above instructors are carrying on their work are as follows:

LIST OF SCHOOLS IN JOHNSON COUNTY—1927
(See map at page 160 for location)

Dist.	Name of School
1	Hagerhill†
2	West Van Lear‡
3	Bend of John's Creek
4	Lower Daniel's Creek
5	Upper Daniel's Creek
6	Upper Miller's Creek
7	Head of Greasy
8	Pigeon Roost
9	Three Forks Greasy†
10	Hurricane Creek
11	Two Mile†
12	Offutt‡
13	White House†
14	Hammond
15	Chestnut
16	West River
17	Thelma
18	Buffalo†
19	Concord
20	Slone
21	Thealka
22	(Consolidated with 21 as H. S. Howes Community School)*§
23	Mingo*†
24	Baker Branch
25	Wiley Branch
26	George's Creek
27	Forks of Hood (Rockhouse)
28	Mouth of Rush
29	Rush Fork†
30	Sitka
31	Froghonery

284   HISTORY OF JOHNSON COUNTY

Dist.	Name of School	Dist.	Name of School
32	Sycamore	61	Green Valley
33	Sip	62	Hurricane Branch
33	Lower Hood	63	Oil Springs*‡
34	Puncheon	64	Bill Rice
35	Upper Franks Creek	65	Green Rock
36	Lower Franks Creek	66	Riceville
37	Head Tom's Creek	67	Long Fork
38	Little Mud Lick	68	Mill Creek
39	Ramey Branch	69	Buck Horn
40	Joe's Creek (Puncheon)	70	Asa
41	Flat Gap	71	Denver
42	Patterson	72	Upper Middle Fork
43	None designated (Joe's Creek)	72	Lower Middle Fork
44	Head Mud Lick	73	Lick Fork
45	Red Bush	74	Japan
46	Upper Keaton	75	Rockhouse
47	Lower Keaton	76	Drake
48	Barn Rock	77	East Point†
49	Skaggs	78	VanHoose
50	Beech Branch	79	Barnetts Creek (Fairview)
51	Cuba	80	Staffordsville†
52	McKenzie Branch		Lower Van Lear (Greentown)‡
53	Low Gap		Van Lear City Schools§
54	L. Little Paint		Van Lear Colored School†
55	L. Mine Fork		Paintsville Public and High School§
56	Hargus		John C. C. Mayo College§
57	Pigeon		
58	Davis		
59	Colvin Branch		
60	Mouth Barnetts Creek		

*Consolidated.
†Two Teachers Required.
‡Three Teachers Required.
§Four or More Teachers Required.

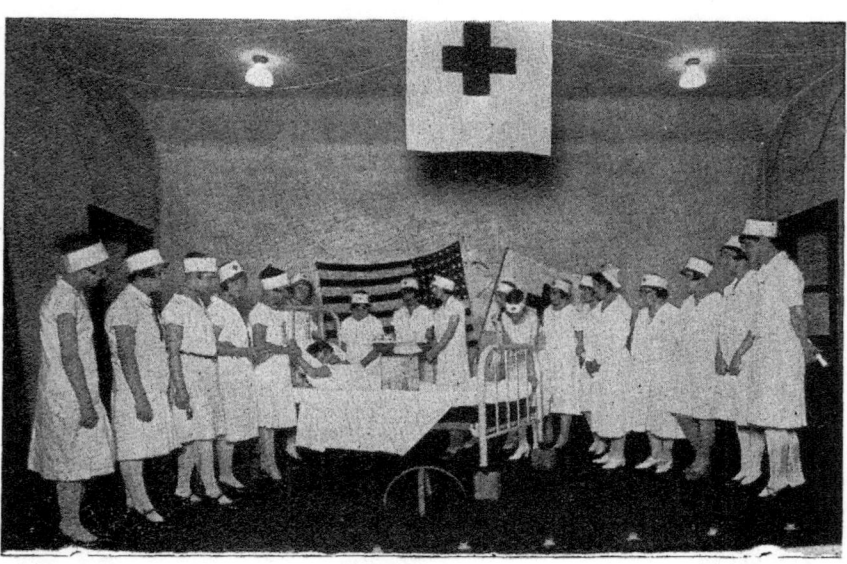

RED CROSS TRAINING IN PAINTSVILLE CITY SCHOOLS

PAINTSVILLE CITY SCHOOL BUILDINGS

Something Any City May Well Be Proud Of. What Town Is There, the Size of Paintsville, That Boasts of a Better or More Modern Plant?

Of the schools named the city schools of Paintsville and Van Lear and John C. C. Mayo College are by far the largest both in attendance and courses offered, each employing from a half-dozen to a score of teachers, who are graduates of the best colleges in the country.

It is impossible to state in so little space or even a book, just how much is being done by these institutions of learning for that section of the State, but anyone visiting them will readily realize that they are as good as may be had in any state, and far above the conditions that some "foreigners," who do not know the conditions of the section, write of for the personal appeal to the reader.

JOHN C. C. MAYO COLLEGE

This college was organized in 1905 with Dr. J. R. Turner, president, and known as the Sandy Valley Seminary until 1918, when the name was changed to the title it now bears to the memory of John C. C. Mayo through whose generosity it was founded.

Although smaller in scale, it did a noble service while under the first name, through the efforts of Professors Skinner, Murril, and Ward, and now lives in the lives of students and graduates sent forth. Mr. Mayo was responsible for the first building constructed, which served for the school for many years. Mrs. Mayo later had the girls dormitory built on the beautiful site overlooking Paintsville and the lower Paint Creek valleys. These two buildings harbored the college until 1918 when Mrs. John C. C. Mayo donated to the M. E. Church, South, which controls the college, the Mayo mansion, offices, and other valuable buildings, with forty acres of land, thereby making it one of the largest and best equipped institutions in the Big Sandy Valley today.

Having received such a gift, probably the largest contribution made by anyone in Eastern Kentucky, the college burst forth under a new name, and due to the untiring efforts of its president, Dr. H. G. Sowards, and his staff of assistants, is today a college offering courses of the highest grade.

Using Dr. Sowards words, "Mayo College is unique in the school field—a Christian school with sound and rigorous requirements in the academic work. Its graduates enter the State University without examination, and many make excellent records in standard universities.

"Mayo's watchword is *Thoroughness;* its motto is *Success Through Service.* So far as the power of environment and persuasion can make it, Christian character is a requirement. This is the highest ideal any school can have. Mayo succeeds by making Christian character a fundamental standard of education."

Mayo has a standard accredited high school class A. No better high school work is offered in Kentucky.

Mayo's Commercial College equips its graduates for business success. Character plus hard work plus Mayo training insures success for any one with the equipment to do the work offered in the commercial college.

Mayo's department of music is one of the strongest in the State of Kentucky. The teachers in this department are college and conservatory trained. Records of former students show that the training received enabled them to make high records in the strongest conservatories.

Mayo's department of expression and physical education gives valuable service in correct English, forceful speech, and healthful living. Public speaking, healthful exercises, and recreations make this department of great value to its students.

Mayo has a grade school taught by normal- and college-trained teachers. Grade work is the foundation of education and is the most important work offered in any school. Unless the work in the grades is thorough, a sound education is impossible. Mayo's grade teachers are carefully trained for their work.

Bible courses, the atmosphere of Christian fellowship, and the evangelistic mission of Mayo College keep before the student the Christian ideal.

Most of the athletics of the school are confined to inter-class, but baseball and football have always been represented by presentable teams.

These are a few of the activities of one of Johnson County's best schools. What better can be had, or offered, by some of the "foreigners" who persist in "knocking" the mountain people of Eastern Kentucky?

REFERENCES TO CHAPTER IX

[1] Ely, William. The Big Sandy Valley, Page 26. 1887. Central Methodist Press, Catlettsburg, Ky.

[2] Ibid.

Administration Bldg. Alice Mayo Hall President's Residence Margaret Hall Mayo Memorial Church

JOHN C. C. MAYO COLLEGE, PAINTSVILLE, KY.

CHAPTER X

RELIGIOUS PROGRESS

NOTE: The purpose of this chapter is not to compare sects, promote the faith of any one denomination, or make attacks on any of them.

In the past there has been too much prejudice in the churches of this country. In some localities, preachers of different denominations would not hear each other preach, or permit their children to attend church if the preacher was not of the denomination of the parents. One church would preach and promulgate the doctrine that if sinners did not join the church of their faith, they were bound for Hades. They did not seem to realize that salvation is a free gift for all who will obey. Some churches would not permit instrumental music, Sunday schools, or modern methods of heating and lighting. The music of the organ or piano was believed to kill the spiritual influence of the church.

It is in view of these facts that this is written, with the idea of a better understanding and a more intelligent good will among the several branches of the Church of Christ. It is well for each to understand what other denominations believe and especially for the young people, who must decide denominational preferences.

The Congregational, the Episcopal, the Lutheran, the Presbyterian, and the Unitarian churches are not discussed as there are no churches of these faiths in the county. There is a Roman Catholic Church located at Van Lear. It has been formed there in the last few years, has a small membership, and has not played a very important part in the religious development of the county, and therefore is not discussed herein.

Those discussed are merely arranged in alphabetical order with no attempt to place them with reference to their respective importance.

It is hoped that these brief sketches will acquaint the reader with the history of his own denomination in the county.

The majority of the early settlers in Johnson County belonged to the best families of Virginia, Pennsylvania, and North Carolina, from which they migrated. During the period of settlement, with their trials and hardships, those pioneers did not forget to worship the Creator. Although they did not build churches at first, due to the urgent need of constructing homes, almost every family reserved one room in the "log-house" for worship. One household would often support a meeting of several days duration, feeding and caring for all who came. In favorable weather, these gatherings were held under some large tree, or shady grove, thereby eliminating the immediate necessity of church houses. This primitive custom has not entirely been abandoned, and many of the present generation can recall when these assemblies were numerous.

With due honor to every householder who made these meetings possible, much of the praise should be given to the early ministers who went into every community up and down Big Sandy for the advancement of the faith of his church. The morals of those good old-time preachers were commendable, and those servants of God who labored hard to win souls to Christ, and received but little or nothing for their toil and anxiety, are worthy the gratitude of their descendants. They did well, according to their knowledge, and many of them knew more than some people now are willing to concede.[1]

As soon as enough dwelling houses had gone up in the county to meet the demands of a steadily increasing population, church houses were built in the more settled districts. By August, 1867, there were about fifteen permanent houses of worship. These included both Baptists and Methodists, but other denominations, up to that time, were scarcely represented in the county. One of the first and best log churches was at Borders Chapel on the edge of the Johnson-Lawrence County line, while another was at Fish Trap on Big Paint, both of which were erected by United Baptists. The first permanent Methodist Episcopal Church, South, was a frame, constructed in Paintsville in 1866, but now replaced by the magnificent Mayo Memorial. The Methodist Episcopal Church, the first brick, was such a neat structure in its time that it was only replaced in the last few years by a more modern and larger church. This one was but slightly in advance of another brick

MAYO MEMORIAL M. E. CHURCH, SOUTH, PAINTSVILLE

of the Reform, Campbellite, or Christian Church, which is still standing in Paintsville.

Religious development in Johnson County has kept pace with that of any other county in Eastern Kentucky, and almost every denomination of the Protestant faith is now represented. A sketch of each is included herewith.

THE BAPTIST CHURCH

The name "Baptist" is the English term for the Greek word *Baptizo* meaning "to dip." Inasmuch as this one branch of the church accepts baptism by the immersion of the whole body in water, they are called Baptists.

They are known for their intense loyalty to personal conviction. They believe that Jesus Christ was baptized by immersion in the river Jordan, and that the early Christians were thus baptized by the apostles, and therefore every believing Christian should be baptized in the same way. "He that believeth and is baptized shall be saved," "Everyone of us shall give an account of himself to God," and "Christ and Him crucified" are among their favorite texts.

Believing that the church should be composed only of regenerate believers, they refuse to baptize children, holding that only people sufficiently mature to make conscious acceptance of Christ as their Savior can be rightly admitted to the church through the ordinance of baptism.

They have no authoritative creed, statements, or symbols, like the Thirty-nine Articles of the Episcopal Church or the Twenty-five Articles of the Methodist Church, or the Westminster Confession of the Presbyterian Church. Their creed is the Bible, and they have not undertaken to formulate its teachings into an authoritative creed. The "New Hampshire Confession of Faith," in the North and South and the "Philadelphia Confession of Faith," in the South, are among some that have been widely published for instruction rather than for enforcement.[2]

The Baptists have at all times, and in all lands, insisted upon the entire separation of Church and State. They believe in "rendering unto Caesar the things which are Caesar's," but only the things which are Caesar's.

The first Baptist church in the United States was established in Newport, Rhode Island, by John Clarke some time between 1638 and 1644. The next one of historical importance was by Roger Williams, who, about the year of 1664, was driven out of Massachusetts—not because he believed in immersion or because of any special religious tenets he held—but because of his extreme individualism in insisting upon the separation of Church and State. Massachusetts had passed laws against Baptists because of their attitude touching these matters in 1644, had imprisoned them in 1651 and banished them in 1669. This was religious persecution by civil authority which Mr. Williams censured from the time he landed in this country. It is not necessary to repeat what almost every history has covered—his activities in stirring up the trouble which finally resulted in his being "railroaded" out of Massachusetts. He went to Providence, was there immersed, became a Baptist and founded Rhode Island, the first state in the Union to guarantee entire religious freedom.[3] It was there, and mainly through him, that the history of the Baptist Church was started in this country.

THE BAPTISTS IN KENTUCKY

As above stated the first important Baptist Church in the United States was established in Rhode Island by Roger Williams, who later lost out in that church and became a Seeker.[4] The Baptist denomination increased rapidly with the early settlement of the colonies and spread over the entire territory known as the New England States.

Virginia was settled by colonists under different conditions. These immigrants were actuated by motives differing from those of the settlers of New England. Not only did they differ in purpose but also in religious beliefs. However, a Baptist denomination was established in the mother state also, but differing in many of its tenets and practices from the one established by Roger Williams. This Virginia church gradually extended west of the Cumberlands.

To understand the Baptists, and to have a correct knowledge of their origin in Kentucky, one must go back to the beginning of the religious pioneers of Kentucky.

Among those first preaching this doctrine in the State were Robert Smith, Lewis Craig, and Squire Boone. Reverend Smith's name is on the records of Mason County, having been listed in May, 1796, while the Reverend Craig is mentioned in October of the same year. In addition to assisting his brother in laying out the Wilderness Road, building the first cabin in Kentucky, marrying the first couple in the State, and being horribly crippled from wounds received in warfare, Squire Boone was also a Baptist preacher, killing Indians during the week and holding services on Sunday. It was he who preached the first sermon ever heard in Louisville.[5]

It is easy to find a direct historical connection with Old South Kentucky Association, which was organized in May, 1788 A.D., in Yates Creek Church in Madison County. This body divided in the year 1801 A. D., and North District Association was organized and embraced all the churches east of the Kentucky River.⁶

About this time, there were two associations, known as the North Licking Association of Separate Baptists, and the South Licking Association of Regular Baptists, differing somewhat from each other.

These two institutions existed side by side, and as they learned more of each, many of the leaders came to the conclusion that the differences in the creeds were not essential or of such vital importance to justify separate organizations. Consequently, many efforts were made to harmonize the beliefs of the two factions. This proposed union of the two churches was a prominent subject of discussion for several years, both separately and jointly. Many conferences were held for the purpose of effecting a compromise and in the endeavor to formulate articles of faith that would be acceptable to both. While the differences were apparently not so great, yet for a long time these conferences failed to effect a union. Frequently all hope of compromise seemed to be lost but finally, in the year 1804, through the untiring efforts prompted by the unconquerable faith of many of the leaders of both factions, articles of faith were agreed upon. The union was established and the new organization, composed of both divisions, launched forth under a name suitable for the new church—a name that would be suggestive of the former history and at the same time would not be offensive to any old prejudices that might exist—"Regular United Baptists." Both divisions of this union held to the same faith and order and in full correspondence with each till some time after the Civil War.

During this time several associations were granted letters from the Union. Burning Springs in 1813; New Salem, 1825; Paint Union, 1837; Union, 1859; Mates Creek, about the year 1867; and Sand Lick, in the year 1876.⁷

Notwithstanding the fact that this united church grew and prospered there were some members who still recalled the old differences and clung tenaciously to the original tenets. These people, though very young at the time of the union, were now facing the sunset of life and as their time evidently became shorter they were less willing to leave old principles, which they held so dear, buried beneath seventy years of history. They were not satisfied with the existing order of things, and had not been at any time, but had acquiesced trusting in their own steadfastness of faith. In their declining years they could not bear the idea of seeing their children taught a form of religion not in conformity with their original opinions, feeling that with the passing of the old members those primitive principles would eventually be forgotten.

In order therefore to perpetuate the original doctrine they at last determined to re-establish the old faith and to re-organize the old denomination. Beginning about the year 1892 and continuing for about five years these various Regular Baptist associations divided over the question of predestination, election, and kindred questions. They divided into what is now known as Primitive or Predestinarian Baptists and Regular Baptists, the Predestinarian Baptists holding and teaching the doctrine of absolute predestination of all things, particular election, limited atonement, etc. The Regular Baptists denied these doctrines and held to the faith taught by Regular Baptists throughout the ages. The Regular Baptists, opposing the Predestinarian Baptists, held to the doctrine of a full atonement of Jesus Christ, predestination according to the righteous purpose of God in Christ, but denying that He predestinated the evil acts of either men or angels. They held that sinners are saved or elected by the washing of regeneration and renewing of the Holy Ghost, through repentance toward God and faith in the Lord Jesus Christ; that sinners are chosen, or elected through sanctification of the spirit and obedience to, and belief of, the truth.[8]

The result of this break in the church is that the Baptists have two branches or bodies of different faith in Eastern Kentucky. One of them, called the Primitive, "Iron-Jackets," or "Predestinarian," believe in predestination—that is, those who believe in a partial or limited atonement, and hold that they are saved or lost, as the case may be, before they were born. The other branch, called Regular Baptists, believe in a full atonement or that Christ died that all have an opportunity to be saved when they comply with the terms of the Gospel.

These two branches of the Baptist faith are strongest in the upper Big Sandy and Kentucky River valleys and in southwestern Virginia. Those strongest in Johnson County are the United Baptists and Regular Baptists, both probably being branches of the original General Association of Kentucky Baptists, but at some time after the union of the "Regular United Baptists," it seems the Regular Baptists dropped the word "united" while the United Baptists dropped the word "regular."

In fundamental doctrine the United Baptists do not differ much from the faith of the Regular Baptists, except that they are anti-missionary, opposed to Sunday schools and to educated and paid ministry, and wash the saints' feet. They have no publishing houses nor denominational literature, other than their annual minutes.[9]

The United Baptists organized the Paint Union, Blaine Union, Zion, and a number of other associations, but all of them were either directly, or indirectly in correspondence until the year 1889, when New Salem and Paint Union dissolved, or dropped correspondence with each other over the question of "Secret Orders." Since that time correspondence between the Regular Baptists and the United Baptists has been disrupted and they have not been able to get together to settle these questions.

BURNING SPRINGS ASSOCIATION

The first churches in Eastern Kentucky were organized by Elder Daniel Williams, the pioneer preacher to the mountains, and bade by him to join North District Association, which body then was in full fellowship with General Association of Kentucky Baptists. It was found difficult to attend the denominational meetings in the Bluegrass, so in the year 1814 these churches were granted letters of dismission from the parent association (in the district) to form Burning Springs Association named for Old Burning Springs Church in Magoffin County.[10] This division was not from doctrinal matters but wholly for convenience. Burning Springs Association prospered, and spread over much of Eastern Kentucky, including also what is now Johnson County. However, after a few years, this body became anti-missionary and hyper-Calvinistic in its teachings, and has remained so. They are now called Hardshells, or believers of the "hard" doctrine.

PAINT UNION ASSOCIATION OF UNITED BAPTISTS

Much has been said and written in recent years about this, the strongest Baptist body in the Big Sandy Valley, and many efforts have been made to find its origin. It holds for the most part that it is the lineal descendant of Apostolic Churches. Below is given a brief account of the brotherhood.

In 1837 it was again deemed advisable to form another association on the waters of the Big Sandy. With this end in view a few brethren under the leadership of Elders William Wells, Wallace Bailey, Elijah Prater, and John Borders met in October, 1837, at Old Union Church on Paint Creek a few miles above Paintsville in Johnson County (which then was part of Floyd) and took steps to organize Union Association of United Baptists. This division was, according to the minutes of both associations friendly and for convenience and effective co-operation. However, there is a tradition among the Burning Springs people that a personal quarrel between two of the leading brethren got into the churches and caused the division. In 1840 the brethren of this association became aware of the fact that there was another Union Association of Baptists in the State, and added the word Paint to their name. So we have Paint Union Association of United Baptists.[11] This body now is the strongest in numbers of any denomination in Johnson County, having about five thousand in the membership of its churches.

A list is given here of the names of the societies or churches with the number of memberships, as taken from the minutes covering the proceedings of the association held at the Middle Fork Meeting-House on Little Sandy, in Morgan County, October, 1837.

Church	Messengers' Names	Members
South Fork	Wm. Lykins, Mathew Adams, Richard Ratliff, John Barker	87
Low Gap	Wm. Coffee, Daniel Reed, Moses and Reuben Howard, James McGuire	68
Burning Springs	Elijah Prater, Wallace Bailey, Mason Williams, Lewis Power, B. Caudill	58
Union	S. P. Simer, Alexander Pelphry, William Ramey, James Davis	87
Bethel	Lewis Skaggs, John Lemaster, Francis Lemaster, Henry Jane	25
Big Blaine	Elias Kazee, Jas. Webb, John Boggs, William Holbrook	53
Georges Creek	Jesse Price, Reubin VanHoose, John and Charles Spencer	50
Middle Fork	Isaac Wilbern, James Henson, John Adkins, John Lewis	42
Open Fork Paint	Henry Dickson	6
Zion	Peter Lykins, Caleb Williams, David Lykins	20
Rockcastle	No letter or messenger.	
Silver Creek	Thomas Kirk, Francis Flinty	76
Stillwater	John Rose, W. Murphy, Washington Swango	32
TOTAL MEMBERSHIP		604

The United Baptists are sometimes ridiculed for their seemingly peculiar customs; but as a rule they are a very devout sect, and the present generation owes much to them for their religious activities in the past century. The following are their Articles of Faith:[12]

1. We believe in only one true and living God, the Creator of the heavens and the earth and all things that are therein contained.

2. We believe in Jesus Christ, the eternal Son of God, who is Head and King of His Church.

3. We believe in the Holy Ghost, the Sealer and Applier of the redemption purchased by Christ.

4. We believe in the Father, Son and Holy Ghost, and these three are one.

5. We believe in the Scriptures of the Old and New Testaments to be the infallible word of God, take it for our only rule of faith and practice, and nothing is to be added or taken from it.

6. We believe in the free atonement of Jesus Christ, and that He tasted death for every man and that salvation is offered to all men and women upon the terms of the gospel.

7. We believe that repentance and faith in the Lord Jesus Christ are necessary previous to baptism and that immersion is the only right way of administering the ordinance.

8. We believe that Christ has but one true gospel church and that it will finally persevere through grace to glory.

REVEREND ARTHUR GREEN
Of the United Baptist Church, Paintsville, Ky.

9. We believe in the communion of the Lord's Supper, that is, taking of the bread and wine, by the Church of Jesus Christ in commemoration of the death and suffering of the Son of God until His second coming.

10. We believe that feet washing is an ordinance of Jesus Christ and ought to be observed and kept up by His church until His second coming.

11. We believe in the sum of the moral law as it stands on record in the book of Exodus.

12. We believe that Jesus Christ is the first resurrection from the dead and that He lives forever.

13. We believe in the resurrection of the just and the unjust.

14. We believe in the final punishment of the wicked and the eternal happiness of the righteous.

Of the early United Baptist preachers in the Paint Union Association, the following were the most prominent and useful men to the church in their day:

The Reverend John Borders was one of the most active and able leaders who served long and faithfully in the ministry. Borders Chapel was named in his honor. Reverend James Pelphry of the Fish Trap Church was a very useful and popular preacher. He married more Johnson County people than any man of his time, and gave nearly sixty years service to his church. Reverend Wallace Bailey, a resident of Magoffin County, was noted throughout the eastern part of the State as a great Baptist divine and did much good in bringing men and women into the church and into an acceptance of Christ.

Reverend George W. Price was a man of wonderful power in the pulpit and did much to make his church the power for good it has been, and is, in the county. Through the many years of service that he saw, he became widely known and consequently greatly loved by the people, and his name is worthy of the record he left, which is still in the memory of the older persons of today. Others of prominence, for the period from 1820 to 1885, were: Reverends William Wells, Benjamin P. Porter, James Williamson, Andrew Johnson, and Goodwin Lykins.

Of those more recently, but who have passed on, honorable mention should be made of the Reverends William Honeycutt, Ali Ward, Moveta Keaton, and "Rhode" Murray.

Having finished discussing those of the past, it is essential to name those who are now filling pulpits, and are active leaders in their districts. Too much space could not be given for many now serving in that capacity, and with due respect to those who may not have been included, but among those deserving special honors are Elders J. Powell Ferguson, Dennis Williams, J. J. Prater, J. Thurman Ferguson, A. R. Green, James Henry Howe, Lafe Walters, Sandy Phillips, Haden Conley, Alonzo Wright, and Joe Hall.

It would be offensive to name the ministers, and say nothing of the singing. In consideration of the type of hymns used by the Baptists, which are sometimes termed "old-fashioned" by the present choirs, the Reverend Bazil Daniel, formerly of the Concord Church, is without a doubt the master of all of them.

The steady progression of the United Baptists can be seen from a comparison of its annual report of the eighty-eighth association, held with the Little Paint Church near Oil Springs, September, 1925, with the one of October, 1837.

Name of Church	Post Office of Church	Membership

FIRST DISTRICT:
1. Union — Paintsville, Ky. — 58
2. Jennies Creek — Denver, Ky. — 152
3. Barnetts Creek — Barnetts Creek, Ky. — 107
4. Low Gap — Kenwood, Ky. — 141
5. Rockhouse — Orient, Ky. — 113
6. Concord — Thelma, Ky. — 248
7. Toms Creek — Mingo, Ky. — 222
8. Locust Grove — Stambaugh, Ky. — 204
9. River — River, Ky. — 145
10. Paintsville — Paintsville, Ky. — 106
11. Georges Creek — Lowmansville, Ky. — 141

SECOND DISTRICT:
12. Burning Springs — Salyersville, Ky. — 117
13. Stinson — Lakeville, Ky. — 55
14. Middle Creek — Ivyton, Ky. — 83
15. Abbot — Bonanza, Ky. — 178
16. Lick Springs — Mash Fork, Ky. — 106
17. State Road Fork — Falcon, Ky. — 47
18. Litteral's Fork — Wheelersburg, Ky. — 66
19. Little Paint — Oil Springs, Ky. — 203
20. Beech Grove — Gifford, Ky. — *
21. Gun Creek — Ivyton, Ky. — 100
22. Half Mountain — Swampton, Ky. — 54
23. Long Fork — Riceville, Ky. — 160
24. Puncheon — Gypsie, Ky. — *
25. Carver — Carver, Ky. — 31

THIRD DISTRICT:
26. Hoods Fork — Davisville, Ky. — 387
27. Little Blaine — Norris, Ky. — 89
28. Sugar Grove — Sip, Ky. — 129
29. Bethel — Red Bush, Ky. — 281
30. Fish Trap — Manila, Ky. — 161
31. Cold Springs — Fuget, Ky. — 138
32. Oil Springs — Kenwood, Ky. — 78
33. White Oak — Dingus, Ky. — *
34. Lebanon — Dingus, Ky. — 63
35. Mt. Olive — Wilbur, Ky. — 122
36. Candy Run — Lucasville, O. — 104
37. Mary — Charley, Ky. — 100
38. Big Run — Lucasville, O. — 17

39. Pine Creek	Lyra, O.	28
40. Beaver Valley	Beaver, O.	40
	Total	4,574

*Not represented last report.

ENTERPRISE ASSOCIATION OF REGULAR BAPTISTS

(Sometimes referred to as "Slab" Baptists.)

No religious history of western Johnson County would be complete without a statement about this intensely virile and evangelistic body. Although it was organized with the county, the causes which led to its organization were without the county and the majority of its churches are in Morgan County.

In 1894 division again tore from the Burning Springs Association a goodly number of its churches and divided others (see page 296). Each side has its version of the affair; but when it is all boiled down, it was a misunderstanding between the "Fathers in Israel" and "The Younger Set." The revolting party protested against the hyper-Calvinistic doctrine of election and predestination, while they themselves were accused of overemphasizing the freedom of the will and favoring "Open-Communication." The revolting party met later in 1894 at Red Bush, Johnson County, and organized the Enterprise Association of Regular Baptists. The years that have followed have been prosperous with them. They number about thirty-five hundred members in their churches. The leading brethren in the organization were Elders W. L. Gevedon, Willis Lykins, W. B. Lykins, Haden Hamleton and W. B. Skaggs. Some of the leading preachers now are Elders W. M. Lester, Asa Hay, W. B. Skaggs, Hood Wallin, Dewey Brown, and R. W. Wallin. This association in 1924 was received into the fellowship of the General Association of Kentucky Baptists.

Their beliefs are as follows:[13]

ARTICLES OF FAITH

Article 1. We believe in one true and living God—Father, Son, and Holy Ghost, equal in essence, power, and glory.

Article 2. We believe that Jesus Christ is the Son of God, and that the Scriptures of the Old and New Testaments are the inspired word of God, and our only rule of faith and practice.

Article 3. We believe that by the offense of one, judgment came upon all men unto condemnation, even so by the righteousness of one the free gift came upon all men unto justification of life by which the grace of God became equally accessible to all men.—Romans 5:18.

Article 4. We believe that sinners are justified by the grace of God received through faith in the Lord Jesus Christ.

Article 5. We believe in the resurrection of the dead both of the just and the unjust, and that the happiness of the righteous and the punishment of the wicked will be eternal.

Article 6. We believe that the church of God is composed only of those who have been partakers of the Holy Ghost and tasted the good word of God and the powers of the world to come.

Article 7. We believe that we have an advocate with the Father—Jesus Christ the righteous and that He is a propitiation for our sins, and not for ours only but also for the sins of the whole world.

Article 8. We believe that those only who have received remission of sins are fit subjects of baptism and that immersion in water is the only mode. —Acts 8:38.

Article 9. We believe that the Lord's Supper and the washing of the Saints' feet are ordinances of the Lord and shall be observed by the Church until Christ's second coming.

Article 10. We believe that the Gospel is the power of God unto salvation to every one that believes, and that is commanded to be preached to every creature, that all men are responsible for the manner in which they hear.

Article 11. We believe that there is but one true church, and that every member thereof is an heir to God and joint heir with Christ, and not one member of this church shall ever perish; and if children, then heirs of God and joint heirs with Christ if so be that we suffer with Him, that we may be also glorified together.—Romans 8:17.

STATISTICAL REPORT OF ENTERPRISE ASSOCIATION OF REGULAR BAPTISTS—1926

Name of Church	Date Organized	Admitted Into Association	Membership	Name of Church	Date Organized	Admitted Into Association	Membership
Grassy Lick		1894	230	Paint Valley	1910	1910	46
New Hope		1894	57	Union	1910	1910	67
Bethany	1886	1894	128	Cope		1910	22
Elizabeth		1894	247	Louisa		1910	58
Perseverance	1916	1894	30	Newcomb Valley	1911	1911	40
Red Bush	1894	1894	169	Eureka		1913	55
Flat Gap		1894	56	Little Gap Union	1913	1913	81
Centerville	1895	1895	134	Smoky Valley	1913	1913	58
South Liberty		1895	176	Sun Light	1906	1913	24
Point Pleasant		1895	123	Richmond		1914	17
Chestnut Grove	1893	1896	40	Isonville		1915	20
Wells Union		1897	67	Pennsylvania	1906	1915	60
New Salem		1898	73	Index	1915	1915	58
Pleasant Run		1900	55	Portsmouth		1920	181
Corinth		1901	47	Fire Brick Chapel	1921	1921	74
Mary	1901	1902	133	Williams Chapel	1921	1921	30
Providence		1904	67	Union Chapel	1921	1921	32
Martha	1903	1904	78	Rocky Branch	1923	1923	19
Jones Creek	1905	1905	57	Cora Chapel	1923	1923	62
Unity		1906	47	Mt. Zion		1923	32
Charity		1908	41	Sandy Chapel	1923	1924	14
Hampshire	1907	1908	79	Big Branch	1924	1924	11
Mauk Ridge		1909	64	Antioch	1886	1925	34
Big Gap	1909	1909	70	Lenox		1925	20
West Wood	1909	1909	142	Lacy Creek	1925	1925	50
Wells Creek	1909	1909	40	Major Chapel	1924	1925	43
Greenville		1910	34	Cisco		1926	11
Brushy Fork	1909	1910	119	North Moreland	1926	1926	20

Total............3,842

THE MISSIONARY BAPTIST CHURCH

The history of the Baptist people in regard to missionary effort has been a curious one. When the idea of sending missionaries to foreign lands was first suggested, it split the church. The anti-missionary party said "If God wants the heathen converted he will convert them without our help." Because of their extreme Calvinism they insisted that the efforts of the missionary societies would be "an unjustifiable encroachment upon the divine sovereignty," for God by his eternal decrees had determined from all eternity who should be saved and who should be lost. And the Baptists who held this view were split off and became a separate denomination.[14]

But the missionary spirit grew and "The Missionary Baptists" considering the United States as a whole are probably the largest branch of the Baptist Church today.

MISSIONARY BAPTISTS OF JOHNSON COUNTY[15]

The first Missionary Baptist Church established in Johnson County was Liberty Church, at Denver, in 1869, by Elders William Jayne and T. J. Rigg. William Jayne was a native of Johnson County, educated in the public schools, taking his high school and college course at Georgetown College, the first Baptist college established in Kentucky. Elder Jayne was converted in 1862 and joined Bethel Church of United Baptists; but, while in Georgetown College he heard ministers of the Missionary Baptists preach and teach the Baptist doctrine and church government as they conceived it to be taught in the New Testament. Being thus convinced he took membership in the Baptist Church at Georgetown while he was a student there. When Flat Gap Church was organized he became one of the charter members by letter from the church at Georgetown. He was principal of Enterprise High School at Flat Gap for many years, doing much preaching and teaching, creating the very religious and cultured citizenship in and around Flat Gap. He died at Lake City, Florida, December 22, 1917, at an advanced age.

Elder T. J. Rigg was a native of West Virginia and began preaching when a boy, having been converted when he was only 15 years of age. He came to Johnson County about 1868 or 1869, only a short time before Liberty Church was organized. He was a man of limited education but of strong and pleasing personality, kindly disposed toward every one, even his enemies, and withal a powerful preacher of the Gospel, emphasizing the doctrine of salvation by grace through repentance toward God and faith in Jesus Christ, as the essentials on man's part to becoming an heir of God and joint heir with Jesus Christ.

Many converts were made and new churches established, principally through his labors, notwithstanding other Baptist preachers aided in the work, among whom should be mentioned H. G. Reynolds, Marion Reynolds, J. W. VanHoose, and Henry Daniel.

One series of meetings among the many held by Elder Rigg was a five-weeks revival with Liberty Church at Denver in 1879, during which there were 69 additions. Many of these converts were men and women past middle age who were the most influential citizens of the community. The soundness of the work done in this meeting is attested by the fact that very few of the converts, comparatively speaking, were ever excluded from membership because of immorality. One of the converts coming into Liberty Church during this meeting was L. F. Caudill who was ordained to preach four years after he was converted, being at the time of his ordination to the ministry, 31 years of age. After serving Liberty, Fair View, and East Point churches as pastor for a few years, he moved to Magoffin County, Kentucky, and established three churches, Mash Fork, Licking River, and Lakeville, leading in the building of a house of worship for each church. When the Home Mission Board of the Southern Baptist Convention established Magoffin Institute he raised most of the $2,000.00 required of the people there to secure the school at Salyersville, the county seat of Magoffin County. He is now supply pastor of the First Baptist Church of Salyersville, preaching at his age, 74 years, when health will permit.

Another convert under the preaching of T. J. Rigg was H. H. Rice, who, after his ordination to the ministry served churches in Johnson County as pastor before moving to Boyd County, Kentucky, where he now lives. Reverend Rice has proved himself to be a useful minister of the Gospel in serving many of the churches of Greenup Association as pastor and evangelist. He now lives near Ashland, Kentucky. (See No. 68 of the Rice family.)

Elder Rigg died August, 1926, at Ashland, Kentucky, after a long and useful life, having attained the ripe old age of 76 years, and he was buried in the Ashland cemetery.

Other active workers and members in the church in Johnson County are H. LaViers, R. C. Thomas, Reverend S. D. Grumbles, J. G. Hager, and A. H. Webb, who submitted a part of the information contained in this chapter.

There are at the present time eight Missionary Baptist churches in Johnson County: Liberty, with a membership of 113, pastor, A. E. Meade; Paintsville, with a membership of 156, pastor, A. H. Webb; Thealka, with a membership of 80, pastor, J. C. Hager; Van Lear Junction, membership 43, pastor, J. C. Hager; Flat Gap, membership 12, (no pastor); Offutt, no report in statistics of meeting of Enterprise Association of 1926 from

RICHARD C. THOMAS
General Superintendent of the Northeast Coal Company's Operations in the
Big Sandy Valley, and an Active Church Worker in the
Missionary Baptist Church

which these statistics were taken; Van Lear, membership 45, (no pastor); Spice Cove, (no report); Paintsville, Thealka, Van Lear and Van Lear Junction have Sunday schools with enrollments as follows: Paintsville, 175; Thealka, 77; Van Lear, 154; Van Lear Junction, 96.

The Missionary Baptist churches of Johnson County, for the year 1926, contributed the following amounts for local support and co-operative work: Paintsville, $5,118.71; Van Lear, $1,453.50; Thealka, $489.37; Van Lear Junction, $470.82; Liberty, $75.80; Total $7,608.20.

Their Articles of Faith are as follows:[16]

ARTICLES OF FAITH
I. *The Scripture*

We believe that the Holy Bible was written by men divinely inspired, and is a perfect treasure of heavenly instruction; that it has God for its author, salvation for its end, and truth without any mixture of error for its matter; that it reveals the principles by which God will judge us and therefore, is, and shall remain to the end of the world the true center of Christian union, and supreme standard by which all human conduct, creeds, and opinions shall be tried.

II. *The True God*

We believe the Scriptures teach that there is one, and only one, living and true God, an infinite, intelligent spirit whose name is Jehovah, the Maker and Supreme Ruler of heaven and earth; inexpressibly glorious in holiness and worthy of all possible honor, confidence and love; that in the unity of the Godhead there are three persons, the Father, the Son and the Holy Ghost; equal in every divine perfection and executing distinct but harmonious offices in the great work of redemption.

III. *The Fall of Man*

We believe that the Scriptures teach that man was created in holiness, under the law of his Maker; but by voluntary transgression fell from that holy and happy state; in consequence of which all mankind are now sinners not by constraint but by choice; being by nature utterly void of that holiness required by the law of God, positively inclined to evil and therefore under just condemnation. Jesus, who by the appointment of the Father, freely took upon him our nature, yet without sin; honored the divine law by His personal obedience and by His death made a full atonement for our sins; that having risen from the dead He is every way qualified to be a suitable, a compassionate and all-sufficient Savior.

IV. *Justification*

We believe the Scriptures teach that the great gospel blessing which Christ secures to such as believe in Him, is justification; that justification includes the pardon of sins and the promise of eternal life not on principles of righteousness which we have done, but solely through faith in the Redeemer's blood; by virtue of which faith His perfect righteousness is freely imputed to us of God; that it brings us into a state of most blessed peace and favor with God, and secures every other blessing needful for time and eternity.

V. The Freeness of Salvation

We believe the Scriptures teach that the blessings of salvation are made free to all by the gospel; that it is the immediate duty of all to accept them by a cordial, penitent and obedient faith; and that nothing prevents the salvation of the greatest sinner on earth but his own inherent depravity and voluntary rejection of the gospel which rejection involves him in an aggravated condemnation.

VI. Regeneration

We believe that the Scriptures teach that in order to be saved, sinners must be regenerated or born again; but regeneration consists in giving a holy disposition to the mind; that it is effected in a manner above our comprehension by the power of the Holy Spirit, in connection with divine truth, so as to secure our voluntary obedience to the gospel; and that its proper evidence appears in the holy fruits of repentance and faith and newness of life.

VII. Repentance and Faith

We believe the Scriptures teach that repentance and faith are sacred duties, and also inseparable graces wrought in our souls by the regenerative spirit of God, whereby being deeply convinced of our guilt, danger and helplessness, and of the way of salvation by Christ, few turn to God with unfeigned contrition, conversion and supplication for mercy; at the same time heartily receiving the Lord Jesus Christ as our prophet, priest and king and relying on Him alone as the only and all-sufficient Savior.

VIII. God's Purpose of Grace

We believe the Scriptures teach that election is the eternal purpose of God, according to which He graciously regenerates, sanctifies and saves sinners; that being perfectly consistent with the free agency of man, it comprehends all the means in connection with the end; that it is a most glorious display of God's sovereign goodness, being infinitely free, wise, holy and unchangeable, that it utterly excludes boasting and promotes humility, love, prayer, praise, trust in God and active imitation of His free mercy; that it encourages the use of the means in the highest degree; that it may be ascertained by its effects in all who truly believe the gospel; that it is the foundation of Christian assurance and that to ascertain it with regard to ourselves demands and deserves the utmost diligence.

IX. Sanctification

We believe the Scriptures teach that sanctification is the process by which, according to the will of God, we are made partakers of holiness; that it is carried on in the heart of believers by the presence and power of the Holy Spirit, the Sealer and Comforter, in the continual use of the appointed means—especially the Word of God, self-denial, watchfulness, and prayer, and in the practice of all godly exercises and duties.

X. Preservation

We believe the Scriptures teach that such only are real believers as endure unto the end; that their preserving attachments to Christ is the grand mark which distinguishes them from superficial professors; that a special providence watches over their welfare; and they are kept by the power of God through faith unto salvation.

XI. The Law and the Gospel

We believe the Scriptures teach that the law of God is the eternal and unchangeable rule of His moral government; that it is holy, just and good; and that the inability which the Scriptures ascribe to fallen man to fulfill its precepts arises entirely from his sinful nature; to deliver him from which and to restore him through a mediator to unfeigned obedience to the holy law, is one great end of the gospel, and of the means of grace connected with the establishment of the visible church.

XII. A Gospel Church

We believe that the Scriptures teach that a visible church of Christ is a congregation of baptized believers, associated by covenant in the faith and fellowship of the gospel; observing the ordinances of Christ; governed by the laws; and exercising the gifts, rights, and privileges invested in them by His word; that its only Scriptural officers are bishops or pastors, and deacons, whose qualifications, claims, and duties are defined in the epistles of Timothy and Titus.

XIII. Christian Baptism

We believe the Scriptures teach that Christian baptism is the immersion in water of a believer in Christ, on authority of a New Testament church by an authorized administrator in the name of the Father, and Son, and Holy Ghost; to show forth in a solemn and beautiful emblem, our faith in the crucified, buried and risen Savior, with its effects in our death to sin and resurrection to a new life; that it is prerequisite to the privileges of a church relation and to the Lord's Supper.

XIV. The Lord's Supper

We believe the Scriptures teach that the Lord's Supper is a provision of bread and wine, as symbols of Christ's body and blood, partaken of by members of the church in commemoration of the suffering and death of their Lord, showing their faith and participation in the merits of His sacrifice, and their hope of eternal life through His resurrection from the dead, its observance to be preceded by faithful self-examination.

XV. The Christian Sabbath

We believe that the Scriptures teach that the first day of the week is the Lord's day, or Christian Sabbath, and is to be kept sacred to religious purposes by abstaining from all secular labor, except works of mercy and necessity, by the devout observance of all means of grace, both private and public, and by preparation for that rest that remaineth for the people of God.

XVI. Civil Government

We believe that the Scriptures teach that civil government is of divine appointment for the interest and good order of human society; and that magistrates are to be prayed for, conscientiously honored and obeyed, except only in things opposed to the will of our Lord Jesus Christ, who is the only Lord of the conscience and the Prince of the kings of the earth.

XVII. Righteous and Wicked

We believe that the Scriptures teach that there is a radical and essential difference between the righteous and wicked; that such only as through faith are justified in the name of the Lord Jesus and sanctified by the spirit of our God are truly righteous in His esteem; while all such as continue in impenitence and unbelief are in His sight wicked and under the curse; and this distinction holds among men both in and after death.

XVIII. The World to Come

We believe that the Scriptures teach that the end of the world is approaching, that at the last day Christ will descend from heaven and raise the dead from the grave for final retribution; that a solemn separation will then take place; that the wicked will be adjudged to endless punishment and the righteous to endless joy, and that this judgment will fix forever the final state of men in heaven or hell on principles of righteousness.

CHURCHES OF THE ENTERPRISE ASSOCIATION OF BAPTISTS
1924

Churches	Members	Churches	Members
Allen	40	Mine Fork	
Beaver Valley	10	Mt. Beulah	15
Bloomington		Mouth Card	70
Elk Foot		North Benson Memorial	16
Elkhorn City	29	Offutt	57
Feds Creek	112	Paintsville	120
Flat Gap	13	Peters Creek	
Inez	20	Pikeville	110
Irene Cole Memorial	108	Riceville	25
Ivyton	30	Salyersville	191
Lakeville	65	Spice Cone	
Liberty	114	Thealka	45
Licking River	42	Van Lear	135
Little Paint		Van Lear Junction	32
McVeigh	53		
Mash Fork	80	Total	1,532

FREE-WILL BAPTISTS

The Free-Will Baptists organized a church in Johnson County —the second of the denomination in Kentucky—sometime previous to 1885. Reverend Thomas Williams became their pastor, and several of the most influential people of the vicinity of Paintsville joined the church, among them Daniel Wheeler, Wiley Williams, John Richmond, the VanHooses, and other noted people.[11]

The first church of this faith in Johnson County was organized at the mouth of Rush Fork of Tom's Creek. The organizers had been members of the United Baptist Church at the place now called Mingo. In this United Baptist Church some question of discipline had arisen creating quite a dissension among the leaders. The question itself was perhaps of minor importance, no doctrinal principle being involved, but, as frequently happens, the rivalry between the factions became greater as the discussion progressed and it was soon evident that the church itself must take a position on the question The minority party was fully convinced of the correctness of its

BURNS CONLEY

position, and, rather than sacrifice opinion and possibly some exercise of free-will, it withdrew from the church membership.

This ended the controversy so far as the Mingo Church was concerned, but the church suffered the loss of some of its most valuable members. The party withdrawing intended to organize another Baptist Church of like faith and order and of the same denomination. Efforts along this line were duly made, but it soon found that "organization" was more powerful than at first supposed and that the principle of worshipping "according to the dictates of conscience" was more of an ideal than a reality. This came about when recognition by the association was sought. Under the rules of the Paint Union Association recognition could not be granted until the newly organized church made reconciliation with the Mingo Church. This eliminated all hope of organizing a United Baptist Church. Some of the party became discouraged and returned to the old church but others were determined to stand by their principle of free-will in matters of worship. They communicated with some Free-Will Baptist Church in the state of Ohio, which more than likely was a branch of the regular "Free-Will" Baptist Church that originated in Wales in 1701, and the result was that this denomination was organized within Johnson County.

The rightness or wrongness of the question involved is not considered in these statements. The purpose is merely to outline briefly some of the initial steps that led up to the organization of the first church of this denomination. It might be said, however, that the founders were consecrated to the belief that each individual should be permitted to worship under the guidance of his own conscience. They were among the best citizens of the community. They were sincere in their convictions and the new church was dedicated on the principle of free-will in all matters religious.

Some of the noted preachers in this church were James, Nathan, and Eliphus VanHoose, who were among the organizers of the church above mentioned on Tom's Creek. Both Nathan and Eliphus were influential in pulling away from the United Baptists, but Eliphus was the backbone of this church for many years. Some of the Butlers on Mud Lick were backers of this denomination for a period.

Of the present ministers in this church, mention should be made of H. B. Conley, John Elliot Conley, Millard VanHoose, S. F. Williams, Wise Reed, F. S. VanHoose and Irvin Rice.

A beautiful church building was erected on Third Street in Paintsville by this denomination in 1926. They are becoming very strong in Johnson County.

THE DISCIPLES OF CHRIST
By Hampton Adams, A.B., M.A., B.D.

This communion of people is usually known in Kentucky as the "Christian Church." In some places "Church of Christ" is the designation. But "Disciples of Christ" is the name which many members of the church prefer, and it is the name by which this body is known in interdenominational circles. "Christian Church" is the corporate name of the followers of Barton W. Stone, that group of the disciples of Stone who never united with the Campbellian forces. "Church of Christ" is the name assumed by the "Antis," those who withdrew from the Disciples of Christ because they could not endorse the use of the organ in public worship and the existence of Sunday schools and missionary societies, organizations which they thought were not prescribed in the Bible.

In 1807 Thomas Campbell left his home in Ireland to seek restoration of his health in America. He did not suspect that he would become one of the mightiest spiritual influences in the new country and that from the impetus of his conviction a religious body would issue, destined to be one of the major Christian communions of the world.

Thomas Campbell was a scholar. He was educated in Glasgow University and Divinity Hall. But he was more than a scholar. He was a man of warm and wide spirit. Sectarianism clouded the churches of Scotland in his day. There were many sects who had broken with the Established Church, and they endeavored to prove their religious fervor by the bitterness of their opposition to the Established Church. If there happened at any time to be a lull in their hostilities with the great object of their scorn they turned upon one another. The soul of Thomas Campbell was not blighted by the dimness characteristic of his time. Divisions in the Church were a source of sadness to him. Undoubtedly he expected something different from the narrowness and bigotry of Scottish churches when he set sail for America. But he was to be disappointed.

Upon his arrival in America, Thomas Campbell identified himself with the Chartiers Presbytery which included Washington County, Pennsylvania, and some adjacent territory. He began immediately to serve the Seceder Church through this Presbytery.

He was sent into Western Pennsylvania to preach and to administer the Lord's Supper. While on this tour he found Presbyterians who had not affiliated with the Seceder Church who desired the privilege of the Lord's Table. With his fine catholic spirit he invited them to commune. However, this invitation gave offense to the Seceders and he was reported to the Presbytery.

The Presbytery censured Thomas Campbell. He appealed to the Synod of North America. The Synod criticized the manner in which the Presbytery had dealt with the case but the censure was allowed to stand. Thomas Campbell decided to abide by the decision of the Synod, but antagonism to him did not abate so that within a short time he renounced the Synod and withdrew from the Seceders Church.

In 1809 he organized "The Christian Association of Washington." This was not a church; at least it was not intended to be. It was a voluntary association of people who were ready to follow the slogan of Thomas Campbell, "Where the Scriptures speak, we speak; and where the Scriptures are silent, we are silent."

About this time Mr. Campbell wrote "A Declaration and Address" in which he gave reasons for the newly formed association. In this document he affirmed that theology should not be made a basis of fellowship among followers of Christ. He pleaded for the union of God's people upon a New Testament basis. He urged that nothing be put into the worship of the church which is not found in the New Testament.

It was not the will of Mr. Campbell that another denomination be created, and he insisted that the brethren of The Christian Association of Washington petition the Synod of Pittsburgh for "Christian and Ministerial Communion." The petition was refused.

When Thomas Campbell was reading the proof sheets on his "A Declaration and Address," his son Alexander Campbell arrived in America. The father and son were very happy to find that their theological thinking in the months of their separation had taken the same direction and that they were then agreed on the fundamental principles of their faith.

The Synod of Pittsburgh refused the petition of The Christian Association of Washington in 1810. The Brush Run Church was organized in 1811. On June 12, 1812, Alexander Campbell was rebaptized by immersion. His father and the majority of the members of the Brush Run Church followed his example.

In 1813 the Brush Run Church affiliated with the Baptist communion by being admitted into the Redstone Association. It was understood that the Brush Run Church would not be required to submit to the Philadelphia Confession but would "be allowed to teach and preach whatever they learned from the Holy Scriptures."

However, the union with the Baptist Church did not prove congenial either to the Baptist or to the followers of the Campbells. Alexander Campbell precipitated bitter opposition within the Baptist Church in 1816 when he preached his famous sermon on the Law, affirming that the Old Testament was primarily for the Jews while the New Testament is authority for followers of Christ. By 1823, opposition to the Campbells and their followers became very bitter and plans were made to expel them from the Redstone

Association. In 1826, ten churches of the Redstone Association excommunicated fourteen churches of the same association for being in sympathy with the reformation ideals of the Campbells. In 1832, Alexander Campbell was refused admittance into Baptist pulpits in New York, Philadelphia and elsewhere. In the autumn of 1832 the Dover Association of Virginia excommunicated six preachers. This event marks the final separation between the Baptists and the Reformers.

Barton W. Stone was the leader of another group of people who had about the same conception of Christian faith and practice as Thomas Campbell, Alexander Campbell, and those who had associated themselves with them. Stone and several other Presbyterian ministers of the Lexington (Ky.) Presbytery withdrew and organized the Springfield Presbytery. In 1804, after about three years' existence, the Springfield Presbytery was dissolved by Stone's writing its "Last Will and Testament." Then Stone and his followers definitely avowed their intention of wearing no name but "Christian" and of having no creed but the Bible.

It was in the early days of January, 1832, that the two groups led respectively by the Campbells and Stone, met in Lexington and consummated a union. However, the followers of Stone outside Kentucky did not come into the union.

This movement, begun in protest of sectarian spirit and with the purpose of making the Bible the sole guide to faith in Jesus Christ, has grown until the Year Book for 1926 shows for the Disciples of Christ a total membership of about a million and a half.

The limits of so brief a paper have made it impossible to deal adequately with this great brotherhood. From small beginnings it has grown to be one of the great religious bodies of America. It has its internal problems today just as every other great communion has. Therefore a group of doctrines could not be stated as being the accepted beliefs of all the communicants. However, it can be said that with exceptions granted only to a minority, the Disciples of Christ have remained true to the spirit that was evidenced in the Campbells in their passion for the unity of the people of God. This spirit has been propagated by means of the great evangelistic zeal which has characterized the Disciples in every decade of their history.

This association, which is commonly referred to locally as the "Campbellite Church," is strongest within the county in the East Point and Buffalo sections of Johnson County. It is noted especially for the choirs in its churches, and it justly boasts of this feature, for better instructed and more beautiful singing cannot be had anywhere.

DR. JOHN P. WELLS

It is said by some that Samuel Hannah founded the first "Campbellite Church" in Johnson County. The proof of this statement is lacking, however, and the County Court Orders of Floyd County show that Samuel Hannah, a *Baptist* minister, was allowed to solemnize the rights of matrimony on August 19, 1829.

The leaders now active in this Church in the county are the Reverends J. L. Harrington, James "Jemes" Hall, and J. A. Parker.

INTERNATIONAL BIBLE STUDENTS ASSOCIATION

The I. B. S. A., as it is familiarly called, began its development in 1875, although it was not until some years later that it was duly incorporated. The late Pastor Charles T. Russell, whose Sunday sermons were being published in over two thousand newspapers at the time of his death in 1916, was perhaps the most prominent individual in the organization and development of the International Bible Students Association and was repeatedly chosen as its president.

This organization is made up of deeply devoted Christian men and women from every denomination and from every race and nation and today maintains branches in practically every country on earth. It is said that its growth has been more rapid and phenomenal than that of any similar organization in the history of Christianity. Immense printing and publishing establishments are owned and operated in Brooklyn, N. Y.; Madgeburg, Germany, and Berne, Switzerland, with smaller plants scattered throughout America and Europe. So great has been the demand for International Bible Students Association literature that the Brooklyn plant alone printed and distributed 6,499,453 books during 1927 besides furnishing to subscribers a total of 1,576,300 copies of the Watch Tower and 1,864,900 copies of the Golden Age to American subscribers, together with 6,499,453 free handbills and tracts distributed to the public.

The organization is unique in that it pays no salaries; has no membership roll; solicits no moneys and makes no assessments, but is maintained wholly by voluntary contributions of time and money. Its sole object is to familiarize the peoples of the earth with the teachings of the Bible and the fulfillment of prophecy, and it therefore stands free from all creeds and sects of men, adhering strictly to the Bible as God's revealed Word of Truth.

Dr. Jno. P. Wells has been prominently identified with the International Bible Students Association for more than fifteen years, working in Johnson County, and has traveled extensively in public lecture work for this organization.

Following is a brief epitome of the things this organization believes and teaches:

TO US THE SCRIPTURES CLEARLY TEACH

THAT JEHOVAH is the only true God, the Maker of heaven and earth, and is from everlasting to everlasting; that the Logos was the beginning of his creation; that the Logos became a man; that he is now the Lord Jesus Christ in glory, clothed with all power in heaven and earth.

THAT GOD created the earth for man, created perfect man for the earth and placed him upon it; that man wilfully disobeyed God's law and was sentenced to death; that by reason of Adam's wrongful act all men are born sinners and without the right to life.

THAT JESUS was made a human being in order that he might become the Redeemer of man; that he gave his life a sacrifice for man and thereby produced the ransom price; that Jesus the divine arose from the dead, ascended into heaven, and presented the value of his human sacrifice as the redemptive price for man.

THAT for many centuries God, through Christ, has been selecting from amongst men the members of his church, which constitutes the body of Christ; that the mission of the church is to follow in the footsteps of her Lord Christ Jesus, grow in his likeness, give testimony to the name and plan of Jehovah God, and ultimately be glorified with Christ Jesus in his heavenly Kingdom; that Christ, Head and Body, constitute the "seed of Abraham" through which all the families of the earth shall be blessed.

THAT THE WORLD HAS ENDED; that the Lord Jesus has returned and is now present; that Jehovah has placed Christ Jesus upon his throne and now commands all nations and peoples to hear and obey him.

THAT THE HOPE of the peoples of earth is restoration to human perfection during the reign of Christ; that the reign of Christ will afford opportunity to every man to have a fair trial for life and those who obey will live on earth forever in a state of happiness.

THE METHODIST EPISCOPAL CHURCH

The term "Methodist" was at first a nickname. It was applied derisively to a group of Oxford students, John and Charles Wesley among the number, because in their determination to deepen their Christian life they lived methodically. They read the Scriptures and prayed and took communion; they visited the sick, the poor, the imprisoned, and performed other acts of Christian service, according to a settled rule and program. They were so exact and conscientious in it that their fellow students called them "Methodists" as distinguished from men who lived by mood and impulse. They accepted the title, and it has come to be the honorable designation of this great branch of the church.

The word "Episcopal" is added, because it is governed by bishops, like the Episcopal Church.

The beginning of this church dates back to the time of the Revolution in America and the French Revolution, and is a result of the indefatigable labors of John Wesley, who was one of the greatest religious leaders of modern history. John Wesley was a man of culture and scholarship as well as a flaming evangelist. He was a graduate of Oxford and a fellow of Lincoln College.

In his evangelistic tours he traveled over two hundred and fifty thousand miles, and preached over forty thousand sermons.[18] Wesley and his followers succeeded in spreading the Methodist spirit internationally. It expanded to America, and by 1800 had spread into the interior. The records of Mason County, Kentucky, refer to Henry Burchett (June, 1789), Richard Bird (August, 1794), and Joseph Moore (October, 1796), as being Methodist preachers, who no doubt aided in spreading this doctrine west of the Cumberlands.

Methodism was first introduced into the Big Sandy Valley by a company of Methodist people who moved from Tazewell County, Virginia, about the year 1795. In this company was Cornelius McGuire, a local preacher, who organized the first Methodist class, in the house of Henry Stratton, in Floyd County, in 1796. This point was about ten miles above Prestonsburg. Mr. McGuire, assisted by godly laymen, conducted services in several communities by the year 1809.

In 1809 Cornelius McGuire carried a petition to the Western Annual Conference, which met in Cincinnati, Ohio, September 30th, Bishop Asbury presiding, largely signed, praying the conference to send a preacher to the Big Sandy Valley. On the strength of this petition the Sandy River Circuit was formed, being a part of the Kentucky District, and Benjamin Edge was appointed preacher in charge, and James Ward presiding elder.

This year, Mr. Edge traveled up and down the valley preaching and holding services wherever he could find people to preach to, and organized several churches. Almost the entire valley was then a wilderness, very sparsely settled, with only paths in which to travel. These paths, many of them, were so difficult to follow without a guide, that Mr. Edge procured from a blacksmith an iron rod with a sharp point, with which he marked the trees where the paths parted, that he might, when alone, not get lost.

The old circuit rider who went from place to place, preaching in schoolhouses, in the homes of the people, in tents or out of doors, wherever a congregation could be gathered, often had little theological training or literary equipment. He carried a Bible, a hymn book, a copy of Methodist discipline, and perhaps a volume of Wesley's sermons in his saddle bags, placing his main reliance upon the sincerity and fervor of his own heart as he called upon men to forsake their evil ways and follow Christ. It was a time when books were not common as they are now, when newspapers and magazines were not in general circulation, and these unschooled men found ready acceptance for their message. They rendered a noble service in laying the foundations of the Kingdom of God out in thousands of neglected communities on the frontiers.[19]

This year (1809) the Kentucky District showed a net increase of seven hundred and forty-five white, and one hundred and twenty-eight colored members. This circuit, according to official record, "extended from the headwaters of the Kentucky River to the mouths of the two Sandys, a distance of five hundred miles, with two additional appointments in the state of Ohio, in what was called the French Grant."

At the conference in 1810, held at the Brick Chapel in Shelby County, Kentucky, with Bishops Asbury and McKendree both present, John Johnson was appointed to the Sandy River Circuit, with John Sale as presiding elder of the district. During this year, numerous preaching places were established, and the work prospered to a remarkable degree. The increase was eleven hundred and twenty-five, of which one hundred and eighteen were colored.

The session of the conference for 1811 was held in Cincinnati, Ohio, commencing October 1st, with both Bishops Asbury and McKendree present. At this session Marcus Lindsey was appointed to the Sandy River Circuit, and John Sale continued on the Kentucky District. Mr. Lindsey was one of the most distinguished preachers of his day. At the close of this year Mr. Lindsey reported four hundred and sixty-five white and twenty-five colored members on the Sandy River Circuit. It was a year of remarkable prosperity.

PAINTSVILLE CHURCH ORGANIZED

It was some time during the summer of this year (1812) that the Paintsville Society was organized by Mr. Lindsey, the preaching place being the home of John Auxier, which afterwards was bought by, and became the home of Moses Preston, familiarly called "Cobe" Preston. This house was situated in the bottom in the east end of Paintsville, and will be remembered by all the old people now residing in Paintsville. This house continued to be the preaching place as long as Mr. Auxier lived there, and for several years after it became the home of Mr. Preston. In this organization were some of the most prominent people of the community.

In 1812 the name of the conference was changed from "Western" to "Ohio" and the session met in Chillicothe, Ohio, beginning October 1, Bishops Asbury and McKendree both being present. John Sale was returned as presiding elder of the Kentucky District, and the Sandy River Circuit was divided, the eastern portion being called Big Sandy Circuit, and the western portion Little Sandy Circuit. Jonathan Stamper was appointed to the Big Sandy Circuit, but having enlisted as a soldier against the Indians did not reach the work until the month of December. Jonathan Stamper was one of the great men of his day, a preacher of commanding ability, and the impress of his powerful sermons and debates on Calvinism still abide in the church.

In the years following, some of the most distinguished men in the church preached to the Paintsville Society, among the number H. H. Kavanaugh, William Landrum, William Bickers, Samuel Kelley, Marus L. King, Jeremiah Farmer, Samuel Black, Joseph H. Wright, Edward Vertegans, George B. Poage, C. M. Sullivan, Stanton Field, and many others of like distinction.

Among citizens of that section who were influential and zealous in organizing and maintaining the church, mention should be made of Lewis Mayo, who was a power for good, and perhaps the most influential laymen in the Big Sandy Valley. He conducted prayers and class meetings, and was a ready and willing worker and contributor at all times and in all places.

Reverend Alexis Howes, a local preacher, from whom the Howes family descended, was a man of great influence, preaching, exhorting, and holding prayer meetings, and using his means for the promotion and growth of the church. His son, Reverend John Howes, also a local preacher, followed in the footsteps of his venerable father, and was a man of large influence and great usefulness to the church.

Reverend Chas. J. Howes, whose father and grandfather were both preachers as above mentioned, was an able preacher, standing among the leaders of the Kentucky Conference, Methodist Episcopal Church. Mr. Howes not only represented his church in a General Conference but was made one of the secretaries of that body.

Mr. Howes' younger brother, Reverend G. Winn Howes, although prepared for and having practiced law for a few years, was an able expounder of the word in the Methodist Episcopal Church. The Howes family furnished a larger number of Methodist preachers than any other family in the Big Sandy Valley. Moses Preston, in whose house preaching was held for many years, and his good wife were ardent friends of the church, and in their home the itinerant preacher always found a warm, hearty welcome. Daniel Hager and his wife also gave a warm welcome to their home for the itinerant preacher, and their influence and means did much to strengthen and build up the church. Lewis Todd and his wife were two of the most zealous, ardent, and liberal supporters of the church, their activity and liberality knowing no bounds. Squire Todd was a man of high character, of a liberal spirit, and his good wife was never happier than when entertaining Methodist brethren and sisters. There were also the families of Samuel Friend, D. B. Wells, and John Vaughan, all of whom were loyal to the cause, and could always be depended upon to actively support the institutions of the church.

There were, in fact, so many of this type, including John Auxier, in whose house the church was organized, that it would require too much space to mention them all here.

SEPARATION

At the General Conference of the year 1844, held in New York, the agitation on the subject of slavery and abolition in a portion of the church reached a climax, and the delegates of the conference in the slave-holding states offered the "Declaration of the Southern Delegates" which resulted in a mutual and friendly division of the church. The Plan of Separation, as it was called, was adopted June 8, 1844. It provided that all the churches in the South should remain under the unmolested pastoral care of the Southern Church, and that the ministers of the Methodist Episcopal Church (North) should in no wise attempt to organize churches or societies within the limits of the Church, South, and vice versa, conferences adhering, by a vote of a majority, to the Methodist Episcopal Church; provided, also, that this rule should apply only to societies and conferences bordering on the line of division, and not to interior charges. It also specified that ministers might without blame attach themselves to either church.[20]

Both branches of the church retained the twenty-five articles of faith which John Wesley abridged from the thirty-nine articles of religion of the English Church. They have never been changed, and are as follows:[21]

I. Of Faith in the Holy Trinity

There is but one living and true God, everlasting, without body or parts; of infinite power, wisdom, and goodness; the Maker and Preserver of all things, both visible and invisible. And in unity of this Godhead, there are three persons of one substance, power, and eternity; the Father, the Son, and the Holy Ghost.

II. Of the Word, or Son of God, Who Was Made Very Man

The Son, who is the word of the Father, the very and eternal God, of one substance with the Father, took man's nature in the womb of the blessed Virgin; so that two whole and perfect natures, that is to say, the Godhead and manhood, were joined together in one person, never to be divided, whereof is one Christ, very God and very man, who truly suffered, was crucified, dead, and buried, to reconcile his Father to us, and to be a sacrifice, not only for original guilt, but also for actual sins of men.

III. Of the Resurrection of Christ

Christ did truly rise again from the dead, and took again his body, with all things appertaining to the perfection of man's nature, wherewith he ascended into heaven, and there sitteth until he returneth to judge all men at the last day.

IV. Of the Holy Ghost

The Holy Ghost, proceeding from the Father and the Son, is of one substance, majesty, and glory, with the Father and the Son, very and eternal God.

V. *Of the Sufficiency of the Holy Scriptures for Salvation*

Holy Scripture containeth all things necessary to salvation; so that whatsoever is not read therein, nor may be proved thereby, is not to be required of any man, that it should be believed, as an article of the faith, or be thought requisite or necessary to salvation. In the name of the Holy Scripture, we do understand those canonical books of the Old and New Testament, of whose authority was never any doubt in the church.

Of the names of the Canonical Books: Genesis, Exodus, Leviticus, Numbers, Deuteronomy, Joshua, Judges, Ruth, The First Book of Samuel, The Second Book of Samuel, The First Book of Kings, The Second Book of Kings, The First Book of Chronicles, The Second Book of Chronicles, The Book of Ezra, The Book of Nehemiah, The Book of Esther, The Book of Job, The Psalms, The Proverbs, Ecclesiastes, or the Preacher, Cantica, or Songs of Solomon, Four Prophets the Greater, Twelve Prophets the Less.

All the books of the New Testament, as they are commonly received, we do receive and account canonical.

VI. *Of the Old Testament*

The Old Testament is not contrary to the New; for both in the Old and New Testament everlasting life is offered to mankind by Christ, who is the only Mediator between God and man, being both God and man. Wherefore they are not to be heard, who feign that the old fathers did look only for transitory promises. Although the Law given from God by Moses, as touching ceremonies and rites doth not bind Christians, nor ought the civil precepts thereof of necessity to be received in any commonwealth; yet, notwithstanding, no Christian whatsoever is free from the obedience of the Commandments which are called moral.

VII. *Of Original or Birth Sin*

Original sin standeth not in the following of Adam (as the Pelagians do vainly talk), but it is the corruption of the nature of every man, that naturally is engendered of the offspring of Adam, whereby man is very far gone from original righteousness, and of his own nature inclined to evil, and that continually.

VIII. *Of Free Will*

The condition of man after the fall of Adam is such, that he cannot turn and prepare himself by his own natural strength and works to faith, and calling upon God; wherefore we have no power to do good works, pleasant and acceptable to God, without the grace of God, by Christ preventing us, that we may have a good will, in working with us, when we have that good will.

IX. *Of the Justification of Man*

We are accounted righteous before God, only for the merit of our Lord and Savior Jesus Christ, by faith, and not for our own works or deserving; wherefore, that we are justified by faith only, is a most wholesome doctrine, and very full of comfort.

X. *Of Good Works*

Although good works, which are the fruits of faith, and follow after justification, cannot put away our sins, and endure the severity of God's judgment; yet, are they pleasing and acceptable to God in Christ, and spring out of a true and lively faith, insomuch that by them a lively faith may be as evidently known, as a tree discerned by its fruit.

XI. *Of Works of Supererogation*

Voluntary works, besides, over and above God's commandments, which they call works of supererogation, cannot be taught without arrogancy and impiety. For by them men do declare, that they do not only render unto God as much as they are bound to do, but that they do more for his sake than of bounden duty is required; whereas, Christ saith plainly, when ye have done all that is commanded you, say, we are unprofitable servants.

XII. *Of Sin after Justification*

Not every sin, willingly committed after justification, is the sin against the Holy Ghost, and unpardonable. Wherefore the grant of repentance is not to be denied to such as fall into sin after justification; after we have received the Holy Ghost, we may depart from grace given, and fall into sin, and by the grace of God rise again, and amend our lives. And therefore they are to be condemned who say they can no more sin as long as they live here, or deny the place of forgiveness to such as truly repent.

XIII. *Of the Church*

The visible Church of Christ is a congregation of faithful men, in which the pure word of God is preached, and the sacraments duly administered according to Christ's ordinance, in all those things that of necessity are requisite to the same.

XIV. *Of Purgatory*

The Romish doctrine concerning purgatory, pardons, worshipping, and adoration, as well of images as of relics, and also invocation of saints, is a fond thing vainly invented, and grounded upon no warrant of Scripture, but repugnant to the word of God.

XV. *Of Speaking in the Congregation in Such a Tongue as the People Understand*

It is a thing plainly repugnant to the word of God, and the custom of the Primitive Church, to have public prayer in the church, or to minister the sacraments in a tongue not understood by the people.

XVI. *Of the Sacraments*

Sacraments ordained of Christ, are not only badges or tokens of Christian men's profession; but rather they are certain signs of grace, and God's good will towards us, by the which he doth work invisibly in us, and doth not only quicken, but also strengthen and confirm our faith in him.

There are two sacraments ordained of Christ our Lord in the Gospel; that is to say, Baptism and the Supper of the Lord.

Those five commonly called sacraments; that is to say, Confirmation, Penance, Orders, Matrimony, and Extreme Unction, are not to be counted for Sacraments of the Gospel, being such as have partly grown out of the corrupt following of the apostles, and partly are states of life allowed in the Scriptures, but yet have not the like nature of Baptism and the Lord's Supper, because they have not any visible sign or ceremony ordained of God.

The sacraments were not ordained of Christ to be gazed upon, or to be carried about; but that we should duly use them. And in such only as worthily received the same, they have a wholesome effect or operation; but they that receive them unworthily, purchase to themselves condemnation, as St. Paul saith.

XVII. Of Baptism

Baptism is not only a sign of profession, and mark of difference, whereby Christians are distinguished from others that are not baptized; but it is also a sign of regeneration, or the new birth. The baptism of young children is to be retained in the church.

XVIII. Of the Lord's Supper

The Supper of the Lord is not only a sign of the love that Christians ought to have among themselves one to another, but rather is a sacrament of our redemption by Christ's death: Insomuch, that to such as rightly, worthily, and with faith receive the same, the bread which we break is a partaking of the body of Christ; and likewise the cup of blessing is a partaking of the blood of Christ.

Transubstantiation, or the change of the substance of bread and wine in the Supper of the Lord, cannot be proved by Holy Writ; but is repugnant to the plain words of Scripture, overthroweth the nature of a sacrament, and hath given occasion to many superstitions.

The body of Christ is given, taken, and eaten in the Supper, only after an heavenly and spiritual manner. And the means whereby the body of Christ is received and eaten in the Supper, is faith.

The sacrament of the Lord's Supper was not by Christ's ordinance reserved, carried about, lifted up, or worshipped.

XIX. Of Both Kinds

The cup of the Lord is not to be denied to the lay-people; for both the parts of the Lord's Supper, by Christ's ordinance and commandment, ought to be administered to all Christians alike.

XX. Of the One Oblation of Christ, Finished Upon the Cross

The offering of Christ once made, is that perfect redemption, propitiation, and satisfaction for all the sins of the whole world, both original and actual; and there is none other satisfaction for sin but that alone.

Wherefore, the sacrifice of masses, in the which it is commonly said that the priest doth offer Christ for the quick and the dead, to have remission of pain or guilt, is a blasphemous fable, and dangerous deceit.

XXI. Of the Marriage of Ministers

The ministers of Christ are not commanded by God's law either to vow the estate of single life or to abstain from marriage; therefore it is lawful for them, as for all other Christians, to marry at their own discretion, as they shall judge the same to serve best to godliness.

XXII. *Of the Rites and Ceremonies of Churches*

It is not necessary that rites and ceremonies should in all places be the same, or exactly alike; for they have been always different, and may be changed according to the diversity of countries, times, and men's manners, so that nothing be ordained against God's word. Whosoever, through his private judgment, willingly and purposely, doth openly break the rites and ceremonies of the church to which he belongs, which are not repugnant to the word of God, and are ordained and approved by common authority, ought to be rebuked openly, that others may fear to do the like, as one that offendeth against the common order of the church, and woundeth the consciences of weak brethren.

Every particular church may ordain, change, or abolish rites, and ceremonies, so that all things may be done to edification.

XXIII. *Of the Rulers of the United States of America*

The president, the congress, the general assemblies, the governors, and the councils of state, as the delegates of the people, are the rulers of the United States of America, according to the division of power made to them by the Constitution of the United States, and by the constitutions of their respective states. And the said states are a sovereign and independent nation, and ought not to be subject to any foreign jurisdiction.

XXIV. *Of Christian Men's Goods*

The riches and goods of Christians are not common as touching the right, title, and possession of the same, as some do falsely boast. Notwithstanding, every man ought, of such things as he possesseth, liberally to give alms to the poor, according to his ability.

XXV. *Of a Christian Man's Oath*

As we confess that vain and rash swearing is forbidden Christian men by our Lord Jesus Christ and James his apostle; so we judge that the Christian religion doth not prohibit, but that a man may swear when the magistrate requireth, in a cause of faith and charity, so it be done according to the prophet's teaching, in justice, judgment, and truth.

After the General Conference of 1844, the Paintsville Circuit fell in the bounds of the Methodist Episcopal Church, South, and as such the Paintsville Society has had an unbroken continuity. In 1860 the congregation began the erection of a church house in Paintsville, but before its final completion, lacking only the seats and pulpit, and for which the lumber was in the house, the war came on, and before its close, the torch of an incendiary reduced it to ashes. Prior to this time, and for some years afterwards, the congregation worshipped in private houses, in the schoolhouse, and after the erection of the court house, in that building.

M. E. CHURCH (NORTH) IN PAINTSVILLE

During the Civil War, about 1864, a minister of the Methodist Episcopal Church began to preach in Paintsville, and sometime afterward organized a society there, in violation of the Plans of Separation, which organization included some members who had

H. G. SOWARDS

formerly belonged to the M. E. Church, South, thus weakening that society for the time being, and this new organization soon became prosperous, and so continues to-day.

But the Church, South, continued; godly men were sent to preach the word and minister to the people; a neat brick church house was erected, the progress of the church was steady, and many souls were born into the Kingdom at her altars. During the latter part of the nineteenth century, such preachers as Samuel W. Mullen, Richard Claughton, J. H. Hager, R. C. Wiseman, Thos. S. Brown (1847), Hiram Moore, Ernest Robinson, and many others broke to them the Word of Eternal Life. Among the efficient laymen were Frank Preston, John W. Castle, B. F. Hager, John P. Wells, John D. Preston, T. J. Mayo, and a host of others.[12]

Of those who have served the Paintsville Church recently in the Western Virginia Conference, Dr. H. G. Sowards is among the outstanding ministers. He came to Paintsville about 1915 as pastor of the Mayo Memorial Church, and after serving a number of years, he was chosen as President of John C. C. Mayo College, and his management of that institution of learning has been very successful. Although kept very busy in this capacity, he has found time to give to both college and church.

Having devoted three or four years to organizing the college, in which the work was such that he could not serve as pastor, he in 1926 again accepted the pastorate of the same church at the request of church members, continuing as president of the college. The popularity of only a very few preachers increases with time in any certain locality, but Dr. Sowards is one of the exceptions to this rule. Not only the people of Paintsville and Johnson County but the people of the entire Big Sandy Valley are numbered among his friends, and, using the statement of a friend, "He improves with age; the longer he stays in Paintsville the better they like him."

The Methodist Church is noted for its splendid Christian zeal, what it has contributed toward the formation of Christian character, and for its almost perfect organization.

REFERENCES TO CHAPTER X

[1] Ely, William, The Big Sandy Valley, Page 432, 1887.

[2] Brown, Charles R., The Larger Faith, Page 19. The Jordon and More Press, Boston, 1923.

[3] Ibid. Page 20.

[4] Armitage, Thos. D., History of Baptists.

[5] The Louisville Times.

[6] Spencer, J. H., History of Kentucky Baptists, Pages 118-119, Vol. II.

[7] Hall, Rev. Joe, Whitesburg, Ky.

[8] Ibid.

[9] Webb, Rev. A. H., Paintsville, Ky.

[10] Spencer, J. H., History of Kentucky Baptists, Pages 509-511, Vol. II.

[11] Ibid.

[12] Minutes of the Eighty-eighth Annual Meeting, Paint Union Association of United Baptists.

[13] Minutes of the Thirty-third Annual Session of the Enterprise Association of Regular Baptists.

[14] Brown, Charles R., The Larger Faith, Pages 23-24. The Jordan and More Press, Boston, 1923.

[15] Written by L. F. Caudill, Salyersville, Kentucky.

[16] Forty-seventh Annual Session of Enterprise Association of Baptists.

[17] Ely, William, The Big Sandy Valley, Page 430, 1887. Central Methodist, Catlettsburg, Ky.

[18] Brown, Charles R., The Larger Faith, Page 107. The Jordon and More Press, Boston, 1923.

[19] Ibid. Page 109.

[20] McTyeire, Holland N., D.D., History of Methodism, Page 638, 1884.

[21] Rowe, Gilbert T., The Doctrines and Discipline of the Methodist Episcopal Church, South, Pages 17-28, 1926.

[22] Meek, Zephaniah, Centennial Souvenir, M. E. Church, South, 1909. Also Redford's History of Methodism in Kentucky.

AN ADDITIONAL GROUP OF PAINTSVILLE BUSINESS MEN
B. F. ROBERTS   PAUL C. HAGER   HARRISON WHEELER
W. L. PRESTON   FRANK J. CONLEY   S. A. WEBB
RALPH STAFFORD   DR. H. G. HAZELRIGG

CHAPTER XI
INDUSTRIAL DEVELOPMENT

Nature has bequeathed to mankind legacies of inestimable value, but in all her generous donations it can be truthfully stated that no section of the country—North, East, South or West—abounds in natural wealth more than does the Big Sandy Valley. Resources that stand out conspicuously are the wonderful topography of the country; the rich, indigenous soil; coal beds, oil wells and gas; timber; fire clay; building stone; road materials; glass sand; sufficient rainfall throughout the year; the mean temperature; and the ideals of the native population.

Johnson County is in the center of the Big Sandy Valley, and enjoys all the benefits of its bordering counties. It is rich in the above-mentioned resources, and their development is yet in its infancy. Marked progress is already being made, and as time passes, men of means seeking location for profitable investment, will find this "land of wealth" attractive.

The hills that form such a large and conspicuous part of the country are vast storehouses for Nature's gifts to man. To the transient traveler passing by train along the placid waters of the river, whose course in the main follows the formation of the ranges, it seems almost incredible what is hidden beneath the rocks and that behind and beyond these steep ramparts of rock which limit the vision, there lies a fair and more or less level and rolling country; but the visitor who penetrates beyond these barriers finds that such is the case, and that spread before him is a land of such surpassing beauty and varied charm interspersed here and there with round knolls, gently sloping hills and unrivaled beauty, that his visit can be but one of continued delight.

From its native wilds to a country abounding in everything that man needs to satisfy his fondest desires, materially speaking, is the beginning of the development of Johnson County's industries.

COAL

Coal was first discovered and used in the Big Sandy Valley by Dr. Thomas Walker on April 13, 1750, during the course of his explorations.[1] (See page 44.)

As far back as 1845 companies were formed, and came to the Big Sandy Valley to mine the coal found in such abundance as to attract the attention of capitalists, but for the lack of transportation and market, and after several years of struggling, abandoned the undertakings. For a period of fifty years, only local mines along the river were worked to supply domestic needs and furnish steamers with the fuel to run them. Among this class of operators was Daniel Wheeler who had an opening near Concord. None of these enterprises ever brought a fortune to the owners or prosperity to the valley, though a few furnished a living for the men working them.[2]

The first operation of any magnitude in the valley was at Peach Orchard (now Richardson), begun about 1847 by a bunch of Cincinnati capitalists. All shipments were made down the river by boat. Fair headway was made for fourteen years, when all work had to be abandoned because of the Civil War. Nothing was done toward re-opening the mines there after the close of the War for many years. The Company's mill and general store were continued, grinding grain and furnishing supplies for the farmers, with the idea of renewing the coal business as soon as there was a market and a means of transportation.

Through the untiring efforts of George S. Richardson and others, the Chatterawha Railroad was completed in 1882 from Ashland to Richardson. Mining of the Peach Orchard coal was resumed, and for many years was the only mine operated on what was an extensive scale at that time.

In 1887 and 1888, the Chatterawha Railroad was extended to White House to reach the cannel coal mines at that place. This was the first large operation within the county, those mentioned above being in Lawrence. Several mines within the vicinity of White House were soon started at River, Offutt, and Williamsport. These operations produced the county's output for many years. Although the output seemed large then, it was only a drop in the bucket as compared to present tonnage. It did not increase much after the railroad was extended on through the county in 1903. A few more mines were started, one at Leslie, one at the mouth of Greasy, and another at Dog Hollow just below the present post office at Thealka.

It is true that the people hung back and that for a long time they were content to get out coal for local consumption, and without much concern for the foreign market. The real development of Big Sandy's coal fields started in the year of 1906.

The following report[3] showing the total production of mines in the Big Sandy District and number of mines operating, years 1906 to 1925, inclusive, will give a comprehensive idea of the consistent growth of this field, of which Johnson County is a part:

Year	No. of Mines	Tons Produced
1906	No Record	124,570
1907	No Record	255,000
1908	No Record	343,824
1909	No Record	469,390
1910	31	986,726

WIVES OF LEADERS
Those Who Succeed in Their Professions and Aid Materially the Industries of Their Section, Owe a Part of the Honor to the Wives, Whose Companionship, Opinions and Advice Are a Wonderful Help and Inspiration to Husbands

MRS. MITCHEL HALL MRS. B. F. ROBERTS MRS. E. E. ARCHER
MRS. G. H. RICE MRS. V. D. SPLANE MRS. HARRY LAVIERS
MRS. PAUL B. HALL   MRS. E. J. EVANS

Year	No. of Mines		Tons Produced
1911	33		1,289,876
1912	42		2,004,487
1913	43		2,665,321
1914	47		2,981,234
1915	51		3,316,185
1916	55		4,440,322
1917	76		4,095,764
1918	118		4,352,591
1919	129		5,062,934
1920	145		5,684,935
1921	162	(Subnormal year)	3,997,104
1922	177		6,133,077
1923	180		7,464,185
1924	180		8,526,431
1925	178		10,822,260
Total			75,016,216

From the above table, it can be seen that a very different state of affairs now exists, and that owners, railroads, corporations, and individuals have alike taken on a spirit more adventurous and are looking forward with confidence to the greatest extension of productive activities in their history. This growth is due to the progressive ideals of those actively engaged in the industry in this region.

It is interesting to note that the idea of quality coal is not a new one in the district but had its original inception with the earliest pioneers of the industry. While the black diamond has been marketed all these years, it seems just the beginning of what promises to become a second Pittsburgh section, when one considers the vast area yet undeveloped. The Big Sandy Division comprises some one and three-quarter million (1,750,000) acres. This region will bear approximately twelve and a half billion (12,500,000,000) tons of coal. This figure includes only coal seams which under the present highly competitive market conditions are considered economical for operation. If all seams were taken into consideration these figures would show twice the coal reserve indicated, or about twenty-five billion tons of coal.

From a transportation viewpoint 34 per cent of this region can be termed developed. In other words, 4,290,970,000 tons can be removed with the present transportation facilities. The remaining 66 per cent, approximately 8,209,303,000 tons, remain dormant until further railroad development is had.[4]

This vast area of practically inexhaustible reserve of highgrade by-product, is probably Johnson County's most valuable asset. It has some of the best coal in the Big Sandy Region. The Miller's Creek seam is a hard, firm, large block coal, making a most picturesque open grate fire and highly desirable for domestic use, and stands especially well transportation and storage handling with a very low percentage of breakage. It is also a very high-grade coal for industrial usage, with a high percentage ration of combustible material, quick to ignite and slow to consume. This coal is also low in ash and sulphur content and high in heat unit efficiency.

The "Yellow Jacket" coal is all the name implies. The limited cannel coal produced is an extraordinary quality because of its low ash content. It is much in demand because of its especial adaptability for open grate fires, since it is free from black, and ignites easily, giving out much heat. This unique solid fuel, high in volatiles for gas making, and the delight of every lover of an open grate fire, is broadly distributed throughout the county.

Coal is the invitation to industry, wealth and opportunity. It gives to a section the promise of supremacy, through which Johnson County is fast coming to the front.

The whole development has brought about a complete transformation from the small mining camps in the county to prosperous communities. Beautiful churches, excellent school facilities, up-to-date buildings, modern business houses, paved streets and sidewalks have supplanted the one-time camp of crowded one-room unsanitary houses where tin cans, garbage, refuge, pigs, cows, and chickens made themselves at home in the house and street, and which some uninformed outsiders persist in referring to in connection with the "mountains."

JOHN C. C. MAYO [5]

No real changes were noticeable in the coal business in the county until the coming of John C. C. Mayo of Paintsville, Kentucky. One cannot write of the coal industry without linking with it the name of Mayo, in whose fertile brain first originated the idea of the coal development on a large scale in Eastern Kentucky. It is with pride that an appreciation is here expressed for the man responsible for its development and who first directed the eyes of the nation to the latent possibilities of wealth contained in the mountains of this vast empire in the form of rich coal deposits. That man had an abiding faith in the coming greatness of his native hills in the production of this coal.

Mr. Mayo received his early education in the common schools in his native county of Johnson, later taking a college course at Millersburg College, Millersburg, Kentucky. He returned to Johnson County where he taught in the public schools of his county for a number of years. It was during these years while he instructed the youth of his county that he conceived the idea of the development of the coal resources of the Big Sandy Valley and grasped the vision of the great possibilities of the potential wealth contained in the rugged hillsides. He then began to acquire mineral rights and soon interested Eastern capital in the valley.

AUXIER, KY.

A Model Mining Town of the Northeast Coal Company, Six Miles South of Paintsville

INDUSTRIAL DEVELOPMENT 345

He began his career in a region marvelously rich in resources, but utterly remote from all industrial developments and he closed his life before he was fifty years old, with innumerable friends in all parts of the Commonwealth, rich in worldly goods, and leaving for his children the priceless heritage of a useful and honorable career.

Thirty-five years ago Eastern Kentucky, figuratively speaking, was distant, detached, and unknown. In this section, as in most sections then, the years had passed in their splendid march of progress, and civilization had stood still between the Big Sandy and Cumberland. A hundred years had been but as a watch in the night. All the marvelous wealth of the section was unknown or unvalued. John Mayo came into manhood amid circumstances, customs and surroundings that a century had not changed. And the marvel of it was, that then he dreamed his dream of future development, his fancy, free and unfettered, went out into the great world beyond and brought him visions of railroad and mine and mill; visions of highways thronged with travel, of fields the richer grown from reaping cities, busy, great and prosperous, amid his mountain wilderness.

A country school teacher, poor as the poorest, obscure as the humblest, gifted only with genius, strong with the strength of a great purpose, without money, and without acquaintance, he set about making his dream come true.

Twenty-five years was too short a time for him. He did his work as best he could. The untimely shadows closed about him all too soon. But he lived to reap much of the great harvest which he sowed through the years of constant struggle with scorn and skepticism, and of wonderful accomplishments in the face of difficulty that seemed unsurmountable.

His abilities were such that he made the skeptic see, as he saw, the inexhaustible riches sealed in these remote hills, and he changed the men who laughed at his faith into enthusiastic converts to his plan. Through all those years he worked, and worked without rest, to develop Eastern Kentucky along the large and lofty lines of his prophetic visions. He was an empire-builder, as was Clive and Rhodes and Hill and McKenzie, and what was done by these great men for India and South Africa, for our great Northwest and for Canada's imperial domain, John C. C. Mayo did for Eastern Kentucky. He possessed all the mental attributes of the great empire builder. He could see the harvest ere the grain was sown and on the midnight sky of rain could paint the golden morrow.

Through the struggles to obtain recognition for one of the greatest coal fields in the world, a struggle filled to an unusual extent with delays, defeats, doubt and difficulties, his hope ever held high, his courage never wavered, and his faith was unfaltering. He was strong with the faith of the hills; far-sighted from gazing on horizons that stretched from the mountain tops; keen-witted, industrious, forcible, shrewd, practical and magnetic, he laid broad and deep and strong the foundations of an industrial empire whose mighty fabric shall be a growing memorial for one of Kentucky's greatest sons.

It is not too much to say that this one man transformed and transfigured the whole of Kentucky's mountain section; and indeed opened a great new region for industrial America.

His life was dedicated to fulfilling the splendid vision of his early manhood and he lived to see his beloved hills unseal their hidden riches in ampler measure than he had ever foretold. He saw the railroads stretch their shining steel, following where his feet had found the way to the coal. He saw the hillsides blossom into busy cities, and he saw his own genius unfetter Eastern Kentucky, strike from her feet immemorial shackles, and set her on her course to progress.

He lived to see the empire of his dreams become an empire of reality, greater, and richer in its boundless possibilities than even he had dared to hope or to dream.

During the years since his departure and in those that are to come, as more and more the great coal empire of Eastern Kentucky comes into its own, the splendid achievements of Mr. Mayo are being realized, and they will continue to loom into plainer view. His great abilities find readier recognition, and his rare qualities of head and heart bear deeper impress upon his people. His county, his State, and his country were immeasurably richer because of his life and his work. His friends and his family are most desolate indeed without him. His career closed in 1914, but every train-load of the black diamond going forth from the Big Sandy coal fields today is his monument, and so long as it is marketed, it will perpetuate his name.[6]

Johnson County ranks eleventh among the twenty odd counties producing coal in the Eastern Kentucky field. A list of the separate coal operations in the county is as follows:

Name of Corporation	Address	Name of Coal
Consolidation Coal Co.,	Van Lear	No. 1, Miller's Creek Block
Northeast Coal Co.,	Paintsville	No. 1, Yellow Jacket
Royal Collieries Mine,	Offutt	No. 1
Ayers Lang Coal Co.,	Offutt	Chattario
Greasy Creek Coal Co.,	Offutt	No. 1
Greenrock Coal Co.,	Riceville	No. 1
Denver Coal Co.,	Denver	No. 1
High Grade Block Coal Co.	Denver	No. 2
Line Branch Coal Co.,	Hager Hill	No. 1

JOHN C. C. MAYO

Of this list, the first two are the larger-producing operations.

THE CONSOLIDATION COAL COMPANY. The Miller's Creek Division operations of this Company are located at Van Lear, about four miles from Paintsville. The Company owns in this division approximately 33,000 acres lying in Johnson and Martin counties, but principally in Johnson County. There are five mines in operation, Mines Nos. 151, 152, 153, 154, and 155. All are in the famous Miller's Creek No. 1 seam and the coal is known as "The Miller's Creek Block Coal." The extreme hardness of the splendid coals in this particular locality permits ready preparation into block sizes, many too large for any man's single strength, with the resultant egg and nut sizes and a very small percentage of slack. The block coal from this district attained a very quick popularity, and in many cases has displaced the use of anthracite in the markets of the middle west. Its distinctive features are its hardness, especially desirable in transportation and storage, its quick ignition, slow consumption, and its extremely small percentage of non-combustible material. It is especially adaptable to domestic use in either wood stoves, open grates, and all kinds of coal stoves, and its free-burning nature makes it almost fool-proof, since it requires but little draft from below or through the fire bed.

The egg and nut sizes are very popular in city use in domestic furnaces and cooking ranges, since a quick heat is easily secured for either cooking or heating. The smaller sizes are very much in demand for boiler use, both stationary and locomotive, where free-burning coals are required.

The seam of this Miller's Creek coal varies in thickness from three feet to four and one-half feet, with an average not exceeding forty-two inches, and invariably clean.

The mines are all electrically equipped. The coal is machine mined and is cut on the bottom. Haulage is done with electric locomotives entirely. Large tipples at each of the mines prepare the coal for market in the following sizes: Block, 4-inch lump, 2-inch lump, egg, nut, nut sea slack, and slack. The structure of the coal is such that about fifty-five per cent of the output is 4-inch lump.

The Company is one of the steadiest producers on the Big Sandy. During the slack run or dull market, coal is stored on the ground at the different mines, thus giving the miners more regular employment than mines where this is not done.

THE NORTHEAST COAL COMPANY. This Company has coal operations at Thealka, near Paintsville, and White House, both in Johnson County, and another at Auxier, Floyd County, at which place the mines have workings extending into Johnson

County. Two and three mines are operated at each place. All are served by the Big Sandy Division of the Chesapeake and Ohio Railroad. These mining towns are marvels of beauty, convenience and comfort. The homes of the men employed by this Company are supplied with every convenience—even better than is to be had in many cities and county seats.

This Company employs native labor exclusively, and treats its men with kindest consideration for themselves and families. Consequently labor troubles are at the minimum with them, as their employes are happy and contented. By the liberal policy of the Company toward its men, it has no trouble in holding in its employ the best of labor. It has men in its employ who have been with the Company since it first began operations in the county, and it is to be remembered that this Company was one of the pioneer operators of the valley.

It is strong in religious and educational matters, and the best of schools and churches are maintained in all its towns so that the children of miners are provided with the best of advantages, both educationally and religiously.

Up-to-date stores are conducted in each town of this corporation where miners have the advantage of buying the best of all kinds of foods and other supplies necessary for the sustenance of life and the maintenance of happiness, at the lowest possible cost.

A. D. W. Smith of Philadelphia, is president of this corporation. Although he is not a local man, the county owes much to him for its progress, and he is deserving of a place among the really great coal men of the State.

Henry LaViers is general manager of the Company, and a citizen of Paintsville. He is an experienced coal man and his able management is pleasing to both the owners and employes.

Mr. LaViers has also served two terms as president of the Northeast Kentucky Coal Association, an organization of Eastern Kentucky coal men, very active in the interest of the bituminous coal industry of that section. He started in the coal business at the bottom—a pick and shovel miner. He worked himself up to the top of the ladder with only himself to depend on, and is now regarded as one of the best coal men in Kentucky. In addition to boosting school and church activities, he is a member of every local organization which stands for the upbuilding of the community and the welfare of its people. (See page 363 for photo.)

R. C. Thomas is superintendent of the Big Sandy operations of the Northeast Coal Company. He is experienced in the coal business and a man of sterling character. He is not only popular with the employes of the Company, but with all who know him, inasmuch as he is a high-class Christian gentleman and interested in all causes for the betterment of mankind. He has served as

E. R. PRICE

For Fifteen Years Connected with the Miller's Creek Division of the Consolidation Coal Company, Several Years as Manager. No Manager of This Division Ever Co-operated with the Citizens of Paintsville and Johnson County as Did Mr. Price

president of the Paintsville-Van Lear Rotary Club. He is a singer of rare ability and his time is freely given to all church and religious activities of the city, although he is a very busy man. (See chapter on Religious Progress for photo.)

OIL AND GAS DEVELOPMENT
THE ORIGIN OF OIL'

The story of oil runs back into the early stages of the earth's history. The first chapters of the account were written in the records of the ancient seas. These seas periodically advanced and receded, so that in their extreme expanse, they mingled the waters of the Equator with those of the Arctic; but always, whatever their size, rivers flowed down to the seas throughout the ages, and then, as now, carried with them great quantities of mud and sand to be spread out by currents and tides over the entire sea bottom. Each day and each year through millennium, new deposits were distributed, layer upon layer over the sea floor. Thus were built up the thick series of shales and clays and sandstones which characterize the formations penetrated by our oil and gas wells.

Lacking any other reasonable explanation, we must accept the geologist's conclusion that the sea-bottom muds and sands of a geological yesterday, squeezed by the weight of thousands of feet of overlying muds and sands, crumbled and broken and finally thrust above the sea level by the movement of the earth's crust around and beneath them, became the shales, limestones, and sandstones of today. And we accept their conclusion that the organic mud, the mass of marine life, and plant and animal life which came into the seas with the river silts, together with the immense masses of tropical plants carried thither by the changing seas are the principal source materials of petroleum. These masses of plant and animal life, buried by subsequent deposits of mud, sand, and shale, sealed from the air, and further protected from ordinary decay by the brine of the ocean itself, were subjected to a slow decomposition which finally yielded among other products the petroleum of commerce.

But petroleum, so formed and disseminated uniformly through great bodies of organic mud, was not available to man. It had still to be concentrated, to accumulate in a definite limited reservoir such as the pore spaces between the grains of a bed of sand, or more rarely, the cracks and crevices of a limestone, when it can issue under pressure into the well which the operator drills into the reservoir. This concentration of petroleum is accomplished in part by great pressure which transforms the mud into a dense shale, at the same time driving the oil into the more open, non-comprehensible sands, and in part by water moving down through the bed from its outcrop on the earth's surface, or rising upward with the water under pressure from greater depth, and also by pressure caused by the upheavel of the substructures of the earth itself, until the oil or gas finally accumulate in a rock fold, or against the faulted broken edge of a sand bed, whence the water cannot dislodge it.

EARLY HISTORY OF OIL

There is evidence of ancient writers that oil and asphalt were known and used by man. Herodotus in writings of date about 450 years B.C., refers to a well in Persia as follows: "From this well they got bitumen, salt, and oil, producing it in a way which I shall now describe. They draw with a sweep, or the like, and instead of a bucket they make use of the half of a wine skin; with this the man dips and after drawing, pours the liquid into a reservoir wherefrom it passes into another, and there takes three different shapes. The salt and bitumen collect and harden, while the oil is drawn off into casks." In 75 B.C. Pliny states that the water from a well at Babylon, "Was taken from the wells to the works, and there heated by the great heat of the sun, and condensed partly into liquid bitumen and partly into salt." We learn from ancient history that the Egyptians used bitumen obtained from crude oil for embalming, and Abraham mentions in the Bible its use by the Sumerians, and we have little doubt but that Noah used pitch in caulking the Ark, but regardless of these facts, it can be proved that oil was a useful article of general commerce, and was even used in heating and lighting two thousand years before Columbus discovered America. The American Indians used the oil for treatment, medicine, light and heat—a fact to which George Washington attests in his writings and will. Washington became so impressed with the uses of the oil and

A MINE OF THE CONSOLIDATION COAL COMPANY AT VAN LEAR, KY.

of the many possibilities for other uses that he acquired a large boundary of the lands upon which some of the oil springs of Northwestern Pennsylvania were located, and he further wrote that Indians had dug great pits at the springs along what is now called Oil Creek, and shored them up with timbers to collect the oil.

Martin Beatty of Abingdon, Virginia, brought in the first oil well in Kentucky in 1819, on the South Fork of the Cumberland River close to the Tennessee state line in what is now McCreary County, then Wayne County.[8] Beatty had been drilling a shallow well for salt, which then was a necessity of more importance than oil, and was disgusted when he struck oil, for his chances of recovering salt brine from such a well were spoiled.

Cumberland County, forty miles to the west, followed in 1828 with flowing oil production—as before, the result of salt-water well prospecting. This well came to be known widely as the Great American Well. The man who drilled it, whose name has since been lost, said that he would either get salt water or drill into hell. He did what he promised, but instead of getting the salt water, he got oil and gas which caught fire, causing him to think that he had opened up the infernal regions below. He acknowledged that he had failed in getting salt, and was so thoroughly convinced of his failure, that he did not remain to sell his belongings, but immediately left to return in disgust to his native hills of Pennsylvania. The oil from this phenomenal well flowed unrestrained down the little branch in which it was drilled into Cumberland River, to a point forty miles below Burkesville, where a grass fire ignited it. There resulted the unusual phenomenon of a burning river, for the flames crept back little by little to the mouth of the well.[9]

About the same time (1828) crude oil was being obtained from the natural oil springs in Johnson County, Kentucky.

That these springs are no myth, can readily be ascertained by any who desire to see them in person, as the oil from them is still flowing. It is stated that this oil was gathered and sold as "rock oil" for medicinal purposes, and was recommended for many ailments, including ridding hogs and other animals of vermin. It is a fact that crude oil is a good remedy for colds, croup, bruises, sprains, etc.

But for all this, oil did not come into world-wide fame or into extremely common and general use until Drake drilled his historic well in 1859. Edwin L. Drake, a railroad conductor, who had been a victim of a stock-selling project that had started from the sale of "rock oil" obtained from some oil springs near the town of Titusville, Pennsylvania, was not satisfied when profits and dividends failed to materialize. He got on the trail of the promoters of the "wild-cat" stock and made it so uncomfortable for them, that they got rid of him by turning over some of the leases to him and suggesting that he go on the ground and work out a better plan. After looking over the situation, he conceived the idea that if oil seeped to the surface, a better and quicker way to get it was to drill for it. Before he tried drilling, he experimented long with trenches and pits to draw in the oil, but naturally with small success. After getting together a little money and some crude tools used for drilling salt wells, he started a crew to drilling. On the afternoon of August 2, 1859, the well had reached a depth of 69 feet, where they quit for the day. When they returned to work the next morning, the well was nearly full of oil. The discovery had been made. The news spread, and soon the village of Titusville was literally swamped with transients. The oil industry started off with a bang and grew lustily. Drake was confident, at first, that he had tapped the one and only vein, but was shocked when others found oil at points miles from the site on Oil Creek. Drake left the oil field with a small fortune, but went to New York and lost it all, and ended up as a ward of the State and is buried in Woodlawn Cemetery at Titusville.

The first flowing well was drilled on Pithole Creek about ten miles south of Titusville. There is much to be said of the famous Pithole, as it soon became the center of an oil-boom and rush, reaching a population of many thousands, and its fame spreading to the four corners of the earth, only to go to the ruins as fast as it had grown, when the wells began to fail.

Such were the beginnings of the oil industry, which in one generation has revolutionized society, and become, almost if not, the biggest business in the world. From Oil City and Pithole City went forth the nucleus of that ever-increasing army of oil scouts and prospectors, which scattering to Bradford and thence southwesterly into West Virginia, Ohio, and Kentucky, and finally overrunning the continent into all states where it was thought that oil might be found, and so into all parts of the world—an army of men "optimistic as a new seed catalog" and "nervy enough to give swimming lessons to a fish."

These old-time prospectors of Pennsylvania drifted down through the fields of West Virginia, and although geology was not much thought of in that day, so far as its practical application to the discovery of oil was concerned, still in a way these old-time prospectors applied practical geology, because they observed that the formation and hills along the way down through West Virginia and into Kentucky had the same general appearance as some places back in Pennsylvania. They also saw the line of the oil springs and seepages passing en route to Kentucky.

Having decided that Kentucky looked favorable for production these prospectors proceeded to put down some test wells. In those early days there were, of course, no pipe lines or other means of

A MINE OF THE NORTHEAST COAL COMPANY, THEALKA, KY.

transportation for the oil, and while it appears from the best information obtainable that these old-time prospectors struck oil in every well they drilled, they failed to market the product, and the wells were gradually abandoned, as a few years after the Civil War, oil became very cheap in price. Among these old-time wells, perhaps, the Brainard well on Big Paint Creek, about ten miles west of Paintsville, is the most famous. Other old wells are the Bracken, which, after being shot in recent years, is now a paying producer, the Colvin Branch, and the Black wells.

Considerable activity was manifested in Johnson County during and just after the Civil War, and several test wells were put down which old reports claim were good wells, all of which still have oil in them. The lack of transportation facilities continued to be a damper on the progress of this business, and it gradually dwindled until by 1897, only 322 barrels of oil were produced from the whole State of Kentucky. The industry, however, with more settled business conditions in 1898, began to assume larger proportions, and in that year approximately 6,000 barrels of oil were produced. From that time on, prospecting and developing for oil were steadily carried on, and the million-barrel production mark was reached in 1905.

The little financial flurry of 1907, 1908, and 1909 again witnessed the falling off of production, after which time, the industry has steadily increased.

THE JOHNSON-MAGOFFIN OIL FIELD[10]

The discovery work which led to the opening and final development of the great Eastern Kentucky oil fields began in the year 1917. During October of that year, the Bed Rock Oil Co., on first test, found a large gas well on the Mine Fork Dome, near the head of Pigeon Creek, in Johnson County.

The Bed Rock Company was organized by David Browning, a native of Webster County, Kentucky, for the purpose of making tests on three well-defined structures, which had been located and mapped by geologists Iley B. Browning and Phillip Russell, who made the locations. Later in 1918 other gas wells were completed just over the line in Magoffin County. On February 1, 1919, gas was marketed from nine wells, being piped to Central Kentucky cities.

On September 4, 1919, the first real oil well was completed in Magoffin County on the Milt Wheeler farm, one-half mile south of Wheelersburg, by the Bed Rock Oil Company. This initial well flowed 60 to 75 barrels daily. This pioneer company on September 9th, at the suggestion of G. M. Davison, president, celebrated by an old-fashioned barbecue, which was attended by the entire population of that section, as well as oil men and scouts of many producing companies. The excitement occasioned by the celebration of a better than 60-barrel well on so large and pronounced a structure as the Mine Fork Dome, brought oil operators, geologists, and speculators, who follow all new fields, in great numbers and lease values increased daily in the north part of Magoffin County and Western Johnson County.

About the same time (1917) Mr. A. B. Ayers of the Union Gas & Oil Company had found several gas wells and three oil wells, about ten miles north of the Wheeler well, on the north side of the great Flat Gap - Red Bush Dome, near the Johnson-Lawrence line. To the Union Gas & Oil Company the same credit is due, as a pioneer of the Blaine-Keaton Fork oil field, that is given to the Bed Rock Oil Company of the Magoffin pool.

Two other wells were drilled in the fall of 1919 on Mine Fork, west of Wheelersburg, by the Bed Rock Oil Company, and in December of that year, what was known as the Sobel well was completed two and one-half miles south of the initial well, which proved the extent of the pool. March, 1920, the fourth important well was completed by the Browning Petroleum Company on the L. C. Bailey lease, which proved to be a 90-barrel well. Immediately following this the C. C. Meade well, drilled by Iley B. Browning was completed, and on June 15, 1920, the Cumberland Pipe Line Company completed a line to the Bailey lease and the first oil was run from the Oil Springs pump station.

At this time the price of Somerset oil was at its height and the rush drilling and completion of new wells were so rapid that in six months several hundred had been completed and connected with the pipe line. The number of oil companies operating in the field became so numerous and completion of wells so rapid that it would be unreasonable to name them all. A few figures, however, would not be out of place. In the Oil Springs sections of Johnson County and Magoffin County, there were 676 producing wells in 1923, and 501 at the same time in the Blaine field in Johnson and Lawrence counties. In 1924 Blaine had 836, Oil Springs 849. In 1925 there were 1,073 in the Blaine field, and 943 in the Oil Springs field. And in 1926 there were 1,224 in the Blaine field, and 1,022 in the Oil Springs field.

In 1923 these fields (Johnson, Magoffin and Lawrence) produced 2,841,670 barrels of oil. In 1924 they produced 2,751,835. In 1925 they produced 2,597,340. In 1926 they produced 2,375,410 barrels at a value of more than $6,000,000.

There have been outlined two Weir sand pools (Mine Fork and Keaton Fork) in Johnson, Magoffin and Lawrence counties, and four Berea sand oil pools (Paint Creek, Busseyville, Fallsburg, and Louisa) in Johnson and Lawrence counties, and five large gas pools (Beaver Creek, Ivyton, Win, Red Bush and Flat Gap) producing from the Maxton and the Weir sands."[11] The real pay sand which is found about 250 feet below the Mississippi lime at

HENRY LaVIERS
General Manager of the Northeast Coal Company

a depth of from 900 to 1,200 feet, according to surface elevation, belongs to the Big Injun family of sands, so productive in West Virginia and Pennsylvania.

The oil and gas from the Berea sand oil pools are produced from a broad anticlinal structure which is locally called the Paint Creek Anticline and Fault, but which is known in the state of West Virginia as the Chestnut Ridge Anticline, and which passes squarely through Johnson County, Kentucky, crosses the Big

"SHOOTING" A WELL IN THE JOHNSON-MAGOFFIN OIL FIELD

Sandy River near the mouth of Buffalo and Greasy creeks and extends north of Paintsville, crossing the headwaters of Tom's Creek and thence across Big Mud Lick Creek, Little Mud Lick Creek, and Big Paint Creek, the fault having its greatest down-throw near Fishtrap on Big Paint Creek, and thence crossing Little Paint Creek into Magoffin County."[13]

There are many small local structures along the crest and far down the flanks of this anticline, and so much test work has been done in a systematic way, that the productive sands have been found and the areas outlined along the way. Of the sands penetrated in sections along the Paint Creek Anticline and Fault, the Berea Grit, at a depth of from 800 to 1,000 feet, showed the best results over a wide area. Paying wells have been drilled in this Berea sand right in the town of Paintsville, on Tom's Creek, in and around Staffordsville, on Big Mud Lick Creek, on the upper waters of Big Paint Creek, including its tributaries, Colvin Branch, Gullett Branch, McKenzie Branch and Barnetts Creek.

The field from which the product is obtained from the Weir sand, lies along the border of Johnson and Magoffin counties, on a formation running generally in a north and south direction. This formation extends all the way from Lawrence County by way of Keaton's Fork, Laurel Creek, headwaters of Big Blaine, crossing upper Big Paint Creek, Little Paint Creek and waters of Mine Fork, and butts squarely into the Paint Creek Anticline, thus forming the great Paint Creek Dome; thence across headwaters of State Road Fork, Mash Fork, other waters of Licking River, and extending into Floyd County.

The Berea field produces a better grade of oil than the Weir, while the latter is not regarded of so long a life, though the production is larger than the Berea, running as high as 100 barrels per day in a well or two.

GAS

For a long time the largest developed natural gas fields of Eastern Kentucky were the Menifee and Martin County fields. The first of these fields, that in Menifee County, lies just east of the Central Bluegrass boundary. It is an old shallow field, the gas being taken from the Corniferous limestone which is the present oil-producing formation of the Estill, Lee, and Bath County fields to the south and northeast. The gas was secured at depths of from 450 feet to 680 feet, which made the field, from an operator's standpoint, one of unusual attraction. Practically all the gas from this field was used by the Central Kentucky Natural Gas Company, which supplied almost all of the Central Kentucky towns. Due to the heavy drain upon its volume, this field greatly depreciated,

GASOLINE PLANT OF OLIVER JENKINS, LOCATED IN THE JOHNSON-MAGOFFIN OIL FIELD

and soon other fields in counties further to the east had to be developed.[13]

The Martin County gas field, sometimes called the Inez field, after Inez, the county seat, and often included with the West Virginia fields under the appellation of "Triple State Field," was next to be developed to a large extent. This field was by no means new, some of its first wells having been drilled in 1897. In contrast to the Menifee gas field, the Martin County field is a rather deep field, the productive gas sands being the "Big Lime" sand streak and the "Big Injun" sand. The formations average in depth below the surface between 1,100 feet and 1,500 feet.[14]

The Martin field has been a great producer, but like the Menifee field, it has been rapidly depreciating for several years, with the result that other fields had to be developed.

Among these have been the Lawrence, Johnson, and Floyd County fields, the last of which is the most important at this time, or at least more systematic developing is going on in that section. Several sections of Johnson County have proven to be gas-bearing territory, though, with gas flows of one-half million feet per day. Wells of this capacity have been paying better dividends than oil at the present price of oil. A great many gas wells have been drilled in the Red Bush and Flat Gap pools. The Staffordsville section is rich in natural gas. Good flows have been encountered in that neighborhood, which if properly handled, would have supplied gas for a number of towns the size of Paintsville, whereas, most of this gas has been wasted.

Johnson County has many thousand acres of potential oil and gas territory which has never been tapped by the drill. Gas is encountered in some quantity in any section where drilling is done, and Johnson will, no doubt, in a few years become a great gas-producing county. The fact in the case is that Johnson County remains unexplored, comparatively speaking, in the search for either oil or gas, the surface merely being scratched. There are several sands known to exist in the county which have been proven rich producers in either oil or gas in other counties, which have never been tapped here. These are the deeper sands, and consequently more expensive to drill, than the shallow sands where oil and gas are now being produced in Johnson and Magoffin counties. For this reason tapping of the lower sands has been delayed. Deep drilling is essential to the complete development of the oil and gas industry of Johnson County.

OIL PRODUCTION—JOHNSON COUNTY

Producing "Sand" Mississippian sandstone, principally the Weir, and to slight extent the Berea, of Waverly age. No deep sands producing.

(Reports from April, 1920, to September, 1925, from New Oil Pools of Kentucky, 1926, the Kentucky Geological Survey, W. R. Jillson, director. Those from the latter date to December, 1927, taken from records of the Kentucky State Tax Commission. None certified after October, 1926, pending a suit in the Federal Courts.)

	1920 Barrels	Value
April	447.98	$ 1,899.92
May	823.90	3,295.60
June	1,642.87	6,571.48
July	2,800.07	11,200.28
August	4,421.08	17,684.32
September	6,186.93	26,294.45
October	8,483.72	37,060.72
November	9,524.15	41,910.49
December	11,018.48	46,067.01
Total	45,349.18	$ 191,984.27
	1921	
January	14,119.46	$ 34,200.55
February	14,069.95	24,610.63
March	18,846.24	32,898.76
April	21,176.37	44,781.82
May	25,661.76	44,685.36
June	24,486.12	24,167.04
July	27,153.24	26,696.81
August	33,726.94	41,267.80
September	30,157.57	56,063.11
October	34,538.17	90,687.97
November	31,759.13	83,843.70
December	39,873.09	85,297.66
Total	315,568.04	$ 589,201.21
	1922	
January	39,713.30	$ 84,937.11
February	40,916.23	87,606.38
March	50,050.06	107,280.14
April	47,379.54	101,530.77
May	53,457.29	127,730.89
June	53,078.97	126,906.55
July	60,774.94	115,062.77
August	63,966.95	120,975.34
September	63,842.50	120,598.30
October	61,322.26	119,476.35
November	68,895.07	134,299.49
December	63,370.65	139,467.40
Total	666,767.76	$1,385,871.49
	1923	
January	75,305.58	$ 203,154.75
February	70,223.50	199,909.26
March	72,627.39	181,302.62
April	68,734.86	154,214.60
May	75,152.94	153,313.77
June	83,026.38	132,875.89
July	58,846.90	94,017.02
August	106,802.53	170,736.84
September	100,737.66	146,133.56

	Barrels	Value
October	104,346.86	$ 140,893.65
November	98,795.13	133,402.78
December	100,406.26	169,371.82
Total	1,015,005.99	$1,879,326.56
	1924	
January	96,822.30	$ 226,274.59
February	94,324.45	234,582.66
March	102,727.64	255,433.76
April	100,547.84	225,106.52
May	102,636.80	229,866.49
June	102,396.62	188,551.25
July	103,385.12	174,848.19
August	95,895.50	162,266.72
September	96,387.58	162,995.58
October	98,280.85	166,164.89
November	91,366.74	154,539.01
December	93,903.97	158,803.79
Total	1,178,675.41	$2,339,433.45
	1925	
January	90,715.41	$ 198,771.00
February	82,882.54	202,354.45
March	91,600.20	223,726.05
April	86,773.75	198,963.24
May	86,825.66	225,213.08
June	83,616.45	216,883.19
July	90,658.68	235,016.77
August	81,285.96	190,519.12
September	84,202.96	197,224.82
October	85,634.70	187,594.26
November	82,471.46	193,034.55
December	79,654.52	186,326.04
Total	1,026,322.29	$2,455,626.57
	1926	
January	80,328.21	$ 188,077.36
February	74,532.93	181,851.72
March	81,777.36	199,546.82
April	80,009.13	195,217.82
May	78,299.59	206,765.05
June	83,042.76	219,296.00
July	83,283.62	219,915.43
August	82,152.65	216,904.15
September	82,916.63	219,057.93
October	82,917.47	218,913.31
November	78,384.70	183,521.16
December	80,638.89	188,775.48
Total	968,283.94	$2,437,842.23

E. J. EVANS
A Progressive Oil Developer and Operator of Johnson County

	1927		TOTALS		
	Barrels	Value		Barrels	Value
January	79,296.64	$ 174,452.61	1920	45,349.18	$ 191,984.27
February	73,225.13	120,821.46	1921	315,568.04	589,201.21
March	77,032.97	115,549.46	1922	666,767.76	1,385,871.49
April	74,172.10	111,258.15	1923	1,015,005.99	1,879,326.56
May	70,189.02	105,283.53	1924	1,178,675.41	2,339,433.45
June	71,164.20	106,746.30	1925	1,026,322.29	2,455,626.57
July	74,418.41	111,627.62	1926	968,283.94	2,437,842.23
August	73,237.60	109,856.40	1927	862,908.92	1,374,183.20
September	67,869.40	101,804.10			
October	69,019.53	103,529.30	Grand total	6,078,881.53	$12,653,468.98
November	65,776.42	105,242.27			
December	67,507.50	108,012.00			
Total	862,908.92	$1,374,183.20			

ROCK ASPHALT

Eastern Kentucky is becoming known throughout the State and nation as one vast mineral bed, and Johnson County seems to be right in the center of these natural riches. As development progresses new and interesting facts are being brought to light. Not only is Johnson County rich in coal, oil, and gas, but it has recently been brought to light that the county is underlaid with deposits of rock asphalt, which may prove to be of commercial value at some future date. These asphalt deposits, however, are not a new discovery. More than fifty years ago Daniel Lemaster with his associates were gathering the lighter oil from the outcrop and transporting it to market, the mode of transportation, at that time, being by ox teams and flatboats. As a further evidence of an early knowledge of this deposit, many old deeds and leases recorded in the Johnson County clerk's office, and dating back more than fifty years refer to it and reserve it in the sale of lands.

Some seven or eight years ago, Doctor Willard Rouse Jillson, Kentucky State Geologist, examined asphalt impregnated sandstone in the cliffs of Big Paint Creek gorge, near Low Gap Branch, and at other points along the creek and its tributaries, but reported the deposits not thick enough to be commercially profitable, due to the excess overburden.

Since Doctor Jillson visited these fields, oil well logs show the bed to be twelve feet thick in places, and other geologists who have made investigations bear out the reports of an extensive field. The main deposit lies mostly in the Little Paint Creek region beginning in the Fish Trap section of Big Paint Creek, and extending into the Little Paint section of Magoffin County.

Samples of the rock asphalt found in this county have been analyzed in laboratories and tested almost perfect with samples of rock asphalt now being used for hard-surfacing roads throughout the country. Paintsville business concerns have displayed some of these samples, which are of sandstone richly impregnated with asphalt, and represented as exact replicas of millions of tons of the mineral.

A wilderness of small timber, coupled with precipitous walls of rock, bad roads, and no railroad, with frequent high water, make traveling in the Paint Creek gorge difficult except during the dry periods of the year. In view of this fact and considering the heavy overburden of rock, asphalt production in this gorge would have to be a mining proposition, and as such the deposits have not, as yet, been regarded as commercial. Underneath the asphalt, well logs indicate, lies a seam of good coal, ten inches in thickness. This, engineers say, would make the mining proposition a practical scheme, as the coal and asphalt could be taken out in one operation.

Rock asphalt is one of the most valuable materials known for the surfacing of roads, and in this day of road construction throughout the nation, the development of the field should become a paying investment to promoters of a company for that purpose. In addition to its adaptability as a road-building material, rock asphalt can be utilized for the manufacture of numerous products used daily, one of which is asphalt roofing.

A more intensive survey of these rock asphalt deposits of Johnson County may prove that the material exists in practically unlimited quantities, destined to prove of immediate economic advantage to road building in Eastern Kentucky.

TIMBER AS AN INDUSTRY

Timber was Big Sandy's first industry. Before the advent of the railroad and the opening of mines and oil wells in Johnson County, lumbering was the chief industry of the section, and many of the older citizens realized large fortunes from the sale of timber and timber products.

The method of logging and transporting the products of our virgin forests to market was looked upon as "the good old days," and is the background of many fond recollections of the older citizens of today. Lumber camps were established in the forests usually by logging companies where men and cattle worked in "bluffing" logs from the hills into small streams which floated them to the river. To be a good ox driver in this industry was an accomplishment at that time, in which the Blantons, McKenzies, and Lemasters on Big Paint excelled. After getting the logs into the creeks, either splash dams were constructed or the first rise

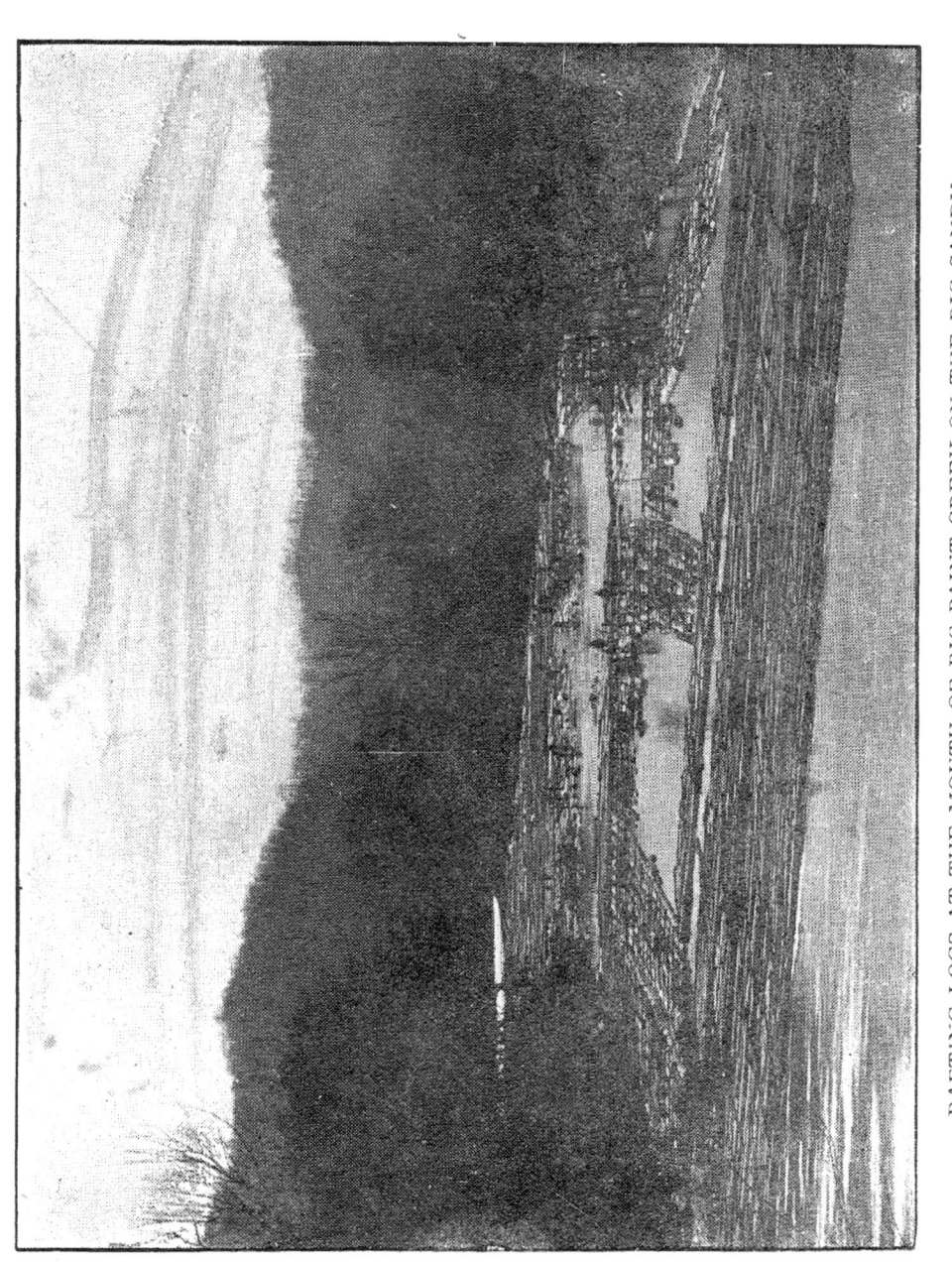

RAFTING LOGS AT THE MOUTH OF BIG PAINT CREEK ON THE BIG SANDY IN THE DAYS OF OLD

was awaited to float them out. Workmen followed the stream on the crest of the tide and drifted the logs to the mouth of the creeks, where they were caught by means of booms, and later rafted together into rafts of from 100 to 150 logs. Large oars were placed on each end of the raft, and with a man at each oar the raft of logs was then started for the mouth of Big Sandy at Catlettsburg on the Ohio River where they were sold and cut into lumber.

This trade in timber on the Big Sandy was a small affair until 1840, when it began to assume great magnitude, and continued to grow rapidly. By 1850 the number of logs cut and carried to market had annually quadrupled in number, and had considerably increased in price. In 1860, just preceding the beginning of the Civil War, the run in timber had increased fourfold since 1850. From 1861 to 1865, inclusive, the trade almost entirely ceased, except in furnishing timber for gunboats. In 1866 the cutting and running of timber to market received a wonderful impetus. This was in part due to the increased demand for lumber to supply the demand caused by four years devoted to destructive war. By 1875 or 1880 the trade had grown so great that firms representing heavier capital began to be formed at Catlettsburg. The amount of money paid out annually at Catlettsburg for timber and lumber had increased from an insignificant sum in 1840 to $1,500,000 in 1886, the quantity of timber run and its cash value increasing year by year.[15] This supply continued to be as prolific for another quarter of a century, and even fifteen years ago the river and creeks were black with saw-logs during highwaters, but such was not to be for all time, and now it is seldom a raft can be seen wending its slow course down the Big Sandy River toward the Ohio.

While the greater bulk of timber in Johnson County has been cut, there are several forests of virgin timber yet untouched in several sections within its boundary. This, however, is in isolated sections and will remain unmarketed until reached by railroad or highway. The timber that is available and being marketed now is worked into lumber by local mills, and the lumber shipped by rail or consumed locally.

(For kinds and grades of timber see page 151 under Times and Customs.)

Since the expansion of the mining industry in the county, much of the timber is being worked into mine posts, caps, ties, etc. Any kind of timber down to a very small size can be used for this purpose, and as a consequence the mountain slopes adjacent to these operations and along the railroad lines are almost bare; which, combined with the fact that no attention has been given to the subject of forestry, and no effort made to replace the timber on the hills, has left them practically denuded. Of the more prominent men engaged in the timber business of Johnson County, mention should be made of the Auxiers, Borders, Burgesses, Mayos and Prestons in the earlier days, while Geo. W. Preston, John Teass, Ashley Ward, John Kelley, E. P. Davis, Jesse Stafford, Sr., and many others were very prominent in the trade while it was at its height in Johnson County.

FARMING

Farming in Johnson County, except for average crops of corn and the raising of a few hogs and cattle, has never been extensive, as compared to the Bluegrass section of the State. It is readily apparent that in a region of such great relief, agriculture should not be expected to attain more than a modicum of success. Residual soils, generally silt or sandy clay loams, are now thin and of low productivity. Hillsides facing east and north generally show a deeper soil and are therefore better fitted for tilled lands than those exposed to the west and south which exhibit a closer adaptation to grass and retimbering. Nearly all of the old hillside fields are washed badly. They are, in fact, generally too steep for cultivation.

The residual or "bottom" soils are the best in this region. Along the main course of the larger streams, the soils of the flood plain are deep, well watered and fairly productive. Consisting generally of heavy sandy clay loams, they are usually deficient in calcium carbonate, phosphorus and other important soil constituents. When drained they are reasonably productive, particularly if flood waters occasionally leave a good silt cover. In all low and poorly drained places, these soils remain heavy and unproductive. The comparative values of the residual and transported soils are well known to the farmer who, until recently, has generally insisted on placing the public roadway in the waters of the small creek or branch, whenever possible, so that every bit of tillable bottom soil might be conserved.[16] These level lands that have been properly cared for have remained in cultivation and are fairly productive. Those that have not been looked after by the farmer of the past who did little to retain the soil, knowing that he could obtain more land when his holdings were worn out, constituted the greater part. As a consequence the lowlands were abandoned, insofar as cultivation was concerned, and the steeper slopes and river banks were invaded by the axmen, and then still steeper slopes, so that very much of the land now being cleared is too steep for cultivation under present methods of farming and should be kept in forest.

Newly cleared land, though steep, produces a good crop—mostly corn—for the first two or three years, after which time it becomes leached and washed. Though the productivity got exceedingly low, those pioneer farmers, with their characteristically

A RIVER BOTTOM ALONG THE BIG SANDY
(A Winter Scene)

One of the Many Large Bottoms, in Johnson County, Suitable for Farming and Grazing

INDUSTRIAL DEVELOPMENT

American disregard of the future, often tilled these hillsides many years after clearing.

Those obsolete methods of cultivating the lands and handling of the crops are now being superseded by more modern and up-to-date facilities. County agricultural agents, backed by the county, the State College of Agriculture, and the Federal Department of Agriculture, have succeeded in introducing better stock, and in showing the farmers that their lands could furnish them a better living through grazing and feeding flocks of sheep and droves of cattle, the raising of poultry and keeping of bees, dairying, truck farming, and fruit culture. Many acres of young orchards are being set out on the hillsides. As some of the slopes are cleared of their fine hardwood timber, and the softer woods utilized as fuel, instead of the continuous cultivation after two or three crops from the time of clearing, landowners are planting apple and peach trees. Fred VanHoose of the Tom's Creek section has one of the best orchards in Kentucky.

These hills are being honeycombed for their wealth of fuel, and their surfaces are being made to bear abnormal crops which can be harvested annually.

While the hills are being converted into orchards and grazing lands, the bottoms are being better taken care of with cowpeas, soy beans, and fertilizers. Although production of farm products within the county is not what it was twenty years ago, partly because of farm labor shifting to public works furnished by the coal, oil, and gas development, much activity is still in progress on the farms of Johnson County.

In 1924 the county had 17,057 acres of corn cultivated, raising 281,999 bushels as compared to 23,658 acres, 433,515 bushels, in 1919. It had 3,512 acres in grass, raising 3,875 tons of hay in 1924, as compared to 3,447 acres, 3,272 tons, in 1919. There were 43,686 apple trees bearing 77,999 bushels in 1924 compared to 37,768 trees, 66,398 bushels, in 1919.[17] Potatoes, molasses, and wheat are also raised to some extent, but all consumed locally.

(For additional data on agricultural products see page 151.)

RAILROADS

THE CHATTAROI

The Chattaroi (Chatterawha) Railroad Company was incorporated March 11, 1873, by John H. Carlisle of Cincinnati, Ohio, George S. Richardson, a business man from Massachusetts, and others. On April 1, 1880, the first shovel of dirt was turned toward the actual construction of the railroad at Ashland, which at that time was a small town of fifteen hundred population.

The road was at first commenced as a narrow gauge, but before completion the standard gauge was adopted.[18] Grading and construction work continued during the fall and winter of 1880 and 1881. On April 10, 1881, rail was laid into the town of Louisa and the first locomotive with material and cars reached there on that date.

Three miles above Louisa, the road left the river, due to a fearful opposition from the landowners between Three-Mile and George's Creek, going up Three-Mile Creek, crossing over and up Griffith's Creek to the Peach Orchard Tunnel, which was seven-eighths of a mile long. A series of switchboards was necessary to bring the grade down to the level of the Peach Orchard mines. The road was completed to this point in the winter of 1882 and spring of 1883 and was operated between Ashland and Peach Orchard, a distance of about forty-five miles. As soon as it was opened to this point, it was taxed to its utmost to provide transportation for the Peach Orchard coal. Shortly afterward the line was continued down Gates Creek, coming out again onto the Big Sandy at Richardson, May 1, 1883. In 1888, the line was changed and a new line built up the river route from Walbridge to Richardson, and shortly thereafter the original or old line was abandoned.[19]

OHIO AND BIG SANDY RAILROAD

In 1887 the road was built from Richardson to White House, a distance of eight miles, under the charter of Ohio, Kentucky, and Virginia, and intended to become a link in a through line from Chicago to Charleston, which was destined to make the Sandy Valley one of the most prosperous regions of Kentucky. Although completed to White House in 1888, the road was not connected with the Chattaroi Railroad until along in the early nineties.

On April 2, 1902, the Chesapeake and Ohio Railroad Company began the extension of this line under the charter of the Big Sandy Railroad Company from White House to Elkhorn City. Work of grading and track laying was pushed along as rapidly as possible and was completed into Elkhorn City about 1907.

The motive power of this old road consisted of six locomotives, four eight-wheel passenger engines and two light Baldwin Moguls Nos. 6 and 7. Box cars were fifteen tons capacity and coal cars of from nine to twelve hundred bushels which were not too heavy at that time for the sixty-pound rail that was used.

Some of the first officials of the road were: J. H. Carlisle, F. H. Oliphant, Charles H. Rockwell, Colonel George S. Richardson, Colonel Jay H. Northup, superintendents; W. R. Morris, master mechanic, and L. S. Stewart, trainmaster. Among some of the first conductors to run trains on the Chattaroi were Phillip

ALONG THE C. & O. IN JOHNSON COUNTY

C. Montague, Samuel D. Lawrence, John Songer, and Charles Richardson.

Of those who ran the old Chattaroi engines only two are known to be living today, namely: Thomas C. Songer and George Stewart, who reside in Ashland. Some of the older men who have long since made their last run and entered the Grand Terminal Above are F. G. Merriman, Andrew Berry, Bolivary L. Wesley, Oscar West, and Charles Conway.[20]

Below are some of the legislative acts with regard to this road in Johnson County:

Chapter 1436, Page 749, Acts 1888.

"AN ACT passed and approved May 3, 1888, authorizing the county levy court to ascertain the amount that may be paid by the Charleston, Cincinnati, and Chicago Railroad Company for the right of way for its railroad through the county, including the cost of condemnation. A similar act was passed and approved May 21, 1890, but also specified that taxes levied upon any railroad may be applied to the payment of the cost of the right of way, and interest thereon." (See page 1199, Chapter 1678, Acts 1890.)

Chapter 1692, Page 1225, Acts 1890.

"AN ACT passed and approved May 21, 1890, authorizing the county to subscribe to the capital stock of the Ohio and Big Sandy Railroad Company."

This act was repealed by legislative action and approved May 27, 1890. (See Page 1686, Acts 1890, Chapter 1910.)

Chapter 1909, Page 1684, Acts 1890.

"AN ACT passed and approved May 27, 1890, authorizing the county to have the power to exempt from all county taxation the property of the Ohio and Big Sandy Railroad Company."

THE CHESAPEAKE AND OHIO (BIG SANDY DIVISION)

This chapter has now brought the reader up to the present-day operation of the Big Sandy Division. This road traverses the beautiful Big Sandy Valley for a distance of 128 miles, leaving the main line at Big Sandy Junction and following the river to Elkhorn City, where it connects with the C. C. & O. for points south. The Big Sandy Division also has about 103 miles of branch lines, with the 128 miles of main line, nineteen of which is double tracked, making a total of about 250 miles.

There are now in operation 120 coal mines with daily rating of 931 cars of which the average production is 800 cars daily. The loading on Big Sandy District has attained the average of

4,500 to 5,000 cars weekly, which is a continuous increase and the present prospects are that this field will attain a daily average of 1,000 cars during the year of 1927."

This road passes through the heart of Johnson County, following the river all the way, except for a short cut-off above White House. Railroad stations within the county are: Patrick (formerly Chestnut), White House, Offutt, Buskirk (formerly Buffalo), Paintsville, Dawkins, Van Lear Junction, East Point.

At the Paintsville Station is located a roundhouse, watering station, coaling tipple for the engines, and the largest yards on this division, necessary inasmuch as it is about midway of the valley and trains are laid up and made up for both east and west directions in these yards.

An idea of the traffic passing through these yards and over this division may be had when one considers the fact that in addition to the "coal drags" carrying the above-mentioned 1,000 cars of coal daily, there are now scheduled daily four passenger trains, two local freights east, and two west, two manifest freights, and two shifters of three eight-hour shifts, besides the "extras." Instead of the light Baldwin No. 6 engines used in the early stages of the road, Mallies (16 driving wheels), Mikes, and G-7's and 9's now furnish the power to propel these trains.

It would be unreasonable to try to give names of those who are now conducting the activities of this road, but out of respect to him, mention should be made of Uncle Billy Myers, known by most every individual in the valley, who recently retired as conductor in the passenger service.

THE MILLER'S CREEK RAILROAD

This railroad was built about 1909 by the Baltimore and Ohio Railroad Company to market the coal on the holdings of the Consolidation Coal Company on Miller's Creek. It connects with the Chesapeake and Ohio at Van Lear Junction, crosses the Big Sandy River, and extends up Miller's Creek to the head, a distance of approximately seven miles. It only serves the above-mentioned coal company, and has about six trains daily. The Interstate Commerce Commission permitted the Chesapeake and Ohio to purchase this road from the Baltimore and Ohio in 1926, and it is now operated by the last-named company.

THE BIG SANDY AND KENTUCKY RIVER RAILROAD

In the development of the timber resources of the more remote sections of Johnson County, railroad transportation was necessary. In an effort to open up one of the best tracts of timber in that section, some business men from Ashland, led by the Vansant-Kitchen Lumber Company, Mr. Dawkins, and others, built the B. S. & K. R. Railroad from the C. & O. Railroad at Dawkins Station up Jenny's Creek to Royalton in Magoffin County in 1912.

C. & O. RAILROAD YARD AT PAINTSVILLE, KY.

INDUSTRIAL DEVELOPMENT 389

This railroad opened up an isolated territory, and as a result many millions of board-feet of lumber have been marketed. Traffic is very light on it, due to the fact that very little coal is mined along the route, and lumber is its chief dividend.

ALONG THE C. & O. UP BIG SANDY

In the last four years this road has been extended into Breathitt County, making it about thirty miles in length. Principal stations are Dawkins, Johnson, Blair, Denver, Swamp Branch, Riceville, Ivyton, and Royalton.

NARROW-GAUGE ROADS

Two narrow-gauge railroads have been built in the county, but are now a thing of the past. One was constructed from Offutt and extended up Greasy and Two-Mile creeks to reach the cannel coal mines at Williamsport. The other was a lumber road with its terminus also at Offutt and extended up Greasy Creek and over on Rockcastle Creek in Martin County. The first was built thirty-odd years ago, and the latter about twenty years. Their source of supplies exhausted, they discontinued to operate about 1920 and the tracks have been taken up.

ROADS AND HIGHWAYS

From the very first, the mightiest of all religions went forward upon the highways of travel. The Appian Way, most famous of Roman highways, was called by Horace Bushnell "the Queen of Roads." In establishing Christianity Paul and other early Christians made great one of the famous twenty-nine military roads radiating from Rome. "And so we came to Rome . . . the brethren . . . . came to meet us as far as the Market of Appius." And it came to pass that Rome, having the greatest road, built later the greatest church, St. Peter's. Or, in other words, the greatest church built at the end of the greatest highway.[22]

The history of roads in Eastern Kentucky is merely a repetition of that of any other region, and of all new territories. The "buffalo trace" became the "Indian path," and this in turn became the saddle road, which widened and grew into wagon roads, later to become hard-surfaced highways over which travel can now be seen steadily and constantly rolling.[26]

The first known trail in the Big Sandy, which in reality was more of a path meandering with the streams and ridges, was the immigrant trail of the early home-seekers and adventurers that left the Wilderness Road in Virginia, and following up the Clinch, Powell, Holston, and New rivers, and over the heads of the Tug and Levisa forks, through the "Breaks" and Pound Gap and on down the Big Sandy to the Ohio. This later, through the acts of the Virginia and Kentucky legislatures, became the first turnpike in Eastern Kentucky, and known as the Virginia Road.

The next turnpike in that section was one from Mt. Sterling to the Big Sandy River, to connect with the Virginia Road. The legislative act to open this road was passed December 13, 1802. James Trotter, William Kelly, Richard Menifee, Joseph H. Davies, and Benjamin Howard were included as the commissioners to open it.

Following closely on this, another act was passed February 4, 1817, to open a turnpike from Mt. Sterling via Prestonsburg to the State line and Cumberland Mountain. Alex Lackey, John Jameson, and Daniel Peyton were named as commissioners. It evidently took several years to establish this road, as many acts were passed in succeeding legislatures regarding it. The Floyd County Court order books have several orders with reference to it,

BRIDGE ON THE MILLER'S CREEK RAILROAD
OVER THE BIG SANDY AT VAN LEAR, KY.

INDUSTRIAL DEVELOPMENT 393

one of which was the appointment of Mason Williams as a commissioner on May 22, 1821.

In June, 1830, the County Court of Floyd County passed an order establishing a road from Prestonsburg via Paintsville to Little Sandy Salt Works, which also had a number of orders about it later. Coaches and chariots, carriages of two and four wheels, and horseback were the methods of transportation over these roads in those days.[24]

With the exception of one other road leading up Licking River, and thence to the Big Sandy, the above-mentioned roads constituted the main public highways of Eastern Kentucky until the State primary system of roads was adopted in 1920.

Each county court, acting on the request of a few citizens, continually added local roads within the county. Two-thirds of all orders passed by these courts pertained to roads which, not being indexed, are very confusing to researchers in going through the order books. Upon request, some three respectable persons were appointed to view and lay out the desired road, which usually followed the creek bed or meandered with the contours of the hills to avoid all good lands suitable for cultivation. If the commissioners reported favorably to the next court, a surveyor, at that time meaning a foreman or overseer, was appointed to call on all the hands in his community to aid in opening the road. All roads were constructed in this way previous to 1920 and the result was a narrow wagon trail that could be used about two-thirds of the year.

These roads served the people for many years during the period of the sled, wagon, and buggy, but with the coming of the Ford, conditions changed considerably. People began to realize the advantages of improved roads in transportation, marketing farm products, bettering living and working conditions, increasing value of real estate, offering recreational opportunities and a wider view of life, with the result that the better road sentiment is unanimous.

Not much can be said of these early wagon trails for all of them were earth, very narrow, with poor grades and alignment, and in the spring after heavy rains, transportation was almost impossible, except by horseback or two-mule teams hauling a small load in a wagon. And it is with regret that some roads up the smaller valleys and less populated places are still in this condition and will be for some time to come, as it will not be feasible to improve all of them.

The order books of Johnson County Court are full of the establishment of these different dirt roads, too numerous to mention. Next are given the legislative acts pertaining to roads in general in the county:

Chapter 807, Page 471, Acts 1856.

AN ACT for the protection of the public roads in Johnson County.

"Be it enacted by the General Assembly of the Commonwealth of Kentucky, That any person or persons in the counties of Lawrence, Johnson, Floyd or Pike, who shall haul saw-logs or other timber, or cause the same to be done, on any of the public roads in either of the counties aforesaid, and shall by said hauling, injure, damage, or render the same more difficult of travel, shall within twenty days repair the same, so as to leave said road in as good order as when said hauling was commenced; and for said failure, he or they so offending shall pay a fine of not less than five dollars, nor more than twenty dollars, to be recovered by warrant before a justice of the peace, in the county and district in which said offense was committed, or by presentment of the grand jury; and all of said fine shall be turned over to the county judge to be applied to the improvement of the public roads in said county."

Approved March 10, 1856.

Chapter 1100, Page 533, Acts 1884.

AN ACT to create the office of road commissioner.

An act was passed and approved April 24, 1884, creating the office of road commissioner in the county, to be appointed by the Governor, and to hold office for terms of four years. There are seven sections to this act.

Chapter 18, Page 314, Acts 1886.

AN ACT regulating the jurisdiction of justices of the peace.

"Be it enacted by the General Assembly of the Commonwealth of Kentucky, That the justices of the peace of Floyd and Johnson counties shall have concurrent jurisdiction with the county courts of said counties over all failures to work upon the public roads, as now provided for by general laws.

"2. All acts and parts of acts inconsistent with the provisions of section one of this act are hereby repealed.

"3. This act shall take effect and be in force from and after its passage."

Approved January 20, 1886.

Chapter 379, Page 979, Acts 1886.

AN ACT passed and approved March 23, 1886, for the working of persons committed to the custody of the jailor. Also allowing the jailor to place said persons in ball and chain, for disobedience. This act was amended March 24, 1888 (see Chapter 640, Page 382), to allow their being worked on the public roads, street or alley, provided the person was a resident of the county at the time he was tried.

Chapter 1044, Page 81, Acts 1888.

AN ACT to amend the act providing for the appointment of road commissioner, repealing sections two and three of the original act, and extending his supervision, and defining his duties regarding contracts, reports, and salary.

Chapter 1445, Page 510, Acts 1890.

AN ACT passed and approved May 12, 1890, amending the act regarding the working of prisoners on the roads, so that a road surveyor may not have to work but give bond instead; and that persons may be worked in any district that is specified by the county clerk.

Chapter 931, Page 1040, Acts 1890.

AN ACT was passed and approved April 19, 1890, submitting to the voters of the county, a road law, to be voted on in the August election of that year. This was a very lengthy act, containing between four and five thousand words, and too voluminous to be included here. Its general provisions are given below.

It authorized the dividing of each magisterial district into road precincts; provided for the appointment of a surveyor or overseer for each district to hold for a term of two years, and for the clerk to purchase a book in which to keep the boundaries of the precincts, the name of the surveyor and dates of his term of office; named the duties of the surveyor, and the duties of the clerk and sheriff regarding the appointment of the surveyor; provided for the filling of vacancies; stated who was liable to work the road (all male persons between the ages of sixteen and fifty years, except ministers of the gospel and persons exempted by the county court due to physical condition), for how long, when (ten days, of eight hours each, in each calendar year, if that amount were necessary), the time and place to meet, tools to bring, and that notice of three days would be given in advance, and a certificate giving the time the hand worked afterward. It further provided for punishment by fine for failure to work as notified, the obtaining of teams by the surveyor, the obtaining of material from the adjoining landowner, the duties of the county judge. the widening of roads (not to exceed fifty feet), the opening of new roads (at the same time providing for the working of all those living within one-half mile of the proposed road in addition to the required ten days work), the crediting to his poll tax for work that a person may have done over the ten days, except for the opening of new roads, the marking of roads, the placing of indictments against road surveyors under the jurisdiction of the county court; fees of the justices of the peace and their duties in regard to the provisions of the act the working out of taxes on roads by delinquent tax-payers, the keeping of a separate "Road Fund" by the county treasurer to be paid out only on order of the county judge or one of the surveyors, and fines for those obstructing the public roads. It also provided that no person should be required to work more than two days in any one week, except delinquent tax-payers, or on any election day; that chapter ninety-four of the General Statutes apply to all cases not included in said act; and that all existing laws in conflict, as well as the act creating the office of road commissioner, be repealed.

Another act authorizing the printing of two hundred copies of the county's road laws was passed and approved May 3, 1890. (See Page 102, Acts 1890.)

This road law is still in effect, but is not enforced to any extent.

Until about 1900 or 1901 there was not a foot of paving or surfaced road in Johnson County, even in the town of Paintsville. In the summer citizens of the town even were choked with dust, and in winter the streets resembled a hog wallow of mud, requiring four strong horses to draw an ordinary load. A few of the public-spirited citizens recognized the disadvantages accruing by reason of the town's unpaved, muddy streets, and agitation for paving was started which finally resulted in the streets being paved with vitrified brick, from Main to Third Street, north and south, and from Bristlebuck to Grabnickle, east and west. In 1913 paving was extended through Bristlebuck and Grabnickle by the Sam Collier Paving Company, of Ashland, and in 1925 more outlying streets were completed with rock asphalt surfacing by a Mr. Black of Frankfort, and in 1926 all remaining streets and most of the alleys were concreted by E. J. Knepfle's Sons, giving Paintsville more pavement than any town, population considered, in Eastern Kentucky, and possibly than any in the State.

Nothing was done toward improving the roads of the county, until what was known as the Old State-Aid System was passed in 1914. Under this law the State sent inspectors to the county in 1915 and 1916-17 and the roads from Paintsville toward Dawkins and Thealka were partially improved and graded.

THE MAYO TRAIL

Section 5, Chapter 17, Page 87, Acts 1920.

"A primary system of State highways is hereby established which will give to each county in the State at least one main thoroughfare and the roads thus established as a system of primary roads shall be as follows:

"Project No. 6—From Ashland to Pineville, via Catlettsburg, Louisa, Paintsville, Prestonsburg, Pikeville, Whitesburg, and Harlan."

After the death of John C. C. Mayo in the spring of 1914, a meeting of leading citizens of the Big Sandy was called and assembled in Paintsville for the purpose of naming something in his honor that would forever perpetuate his name. As a consequence, the great and main highway up the Big Sandy, which later became Kentucky State Project No. 6 of the primary system of highways and referred to in the last-named act, and United States Route No. 23 of federal roads, was designated to bear the name of Eastern Kentucky's greatest financier, and is now called the Mayo Trail.

"Here we pause to pay tribute to the man whose spirit vanished in the prime of his greatest activities, the man from whom this trail derives its name, the man whose generous spirit, irresistible determination and unaltered purpose spoke and unlimited riches pursued him, the man whose courage and matchless energy gripped the hands of timid capital and eastern syndicates, the man who led men of his own type into this valley of industrial dry bones, the man whose skill and efficiency laid the cornerstone of development and the foundation of every commercial enterprise from the Ohio River to the Cumberland, the man whose accomplishments in finance and educational institutions would build a city in itself, the man whose mere personality and faith moved a child mountain and unlocked the resources and riches of the land which he loved—the man who triumphed gloriously over every opposition which he met in the way. His name in itself is an inspiration and stands out like the Flaglers of Florida who built Miami, and Yahn of Oregon who built the Columbia Highway and graced the city of Portland with a four-square skyscraper which bears his name. So, also, the last vision which materialized in the fertile brain of this financial genius was that of the trail which he saw not with the natural eye. To this name, we the people of the Big Sandy Valley and the Cumberland pay our deepest and most sincere respects in memory of the man who stands uppermost in the hearts of the people, who bore every evidence of charity, the greatest of gifts from a divine standpoint. He gave abundantly and freely unto all who came."[25]

This highway begins at Ashland in Boyd County at the mouth of Big Sandy and runs a southerly course to Pound Gap at the head of the river at the Virginia state line, branching also at Jenkins by way of Whitesburg and Harlan to Pineville where it connects with the Dixie Highway. It passes through Boyd, Lawrence, Johnson, Floyd, Pike, Letcher, Harlan and Bell counties, touching the county-seat towns of Catlettsburg, Louisa, Paintsville, Prestonsburg, Pikeville, Whitesburg, Harlan, and Pineville.

The tourist in Kentucky has not seen Kentucky until he has traversed some of the finished portions of the Mayo Trail, where the State is chiseling, from the rocks of the hills and cliffsides, a great highway, 250 miles in length, through a section until recently impassable to automobiles.

The trail is perfect for travel during the summer months, and is much used by the people of Eastern Kentucky. Grading and drainage has been completed along its entire route with the exception of small stretches in Floyd, Pike, Letcher, and Harlan counties. Hard-surfacing has been completed in Boyd and Bell counties, and partially completed in Harlan and Johnson counties, with all bridges completed or under construction.

The progress of State and federal construction on the Mayo Trail to date is outlined below:

The survey from the Lawrence County line at Lowmansville to Paintsville was made by the State Highway Department, and paid for by Johnson County, in the fall of 1922. J. S. Bentley was in charge of the locating party.

The contract for building the same stretch of road of 11.275 miles as Grade and Drain was awarded to M. A. Wheeler, of Knoxville, Tennessee, on May 14, 1923, at an estimated price of $212,189.32 with the time of completion to be by June 14, 1924. Many delays were encountered and it was not completed until September 16, 1926, at a total cost of $253,368.19, less engineering and contingencies which when added made a final estimate of $270,510.77. The grading and draining of this project was officially known as State Project No. 6-A, and Federal Aid Project No. 77.

The road from the Floyd County line at East Point to Paintsville, officially known as State Project No. 6-B, was surveyed also by J. S. Bentley, in May, 1920. Failing to get the promise from the State Highway Commission for an early letting on this road, the county, with aid from the town of Paintsville and local subscriptions, constructed a 20-foot concrete road in the fall of 1923 on the stretch from the Big Paint Creek bridge to the Chesapeake and Ohio depot.

This road was paved by contractors of Covington, Kentucky, and was under the direct supervision of Stanley Temple and W. D. Auxier, of Paintsville. The remainder of this highway, 5.289 miles, was let to contract August 5, 1924, and awarded to Walton, Suddith, Waugh Company of West Virginia at an estimated price of $106,382.41. It was completed as a grade and drain project January 15, 1927, with a total cost of $112,760.16.

The completion of this road finished the grading and draining of the Mayo Trail all the way across the county. Although it was much used by the Big Sandy people, it could not be traveled to

CONCRETE BRIDGE ON THE MAYO TRAIL ON TOM'S CREEK

THE MAYO TRAIL NEAR PAINTSVILLE, KY.

any advantage during the winter months till it was hard-surfaced. This was begun in the summer of 1927. State Project No. 6-D, from Paintsville to Turner's Branch, a distance of 1.342 miles, was awarded to the Hatfield Construction Company of Huntington, West Virginia, at an estimated cost of $37,799.79. This stretch of reinforced concrete road was completed and opened to traffic in October, 1927.

State Project No. 6-C, from the Paintsville depot to Dawkins, a distance of 1.445 miles, was awarded to the same firm at the same time for $46,975.83, using reinforced concrete, but work was not begun till in September which was completed in December, 1927.

THE GARRETT HIGHWAY

Section 5, Chapter 17, Page 87, Acts 1920.

"A primary system of State highways is hereby established which will give to each county in the State at least one main thoroughfare and the roads thus established as a system of primary roads shall be as follows:

"Project No. 34—From Paintsville to Salyersville."

Amended February 29, 1924, Chapter 171, Page 516, Acts 1924, to read as follows:

"Project 34—From Paintsville to Salyersville, and then from Paintsville through Martin County, to or near the mouth of Wolfe Creek on the Kentucky-West Virginia State line, by way of Inez, Himlerville, and Warfield."

Equally important as the Mayo Trail to the Sandy Valley, especially to those south of Paintsville, is the Garrett Highway, named for Honorable Green Garrett, chairman of the Kentucky State Highway Commission from 1920-1924, running from Mt. Sterling in Montgomery County where it connects with the Midland Trail, passing through Montgomery, Menifee, Morgan, Magoffin, Johnson and Martin counties, connecting towns of Mt. Sterling, Frenchburg, West Liberty, Salyersville, Paintsville and Inez, intersecting with West Virginia State Route No. 8, at Kermit, which affords another outlet for the Big Sandy over paved roads to all sections. At Mt. Sterling this highway gives Eastern Kentucky another outlet to all sections of Kentucky and on to the south. It furnishes a shorter route for the upper Big Sandians to the Bluegrass, and to Lexington and Louisville.

This route is also noted for its scenic beauty. Passing through both the lowland or Bluegrass section and the highlands, any tourist is delighted with the changing scenery. The building of this main highway from the Bluegrass to the hills, or mountains, as some outsiders take pleasure in calling them, has gradually eliminated the prejudice that once existed between the two sections.

The greater part of the Garrett Highway has been graded. A stretch in Magoffin and Morgan counties is now under construction and will be completed by the fall of 1928. One piece of road in Johnson County from the mouth of Buffalo Creek to the Martin County line is the only ungraded section. Grading was begun on this section in 1928. Martin County has completed grading from Inez to the Johnson County line, and has under construction from Inez to the West Virginia state line.

The Garrett Highway is officially known as State Project No. 32 from Mt. Sterling to West Liberty, as No. 28 from West Liberty to Salyersville, and as No. 34 from there to the West Virginia line.

Construction progress through Johnson County is as follows: The section from the Magoffin County line to intersect the Mayo Trail near Paintsville, officially known as State Project No. 34-A, and Federal Aid Project No. 76, was surveyed first by I. C. Jolly in 1920, and revised by J. S. Bentley, in June, 1922, both locating engineers of the State Highway Department but paid by the county. The contract for grading was let to the Dempster Construction Company of Knoxville, Tennessee, August 16, 1922, at a contract price of $161,318.05 and completion to be by June 1, 1924. It was actually completed December 1, 1924, with a final estimate of $264,524.13, which did not include engineering and contingencies. This added, made a total cost of $287,270.32 not including the bridge over Big Paint Creek at the mouth of Barnetts Creek, which cost $13,876.09.

The next section from Paintsville to the Martin County line, known as State Project No. 34-C and Federal Aid Project No. 139 A-C, was surveyed by J. C. St. Clair for the Highway Department at the expense of the county, in September, 1924.

One stretch of this road from the bridge over the Big Sandy River to the mouth of Buffalo Creek, a distance of 1.747 miles, was awarded for grading to the Sutton Construction Company of Ashland, Kentucky, August 25, 1925, for $36,096.46. It was completed August 19, 1926, at a cost of $36,635.56. The bridge over the Big Sandy was built by the Champion Bridge Company in 1921, for $50,000.00 and paid for by the county, but to apply on the county's share of expense in completing the rest of the road.

Two contracts for surfacing on the Garrett Highway have been let in the county by the State Highway Commission. The first on State Project No. 34-B from Turner Branch to the mouth of Mud Lick Creek, a distance of 2.092 miles. It was let and contracted as reinforced concrete to the Hatfield Construction Company, of Huntington, West Virginia, in July, 1927, at an estimated price of $55,780.28, and was completed in October of the same year.

ALONG THE GARRETT HIGHWAY IN JOHNSON COUNTY

The remainder of the highway from Paintsville to the Magoffin County line, a distance of 7.352 miles, known as State Project No. 34-D, was awarded for traffic-bound sandstone to the Wilmore Construction Company of Wilmore, Kentucky, in September, 1927, for $39,305.20.

OTHER JOHNSON COUNTY ROADS ON THE PRIMARY SYSTEM THAT HAVE NOT RECEIVED STATE AID

Page 954, Chapter 252, Acts 1926.

"Be it enacted by the General Assembly of the Commonwealth of Kentucky, That there is hereby established as a part of the primary system of highways in this Commonwealth the following route, to-wit:

"From the depot in White House, Johnson County, Kentucky, going up Lick Creek a distance of two or two and one-half miles to the head of Lick Creek, intersecting with the Garrett State Highway."

This road is officially known as State Project No. 184.

Page 994, Chapter 315, Acts 1926.

"Be it enacted by the General Assembly of the Commonwealth of Kentucky, That there be and there is established as a part of the primary road system of the Commonwealth of Kentucky the following to be designated as Project No. 32 from Paintsville, Johnson County, Kentucky, to West Liberty, Morgan County, Kentucky, as follows: Beginning at the mouth of Mud Lick Branch at the point of intersection with Project No. 34, thence up Mud Lick Creek by way of Red Bush post office and Relief post office; then by Elk Fork and Licking River to West Liberty."

This project is officially known as State Project No. 183.

Senate Bill No. 45—January 31, 1928.

AN ACT establishing a State primary road project leading from Paintsville, Johnson County, to Royalton, Magoffin County.

"Be it enacted by the General Assembly of the Commonwealth of Kentucky, That there is hereby established and created as a part of the primary system of the State highways of the Commonwealth of Kentucky a road beginning at Paintsville at or near the Paintsville National Bank; thence bridging Paint Creek to Henclip; thence up the same and through a low gap to Jennies Creek; thence up Jennies Creek to the forks; thence up the right-hand fork of Jennies Creek via Denver, via Riceville, to Royalton, Magoffin County.

"Subject to all the conditions set out provided for in Chapter 17 of the Acts of the General Assembly of the Commonwealth of

HISTORY OF JOHNSON COUNTY

Kentucky, establishing and creating a primary system of State highways."

Senate Bill No. 108—January 31, 1928.

AN ACT to establish a State Primary Road Project from Project No. 34 near Paintsville, in Johnson County, Kentucky, via Davis Branch and the Big Sandy River to intersection of State Highway Project Nos. 39 and 195.

"Be it enacted by the General Assembly of the Commonwealth of Kentucky, That the road leading from a point in State Highway Project No. 34 approximately one-half mile east of Paintsville, in Johnson County, and running thence southeastwardly, via Davis Branch, lower Van Lear, and Big Sandy River to mouth of John's Creek, and up said John's Creek, to the intersection of State Highway Project Nos. 39 and 195, approximately .... miles in length. be and the same is hereby established and designated as a part of the primary system of State highways of the Commonwealth of Kentucky.

"That the construction, maintenance, supervision and control of said road shall be subject to all the terms and conditions as set out and provided for in Chapter 17, Acts of the General Assembly of 1920, establishing and creating a primary system of State highways."

House Bill No. 52—January 11, 1928.

AN ACT establishing a road project from the Mayo Trail, via White House depot so as to intersect with the Garrett Highway, Project No. 34, at the head of Lick Creek.

"Be it enacted by the General Assembly of the Commonwea'th of Kentucky, That the following road be added to the primary system of roads, beginning at the Mayo Trail at the mouth of the Harrison Young Branch in Lawrence County, thence up said branch to the gap at Dave Chandlers, thence to the head of the Muddy Gut Creek, thence down said creek to Big Sandy River, thence up said river to a point known as the County Road Fork opposite the upper end of the Chesapeake and Ohio depot, thence crossing said river by bridge to Chesapeake and Ohio depot, thence down said river to the mouth of White House Creek, thence running up said creek with the old railroad bed to the forks, thence up the right-hand fork of said creek so as to connect with Project No. 34, the Garrett Highway, at the head of Lick Creek, that the construction, maintenance, supervision, and control of said road shall be subject to all the terms and conditions as set out and provided for in Chapter 17, Acts of the General Assembly of 1920, establishing and creating a primary system of State highways."

THREE IN ONE
The Mayo Trail, The C. & O. Railroad, and the Big Sandy River Near Paintsville

INDUSTRIAL DEVELOPMENT 411

House Bill No. 53—January 11, 1928.

AN ACT establishing and making the road beginning at the Mayo Trail, Project No. ...., at the Walker place in Johnson County and extending via Sitka and Sip, Kentucky, to Project No. 49 in Lawrence County, a part of the primary system of the State highways of the Commonwealth of Kentucky and designating said road as Project No. ....

"Be it enacted by the General Assembly of the Commonwealth of Kentucky, That the road leading from the Mayo Trail, Project No. ...., at the Walker place in Johnson County on the Rush Fork of Tom's Creek and extending up Rush Fork and down Goose Creek to Sitka, thence via Sip, Hood's Fork Creek to intersect State Highway Project No. 49 at Blaine in Lawrence County, Kentucky, be and the same is hereby established as a part of the principal system of State highways of the Commonwealth of Kentucky and the construction, maintenance, supervision, and contract of said road shall be subject to all the terms and conditions set out and provided for in Chapter 17, Page 76, of the Acts of 1920, establishing and creating a principal system of State highways."

Said road shall be designated as Project No.——.

House Bill No. 54—Wednesday, January 11, 1928 (same as Senate Bill No. 45).

House Bill No. 56—Wednesday, January 11, 1928 (same as Senate Bill No. 108).

House Bill No. 300—January 24, 1928.

AN ACT relating to roads and highways and establishing Road Project No. .... as a part of the primary road system of the State, said road project beginning near the Oil Springs post office and running to Riceville, and designating said road as State Project No. ....

"Be it enacted by the General Assembly of the Commonwealth of Kentucky, That there be and is hereby established as a part of the primary system of State highways, a road beginning at the Garrett Highway, near Oil Springs post office, thence running a southeastern direction up Little Paint Creek, passing Ballot post office, to the head of Green Rock Fork; thence down Green Rock Fork to Riceville, a station on the Big Sandy and Kentucky River Railway. Said road being approximately five and one-half miles long, and that same shall be designated as Road Project No. ...."

House Bill No. 710—February 28, 1928.

AN ACT to establish a road on the primary system of public highways from Project No. 34 at the Lick Gap in Johnson County, Kentucky, thence out the ridge to the gap at the head of Trace Fork at the Martin County line, then down Trace Fork to Rock House Creek, thence down Rock House Creek intersecting with Project No. 34 near Tomahawk, Martin County, Kentucky.

"Be it enacted by the General Assembly of the Commonwealth of Kentucky, That there be and is hereby a road project established on the system of public highways leading from Project No. 34 at Lick Gap via Trace Gap down Trace Creek to Rock House Creek; thence down Rock House Creek so as to intersect with Project No. 34 at or near Tomahawk, Martin County, Kentucky.

"That the construction, maintenance and supervision and control of said road shall be subject to all the terms and conditions as set out and provided for in Chapter 17, Acts of the General Assembly of 1920, establishing and creating a primary system of State highways."

A tabulation of all highway construction and maintenance costs expended by the county, State, and federal governments in road improvement in Johnson County is given herewith. It does not include costs of right of way and surveys which were paid for by the county.

It can be seen from the table of expenditures that completed construction cost $721,348.68 of which the county only put up $155,500.00. This was all contracted under the administration of Judge Beecher Stapleton, who was judge of the county from 1922 to 1926, and no doubt the greatest sponsor of good roads that the county has ever had. Although he met with continual right-of-way troubles and opposition from a public uneducated to good roads, he kept everlastingly at it, and the following report is evidence of his labors as a good-roads official:

JUDGE BEECHER STAPLETON
County Judge of Johnson County 1922-1926

TABULATION OF STATE HIGHWAY CONSTRUCTION AND MAINTENANCE

Johnson County

As of March 1, 1928

Completed Construction

Project No.	Length	Type	From	To	Actual Total Cost	County Exp.
FA 76	9.288	G & D	Magoffin County Line	Turner Branch	$301,146.41	$ 50,000.00
FA 77	11.275	G & D	Paintsville	Lawrence County Line	270,510.77	65,000.00
FA 139-A	1.747	G & D	Paintsville	Buffalo Creek	36,635.56	20,000.00
FA 139-B	(Engineering charges on proposed extension toward Inez)				295.78	
SP 6-B	5.272	G & D	East Point	Paintsville Depot	112,760.16	20,500.00
	27.582			Sub Total........	$721,348.68	$155,500.00

Projects Under Construction

Project No.	Length	Type	From	To	Estimated Total	Cost
SP 6-C	1.445	Rein. Con.	Dawkins	Paintsville Depot	$ 46,975.83	$ 126,196.25
SP 6-D	1.342	Rein. Con.	Paintsville	Turner Branch	37,799.79	
SP 34-B	2.092	Rein. Con.	Turner Branch	Mud Lick Creek	55,780.28	
SP 34-D	7.352	T. B. Sand.	Magoffin County Line	Mud Lick Creek	39,305.20	39,305.20
FA 139-C	9.873	G & D	Buffalo Creek	Martin County Line	204,847.91	20,000.00*
				Sub Total........	$384,709.01	$ 185,501.45
						1,106,057.69
Total actual and estimated construction..................						12,733.08
Total actual maintenance costs..................						
Grand Total Construction and Maintenance........						$1,118,790.77

*Also Credited with Bridge for $50,000.00.

Of course he had to have the co-operation of State officials to accomplish what he did, and in this respect due consideration is given to Mr. Green Garrett while chairman of the Highway Commission, and to Former Governor Wm. J. Fields, who was Eastern Kentucky's greatest friend to date as an official.

Judge Stapleton's successor, John W. Butcher, has kept up the work, but the county has had to advance most of the money expended under his administration for road purposes. This, however, was advanced on a guarantee of the Highway Commission of $3.00 for every one dollar put up by the county, which when fulfilled will give the county approximately an additional $450,000.00 worth of roads.

To finance the county's share of this road expense, Johnson County has floated two bond issues. The first for $200,000.00 was voted in 1920 and the second of $150,000.00 was voted by a majority of 16 to 1 in December, 1926.

When the highway system for Eastern Kentucky is completed, Paintsville, in the center of the Big Sandy Valley, will be the best served town in that section in the way of good roads. The Mayo Trail passes through the city running north and south while the Garrett Highway passes through east and west, which in a business way will mean much to the town.

BANKS

While this history is not intended to discuss or promote, in the way of advertisement, any business organization in the county, an account of the industrial development would not be complete without mentioning the two financial institutions of Paintsville, which have been very important in the development of Johnson County's resources.

With the development of the coal industry in the Big Sandy Valley, and the advent of railroads, new towns were quick to spring up, while the old ones took new life. It soon became apparent that banks were needed to care for the business of these growing communities and the others that would inevitably follow. Quick to see the need of the times, John C. C. Mayo, John E. Buckingham, and other pioneer leaders of that time, organized and established the Paintsville National Bank.

THE PAINTSVILLE NATIONAL BANK

The Paintsville National Bank, known through Eastern Kentucky as the "Old Reliable," was chartered by the Treasury Department January 20, 1902. It has had over twenty-five years of steadily increasing business, and today is one of the outstanding financial institutions of the whole State of Kentucky. At the close of business in December, 1927, the total assets of this solid financial institution were over two and one-half millions of dollars. The bank has been a leader in Eastern Kentucky commercial and financial affairs for over a quarter of a century, and has wisely and conservatively used its power for constructive development of the Big Sandy Valley.

When the bank began business in 1902, it had a capital of only $25,000.00. But, it was ably and conservatively and soundly managed. The organizers were Dan Davis, I. R. Turner, John C. C. Mayo, Dan M. Hager, Jno. H. Preston, Jas. D. Johnson, John E. Buckingham, and F. M. Williams. This group of men were leaders in their line, and stood out in the community as men of character and integrity, and immediately the bank held the abiding confidence of the community. There was no railroad in the valley then above White House. In the year of 1903, the active and sound development of the valley began. The Chesapeake and Ohio extended its line from White House to Elkhorn City to connect with the Carolina, Clinchfield, and Ohio Railroad, giving through transportation from the Ohio River to the South Atlantic Seaboard. In that year, the great coal resources of the valley were tapped, and millions of dollars poured into the valley for development. The Consolidation Coal Company, the Elkhorn Coal Corporation, the North-East Coal Company and a number of other strong developers came into the valley and began their work.

The Paintsville National Bank co-operated to the fullest with all of these agencies, and played a very important part in the program. So ably and conservatively and actively were its affairs managed that its business began to grow by leaps and bounds.

In November of 1903, to meet the requirements of the rapidly developing country, the capital of the bank was increased to $50,000.00. In March, 1904, the capital was again increased, this time to $100,000.00. In 1908, the business of the community had so expanded that the officers and directors of the bank felt that another increase should be made, and the capital was raised to $150,000.00. In June, 1910, the capital was increased to $175,000.00, and in April, 1913, another increase was made to $200,000.00.

In these various increases of capital stock, the bank added to its stockholders some of the most substantial business men of the entire Sandy Valley. The surplus of the bank grew steadily until it amounted to $200,000.00, giving the institution a working capital of $400,000.00.

The officers and stockholders of the bank are men of affairs, progressive, yet conservative, and have the confidence of the entire valley.

No bank, or commercial institution, can rise in success and service above the skill, knowledge, and ability of those who manage it. All through the years, the Paintsville National Bank has been in the hands of experienced bankers and business men who have succeeded in their own affairs, and have given unstintedly of their time and talent for the success and progress and safety of this reliable and progressive institution. The bank has been a powerful factor in progress and development, because the men behind it were men of vision and skilled in the handling of business affairs. In 1905, the bank built the commodious banking quarters in which it now conducts its business. At the time it was thought that this building would answer the requirements of any financial institution for at least fifty years. But the business of the bank has so grown and expanded that the directors purchased the lot at the corner of Main and College streets where sometime in the near future a new and modernly equipped banking house will be erected.

Below is given one of the statements of this bank which is an indication of the resources of this institution, in addition to the wealth of Johnson County.

Charter 6100   Reserve District No. 4

REPORT OF THE CONDITION OF THE PAINTSVILLE NATIONAL BANK IN THE STATE OF KENTUCKY, AT THE CLOSE OF BUSINESS ON DECEMBER 31, 1927

RESOURCES

Loans and discounts	$1,665,600.06
Overdrafts, unsecured	909.25
U. S. Government securities owned:	
Deposited to secure circulation $149,500.00	
All other United States Government securities 2,048.75	151,548.75
Other bonds, stocks, securities, etc., owned	228,369.97
Banking house, $10,620.00; furniture and fixtures, $9,208.39	19,828.39
Real estate owned other than banking house	25,000.00
Lawful reserve with Federal Reserve Bank	88,671.53
Cash in vault and amount due from national banks	260,226.00
Amount due from State banks, bankers, and trust companies in United States	20,435.93
Checks on other banks in the same city or town as reporting bank	14,573.78

(Total............$295,235.71)

Miscellaneous cash items	4,216.57
Redemption fund with United States Treasurer and due from United States Treasurer	10,000.00
United States Government securities borrowed	50,500.00
Other assets	6,032.74
Total	$2,545,912.97

LIABILITIES

Capital stock	$ 200,000.00
Surplus fund	200,000.00

JOHN E. BUCKINGHAM

Undivided profits	$30,722.42	
Reserved for dividends	20,000.00	$ 50,722.42
Circulating notes outstanding		193,200.00
Amount due to national banks		32,839.89
Amount due to State banks, bankers, and trust companies in the United States		5,818.40
Certified checks outstanding		1,747.64
Cashier's checks outstanding		6,685.25

(Total............$47,196.18)

Demand deposits subject to reserve:
Individual deposits subject to check	930,895.26
Certificates of deposit due in less than 30 days	35,399.45

(Total demand deposits............$996,294.71)

Time deposits subject to reserve—Savings deposits	837,220.09

(Total of time deposits subject to reserve............$837,220.09)

United States deposits, including War Loan deposit account and deposits of United States disbursing officers	779.57
United States Government securities borrowed	50,500.00
Total	$2,545,912.97

STATE OF KENTUCKY,
COUNTY OF JOHNSON, ss:

I, Jas. W. Turner, cashier of the above-named bank, do solemnly swear that the above statement is true to the best of my knowledge and belief.

JAS. W. TURNER,
Cashier.

Subscribed and sworn to before me this 8th day of January.

EXER ROBINSON,

Correct—Attest:

Notary Public.

J. H. HOLBROOK,
W. H. SLONE,
GEO. W. PRESTON,
Directors.

Other officers and directors, not included above, are John E. Buckingham, president; George W. Preston, vice-president; James W. Turner, H. LaViers, Harry Davis, and Paul B. Hall, directors; W. D. Spencer, assistant cashier; E. R. Ward, assistant cashier.

A commercial institution is known by those who manage it. In view of this fact, a statement is given below of those who have been at the helm of the Paintsville National Bank.

JOHN C. C. MAYO. "He was born, he lived, he died," all this can be said about any man, but more than this can be said, and is included in many places herein, about John C. C. Mayo. See pages 342, 399.

JOHN E. BUCKINGHAM. Closely associated as an intimate friend and in business with Mr. Mayo, was John E. Buckingham. Mr. Buckingham, a native of Johnson County, was one of the original organizers of the Paintsville National Bank. He was its cashier when the bank opened for business, and continued in different executive positions until 1917 when he was made president. Through his ability and influence his financial interests spread rapidly, and shortly thereafter he organized and established the First National Bank of Jenkins, the First National Bank of Fleming, the Bank of Wayland, the Beaver Valley State Bank at Weeksbury, and assisted in the reorganization of the Ashland National Bank, Ashland, Kentucky. Mr. Buckingham became, and still remains, the executive head of these institutions, which, linked together, comprise the strongest combination of financial resources in the State of Kentucky outside of Louisville.

Mr. Buckingham accomplished these achievements not by stepping on somebody's head, but by sheer merit. He is absolutely sincere in everything he does or says. When he says a thing he means it; there is no lip service with him. When he does a thing, he does it because he is thoroughly convinced that it is the right thing to do.

Loyalty, thoughtfulness, and friendliness are predominating traits of his character. Of all his excellent traits, the outstanding ones are his unselfishness and sincerity. However, this does not mean that he is not essentially a friendly man. He is very kind, and has the happy faculty, to an uncommon degree, of making friends and keeping them. He always is eager to be of service to his friends and his community, and he is never too busy or too tired to do a favor, or to go far out of his way to help in a more substantial manner. Many a man in the banking business has gotten his start through Mr. Buckingham. He is an exceptional man. For more of Mr. Buckingham's life see Section II.

JAMES W. TURNER. Mr. Turner, director and cashier of the Paintsville National Bank, is one of the largest stockholders in this institution, and for twenty-five years has given its affairs his best abilities. He is a native Big Sandian, having been born and reared in Paintsville, and loves the valley and its people. He is thoroughly familiar with the principles and practice of banking and is interested in other financial and business enterprises in Eastern Kentucky. Mr. Turner is closely identified with the business interests of the section, and in the development of the natural resources. Being a banker and therefore in close touch with commercial, industrial, financial and economic conditions, he has worked with laudable zeal and marked ability to develop these resources in Johnson and adjoining counties. He is possessed of a firm faith and confidence in the people in the county and in return they confide in him. Aside from his business responsibilities Mr. Turner devotes much of his time to every worthy cause looking toward the betterment of the people and the advancement of the city, county, and valley; in fact, everything that is for the ad-

JAMES W. TURNER

vancement of Eastern Kentucky finds a hearty response in Mr. Turner. He is recognized as one of Eastern Kentucky's leading citizens.

Mr. Turner's reputation as a level-headed business man and a general good-fellow is not confined to his native heath but he is well and favorably known throughout the State. Regardless of whether one calling on him may wear overalls or broadcloth he will always find a welcome smile and a warm handclasp in "Jim" Turner. He is a big man, but small enough to recognize and appreciate the people of his home and section.

Honest to the core, courageous to the limit, brilliant far beyond the capacity of most intellects, sympathetic in the extreme—admirable and lovable—that is James W. Turner.

THE SECOND NATIONAL BANK

The Second National Bank (formerly The Paintsville Bank and Trust Company) was established in 1910. It was first chartered as a State bank, and began business in an old building on the site of the present home. It met with success and soon started on a course of growth and progress; and its lack of facilities to care for the increasing demands upon its services made it apparent to its officers that new and enlarged banking quarters would be required to properly and efficiently handle the volume of business. To meet the needs, it was determined by the directors to erect a modern banking house. This building was completed several years ago, and is an accomplishment on the part of the officers.

In its new home the bank is adequately equipped to meet every demand for a town the size of Paintsville, and its facilities have been enlarged to care for any exigency that may arise.

Several men have been cashier of this bank, some of whom were Claude Buckingham, James Williams, Beecher Stapleton, Ray Turner, and D. H. Dorton, the present cashier.

On July 1, 1922, this institution was reorganized and the present management took charge of the bank. Below is a statement of the condition of the Paintsville Bank and Trust Company as of June 30, 1922, the date on which this change in control was made. H. S. Howes was president; C. T. Rule, vice-president; Ray Turner, cashier; and the directors were as follows: Dr. J. H. Holbrook, John E. Buckingham, H. LaViers, James W. Turner, C. T. Rule, Dr. G. V. Daniel, R. A. Patrick, Ray Turner, and H. S. Howes.

STATEMENT OF CONDITION OF PAINTSVILLE BANK AND TRUST COMPANY, AS OF JUNE 30, 1922

ASSETS

Loans and discounts	$319,842.26
Bonds and securities	12,820.51
Real estate, banking house and furniture and fixtures	21,123.92
Other assets	67.70
Cash in vault and due from banks	29,585.06
Total	$383,439.45

LIABILITIES

Capital stock	$ 50,000.00
Surplus fund	10,000.00
Undivided profits	4,304.08
Bills payable and rediscounts	30,952.18
Deposits	288,030.90
Other liabilities	152.29
Total	$383,439.45

As a State bank and under the former managements, the Second National Bank was a growing institution, but its greatest growth has been reported since the present management took charge of affairs.

On January 3, 1927, this financial institution changed from a State bank to a national bank and its growth since has been in keeping with the territory. It is a progressive business, managed by progressive men. The directors are composed of some of the best and most responsible business and professional men in the county. They are: C. T. Rule, G. H. Rice, W. B. Bailey, W. S. Wheeler, R. A. Patrick, G. V. Daniel, and W. H. Conley. The officers are: C. T. Rule, president; G. H. Rice, vice-president; D. H. Dorton, cashier, and Frank Chandler, assistant cashier.

Following is a statement of this bank as of December 31, 1927. Compare this with the one of June 30, 1922, and note how it is growing.

Charter No. 13023   Reserve District No. 4

REPORT OF CONDITION OF THE SECOND NATIONAL BANK AT PAINTSVILLE, IN THE STATE OF KENTUCKY, AT THE CLOSE OF BUSINESS ON DECEMBER 31, 1927

RESOURCES

Loans and discounts		$500,069.43
Overdrafts, secured		109.95
Other bonds, stocks, securities, etc., owned		178,502.88
Banking house	$19,655.80	
Furniture and fixtures	4,457.35	24,113.15
Lawful reserve with Federal Reserve Bank		37,101.32
Cash in vault and amount due from national banks		37,686.00

D. H. DORTON
Cashier of the Second National Bank, Paintsville, Ky.

Amount due from State banks, bankers, and trust companies in
United States ....$ 62,339.91
Checks on other banks in the same city or town as reporting bank   6,631.16
Total of Items 9, 10, 11, 12, and 13... 106,657.07

Total $848,250.22

LIABILITIES

Capital stock paid in ....$ 75,000.00
Surplus fund 40,000.00
Undivided profits 2,893.06
Certified checks outstanding 123.28
Cashier's checks outstanding 17,932.10
    (Total............$22,555.38)
Demand deposits (other than bank deposits) subject to reserve.... 409,078.66
Certificates of deposit due in less than 30 days...................   2,450.00
State, county, or other municipal deposits secured by pledge of
assets of this bank or surety bond...   6,073.28
    (Reserve............$417,601.94)
Savings deposits (including time certificates of deposit other than
for money borrowed) $290,199.84

Total $848,250.22

STATE OF KENTUCKY,
 COUNTY OF JOHNSON, ss:

 I, D. H. Dorton, cashier of the above bank, do solemnly swear that the above statement is true to the best of my knowledge and belief.

              D. H. DORTON,
                    Cashier.

 Subscribed and sworn to before me this 5th day of January, 1928.

             FRANK CHANDLER,
                   Notary Public.

Correct Attest:
    C. T. RULE,
    W. B. BAILEY,
    G. H. RICE.

REFERENCES TO CHAPTER XI

[1] The Paintsville Herald, December 20, 1923.
[2] Ely, William, The Big Sandy Valley, page 309, 1887.
[3] NeeKamp, C. J., Article in The Paintsville Herald, March 10, 1927.
[4] Ibid.
[5] Taken in part from "An Appreciation of John C. C. Mayo," by C. W. Watson and J. H. Wheelwright, Louisville (Ky.) Post, May 18, 1914.
[6] For more of the life of John C. C. Mayo, see page 399 herein. Also the Price family.
[7] Written by Ralph Stafford in The Paintsville Herald, March 10, 1927.
[8] Jillson, W. R., Oil and Gas Resources of Kentucky, page 4, The State Journal Co., Frankfort, Ky., 1920.
[9] Ibid, page 5.
[10] Written by David Browning in The Paintsville Herald, December 20, 1923.
[11] Registrar of the Kentucky Historical Society.
[12] See the map of the Structural Geology of Johnson County as issued by the Kentucky Geological Survey, 1921.
[13] Oil and Gas Resources, Industrial Review, The Paintsville Herald.
[14] Ibid.
[15] Ely, William. The Big Sandy Valley, pages 322 and 326, 1887.
[16] The Truth about Kentucky, Department of Agriculture, Frankfort, pages 119 and 121, 1924-25.
[17] Ibid, page 190.
[18] Ely, William, The Big Sandy Valley, page 316, 1887.
[19] Daniel, M. D., C. & O. Employes Magazine. Also Paintsville Herald, October, 1927.
[20] Ibid.
[21] Ibid.
[22] Roberts, Dorothy Louise, Harlan, Ky. The Influence of Highway Transportation upon the Religious Life of the Community.
[23] Industrial Review, The Paintsville Herald.
[24] Jillson, W. R., The Big Sandy Valley, page 128, J. P. Morton & Co., Louisville, Ky., 1923.
[25] Layne, John S., Article in The Paintsville Herald, 6-23-27.

CHAPTER XII
HISTORIES AND PUBLICATIONS

History may be called the most neglected of the sciences. Industry has provided for the development of physics and chemistry and in its large, well-equipped laboratories great men have been produced. Various foundations have fostered the increase in knowledge in biology, pathology, and medicine and every facility is offered the researcher in his valuable study of life, of disease, and its cure.

The historian is left to grope alone. He is a kind of step-child of the sciences, due to the fact that history has no motive power of its own, will not cure a disease, and will not provide bumper crops. But it has a motivating force on humanity. The light of the past is a guide to the future. The civic ills of other times may be avoided by its study. It is a food of a mental kind, the knowledge and experience of former generations.

Kentuckians know too little of Kentucky history. Kentucky lore is learned pleasingly from study of what the early Kentuckians used in their work and their play. Appreciation of what the forefathers had to contend with, what they contrived for their use and amusement in a pioneer setting, is of value to the older and younger Kentuckians.

Through the influence of the increasing historical societies the public is cultivating a taste for popular literature. They are demanding thoughtful fiction of the better sort, works on travel, and especially books dealing with history and biography.

While there have been many good histories issued of the Bluegrass section of Kentucky, very few have been published of Eastern Kentucky.

The first of any importance was *The Big Sandy Valley*, by William Ely, published through the co-operation of Zephaniah Meek in 1887. This was a history of families and individuals from their entrance into the valley up to 1887 together with the times and customs through that period. A book of 500 pages embellished with occasional illustrations, the history is a valued possession. Its author, once editor of the Weekly Progress, was an interesting writer and spent a number of years in writing the history, traveling throughout the valley, much of it on horseback, to gather data.

Unlike most histories, *The Big Sandy Valley* does not give events in chronological order, nor does it relate the history of the people collectively, or politically, but rather does it give a personal history of the people of the valley and their achievements individually, serving to keep alive the valley's early history, and at the same time, interesting intimate personal touches on the lives of our forebears, the pioneer settlers.[1]

It was printed by the Central Methodist Press of Catlettsburg, and although more of a genealogy than a history, it was a wonderful publication for that time. The printing and binding would compare with modern work. A few copies of this book may still be had from Davis Meek, Catlettsburg, Kentucky, for $1.50 each.

Several brief sketches have been prepared annually for the official publication of the Kentucky Department of Agriculture. One of the best of these was prepared by John C. C. Mayo in 1900. It is included herein under the chapter "Times and Customs."

The Founding of Harman's Station, by William Elsey Connelley was the next narrative of importance. It was published in 1910 and describes at length the founding of this early settlement, and gives an account of the Indian captivity of Mrs. Jennie Wiley and the exploration and settlement of the Big Sandy Valley in the Virginias and Kentucky, to which is affixed a brief account of the Connelly family and some of its collateral and related families in America. This book, of 177 pages, is only one of Mr. Connelley's books, as he has issued several books and papers on Eastern Kentucky and Kansas. He now resides at Topeka, Kansas, where he is secretary of the Historical Association, but was reared in Johnson County, Kentucky. (See the Conley family.)

Another book entitled *The Big Sandy Valley* was written by Dr. Willard Rouse Jillson, Kentucky State geologist, historian, and poet, in 1923. It was a very comprehensive history of that section, and brought to light for the first time the importance of the remote and beautiful valley in the pioneer history of the Commonwealth. Dr. Jillson gave a brief geological history of the Big Sandy Valley, and presented its historical development in some detail, including first explorations, border warfare, and settlement. This regional history closed with the year 1850, and was published by the John P. Morton Company of Louisville, Kentucky. Dr. Jillson has been the author of many books pertaining to Kentucky. He was formerly on the faculty of the University of Kentucky as professor of geology, and is a member of the American Historical Association, the Kentucky State Historical Society, and the Filson Club of Louisville.

The Paintsville Herald has published, from time to time, many articles of historical importance on Johnson County and the Big Sandy Valley, the best of which were its editions of December 20, 1923, and March 10, 1927, and referred to herein under "Newspapers."

Life Among the Hills and Mountains of Kentucky was gotten up by W. R. Thomas of Allen, Kentucky, and published by the Standard Printing Company of Louisville, Kentucky, in 1926. This

book contains brief sketches of forty counties of the eastern part of Kentucky, giving the mode and manner of living in bygone days, and discussing the hardships and turmoils of the hardy pioneers. It deals at length with the folklore, short vision, and illiteracy of some sections, but these are conditions which existed twenty years ago, and are not found today, any more than in remote places in any other state.

Johnson County, Kentucky (this publication). Of late years there has been a lamentable tendency noticeable in the larger cities, especially of the East, and some right in the Bluegrass section of Kentucky, which apparently looks upon every one as a barbarian who does not live within sight of the Statue of Liberty, on Manhattan Island, in Hollywood, Palm Beach, or on Michigan Boulevard. Particularly have the sneers of mis-led "foreigners" and "outsiders" been directed, through motion pictures and writings of newspaper reporters, toward the communities which nestle among the tree-clad hills of Eastern Kentucky.

Eastern Kentucky does lack some things, just as do all other sections of the country. Go back into the most remote spots and perhaps one will find unusual conditions, which, at their worst, however, will not compare with the gunmen of Chicago's gang war, or the Metropolis' Chinatown; but these are by no means typical. The streets of Manhattan may be filled with cultured people, but not more cultured than are found in Eastern Kentucky; their patriotism may be of a high type, but there is none of it so high that citizens of this section cannot equal or surpass it; they may be proud of themselves, but let them try to show a purer strain of real American blood than these people. Better live in the hills of Kentucky, where some persons cannot spell "mosquito" than in the flats of New Jersey where nobody can dispel them.

"Outsiders" who venture into the territory are surprised and even shocked to find that Eastern Kentucky is just as peaceful and safe to live in as the place from which they came. They do not find everybody "toting" a gun, or the people rough, and ready to "coldcock" them at every turn. It is quite interesting to a native lover of the section to hear the newcomers make such statements: "Well, it is different from what I expected, why, I expected to find feuds; to find people more ignorant than anywhere else; to find nothing but muddy roads; in fact I expected to experience quite a bit of excitement."

Teachers, ministers and other professional characters, who have come to assist the "mountaineer," say they are worthy of all assistance given them and in many instances the native is superior in intelligence and intellect to the representatives who are sent to help them.

After all, the things that have been written and told of the region, for their sympathetic appeal and sensational reading material have not been true. It is a great country, where any law-abiding citizen may live in safety, and prosper. It is just these things that the author puts forth by presenting all records and activities in book form so that they may be available to any one seeking true and impartial information of the Big Sandy Valley.

Four years, beginning in May, 1924, were required to gather the data contained herein. All records, pertaining to Johnson County and the Big Sandy Valley on file with the Kentucky State Library, the Kentucky State Historical Society, the Kentucky Geological Survey, and the county court records of Mason, Floyd, and Johnson counties were examined in the preparation of this work, not mentioning the numerous references acknowledged herein.

The work was begun by tracing the lineages of four families; namely, Davis, Hall, Price, and Rice. It was soon evident that these families had married into and were related to all the larger families of Johnson County. When their genealogies had been traced and some remarks added of each person of prominence a book on genealogy had been secured. Every family has something of historical importance connected with it which some member takes pride in passing on down through the generations, and when these were submitted with the lineages a little history had been gathered. Using this as base material it was seen that if this were combined with the official records a complete history could be written of the county.

Having been born and reared within its boundary, having a personal knowledge of its topography, environment, and surroundings, and knowing the traits, character, education, religion, and customs of the people, and at present residing in Frankfort where most of the records are available, and therefore in a better position than an outsider to do so, it has been a pleasure to prepare a compilation of Johnson County, that no other local person has attempted. The value and merit of the book from a historical standpoint, and as a reference to the county, are left to the reader.

NEWSPAPERS

In 1852 a printer by the name of Smith came to Catlettsburg, and started the first newspaper ever published in the Big Sandy Valley. It was called the Big Sandy News, and was published for less than two years, and suspended for lack of patronage.

In like manner numerous newspapers were started and suspended in the valley, most of which were published at Catlettsburg. Among those standing the test for any length of time were:

the Sandy Valley Advocate, established 1859; the Herald, established 1863; the Christian Observer, published by Zephaniah Meek; the Central Methodist, which took the place of the Christian Observer; the Tribune, established 1865; the Enquirer, established 1874; the Index, published sometime in the seventies; the Kentucky Democrat, largest paper edited in the Big Sandy in that time, established by T. D. Marcum in 1878; the Advance, founded at Paintsville in 1880; the Chatterawha News, succeeding the Advance at Louisa in 1881; the Monthly Progress, 1881; the Weekly Progress, 1882; the Enterprise, of Pikeville, in 1882 or 1883; the Banner, at Prestonsburg, 1883; the Lawrence Index, Louisa, about the same time; and the Times, which succeeded the Lawrence Index in 1885, and afterwards changed to the News.'

As above stated the Advance was founded by Howes & Borders at Paintsville in 1880, and after nine months was moved to Louisa, Howes dropping out as a partner. This paper was non-political.

Other papers published at Paintsville have been the Paintsville Paragraph, succeeded by the Paintsville Commercial, 1893; the Times, a Democratic paper that was the only one in the county in 1896; the Paintsville Courier in 1898; the Commercial, in 1901, 1902; the Herald and Leader, in 1904, 1906, and 1908; the Herald (only) in 1910 and on up to the present. The Paintsville Post appeared under the leadership of Messrs. John and Martin Wheeler from 1916 to 1920 when the plant was destroyed by fire.

THE PAINTSVILLE HERALD

Greatest of all these in both time and circulation has been the Paintsville Herald. The story of the rise of this newspaper does not read like a romance, but out of the numerous ups and downs, it has risen to a commanding position in the business affairs of Paintsville and Eastern Kentucky. The Herald was established May 2, 1901, as a part of the Commercial. The Commercial was of few years duration, and the Herald took its place.

This weekly paper has had a great mission to fill, but naturally has fallen short of some of its ideals, not because of lack of good motives, but because of sheer mechanical inability to do what it would like to have accomplished.

It has had a local touch and flavor which the dailies have not had. It has always entered the homes of Eastern Kentucky as a friend to those of that section, carrying its message of cheer, and giving the news to each family, ever ready to defend them against adverse criticism from the outside, and boosting every project tending toward the upbuilding, prosperity, and happiness of the people it serves. It has never catered to criminal news but endeavored to sift the important news that would aid in the advancing and industrial progression of the community. In so doing it has served and is serving a good cause for the common good of Johnson County, and is filling a place which no outside paper can fill.

It was under the guidance of Warren M. Meek for a few years after its establishment, but soon afterwards the present publisher became its owner, and with the assistance of one or two valued employes, the fight was started, which has brought them much praise. The Herald during its twenty-six years of existence has constantly improved and today is the oldest business establishment in Paintsville, with a modern plant. It is read each week by thousands of readers in Eastern Kentucky, and by many in all states of the Union. It is a firmly established, solid business institution, doing business in competition with foreign printing houses, but covering a field all to itself in the newspaper business.

The largest department of the Herald plant is its complete job printing department, which supplies most of the printing for the various business establishments and coal and oil operations in Eastern Kentucky. In fact, this plant is probably the largest and best equipped for all kinds of printing and for the publication of a weekly newspaper in Kentucky, second only to those of the large dailies. Linotypes are used for composition, which include models 1, 5, and 14. Other equipment includes a Babcock newspaper printing press and folder combined, driven by individual motor; three late model Chandler and Price job printing presses; power saw trimmer; complete stereotyping outfit; power perforator and stitchers, as well as everything necessary in a modern plant.

The paper contains twenty pages regularly, and more when advertising demands. In connection with advertisements, mention should be made of their relation to history. Anyone may pick up a paper for a given date, and depict the times and customs for that date. One may learn that music is being furnished by the phonograph or radio. Theatrical advertisements reveal the state of the stage and the films. From them posterity may get a graphic picture of present- or past-day customs and manners, and so on. The vast fund of knowledge contained in newspapers is most valuable as current history. It makes keeping up with the times a simple matter. By reading Paintsville's best and only paper, the reader will always be informed of conditions there at any time.

Of the many achievements of the Paintsville Herald, three have been outstanding. The first was a special edition of December 20, 1923. The second was receiving the silver loving cup which was awarded it, for being Kentucky's best weekly newspaper, by the Kentucky Press Association at its meeting in June, 1926. The third was the publication of its Industrial Edition on March 10, 1927, said to be the largest edition of any Kentucky newspaper to

CHAS. A. KIRK
Editor of the *Paintsville Herald*, Paintsville, Ky.

date. This edition contained 180 pages, 12 sections of eight pages, 4 pages of comics, 5 sections of 16 pages each of rotogravure, 683 pictures, 10,000 copies were printed. Each copy cost 74 cents to produce but was sold to the public for 25 cents per copy. This did not include regular subscribers who received it free of cost. The Herald and Editor were complimented by newspapers the country over. The future of the Herald looms bright with many promises, and secure with solid realities.

The theory that the reader makes the newspaper does not absolve the editor from all responsibility. The people really demand editorial leadership in all public affairs, as much as an army demands generals. With good leadership the people will do what is right. With bad leadership they will go wrong. With no leadership they will blunder along and go wrong as often as they go right. Leadership is in the individual, not in the leaderless multitude. The editor of the country paper or small-town weekly or daily is nearer the real community consciousness than any other, and mostly directs it aright.[3]

To this distinction goes the name of Mr. Chas. A. Kirk, owner, editor, and publisher of the Herald. Using his own language, thirty years ago he, then a lad of fourteen, landed in Paintsville with his earthly belongings under one arm, which consisted of one blue shirt and a 15-cent straw hat. He started to work for the old Paintsville Commercial at a salary of one dollar a week. He later purchased the paper and with an old Washington hand press and a marble slab for a composing stone mounted on a drygoods box, he started upon his journalistic career which was fraught with many knocks and with many hostile influences, but by keeping "everlastingly at it" he succeeded, and today each paper mailed weekly is a monument to his efforts.

To run a newspaper all a fellow has to do is to be able to write poetry, discuss the tariff and money questions, umpire a baseball game, report a wedding, saw wood, describe a fire so that the readers will shed wraps, make $1 do the work of $10, shine at a dance, abuse the liquor habit, subscribe to charity, go without meals, attack free silver, wear diamonds, invent advertisements, sneer at snobbery, overlook scandal, appraise babies, describe the good-looking graduates, delight potato raisers, minister to the afflicted, heal the disgruntled, fight to a finish, set type, mold public opinion, and stand in with everybody and everything.

Mr. Kirk has stood the test, having spent the greater part of his life in the newspaper business. An editor has more to do with the upbuilding of a community than any other one individual, and acting in this capacity, he has done himself justice as evidenced by the progressive, moral, and law-abiding citizens of Paintsville and Eastern Kentucky.

While success has attended Mr. Kirk's efforts, he still is possessed of those characteristics that attract to him an ever-widening circle of friends.

The Herald is now rounding out its twenty-seventh year of service and boosting of Paintsville and the Big Sandy Valley. These many years have been strenuous ones but not without their pleasures to the Herald force. As a representative newspaper of its territory, the Herald speaks for itself. The Herald has the largest foreign and local advertising patronage of any weekly in the State, and its circulation is rapidly increasing. This has been brought about by issuing each week the best newspaper possible to produce. Almost everyone in its territory is a reader as well as a booster of the Herald and this fact alone is ample reward for the years of hard work spent in building up such a newspaper. "Keeping Everlastingly At It Brings Success," is a motto the manager has always strictly adhered to.

Towns and their newspapers usually lag or lead together. Progressive journalism is the unfailing tonic of the dull community but it is equally true that a lifeless newspaper can seriously retard the development of its community. There is no better community asset than a home newspaper equal to the needs of that community. While a poor newspaper is better than none to the individual reader, that does not hold true for the town.

What can a good newspaper do for its community? It can serve as the town's messenger to the outside world. It must take the leadership in all community projects if they are to be successful. It is the infallible line of communication between local government and citizen. It is to the newspaper that all organizations turn for assistance in public welfare work; and without that assistance they face failure.

The newspaper reaps the reward of its initiative by sharing in the general improvement of business and community affairs it has been instrumental in bringing about. The good newspaper deems it a pleasure to serve its community and its readers and is fully aware that it is only through giving a full measure of service that it can progress and prosper.

REFERENCES TO CHAPTER XII

[1] The Big Sandy News, Louisa, Ky., April, 1928.
[2] Ely, William. The Big Sandy Valley, pages 328-333. 1887.
[3] The Saturday Evening Post, April, 1927.

CHAPTER XIII
SERVICE MEN

Practically every history relates the events in general of each war in which the United States has participated, but a very few books give any lists of the names of those who served.

The following is a list of Revolutionary Soldiers as taken from the official order books of Mason, Floyd, and Johnson counties.

Revolutionary Soldiers Floyd County	Date Applied for Pension	County Court Order Book	Page
Thomas C. Brown	September 17, 1832	6	111
William Brown	September 26, 1825	4	314
Edward Burgess	December 21, 1819	3	139
Edward Burgess		–	
Richard Cains	June 16, 1818	3	27
James Camron	November 27, 1826	5	183
James Camron	September 17, 1832	6	111
Thomas Cassady	July 14, 1834	6	250
Bazil Castle		1(Johnson Co.)	
Samuel Clark	January 20, 1834	6	209
David Conley		4	181
Henry Conley		–	
Zachariah Davis			
Abiud Fairchild	———(See Fairchild family)–		
William Ferguson	May 20, 1818	3	21
William Fitzgerald		–	
James Flannery		1(Johnson Co.)	
John Flannery		1(Johnson Co.)	
Isaac Flatwood		4	131
Thomas Francis		1(Johnson Co.)	
John Hall (Wife Bareba)	January 21, 1836	7	238
John Hall (Wife Bareba)	June 2, 1838(Cert. No. 30346)	–	
Thomas Hamilton	September 26, 1826	5	182
William Haney	May 23, 1826	4	362
James Harris	June 17, 1833	6	168
Samuel Harris		–	
Pawley Jacobs			
William Jacobs			
Thomas Johns		–	
John Justice	September 18, 1820	–	
Simeon Justice	June 15, 1818	3	26
Simeon Justice	February 21, 1820	–	
Simeon Justice	September 18, 1820	–	
John Kelly	May 18, 1818	3	17
Thomas Lovelady	August 25, 1823	4	178
Reuben Mathews	May 19, 1818	3	19
John Moore	February 18, 1834	6	218
John Moore		7	78
John Moore		–	240
John Mullins		–	154
Thomas Murry		4	147
John Porter Sr.	November 18, 1833	6	193
James Pratt	———(Died Oct. 8, 1854)	–	
Mack Preston	December 21, 1819		
Nathan Preston		4	169

Revolutionary Soldiers Floyd County	Date Applied for Pension	County Court Order Book	Page
John Smith		4	137
Peter Sullivan	May 23, 1825	4	287
Thomas Wadkins	February 17, 1834	6	212
George R. Walker (Wife Lucy)		–(Johnson Co.)	—
Benedict Watkins	August 20, 1832	6	107
Richard Wells		7	327
Alexander Young		5	205

WAR OF 1812

Very little information which actually affected the Big Sandy Valley was obtained, and so far as is known, there are no accounts or lists available of the names of those who served. (See the Wells family history, included herein, for some information of the War of 1812.)

THE CIVIL WAR

There is an official book on file at the County Clerk's office at Paintsville, Kentucky, giving the names of those from Johnson County who served in this war. As they are arranged according to infantries, etc., and are available to those interested, the list has not been included here.

The Big Sandy Valley was not immune from the ravages of war during the stirring days of the Civil War. James A. Garfield, who was later elected President of the United States, spent several months in this region in charge of Union soldiers. He was sent to the valley to dislodge General Humphrey Marshall who was encamped at Prestonsburg in charge of Confederate soldiers. During the campaign Garfield camped near Paintsville, later moving to Middle Creek where he engaged Marshall in battle, driving the Confederates into Virginia. At Hagerhill, near Paintsville, can still be seen faint traces of the old breastworks thrown up by Marshall's men.

The following interesting story of Garfield's activities in the Big Sandy Valley is taken from an article prepared by Judge John F. Hager of Ashland, Kentucky, for the Paintsville Herald:

"On January 6, 1862, Garfield arrived near Paintsville. Marshall had first cast up breastworks in the narrows just above the present C. & O. Station at Paintsville but later chose and fortified a position on the crest of Hagerhill a mile to the southwest. Fearing advance by flank movement on his left and rear, Marshall fell back to the forks of Middle Creek, and Garfield moved to his new front on the 10th of January. Skirmishing began at 11:00 a. m., and the engagement continued until dark, both sides claiming a victory and both withdrawing from the field of battle, Marshall taking his force to Virginia and Garfield to Paintsville, and later to Pikeville and on March 16 his force of 750 attacked a battalion of Virginia militia occupying Pound Gap and drove them away and burned the log huts built for winter quarters.

"The battle casualties at Middle Creek were not great, Garfield's report showing two killed and 25 wounded and Marshall reported 11 killed and 15 wounded.

"That occupation of Eastern Kentucky was considered important to the cause of each belligerent and was achieved by the Federal forces—a triumph which resulted in promotion of Garfield who took oath of office as brigadier general in what is now known as the Bowles home in Pikeville. The highest stage ever known in Big Sandy waters was in the winter of 1862. Garfield's campaign could not have been conducted in these wintry months without the transportation afforded by 'Sunday' steamboats, the flagboat and admiralship so to speak being the 'Sandy Valley,' a boat of great speed owned by Judge Arch Borders and of which Captain Hi Davis was the efficient and chief pilot.

"General Garfield while yet at Pikeville was ordered to report to General Buell who had gone to the relief of General Grant at Pittsburgh Landing, so called by the Confederates of Shiloh as designated by the Federals. He arrived there April 7, 1862, in time to take part in the second day's contest.

"General Marshall was then about fifty years of age, a graduate for courage at Buena Vista in the Mexican War, was a member of Congress from the Louisville District for four terms and minister to China under President Filmore. As lawyer he had no superior and few equals. He was famous as an orator and possessed the remarkable talents of the Marshall family for eloquence and power in the forum. Personally he was not adapted to mountain warfare, owing to his great size, being over six feet in height and weighing well above 300 pounds, despite the fact of a ribald boast of his soldiers in singing, 'Humphrey Marshall, he's our boss, big as hell, and brave as a hoss.'

"He later resigned from the Confederate army believing he had been illy treated by President Davis in not receiving support which he deserved and the necessities of his command required. He practiced law at Louisville after the close of the war, and until death was ranked by fellow-members of the bar and judges as greatest among the great lawyers of the Louisville bar."

It is not necessary to write further respecting the career of General Garfield after leaving Eastern Kentucky. His high and honorable achievements, military and civil, are embodied in the history of our own times.

SPANISH-AMERICAN WAR

Nothing has been shown regarding this war, as there is also a book on file at the County Court Clerk's office at Paintsville, which is available to those interested.

THE WORLD WAR

Anything that would be written in words would not be enough to say of the time that in 1918 gave peace to a world of turmoil and destruction, and in memory of our comrades and loved ones who paid the extreme penalty and are now at rest in Flanders Field—in memory of the twenty-five boys from Johnson County who never returned. To them there is no death; they live forever in the memory of their glorious achievements.

With all thankfulness we look back to that Armistice Day which ended the World War. We remember how the load of anxiety fell in a moment from a world of men's and women's hearts; how a war-torn world turned back to peace with profound gratitude to the God who gave it and to the men who paid for it with their lives.

War produces the greatest extremes in human life. It brings men to sanity; yet it drives them mad. It reveals them magnificent in sacrifice and revolting in brutality. There is some truth in the war prophet's doctrine who said war does breed splendid and essential virtues; but it breeds them at too terrible a cost. Peace must breed and can breed these same virtues without that cost.

"Under the quiet sod or beneath the murmuring waves their bodies sleep in peace. But in the destinies of men their souls go marching on."[1]

"Solemnly with love, honor, and respect, do we hereby dedicate this memorial to the memory of the soldiers, sailors, marines, and nurses, who gave their lives in the cause of this great nation." Such are the words inscribed on a beautiful memorial erected to the memory of the World War victims from Johnson County who lost their lives in encounters at Argonne Forest, St. Mihiel, Soissons, Montfaucon, Bouresches, Belleau Wood, Chateau-Thierry, and Cantigny, by the Johnson County Post No. 117, The American Legion, at Paintsville, Kentucky. To date, this is the only memorial of its kind in all Eastern Kentucky.

Too much praise could not be written for every man in the service, and especially for those who distinguished themselves by acts of bravery on the battlefields of France. In addition to those who paid the extreme sacrifice, and to those who were wounded, three men received special citations. An account of each and their citations follow.

HERBERT (HEBER) WARD[2]

Herbert Ward has a World War record that but few equal. He enlisted in the United States Army, May 12, 1916, at Columbus, Ohio, and after a short period of training in the States, including

AMERICAN LEGION'S MEMORIAL AT PAINTSVILLE, KY.

service on the Mexican border, sailed for France, June 12, 1917, and returned to the States disabled on June 16, 1919.

Mr. Ward served overseas with Company C, 28th Infantry, and was made Corporal, August 25, 1917, and Sergeant, April 3, 1918, with which rating he was discharged from the service. While in France he served on the following fronts: Luneville Sector, Toul Sector, Cantigny, Saizeras, Montdidier-Noyon, Aisne-Marne, St. Mihiel, and Meuse-Argonne. While at Soissons, Mr. Ward was severely wounded in the head, the bullet entering the skull above the right eye and on account of lodging so close to the brain an operation was not advisable and the bullet remains in his skull. While in action in the Argonne he was hit by a bullet either from a machine gun or rifle, the bullet entering his right hip and coming out just back of the left hip.

Mr. Ward received the First Division Citation (Fourragere); the Distinguished Service Cross, and was recommended for a Medal of Honor, which recommendation is still pending. He is one of the three men in Johnson County receiving the Distinguished Service Cross.

SERGEANT HERBERT WARD,
Paintsville, Kentucky.

DISTINGUISHED SERVICE CROSS
Citation

Herbert Ward (Army Serial No. 57104), Sergeant, Company C, Twenty-eighth Infantry, First Division. For extraordinary heroism in action near Berzy le Sec, France, July 19, 1918. After his platoon leader had been wounded, Sergeant Ward reorganized the platoon under heavy fire, and led it to its objective. He then led forward a patrol to locate the enemy positions, during which reconnaissance he was wounded by a machine-gun bullet; the ball lodged above the right eye. After receiving first aid he returned to his unit for duty. During a subsequent attack in the Argonne, he was again wounded.
General Orders No. 39,
War Department, Washington,
June 25, 1920. Page 5.

CAPTAIN MALCOLM RICE,
Hagerhill, Kentucky.

DISTINGUISHED SERVICE CROSS
Citation

The Commander in Chief of the American Expeditionary Forces, in the name of the President, has awarded the Distinguished Service Cross to the following named officer, for the act of extraordinary heroism described below:

"Capt. Malcolm Rice, Eighteenth Infantry, for extraordinary heroism in action near Exermont, France, October 1-8, 1918; during the advance on October 8, Captain Rice was severely gassed, and although suffering

greatly from the effects thereof, he remained with his company for four days, after which he was forced to evacuate on account of temporary blindness.
Official Bulletin,
Feb. 11, 1919. Page 39.

FRENCH ORDER FOR DECORATION OF CROIX DE GUERRE
P. C.—GRAND QUARTER GENERAL
          DES   5-16-19
Armees Francaises de l'Est
    ETAT-MAJOR
BUREAU DU PERSONNEL
      (Decorations)   ORDRE No. 15, 170 "D" (EXTRAIT)

Apres approbation du General Commandant en Chef les Forces expeditionnaires Americaines en France, le Marechal de France Commandant en Chef les Armees Francaises de l'Est cite a l'Ordre de la BRIGADE:

Capitaine Malcolm Rice, du 18° Regiment d'Infanterie Americain:

"Officier doue de belles qualites militaires mises en relief par un profond sentiment du devoir. S'est distingue dans les operations de SOISSONS, en conduisant sa compagnie jusqu'au moment ou il fut grievement blesse."

                Au Frand Quartier General, le 30 Mars 1919
                    Le MARECHAL DE FRANCE
COMMANDANT EN CHEF LES ARMEES FRANCAISES DE L'EST,
                        PETAIN
POUR EXTRAIT CONFORME:
    Le Lieutenant-Colonel,
        Chef du Bureau du Personnel,

KIRK FAIRCHILD, 107046,
    Hagerhill, Kentucky.

                    CROIX DE GUERRE
                          Citation

Kirk Fairchild, 107046, private, Company B, Fourth Machine-gun Battalion, Second Division.

French Croix De Guerre, with gilt star, under order No. 11, 466 "D," dated November 11, 1918, General Headquarters, French Armies of the North and Northeast, with the following citation:

"All the men of his squad having been killed or wounded, he remained valiantly at his post in spite of his own wound, and continued to fight until the end of the attack."

JOHNSON COUNTY DEATHS—WORLD WAR

James W. Akers, Lieut.	John W. Lackey	James H. Slone
John Arms	John W. Lemaster	Flem Stapleton
Charles Blair (Challie)	Estel Messer	Bill Walters
Turner Branham	Fred C. Pinson	Ora Ward
Charley Conley	Chester Reed	Lindsey Wireman
Curtis M. Conley	Warren G. Rice, Lieut.	John Pelphry
Budd Elswick	Benjamin R. Ross	Leonard Perry
Elzie Estep	James L. Rowland	
Elwood Hampton	Emery Skaggs	

HERBERT WARD

SERVICE MEN 453

JOHNSON COUNTY WOUNDED—WORLD WAR

Ben Adams, Sergt.
Ora K. Blanton
William M. Blevins, Corp.
Jesse Boggs
Frank Burton
Wiley Burton
Henry Byrd
Herbert Castle
James Caudill
James M. Chandler
John Henry Chandler
Roy Clark
Grover C. Collins
Ed. Daniels
Jesse Davis
Arthur Dixon
Clellie Dye
Kirk Fairchild
Lloyd Fairchild, Corp.
Wiley V. Hall
Luther Harmon
Irwin Hitchcock
Wiley Hitchcock
John Jervis
John L. Jones
Ben Keaton
Wm. McKenzie
Yancy Melvin
Elbert Murray
Wasselle Pellex
Walter Pelphrey
George Perkins
Jeffrey Perry
Cyrus Preston
Russell Preston, Ccrp.
James A. Rice, Corp.
Malcolm Rice, Lieut.
Dewey Robinson, Lieut.
Benjamin F. Ross
Mason Ross
Elzie Salyer
Herbert Salyer
Hoadley Salyers
Charlie F. Sebastian
James H. Slone, Corp.
Willie Smith, Sergt.
Monroe Stambaugh
Elliott Stanley
John Stricklin, Corp.
Thomas H. Terry
Bert Thomas
McCoy Trimble, Corp.
Claude VanHoose, Corp.
Hancel VanHoose
Herbert Ward, Sergt.
Lorenzo Ward
Roscoe Watson
Heskell Webb

LIST OF SERVICE MEN FROM JOHNSON COUNTY, KENTUCKY WORLD WAR 1917-1918

*Volunteers, ‡Enlisted, †Volunteers in United States Navy, §S. A. T. C.

Ben Adams
John D. Adams
Kelly Adams
James W. Akers
Frank Arms
John Arms
Alger Bailey
Elbert C. Bailey
Emmet Bailey
Emit Bailey
Harrison W. Bailey
Melvin Bailey
Wm. H. Bailey
Arnett Baldridge
Freddie Baldwin
Robert Baldwin
Henry W. B. Bayes
Ray Bayes
Elbert Beers
Carl Beggs
Challie Blair
Posey G. Blair
Robert Blair
Thomas Blair†
Vernie Blair
William Blair
William J. Blair
Walter L. Bland
Anderson Blanton
General S. Blanton
George W. Blanton
John M. Blanton
Kendrick Blanton
Miller F. Blanton
Ora K. Blanton
William Blanton
Everett Blevins
Frank Blevins
James Blevins
William M. Blevins
Jesse Boggs
Henry Bohanon
Glenn Borders
Lewis Borders
Virgil Borders
Herschel Boyd
Hilliard Boyd
Chester Bradley
Eddie Bradley§
Roscoe Branham
Turner Branham
Charlie Brown
Elbert Brown
Hasten Lee Brown
Isaac Brown (Col.)†
William Robert Brown (Col.)
Jesse Burchett†
Julius Burchett
Lonnie Burchett
John P. Burke
Walker Burke
Walter Burke
Frank Burton
Wiley Burton
Henry Byrd
Golbert Candell
Elbert Castle
Harrison Castle
Herbert Castle
Link Castle (Deserter)
Oakley Castle
Walter Castle
Archie M. Caudill
Gilbert Caudill
James Caudill
Lonnie Z. Caudill
Mathew Caudill
Albert Centers
James M. Chandler
John Henry Chandler
George Charlie
J. R. Childers
Roy Clark
John Allen Coldiron
Dennis Collins
Grover Collins

James Collins
Norman Collins
Perry Collins
Frank Collinsworth
Bruce Colvin
Charley Colvin
Harve Colvin
Ben F. Conley
Burll Conley
Charles B. Conley
Charles R. Conley
Charlie Conley
Curtis M. Conley
Dona Conley
Everett Conley
Forest Conley
George W. Conley
Heber Conley
Lindsey Conley†
Morris Conley
Othie B. Conley
Paris Conley
Sherman Conley
Edward B. Connolley†
John Hays Cordial
Crassford Crace
Lonzie Crace
Thomas Crum
Frank J. Daniel
Edward Daniels
Jesse Davis
John C. Davis
Anthony F. Dills‡
Jesse B. Dills
Arthur Dixon
James Franklin Dixon‡
Hubert Dixon
Harrison Duty
Clellie Dye
Bud Elswick
Elzie Estep
Jimmie Estep
Proctor J. Evans*
Dennie Fairchilds
Kirk Fairchilds†
Lloyd Fairchilds
Sun Fairchilds
Troy Fairchilds
Walter Fairchilds
Clyde Fannin
Braddus Faulkner
Proctor James Fife
Roy Fitch
Sherman Fitch†
Carl Fitchpatrick
James M. Flannery
Ulyssis G. Fletcher
William Franklin
Harry Frazier
James L. Frazier
Marvin Gillman

Joseph Gonnicks
Andrew Greathouse
Mathew Guliett
Cutis L. Gullet
Thomas H. Hackworth
Deed Hall
James W. Hall
Mitchel Hall§
Paul Bryan Hall*
Wiley B. Hall
Wiley V. Hall
Wm. Bradley Hamilton
Elwood Hampton
William Hampton†
Proctor Hannah
  (Deserter)
Wayne Hannah
Luther Harmon
Will Haskell
George Paul Helton
Challie Hitchcock
Irwin Hitchcock
Wiley Hitchcock
Arthur C. Holbrook
Arthur Grant Holbrook
Charles Holbrook
Charles W. Holbrook‡
Edgar Howes†
R. G. Howes*
Donovan Huff
Andrew J. Hughes
James Ballard Hughes
Winifred Hurt
James Jackson
Logan Jackson
Ora C. Jayne
John Jervis
Garfield Jockson
John Johnson
John L. Jones
Walter Kastro
Ben Keaton
Floyd King
Paul Krockinpnicki
John W. Lackey
Edward Paul Lavender*
Harry LaViers§
Russell Lee†
Ben F. Lemaster
Earn Lemaster
  (Deserter)
Flem Lemaster
Floyd Lemaster
J. Walter Lemaster
John W. Lemaster
Luther Lemaster
Roscoe M. Lemaster
Roy H. Lemaster
Stephen L. Lemaster
Oscar Lemley
John L. Lester†

Gordon Litteral
Harvey Litteral
Harvey G. Litteral
J. Benson Litteral
Lonnie Litteral
Oscar Lovely
Fred Lowe
Mason Lyons
Arthur (Son) Mahan
Scott May‡
Grats McCarty
John McCourt Jr.
German McKenzie†
Harvey L. McKenzie†
Haskell McKenzie
Jay McKenzie
William McKenzie
Bob Meade
Guy Meade
Robert Meade
Thomas Meade
Clyde Melvin
Yancy Melvin
Estill Messer
Bernard H. Mieman
  (Covington)
Mance Montgomery
Robert Moore
Elbert Murray
Walter Murrey
Jeff Need
Alfred Osborne
James H. Osborne
Proctor Osborne
Frank Pack
Tracy Pack
Samuel Herschell
  Patrick
Wassell Pellix
John Pelphry
Walter Pelphry
Willie Pelphry
James Penix
Shade Penix
Rancie Pennington
Sherman Pennington
George Perkins
Jeffrey Perry
Leonard Perry
William J. Perry
Emeron Picklesimer
Emerson Picklesimer
Henry Picklesimer
Oakley Picklesimer
Sanford Picklesimer
James Tildon Pigg
Fred C. Pinson
Clyde Preston†
Cyrus Preston
Earnest R. Preston†
Martin Preston

SERVICE MEN

Russell Preston
Clarence Price
Green Price
Wiley W. Price†
Cleve Puckett
Butler Ramey
Joe Ramey
Rova F. Ramey
Paris Ratliff
Chester Reed
Dave Reed
Frank Reed
Jeff Reed
Milton Reed
Alex Rice
Francis M. Rice
George Dewey Rice
German W. Rice
Heber Rice
Hobart Rice
James A. Rice
Malcolm Rice
Oscar Rice
Robert Rice
Samuel P. Rice
Warren G. Rice
Gus Riffit†
Oscar Ritchie
Bert (Pat) Roberts
Carmen Roberts
John Logan Roberts
Norman Roberts
Dewey Robinson
Charles G. Rose*
Benjamin F. Ross
John Franklin Ross
Mason Ross
James L. Rowland
Estill Rule
Crayton G. Sagraves
Elzie Salyer
Freeman Salyer
Hedley Salyer
Herbert Salyer
Minyard Salyer
Noah C. Salyer
Ramson Salyer

Tony Salyer
Arthur Salvers
Clinton J. M. Salyers
Dock Salyers
George Savco
Sherman Scarberry†
John C. Schroeder
Chalie F. Sebastin
Emery Skaggs
Peter Skaggs
  (Deserter)
James Henry Slone
William P. Slone
Binnie Smith
Willie Smith
Earnest C. Sneed†
Wm. Harrison Sparks
Bernard Spears
Marion Spears
  (Deserter)
Bernie Spencer
Walter Spencer
Noah Spradlin
Charley Stafford
Albert Stambaugh
Fred Stambaugh
Hubert Stambaugh†
Hubert C. Stambaugh
Monroe Stambaugh
Elliot Stanley
Dock Stapleton
Flem Stapleton
Millard Stapleton
Sammie Stapleton, Jr.
Willie Stapleton
Earl Stone
John W. Strictlin
Benjamin E. Strother
Francis M. Tackett
Paris Tackett
Thomas Tackett
Bert Taylor
Demra Taylor
Mrs. Norma Terry
Thomas Henry Terry
Bert Thomas
James V. Trible

Patrick Trible
Bruce Trimble
Harry V. Trimble
James H. Trimble
James V. Trimble
McCoy Trimble
Paris L. Trimble
Thomas E. Trimble
Claude Van Hoose
Dan Van Hoose
Hancel Van Hoose
Hobart Van Hoose§
Kirk Van Hoose
Woodward R. Wallen
George N. Walters
Ingram Walters
William Walters
Edgar W. Ward
Heber Ward
Jeff M. Ward
Lorenz Ward
Ora Ward
Roma Grey Ward
William J. Ward
Roscoe Watson (Probably killed in action)
Hescel Webb
Charles M. Wells
Hubert Wells
Zephaniah Wells
Chas. Orion Wheeler*
John Wheeler
Orrell Wheeler
Willie James Wheeler
Wm. Cash Whittaker
Henry Wilbur†
Jess Wilcox
Charles N. Williams
Estill M. Williams
Milligan Williams‡
Oka Lee Williams
Ralph B. Williams
Lindsey Wireman
Albert Wolf
Earnest Woods
John W. Woyno
Benjamin H. Young.

REFERENCES TO CHAPTER XIII

[1] Hall, Dr. Paul B., Armistice Day Address at Paintsville, Kentucky, November 11, 1927.
[2] C. & O. Employes Magazine, February, 1928.

CHAPTER XIV
APPENDIX
TAX LIST—1925

Note: Original spelling of names has been retained in most cases.

Abromonick, Eli
Adams, Alma
Adams, Ashland
Adams, Ben
Adams, Bill
Adams, Derum
Adams, Ed
Adams, Elbert
Adams, Fonzo
Adams, Frank
Adams, Fred
Adams, Fred R.
Adams, Garrett
Adams, Hardin
Adams, H. B.
Adams, Henry
Adams, Jack
Adams, James H.
Adams, Jincy
Adams, J. M.
Adams, Joe
Adams, John
Adams, K. B.
Adams, Lester
Adams, Marcus
Adams, Miles
Adams, Paris
Adams, R. D.
Adams, Rosabelle
Adams, Ross
Adams, Wesley
Adams, Will
Adams, Willie
Adair, Willie A.
Adkins, Buddy
Adkins, George
Adkins, James
Adkins, Jerry
Adkins, J. H.
Adkins, Lester
Adkins, Nancy
Adkins, W. P.
Akers, James
Akers, J. E.
Akers, Logan
Akers, Millard
Akers, Russell
Akers, T. B.
Akers, W. S.
Allen, Jeff
Allen, Sally

Anderson, Frank
Archer, E. E., Dr.
Arms, Dan
Arms, Elijah
Arms, Everett
Arms, Henry
Arms, J. B.
Arms, Jesse
Arms, John (Dist. 1)
Arms, John (Dist. 2)
Arms, Milford
Arms, Morris
Arms, Oliver
Arms, Oscar
Arms, Sam K.
Arms, Sanford
Arms, Son
Arms, Willie
Arnett, Fanny
Arnett, Homer
Arnett, Morris
Arrowood, A. J.
Arrowood, Diliah
Arrowood, G. D.
Arrowood, H. F.
Arrowood, Irvin
Arrowood, J. M.
Arrowood, Liss
Arrowood, Lon
Arrowood, Melvin
Arrowood, Willie
Arrowood, W. J.
Atkinson, B. H.
Atkinson, Charley
Atkinson, Frank
Atkinson, Fred
Atkinson, Julia F., Mrs.
Atkinson, Stella
Atkinson, W. T., Dr.
Austin, Elmer
Austin, Fanny
Austin, F. M.
Austin, J. M.
Auxier, A. E.
Auxier, Annie Lee
Auxier, Dick
Auxier, Down
Auxier, G. G.
Auxier, Henry J.
Auxier, I. L.
Auxier, James W.

Auxier, J. B.
Auxier, J. J.
Auxier, J. K. P., Sr.
Auxier, J. K. P., Jr.
Auxier, J. S.
Auxier, Louisa
Auxier, Milt
Auxier, R. C.
Auxier, Sam
Auxier, S. L.
Auxier, Tobe
Auxier, W. D.
Bailey, Alger
Bailey, Charley
Bailey, C. M.
Bailey, D. B.
Bailey, Dury
Bailey, Estill
Bailey, Everett
Bailey, Fred
Bailey, Hampton
Bailey, Harrison
Bailey, Hige
Bailey, J. F.
Bailey, J. F., Judge
Bailey, J. T.
Bailey, L. C.
Bailey, Lilly
Bailey, Santford
Bailey, T. B.
Bailey, W. B.
Bailey, W. R.
Baker, Sam
Balden, Willie
Baldin, Fred
Baldin, John
Baldin, McKinley
Baldridge, Ben
Baldridge, Garfield
Baldridge, G. E.
Baldridge, Irvin
Baldridge, Liss
Baldridge, Robert
Baldridge, Susan
Baldridge, Thomas
Baldridge, Tom
Baldwin, Clint
Baldwin, Dock
Baldwin, Fred
Baldwin, John F.
Baldwin, Luther

APPENDIX 457

Baldwin, S. A.
Baldwin, Wince
Banks, Elza
Banks, Robert
Baranaski, John
Barber, Curtis
Barber, Henry
Barker, Alfred
Barker, Alonzo
Barker, Eli
Barker, Hardy
Barker, Jassitt
Barker, John
Barker, Lon M.
Barker, Walter
Barker, W. L.
Barnett, Andy J.
Barnett, F. A.
Bartelle, Benny
Barton, Green
Bayes, Charley
Bayes, Denny
Bayes, Dord
Bayes, D. S.
Bayes, Elijah
Bayes, Floyd
Bayes, Frank
Bayes, J. B.
Bayes, J. J.
Bayes, J. M.
Bayes, John
Bayes, Leander
Bayes, Lois
Bayes, Mark
Bayes, Martha
Bayes, Mary
Bayes, Mary, Mrs.
Bayes, Nat
Bayes, Newt
Bayes, Newton
Bayes, Pete
Bayes, Printice
Bayes, Sam
Bayes, Warren
Bayes, W. M. H.
Bayes, Worth
Beers, E. W.
Belcher, J. N.
Belcher, Julia
Berlin, E. W.
Berns, John
Berry, E. C.
Berry, Garfield
Bewis, Richard
Bigford, George R.
Bigford, Ora
Bill, Charley
Billows, Milton J.
Black, H. G.
Blackburn, Linzie

Blair, Alamander
Blair, Albert
Blair, Albert H.
Blair, Alonzo
Blair, Andy
Blair, Andy
Blair, B. J.
Blair, Burns
Blair, C. E.
Blair, Charles
Blair, Charley
Blair, Coonie
Blair, Crate
Blair, Crate
Blair, Crosford
Blair, Cyrus
Blair, Dave
Blair, Dee
Blair, Denny
Blair, Dewey
Blair, Dicy
Blair, Earl
Blair, Edgar
Blair, Elliot
Blair, Everett
Blair, Farmer
Blair, Floyd
Blair, F. P.
Blair, Frank (Little)
Blair, Frank (Big)
Blair, Furman
Blair, G. A., Mrs.
Blair, George N.
Blair, George W.
Blair, Grant
Blair, Green (Paintsv.)
Blair, Green (Dist. 3)
Blair, Hallie
Blair, Harlan
Blair, Harland
Blair, Harry
Blair, Harry H.
Blair, Herbert
Blair, James
Blair, James F.
Blair, Jesse
Blair, Jesse (Dist. 3)
Blair, J. F.
Blair, John
Blair, John B.
Blair, John N.
Blair, J. M. W.
Blair, Joseph
Blair, Joseph M.
Blair, Leander
Blair, Levi
Blair, Lewis
Blair, Lincoln
Blair, Lindsey
Blair, Liss

Blair, L. J.
Blair, Lonnie
Blair, Martha Jane
Blair, Millard
Blair, Mitchell
Blair, Nat
Blair, Ned
Blair, Paris
Blair, Reese
Blair, Robert
Blair, Sarah, Mrs.
Blair, Sherman
Blair, Taylor
Blair, Tom
Blair, Verner
Blair, Vernie
Blair, Walter
Blair, Walter
Blair, Warnie
Blair, Watt
Blair, W. F.
Blair, W. H.
Blair, William
Blair, W. M.
Blair, W. M. F.
Blair, W. S.
Blankinship, Lenad
Blankinship, Paulie
Blankinship, R.
Blanton, A. J.
Blanton, Al
Blanton, Alamander
Blanton, Arch
Blanton, Bessie
Blanton, Branch
Blanton, Callie
Blanton, C. Giney
Blanton, Challie
Blanton, Clifford
Blanton, Ed
Blanton, Edward
Blanton, Everett
Blanton, Fonzo
Blanton, George
Blanton, George B.
Blanton, Gilbert
Blanton, Granville
Blanton, Grover
Blanton, G. S.
Blanton, Hade
Blanton Hansford
Blanton, Harry
Blanton, Harry (Dist. 3)
Blanton, Hendrick
Blanton, Henry
Blanton, Herbert
Blanton, James
Blanton, James F.
Blanton, James P.
Blanton, J. F.

Blanton, J. M.
Blanton, John
Blanton, John Ed.
Blanton, John M.
Blanton, Jov
Blanton, Kendric
Blanton, Leck
Blanton, Lewis
Blanton, Lige
Blanton, Manford
Blanton, Mary
Blanton, Mary (Dist. 1)
Blanton, M. D.
Blanton, Millard
Blanton, Millard F.
Blanton, Oliver P.
Blanton, Ollie, Mrs.
Blanton, Ora
Blanton, Oscan
Blanton, Oscar
Blanton, Paris
Blanton, Rosco
Blanton, Rose
Blanton, Sallie
Blanton, Sam
Blanton, Sherman
Blanton, S. J.
Blanton, S. L.
Blanton, S. W.
Blanton, W. A.
Blanton, Walter
Blanton, Walter (Dist. 3)
Blanton, W. H.
Blanton, Willie
Blanton, W. R.
Blevins, Albert
Blevins, Andy
Blevins, Bailey
Blevins, Ben
Blevins, Charley
Blevins, Dennis
Blevins, Dick
Blevins, Earl
Blevins, Eli
Blevins, Elias
Blevins, Elisha
Blevins, Elzie
Blevins, Emma, Mrs.
Blevins, Floyd
Blevins, Frank
Blevins, George
Blevins, George W.
Blevins, Glen
Blevins, Guss
Blevins, James
Blevins, Jams
Blevins, Janes
Blevins, J. H.
Blevins, J. T.

Blevins, Laura
Blevins, Lewis
Blevins, Lias (Elias)
Blevins, Licas
Blevins, Lonzo
Blevins, Louis
Blevins, Luke
Blevins, Mack
Blevins, Sam
Blevins, Sam (Poor Bear)
Blevins, Smith
Blevins, Sonny
Blevins, W. B.
Blevins, W. R.
Blim, Frank
Blim, James C.
Boberick, Wassel
Boggs, Bert
Boggs, Charley
Boggs, H. L.
Boggs, J. A.
Boggs, Loe
Boggs, W. G.
Bond, J. D.
Booker, Henry
Booth, Charley
Booth, Garfield
Borders, H. A.
Borders, John
Borders, Johnnie
Borders, Mary R.
Borders, Nathan
Borders, Patrick
Boss, W. P.
Bowe, Susan
Bowe, W. C.
Bowen, Bud
Bowen, George
Bowen, Jack
Bowen, James
Bowen, John W.
Bowen, Johnny
Bowen, Morgan
Bowen, Samuel
Bowen, Willie
Bowens, Aug
Bowens, Henry
Bower, Mack
Bowling, Clay
Bowling, Clayton
Bowling, Jim
Bowling, Joe
Bowling, Lee
Bowling, Lige
Bowling, Mouse
Bowling, Paris
Bowling, Proctor
Boyd, Anderson
Boyd, Bryan

Boyd, Charley
Boyd, Croker
Boyd, George W.
Boyd, G. V.
Boyd, Hershall
Boyd, Hillard
Boyd, Joe
Boyd, John
Boyd, Julia, Mrs.
Boyd, Mastin
Boyd, Milt
Boyd, R. C.
Boyd, Russell
Boyd, W. C.
Boyd, W. S.
Bradley, Eddie
Bradley, L. M.
Bradley, Wm.
Bragg, Arthur
Brandenburg, Clay
Brandenburg, W. C.
Branham, Arthur
Branham, Harrison
Branham, Jeff
Branham, John
Branham, Joseph
Branham, J. T.
Branham, Sarah
Branham, Steeve
Branham, Tandy
Branham, Turner
Branham, William
Brewer, J. J.
Brooks, A. L.
Brooks, S. L.
Brown, A. J.
Brown, Aaron
Brown, Andrew
Brown, Billy
Brown, Canada
Brown, C. H.
Brown, Daniel
Brown, D. D.
Brown, D. K.
Brown, D. L.
Brown, Earnest F.
Brown, Ed
Brown, Elizabeth
Brown, E. M.
Brown, Estole
Brown, F. A.
Brown, Frank B.
Brown, G. B.
Brown, Geo. Dewey
Brown, George M.
Brown, G. H.
Brown, Glen
Brown, Hasten
Brown, Henry
Brown, James B.

APPENDIX 459

Brown, J. B.
Brown, J. J.
Brown, J. M.
Brown, Joe
Brown, Lawrence
Brown, Lewis
Brown, M. C.
Brown, Roscoe
Brown, Roy
Brown, S. H.
Brown, T. A. (Estate)
Brown, T. C.
Borwn, Tom
Brown, Tom C.
Brown, Wesley
Brown, W. H.
Brown, W. M.
Browning, N. M.
Bryant, Clark
Bryant, Frank
Bryant, James
Bryant, Jesse
Bryant, Manford
Buckingham, Claude
Buckingham, Elizabeth
Bunyard, Logan
Burch, Will Jessie
Burchett, A. J.
Burchett, Amanda
Burchett, Charley
Burchett, George
Burchett, George W.
Burchett, Gross
Burchett, Ham
Burchett, Harmon
Burchett, Isaac
Burchett, James
Burchett, Landrum
Burchett, Lydia
Burchett, Pricilla
Burchett, Proctor
Burchett, Noah
Burchett, T. H.
Burchett, Tobbie
Burchett, William
Burchett, Willie
Burchett, W. J.
Burgess, Frank
Burgess, Will
Burk, John
Burk, Ora
Burke, B. H.
Burke, Carl
Burke, C. W.
Burke, J. P.
Burke, Mart
Burke, S. J.
Burke, Tom L.
Burke, Walker
Burke, Walter W.

Burkett, Sam
Burton, Dinnis
Burton, E. L.
Burton, Foster
Burton, Frank
Burton, L. T.
Burton, P. A.
Burton, Roscoe
Burton, T. J.
Bush, Ellen
Bush, John
Butcher, Ballard
Butcher, Beecher
Butcher, Bud
Butcher, Garfield
Butcher, George W.
Butcher, Harmon
Butcher, Henry M.
Butcher, H. H.
Butcher, Hulda
Butcher, James
Butcher, J. K.
Butcher, J. K., Mrs.
Butcher, John W.
Butcher, Jonny
Butcher, Lewis
Butcher, Mark
Butcher, Melvin
Butcher, Rich
Butcher, Simon
Butcher, Son
Butcher, Thomas
Butcher, Wilber
Butcher, Willie
Butler, Colfax
Butler, Earl
Butler, Ella
Butler, Gus
Butler, J. P.
Butler, Mary
Butler, Tom
Butler, Virgil
Caines, Robert H.
Campton, James L.
Canes, R. H.
Canpigotta, Frank
Canpigotta, John
Cantrell, Alma
Cantrell, Alna
Cantrell, Ben
Cantrell, Charley
Cantrell, Claud
Cantrell, Coy
Cantrell, Dewey
Cantrell, Dock
Cantrell, Elijah
Cantrell, George
Cantrell, Goble
Cantrell, Henry
Cantrell, Henry, Jr.

Cantrell, H. F.
Cantrell, Ira, Jr.
Cantrell, James
Cantrell, James (Dist. 1)
Cantrell, J. H.
Cantrell, Jim
Cantrell, J. K.
Cantrell, John E.
Cantrell, John Riley
Cantrell, Loman
Cantrell, Mace
Cantrell, Mance
Cantrell, Mary
Cantrell, Newt
Cantrell, Noah
Cantrell, Ollie
Cantrell, Roy
Cantrell, R. P.
Cantrell, Sam
Cantrell, Sanford
Cantrell, Shade
Cantrell, Tom
Cantrell, Tom (Dist.)
Cantrell, William
Carpenter, Eli
Carpenter, J. C.
Carpenter, L. C.
Carroll, John
Carter, Cecil
Carter, George W.
Carver, W. H.
Castle, Alijah
Castle, Ambers
Castle, Amos
Castle, Arch
Castle, Arnold
Castle, Asbury
Castle, Bazwell
Castle, B. L.
Castle, Burns
Castle, Cap L.
Castle, Capt.
Castle, Charley
Castle, Clem
Castle, Clyde
Castle, Con
Castle, Corbett
Castle, Crag
Castle, Dovie
Castle, Dow
Castle, Emma
Castle, Emma, Mrs.
Castle, Faris
Castle, Frank
Castle, Garfield
Castle, Garrett
Castle, Gladys
Castle, Gladys, Mrs.
Castle, Hard

Castle, Harper
Castle, Harrison
Castle, Harrison (B. L.'s Son)
Castle, Harry
Castle, Hays
Castle, Herbert
Castle, H. H.
Castle, Irvin
Castle, Isaac
Castle, Jackson
Castle, James
Castle, James (Dist. 1)
Castle, James B.
Castle, James C.
Castle, James G.
Castle, Jerome
Castle, Jesse
Castle, Jim J.
Castle, J. M.
Castle, Joaly
Castle, Joe
Castle, John
Castle, John C.
Castle, John M.
Castle, Jonah
Castle, Joseph
Castle, J. S.
Castle, Kie
Castle, Lafe
Castle, Lewis
Castle, Lindsey
Castle, Lorenda J.
Castle, Lum
Castle, Lydia
Castle, Mantford
Castle, Margaret
Castle, Marion
Castle, Marion
Castle, Mart
Castle, Martin M.
Castle, Marvin
Castle, Mary J.
Castle, Mary
Castle, Milty
Castle, Monroe
Castle, Mose
Castle, Nathan
Castle, Noah
Castle, Nonnie J.
Castle, Oscar
Castle, Pop (Aunt)
Castle, Pricey
Castle, Proctor
Castle, Robert
Castle, Robert (Dist.1)
Castle, Robert, Jr.
Castle, Ross
Castle, Sam
Castle, Sam D.

Castle, Sarah Jane
Castle, Satirra
Castle, Sulivan
Castle, Sun
Castle, Tom
Castle, Tom F.
Castle, Tommie
Castle, Walter
Castle, William
Castle, William W.
Castle, Willie
Castle, W. M.
Castle, W. R.
Castle, W. R., Dr.
Castle, W. R., Mrs.
Caudill, Able
Caudill, Alfred
Caudill, Allen
Caudill, Archy M.
Caudill, Charley
Caudill, Ed
Caudill, Edgar
Caudill, Edmund
Caudill, Elzy
Caudill, Foster
Caudill, Frank
Caudill, Garnett
Caudill, George
Caudill, Henry
Caudill, James
Caudill, Jesse
Caudill, J. M.
Caudill, John
Caudill, John D.
Caudill, John N.
Caudill, J. W.
Caudill, Lou, Mrs.
Caudill, Lundy
Caudill, Luther
Caudill, Marion
Caudill, Mathew
Caudill, Mathie
Caudill, Menifee
Caudill, Monroe
Caudill, Morton
Caudill, Roy
Caudill, Sarah E.
Caudill, Terry
Caudill, Thomas
Caudill, W. B.
Caudill, W. H.
Cecil, G. E.
Cecil, Oscar
Centers, Albert
Centers, Billy
Centers, James
Centers, Lewis
Centers, W. P.
Chaffins, Ren
Chaffins, Shade

Chambers, G. C.
Chandler, Alfred
Chandler, Catherine
Chandler, Charley
Chandler, Columbus
Chandler, D. J.
Chandler, D. K.
Chandler, Frank
Chandler, Hans
Chandler, Harry
Chandler, Henry
Chandler, H. G.
Chandler, Lafe
Chandler, Lucy
Chandler, S. M.
Chandler, Virgil
Chandler, W. N.
Charles, Pete
Cheek, Charley
Childers, Bill
Childers, Charley
Childers, Jack
Childers, John
Childers, Perry, Sr. (Tip)
Childers, Perry, Jr. (Joe)
Childers, Willie
Childers, Wince (Spud)
Chochran, Bruce
Church, Alf
Church, Pat
Clark, Bob
Clark, Eva (Rice)
Clark, George
Clark, George W.
Clark, Henry, Jr.
Clark, James
Clark, James H.
Clark, Logan
Clark, Morgan
Clark, Ray
Clark, Samuel
Clark, Wheeler
Clark, Will
Clark, Willie
Clay, Elmon
Clay, Henry (Paintsv.)
Clay, Henry
Clay, Irvin
Clay, Lloyd
Click, Joe
Coalgrove, Lewis
Cockran, Bruce
Cockran, J. D.
Cockran, John W.
Cockran, Loman
Cockran, Roy
Cockran, Sam
Cockran, Thurman

APPENDIX 461

Coffee, Ballard
Collier, Elmer
Collier, Henry
Collier, J. M.
Collier, John
Collier, Sam
Collier, Sarah
Collins, A. B.
Collins, Andrew
Collins, Bailey
Collins, C. B.
Collins, Charley
Collins, Cordie
Collins, Dewey
Collins, D. W.
Collins, Frank
Collins, Frank P.
Collins, Garfield
Collins, Garland
Collins, George
Collins, G. W.
Collins, Henry
Collins, James A.
Collins, John
Collins, Lloyd
Collins, Malcolm W.
Collins, Manford
Collins, Marion
Collins, McKinley
Collins, Nelson
Collins, Pete
Collins, Polk
Collins, R. C.
Collins, Robert
Collins, Sam
Collins, Sam F.
Collins, Sanford
Collins, Shell
Collins, Sonnie
Collins, Virgil
Collins, Wiley
Collins, Will
Collins, Willie
Collins, W. L.
Collins, W. M.
Collins, W. N.
Collins, W. P. (Perry)
Collins, Zack
Collinsworth, Frank
Collinsworth, Noah
Collinsworth, Oscar
Collinsworth, W. M.
Columbus, James
Columbus, John W., Sr.
Columbus, John W., Jr.
Colvin, Albert
Colvin, Bruce
Colvin, Charley
Colvin, Foster
Colvin, Harve

Colvin, Henry
Colvin, Isaac
Colvin, John H.
Colvin, Mollie
Colvin, Oscar
Colvin, Ray
Colvin, Roy
Colvin, Sarah
Colvin, S. F.
Colvin, Tallie
Colvin, Tom
Colvin, Tom (Dist ?)
Combs, B. C.
Combs, Ben
Combs, Bob
Combs, Burns
Combs, Leslie
Condor, W. L.
Conley, Addie
Conley, Arzie
Conley, Ballard
Conley, Bascom
Conley, Ben F.
Conley, Ben F., Jr.
Conley, Bertha L.
Conley, B. F.
Conley, B. H.
Conley, Brooke
Conley, Buell
Conley, Burnice
Conley, Burns
Conley, Calista M.
Conley, C. F.
Conley, Charley
Conley, Charley C.
Conley, Claud
Conley, Coonie
Conley, Cordie
Conley, Cyrus
Conley, D. B.
Conley, Den (Pippins)
Conley, Den, Jr.
Conley, Dude
Conley, Earl
Conley, Eddie
Conley, E. M.
Conley, Eugene
Conley, Eula
Conley, Everett
Conley, Flem
Conley, Forest
Conley, Frank
  (Paintsville)
Conley, Frank
Conley, Frank J.
Conley, G. E.
Conley, George
Conley, George B.
Conley, George W.
Conley, George W. (Sug)

Conley, G. L.
Conley, Grace, Mrs.
Conley, Haden
Conley, Hargus
Conley, Harrison
Conley, H. B.
Conley, H. C. H.
Conley, Herschell
Conley, H. M.
Conley, Hobart G.
Conley, Irvin
Conley, I. W.
Conley, James
Conley, Jane
Conley, Jane, Mrs.
Conley, J. M.
Conley, John
Conley, John (Dist. 1)
Conley, John C.
Conley, John F.
Conley, John J.
Conley, Konah
Conley, Larence
Conley, L. D.
Conley, Len
Conley, Lewis
Conley, Lindsey
Conley, Lindsey, Jr.
Conley, Lonzo
Conley, Luther
Conley, Margarette,
  Mrs.
Conley, Mary, Mrs.
Conley, Mason
Conley, Maxie
Conley, Millard
Conley, Millard (Dist. 1)
Conley, M. L.
Conley, Noah
Conley, Ollie
Conley, Paris
Conley, Proctor
Conley, Raleigh
Conley, Ralph
Conley, Raymond
Conley, Robert
Conley, Roscoe
Conley, Russell
Conley, Sam
Conley, S. C.
Conley, Sherman
Conley, Tallie
Conley, T. J.
Conley, Tom
Conley, Tom (Dist. 3)
Conley, Troy
Conley, Vern
Conley, Walter
Conley, Walton

Conley, Wayne
Conley, W. G.
Conley, Wick
Conley, W. J.
Conley, Worth
Conley, W. P.
Conley, W. S.
Conley, W. W.
Connard, Frank
Cook, J. A.
Cooper, Annie
Cooper, C. M.
Cooper, C. M., Mrs.
Cooper, Frank
Cooper, J. F.
Cooper, J. H.
Cooper, Ollie
Copley, S. N.
Copley, S. W.
Corder, C. B.
Corder, D. M.
Corder, Emma, Mrs.
Cordial, A. J.
Cordial, Alonzo
Cordial, Ben
Cordial, E. H.
Cordial, George W.
Cordial, G. V.
Cordial, Jenny
Cordial, Jesse
Cordial, Lonzo
Cordial, R. C.
Cordial, Samuel
Cordial, Susan
Coulson, Joe
Cox, B. H.
Cox, B. H., Jr.
Cox, Green
Cox, Thurs Ann
Cox, W. H., Sr.
Cox, W. S., Jr.
Crace, Charlie
Crace, Crosford
Crace, Jason
Crace, Lonzo
Crace, W. L.
Craft, Charles
Craft, Franklin
Craft, N. W. B. (Heirs)
Creslip, E. E.
Creslip, Fred
Creslip, George A., Jr.
Creslip, George A., Sr.
Creslip, Lonnie
Creslip, Willie E.
Crider, Alf
Crider, Grover
Crider, Maymie
Crider, Willie
Crider, W. M.

Crum, Adam
Crum, John W.
Crum, Millard
Crum, Paul
Crum, S. V.
Crum, William
Culwell, Dennis
Culwell, Harrison
Culwell, Jerry
Culwell, Millard
Culwell, W. M.
Cumbo, W. A.
Curnutte, August
Curtis, Hiram
Curtis, John
Curtis, Johny
Curtis, R. M.
Curtis, Thurman
Cyrus, Ben
Dale, Hardin
Dale, Jesse
Dale, John
Dale, Louis
Dale, Sheridan
Dale, Tony
Dale, Walter
Daniel, Alamo
Daniel, Amanda
Daniel, Anderson
Daniel, Anna, Mrs.
Daniel, Arbie
Daniel, Arby
Daniel, Artho
Daniel, Bee
Daniel, Boram
Daniel, Burns
Daniel, Call
Daniel, Catherine
Daniel, Cecil
Daniel, Charley
Daniel, Charlie
Daniel, Charlotte
Daniel, Con
Daniel, Crate
Daniel, C. S.
Daniel, D. H., Dr.
Daniel, Don
Daniel, Ed
Daniel, Edgar
Daniel, E. L.
Daniel, Elizabeth
Daniel Elmer
Daniel, Erchell
Daniel, Estill
Daniel, Everett
Daniel, Eugene
Daniel, F.
Daniel, F. C.
Daniel, F. H.
Daniel, Forest

Daniel, Frank
Daniel, Frank
Daniel, Frank, Jr.
Daniel, F. S.
Daniel, Grant
Daniel, Gus
Daniel, G. V.
Daniel, G. V., Dr.
Daniel, H. A.
Daniel, Ham
Daniel, Harrison
Daniel, Harry
Daniel, Harry
Daniel, Herbert
Daniel, Hobert
Daniel, Irvin
Daniel, Isom
Daniel, Isom
 (Dave's Son)
Daniel, Isom P.
Daniel, James
Daniel, James
Daniel, Jay
Daniel, J. B.
Daniel, J. B. (Dist. 1)
Daniel, J. D.
Daniel, Jeff
Daniel, J. F.
Daniel, J. F. (Dist. 5)
Daniel, J. G.
Daniel, J. H.
Daniel, J. M.
Daniel, Joe, Jr.
Daniel, John
Daniel, John A.
Daniel, John C.
Daniel, John L.
Daniel, John V.
Daniel, Joseph
Daniel, Joseph
Daniel, Josie
Daniel, J. R.
Daniel, Julius
Daniel, J. W.
Daniel, Lafe
Daniel, Larence
Daniel, Lawrence
Daniel, Leonard
Daniel, Leonard
Daniel, Leonard (P'ville)
Daniel, Lonzo
Daniel, L. T.
Daniel, Lucinda
Daniel, Luther
Daniel, Major
Daniel, Margaret
Daniel, Marion
Daniel, Mary L., Mrs.
Daniel, Matilda
Daniel, Milroy

APPENDIX 463

Daniel, Milt
Daniel, M. L.
Daniel, Norman
Daniel, Ora
Daniel, Paris
Daniel, Ransom
Daniel, Rebecca
Daniel, Roscoe
Daniel, Samantha
Daniel, Scott J.
Daniel, Sizemore
Daniel, Tom
Daniel, Valentine
Daniel, Verlan
Daniel, Veslon
Daniel, Virgil
Daniel, Warren
Daniel, W. B.
Daniel, W. B. (Dist. 1)
Daniel, W. E.
Daniel, W. H.
Daniel, Willard
Daniel, Willie
Daniel, W. M.
Davis, Adron
Davis, Albert
Davis, Ben
Davis, Bob
Davis, C. F.
Davis, Charles G.
Davis, Clara
Davis, Clarence
Davis, Dan B.
Davis, Earnie
Davis, Ed
Davis, Elias
Davis, Emma
Davis, Enoch
Davis, Frank
Davis, George
Davis, Grant
Davis, Harry
Davis, Henry
Davis, Henry W.
Davis, Herbert
Davis, Irvin
Davis, J. D.
Davis, Jeff
Davis, Jesse
Davis, Jim
Davis, John
Davis, Johnnie
Davis, J. W.
Davis, Leck
Davis, Lewis
Davis, Lindsey
Davis, Lon
Davis, Lucy
Davis, Marcus
Davis, Martha Jane
Davis, Mary L.
Davis, Mat
Davis, Proctor
Davis, R. L. (Estate)
Davis, Roscoe
Davis, R. T. (Estate)
Davis, Sam
Davis, S. J.
Davis, T. J.
Davis, Vina
Davis, Vint
Davis, Willard
Davis, William
Davis, W. R.
Dawson, Albert
Dawson, Elmer
Dawson, Frank
Dawson, Jim
Dawson, Nick
Dawson, Richard
Dawson, Theodore
Dehart, L. C.
Delong, Ben
Delong, Harrison
Delong, I. R. E.
Delong, James
Delong, John F.
Delong, Marion
Delong, Willie
Dent, C. P.
Dickerson, Gus
Diles, E. D.
Diles, James
Dills, Buren
Dills, Canes
Dills, Earnest
Dills, George (Est.)
Dills, Jesse
Dills, Leonard
Dills, Net
Dills, Ray
Dills, Roy
Dills, Tom, Mrs.
Dills, Zina
Ditty, Will
Dixon, C. C.
Dixon, Della
Dixon, Eugene
Dixon, Guy
Dixon, Haska
Dixon, Hubert
Dixon, John
Dixon, Lenzie
Dixon, Lonzo
Dixon, Orin
Dixon, Rolla
Dixon, Sarah M., Mrs.
Dixon, Tobe
Dixon, Will
Dofas, John
Dollarhide, Rich
Dollarhide, Win
Dorton, A. G. T.
Dorton, D. H.
Dorton, John A.
Dorton, J. R.
Dorton, Thurman
Dotson, R. H.
Doust, George
Ducan, G. W.
Duff, Barney
Duncan, J. M.
Duncan, Mart
Duncan, Scott
Duton, B. J.
Duton, Elias
Duton, Joe
Duton, John
Duton, M.
Duty, James
Duty, Russell
Duty, Will
Dye, Henry
Ealey, Charles
Ealey, David
Ealey, George
Ealey, James
Ealey, Luther
Ealey, Ruth
Ealey, William
Eaton, Lillie
Elliot, Sarah A.
Elliot, Sarah A. (Rice)
Estep, Ambrose
Estep, Curtis
Estep, C. W.
Estep, Edgar
Estep, Elzie
Estep, George
Estep, George H.
Estep, George W.
Estep, Hansford
Estep, Hattie
Estep, James
Estep, James (Dist. 5)
Estep, J. H.
Estep, John R.
Estep, L. F., Mrs.
Estep, Mary
Estep, Okla
Estep, Oscar
Estep, Paris
Estep, Polly Ann
Estep, Roy
Estep, Sadie
Estep, Scott
Estep, S. H.
Estep, Shade
Estep, Sheridan
Estep, Tom

Estep, Thomas J.
Estep, Walas
Estep, W. H.
Evans, Ed
Evans, E. J.
Evans, George N.
Evans, James H.
Evans, Mont
Evans, Proctor
Evans, W. D.
Fairchild, A. M.
Fairchild, Charles
Fairchild, D. M.
Fairchild, Ed
Fairchild, Elmer
Fairchild, Elzie
Fairchild, Enoch
Fairchild, Grant
Fairchild, Henry
Fairchild, Ireland
Fairchild, James
Fairchild, James H.
Fairchild, Jesse
Fairchild, Jessie
Fairchild, J. F.
Fairchild, Joe
Fairchild, John
Fairchild, John M.
Fairchild, John R.
Fairchild, John R., Dr.
Fairchild, Larence
Fairchild, Laurence
Fairchild, Laura
Fairchild, Levi
Fairchild, Lindsey
Fairchild, Lonzo
Fairchild, Mary
Fairchild, M. B.
Fairchild, Millard
Fairchild, N. C.
Fairchild, Nim
Fairchild, Paris
Fairchild, Ray
Fairchild, Roy
Fairchild, Siss
Fairchild, Susan
Fairchild, Walter
Fairchild, Warnie
Fairchild, Wesley
Fairchild, Will
Fairchild, William
Fannin, B. B.
Fannin, Clyde
Fannin, Fred
Fannin, Grover
Fannin, Henry
Fannin, Lena
Fannin, Lenard
Fannin, Newt
Fannin, Vincil

Fannin, Vincil, Mrs.
Fannin, Willie
Farmer, Alex
Farmer, Lou
Farmer, Robert
Farris, Guss
Fenning, Henry P.
Fergerson, Carrie
Fesker, H. D.
Fetter, Allice Mayo
Feuter, Charles J.
Fields, Jeff
Fields, Milam
Fields, Robert
Fields, Thomas
Fife, F. H.
Fiffe, Alma
Fiffe, Cecil
Fiffe, Felix
Fiffe, Henry
Fiffe, James F.
Fiffe, James M.
Fiffe, J. H.
Fiffe, J. J.
Fiffe, J. M.
Fiffe, L. F.
Fiffe, Merida
Fiffe, Noah
Fiffe, Noah M.
Fiffe, Pailey
Fiffe, Proctor
Fiffe, Steve
Fiffe, W. H.
Fitch, C. P.
Fitch, J. C.
Fitch, Mack
Fitch, Oscar
Fitch, Roy
Fitch, Sherman
Fitch, S. U.
Fitch, W. E.
Fitchpatrick, Albert
Fitchpatrick, A. M.
Fitchpatrick, Charles
Fitchpatrick, Elza
Fitchpatrick, Hebern
Fitchpatrick, James M.
Fitchpatrick, J. H.
Fitchpatrick, Luther
Fitchpatrick, Manuel
Fitchpatrick, Manuel, Mrs.
Fitchpatrick, Martha
Fitchpatrick, Mason
Fitchpatrick, Tom
Fitchpatrick, Troy
Fitchpatrick, Roy
Fitchpatrick, Will, Sr.
Fitchpatrick, Wm., Jr.
Fletcher, Eugene

Fletcher, Jesse
Fletcher, Pat
Ford, James
Ford, M. L., Mrs.
Foster, Bud
Foster, Burt
Foster, Camel
Foster, Canbell
Foster, James
Fowler, Otto
Fox, H. M.
Frail, J. H.
Frailey, Burley
Frailey, James
Frailey, Thomas S.
Fraley, Fonzo
Fraley, James
Fraley, Joe
Fraley, John
Fraley, Logan
Fraley, Millard
Fraley, U. S.
Frances, J. T.
Francis, J. W.
Francis, Kennis
Francis, M. U.
Francis, Tom
Francis, W. B.
Franklin, Galen
Franklin, H. C.
Franklin, James
Franklin, John
Franklin, Mack
Franklin, Mary
Franklin, Toral
Franklin, Walker
Frazier, Allie
Frazier, D. W.
Frazier, Ed
Frazier, Ellen
Frazier, Eulah
Frazier, Garland
Frazier, Harry
Frazier, J. H.
Frazier, J. T.
Frazier, M. L.
Frazier, Steve
Frazier, Willie
Freeman, James
Freeman, Manuel
Freeman, William
French, Lloyd W.
Friend, C. S.
Furguson, A.
Furguson, Ben
Furguson, Con
Furguson, Cossie
Furguson, Foster
Furguson, George
Furguson, Hade

APPENDIX 465

Furguson, J. Powel
Furguson, L. P.
Furguson, Nelson
Furguson, Ora
Furguson, W. H.
Furguson, Willie
Furguson, Wince
Gambill, E. H.
Gambill, James M.
Gambill, J. C.
Gambill, J. H.
Gebroski, Paul
Gebroski, Steve
Gee, Thomas
Geiger, Marion
Geiger, O. C.
Gelem, Wese
George, Bradley
George, Esta
Gibbs, Frank
Gibbs, George W.
Gibbs, R. B.
Gibson, B. L.
Gibson, John M.
Gibson, Lee
Gibson, Minnie
Gibson, Nath
Gilbert, W. H.
Gilkerson, Ed
Gillem, G. W.
Gillespie, R. G.
Gillippie, R. G.
Gillmore, John
Gilskr, John
Glispie, Anna
Gobeen, Edgar
Goble, Abe
Goble, A. J.
Goble, Anderson
Goble, Ben
Goble, C. C.
Goble, John
Goble, John W.
Goble, Leze
Goble, Maud
Goble, Nelson
Goble, Raleigh K.
Goble, Tom
Goble, W. H.
Goff, Charles
Goodman, Ed
Gordon, George W.
Gouch, Harvey
Green, Arthur
Green, Bascom
Green, Delbert
Green, E. M.
Green, Farris
Green, Foster
Green, Fred

Green, George, Jr.
Green, G. W.
Green, Henry C.
Green, Jeff
Green, J. F.
Green, Jiles
Green, J. J.
Green, J. L.
Green, J. M.
Green, John
Green, John C.
Green, L. C.
Green, Leander
Green, Lomie
Green, Lon
Green, Lonnie
Green, Martha
Green, Martin
Green, M. L.
Green, Paul
Green, Proctor
Green, Sam
Green, Sam (Dist. 1)
Green, Shadie
Green, Virgil
Green, Walter
Green, W. F.
Green, William
Green, William, Jr.
Green, Willie
Green, W. M.
Greer, Joe
Greer, Malissa
Greer, S. W.
Griffith, Chester
Griffith, Lawrence
Griffith, Lon
Griffith, Wallis
Grim, Minyard
Grim, Shady
Groves, Eli
Groves, Emmet
Gullett, Arthur
Gullett, Bud
Gullett, Charles
Gullett, Charlie
Gullett, Cyntha
Gullett, Daniel
Gullett, Harrison
Gullett, Harry
Gullett, J. B.
Gullett, J. J.
Gullett, Leck
Gullett, Lomie
Gullett, Mack
Gullett, Mary
Gullett, Oscar
Gullett, Roscoe
Gullett, Sherman
Guning, Bell

Hackworth, J. E.
Hackworth, Martin
Hackworth, Roy
Hager, Ben F.
Hager, B. F. (Estate)
Hager, C. G.
Hager, C. M
Hager, Dan M.
Hager, Dan M., Mrs.
Hager, Dick
Hager, Eugene
Hager, Exer
Hager, Frank P.
Hager, Fred
Hager, Geo. W.
Hager, Morgan
Hager, Paul C.
Hager, Russell
Hale, Lizzie
Hall, Albert
Hall, Alonzo
Hall, A. M.
Hall, Bert
Hall, Calloway
Hall, Cart
Hall, Curt
Hall, D. P.
Hall, Elizabeth
Hall, Elzie
Hall, Grant
Hall, Isom
Hall, James
Hall, James N.
Hall, James T.
Hall, J. C.
Hall, J. D.
Hall, Jerry
Hall, J. G.
Hall, J. Melvin
Hall, John
Hall, John M.
Hall, J. P.
Hall, Lenard
Hall, Lon
Hall, Lonnie
Hall, Lloyd M.
Hall, Martha
Hall, Martin
Hall, Martin M.
Hall, Mary J.
Hall, Monroe
Hall, Paul B., Dr.
Hall, Rosa
Hall, S. H.
Hall, Vela (Aunt)
Hall, Walbridge
Hall, Wiley
Hall, Will
Hall, Willie
Halton, Bill

Halton, Dakota
Halton, John
Hamilton, Bud Goble
Hamilton, Enry, Jr.
Hamilton, F. P.
Hamilton, Isaac
Hamilton, Jeff
Hamilton, John
Hamilton, Thurman
Hamilton, W. M.
Hamilton, W. W.
Hammond, J. W.
Hamons, John
Hampton, Ed
Hampton, Harry
Hampton, W. H.
Haney, Clay
Haney, Floyd, Jr.
Haney, Floyd, Sr.
Haney, Will
Hannah, A. J.
Hannah, Bill
Hannah, Enoch
Hannah, J. H.
Hannah, Johnie
Hannah, Millard
Hannah, Proctor
Hannah, Ross
Hannah, Walter
Hannah, Wayne
Hare, J. E.
Harless, Lacy
Harmon, Adam
Harmon, Henry
Harmon, Josie
Harper, J. H.
Harris, Charles
Harris, E. F.
Harris, J. B.
Harris, Jim
Harris, Mary
Harris, Milt
Harris, Olna
Harris, R. H.
Harris, Willie
Harris, W. W.
Harrison, L. D.
Harrison, W. M.
Hatcher, J. M.
Hatcher, Lucy, Mrs.
Hatfield, John
Hatfield, Irvin
Hays, Arch
Hays, Herbert
Hays, J. H.
Hays, Lon
Hays, Mart
Hazelrigg, H. G., Dr.
Hazelrigg, Murah
Hazlett, Ballard

Hazlett, Clyde
Hazlett, John
Hazlett, John A.
Hazlett, Noah
Hazlett, Sam
Hazlett, Taylor
Hazlett, Tom
Heddleson, L. R.
Helton, Charles
Helton, Den
Helton, Paul
Hensley, A. J.
Hensley, Robert
Henzman, C. B.
Hickman, Fred
Hicks, Ben
Hill, J. C.
Hill, Richard
Hill, Selina
Hilton, David
Hilton, Dewey
Hilton, George
Hilton, Greenville
Hilton, Kelse
Hinkle, Cobb
Hitchcock, Allice
Hitchcock, Ben
Hitchcock, Bennie
Hitchcock, Caleb
Hitchcock, Cecil
Hitchcock, Challie
Hitchcock, Charley
Hitchcock, D. S.
Hitchcock, Ellen
Hitchcock, Elijah
Hitchcock, Estill
Hitchcock, G. B.
Hitchcock, General
Hitchcock, Grant
Hitchcock, Jessie
Hitchcock, John
Hitchcock, Johnie
Hitchcock, Mary Jane
Hitchcock, Virgie
Hitchcock, Wiley
Hite, Garfield
Hite, James
Hite, Lula
Hite, Molley
Hobbs, Bill
Hobson, Mary
Hobson, Millard
Hobson, Priscilla
Hobson, T. W.
Holbrook, A. M.
Holbrook, Arthur
Holbrook, Cam
Holbrook, C. W.
Holbrook, Detroit
Holbrook, Dewey

Holbrook, G. W.
Holbrook, Harry
Holbrook, Herbert
Holbrook, J. H., Dr.
Holbrook, John
Holbrook, John F.
Holbrook, John H.
Holbrook, J. R.
Holbrook, J. S.
Holbrook, Keneth
Holbrook, L. D.
Holbrook, Mary
Holbrook, P. T.
Hollett, Charles
Holt, Mont
Honaker, Sam
Honeycutt, Esaw
Honeycutt, Janes
Honeycutt, Johny
Honeycutt, Malcom
Honeycutt, Nathan
Horn, Albert
Horn, Belle
Horn, Earl
Horn, Jesse
Horn, John
Horn, Julia
Horn, Lonzo
Horn, Norman
Horn, Roba
Horn, Son
Horn, Walker
Houston, John
Howard, Campbell
Howard, James
Howard, Joe
Howard, John R.
Howard, Lewis
Howard, Lina
Howard, Stephen
Howard, Victoria
Howe, Don
Howe, J. H.
Howell, Lanthorn
Howes, E. F.
Howes, Ethel
Howes, Fred
Howes, H. S. (Estate)
Howes, John F.
Howes, R. G.
Howes, Sarah E., Mrs.
Howes, Turner
Howley, W. S.
Huff, Frank
Huff, Millard
Huff, Quiller
Huff, Roy
Hughes, Andy
Hughes, George
Hughes, John

Hughes, Lila
Hughes, P. L.
Hughes, R. H.
Hughes, W. H.
Hunley, Bill
Hunley, Charles
Hunt, Jim
Hurt, Abe
Hurt, Bascom
Hurt, Ben
Hurt, Bill
Hurt, George
Hurt, Sam
Hyden, Ballard
Hyden, Ed
Hyden, Mack
Hyden, Richard
Hyten, Will
Ingram, Jimmie
Irvin, W. H.
Irvin, W. H., Mrs.
Jackson, A. L.
Jackson, Arlie
Jackson, Elisha
Jackson, Frank
Jackson, Henry
Jackson, Ira
Jackson, Isiah, Jr.
Jackson, James
Jackson, J. J.
Jackson, John Allen
Jackson, Nathan
Jackson, Robert
Jackson, Stanford
Jackson, Tony
Jackson, Walter
Jacobs, Henry
Jacobs, Lou
Jarrell, Finley
Jarrell, Golda
Jasper, Robert
Jayne, Andy
Jayne, Earnest
Jayne, Irvin
Jayne, Jessie
Jayne, Joe
Jayne, Julia
Jayne, J. W.
Jayne, Sarah
Jenkins, Ira
Jenkins, Martha
Jenkins, Oliver
Jennings, Calista
Jennings, Conali
Jennings, Elbert
Jennings, Emerson
Jennings, J. P.
Jerey, Mick
Johnson, Arminta
Johnson, Buell

Johnson, Catherine
Johnson, Charles J.
Johnson, Charlie
Johnson, Colfax
Johnson, David
Johnson, Dewey
Johnson, E. O., Dr.
Johnson, Farry
Johnson, Frank
Johnson, Grant
Johnson, James
Johnson, Janes
Johnson, Jimes
Johnson, J. M.
Johnson, John
Johnson, J. R.
Johnson, Julius
• Johnson, Levi
Johnson, Lydia M.
Johnson, Mahala J.
Johnson, Nancy
Johnson, Otto
Johnson, Robert
Johnson, S. J.
Johnson, Stonewall
Johnson, W. A.
Johnson, Walter
Johnstone, W. E.
Jones, A. R.
Jones, Brownlow
Jones, Delbert
Jones, Eleanor
Jones, E. T.
Jones, F. A.
Jones, Giddie
Jones, John A.
Jones, L. B.
Jones, Lennie
Jones, Lewis
Jones, L. H.
Jones, Lyman
Jones, Malissa
Jones, Nathaniel
Jones, Reedye
Jones, Silvester
Jones, Walter
Jones, Wilda
Jordon, Carl
Joseph, J. B.
Joseph, Woodson
Justice, Fraley
Justice, John
Justice, Lindy
Justice, Lucy
Justice, W. C.
Kane, Dave
Kazee, Charley
Kazee, Edgar
Kazee, John
Keaton, J. W.

Keaton, Lant
Keaton, Louis
Keaton, Mariana
Keaton, Martha
Keaton, Rebecca
Keaton, Tom
Kelly, A. M.
Kelly, Dewey
Kelly, George
Kelly, Hendrick
Kelly, Joel
Kelly, John S.
Kelly, Luther
Kelly, Millard
Kelly, Sherley
Kelly, S. Q.
Kelly, Wayne
Kelly, W. M.
Kennard, Ben F.
Kennard, Frank
Kennard, G. W.
Kennard, J. N.
Kennard, R. A.
Kennard, R. L.
Kennard, W. A.
Kerns, Clarence
Kilburn, George W.
Kimber, B. H.
Kimber, J. H.
Kimbler, Albert
Kimbler, Alonzo
Kimbler, Jane
Kimbler, J. B.
Kimbler, J. M.
Kimbler, J. W.
Kimbleton, Jim
Kimbleton, J. M.
Kimbleton, T. H.
Kimbleton, W. A.
King, Charley, Sr.
King, Charley
King, James
King, Jessie
King, Lloyd
King, Milt
King, Raymond
King, S. P.
King, Tallie
Kirk, A. J., Jr.
Kirk, A. J., Sr.
Kirk, Chas. A.
Kirk, Conrad R.
Kirk, Edna J.
Kirk, Holmes
Kirk, M. C.
Kirk, Raymond
Kistner, Louisa
Kistner, Malcolm
Kistner, Norris
Kistner, Samuel

Knapp, G. A.
Kretzer, Burdett
Kretzer, Will
Lambert, James
Laubert, Garden
Laubert, John
Lavender, Eddie
Lavender, Henry
Law, Harry
Lawson, Ranzie
Layne, M. L.
Lee, Ed
Leedy, Dan
Leek, Sam
Lemaster, A. B.
Lemaster, A. L.
Lemaster, Alfred
Lemaster, Alice
Lemaster, Arthur
Lemaster, Bascom
Lemaster, C. M.
Lemaster, Dan
Lemaster, Dock
Lemaster, Earnest
Lemaster, Ed
Lemaster, Edgar
Lemaster, E. F.
Lemaster, E. G.
Lemaster, E. L.
Lemaster, Ellen
Lemaster, Elliot
Lemaster, Eunice
Lemaster, Everett
Lemaster, F. H.
Lemaster, Flem
Lemaster, Floyd
Lemaster, Fred
Lemaster, Galem
Lemaster, George
Lemaster, H. C.
Lemaster, Hollie
Lemaster, J.
Lemaster, James B. (Estate)
Lemaster, James D.
Lemaster, Jasper
Lemaster, J. B.
Lemaster, Jeff
Lemaster, Jermitta
Lemaster, J. M.
Lemaster, John
Lemaster, J. R.
Lemaster, L. F.
Lemaster, Lilly
Lemaster, Lloyd
Lemaster, Logan
Lemaster, Lunda
Lemaster, Luther
Lemaster, Mace
Lemaster, Mandy

Lemaster, Martha
Lemaster, Martin
Lemaster, Mildred
Lemaster, Milton
Lemaster, Monroe
Lemaster, Oscar
Lemaster, Pae
Lemaster, Perlie
Lemaster, Phoebe
Lemaster, Powell
Lemaster, Roscoe
Lemaster, Roy
Lemaster, Sam
Lemaster, Sant
Lemaster, Sarah
Lemaster, Sherman
Lemaster, S. L.
Lemaster, S. M.
Lemaster, Sola
Lemaster, Thomas J.
Lemaster, Thurman
Lemaster, T. M.
Lemaster, Tommie
Lemaster, Tommie E.
Lemaster, W. D.
Lemaster, W. E.
Lemaster, W. H.
Lemaster, Willie
Lemaster, W. J.
Lemaster, W. L.
Lemaster, W. R.
Lenis, Charles
Lenis, Floyd
Leslie, Arthur
Leslie, Calinda
Leslie, D. B.
Leslie, Myrtle
Lester, C. L.
Lester, Ira
Lewis, Cecil
Lewis, Frank
Lewis, Jerry
Lewis, Martha
Lewis, Pauline, Mrs.
Lewis, Robie
Lewis, Sylvie
Lilly, Bud
Lilly, Marion
Lilly, Mont
Lilly, Onda
Lilly, Samp
Litteral, Benson
Litteral, Bert
Litteral, Dan
Litteral, Flem
Litteral, H. C.
Litteral, H. H.
Litteral, H. P.
Litteral, John E.
Litteral, Joseph

Litteral, Julia, Mrs.
Litteral, Martha, Mrs.
Litteral, Roy
Litteral, Sarah C,. Mrs.
Litteral, Virgie, Mrs.
Litteral, Warren
Litteral, W. C.
Litteral, W. J.
Little, William
Litton, W. M.
Litz, Chas. D.
Lockhart, Jim
Lockwood, B. G.
Lockwood, H. B.
Lockwood, S. J.
Logan, Marshall
Long, Alfred
Long, Charley
Long, Darwin J.
Long, F. G.
Long, Floyd
Long, James
Long, Lundy
Long, W. W.
Lovely, Oscar
Lowe, Fred
Lyons, Abraham
Lyons, A. M.
Lyons, Arminta
Lyons, Arnold
Lyons, Clinton
Lyons, C. T.
Lyons, Edward
Lyons, Essie
Lyons, Evaline
Lyons, F. M.
Lyons, Forest
Lyons, George
Lyons, Guy
Lyons, Ham
Lyons, Harry
Lyons, H. B.
Lyons, James
Lyons, Jessie
Lyons, J. L., Dr.
Lyons, John
Lyons, Kesiah, Mrs.
Lyons, Lafayette
Lyons, Landon
Lyons, Lewis C.
Lyons, Manford
Lyons, Martela
Lyons, Proctor
Lyons, R. C.
Lyons, Roscoe
Lyons, Sam
Lyons, Sanford
Lyons, Sarah
Lyons, Sherman
Lyons, Vinson

APPENDIX 469

Lyons, Willie
Maggard, J. C.
Mahan, Ben F.
Mahan, Earl
Mahan, Harry
Mahan, John
Mahan, Mace
Mahan, Sam
Mann, S. L.
Marcum, Josh
Marcum, W. M.
Marshall, A. J.
Marshall, Asa
Marshall, John
Marshall, Willis
Martin, D. J.
Martin, Scott
Matney, J. H.
Matney, Mary
May, Ballard
May, Claude
May, Curtis
May, Eddie
May, Hannie
May, H. H., Mrs.
May, John M.
May, Price
May, R. L.
May, S. D.
May, Willie
May, W. P.
Mayhew, George W.
Maynard, England
Maynard, Harrison
Maynard, Rufus
Maynard, W. J.
Mayo, Andy
Mayo, Charles
Mayo, John
Mayo, Margaret
Mayo, Milton
Mayo, Rida, Mrs.
Mayo, Robert
Mayo, W. J.
Mays, Andy
McBrayer, C. H.
McCalister, James
McCarty, Burns
McCarty, Clifton
McCarty, Forest
McCarty, George
McCarty, Gratts
McCarty, James F.
McCarty, Jessie
McCarty, John
McCarty, John H.
McCarty, Oscar
McCarty, Paris
McCarty, Robert
McCarty, Sarah

McCarty, W. M.
McCloud, Arminta
McCloud, George
McCloud, Mary
McCloud, Phonzo
McCloud, Rachael
McCloud, W. I.
McClure, Dewey
McClure, Fred
McClure, Margaret
McCourt, John
McCourt, Tom
McCoy, Abe
McCoy, Bud
McCoy, Lizza
McDail, Joe
McDowell, John
McDowell, Milton
McFaddin, Claud
McFaddin, Ed
McFaddin, George
McFaddin, Isaac
McFaddin, Laud
McFaddin, Ross
McFaddin, W. M.
McFarland, Sina
McIntosh, Paris
McKay, Mack
McKenzie, Albert
McKenzie, Albert, Mrs.
McKenzie, Bee
McKenzie, Bert
McKenzie, Bert L.
McKenzie, Burns
McKenzie, Charles
McKenzie, Charley
McKenzie, Dan
McKenzie, Dennie
McKenzie, Dock
McKenzie, Dock Will
McKenzie, E.
McKenzie, Elzie
McKenzie, E. M.
McKenzie, Floyd
McKenzie, Forest
McKenzie, George
McKenzie, Germ
McKenzie, Hallick
McKenzie, Hallie
McKenzie, Harrison
McKenzie, Harry
McKenzie, Haskell
McKenzie, Henry
McKenzie, Hereford
McKenzie, H. P.
McKenzie, I. W.
McKenzie, Jack
McKenzie, James
McKenzie, Jay

McKenzie, J. D.
McKenzie, Jethro
McKenzie, J. M. H.
McKenzie, Joe
McKenzie, Joe Lee
McKenzie, J. T.
McKenzie, Kate
McKenzie, Lindsey
McKenzie, Lou
McKenzie, Lydia
McKenzie, Margaret
McKenzie, Matilda
McKenzie, Merida
McKenzie, Minnie
McKenzie, M. O.
McKenzie, N. A.
McKenzie, O. B.
McKenzie, Oscar
McKenzie, Powell
McKenzie, Rachael
McKenzie, Ray
McKenzie, Rilda
McKenzie, Roba
McKenzie, Sebastan
McKenzie, Talbert
McKenzie, T. F.
McKenzie, T. J.
McKenzie, Tobe
McKenzie, Trigg
McKenzie, Vertresa
McKenzie, W. E.
McKenzie, W. H.
McKenzie, Willie
McKenzie, Willie (Andy's Son)
McKenzie, W. M.
McKenzie, W. R.
McNeal, H. R.
Meade, C. C.
Meade, Curtis
Meade, Fred
Meade, George
Meade, Gus
Meade, James
Meade, Jeff
Meade, John
Meade, John A.
Meade, John C.
Meade, J. R.
Meade, L. G., Dr.
Meade, Lindsey
Meade, L. L.
Meade, Lloyd
Meade, Milt
Meade, Nollis
Meade, Paris
Meade, R. C.
Meade, Robert
Meade, Sam
Meade, Susan

Meade, Taylor
Meade, Thomas
Meade, W. R.
Meadows, Ben
Meadows, Milt
Meddings, George
Meddings, Lawrence
Meddings, Stanley
Medley, Will
Meek, Aaron
Meek, Asa
Meek, B.
Meek, Bud
Meek, Clint
Meek, Curtis
Meek, Davis
Meek, Delda
Meek, Elias
Meek, Flem
Meek, G. B.
Meek, Harrison
Meek, Harry
Meek, Isaac
Meek, Jack
Meek, James
Meek, Jess
Meek, J. N.
Meek, John
Meek, John C.
Meek, Jonathan
Meek, Lafe
Meek, Robert
Meek, Rosalee
Meek, Shady
Meek, William
Meek, Winifred
Melvin, Ad
Melvin, Billie
Melvin, Clyde
Melvin, George
Melvin, John
Melvin, Ray
Melvin, R. L.
Messer, John
Messir, W. A.
Michael, Harry
Miles, Fred
Miller, E.
Miller, Eugene B.
Miller, Frank
Milles, Burnard
Millis, J. L.
Millis, John
Millis, Willis
Moffitt, G. K.
Moffitt, J. C.
Moles, Frank
Moles, Jeff
Mollett, Ali
Mollett, Ben

Mollett, Eddie
Mollett, Elias
Mollett, Elijah
Mollett, G. W.
Mollett, Jacob
Mollett, Jake
Mollett, James
Mollett, J. C.
Mollett, John B.
Mollett, Lafe
Mollett, Lydia
Mollett, Rafe
Mollett, Ratice
Mollett, Willie
Mollett, W. T.
Montgomery, James
Montgomery, J. W.
Moore, Aaron
Moore, Bill
Moore, Bryce
Moore, F. M.
Moore, George W.
Moore, G. K.
Moore, James
Moore, James W.
Moore, John
Moore, John D.
Moore, P. H.
Moore, Scott
Moore, Tom
Moran, Tom
Mullins, Jerry
Mullins, Ralph
Mullins, Will
Mullins, Wince
Murphy, A. J.
Murphy, Bob, Mrs.
Murphy, Dewey
Murphy, Everett
Murphy, James C.
Murphy, Lloyd
Murphy, Norman
Murphy, Pat
Murray, Alvin
Murray, Arba
Murray, Arby
Murray, B.
Murray, Bethley
Murray, Cas
Murray, C. B.
Murray, Clint
Murray, Edgar
Murray, Elbert
Murray, Elzie
Murray, Emett
Murray, Farris
Murray, Frank
Murray, Fred
Murray, Fred, Jr.
Murray, Jeff

Murray, Jesse
Murray, J. P.
Murray, Leo
Murray, Lloyd
Murray, Lonzo
Murray, Matilda
Murray, Ray
Murray, R. H.
Murray, Roy
Murray, Sarah
Murray, S. R.
Murray, Tom
Murray, Winifred
Music, Abe
Music, Alex
Music, Amos
Music, Andrew
Music, Arch
Music, Ben
Music, Buck
Music, D. Mart
Music, Earl
Music, E. R.
Music, George Dewey
Music, Harland
Music, Henry
Music, Irvin
Music, Jake
Music, James
Music, James A.
Music, Jeff
Music, John
Music, John A.
Music, John D.
Music, John E.
Music, Johnny
Music, J. W.
Music, Lewis
Music, Martin
Music, Melvin
Music, Nute
Music, S. M.
Music, Tom
Music, W. H.
Mynlier, Fred
Neeby, A. B.
Nehez, Steve
Nelan, Robert
Nelson, E. B.
Nelson, J. W.
Nelson, Ralph
Nelson, Will
Newman, John G.
Newsom, Jarvey
Nickell, Albert
Nickell, J. A.
Nickell, Lee
Nickell, Loss
Nickell, W. M.
O'Bryan, Clyde

APPENDIX 471

O'Bryan, Ed
O'Bryan, Harry
O'Bryan, J. U.
O'Bryan, Lula
O'Bryan, Millard
O'Bryan, William
Ollie, Sam
Oppenheimer, Ralph
Oppenheimer, Rudolph
Oppenheimer, Silas
Oppenheimer, Wm. O.
Orr, B. A.
Orsagus, Jim
Osborne, A. J.
Osborne, A. M.
Osborne, Calvin
Osborne, Clint
Osborne, David, Dr.
Osborne, Marion (Dock)
Osborne, Ellen
Osborne, Harrison
Osborne, John
Osborne, Lee
Osborne, Mac
Osborne, Malissa
Osborne, Proctor
Osborne, Thomas
Osborne, Walter
Osborne, Willie
Owens, Kelly
Owens, Lee
Pace, C. F.
Pack, A. B.
Pack, A. T.
Pack, Charles
Pack, Charley
Pack, Dick
Pack, E. L.
Pack, Elzie
Pack, G. W.
Pack, Henry
Pack, Hubert
Pack, Kennie
Pack, James
Pack, Jay
Pack, J. W.
Pack, L. C.
Pack, Lee
Pack, Remmie
Pack, R. M.
Pack, Vinson
Pack, Walter
Pack, W. M.
Page, Garley
Painter, Howard
Panigan, L. J.
Parrigan, L. J.
Parson, Ben
Parson, Coger

Parson, Linzie
Parter, Ben, Mrs.
Parter, Paul
Patrick, Ben
Patrick, Bradley
Patrick, Challie
Patrick, Charley
Patrick, Clista A.
Patrick, C. M.
Patrick, Doke
Patrick, Herschell
Patrick, Johnson
Patrick, K.
Patrick, Kelley
Patrick, Noah
Patrick, Oscar F.
Patrick, Pite
Patrick, R. A.
Patrick, R. C.
Patrick, Sam
Patrick, S. H.
Patton, F. D.
Patton, R. A.
Patton, Thomas D.
Peffer, G. G.
Pelix, James
Pelphrey, Amos
Pelphrey, Ben F.
Pelphrey, Challie
Pelphrey, Charles
Pelphrey, Clark
Pelphrey, Dan
Pelphrey, Dock
Pelphrey, Frank
Pelphrey, Harris
Pelphrey, Harry
Pelphrey, Jesse F.
Pelphrey, Jesse, Jr.
Pelphrey, J. H.
Pelphrey, John
Pelphrey, **Laura**
Pelphrey, Lula
Pelphrey, Millard
Pelphrey, Milt
Pelphrey, Obie
Pelphrey, Paris
Pelphrey, Roy
Pelphrey, Smith
Pence, D. B.
Pendleton, Billie
Pendleton, Grover
Pendleton, James, Sr.
Pendleton, R. T.
Pendleton, Trigg
Pendleton, Turner
Pendleton, W. J.
Pendleton, William
Penix, Fanny
Penix, James
Penix, J. C.

Penix, John
Penix, Leonard
Penix, Mary
Penix, Paris
Penix, R. A.
Pennington, Arthur
Pennington, Media, Mrs.
Perce, C. M.
Perkey, Buddy
Perkey, Jam
Perkins, Billie
Perkins, Earl
Perkins, Willie
Perkins, Willie, Mrs.
Perposki, Pite
Perry, Albert
Perry, C. E.
Perry, Dave
Perry, Elbert
Perry, F. M.
Perry, George
Perry, George C.
Perry, G. C., Mrs.
Perry, Hade
Perry, Harlan
Perry, James
Perry, Jeff
Perry, Laura
Perry, Mitchel
Perry, Ralph
Perry, Roy
Perry, T. H.
Perry, W. E.
Perry, W. T.
Phelps, Jay
Phelps, John
Phelps, Lee
Phelps, Lon
Phelps, Sam
Phelps, Thomas
Phillips, Ala
Phillips, D. A.
Phillips, Talbia
Phillips, M. P.
Phillis, A. W.
Pickerell, H. B.
Pickle, James
Pickle, Johnnie
Picklesimer, Albert
Picklesimer, Dorman
Picklesimer, Elbert
Picklesimer, Ella
Picklesimer, Elzie
Picklesimer, Farmer
Picklesimer, Frank
Picklesimer, G. A.
Picklesimer, Henry
Picklesimer, Homer D.
Picklesimer, Jennie

Picklesimer, Jim
Picklesimer, J. H., Rev.
Picklesimer, J. J.
Picklesimer, John H.
Picklesimer, Johnny
Picklesimer, Kelly
Picklesimer, Lucy Ann
Picklesimer, Maggie
Picklesimer, Maurice
Picklesimer, M. M.
Picklesimer, Rafe
Picklesimer, R. W.
Picklesimer, Sam
Picklesimer, Sanford
Picklesimer, Sherman
Picklesimer, Simon
Picklesimer, Smith
Picklesimer, U. G.
Picklesimer, Virgie
Picklesimer, Virgil
Picklesimer, W. R.
Pigg, Dennie
Pigg, S. M.
Pinson, Sallie C., Mrs.
Plumer, Isiah
Plummer, Charles
Plummer, John
Pol, Albert
Poole, A. E.
Porter, Arbie
Porter, B., Mrs.
Porter, Ben, Mrs.
Porter, John
Porter, Paul
Powell, Earl
Powell, Glen
Powers, Billy
Powers, Brayden
Powers, Garfield
Powers, George
Powers, G. W.
Powers, Jerry
Prater, Cap
Prater, E. H.
Prater, Lack
Prater, Laura
Prater, Sherman
Prater, Wardie
Prater, Wilber
Prater, Will
Pratt, Tom
Preston, A. C.
Preston, Acy
Preston, Arthur
Preston, Az
Preston, Ballard
Preston, Bert
Preston, Bird
Preston, Bruce
Preston, Carson

Preston, Charles
Preston, Charles E.
Preston, Charley
Preston, Clate
Preston, Claton
Preston, Claude
Preston, Clell
Preston, Clell, Jr.
Preston, Clyde
Preston, C. W.
Preston, Cyrus
Preston, Dan
Preston, Dan E.
Preston, D. Lynn
Preston, Earl
Preston, Earnest
Preston, Edgar
Preston, E. H.
Preston, Elijah
Preston, Ella
Preston, E. P.
Preston, F. B.
Preston, F. M.
Preston, Forest
Preston, Fred
Preston, George
Preston, George W.
Preston, G. L.
Preston, Glance
Preston, Glenn F.
Preston, Guy
Preston, Guy W.
Preston, Harry
Preston, Herbert
Preston, Hop
Preston, Hopkins
Preston, Irvin
Preston, Isaac
Preston, James
Preston, James L.
Preston, J. B.
Preston, J. C.
Preston, J. E.
Preston, Jebb
Preston, Jess W.
Preston, Jesse
Preston, Jim
Preston, Joe
Preston, John
Preston, John E.
Preston, John H.
Preston, John L.
Preston, John W.
Preston, Julia
Preston, J. W.
Preston, Lafe
Preston, L. B.
Preston, L. M.
Preston, Lon E.
Preston, Margaret

Preston, Marvin
Preston, McKinley
Preston, M. G.
Preston, Mildred
Preston, Mitchel
Preston, N. M.
Preston, Ora
Preston, Ora May
Preston, Paris
Preston, Russell
Preston, Samuel
Preston, Sanford
Preston, Solomon
Preston, Perry ("Tip")
Preston, Perry ("Joe")
Preston, Thomas J.
Preston, Vina
Preston, Waitman
Preston, Warren H.
Preston, Warren L.
Preston, W. H.
Preston, William
Preston, William R.
Preston, W. J.
Preston, W. L.
Preston, W. M. ("Bill Dock")
Preston, W. M. ("Bug")
Preston, Winfield
Preston, W. R.
Preston, W. S.
Price, B.
Price, Ballard
Price, C. C.
Price, Charley
Price, Clarence
Price, E. R.
Price, Fannie
Price, Flossie, Mrs.
Price, Frank
Price, George W.
Price, G. M.
Price, Green
Price, Harlin
Price, Henry
Price, Jeff
Price, Jesse
Price, John
Price, L.
Price, Lon
Price, Malcolm
Price, Martin L.
Price, M. L.
Price, N. J.
Price, N. K.
Price, Otto
Price, Russell
Price, R. W.
Price, Sarah

APPENDIX 473

Price, W. S.
Prince, George
Prince, Harlan
Prince, James M.
P'Simer, James
Puckett, Charley
Puckett, Clem
Puckett, Lacy
Puckett, Rosa
Pugh, C. W.
Radcliff, Arthur
Radcliff, Clark
Radcliff, Eli
Radcliff, Elliot
Radcliff, Esan
Radcliff, Frank
Radcliff, George
Radcliff, James
Radcliff, John E.
Radcliff, Leander
Radcliff, Lonnie
Radcliff, Millard
Radcliff, Topsy
Radcliff, Warran
Ramey, Asa
Ramey, Dallas
Ramey, Don
Ramey, Elex
Ramey, Elizabeth
Ramey, Evalina
Ramey, Fairy
Ramey, Frank, Dr.
Ramey, G. W.
Ramey, John
Ramey, L. C., Mrs.
Ramey, N. L.
Ramey, Owen
Ramey, Sandy
Ramey, Sarah
Ramey, S. M.
Ramey, T. J.
Ramey, W. E.
Ramey, Willey
Ramsey, P. W.
Randolph, Herschell
Ratliff, A. D.
Ratliff, Alfred
Ratliff, Bud
Ratliff, Cap
Ratliff, Dick
Ratliff, Ed
Ratliff, Ernie
Ratliff, Fred
Ratliff, Jesse
Ratliff, Lydia M.
Ratliff, Paris
Ratliff, Press
Ratliff, Sam
Ratliff, Sandy
Ratliff, Walker

Ratliff, W. H.
Ratliff, William
Reed, Albert
Reed, Arthur
Reed, Ben F.
Reed, Docky
Reed, George
Reed, George W.
Reed, James
Reed, Jeff
Reed, Johny
Reed, Milt
Reed, Walter
Reed, William
Reynolds, Eugene
Reynolds, J. J.
Reynolds, Leslie
Rhidford, Maud
Rice, Alex
Rice, Alger
Rice, Alonzo
Rice, Amanda
Rice, Archie M.
Rice, Barton
Rice, Bascom
Rice, B. G.
Rice, Brice
Rice, C. C.
Rice, Charley
Rice, Charley L.
Rice, Dave
Rice, Dewey
Rice, Elizabeth
Rice, Everett
Rice, F. M.
Rice, Forest
Rice, Fred
Rice, Ganes
Rice, G. B.
Rice, George B.
Rice, George M.
Rice, George W.
Rice, G. H.
Rice, G. H., Mrs.
Rice, German
Rice, Grant, Dr.
Rice, Harry
Rice, H. B., Mrs.
Rice, Hebern
Rice, H. M.
Rice, Irvin
Rice, Isaac G.
Rice, James C.
Rice, J. B.
Rice, J. C.
Rice, J. E.
Rice, John
Rice, John C.
Rice, John R.
Rice, J. P.

Rice, Julia, Mrs.
Rice, Kate
Rice, Leck
Rice, Link
Rice, Lon
Rice, Luther
Rice, Luther, Jr.
Rice, Malinda
Rice, Manford
Rice, Martha E.
Rice, Martha J.
Rice, Martin N.
Rice, Maude
Rice, Mintie
Rice, Mitchel
Rice, Mose
Rice, Nathaniel J.
Rice, Norman R.
Rice, Oscar
Rice, S.
Rice, Sherman
Rice, Smith
Rice, Stella
Rice, Thomas
Rice, Wade
Rice, Walter
Rice, Wayne
Rice, W. E.
Rice, W. H.
Rice, Will
Rice, William
Rice, Wilson
Rice, Y. B.
Richardson, Woods
Richmond, Chester
Richmond, H. B.
Richmond, Henry
Richmond, Lige
Richmond, Willie
Richmond, W. R.
Rickman, George
Riffe, Austin
Riffe, Howard
Rigsby, Cordilla
Rigsby, D. P.
Rigsby, Lon
Rigsby, Proctor
Rigsby, Squire
Rigsby, Watt
Rigsby, W. T.
Rister, Green
Ritchie, Donna
Ritchie, Dudley
Ritchie, Lillie
Rivers, Bert
Rivers, George
Rivers, John
Rivers, S. R.
Rivers, Susan
Rivers, Susan J.

Rivers, W. D.
Rivers, W. F.
Roberts, Bailey
Roberts, B. F.
Roberts, B. J.
Roberts, Carmon
Roberts, Charley
Roberts, D. H.
Roberts, D. H., Mrs.
Roberts, Earl
Roberts, Elza
Roberts, Everett
Roberts, Fred
Roberts, Ida
Roberts, Joe
Roberts, John
Roberts, Norman
Roberts, Pat
Roberts, Tallie
Roberts, T. J.
Roberts, Veirre
Roberts, Vern
Roberts, Verne
Robinson, B. F.
Robinson, George W.
Robinson, H. D.
Robinson, Homer
Robinson, John
Robinson, John B.
Robinson, John W.
Robinson, J. W.
Robinson, Loulie
Robinson, M. H.
Robinson, Paulina, Mrs.
Robinson, Proctor
Robinson, T. S.
Robinson, Willie
Robinson, W. L.
Robinson, W. T.
Roman, Fleet
Rose, Arby
Rose, Charles
Rose, J. M.
Rose, John
Ross, D. S.
Ross, Eliphus
Ross, John
Ross, Mason
Ross, Mitchel
Ross, M. S.
Ross, Oscar
Ross, R. M.
Ross, S. P.
Ross, W. H.
Rowland, Armstrong
Rowland, Fred
Rowland, J. F.
Rowland, J. H.
Rowland, John
Rowland, Richard

Rowland, W. L.
Rule, C. T.
Russell, Ed
Russell, Harry B.
Ruth, James B.
Sadler, J. M.
Sadler, Millard
Sadler, Priscilla
Sadler, Thomas
Sadler, Victor
Sagraves, Ashley
Sagraves, Dora
Sagraves, Ivel
Sagraves, Vinson
Sales, Howard C.
Salmon, Eddie
Salmon, James
Salmon, John
Salmon, Martin
Salmon, Nancie
Salmon, Rich
Salmon, Thomas
Salmon, W. G.
Salyer, A. L.
Salyer, Alafair
Salyer, Alson
Salyer, A. M.
Salyer, Ambers
Salyer, Ben
Salyer, Ben F.
Salyer, B. J.
Salyer, Buel
Salyer, Charley
Salyer, Claud
Salyer, Clint
Salyer, Cranston
Salyer, Dedie
Salyer, Dewey
Salyer, D. J.
Salyer, Dock
Salyer, Earn
Salyer, Edward
Salyer, Estill
Salyer, Ezra
Salyer, Fonzo
Salyer, Frank
Salyer, Freeman
Salyer, George
Salyer, George W.
Salyer, Grandville
Salyer, Green
Salyer, Hardy
Salyer, Harlan
Salyer, Harry B.
Salyer, Haston
Salyer, Hatton
Salyer, H. C.
Salyer, Hendrick
Salyer, Herbert
Salyer, Hobart

Salyer, Hope
Salyer, H. S.
Salyer, Isaac
Salyer, Isom
Salyer, Jake
Salyer, James C.
Salyer, James H.
Salyer, J. D.
Salyer, J. F.
Salyer, J. H.
Salyer, J. L.
Salyer, J. Lee
Salyer, J. M.
Salyer, John
Salyer, John M.
Salyer, Joseph
Salyer, Lawrence
Salyer, Logan
Salyer, Lon
Salyer, Lona
Salyer, Lonnie
Salyer, Lorraz
Salyer, Louana
Salyer, Manford
Salyer, Mart
Salyer, Manuel
Salyer, Manuel, Mrs.
Salyer, Martin
Salyer, Martha
Salyer, Mary
Salyer, M. D.
Salyer, Millard
Salyer, Minyard
Salyer, Monroe
Salyer, Oma
Salyer, Ornibus
Salyer, Oscar
Salyer, Patton
Salyer, Raba
Salyer, R. C.
Salyer, Roscoe
Salyer, Ross
Salyer, Savilla
Salyer, S. B.
Salyer, Sol
Salyer, Stanley
Salyer, T. A.
Salyer, Tennie
Salyer, Tom
Salyer, Troy
Salyer, Wallis
Salyer, Walter
Salyer, W. E.
Salyer, W. H.
Salyer, Will
Salyer, William
Salyer, Wilson
Salyer, Zack
Saneder, Frank
Saylor, Arthur

APPENDIX 475

Saylor, Dennie
Saylor, Dock
Saylor, Garlie
Saylor, Hobert
Saylor, J. M.
Saylor, Lige
Saylor, Mathew
Saylor, Nancy
Saylor, Sol
Saylor, Zack
Scarberry, Alfred
Scarberry, Elwood
Scarberry, Garfield
Scarberry, George
Scarberry, Lina
Scarberry, Malcolm
Scarberry, Missouri
Scarberry, Ray
Scarberry, Sherman
Scott, Clarence
Scott, Gale
Scott, Hebern
Sellers, Floyd
Selvage, Add
Selvage, Alfred
Selvage, Cal
Selvage, Clate
Selvage, Dennis
Selvage, George
Selvage, Harry B.
Selvage, John
Selvage, Kelly
Sestes, C. W.
Sestes, Walter
Shelingberg, Clyde
Sherman, Alfred
Sherman, Buck
Sherman, Eliga
Sherman, Ezra (Doke)
Sherman, Fred
Sherman, H. R.
Sherman, Jack
Sherman, Lou, Mrs.
Short, Ed
Short, Elizabeth
Short, German
Short, Granderson
Short, Herbert
Short, Herschall
Short, J. D.
Short, Leanord
Short, Louisa
Short, Mary J.
Short, Wellman
Short, W. M.
Shrout, E. D.
Siler, L.
Simpson, Luther
Simpson, Thomas
Singer, E. J.

Sites, Pete
Sizemore, Emma
Sizemore, Evenea
Skaggs, Alonzo
Skaggs, Amos
Skaggs, Andy
Skaggs, Buel
Skaggs, Cornellius
Skaggs, D. E.
Skaggs, D. R., Dr.
Skaggs, D. U.
Skaggs, E. L.
Skaggs, Elisha
Skaggs, France
Skaggs, Hardy
Skaggs, H. C.
Skaggs, Henderson
Skaggs, H. M.
Skaggs, Jerry
Skaggs, J. H.
Skaggs, J. S.
Skaggs, Laura
Skaggs, Leander
Skaggs, Lloyd
Skaggs, Minna
Skaggs, M. L.
Skaggs, S. U.
Skaggs, T. G.
Skaggs, W. B.
Skaggs, W. E.
Skaggs, Wort
Skeens, Bob
Skeens, Frank
Slone, George
Slone, Jasper
Slone, J. M.
Slone, John
Slone, Manuel
Slone, Marion
Slone, M. H.
Slone, Milburn
Slone, Proctor
Slone, W. H.
Slone, W. P.
Smith, Allie
Smith, Bill
Smith, Charles M.
Smith, Frank
Smith, Ira
Smith, Jack
Smith, J. D.
Smith, J. H.
Smith, J. M.
Smith, John G., Mrs.
Smith, J. S.
Smith, K.
Smith, L. A.
Smith, Lige
Smith, Ora
Smith, Paris

Smith, Seldon
Smith, Thomas
Smith, Will
Smith, W. L.
Snipps, Billard
Songer, J. B.
Sourd, Leslie
Sowards, H. G.
Sowards, Leonard
Sparks, Alonzo
Sparks, Charles
Sparks, Dan
Sparks, Edward
Sparks, E. L.
Sparks, Estill
Sparks, Grover
Sparks, Harry
Sparks, Henry
Sparks, Herbert
Sparks, Jess
Sparks, Jesse
Sparks, J. H.
Sparks, John
Sparks, Lafe
Sparks, Liss
Sparks, Oakley
Sparks, Olna
Sparks, Powell
Sparks, S. C.
Sparks, Therman
Sparks, Tolvie
Sparks, Tom
Sparks, W. H.
Sparks, Will
Spears, Alford
Spears, Alfred
Spears, Aubern
Spears, Dock
Spears, Edgar
Spears, Ep
Spears, Everett
Spears, F. M.
Spears, Garfield
Spears, George W.
Spears, Heber
Spears, Henry C.
Spears, Henry, Jr.
Spears, Isaac
Spears, J. A.
Spears, Jacob
Spears, Joe
Spears, John L.
Spears, Lacy
Spears, Lewis
Spears, Linzie
Spears, Lucy Akers
Spears, Manuel
Spears, Marcus
Spears, Marion
Spears, Martin

Spears, P. D.
Spears, Richard
Spears, Russell
Spears, Sam
Spears, Sheard
Spears, Walter
Spears, Wilber
Spears, Will
Spears, W. M.
Spears, W. R.
Spencer, Bernie
Spencer, Cyrus
Spencer, Jasper
Spencer, Jessie
Spencer, John
Spencer, Malcolm
Spencer, R. C.
Spencer, T. J.
Spencer, Watt
Spencer, W. C.
Splane, V. D.
Spradlin, Albert
Spradlin, Arminta
Spradlin, Ben Ike
Spradlin, Ben J.
Spradlin, B. F.
Spradlin, B. L.
Spradlin, Britain
Spradlin, Charley
Spradlin, Clemmons
Spradlin, Crate
Spradlin, Den
Spradlin, Dord
Spradlin, Earl
Spradlin, Ellen
Spradlin, Elliot
Spradlin, Elzie
Spradlin, Frank
Spradlin, George B.
Spradlin, George W.
Spradlin, Grant
Spradlin, Henry
Spradlin, H. S.
Spradlin, Ida
Spradlin, James H.
Spradlin, John
Spradlin, Manford
Spradlin, Moses
Spradlin, Noah
Spradlin, Oliver
Spradlin, Rafe
Spradlin, Sam
Spradlin, Sant
Spradlin, Tom
Spradlin, Walter
Spradlin, Walter F.
Spradlin, Wayne
Spradlin, Winifred
Sprigs, Burl
Sprigs, James

Stacy, Garfield
Stacy, G. W.
Stafford, Burl
Stafford, Carl
Stafford, C. C.
Stafford, Crate
Stafford, Frank
Stafford, G. M., Dr.
Stafford, Harry G.
Stafford, Harvey
Stafford, H. M.
Stafford, H. M., Mrs.
Stafford, Jesse, Jr.
Stafford, Jesse, Sr.
Stafford, J. H.
Stafford, John Frew
Stafford, Johny
Stafford, Lula
Stafford, Ralph
Stafford, Ray
Stafford, R. B.
Stafford, Robert
Stafford, T. R.
Stafford, W. T.
Staggs, Charles
Stambaugh, Albert
Stambaugh, B. H.
Stambaugh, Bruce
Stambaugh, Carl
Stambaugh, C. H.
Stambaugh, Charley
Stambaugh, Forest
Stambaugh, Frank
Stambaugh, Fred
Stambaugh, Garfield
Stambaugh, Garfield, Jr.
Stambaugh, G. C., Jr.
Stambaugh, George
Stambaugh, G. T.
Stambaugh, Harry
Stambaugh, Herbert
Stambaugh, Hervie
Stambaugh, J. B., Mrs.
Stambaugh, J. C.
Stambaugh, Jerry
Stambaugh, J. M.
Stambaugh, Joe
Stambaugh, John
Stambaugh, Johnt
Stambaugh, J. V.
Stambaugh, J. Vernir
Stambaugh, Lafe
Stambaugh, Lewis
Stambaugh, Mary M.
Stambaugh, Minnie
Stambaugh, M. L.
Stambaugh, Morgan
Stambaugh, Morris
Stambaugh, Paris

Stambaugh, Rado
Stambaugh, Ralph
Stambaugh, Sam
Stambaugh, Taylor
Stambaugh, Thomas
Stambaugh, Troy
Stambaugh, Walie
Stambaugh, W. F.
Stambaugh, W. G. H.
Stamper, George
Stanford, Enoch
Stanford, Willie
Staniford, Caroline
Staniford, Elijah
Staniford, Ernie
Stanley, Bascom
Stapleton, Albert
Stapleton, Alf
Stapleton, Ashland
Stapleton, Beecher
Stapleton, Beecher, Jr.
Stapleton, Bob
Stapleton, C. E.
Stapleton, Clarence
Stapleton, Cleve
Stapleton, Clyde
Stapleton, Crate
Stapleton, Dock
Stapleton, Dora
Stapleton, Earl
Stapleton, F. L.
Stapleton, Green
Stapleton, Gypsie
Stapleton, Haden
Stapleton, Hager
Stapleton, Hansford
Stapleton, Henry
Stapleton, H. H.
Stapleton, J. A.
Stapleton, J. H.
Stapleton, J. W.
Stapleton, Lammie, Jr.
Stapleton, Leona
Stapleton, L. F.
Stapleton, Lon
Stapleton, Madgie
Stapleton, Manossa
Stapleton, Marion
Stapleton, Mary E.
Stapleton, M. J.
Stapleton, M. V.
Stapleton, Ned
Stapleton, North
Stapleton, Paris
Stapleton, Proctor
Stapleton, Proctor, Mrs.
Stapleton, Sam, Jr.
Stapleton, Sam, Sr.
Stapleton, Sandy

APPENDIX 477

Stapleton, S. D.
Stapleton, S. L.
Stapleton, Vina
Stapleton, W. A.
Stapleton, Wayne
Stapleton, Will
Stapleton, Willie
Steel, Ed
Steel, Joe
Steel, Will
Stenson, Albert
Stenson, Orvil
Stenson, Roscoe
Stenson, Rufus
Step, Maranda
Stephenson, N. S.
Stevens, W. B.
Stewart, Walter
Stone, Allie
Stone, B. M.
Stone, Brother
Stone, Earl
Stone, Ira
Stone, L. A.
Stralton, J. K.
Stralton, Louis
Stricklin, Henry
Strother, John R.
Strother, Rush
Strow, Harry L.
Sturgill, J. M.
Sturgill, Lettie
Sturgill, Luther
Sturgill, Millard
Sturgill, N. R.
Sublett, A. J.
Sublett, Brookie
Sublett, Charlotte
Sublett, Dallas
Sublett, Lode, Mrs.
Sublett, Mat
Sublett, Monroe
Sublett, Tandy
Swager C. E., Mrs.
Swinger, C. E.
Sybert, Grant
Tackett, A. J.
Tackett, Alton
Tackett, Britain
Tackett, Charles G.
Tackett, Chat
Tackett, Cora
Tackett, Craig
Tackett, D. C.
Tackett, Elijah
Tackett, Elzie
Tackett, Floyd
Tackett, F. M.
Tackett, George W.
Tackett, Harlan

Tackett, H. C.
Tackett, James
Tackett, Jesse
Tackett, J. H.
Tackett, J. L.
Tackett, John F.
Tackett, John M.
Tackett, Johny
Tackett, Malissa Jane
Tackett, Morris
Tackett, Mose
Tackett, Mose, Jr.
Tackett, Paris
Tackett, Sam
Tackett, Sam H.
Tackett, Simon
Tackett, Ted
Tackett, Wayne
Tackett, W. K.
Talson, James
Tate, Frank
Tate, Lina V.
Taylor, A. C.
Taylor, Anna
Taylor, Bascom
Taylor, Dave
Taylor, David
Taylor, D. C.
Taylor, George
Taylor, Harry
Taylor, Jemima
Taylor, Jim
Taylor, Mary, Mrs.
Taylor, Robert
Taylor, Will
Taylor, W. S.
Teass, John W.
Terry, John
Thomas, Bert
Thomas, Ed
Thomas, E. L.
Thomas, Harry
Thomas, Joe H.
Thomas, Lou
Thomas, R. C.
Thomasson, H. D.
Thompson, A. J.
Thompson, John
Thompson, Sam
Thompson, W. B.
Thompson, Willard
Thomson, W. J.
Tolliver, D. S.
Tolliver, John
Travis, Henry
Travis, John
Travis, Jonathan
Travis, W. M.
Trimble, Bob
Trimble, Bowe

Trimble, Bruce
Trimble, Buell
Trimble, Charlie
Trimble, Conroy
Trimble, Cynthia
Trimble, D. N.
Trimble, Elzie
Trimble, Floyd
Trimble, Grant
Trimble, Green
Trimble, H. B.
Trimble, James H.
Trimble, James V.
Trimble, J. M.
Trimble, Joe H.
Trimble, John G.
Trimble, Lando
Trimble, McCoy
Trimble, Newton
Trimble, Paris
Trimble, Pierce
Trimble, Rexford
Trimble, Salam
Trimble, Serina, Mrs.
Trimble, Sherman
Trimble, Tom
Trimble, W. H.
Trimble, Wince
Trimble, W. J.
Truitt, Ed
Trusty, Elihu
Tryon, Will
Turner, Douglas
Turner, Earnest (Dick)
Turner, Frank
Turner, James W.
Turner, Ray
Underwood, M. B.
Vance, Ben
Vanhoose, Aaron
Vanhoose, A. J.
Vanhoose, Albert
Vanhoose, Albert J.
Vanhoose, Arley
Vanhoose, Arthur
Vanhoose, Bascom
Vanhoose, Ben H.
Vanhoose, Bert
Vanhoose, Brownlow
Vanhoose, Bryan
Vanhoose, Burns
Vanhoose, C. B.
Vanhoose, Claude
Vanhoose, Dan
Vanhoose, David
Vanhoose, D. B.
Vanhoose, D. C.
Vanhoose, D. G.
Vanhoose, D. J.

Vanhoose, D. L.
Vanhoose, Earl
Vanhoose, Ed
Vanhoose, Ella
Vanhoose, Elro
Vanhoose, Erma
Vanhoose, Farris
Vanhoose, F. C.
Vanhoose, Frank
Vanhoose, Fred
Vanhoose, F. S.
Vanhoose, George
Vanhoose, Guy
Vanhoose, Harry, Sr.
Vanhoose, Henry
Vanhoose, H. J.
Vanhoose, Huy
Vanhoose, Ivan
Vanhoose, James
Vanhoose, J. B.
Vanhoose, Jeff
Vanhoose, Jesse
Vanhoose, J. M.
Vanhoose, John
Vanhoose, John (Zigler)
Vanhoose, John Q.
Vanhoose, John W.
Vanhoose, Kennis
Vanhoose, Lafe
Vanhoose, L. C.
Vanhoose, Lee
Vanhoose, L. F.
Vanhoose, Life
Vanhoose, Lint
Vanhoose, Lon
Vanhoose, Malinth
Vanhoose, Maranda
Vanhoose, Martin
Vanhoose, McKinley
Vanhoose, M. F.
Vanhoose, Millard
Vanhoose, Milt
Vanhoose, Nan, Mrs.
Vanhoose, Noah
Vanhoose, Paul
Vanhoose, Proctor
Vanhoose, Rascus
Vanhoose, Richard
Vanhoose, Sam
Vanhoose, Sarah
Vanhoose, Scott
Vanhoose, Tom T.
Vanhoose, Verner
Vanhoose, Virgie
Vanhoose, Virgil
Vanhoose, Walter
Vanhoose, Willie
Vanhoose, W. U.
Varner, George

Vaughan, Ben H.
Vaughan, Fred A.
Vaughan, G. B.
Vaughan, Mary E.
Vaughan, Mollie
Vaughan, Roscoe
Vaughan, Walter
Vaughan, W. H.
Vaughan, W. H., Mrs.
Verbonic, Phillip
Vice, O. B.
Vincil, Martha
Vincil, Roy
Vires, Alex
Vires, Dolla
Virgin, D. W.
Walker, J. F. (Estate)
Walker, J. L.
Walker, J. W., Judge
Walker, Lon
Walker, Lou
Walker, Mirt
Walker, Theadore
Walker, U. S.
Wallace, Robert
Wallen, Hood
Wallen, R. B.
Wallen, R. W.
Wallen, William
Walters, Allie
Walters, C. F.
Walters, Charles
Walters, Clark
Walters, Earnest
Walters, Emma
Walters, Glen
Walters, Jim
Walters, J. M.
Walters, John E.
Walters, Leonard
Walters, Mitchell
Walters, Pigg
Walters, Proctor
Walters, Talbee
Walters, U. S.
Walters, Weddington
Walters, William
Walters, W. J.
Ward, Aaron
Ward, A. J.
Ward, Alex
Ward, A. M.
Ward, Amanda M.
Ward, Antony
Ward, Arbia
Ward, Artey
Ward, Arthur
Ward, As
Ward, Asberry
Ward, B. C.

Ward, Ben
Ward, Bill
Ward, Biran
Ward, Bish
Ward, C. C.
Ward, C. D.
Ward, Colba
Ward, Crate
Ward, Dan
Ward, Dan W.
Ward, Dewey
Ward, Dock
Ward, Edgar
Ward, Elias
Ward, Elliot
Ward, Eugene
Ward, Frank
Ward, Fred
Ward G.
Ward, Galand
Ward, Garfield
Ward, George
Ward, German
Ward, Grant
Ward, Green
Ward, G. W.
Ward, Henry
Ward, Herbert
Ward, Ira
Ward, J. B.
Ward, J. C.
Ward, J. D.
Ward, Jeff
Ward, Jeptha
Ward, Jerry
Ward, Jessie
Ward, Jim
Ward, J. N.
Ward, John
Ward, John C. (River)
Ward, John H.
Ward, John V.
Ward, John W.
Ward, Josie
Ward, J. P.
Ward, J. W.
Ward, Katherine, Mrs.
Ward, Leonard
Ward, Levinna
Ward, Lon
Ward, Lorenz
Ward, Marvin
Ward, Mary
Ward, M. L.
Ward, Ollie
Ward, Paris
Ward, R. G.
Ward, Shade
Ward, Shade, Jr.

APPENDIX 479

Ward, Sherman
Ward, Simon
Ward, Smith
Ward, Steven
Ward, S. W., Sr.
Ward, S. W., Jr.
Ward, T.
Ward, Tom
Ward, Virgil
Ward, Walter
Ward, W. D.
Ward, W. H.
Ward, Will
Ward, William
Ward, W. J.
Ward, W. J., Jr.
Ward, Z. C.
Watkins, Bert
Watkins, R. D.
Watkins, Sam
Watkins, W. D.
Watson, Tom
Webb, A. J.
Webb, Alex
Webb, Alexander
Webb, Ballard
Webb, Boone
Webb, Bozer
Webb, Charley
Webb, Clayton
Webb, Coonie
Webb, Dave
Webb, Dick
Webb, Dugan
Webb, Elmon
Webb, Filmore
Webb, Garland
Webb, Harry
Webb, Haskell
Webb, Herbert
Webb, Jane
Webb, J. B.
Webb, John
Webb, Leander
Webb, Leonard
Webb, McKinley
Webb, Melvin
Webb, Nora
Webb, Proctor
Webb, Roe
Webb, Roy
Webb, S. A.
Webb, Shelby
Webb, Susan
Webb, Walbridge
Webb, Willie
Webb, W. J.
Weddington, J. T.
Weddington, Lee
Welch, Authie

Welch, Elizabeth
Welch, E. P.
Welch, Hobert
Welch, John
Welch, Lige
Welch, T. J.
Welch, U. G.
Wellman, Mary
Wells, Alex
Wells, B. H.
Wells, Burnard
Wells, Calvin
Wells, Charles M.
Wells, C. J.
Wells, Cynthia
Wells, Ed
Wells, Elizabeth
Wells, Ella
Wells, G.
Wells, G. C.
Wells, George
Wells, Green
Wells, H. B.
Wells, Herbert
Wells, Hubert
Wells, Ireland
Wells, Jake
Wells, J. G.
Wells, Jim
Wells, J. K.
Wells, Joe
Wells, John B.
Wells, John L.
Wells, Joseph
Wells, J. P., Dr.
Wells, Kelly
Wells, Lafe
Wells, Lige
Wells, M. A.
Wells, McKinley
Wells, Melvina
Wells, M. L.
Wells, M. L. K.
Wells, Richard
Wells, Sam
Wells, Shade
Wells, Sherman
Wells, Willie
Wells, Z.
Wess, Anne
Wheatley, Grant
Wheatley, J. B., Mrs.
Wheatley, John Brown
Wheatley, William G.
Wheeler, Arbie
Wheeler, B. I.
Wheeler, B. J.
Wheeler, B. R.
Wheeler, C. B.
Wheeler, C. C.

Wheeler, Cecil
Wheeler, Clarence
Wheeler, C. O.
Wheeler, C. W.
Wheeler, Dan
Wheeler, Dan W.
Wheeler, Delida
Wheeler, Dennis
Wheeler, D. J.
Wheeler, Ed
Wheeler, Elizabeth
Wheeler, F. P.
Wheeler, Franklin
Wheeler, George
Wheeler, G. M.
Wheeler, G. P.
Wheeler, G. W.
Wheeler, Harrison
Wheeler, Henderson
Wheeler, Herbert
Wheeler, H. F.
Wheeler, H. M.
Wheeler, Jasper M.
Wheeler, John B.
Wheeler, John W.
Wheeler, J. W.
Wheeler, Leo
Wheeler, Levisa
Wheeler, L. H.
Wheeler, Linville
Wheeler, Lura
Wheeler, Martin
Wheeler, Milt
Wheeler, M. O.
Wheeler, M. U., Mrs.
Wheeler, Nancy Jane
Wheeler, Orion
Wheeler, Shank
Wheeler, Sherman
Wheeler, S. S.
Wheeler, Tobe
Wheeler, Troy
Wheeler, U. S.
Wheeler, William
Wheeler, William F.
Wheeler, W. J.
Wheeler, W. S.
Wheeler, W. V., Sr., Mrs.
White, F. C.
White, Grant
White, John
White, W. M.
Whittaker, Francis
Whittaker, Frank
Whittaker, H. C.
Whittaker, Martin
Whittaker, Mathew
Whittaker, Tom
Whorton, Era, Mrs.

Wilcox, Everett
Wilcox, Henry
Wilcox, Jesse
Wilcox, John
Wilcox, John W.
Wilcox, Lewis
Wilcox, Lyda
Wilcox, Sam
Wilcox, Tom
Wiley, Adam
Wiley, Beth
Wiley, Carl
Wiley, D.
Wiley, Elizabeth
Wiley, J. M.
Wiley, Leonard
Wiley, Malcolm
Wiley, Martin
Wiley, R. W.
Wiley, Sarah
Wiley, Tobe
Wiley, Wallace
Wilhite, R. M., Dr.
Williams, A. B.
Williams, A. C.
Williams, Albert
Williams, Aleck
Williams, Alfred
Williams, Amos
Williams, Arthur
Williams, Ashley
Williams, Bee
Williams, Benford
Williams, Beverly
Williams, B. S.
Williams, Bum
Williams, Cecil
Williams, C. H.
Williams, Charles
Williams, Charles M.
Williams, Charlie
Williams, C. J.
Williams, Corwin
Williams, Dennis
Williams, Dewey
Williams, Donce
Williams, E. F.
Williams, Eliphus
Williams, Elmira
Williams, E. M.
Williams, Everett
Williams, Fanny
Williams, Floyd
Williams, Frank
Williams, Frankie
Williams, Fred
Williams, George
Williams, G. P.
Williams, Haden
Williams, Hallie
Williams, Hamilton
Williams, Harvey
Williams, Hasten
Williams, Isaac
Williams, J. A.
Williams, James
Williams, James B.
Williams, J. C.
Williams, Jennie
Williams, Jesse
Williams, J. M.
Williams, John
Williams, John S.
Williams, K. W.
Williams, Lackey
Williams, L. B.
Williams, Leo
Williams, Leslie
Williams, L. O.
Williams, Luke P.
Williams, Lundy
Williams, Marcus
Williams, Millard
Williams, Milton
Williams, M. K.
Williams, M. L.
Williams, Myrtle
Williams, N. N.
Williams, N. W.
Williams, Oka L.
Williams, O. M.
Williams, Oral
Williams, Oscar
Williams, Oscar P.
Williams, Powell
Williams, Preston
Williams, Ralph B.
Williams, Roslin
Williams, S. F.
Williams, S. J.
Williams, S. M.
Williams, S. P.
Williams, T.
Williams, Taylor
Williams, Thedmore
Williams, Thomas
Williams, Tom
Williams, Tommy
Williams, Toy
Williams, U. S.
Williams, V. S.
Williams, W. A.
Williams, Wallace
Williams, Walter
Williams, W. E.
Williams, W. H.
Williams, Winnie
Williams, W. W.
Wilson, A.
Wilson, Albert
Wilson, Charley
Wilson, James
Wilson, O. N.
Wireman, Abe
Wireman, Lester
Wireman, Walter
Witten, Alonzo
Witten, Argalis
Witten, Cue
Witten, E. D.
Witten, F. M.
Witten, Frank
Witten, French
Witten, Ham
Witten, Hattie
Witten, Hobert
Witten, Lando
Witten, Milt
Witten, Rebecca
Witten, R. H.
Witten, Robert
Witten, T. F.
Witten, Tom
Witten, William
Witten, Willie
Witten, W. P.
Woods, Bazil
Woods, Ben F.
Woods, C. A.
Woods, Dennie
Woods, Earnie
Woods, Emma
Woods, Jasper
Woods, Lizzie
Woods, Will
Woodyard, Wiley
Woollum, J. M.
Worland, George P.
Worland, Jim Bob
Worthington, Clyde
Wright, C. C.
Wright, David
Wright, Floyd
Wright, James
Wright, James H.
Wright, J. C.
Wright, J. H.
Wright, Lonnie
Wright, Marion
Wright, Merida
Wright, Surilda
Wright, W. P.
Wyatt, C. A.
Yates, Chat
Yates, Clint
Yates, James
Yates, Rob
Yates, Sam
Yates, W. C.
Young, Ben

APPENDIX 481

Young, Bert
Young, Bill
Young, Charlotte
Young, Garfield
Young, George

Young, Gilbert
Young, James
Young, J. H.
Young, John L.
Young, J. S.

Young, Mary A.
Young, Monroe
Young, Thomas
Young, Zack
Zeloski, Mike

JOHNSON COUNTY VOTING PRECINCTS 1925

Number
1 Ward 1 (Paintsville)
2 Ward 2 (Paintsville)
3 Barnetts Creek
4 Jenny's Creek (Holly Br.)
5 Whitehouse
6 Buffalo
7 Mingo
8 Flat Gap
9 Little Gap
10 Low Gap
11 East Point
12 Sitka
13 Red Bush

14 Oil Springs
15 Lower Van Lear (No. 1)
16 Muddy Branch (Thealka)
17 Sycamore
18 Middle Van Lear (No. 2)
19 Greasy
20 Riceville
21 Offutt
22 Hagerhill
23 Upper Van Lear (No. 3)
24 Volga (Mud Lick)
25 Bridgeford (Paintsville)
26 Stafford
27 Daniels Creek
28 Salyers Fork

COUNTY OFFICIALS

Kentucky has had four State constitutions. The first one was adopted at Danville on April 19, 1792; the second at Frankfort, August 17, 1799; the third at Frankfort, June 11, 1850; and the fourth at Frankfort, September 28, 1891.

Under the first two constitutions, the county governments were run by a county court made up of the justices of the peace. The third one shifted this power creating the office of county judge, while the fourth transferred much of the power previously invested in the State Legislature to the county courts.

The county officials given herewith include those for the county of Mason from the year 1789 to 1799, while Johnson County was a part of Mason; for the county of Floyd from the year 1800 to 1843, while Johnson was also a part of Floyd; and for Johnson County from 1844 to the present.

Floyd County's court house burned in 1808 destroying all the records, and anything official for the period from 1800 to 1808 could not be obtained.

For reasons explained here, no county judges' names will appear previous to 1851:

COUNTY JUDGES
(Johnson County)

	Date Sworn In
James Remey (Ramey)	June 7, 1851
Shadrach Ward	Avg., 1854
Thomas S. Brown	Sept. 6, 1858
Lewis Tcdd	July 29, 1861
John Howes	Feb. 2, 1863
H. E. Conley	March, 1864
H. E. Conley	Oct. 5, 1865
H. S. Vaughan	In Office, 1866
Nathan A. Brown	Sept. 5, 1870
N. A. Brown	Sept. 7, 1874
J. F. Stewart	1884
J. W. Walker	Sept. 6, 1886
J. K. Dixon	April, 1891
J. K. Dixon	1894
W. E. Litteral	1894–1898
W. E. Litteral	1898–1902
H. B. Rice	1902–1906
W. E. Litteral	1906–1910
John W. Wheeler	1910–1914
Fred A. Vaughan	1914–1918
Fred A. Vaughan	1918–1920
James A. Williams	1920
B. Vaughan	1920
H. B. Conley	1921–1922
Beecher Stapleton	1922–1926
John W. Butcher	1926–1930

COUNTY ATTORNEYS
(Mason County)

	Date Sworn In
Thomas Hall	Avg. 27, 1789
Francis Taylor	Nov. 24, 1790
Francis Taylor	Oct. 22, 1793

(Floyd County)

James Cunning	Dec. 27, 1813
James Trimble	June 26, 1815
John M. McConnell	Nov. 29, 1815
Peter Akers	June 16, 1817
Robert Walker	May 17, 1819
James Crawford	March 20, 1820
William Triplett	Nov. 21, 1820
Thompson Ward	June 19, 1821
Thompson Ward	Nov. 21, 1821
Robert Walker	May 28, 1822
James M. Rice	Nov. 26, 1827
Henry C. Harris	Sept. 20, 1830
Henry C. Harris	Sept. 19, 1831
Henry C. Harris	Nov. 19, 1832
Edwin Trimble	Avg. 19, 1833
Samuel K. Friend	Oct. 12, 1840
B. J. Livingston	Nov., 1844

COUNTY ATTORNEYS—Contd.
(Johnson County)

	Date Sworn In
B. J. Livingston	March 4, 1845
Littleton Harris	May, 1845
Littleton Harris	Nov., 1845
Littleton Harris	Nov., 1846
Littleton Harris	Nov., 1847
Hugh Harkins	Nov. 27, 1848
Samuel K. Friend	Nov. 27, 1849
Samuel K. Friend	Nov. 23, 1850
Samuel K. Friend	June 7, 1851
Samuel K. Friend (Per)	Sept. 2, 1851
Samuel K. Friend	Sept. 5, 1854
John S. Mahan	Aug. 7, 1856
Dennis B. Wells	Sept. 6, 1858
Hugh Harkins	Nov. 2, 1863
William W. Howes	March 7, 1864
W. W. Brown	May 30, 1868
W. W. Brown	Oct. 3, 1870
David H. Hamilton	Sept. 7, 1874
T. B. Strong	May 6, 1878
James H. (M?) Mollotte	Sept. 2, 1878
John F. Stewart (Pro tem.)	
John W. Walker (In)	Feb. 12, 1886
G. W. Howes	Aug. 16, 1886
J. F. Stewart	Nov. 1, 1886
J. P. Wells	Oct., 1887
F. P. Conley	Sept. 1, 1890
F. P. Conley	1894
F. P. Conley	1894–1898
J. W. Walker	1898–1902
W. E. Litteral	1902–1906
Sam Stapleton	1906–1910
W. E. Litteral	1910–1914
Sam Stapleton	1914–1918
Sam Stapleton	1918–1922
Sam Stapleton	1922–1926
Sam Stapleton	1926–1930

COUNTY COURT CLERKS
(Mason County)

	Date Sworn In
Robert Rankins	May 25, 1789
Thomas Marshall, Jr.	Sept. 28, 1790
Thomas Marshall, Jr.	Oct. 23, 1792
Thomas Marshall, Jr.	May 28, 1792

(Floyd County)

William James Mayo	Oct., 1808
William James Mayo	Nov. 27, 1810
William James Mayo	Nov. 29, 1815
William James Mayo	Dec. 18, 1820
Jacob Mayo	Sept. 26, 1825
Jacob Mayo	Nov. 15, 1830
Jacob Mayo	April 13, 1835

APPENDIX 483

COUNTY COURT CLERKS—Contd.
(Johnson County)

	Date Sworn In
John Howes	June, 1844
John Howes	June 7, 1851
John Howes	Sept. 5, 1853
John Howes	Sept. 9, 1854
John Howes	Sept. 6, 1858
Daniel Pelphrey	Sept. 3, 1866
Daniel Pelphrey	May 6, 1867
T. J. Mayo	Jan. 11, 1870
C. J. Howes	Sept. 5, 1870
C. J. Howes	July 3, 1871
E. F. Howes	April 6, 1874
Thomas S. Williams	Sept. 7, 1874
G. S. Preston	Sept. 29, 1876
T. S. Williams	Sept. 3, 1877
E. F. Howes	Jan. 31, 1879
E. F. Howes	Aug. 11, 1882
E. F. Howes	June 14, 1886
H. B. Rice	Aug. 21, 1886
P. M. Rule	Sept. 6, 1886
J. K. Dixon	Oct., 1887
George C. Perry	Sept. 1, 1890
George C. Perry	Aug. 7, 1891
F. M. Bayes	1894–1898
J. M. Preston	1898–1902
James M. Price	1902–1906
William P. Davis	1906–1910
Paul C. Hager	1910–1914
Beecher Stapleton	1914–1918
Frank Chandler	1918–1922
Frank Chandler	1922–1926
Walter VanHoose	1926–1930

DEPUTY CLERKS
(Mason County)

	Date Sworn In
Daniel Morgan	May 25, 1789
John Mackin	Oct. 27, 1789
Marshall Key	Sept. 23, 1799
Roger W. Warring	Sept. 23, 1799

(Floyd County)

Henry B. Mayo	Oct. 25, 1809
Jonathan Mayo	Feb. 23, 1813
Jacob Mayo	Dec. 16, 1817
John K. Keach	Nov. 22, 1824
Greenville Lackey	Nov. 15, 1830
Edwin Trimble	Feb. 21, 1831
Winston Mayo	Nov. 21, 1831
James J. Mayo	May 22, 1832
George F. Hatcher	Sept. 19, 1833
James G. Hatcher	Dec. 11, 1837
Greenville Lackey	March 10, 1840
George W. Mayo	July 15, 1840
Edwin Trimble	June 15, 1841

(Johnson County)

Winston Mayo	Sept. 28, 1847
Chas. J. Mayo	Oct. 4, 1852
Dennis B. Wells	Oct. 6, 1853
William W. Howes	May 13, 1855

DEPUTY CLERKS—Contd.

	Date Sworn In
Zephaniah Meek	Jan. 11, 1858
James M. Howes	Sept. 6, 1858
Harmon Conley	June 2, 1862
Wiley J. Williams	June 1, 1863
Samuel B. Hanna	Nov. 3, 1863
Wiley W. Williams	March 17, 1864
B. F. Spradlin	Dec. 5, 1864
E. H. Conley	Feb. 21, 1865
Jerry Wellman	Sept. 3, 1866
Charles J. Howes	July 9, 1869
E. F. Howes	Sept. 5, 1870
Willis E. Riggsby	Sept. 2, 1871
John M. Fergerson	April 1, 1872
John F. Stewart	Nov. 4, 1872
G. W. Howes	Dec. 2, 1872
Willis Riggsbey	Jan. 5, 1874
Mart F. Stafford	Sept. 8, 1874
Johnette Hamilton	June 4, 1877
Frank P. Conley	Jan. 18, 1878
William Green	Jan. 18, 1878
W. W. Bailey	Sept. 2, 1878
G. W. Howes	Jan. 31, 1879
E. F. Howes	Sept. 6, 1880
M. L. K. Wells	Sept. 16, 1880
W. E. Litteral	Nov. 26, 1880
H. S. Howes	Jan. 18, 1881
Jno. Richmond	Dec. 6, 1881
M. L. K. Wells	Aug. 11, 1882
W. W. Bailey	Aug. 11, 1882
B. F. Hager	Oct. 2, 1882
S. M. Rice	Oct. 14, 1882
M. F. Howes	Oct. 14, 1882
T. J. Robertson	Feb., 1873
H. B. Rice	March 20, 1874
E. F. Howes	Nov., 1884
I. R. Turner	Jan. 26, 1886
Fred Stambaugh	March 19, 1886
C. M. Cooper	March 19, 1886
W. D. Cole	June 14, 1886
B. L. Davis	1886
James F. Rice	Oct., 1887
Smith Rice	March, 1889
E. F. Howes	Aug. 27, 1889
Carl M. Dixon	Sept. 1, 1890
Charles D. Trimble	Sept. 1, 1890
J. E. Akers	Dec. 13, 1890
Daniel Wheeler	Aug. 7, 1891
J. E. Akers	Aug. 7, 1891
Carl Dixon	Aug. 7, 1891
Carlos Trimble	Aug. 7, 1891
Henry Butcher	Aug. 7, 1891
James B. VanHoose	Aug. 8, 1891
Milton McDowell	Aug. 8, 1891
T. S. Brown	Aug. 11, 1891
R. M. Miller	Aug. 13, 1891
W. E. Litteral	Aug. 19, 1891
W. A. Williams	Sept. 7, 1891
Bryant Fannin	1918–1922
Clyde Fannin	1922–1926
W. H. McKenzie	1922–1926
I. L. Auxier	1926–1930

HISTORY OF JOHNSON COUNTY

SCHOOL COMMISSIONERS

(Supt. of Schools)

(Floyd County)

	Date Sworn In
Thomas Willon	July 9, 1838
Alex Lackey	July 9, 1838
Henry B. Mayo	July 9, 1838
Samuel Auxior	July 9, 1838
Meredith Patrick	July 9, 1838

(Johnson County)

James Franklin	Sept. 28, 1847
Martin Franklin	March 25, 1850
Garland Hurt	March 25, 1850
Andrew Rule	March 25, 1850
Martin Franklin(Temp)	June 7, 1852
Henry Jane	June 7, 1852
Martin Franklin	July 8, 1852
George Selson	Dec. 6, 1852
James A. Ward	Oct. 14, 1854
Moses Preston	April 2, 1855
James A. Ward	July 7, 1857
Zephaniah Meek	June 7, 1858
Zephaniah Meek	June 4, 1860
Henry S. Vaughan	Feb. 6, 1862
James Perry	March 7, 1864
James Remy	Aug. 7, 1866
James Remy	Sept. 5, 1870
John F. Stewart	Oct. 3, 1870
H. C. Conley	Oct. 7, 1872
W. B. Lemasters	Oct. 6, 1874
James H. Stambaugh	Sept. 1, 1884
G. B. Stapleton	Aug. 16, 1886
B. H. Harris	Sept. 2, 1891
B. H. Harris	1894
George M. Johnson	1898–1902
George M. Johnson	1902–1906
Milton McDowell	1906–1910
Fred Meade	1910–1914
Fred Meade	1914–1918
Fred Meade	1918–1922
Fred Meade	1922–1926
O. W. Cain	1926–1930

BOARD OF EDUCATION

	Date Sworn In
W. R. Richmond (Chmn.)	1926–1930
David Osborn	1926–1930
Grant Rice	1926–1930
J. M. Williams	1926–1930
Samuel Cordial	1926–1930
Fred Hager (Chmn.)	1926–1930
David Osborn	1926–1930
Y. B. Rice	1894
Aaron Moore	1894–1898
Franklin Wheeler	1898–1902

SHERIFFS

(Mason County)

	Date Sworn In
Thomas Warring	May 25, 1789
Henry Lee	March 22, 1791
Miles W. Conway	Aug. 28, 1792
Thomas Dobyns	May 26, 1795

(Floyd County)

James Brown	May 17, 1808
James Brown	Oct., 1808
James Patton	Feb. 28, 1809
William McGuire	Jan. 28, 1811
Thomas Evans	Feb. 22, 1813
Henry Burgess	March 28, 1814
Spencer Adams	July 3, 1815
Robert Howes	Jan. 30, 1817
Robert Howes	Jan. 1, 1818
James Brown	Jan. 18, 1819
William Graves	May 21, 1821
William Stratton	March 22, 1822
Stephen Harper	March 24, 1823
Thomas C. Brown	Jan. 24, 1825
Alex. Lackey	Feb. 26, 1827
Andrew Rule	Feb. 16, 1829
Thomas W. Graham	April 15, 1829
John Hatcher	May 16, 1831
Reuben Marshall	June 17, 1833
Andrew Rule	June 18, 1835
Ichabod McBrayer	June 12, 1837
Andrew Rule	Oct. 9, 1837
Andrew Rule	March 13, 1838
Joel Martin	June 10, 1839
Stephen Hamilton	June 14, 1841

(Johnson County)

Daniel Hager	July, 1844
Shadrach Preston	May 5, 1845
Francis A. Brown	June 28, 1847
James H. Godsey	1848–1849
German W. Huff	June 24, 1849
Joseph Daniel	June 7, 1851
Joseph Daniel	June 7, 1852
Joseph Daniel	Jan. 3, 1853
Alex. W. Nickel	Jan. 16, 1854
Alex. W. Nickel	Feb. 6, 1854
Alex. W. Nickel	Feb. 5, 1855
Alex. W. Nickel	Feb. 18, 1856
Martin Franklin	Jan. 5, 1857
James A. Ward	Jan. 3, 1859
William E. Hill	May 20, 1862
Henry S. Vaughan	March 7, 1864
Alex. W. Nickel	May 19, 1865
A. W. Nickel	Jan. 7, 1866
J. W. Helton	Feb. 3, 1868
J. W. Helton	Sept. 5, 1870
J. W. Davis	March 19, 1872
Samuel G. Wheeler	Sept. 8, 1873
S. Y. Wheeler	Feb. 8, 1876
Geo. W. Auxier	Dec. 11, 1876

SHERIFFS—Contd.

	Date Sworn In
Geo. W. Auxier	Jan. 8, 1879
Lindsey Litteral	Dec. 1, 1879
G. W. Auxier	Jan. 3, 1881
P. M. Rule	Jan. 1, 1883
P. M. Rule	Jan. 5, 1885
H. F. Howes	Jan. 16, 1886
Geo. W. Auxier	Jan. 3, 1887
Geo. W. Auxier	Jan. 7, 1888
H. S. Howes	Jan. 5, 1891
H. S. Howes	Jan. 2, 1892
H. S. Howes	1894
Geo. W. Auxier	1894
S. P. King	1898
Samuel Stapleton	1902
Ashley Ward	1902–1906
Grant Daniel	1906–1910
Henry Ward	1910–1914
Geo. W. Spears	1914–1918
John Stambaugh	1918–1922
Grant Daniel	1922–1926
H. B. Adams	1926–1930

DEPUTY SHERIFFS

(Mason County)

	Date Sworn In
James W. Warring	Dec. 28, 1790
John Williams	Dec. 28, 1790
Edward Dobyns	March 22, 1791
Thornby Berry	March 22, 1791
James Ward	Aug. 28, 1792
Henry Berry	Dec. 26, 1792
James Dobyns	Nov. 26, 1793
Thomas Wood	July 26, 1796
Edw. Dobyns	Feb. 27, 1797
Edw. Dobyns	June 25, 1798
Enoch Dobyns	Dec. 24, 1798
Thomas Williams	Feb. 25, 1799
Thomas Webb	Sept. 23, 1799
John G. McDowell	Oct. 28, 1799

(Floyd County)

Solomon Stratton	Aug. 23, 1808
Thomas C. Brown	Feb. 28, 1809
William Martin	Feb. 28, 1809
Francis Brown	May 22, 1809
John Stratton	Jan. 28, 1811
Jonathan Mayo	Jan. 28, 1811
Mial Mayo	Jan. 28, 1811
Henry B. Mayo	Nov. 25, 1811
David K. Harris	Nov. 23, 1812
John Turman	March 22, 1813
Francis A. Brown	Aug. 23, 1813
Thomas C. Brown	———, ——
Henry B. Mayo	March 28, 1814
James Stratton	March 28, 1814
John McGuire	May 23, 1814
James B. Smith	Sept. 26, 1814

DEPUTY SHERIFFS—Contd.

	Date Sworn In
Henry B. Mayo	Sept. 26, 1814
Wilson Mayo	July 3, 1815
James P. Harris	July 3, 1815
John Howes	Aug. 28, 1815
James Honaker	Sept. 25, 1815
David K. Harris	Feb. 26, 1816
Lewis Mayo	April 22, 1816
Hiram Stratton	July 22, 1816
Robert Walker	Sept. 23, 1816
William Ratliff	Jan. 30, 1817
James Stratton	May 19, 1817
James H. Wallace	June 16, 1817
Lewis Wellman	June 16, 1817
Thomas Price	Dec. 15, 1817
Wilson Mayo	Jan. 18, 1818
James Stratton	Jan. 18, 1818
Lewis Wellman	Jan. 18, 1818
James H. Wallace	Jan. 18, 1818
David K. Harris	May 19, 1818
Mial Mayo	Jan. 18, 1819
Wilson Mayo	Jan. 18, 1819
William Stratton	Jan. 18, 1819
James Stratton	May 17, 1819
Jesse McGuire	May 17, 1820
Hickman Stratton	June 19, 1820
Joseph R. Ward	May 21, 1821
William Stratton	May 21, 1821
Hickman Stratton	June 18, 1821
Jesse McGuire	March 22, 1822
William McGuire	March 22, 1822
Wilson Mayo	March 22, 1822
Jeremiah Patrick	May 27, 1822
William Layne	June 24, 1822
William Stratton	March 24, 1823
Hiram Stratton	March 24, 1823
Jesse McGuire	Nov. 25, 1823
Joseph Gearhart	March 22, 1824
John C. Lacy	May 24, 1824
James Brown	Feb. 28, 1825
Wilson Sullivan	June 27, 1825
Thomas Evans	June 27, 1825
Jeremiah Patrick	June 27, 1825
John B. Lawhorne	Dec. 26, 1825
Geo. Allen, Jr	Feb. 24, 1826
Kelse N. Harris	June 26, 1826
Greenville Lackey	March 26, 1827
James Morgan	March 26, 1827
John B. Lawhorne	June 28, 1827
Jackson Patrick	June 28, 1827
David Morgan	April 15, 1829
George F. Hatcher	June 21, 1830
David Allen	June 21, 1830
Mathew Adams	June 21, 1830
John Conley	June 21, 1830
Henry G. McGuire	June 21, 1830
James G. Hatcher	May 16, 1831
George F. Hatcher	May 16, 1831
Joseph Gearhart	June 20, 1831
George Allen	June 20, 1831
James Franklin	June 20, 1831

HISTORY OF JOHNSON COUNTY

DEPUTY SHERIFFS—Contd.

Name	Date Sworn In
James Hager	June 20, 1831
John G. Hatcher	May 21, 1832
James M. Lackey	June 18, 1832
David K. Butler	June 18, 1832
Martin Franklin	June 18, 1832
George F. Hatcher	June 17, 1833
J. Morgan Lackey	June 17, 1833
James P. Harris, Jr.	June 17, 1833
John B. Harris	June 17, 1833
Joseph S. Harris	June 17, 1833
James P. Harris, Sr.	June 17, 1833
David Young	June 17, 1833
Solomon C. Stratton	June 17, 1833
Thomas C. Brown	June 18, 1833
Isaac B. Friend	June 18, 1835
Jacob Fitzpatrick	July 13, 1835
Harrison B. Rule	July 13, 1835
James Y. Brown	July 13, 1835
David W. Allen	July 13, 1835
James Remy	July 13, 1835
Morgan Puckett	July 11, 1836
James M. Lackey	July 11, 1836
Fleming H. Brown	March 13, 1837
Samuel P. Davidson	June 12, 1837
A. W. Rule	June 12, 1837
Joseph Gearhart, Sr.	July 10, 1837
Morgan Puckett	July 10, 1837
Harry S. McGuire	July 10, 1837
Samuel P. Davidson	Oct. 9, 1837
A. W. Rule	Dec. 11, 1837
Samuel P. Davidson	March 13, 1838
Andrew Wallace Rule	April 9, 1838
Joseph Gearhart	July 9, 1838
Isaac Flanery	July 9, 1838
William B. Perry	July 9, 1838
William Salyers	July 9, 1838
James C. Harris	June 10, 1839
Samuel P. Davidson	June 10, 1839
Solomon C. Stratton	July 8, 1839
John J. Stratton	Sept. 9, 1839
Barton Garrett	March 9, 1840
Andrew W. Rule	March 9, 1840
Morgan Puckett	July 13, 1840
William J. Mayo	Oct. 12, 1840
Soloman C. Stratton	June 14, 1841
Andrew Rule	June 14, 1841
James Menix	July 12, 1841
Edward W. Hill	Sept. 13, 1841

(Johnson County)

Name	Date Sworn In
William J. Hager	July, 1844
A. W. Rule	May 5, 1845
John B. Harris	Sept., 1845
Ivan Spradlin	Dec., 1846
Daniel Hager	June 28, 1847
James H. Godsey	June 28, 1847
Martin Franklin	Feb. 26, 1849
Samuel K. Friend	June 7, 1851
Dennis B. Wells	Aug. 25, 1851
William Stafford	March 2, 1852
Thomas Daniel	Dec. 11, 1852

DEPUTY SHERIFFS—Contd.

Name	Date Sworn In
Thomas Daniel	Jan. 3, 1853
James Delong	July 4, 1853
James E. Castle	Sept. 12, 1853
Henry Chandler	Feb. 21, 1854
Henry S. Vaughan	Feb. 5, 1855
George J. Nicholl	April 2, 1855
Martin Franklin	Sept. 3, 1855
James C. Castle	Aug. 7, 1856
Harmon Conley	March 6, 1859
James A. Ward	Sept. 5, 1859
Shadrach Meek	Feb. 14, 1861
Samuel B. Hanna	Dec. 2, 1862
James Stafford	March 7, 1864
A. J. Vaughan	March 9, 1865
Edward W. Brown	Nov. 3, 1865
George P. Nickel	
William J. VanHoose	Sept. 3, 1866
Philip Cassady	March 6, 1866
B. F. Salyer	Feb. 7, 1867
Jas. C. Castle	Feb. 7, 1867
William Wells	May 14, 1867
A. W. Nickel	July 18, 1867
Charles J. Howes	July 28, 1868
George Delong	Aug. 31, 1868
John W. Walker	Feb. 6, 1869
James A. Porter	Sept. 5, 1870
J. W. Davis	Oct. 2, 1871
J. W. Helton	March 19, 1872
John W. Turner	April 13, 1872
Samuel G. Wheeler	Aug. 6, 1872
G. W. Howes	March 1, 1874
B. F. Spradlin	Feb. 8, 1876
Lindsey Litterall	July 21, 1877
Lindsey Litteral	Jan. 8, 1879
F. M. Picklesimer	Jan. 8, 1879
Henry Howes	Feb. 7, 1879
Millard F. Howes	Jan. 3, 1881
Shade McGlothin	Feb., 1881
Henry H. Hill	Sept. 29, 1881
W. E. Litteral	Sept. 29, 1881
Frank P. Conley	March 13, 1882
W. H. Vaughan	May 26, 1886
William Walker	Jan. 5, 1891
S. P. King	Nov. 8, 1891
William P. Williams	Dec. 19, 1891
J. L. Walker	Dec. 19, 1891

JAILORS

(Mason County)

Name	Date Sworn In
John Williams	March 22, 1791

(Floyd County)

Name	Date Sworn In
John Turman	May 17, 1808
John Turman	Oct., 1808
Thomas Evans	Feb. 27, 1810
Martin Simons	May 28, 1810
William Keaton	May 27, 1811
John Spurlock	Aug. 24, 1812
Hiram Spurlock	Sept. 28, 1812
John Harris	June 27, 1814

APPENDIX 487

JAILORS—Contd.
Date Sworn In
John Havens............Jan. 30, 1817
George Martin.........Sept. 15, 1817
George Martin.........Feb. 19, 1821
James Derosit..........May 23, 1825
James Derosit........March 18, 1833
John Waldeck..........Jan. 11, 1841
(Johnson County)
William Dixon...............July, 1844
German W. Huff........June 7, 1851
Edward Lavendor........Dec. 6, 1852
William Dixon..........Sept. 3, 1853
Martin Franklin........Feb. 21, 1854
John Vaughan..........Aug. 10, 1854
John Vaughan..........Sept. 6, 1858
Ralph Stafford.........May 12, 1862
James P. Selsor..........Jan. 1, 1866
William Dixon..........Sept. 3, 1866
William Dixon.........April 15, 1867
G. W. Rice..............May 1, 1868
David Lyons...........June 24, 1868
William Castle.........Sept. 7, 1868
A. J. Vaughan..........Feb. 7, 1870
William Castle..........Oct. 2, 1871
Shadrock McGlollin.....Aug. 6, 1872
William Castle.........Dec. 15, 1873
Isaac Fitzpatrick.......April 27, 1874
John W. Castle.........Aug. 17, 1874
J. W. Castle............Sept. 2, 1878
J. K. Dixon............Aug. 11, 1882
M. F. Howes...........Nov. 1, 1884
W. W. Vaughan.........Aug. 9, 1886
G. W. Jailor..............Sept., 1890
George Daniel.............1894–1898
John B. VanHoose.........1898–1902
John D. Preston...........1902–1906
George W. Spears.........1906–1910
Noah VanHoose...........1910–1914
Sherman Trimble..........1914–1918
Isaac Slone................1918–1922
John Sparks...............1922–1926
John Marshall.............1926–1930

DEPUTY JAILORS
(Johnson County)
Date Sworn In
James Girtume............July, 1844
Edward F. Hill........March 4, 1845
Lewis Todd...........July 23, 1849
William Mahan........June 29, 1859
Alex. Vaughan..........Dec. 2, 1862
David Lyons...........Oct. 5, 1866
W. F. Walker...........Aug. 8, 1887

CORONERS
(Floyd County)
Date Sworn In
Robert Howes..........Feb. 28, 1809
James Lacy............Oct. 23, 1809
John Howes...........Feb. 24, 1812
John Harris..........Sept. 26, 1814
Mial Mayo............June 19, 1817

CORONERS—Contd.
Date Sworn In
John Hatcher..........Nov. 16, 1819
Alex. Young...........Sept. 20, 1819
James Derosit..........Dec. 22, 1822
Thomas Evans.........June 28, 1824
Soloman Roberson......May 23, 1825
Thomas Evans.........Dec. 26, 1825
Edwin Trimble.........Dec. 15, 1835
Edwin Trimble.........Oct. 12, 1840

(Johnson County)
James Remey..............July, 1844
N. B. Dixon.............June 7, 1851
Andrew Rule...........Sept. 9, 1854
Joseph Bailey..........Sept. 6, 1858
Robert O. Butler........Sept. 2, 1866
E. E. Williams.........Sept. 5, 1870
E. E. Williams..........Aug. 6, 1872
William A. Holbrook....Nov. 2, 1874
A. J. Wiley............Aug. 31, 1886
B. L. Castle.............Sept., 1890
H. M. Gibbs..............1894–1898
J. H. Adams..............1898–1802
Sheridan Gibbs...........1902–1906
J. H. Holbrook...........1906–1910
H. M. Gibbs..............1914–1918
Dr. F. M. Witten.........1918–1922
W. W. Daniel.............1922–1926
W. W. Daniel.............1926–1928
Grant Daniel..................1928

TREASURERS
(Floyd County)
Date Sworn In
William M. Smith.....March 13, 1837
(Johnson County)
Eliphus Preston............July, 1844
Eliphus Preston..........Jan. 5, 1845

SURVEYORS
(Mason County)
Date Sworn In
Henry Lee............May 25, 1789
Henry Lee............Nov. 27, 1789
Henry Lee............Dec. 25, 1792
(Floyd County)
John Graham..................1810
John Graham..........Nov. 27, 1815
John Graham..........Sept. 18, 1820
John Graham..........Nov. 15, 1830
Vincent Dawson.......Sept. 14, 1835
(Johnson County)
James Clay..............Aug., 1844
John B. Auxier...........July, 1845
John B. Auxier.........June 17, 1851
Samuel Hanna.........Sept. 5, 1854
William A. Wheeler.....Sept. 6, 1858
William R. Wheeler.....Sept. 6, 1863

SURVEYORS—Contd.

	Date Sworn In
William R. Wheeler	Sept. 3, 1866
Isaih Fairchild	Sept. 3, 1866
William A. Wheeler	Sept. 5, 1870
Isaac Hicks	Oct. 5, 1874
Jno. Reid	Jan. 6, 1879
Elijah Fields	Dec. 1, 1884
John W. Castle	July 11, 1885
D. Mart Hager	July 11, 1885
Alamander Blair	Aug. 28, 1886
A. E. Auxier	Sept. 7, 1891
John E. Reed	1894–1898
Wayne Colvin	1806–1910
J. A. Caudill	1810–1914
A. E. Auxier	1914–1918
G. G. Auxier	1918–1922
W. R. Richmond	1922–1926
G. G. Auxier	1926–1930

DEPUTY SURVEYORS
(Mason County)

	Date Sworn In
George Lewis	Nov. 24, 1789
William Sudduth	Nov. 24, 1789
Peter Lee	Nov. 24, 1789
John Stewart	Dec. 22, 1789
Caleb Worley	Dec. 22, 1789
John Obanion	May 26, 1790
Nathaniel Mopie	July 27, 1790
Isaac Kennon	April 26, 1791
Robert Johnson	May 22, 1792
Peter Lee	Dec. 26, 1792
Lucas Sullivan	Dec. 26, 1792
Michael Daugherty	Dec. 26, 1792
Isaac Kennon	Jan. 22, 1793
Thomas Davis	Jan. 22, 1793
George Hart	Dec. 24, 1793
Pierce Lamb	March 24, 1795
Christopher Gray	July 28, 1795
Deval Payne	Aug. 26, 1795
John Graham	Jan. 26, 1796
John Campbell	March 22, 1796
Thomas James	May 24, 1796
Daniel Boone	Aug. 23, 1796
William Henry	Aug. 23, 1796
Richard Woodford	Oct. 25, 1796
Enoch Smith	Dec. 26, 1796
Andrew Woodrow	Feb. 27, 1797

DEPUTY SURVEYORS—Contd.

	Date Sworn In
Omer R. Powell	April 24, 1797
Henry Blomit	April 24, 1797
John McIntire	June 26, 1797
William Johnson	Oct. 23, 1797
George Lewis	Dec. 25, 1797
Henry Smith	Dec. 25, 1797
Robert Poog	Feb. 26, 1798
Lewis Gordan	Feb. 22, 1799

(Floyd County)

	Date Sworn In
Jonathan Mayo	Sept. 23, 1811
James Cummings	May 26, 1812
John McGuire	Dec. 25, 1815
Solomon McGuire	Dec. 25, 1815
Stephen Harper	June 24, 1816
Robert Walker	June 24, 1816
John M. McConnell	Jan. 30, 1817
Peter Akers	Nov. 17, 1817
Josph Smith	Nov. 17, 1817
Peter Amyx	Aug. 17, 1819
Wm. Cockrell	Jan. 17, 1820
Enoch Smith	Sept. 17, 1821
Thomas Graham	Jan. 28, 1822
John Graham	Nov. 28, 1825
Sudduth C. Turner	Dec. 14, 1835
Nathaniel Auxier, Jr.	Dec. 14, 1835
Griffith Dickerson	March 14, 1836
James Dixon	July 11, 1836
Benj. F. Branham	Feb. 10, 1840
James Harris	Oct. 12, 1840

(Johnson County)

	Date Sworn In
Nathaniel Auxier, Jr.	Jan. 4, 1846
Reuben Lisinger	Feb. 2, 1852
Samuel Harris	July 5, 1852
Samuel Hanna, Jr.	Jan. 7, 1856
Isaac Hicks	March 1, 1856
Jno. B. Wheeler	Feb. 6, 1865
Isaac Hicks	Sept. 3, 1866
R. M. Wells	Jan. 6, 1879
Mac. McKenzie	Dec. 1, 1884

PAUPER KEEPERS
(Johnson County)

	Date Sworn In
Hiram F. Strong	Oct. 27, 1851
G. W. Wells	Oct. 8, 1872
B. L. Davis	Nov. 2, 1891

TAX COMMISSIONERS
(Assessors)
(Mason County)

	Dist. No.	Date Sworn In
Miles W. Conway	1	August 26, 1789
Arthur Fox	2	August 26, 1789
George Stockton	3	August 26, 1789
William Lamb	2	April 27, 1791
Edward Dobyns	1	August 28, 1792

TAX COMMISSIONERS (ASSESSORS)—Contd.

	Dist. No.	Date Sworn In
William Lamb	2	August 28, 1792
Abraham Drake	3	August 28, 1792
Abraham Drake	3	May 27, 1793
Whitfield Craig	1	May 27, 1793
Miles W. Conway	3	March 22, 1796
William Roe	1	March 22, 1796
George Mitchell	1	January 23, 1797
Joseph Doniphan	1	January 23, 1797
John Stolcoop	?4	—— ——, ——
Anthony Cummins	?4	September 23, 1799
George Farris	4	February 28, 1800
James Wilson	1	February 28, 1800
Stokes Anderson	2	February 28, 1800
G. W. Botts	3	February 28, 1800

(Floyd County)

Harry Stratton	—	—— ——, 1808
John Stratton	—	February 27, 1809
John Stratton	—	February 23, 1810
Jonathan Mayo	—	February 28, 1814
James Stratton	—	February 27, 1815
Wilson Mayo	—	November 19, 1818
Wilson Mayo	—	November 16, 1819
William Graves	—	November 21, 1820
James Kash	—	November 15, 1822
Alex Lackey	—	January 24, 1827
James P. Harris	Upper	March 17, 1828
Thomas C. Brown	Lower	March 17, 1828
James P. Harris	Upper	March 16, 1829
John M. Kelly	Lower	March 16, 1829
Kelsey N. Harris	Upper	May 17, 1830
Nicholas Hackworth	Lower	May 17, 1830
Solomon C. Stratton	Upper	March 20, 1831
Thomas Gratton	Lower	March 20, 1831
Solomon C. Stratton	Upper	December 17, 1832
George F. Hatcher	Lower	February 17, 1834
Samuel C. Stratton	Upper	March 9, 1835
George Martin	Lower	March 9, 1835
Thomas C. Brown	Lower	April 13, 1835
James H. Layne	Upper	January 11, 1836
Nicholas Hackworth	Lower	January 11, 1836
Solomon C. Stratton	Upper	January 9, 1837
Nicholas Hackworth	Lower	January 9, 1837
Nicholas Hackworth	Upper	January 8, 1838
Wallis Bailey	Lower	January 8, 1838
James Martin	Upper	January 14, 1839
Nicholas Hackworth	Lower	January 14, 1839
Alexander Lackey	Upper	January 13, 1840
Electius Howes	Lower	January 13, 1840
John Hatcher	Upper	December 14, 1840
William J. Ramey	Lower	December 14, 1840

(Johnson County)

Martin Franklin	—	March 4, 1845
William R. Wheeler	—	January 5, 1845
John W. Sturgell	—	January 5, 1845
Spencer Hill	—	January 4, 1846
Armstrong Rowland	—	January 4, 1846

TAX COMMISSIONERS (ASSESSORS)—Contd.

	Dist. No.	Date Sworn In
Benjamin Porter	South	January 24, 1848
John Wheeler	North	January 24, 1848
Joseph Daniels	North	January 22, 1849
Henry A. Livingston	South	January 24, 1849
Marcus L. King	South	January 28, 1850
Claybourn Howes	North	February 24, 1851
Armstrong Rowland	South	February 24, 1851
John Colvin	—	June 7, 1851
Asa J. Fairchild (Assistant)	—	February 2, 1852
Charles J. Grim	—	September 5, 1854
Charles J. Grim	—	December 6, 1858
Winston M. Conley	—	May 6, 1867
E. S. Turner	—	May 6, 1867
Jacob Hylton	—	May 6, 1867
Isaac Goble	—	September 5, 1870
Thos. S. Williams	—	October 2, 1871
James F. Walker	—	September 7, 1874
Wiley Rice	—	May 2, 1881
William Honeycut	—	August 28, 1882
William Honeycut	—	May 1, 1885
William J. Bayes	—	September 6, 1886
Thomas J. Dixon	—	September, 1890
J. M. Preston	—	September, 1890
W. E. Litteral (Dept. Asses.)	—	September 8, 1891
A. L. Preston (Dept. Asses.)	—	November 2, 1891
T. J. Dix	—	———, 1894
Samuel Picklesimer	—	1894–1898
H. B. Conley	—	1898–1902
Sheridan Gibbs	—	1902–1906
John R. Williams	—	1906–1910
John R. Williams	—	1910–1914
John Daniel	—	1914–1918
James P. Hall	—	1918–1922
Manuel Salyer	—	1922–1926
W. H. McKenzie	—	1926–1930

MAGISTRATES
(Mason County)

	Dist. No.	Date Sworn In
Edmund Lyne	1	May 25, 1789
Thomas Warring	1	February 25, 1789
Jacob Edwards	2	May 25, 1789
Henry Lee	2	May 25, 1789
George Stockton	3	May 25, 1789
Miles W. Conway	3	May 25, 1789
John Mackin	4	May 25, 1789
Alex. Darlimpdeor	4	May 25, 1789
Arthur Fox	4	May 25, 1789
William Lamb	5	May 25, 1789
Robert Rankins	5	May 25, 1789
John Wilson	1	August 28, 1792
William Lamb	2	August 28, 1792
John Mackins	4	August 28, 1792
Arthur Fox	5	August 28, 1792
George Mitchell	—	December 24, 1793
Philip Thomas	1	January 28, 1794
Thomas Young	2	January 28, 1794
David Morris	3	January 28, 1794

APPENDIX 491

MAGISTRATES—Contd.

Name	Dist. No.	Date Sworn In
Winslow Parker	4	July 27, 1794
John Bartle	5	July 27, 1794
John Guthridge	1	March 24, 1795
John Johnston	2	January 26, 1796
Joseph Doniphan	3	March 26, 1796
John Hunt	5	March 26, 1796
Michael Kassidy	1	July 26, 1796
John Johnston	2	November 2, 1796
Lewis Bullock	3	February 27, 1797
Hugh Fulton	4	June 26, 1797
Andrew Henderson	1	April 22, 1799
David Childs	3	September 23, 1799
John Lain	6	September 24, 1807
James Cunning	—	(in) September 24, 1807 / (out) — 12, 1812
John Hammond	—	May 16, 1808
John Back	—	—— ——, 1808
John Fuget	—	July 26, 1808
Spencer Adams	—	May 16, 1808
Robert Howes	—	May 16, 1808
Spencer Adkins	—	May 16, 1808
James Brown	—	May 16, 1808
Ebenezer Hanna	—	May 16, 1808
Harry Stratton	—	May 16, 1808
James Lacy	—	May 16, 1808
William Martin	—	May 16, 1808
William Graves	—	May 16, 1808
James Kesh	—	May 16, 1808
John Brown	—	May 16, 1808
Thomas Evans	1	October, 1808
John Hanna	2	October, 1808
George Belshe	4	October, 1808
Thomas C. Brown	5	October, 1808
William McGuire	6	October, 1808
James Patton	—	October, 1808
David Peyton	—	October 24, 1808
Joseph Janes	—	October 25, 1808
Henry Burgess	—	November 29, 1808
Harry Stratton	—	November 29, 1808
Spencer Adams	—	February 27, 1809
Robert Howes	—	May 22, 1809
Richard W. Evans	—	May 28, 1810
Samuel Haws (Howes)	—	——, ——
James Brown	—	February 24, 1812
Ebenezer Hanna	—	May 25, 1812
William Martin	—	June 23, 1812
Ambrose Garland	—	(Res.) September 28, 1812
John Brown	6	February 28, 1814
William Graves	—	February 28, 1814
James Kesh	—	March 28, 1814
Alexander Dunbar	4	December 26, 1814
Stephen Harper	6	December 26, 1814
Edward Burgess	6	March 28, 1815
Spencer Adkins	4	August 28, 1815
John Bevins	6	August 28, 1815
Henry B. Mayo	4	September 23, 1816
Alexander Lackey	4	May 19, 1817
Spencer Adams	5	May 19, 1817

MAGISTRATES—Contd.

Name	Dist. No.	Date Sworn In
James Honaker	—	June 16, 1817
John Adams	—	—, —
Thomas C. Brown	—	—, —
James Slater	—	September 15, 1817
James H. Wallace	2	May 18, 1818
John Frazier	2	June 15, 1818
Simeon Justice	2	August 18, 1818
James Roberts	2	August 18, 1818
Reuben Giddens	2	September 21, 1818
Mason Williams	2	January 18, 1819
Alex. Dunbar	2	May 17, 1819
Peter Amyx	2	June 21, 1819
Lewis Welman	2	June 22, 1819
Richard R. Lee	2	September 20, 1819
Edmund Wells	2	November 15, 1819
James Wheeler	2	September 19, 1820
Harry Stratton	2	November 21, 1820
James Lacy	2	—, —
Henry B. Mayo	2	December 18, 1820
James Lacy	3	December 18, 1820
Harry Stratton	3	January 15, 1821
John Howes	3	August 20, 1821
Andrew Rule	3	August 20, 1821
Lewis Power	3	August 20, 1821
Isaac Lykin	3	January 28, 1822
Rhodes Mead	3	June 24, 1822
John Deskins	3	January 29, 1822
John Hatcher	3	November 25, 1822
Reuben Marshall	3	May 26, 1823
Ichabod McBrayer	3	May 26, 1823
George Daniel	3	May 26, 1823
Jasper Hanna	3	May 26, 1823
Solomon McGuire	3	June 23, 1823
William Prater	3	June 23, 1823
Joel Martin	3	August 25, 1823
J. P. Harris	3	December 22, 1823
John VanHoose	3	June 28, 1824
William M. Smith	3	June 28, 1824
Stephen Hamilton	3	August 23, 1824
Mial Mayo	3	November 22, 1824
David K. Harris	3	November 22, 1824
Owen Owens	3	December 27, 1824
Chas. Rumsey	3	June 27, 1825
William Talley	3	November 28, 1825
Jesse McGuire	3	December 26, 1825
Thomas Patrick	5	August 27, 1827
Wilson Mayo	5	August 27, 1827
Shadrach Preston	5	March 17, 1828
Edwin Trimble	5	January 19, 1829
Francis A. Brown	5	February 16, 1829
Solomon Derosit	5	March 16, 1829
Joel Estep	5	January 20, 1829
John Friend	5	May 18, 1829
William Smith	5	May 18, 1829
Samuel K. Friend	5	August 19, 1829
Solomon Derosit	5	August 19, 1829
James Davis	5	November 16, 1829
Jesse McGuire	5	November 16, 1829

APPENDIX

MAGISTRATES—Contd.

Name	Dist. No.	Date Sworn In
Meredith Patrick	5	December 21, 1829
Thomas Patrick	5	December 21, 1829
Nathaniel Auxier	6	December 20, 1830
Daniel Hager	6	March 20, 1831
N. Auxier	6	March 20, 1831
Samuel Clark	6	June 20, 1831
Harry Stratton	6	September 19, 1831
John Halbert	—	—, —
James M. Rice	6	June 18, 1832
Joseph Edwards	6	November 20, 1832
Robert Patrick	6	September 10, 1833
Reuben Marshall	6	September 10, 1833
Wm. McGuire	—	—, —
James Harris	6	June 10, 1834
John Hatcher	6	December 14, 1835
John Remy	6	December 14, 1835
Hugh Harkins	6	December 14, 1835
Andrew Rule	6	1830–1835
Stephen Hamilton	—	—, —
Samuel K. Friend	6	July 11, 1836
German W. Huff	6	December 12, 1836
John B. Barnett	6	September 11, 1837
Ichabod McBrayer	6	September 11, 1837
John P'Simer	6	June 10, 1839
James Franklin	6	June 10, 1839
Joseph Gearhart	6	July 8, 1839
Joel Martin	6	July 8, 1839
Daniel D. Jones	6	1839
Joseph Edwards	6	1839
Low B. Peery	6	1839
James Franklin	6	1839
David Martin	—	—, —
Linsey Layne	6	April 13, 1840
John Hatcher	6	April 13, 1840
William H. Layne	6	April 13, 1840
Morgan Puckett	6	April 13, 1840
Paris Randall	6	July 12, 1841
John Spradlin	6	July 12, 1841

(Johnson County)

Name	Dist. No.	Date Sworn In
Shadrach Preston	—	April, 1844
Francis A. Brown	—	April, 1844
German W. Huff	—	April, 1844
John Stafford	—	April, 1844
Jno. Picklesimer	—	April, 1844
Samuel Auxier	—	April, 1844
James Berry	—	April, 1844
Henry Jayne	—	April, 1844
Nicholas C. Waldeck	—	April, 1844
Elescious Howes	—	April, 1844
Constentine Conley	—	April, 1844
James Delarry	—	—, —
James Remey	—	May 2, 1845
Nathaniel Baker	—	August 5, 1845
Moses Wells	—	August 5, 1845
Shadrach Ward	—	November 26, 1847
George W. Murray	—	September 25, 1848

HISTORY OF JOHNSON COUNTY

MAGISTRATES—Contd.

Name	Dist. No.	Date Sworn In
Lewis Todd	—	November 27, 1849
George Selson	3	January 28, 1850
Houston Littrell	3	June 23, 1850
James Delong	3	—, —
John W. Sturgell	1	August 25, 1851
Joseph Williams	2	August 25, 1851
Hiram McGinnis	3	August 25, 1851
Britton Blair	4	August 25, 1851
Asa J. Porter	5	August 25, 1851
James Castle	6	August 25, 1851
Rhode Murray	4	August 25, 1851
John Wells	6	August 25, 1851
Ira Baker	2	September 22, 1852
Peter Clay	3	September 22, 1852
John Hitchcock	4	September 22, 1852
Jonathan B. Ward	1	October 14, 1854
Andrew Johnson	5	July 2, 1855
John Roberson	2	September 3, 1855
Isaac Hicks	6	September 3, 1855
William Jane	2	—, —
Asa J. Read	4	—, —
William Logan	5	—, —
John Baldridge	6	—, —
Hiram E. Conley	5	December 3, 1855
Britton Blair	4	January 28, 1856
Joseph Bailey	2	February 4, 1856
German W. Huff	3	April 9, 1856
Moses Wells	3	May 5, 1856
Henry C. Wells	6	October 5, 1857
Hazen Swan	2	September 6, 1858
Sebastin Litteral	4	September 6, 1858
Jacob Castle	2	November 7, 1859
William A. Ward	1	February 11, 1860
Daniel Hager	1	July 7, 1862
German W. Huff	1	November 10, 1866
Nathan A. Brown	1	November 10, 1866
C. C. Price	1	May 30, 1867
German W. Huff	3	May 7, 1867
James E. Burges	5	May 30, 1867
Elizea Lemaster	3	May 30, 1867
N. P'Simer	3	May 7, 1867
James E. Burges	5	May 7, 1867
James Nibert	2	—, —
William Brown	2	May 27, 1867
F. S. Stambaugh	3	May 27, 1867
G. W. Rice	3	May 27, 1867
Aperson Castle	2	May 30, 1867
William J. Ward	2	May 30, 1867
William Brown	3	May 27, 1867
David E. Hamilton	3	May 29, 1867
James Preston	2	May 29, 1867
Samuel K. Rice	1	June 18, 1867
Fred Stambaugh	1	May 27, 1867
Thomas J. Welch	5	May 27, 1867
James S. Mollet	6	May 6, 1867
Allen Stapleton	3	May 30, 1867
Moses Wells	5	June 11, 1867

APPENDIX

MAGISTRATES—Contd.

Name	Dist. No.	Date Sworn In
G. W. Rice	1	May 25, 1867
Matthew Caudill	4	June 30, 1867
N. P'Simer	4	July 1, 1867
James W. Huff	1	July 29, 1867
Samuel K. Rice	1	October, 1870
George W. Rice	2	October, 1870
Thomas J. Welch	3	October, 1870
Greenville Preston	4	October, 1870
James Preston	5	October, 1870
Moses Wells, Sr.	6	October, 1870
D. H. Hamilton	1	October, 1870
Allen Stapleton	2	October, 1870
J. W. Huff	3	October, 1870
Frederick Stumbo	4	October, 1870
Robert A. Butler	1	June 5, 1871
John W. Witten	7	June 5, 1871
George W. Rice	—	June 5, 1871
John W. Walker	1	June 5, 1871
J. W. Huff	2	June 5, 1871
Hiram McKenzie	3	June 5, 1871
Thomas Hamilton	3	June 5, 1871
John Richmond	5	June 5, 1871
Joel D. Long	4	June 5, 1871
Greenville Preston	2	June 5, 1871
Mathew Caudill	4	June 5, 1871
M. L. K. Wells	2	June 5, 1871
J. K. Dixon	1	January 1, 1872
Samuel Clark	8	January 1, 1872
Kingston F. Price	1	September, 1872
John W. Witten	1	June 2, 1873
Thomas Hamilton	2	June 2, 1873
F. M. Litteral	4	September, 1879
James Music	8	October 8, 1880
W. J. McKenzie	1	December 6, 1880
Nathaniel Meek	8	August 16, 1881
G. W. Murry	2	August 16, 1881
James Webb	5	May 7, 1883
C. N. Vaughan	1	June, 1883
Levi Blair	4	June, 1883
Mathew Caudill	4	June, 1883
Jonathan Stambaugh	6	June, 1883
Samuel W. Rice	1	June, 1883
Embry Castle	2	June, 1883
Flem Daniel	2	June, 1883
Lafayette McKenzie	3	June, 1883
Thomas Hamilton	3	June, 1883
W. W. Green	5	June, 1883
James Webb	5	June, 1883
Thomas F. Witten	6	June, 1883
Jno. W. Witten	7	June, 1883
William R. Wheeler	7	June, 1883
James A. Ward	8	June, 1883
Nathan Neek	8	June, 1883
Hiram E. McKenzie	3	June 2, 1873
B. L. Davis	8	June 7, 1873
Fred Stambaugh	—	June 21, 1873
K. F. Price	1	July 7, 1873
Green Preston	2	July 7, 1873

MAGISTRATES—Contd.

	Dist. No.	Date Sworn In
Walter Caudill	—	July 7, 1873
William N. Randolph	1	—, —
Joseph Salmon	3	—, —
Henry L. Porter	5	—, —
John J. Arrowood	5	—, —
William P. James	7	June 23, 1874
J. W. Walker	1	—, —
Hiram E. McKenzie	3	—, —
Sam K. Rice	1	October 5, 1874
Henry C. Wells	3	October 5, 1874
B. F. Salyer	4	October 5, 1874
John B. Van Hoose	2	May 15, 1875
James N. Mollet	8	May 26, 1875
John Bartram	2	May 26, 1875
John L. Vaughan	1	May 26, 1875
William Lemaster	3	May 26, 1875
Charles Pack	7	May 26, 1875
Lewis Caudill	4	May 26, 1875
Geo. W. Spears	5	May 26, 1875
Lewis Z. Christain	5	May 26, 1875
B. L. Davis	8	July 8, 1875
Levi Blair	4	December 7, 1885
F. M. Litteral	4	December 7, 1885
F. M. Litteral	4	May 26, 1886
B. L. Davis	8	September 30, 1886
T. J. Roberson	1	June 6, 1887
Flem Daniel	3	June 6, 1887
M. J. Caudill	4	June 6, 1887
W. W. Greer	5	June 6, 1887
Henry P. Meade	8	June 6, 1887
J. L. Blair	1	June 6, 1887
Garfield Castle	3	June 6, 1887
T. J. McKenzie	—	June 6, 1887
Charles Pack	7	June 6, 1887
S. W. Rice	1	June 6, 1887
Samuel Clark	3	June 6, 1887
Plyman Daniel	4	June 6, 1887
Jont Stambaugh	6	June 6, 1887
H. J. Van Hoose	6	June 6, 1887
Ben Hamilton	3	June 6, 1887
J. C. Barker	4	June 6, 1887
R. J. Stambaugh	6	June 6, 1887
Peter Daniel	2	June 1, 1887
W. J. Arrowood	2	June 1, 1887
W. H. Dorton	3	June 1, 1887
Thomas Rezob	3	June 1, 1887
D. H. Ward	4	June 1, 1887
James Webb	5	June 1, 1887
Jesse Caudill	6	June 1, 1887
Emery Castle	6	June 1, 1887
J. W. Witten	7	June 1, 1887
A. J. Hall	8	June 1, 1887
W. L. Combs	6	June 1, 1887
H. S. Spradlin	1	August 31, 1891
Fred Stambaugh	1	August 31, 1891
Samuel Estep	4	August 31, 1891
Jasper Ward	8	August 31, 1891
T. J. Auxier	5	September 2, 1891

APPENDIX

MAGISTRATES—Contd.

	Dist. No.	Date Sworn In
John Witten	1	—, —
Plymon Daniel	1	April 25, 1892
Thomas F. Witten	6	April 28, 1892
W. B. Wheeler	7	December 5, 1892

(No magistrates shown from 1892 to 1914.)

	Dist. No.	
John W. Spradlin	1	1914–1918
R. B. Akers	2	1914–1918
John A. Hughes	3	1914–1918
S. L. Blanton	4	1914–1918
Ed VanHoose	5	1914–1918
Isaiah Plummer	1	1918–1922
J. W. Butcher	2	1918–1922
John A. Hughes	3	1918–1922
S. L. Blanton	4	1918–1922
Harry Stambaugh	5	1918–1922
B. H. Conley	1	1922–1926
J. W. Butcher	2	1922–1926
Nelson Collins	3	1922–1926
S. L. Blanton	4	1922–1926
W. W. Williams	5	1922–1926
William Burgess	1	1926–1930
Wince Trimble	2	1926–1930
Ernest Jayne	3	1926–1930
Harry Stambaugh	4	1926–1930
John B. Mollett	5	1926–1930
Proctor Webb	6	1926–1930

FLOYD COUNTY CONSTABLE DISTRICTS

The first constable districts of Floyd County were laid off March 26, 1816, and given names instead of numbers. They were as follows: Jackson, Red River, Licking, Flatwood, George's Creek, Paint, Town (Prestonsburg), Madison, Salt Lick, Beaver, Harrison, Mud, John's Creek, Ratliff, and Adkins. (See page 147, Order Book No. 2.) The precinct of Jefferson was formed April 22, 1816.

The precinct Kentucky (meaning Kentucky River section) was divided May 19, 1817, into three districts, namely: Carr's Fork, Rockhouse, and Kentucky. Other precincts added were: Liberty, 8-18-1818; Shelby, 9-21-1818; Brushy Fork, 11-16-1818; Monroe, 11-18-1818; and Burgess, 3-16-1819.

On May 15, 1820, the names of the precincts were abandoned for numbers and the districts laid off anew. Eight districts were provided as follows: No. 1 included all that part of the Big Sandy in Floyd County below the White House shoal; No. 2 contained everything up to Miller's Creek; No. 3 provided for the town of Prestonsburg and vicinity; No. 4 took in all of Beaver, Mud, and Island creeks; No. 5 was for all of the Big Sandy above Prestonsburg; No. 6 was confined to that part of the Kentucky River lying in Floyd County; No. 7 included Quicksand Creek, the Elk and Johnson's forks of Licking River; and No. 8 contained all the rest of Licking River.

CONSTABLES DISTRICTS

As laid off by the County Court May 21, 1821.

(See the Chapter on Government for Rest of Districts)

DISTRICT No. 1—To begin at the mouth of Rockcastle on the Tug Fork and to include all the waters of said Rockcastle and from the head thereof a direct line to John Burgess' on the Louisa Fork, thence to Andrew Thompson's on Blaine, thence a direct course to the county line, thence with the county line to the beginning.

DISTRICT No. 2—Beginning at John Burgess' thence up Sandy River to the White House shoal including all the inhabitants on Sandy waters, thence a direct line to Jesse Helton's on Blaine, thence to the road that leads from Floyd Court House to Little Sandy Salt works, thence along said road to the county line and along the county line to the line of number one, thence along the same to the beginning of district number two.

DISTRICT No. 3—Beginning at the head of Rockcastle, thence a direct line to the mouth of Little Paint near the Blockhouse, thence a direct line to John Conley's, thence to Henry Conley's, thence to the dividing ridge between Licking and Sandy waters, thence to the head of Blaine, thence to the county line at number two, thence with the line of number two and number one to the beginning.

DISTRICT No. 4—Beginning at the head of Rockcastle, thence a direct line to Wireman's mill, thence to the mouth of Middle Creek and up the same including all its waters to the head thereof, thence the dividing ridge between Sandy and Licking to the line of district number three, thence with the line of district number three to the beginning.

DISTRICT No. 5—Beginning at the mouth of Middle Creek, thence up Sandy River with the meanders thereof to the mouth of Island Creek, thence a direct line to Aaron Pinson's on John's Creek, thence to mouth of Pond Creek on Tug, thence to the line of number one, thence to the line of number four, and with the same to the beginning.

DISTRICT No. 6—Beginning at the mouth of Middle Creek, thence with the line of number four to the dividing ridge between Sandy and Licking, thence to include all waters of Beaver and Mud creeks, thence to the dividing ridge between Island and Cider creeks, thence to the mouth of Island Creek, thence down Sandy River to the beginning.

DISTRICT No. 7—Beginning at the mouth of Island Creek, thence up Sandy River to the forks at Spencer Adkins, thence to the fork ridge, thence with the same to the State line, thence with the same to the Tug Fork and down said Tug Fork to the mouth of Pond Creek, thence with the line of number five to the beginning.

DISTRICT No. 8—Beginning at the mouth of Island, thence with the line of number six to the State line and with the same to the line of number seven, thence with said line to the beginning.

DISTRICT No. 9—To contain all the waters of Red River and Grassy Creek in this county and from the mouth of Grassy to the county line at the mouth of Blackwater.

DISTRICT No. 10—Beginning at the dividing ridge between Red River and Johnson's Fork of Licking, thence along the dividing ridge between White Oak Creek and Licking River, thence to the mouth of the Rockhouse Fork, thence including the head of the Elk Fork and the head of Little Sandy, thence with the county line of number nine at the mouth of Blackwater, and with said line of number nine to the beginning.

DISTRICT No. 11—To contain all the waters of the Burning Fork of Licking down to the last crossing of the State road thence with the State road to the line of number ten, thence with the line of number ten to the county line at number two, thence with the line of numbers two and three and part of number four to the beginning.

DISTRICT No. 12—To be composed of all the residue of this county lying on the head of Licking River and Quicksand.

Rockcastle Creek added to number two, 8-21-1821.

Upper Coles (? Cloes) added to number seven, 11-20-1821.

Number eleven was added to number twelve, 11-20-1821.

Number eleven renewed to-wit: Beginning at Licking Station and from thence up and including all the waters of Licking above there except William Prater's. 5-27-1822.

Number twelve altered to-wit: From Licking Station down to the line of number ten and including William Prater's. 5-27-1822.

Licking district formed to-wit: Ordered that all the waters on Licking in this county be made one district. 3-24-1823.

FLOYD COUNTY CONSTABLES DISTRICTS LAID OFF ANEW MAY 26, 1823

No. 1—From Lawrence County line, all Sandy and its waters to the mouth of Little Paint including Big Paint up to Kezee's mill.

No. 2—All Big Paint and its waters above Kezee's mill.

No. 3—From the mouth of Little Paint up Sandy to Prestonsburg to include Middle Creek and its waters and all the inhabitants on John's Creek as high as John Williams.

No. 4—From Prestonsburg up Sandy and its waters to the ford above Graham's, and all John's Creek and its waters from John Williams' to Pike County line inclusive.

No. 5—From ford above Graham's all Sandy and its waters to James S. Layne's inclusive, and Beaver as far as Wilson Mayo's.

No. 6—All Sandy and its waters from James Layne's to Pike County line including all Mud and its waters.

No. 7—From Wilson Mayo's up Beaver to William Burnett's inclusive, thence a straight line to Joseph Gearhart's including him and all the waters of both forks below there.

No. 8—All the waters of the left-hand fork of Beaver above number seven and all the right-hand fork above the mouth of Caney including Caney.

No. 9—All the waters of the right-hand fork of Beaver Creek not included in number seven and number eight.

No. 10—All that part of this county being on the waters of Licking in this county.

Number six extended 1-23-1826 down Sandy River from James S. Layne's to Harry Stratton's inclusive of said Stratton.

Number one changed 8-28-1826 to include the left-hand fork of Jenny's Creek with its waters and all the inhabitants.

Number eleven added 8-28-1826 to-wit: Beginning at Garland Burgess', thence running down the river and including all the inhabitants in this county on Sandy River and its waters to the county line except those on Tom's Creek above Samuel Murray's.

CONSTABLES
(Mason County)

	Dist.	Date Sworn In
Daniel Carroll	—	June 23, 1789
Moses Bradley	—	June 23, 1789
Henry Headley	—	January 26, 1790
William Berry	2	December 28, 1790
George Edwards	3	January 24, 1792
Thomas Williams	4	February 28, 1792
Miles W. Conway	5	February 28, 1792
George Headley	1	August 28, 1792
Sanford Mitchell	2	October 23, 1792
Jacob Hester	5	October 23, 1792
Moses Bradley	3	January 22, 1793

APPENDIX 501

CONSTABLES—Contd.

Name	Dist.	Date Sworn In
William Roe	5	January 22, 1793
George Headley	1	March 26, 1793
Hamilton Reed	2	(in) March 26, 1793 / (out) October 25, 1796
Patrick Killen	3	March 26, 1793
Thomas Williams	4	March 26, 1793
John Lewis	2	August 27, 1793
James McKay	3	August 27, 1793
Caleb Brown	5	August 27, 1793
John Price	3	March 24, 1795
Jonathan Stout	4	(in) August 26, 1795 / (out) March 22, 1796
James Lawry	1	October 27, 1795
Jacob Frizzle	5	October 27, 1795
John Harrison	2	March 22, 1796
Thomas Brown	3	(in) March 22, 1796 / (out) July 24, 1797
Adam Brayard	4	May 24, 1796
Reuben Young	5	May 25, 1796
James Hale	1	August 23, 1796
Thomas Webb	3	October 25, 1796
Reuben Young	5	October 25, 1796
William Whaley	2	June 26, 1797
William Bolling	3	July 24, 1797
William Taylor	4	July 24, 1797
Nelson Clift	5	July 24, 1797
John Hall	1	October 23, 1797
John Thelkeld	2	December 25, 1797
Stokes Anderson	3	December 25, 1797
Nathan Low	4	January 22, 1798
James Campbell	1	February 26, 1798
Walter S. Burgess	2	April 23, 1798
Hugh Jackson	3	June 25, 1798
John Greene	4	December 24, 1798
Jonathan Hyatt	5	January 28, 1799
James Hanna	1	April 22, 1799
John Johnston	2	April 22, 1799
French Martin	3	April 22, 1799
William Oderr	3	July 22, 1799
Samuel Boyd	4	July 22, 1799
George Harris	5	July 22, 1799
Stokes Anderson	3	September 23, 1799
John Kenser	1	October 28, 1799
Peter Wallace	2	December 23, 1799

(Floyd County)

Name	Dist.	Date Sworn In
Francis Brown	—	July 25, 1808
James Wheeler	—	July 25, 1808
Thomas Auxier	P'burg	August 22, 1808
John Lain	Lower	August 23, 1808
Henry Burgess	Lower	August 23, 1808
Christopher Patton	Courthouse	August 23, 1808
Robert Howes	2	——, 1808
James Young, Jr.	P'burg	October 25, 1808
John Iliss	2	(in) February 27, 1809 / (out) January 28, 1811
Francis Brown	4	(out) February 27, 1809
James Case	4	(out) February 27, 1809
John Peyton	6	February 27, 1809

CONSTABLES—Contd.

Name	Dist.	Date Sworn In
Spenser Adkins	—	February 27, 1809
Robert Howes	2	May 22, 1809
Hirom Stratton	3	May 22, 1809
Joseph Ford	Upper	August 28, 1809 / September 23, 1811
Lozones, Damron	Shelby	September 23, 1811
John Russell	Hd. Ky. R	October 24, 1809
Samuel Patton	5	October 24, 1809
William Newlin	3	November 28, 1809
William Coffee	Licking	February 26, 1809
Jacob Shoemaker	2	February 28, 1810
William Prater	Licking	(in) May 28, 1810 / (out) June 22, 1812
Edward Burgess	Lower	September 24, 1810
Ambrose Garland	—	November 27, 1810
William Wiley	2	January 28, 1811
John Ramey	2	February 25, 1811
Peter Ford	Upper	February 25, 1811
Sampson Howes	2	March 25, 1811
James Young, Jr	Courthouse	March 25, 1811
Francis Lewis	1	May 27, 1811
John Adams	Ky. R	May 27, 1811
William Cordell	Hd. Ky. R	(in) May 27, 1811 / (out) June 22, 1812
Edward Osburn	5	September 23, 1811
Elijah Adkins	2	November 25, 1811
Jonathan Mayo	5	February 24, 1811
Henry B. Mayo	5	(in) May 26, 1812 / (out) May 23, 1814
Adam Gearhart	Beaver	May 26, 1812
James Cunning	P'burg	June 22, 1812
Harry Stratton	6	June 22, 1812
James Lacy	6	June 22, 1812
Elijah Adkins	1	June 22, 1812
Lazorus Damron	2	June 22, 1812
James Young	3	June 22, 1812
Francis Lewis	4	June 22, 1812
Edward Burgess	5	June 22, 1812
John Williams	6	(in) June 22, 1812 / (out) August 23, 1813
William Adams	Ky. R	June 22, 1812
T. C. Brown	2	(in) June 23, 1812 / (out) February 22, 1813
Peter Ford	Upper	August 24, 1812
James Stratton	7	November 23, 1812
Francis A. Brown	Paint	February 23, 1813
James P. Harris	7	May 24, 1813
Levi Jackson	7	November 22, 1813
Henry B. Mayo	Town	March 28, 1814
Archibald Gibson	Carr's Fk	March 28, 1814
William H. Randall	Red R	March 28, 1814
Jesse Adams	Ky. R	March 28, 1814
Samuel McClintock	Licking	May 23, 1814
John McGuire	Town	May 23, 1814
William Lewis	2	September 26, 1814
David Stout	7	September 26, 1814
Thomas O'Hair	Red R	November 28, 1814
William Ratliff	7	November 28, 1814

APPENDIX 503

CONSTABLES—Contd.

Name	Dist.	Date Sworn In
John Howes	Sandy	December 26, 1814
Welks Frazier	Beaver	January 23, 1815
Henry B. Mayo	P'burg	February 28, 1815 / April 22, 1816
Ignatus Turman	Georges Ck	May 22, 1815
Joseph Nickel	Red R	June 26, 1815
Michael Risnor	Licking	(in) June 26, 1815 / (out) March 24, 1817
Elijah Adkins	Upper	August 28, 1815
William Frazier	Beaver	August 28, 1815
Joseph Ford	Johns Ck / Ratliff	September 25, 1815 / April 22, 1816
John C. Lacey	Red R	(in) December 25, 1815 / (Res.) November 17, 1817
David K. Harris	Town	(in) February 26, 1816 / (Disc.) May 19, 1817
David Hamilton	Salt Lick	March 25, 1816
William Mays	Atkins	March 25, 1816
John McGuire	Harrison	April 22, 1816
John Pritchett	Ky. R / Rockhouse	April 22, 1816 / May 19, 1817
William Ford	Ratliff	May 19, 1817
Leonard Lawson	Ky / Carr's Fk	September 23, 1816 / May 19, 1817
Solomom McGuire	Harrison / Jefferson	January 20, 1816 / December 23, 1816
Mial Mayo	Madison	September 24, 1816
Andrew Nickel	Red R	October 28, 1816
Lewis Wellman	Flatwood	February 25, 1817
Andrew Rule	Paint	(in) February 25, 1817 / (Res.) February 25, 1817
John Patrick	Licking	March 24, 1817
Irvin Adams	Ky. R	May 19, 1817
Silas P. Wooton	Georges Ck	September 15, 1817 / (Res.) November 19, 1817
William Lewis	Licking	November 17, 1817
Thomas Mollett	—	November 18, 1817
Joseph Hanna	Paint	November 19, 1817
James Burgess	Georges Ck	December 15, 1817
David K. Harris	Town	January 19, 1818
Elijah Prater	Licking	January 19, 1818
Peter Amyx	Madison	February 17, 1818
Jesse McGuire	Madison	February 17, 1818
William Trimble	Red R	March 16, 1818
F. A. Brown	Paint	June 15, 1818
Abijah Brown	Rockhouse	June 13, 1818
Mial Mayo	Liberty	(in) August 18, 1818 / (out) September 20, 1819
William Mullins	Shelby	September 21, 1818
Richard F. Giddens	Brushy Fork	November 16, 1818
James W. Brown	Monroe	November 18, 1818 / January 18, 1819
Edward Miller	Flatwood	March 15, 1819
John Kelly	Rockhouse	March 15, 1819
James Marcum	Burgess	March 16, 1819
Benj. Webb	Ky. R	May 17, 1819
Alex. Durbar	Monroe	(in) May 17, 1819 / (out) September 20, 1819

HISTORY OF JOHNSON COUNTY

CONSTABLES—Contd.

	Dist.	Date Sworn In
William Stratton	Monroe	August 16, 1819
Alex. Young	Madison	August 16, 1819
Elijah Hensley	Brushy Fk	August 16, 1819
Mathew Spurlock	Monroe	August 17, 1819 / November 16, 1819
David K. Harris	Town	September 20, 1819
David K. Harris	Monroe	November 16, 1819
Micajah Collier	Shelby	November 16, 1819
Joseph Gearhart	Liberty	December 21, 1819
James Marcum	1	May 15, 1820
John Lacy	2	May 15, 1820
George Martin	3	May 15, 1820
Hiram Spurlock	4	May 15, 1820
William Campbell	5	May 15, 1820
Thomas Mollett	6	May 15, 1820
William Trible	7	May 15, 1820
Elijah Prater	8	May 16, 1820 / June 19, 1820
William L. Stratton	4	November 20, 1820
John Howes	2	May 21, 1821
Francis A. Brown	3	May 21, 1821
Hiram Spurlock	6	May 21, 1821
Francis Lewis	10	May 21, 1821
Brerwell Vaughan	—	May 21, 1821
Robert Walker	7	May 21, 1821
Stephen Preston	2	August 20, 1821
David K. Harris	P'burg	August 20, 1821
William Prater	11	September 17, 1821
Sampson Moore	6	November 19, 1821
John S. Oakley	9	May 27, 1822
A. Harmon	6	November 25, 1822
Clell Kash	10	November 25, 1822
William Lykin	12	November 25, 1822
Mial Mayo	4	(in) May 26, 1823 / (out) August 23, 1824
John Marshall	10	(in) May 26, 1823 / (out) January 13, 1826
Joseph Gearheart	9	May 26, 1823
Jacob Sanders	8	May 26, 1823
Electius Howes	2	June 23, 1823
James Hatcher	6	(in) June 23, 1823 / (out) January 6, 1825
F. A. Brown	1	June 23, 1823
John H. Haywood	Town	(in) August 25, 1823 / (out) January 22, 1827
James Ramey	1	December 22, 1823
David Martin	9	May 24, 1824
William McGuire	4	May 24, 1824
Wilson Mayo	5	August 23, 1824
John Friend	P'burg	August 23, 1824
Zachariah Hale	6	(in) January 6, 1825 / (out) June 27, 1825
James Lacy	3	February 28, 1825
James G. Hatcher	6	February 28, 1825
James Davis	6	August 22, 1825
John Jacobs	9	June 27, 1825
Jeremiah Patrick	10	(in) January 23, 1826 / (out) May 28, 1827

CONSTABLES—Contd.

	Dist.		Date Sworn In
Nicholas Hackwith	6		May 22, 1826
James Owen	11		May 22, 1826
Thomas Daniel	11	(in)	August 28, 1826
		(out)	November 26, 1827
John Spradlin	1		August 28, 1827
Jacob Fitzpatrick	3	(in)	August 28, 1826
		(out)	May 28, 1826
James Ramey	2		September 25, 1827
Francis Whitaker	10		May 28, 1826
M. D. Lycan	Town		May 28, 1827
John B. Whitt	7		August 27, 1827
Aquilla Harman	7		August 27, 1827
Joel Howell	11		November 26, 1827
Landrum Beaty	7		November 26, 1827
James Van Hoose	1	(in)	March 17, 1828
		(out)	November 17, 1828
Nicholas Hackworth	6		March 17, 1828
Carter H. Jacobs	—	(in)	May 19, 1828
		(out)	May 18, 1829
John B. Lauhorn	2		November 17, 1828
Jesse Van Hoose	1	(in)	November 17, 1828
		(out)	November 15, 1830
Jonathan Fitzpatrick	—		May 18, 1829
Burwell Vaughan	6		May 18, 1829
Patrick Talbert	Town	(in)	May 18, 1829
		(out)	May 16, 1831
Nicholas Hackworth	Town		May 18, 1829
Hiram Spurlock	3		August 19, 1829
Thomas Gratton	2		September 21, 1829
John Martin	—		September 21, 1829
Thomas Barkett	4		November 16, 1829
Jesse Hall	11		November 16, 1829
Hugh Patrick	Burning Spring	(in)	May 17, 1830
		(out)	January 17, 1831
James Remy	2		June 21, 1830
Kelsey N. Harris	Town		September 20, 1830
Henry Sherman	1		November 15, 1830
Thomas J. Sanders	—		November 15, 1830
Burwell Vaughan	—		January 17, 1831
Joseph Bailey	Burning Spring		February 21, 1831
Charles W. Friend	Town		May 16, 1831
James Hager	1		November 21, 1831
Eliphus Preston	—		November 21, 1831
John H. Clark	11	(in)	November 21, 1831
		(out)	May 21, 1832
Robert Hatfield	1	(in)	December 19, 1831
		(out)	May 21, 1832
Patrick Vaughan	1		May 21, 1832
Caleb Justice	11		May 21, 1832
James Remy	2	(in)	June 18, 1832
		(out)	May 20, 1833
John H. Haywood	3	(in)	January 21, 1833
		(out)	December 8, 1834
Burwell Vaughan	6		January 21, 1833
William Barnett	2		May 20, 1833
Chas. W. Friend	Town		May 20, 1833
Nicholas Hackworth	3		August 18, 1833

CONSTABLES—Contd.

Name	Dist.		Date Sworn In
Francis Whitaker	10	(in)	May 20, 1833
		(out)	November 18, 1833
Ben Howard	10		November 18, 1833
William Barnett	Paintsville		April 16, 1834
Geo. Wash Bailey	2		December 8, 1834
Edward L. Osborne	3	(in)	December 8, 1834
		(out)	April 11, 1836
Thos. J. Sanders	4		December 8, 1834
Jonathan Fitzpatrick	—		April 13, 1835
Burwell Vaughan	10		April 13, 1835
Thos. Burchett	—		October 12, 1835
Chas. W. Friend	Town		June 12, 1835
Andrew W. Rule	—		October 12, 1835
James O. Wheeler	10		October 12, 1835
Wiley Morgan	—		December 14, 1835
William Remy	6		December 14, 1835
Soloman C. Stratton	Town		December 14, 1835
Robert Hager	3		June 13, 1835
Caleb Justice	—		June 13, 1835
Patrick Vaughan	—		June 13, 1835
Thos. Daniel	6		September 13, 1836
John Justice	4		December 12, 1836
Joseph W. Bailey	5		December 12, 1836
Alexander Clark	6		December 12, 1836
Robert Meade	1		March 13, 1837
Wm. Ramey	—		April 10, 1837
Reuben Marshall	—		April 10, 1837
Jonathan Fitzpatrick	—		June 12, 1837
Robt. Frazier	—		July 10, 1837
Edward L. Osborn	—		July 10, 1837
Jacob Fitzpatrick	—		September 11, 1837
John Waldeck	Town		September 11, 1837
Jonathan Justice	Beaver		October 9, 1837
Thos. Burchett	—		October 9, 1837
Isaac B. Friend	—	(Res.)	December 11, 1837
John Howes	—		December 11, 1837
Solomon C. Stratton	Town	(in)	December 11, 1837
		(out)	July 8, 1839
Wiley Morgan	—		December 11, 1837
Wm J. Burchett	—		April 9, 1838
Spencer Hall	—		April 9, 1838
Thomas Daniel	—		September 10, 1838
Daniel Rowland	Paint		September 10, 1838
Jeremiah Patrick	Burning Spring		January 14, 1839
Alexander Clark	—		January 14, 1839
Wm. H. Remy	—		April 8, 1839
Spencer Hill	—		April 8, 1839
Robert Meade	Mud Ck.		April 8, 1839
John C. Coburn	—		April 8, 1839
Edward Osborn	—		June 10, 1839
Jonathan Fitzpatrick	—		June 10, 1839
Wm. Prater	—		June 10, 1839
James J. Ford	Town		July 8, 1839
Chas. W. Friend	—		October 14, 1839
Jacob Fitzpatrick	—		October 14, 1839
Jonathan Justice	—		October 14, 1839
John Howes	—		January 13, 1840
John H. Layne	—		January 13, 1840

APPENDIX 507

CONSTABLES—Contd.

Name	Dist.	Date Sworn In
Thos. Burchett	—	March 9, 1840
Joseph Ratliff	—	April 13, 1840
Thos. Daniel	—	September 14, 1840
Daniel R. Rowland	—	September 14, 1840
Wm. Salyer	—	February 8, 1841
Jeremiah Patrick	—	February 8, 1841
Wm. Huff	—	February 8, 1841
Samuel Isaac	—	February 8, 1841
John Clark	—	(in) February 8, 1841 / (out) September 13, 1841
Wallace Rule	—	June 14, 1841
Edw. L. Osborn	—	June 14, 1841
Joseph Kelly	—	June 14, 1841
Thomas Howell	Mud Ck	June 14, 1841
Wm. H. Fitzpatrick	—	June 14, 1841

(Johnson County)

Name	Dist.	Date Sworn In
Martin Franklin	1	May, 1845
Arbuth A. Nott	2	May, 1845
Eleazor Lemaster	3	May, 1845
Andrew Daniel	4	May, 1845
Shadrach Ward	5	May, 1845
Aaron Hyden	6	June, 1845
James Mollett	5	June, 1846
John. J. Hager	2	November, 1846
Arbuth A. Nott	1	May 24, 1847
George W. Turner	3	May 24, 1847
James W. Preston	4	May 24, 1847
Ira Baker	5	May 24, 1847
Wm. G. Wells	6	——24, 1847
Samuel W. Porter	2	February 28, 1848
John W. Sturgell	3	February 28, 1848
Robert R. Williams	7	March 27, 1848
Wm. Wells	6	November 27, 1848
John Matney	2	——, ——
John Wheeler	3	June 24, 1849
Wm. Jeff. Ward	4	March 26, 1849
Isaac Hicks	6	May 28, 1849
Wm. W. Howes	1	June 24, 1849
Jacob Cassady	5	August 27, 1849
Joseph Daniel	4	January 28, 1850
Ira West	5	January 28, 1850
Dennis B. Wells	1	January 28, 1850
Levi Blair	1	May 27, 1850
Eleazor Lemaster	3	May 27, 1850
Thomas B. Brown	1	July 22, 1850
Joseph Davis	2	July 22, 1850
Nathan P. Hylton	2	February 24, 1851
James Stafford	1	June 24, 1851
Alex. W. Nickel	3	June 24, 1851
Isaac Rice	4	June 24, 1851
Wiley Spears	5	June 24, 1851
Jas. Stepp	6	June 24, 1851
Samuel E. Bayes	4	March 1, 1852
Thomas Short	5	April 5, 1852
James Spradlin	4	August 5, 1852
Daniel B. Auxier	5	August 5, 1852
James Stafford	1	June 6, 1853

CONSTABLES—Contd.

Name	Dist.	Date Sworn In
Bartley Pack	2	June 6, 1853
Alex. W. Nickel	3	June 6, 1853
George W. Rice	4	June 6, 1853
Thomas Short	5	June 6, 1853
George Johnson	6	June 6, 1853
Elkijah Howes	3	February 6, 1854
Bracken Van Hoose	4	June 5, 1854
Joseph Bailey	3	August 10, 1854
Wm. Webb	4	September 5, 1854
James Stafford	1	May 13, 1855
James W. Preston	2	May 13, 1855
William Jane	5	May 13, 1855
Alex. Cassaday	6	May 13, 1855
Wm. Webb	4	July 2, 1855
Abiud Colvin	4	September 8, 1855
Eliphus Preston	2	March 3, 1856
John H. Ward	2	July 7, 1856
John H. Ward	2	September 1, 1856
Andrew Osborn	3	July 7, 1856
Allen Stapleton	3	July 7, 1856
John Mollett	6	May 4, 1857
James Stafford	1	June 1, 1857
James Butcher	2	June 1, 1857
Joseph Bailey	3	June 1, 1857
John McCarty	5	June 1, 1857
Joseph Bailey	3	July 1, 1857
John Mollett	6	July 1, 1857
Nathan P. Hylton	2	August 4, 1857
Phillip Cassaday	6	August 4, 1857
William Sagraves	3	September 6, 1858
Francis Marion Conley	1	June 6, 1859
Nathan P. Heylton	2	June 6, 1859
William Sagraves	3	June 6, 1859
George W. Blair	4	June 6, 1859
James Music	5	June 6, 1859
Phillip Cassaday	6	June 6, 1859
Wallace M. Spears	5	September 5, 1859
John R. Robinson	5	December 5, 1859
William Butcher	5	April 2, 1860
Jno. W. Walker	1	June 3, 1861
Lawrence Harris	6	June 11, 1861
David Salyer	4	June 24, 1861
Wm. W. Conley	1	August 12, 1861
Jno. Van Hoose	2	December 2, 1862
Wm. P. Jayne	3	May 5, 1863
Mathew Caudill	4	June 1, 1863
Timothy Cunningham	5	July 6, 1863
F. M. P'Simer	3	August 24, 1863
Joe Franklin	5	April 4, 1864
William Sagraves	4	May 19, 1865
John H. Ward	2	August 8, 1865
James Murphy	5	August 8, 1865
William H. Spradlin	1	September 30, 1865
Phillip Cassaday	6	September 30, 1865
James C. Castle	1	March 5, 1866
Wm. H. Spradlin	2	March 5, 1866
John H. Ward	4	March 5, 1866
Richard M. Wells	2	March 5, 1866

APPENDIX

CONSTABLES—Contd.

Name	Dist.	Date Sworn In
Win Wells	5	March 5, 1866
John W. Walker	1	March 24, 1867
Jacob W. Whitten	1	May 27, 1867
William Arrowood	5	May 27, 1867
Josiah D. Hurst	5	May 27, 1867
Calvin Osborn	2	October 12, 1867
Henry C. Wells	5	November 7, 1867
Samuel Estep	1	January 2, 1868
Henry I. Daniel	2	June 7, 1869
G. J. Mayo	2	June 7, 1869
Tiltman Craft	7	March 7, 1870
John W. Davis	1	March 7, 1870
Daniel Bailey	3	June 5, 1871
William Craft	7	June 5, 1871
Robert Alby	1	July 5, 1871
James M. Pelphry	4	July 5, 1871
John W. Bayes	4	August 6, 1872
Daniel J. Rice	1	September —, 1872
Eliphus Preston	2	September —, 1872
Samuel Clark	1	— —, —
Thomas B. Strong	1	May 12, 1873
E. Preston	2	June 2, 1873
John B. Williams	3	June 2, 1873
Peter Crace	4	June 2, 1873
Harry Porter	5	— —, —
Tedman Craft	7	June 2, 1873
Jonathan Roten	5	June 2, 1873
M. L. Chandler	2	June 2, 1873
John B. Williams	3	November 2, 1874
L. M. C. Brown	1	November 2, 1874
R. M. Wells	8	November 30, 1874
John M. Brown	1	April 5, 1874
William W. Preston	8	August 24, 1875
W. J. Arrowood	8	June 4, 1877
John F. Fyffe	3	June 4, 1877
James Milum	1	June 4, 1877
D. J. Clay	4	June 4, 1877
D. W. Vanderpool	7	June 4, 1877
Robert Williams	3	August 7, 1877
Samuel Litteral	—	March 4, 1878
Samuel M. Long	4	May 18, 1878
Jacob Wells	8	July 1, 1878
William Dills	1	August 15, 1879
Henderson Osborn	5	August 15, 1879
Jasper Meek	8	September 15, 1879
William F. Colvin	4	September —, 1879
Jasper Meek	8	October 8, 1880
Silas Scott	6	August 13, 1880
H. S. Castle	7	June —, 1881
R. J. Stambaugh	6	March 7, 1881
Emery Castle	2	August 16, 1881
H. M. Rice	4	September 29, 1881
H. H. Hill	4	February —, 1882
Beaverly L. Castle	6	February —, 1882
Jasper Meek	8	September —, 1882
R. J. Stambaugh	6	August 11, 1882
H. S. Castle	7	March 5, 1883
H. P. Blair	1	June 4, 1883

CONSTABLES—Contd.

Name	Dist.	Date Sworn In
William P. Williams	7	June 4, 1883
William H. Burton	5	June 4, 1883
B. S. Castle	6	June 4, 1883
R. Y. Caudill	4	June 4, 1883
Peter C. Crace	4	October 6, 1884
William P. Williams	7	December 1, 1884
J. H. Milum	1	December 4, 1884
Limuel Jones	7	August 8, 1885
R. J. Stambaugh	6	August 8, 1885
John Holbrook	3	August 8, 1885
John C. Skaggs	3	August 8, 1885
John N. Caudill	4	October 12, 1885
Limuel Jones	7	June 16, 1887
Henry Butcher	8	September, 1888
J. H. Milum	1	June 3, 1889
Frederick Daniel	2	June 3, 1889
J. C. Skaggs	3	June 3, 1889
W. D. Bland	4	June 3, 1889
B. L. Castle	6	June 3, 1889
Samuel Jones	7	November 18, 1890
R. J. Stambaugh	6	November 18, 1890
James H. Holbrook	3	June 1, 1891
William Dills	7	June 1, 1891
James W. Green	7	June 1, 1891
John Akers	8	October 1, 1891
Frank Blair	4	June 29, 1891
R. B. Akers	8	October 1, 1891
Frank Blair	4	June 6, 1892
J. M. Riggsby	3	December 5, 1892
John Stambaugh	6	August 1, 1892
Frank Blair	5	June 6, 1892
John Stambaugh	5	August 1, 1892
J. M. Riggsby	4	December 5, 1892
D. B. Williams	4	June 5, 1893
J. V. Hall	2	June 5, 1893
Shadrach Preston	2	July 18, 1893
William Dills	1	November 21, 1902
George Spears	4	July 30, 1904
James Melvin	1	December 20, 1905
Albert Colvin	3	January 1, 1906
Anderson Daniel	5	January 1, 1906
W. S. Akers	5	January 1, 1906
James H. McCarty	4	January 1, 1906
A. J. Price	1	October 3, 1906
A. J. Price	1	January 6, 1908
Ira Cantrill	4	August 3, 1908
F. H. Williams	4	August 9, 1909
A. J. Price	1	December 6, 1909
Daniel Davis	3	December 6, 1909
McCoy Cantrill	4	December 30, 1909
S. J. Rice	1	December 30, 1909
Ed Rice	5	January 1, 1909
Elliott Ward	2	January 3, 1910
L. L. McCarty	4	August 9, 1910
Frank Caudill	3	December 19, 1910
B. F. Rice	5	December 9, 1911
J. E. Akers	2	February 24, 1912
Herbert Walker	1	August 21, 1912

CONSTABLES—Contd.

	Dist.	Date Sworn In
Monroe Slone	5	October 23, 1912
W. J. Murphey	5	December 28, 1912
A. J. Rice	1	December 24, 1913
W. J. Murphey	5	December 27, 1913
William F. Blair	3	December 29, 1913
Richard Salmon	2	January 5, 1914
Tom Cantrill	4	January 5, 1914
Frank Salyer	3	December 20, 1917
A. J. Price	1	January 7, 1918
W. J. Murphey	5	January 7, 1918
Grover Music	2	January 7, 1918
J. D. McKenzie	4	January 7, 1918
Jesse Blair	3	March 2, 1918
Clark Walters	3	October 7, 1918
Charley Rice	5	December 2, 1918
E. L. Marcum (Dept.)	2	December 16, 1918
W. T. Mollett	2	April 1, 1919
Lewis G. Blair	3	July 26, 1919
Roy Melvin	1	January 2, 1920
Ed O'Brian	1	May 25, 1920
Charles Staggs	2	December 9, 1920
James Smith	1	January 2, 1921
Ferrat Stambaugh	5	January 2, 1921
Lewis G. Blair	3	July 2, 1922
J. A. Rice	1	January 2, 1922
Coy Cantrill	4	January 4, 1922
Joe Castle	1	January 4, 1922
Burns Vanhoose	5	May 15, 1922
Harve Colvin	4	January 7, 1922
Henry Bowens	1	January 7, 1922
O. W. Mullins	4	September 29, 1922
Joe Castle	1	November 2, 1922
Frank Daniels	2	March 7, 1923
John W. Green	1	May 18, 1923
Chat Yates	3	May 21, 1923
Coy Cantrill	4	June 29, 1923
Arby Daniel	5	October 7, 1924
Hobert Witten	5	December 24, 1925
Newt. Fannin	1	December 24, 1925
B. F. Robinson	2	January 4, 1926
George W. Salyer	3	January 4, 1926
James H. Cantrill	4	January 4, 1926
Frank Daniels	2	January 4, 1926
Grant Daniels	1	July 28, 1926
Frank Daniels	2	August 15, 1927
Arthur Vanhoose (Dept.)	5	October 1, 1927
Joe Castle	1	October 12, 1927

Johnson County, is located at preser.., in the twenty-fourth judicial, seventh appellate, thirty-fifth senatorial, ninety-first legislative, and tenth congressional districts. For other districts in which the county has been allotted, see the legislative acts for the respective changes in the chapter "Government."

In the following list of officials no effort has been made to separate them into districts, but all those actually representing

HISTORY OF JOHNSON COUNTY

Johnson County are given, whether they resided in the county at the time or were living in Floyd, Pike, Martin, or any other county, and were elected from the district in which Johnson County was included.

CIRCUIT JUDGES

	Date
Alex Lackey	June 28, 1808
John Graham	June 28, 1808
John Allen	Oct. 26, 1812
G. W. Baylor	Oct. 26, 1812
Alex Lackey	July 25, 1814
John Graham	July 25, 1814
John Trimble	April 24, 1815
Alex Lackey	July 24, 1815
W. J. Barry	Aug. 5, 1816
Samuel L. McKee	April 21, 1817
Benjamin Mills	July 20, 1818
Kinaz Fanow	May —, 1837
Kinaz Fanow	May 22, 1843
George R. McKee	Oct. —, 1844
John White	1845
W. B. Kinkaid	1845
W. B. Kinkaid	1849
James M. Rice	1850
G. Adams	1852
Thomas F. Hazelrigg (pro tem.)	1855
I. W. Moore	Oct. —, 1858
R. Apperson, Jr.	1867
M. J. Ferguson	1870
M. J. Ferguson	1871
James E. Stewart	Oct. 15, 1874
W. C. Ireland	——, 1875
George N. Brown	Aug. 13, 1880
John M. Burns	
J. S. Patton	Jan. —, 1892
A. J. Auxier	Jan. —, 1898
A. J. Kirk	Jan. —, 1904
A. J. Kirk	Jan. —, 1910
J. F. Bailey	Jan. —, 1916
J. F. Bailey	Jan. —, 1922
J. F. Bailey	Jan. —, 1928

CIRCUIT COURT CLERKS

	Date
W. J. Mayo	July 24, 1815
Winston Mayo	May 22, 1843
J. W. Walker	Oct. 15, 1874
A. J. Vaughan (Deputy)	Oct. 15, 1874
C. J. Howes	——, 1875
H. B. Rice	Aug. 13, 1880
G. B. Stapleton	Jan. —, 1892
I. G. Rice	Jan. —, 1898
John W. Wheeler	Jan. —, 1904
F. P. Blair	Jan. —, 1910
D. C. Vanhoose	Jan. —, 1916

CIRCUIT COURT CLERKS—Contd.

	Date
J. Langley Preston	Jan. —, 1922
Winfrey Meek	Jan. —, 1928

COMMONWEALTH ATTORNEYS

	Date
Ralph S. Button	Jan. —, 1892
A. J. Kirk	Jan. —, 1898
John Butler	Jan. —, 1904
John Butler	Jan. —, 1910
I. G. Rice	(Short Term)
W. E. Litteral	Jan. —, 1916
I. G. Rice	(Short Term)
John W. Wheeler	Jan. —, 1922
J. B. Clark	Jan. —, 1928

MEMBERS OF THE KENTUCKY LEGISLATURE

(From Mason County, while Floyd was a part of Mason.)

Representatives	Date
John Wilson	1792
William Ward	1792-3-4-5
John Machir	1792-3-4-5-8-9-1800
John Howe	1796
Winslow Parker	1796
George Lewis	1796
Philemon Thomas	1796-7-8-9
John Pickett	1796, 1801-2
Thomas Foreman	1797
Michael Cassidy	1797-8
Alex K. Marshall	1797-8-9-1800
Gen. Joshua Desha	1797-9, 1800-1-2

(From Floyd County while Johnson County was a part of Floyd.)

John Hibbard	1809
John Bates	1811
David Morgan	1813
Henry Stratton	1813-14
Henry Stratton	1815
Alex Lackey	1816-17-18, 25-26, 30-31, 40
Henry B. Mayo	1819
David K. Harris	1820
Richard R. Lee	1820, May, 1822
James Stratton	1821
Robert Walker	1822
Peter Amyx	1822
Jacob Mayo	1824
Thomas W. Graham	1827
Jacob Heaberlin	1827
Samuel May	1832-3

APPENDIX

MEMBERS LEGISLATURE—Contd.

	Date
Henry C. Harris	1834-5, 38
G. Lackey	1836
Thomas Cecil	1839
John P. Martin	1841-43

(From Johnson County)

Samuel K. Friend	1844
Daniel Hager	1846
John B. Harris	1848
Bernard H. Garrett	1850
James M. Lackey	1851
Garland Hurt	1851-53
Henry G. Hager	1853-55
John B. Auxier	1855-57
Samuel Salyers	1859-61
George H. Whitten	1863
John M. Elliott	1864 (Expelled)
Thomas S. Brown	1865
Alex. Martin	1867-69
Joseph M. Davidson	1871-72
Thomas J. Mayo	1873-75
A. C. Higgins	1876
David Martin	1877-78
J. A. Porter	1879-80
Thomas Y. Fitzpatrick	1881-82
J. P. Wells	1883-84
J. W. Mayo	1885-86
John W. Langley	1887-88
John W. Langley	1889-90
T. S. Kirk	1891-92
T. S. Kirk	1894
W. W. Green	1896
W. W. Green	1897
C. B. Wheeler	1898
J. P. Delong	1900
W. T. Stafford	1902
Fred A. Vaughan	1904
W. T. Cain	1906
Isaac G. Rice	1908
J. W. Turner	1910
M. C. Kirk	1912
W. M. Webb	1914
W. M. Webb	1916
Fred C. Vanhoose	1918
Fred C. Vanhoose	1920
Fred. C. Vanhoose	1922
A. J. Baldridge	1924
A. J. Baldridge	1926
A. J. Baldridge	1928

SENATORS

(Mason County)

	Date
Alex. D. Orr	1792
John Machir	1796-1800

(Floyd County)

	Date
Richard Menifee	1814
Benjamin South	1814-19
Alex. Lackey	1819-23
Henry B. Mayo	1823-27
David K. Harris	1827-34
Samuel May	1834-39
Henry C. Harris	1843-47

(Johnson County)

Walter Chiles	1848-49-50
Sydney M. Barnes	1850-52
Theodore Kohlass	1853-54
Theodore Kohlass	1855-56
James McKee	1857-58
James McKee	1859-60

(No Election 1861-62)

John Power	1863-64
Elijah Patrick	1865-66
D. Y. Lyttle	1867-68
D. Y. Lyttle	1869-70
A. L. Martin	1871-72
A. L. Martin	1873-74
John Hyden	1876
John Hyden	1878
Alex. E. Adams	1879-80
Alex. E. Adams	1881-82
W. J. Caudill	1883-84
W. J. Caudill	1885-86
A. H. Stewart	1887-88
A. H. Stewart	1889-90
A. H. Stewart	1891-92
William Dingus	1894
William Dingus	1896
William Dingus	1898
T. S. Kirk	1900
T. S. Kirk	1902
John W. Combs	1904
John W. Combs	1906
Hillard Smith	1908
Hillard Smith	1910
Hiram M. Brock	1912
Hiram M. Brock	1914
Hiram M. Brock	1916
Hiram M. Brock	1918
Brig. H. Harris	1920
Brig. H. Harris	1922
J. B. Clark	1924
J. B. Clark	1926
Otto C. Gartin	1928

HISTORY OF JOHNSON COUNTY

CONGRESSMEN
10th Dist.

For members of Congress, previous to 1892, see the Biographical Congressional Directory covering the dates from 1774 to 1903, a copy of which is on file at the Kentucky State Library at Frankfort, Ky.

	Date
J. W. Kendall	1892
W. M. Beckner	1894
Marcus Lisle	1894
John M. Kendall	1896
N. T. Hopkins	1897
Thomas Y. Fitzpatrick	1898
Thomas Y. Fitzpatrick	1900
James B. White	1902

CONGRESSMEN—Contd.

	Date
F. A. Hopkins	1904
John W. Langley (Rep.)	1908-1922
A. J. Kirk	1924
Mrs. John W. Langley	1926-27

APPELLATE JUDGES
7th Dist.

	Date
J. H. Hazelrigg	1898-1901
E. C. O'Rear	1902
E. C. O'Rear	1904
E. C. O'Rear	1910
Robert J. Winn	1912
C. C. Turner	1914
Flem D. Sampson	1917
Flem D. Sampson	1925
S. S. Willis	1928

KENTUCKY LAND GRANTS AND ENTRIES, AFFECTING EASTERN KENTUCKY AND JOHNSON COUNTY

This is an index to all the land grants and entries recorded in the State Land Office in Frankfort, and on the County Court Order Books of Mason, Floyd, and Johnson counties, which in any way may have affected the titles or records of Johnson and surrounding counties, as issued under the laws of both the commonwealths of Virginia and Kentucky, covering the period from 1782 to the present. They are included herewith for the use of historical workers, land title attorneys, abstract clerks, genealogists, and others who may be interested in knowing more of their ancestors, as well as for their historical value.

From the chapter on Government, it will be learned that Kentucky was organized first into three counties, Lincoln, Jefferson, and Fayette, only the last of which affected Eastern Kentucky, and therefore no grants are given herein for the other two counties. Fayette later was divided, from which Mason was made, then Floyd from Mason and so on. Grants are left out after the date that each respective county was divided, that could not have possibly affected Johnson County. For example Johnson County was made from Floyd County in 1844, so that no Floyd County grant will appear after that date, but only those of Johnson County.

The initial spelling has been retained, and those failing to find a desired name in its alphabetical order should look in other places, where the name is possibly misspelled. For instance the name "Sellards" may be found under "Cellards."

APPENDIX 515

Every available record known was searched in an effort to have the grants complete. They, however, do not include military warrants, as names of counties are not available, and would necessitate a laborious search. Dr. Willard Rouse Jillson has a thorough alphabetization of them in his publication of Old Kentucky Entries and Deeds, issued in 1926.

REFERENCES

‡County Court Orders, 1826–1924, Kentucky Land Grants, Filson Club Publication No. 33, 1925.
#Virginia Land Grants, 1782-1792, Kentucky Land Grants, Filson Club Publication No. 33, 1925.
▲Land Grants, 1793–1856, Kentucky Land Grants, Filson Club Publication No. 33, 1925.
¶Land Warrants, 1816–1873, Filson Club Publication No. 33, 1925.
†County Court Orders, from County Court Order Books in respective County Seats for date of Grant.
§County Court Orders, Floyd County, Archives Kentucky State Historical Society.
◎Fayette County Entries, Old Kentucky Entries and Deeds, Filson Club Publication No. 34, Jillson, W. R., 1926, The Standard Printing Company.
*Court of Appeals Deeds-Grantees, Old Kentucky Entries and Deeds, Filson Club Publication No. 34 Jillson, W. R., 1926, The Standard Printing Company.
■Court of Appeals Deeds-Attorneys, Old Kentucky Entries and Deeds, Filson Club Publication No. 34, Jillson, W. R., 1926, The Standard Printing Company.

County	Grantee	Book	Page	Date Survey	Acres	Watercourse
¶Floyd	Adams, Benjamin	c	187	11– 5–1816	150	None
‡Floyd	Adams, Gilbert	10	37	7– 5–1842	100	Burn Fk Lick River
#Bourbon	Adams, Richard	12	384	4–18–1787	20,000	Big Sandy
†Floyd	Adams, Stephen	2	199	10–29–1816	—	—
‡Floyd	Adams, William	6	188	3–15–1839	200	R H Fk S Road Fk Licking
¶Floyd	Adkins, Spencer	F	349	11– 5–1819	349	Greasy Cr
‡Floyd	Akers, James	8	272	8–15–1840	100	Little Mud Cr
‡Floyd	Akers, James	6	177	4–12–1839	100	Little Mud Cr
†Johnson	Alby, Robert	2	259	4– 2– 55	100	
◎Johnson	Alexander, William	4	179	5– 3–1785	21,000	Main Fk Sandy R
‡Floyd	Allen, Adam	11	12	1–20–1843	50	Turkey Cr
‡Floyd	Allen, David W	11	1	1–23–1843	100	Hale Fk Cr
‡Floyd	Allen, D. W.	14	234	1– 8–1843	50	Beaver Cr
◎	Allen, William Jr	4	261	1–18–1876	1,000	S Fk Sandy
#Bourbon	Allen, William Jr	11	209	2– 5–1787	3,681¾	Big Sandy
¶Johnson	Alley, Robert	R-2	393	3–14–1851	700	Little Paint Cr
†Johnson	Alley, Robert	2	396	7– 6– 57	200	
					50	
‡Johnson	Alley, Robert	54	205	2–25–1855	250	Sycamore Fk
‡Johnson	Alley, Robert	54	204	5–17–1856	400	Little Paint Cr
‡Johnson	Alley, Robert	84	247	11– 2–1871	25	Rush Fk
‡Johnson	Alley, Robert	60	75	12–15–1859	600	Toms Cr
†Johnson	Alley, Robert	3	119	2–11– 60	100	
‡Johnson	Alley, Simeon	32	251	8–14–1848	100	Mud Lick Cr
†Floyd	Allington, David Sr	2	197	10–29–1816		
†Floyd	Allington, Isaac	2	197	10–29–1816		
†Floyd	Allington, Jacob	2	210	12–23–1816		
*Res. Phil. Pa.	Allison, David	Q	166	3–10–1796	70,000	Big Sandy R
*Petersb'g	Anderson, Daniel	E	111	4–19–1799	1,000	Sandy R
†Johnson	Arms, E. B.	5	611	3– 2– 78	50	
†Johnson	Arms, E. B.	5	612	3– 2– 78	100	
†Johnson	Arms, Elija B	5	581	7–21– 77	4	
†Johnson	Arms, Elijah B	5	196	2–24– 72	33	
‡Johnson	Arms, Elizah	90	,78	3–11–1872	31	Low Gap Fk Barnetts Cr
‡Floyd	Arnett, Ambrose	6	205	10–19–1839	50	M Fk Licking
‡Floyd	Arnett, David	6	203	10–19–1839	150	Bear Br Mine Fk Licking
‡Morgan	Arnett, Reuben	6	206	11–20–1839	200	M Fk Licking R
‡Floyd	Arnett, Stephen	6	204	10–21–1839	150	M Fk Licking
‡Floyd	Arnett, William	6	207	10–19–1839	100	M Fk Licking R
‡Johnson	Arrowood, Garnett D.	53	319	2–24–1854	80	Rockcastle
†Johnson	Arrowood, James D	2	455	6– 7– 58	80	
†Johnson	Arrowood, William	2	455	6– 7– 58	130	
‡Johnson	Arrowood, William	53	318	6– 4–1858	180	Greasy Cr

HISTORY OF JOHNSON COUNTY

County	Grantee	Book	Page	Date Survey	Acres	Watercourse
‡Johnson	Ask, Catesby	69	294	5– 4–1866	10	Lick Cr
‡Johnson	Ausbourn, Edward	53	170	11–29–1853	50	Mud Lick Cr
#Fayette	Austin, Stephen	13	52	2–27–1785	5,000	Big Sandy
@Fayette	Austin, Stephen	3	118	12–29–1783	10,000	N Fk Big Sandy
†Johnson	Auxier, Daniel	2	155	2– 6– 54	200	
‡Johnson	Auxier, Daniel B	43	544	1–26–1853	200	Rockcastle Fk
¶Floyd	Auxier, Eli	c-2	94	2– 4–1836	50	Sandy R
‡Johnson	Auxier, Enoch	35	490	10–18–1850	26	Sandy R
†Johnson	Auxier, George W	2	155	2– 6– 54	200	
¶Johnson	Auxier, Jackson	R-2	127	9–20–1847	300	Long Br
¶Floyd	Auxier, John	A	478	9– 6–1816	50	Mud Lick Fk
¶Floyd	Auxier, John	A-2	132	11– 1–1830	200	Paint Cr
¶Floyd	Auxier, John	T	42	9–17–1824	100	Paint Cr
‡Johnson	Auxier, John	66	454	4–28–1865	112	Scaffold Lick Fk
¶Johnson	Auxier, John Sr	R-2	22	12–20–1848	50	Johns Cr
‡Johnson	Auxier, John B	66	452	4– 7–1865	330	Lynn Bark Fk
‡Johnson	Auxier, John B	37	50	2–28–1850	50	Lick Br
‡Johnson	Auxier, John B	27	100	1– 1–1847	900	Millers Cr
‡Johnson	Auxier, John B	70	465	12– 1–1855	50	Lynn Bark
†Johnson	Auxier, John B	2	226	12– 5– 54	200	
†Johnson	Auxier, John B	2	266	12– 5– 54	200	
†Johnson	Auxier, John B	2	266	12– 5– 54	200	
†Johnson	Auxier, John B	2	226	12– 5– 54	200	
†Johnson	Auxier, John B	2	226	12– 5– 54	200	
†Johnson	Auxier, John B	2	226	12– 5– 54	100	
‡Johnson	Auxier, John B	27	99	1– 8–1846	100	Scofield Lick Fk
‡Johnson	Auxier, John B	35	488	1– 1–1847	300	Miller Cr
‡Johnson	Auxier, John B	27	101	2–28–1845	100	Spice Br
‡Johnson	Auxier, John B	35	487	8–12–1849	200	Brushy Cr
‡Johnson	Auxier, John B	3	178	1– 7– 61	200	
†Johnson	Auxier, John B	3	178	1– 7– 61	200	
†Johnson	Auxier, John B	3	178	1– 7– 61	200	
‡Johnson	Auxier, John B	35	489	10–14–1850	400	Oak Log Cr
†Johnson	Auxier, John B	3	168	10–17– 60	200	
†Johnson	Auxier, John B	3	168	10–17– 60	200	
†Johnson	Auxier, John B	3	168	10–17– 60	200	
†Johnson	Auxier, John B	3	168	10–17– 60	200	
†Johnson	Auxier, John B	3	168	10–17– 60	200	
†Johnson	Auxier, John B	3	338	1–25–1865	200	
‡Johnson	Auxier, John B	18	39	7– 3–1845	100	Keetons Cr
‡Johnson	Auxier, John B	97	543	1– 7–1876	110	Johns Cr
‡Johnson	Auxier, John B	66	453	4–28–1865	500	Mine Fk Rockcastle Cr
‡Johnson	Auxier, John D	61	192	12–12–1860	2,710	Buck Fk Rockcastle Cr
‡Johnson	Auxier, Margaret	65	307	3–11–1865	830	Rolling Fk
§Floyd	Auxier, Michael	(Tract 41)		8– 2–1803	100	At Two Brothers Shoal on Big Sandy
▲Floyd	Auxier, Nathaniel	18	423	12–22–1814	70	W Fk Big Sandy
▲Floyd	Auxier, Nathaniel	18	424	12–23–1814	53	Big Paint Cr
¶Floyd	Auxier, Nathaniel	A-2	395	10–30–1830	50	Paint Cr
¶Floyd	Auxier, Nathaniel	G-2	2	11–27–1835	100	Bearhollow Br
§Floyd	Auxier, Nathaniel Jr	8	312	9– 5–1841	100	Bearhollow
§Floyd	Auxier, Nath'l Sr	8	313	9– 3–1841	100	Bearhollow
¶Floyd	Auxier, Samuel	W	364	9–13–1825	15	Sandy R
‡Johnson	Auxier, Samuel	54	203	6–11–1856	750	R Fk Davels Daniels(?) Cr
†Johnson	Auxier, Samuel	2	155	2– 6–1854	200	
†Johnson	Auxier, Samuel	2	193	8– 7–1854	200	
¶Floyd	Auxier, Samuel	G-2	125	3– 3–1834	150	Sandy R
†Johnson	Auxier, Samuel	2	456	6– 7–1858	200	
†Johnson	Auxier, Samuel	2	456	6– 7–1858	100	
¶Floyd	Auxier, Samuel	T	138	9–12–1825	50	Johns Cr
¶Floyd	Auxier, Samuel	Z	446	7–31–1827	50	Daniels Cr
‡Johnson	Auxier, Sam'l Jr	14	273	9–26–1844	100	Little Paint Cr
‡Johnson	Auxier, Sam'l Sr	43	518	8–23–1849	200	Beech Fk Rockcastle Cr
‡Johnson	Auxier, Sam'l Sr	43	519	8–23–1849	250	Rt Fk Daniel
§Floyd	Auxier, Simon	(Cert. 90)		5– 7–1804	100	Abbott Cr
§Floyd	Auxier, Simon	(Cert. 96)		6– 4–1804	100	Abbott Cr
‡Johnson	Auxier, W. L	118	5	5–28–1894	5	Lt Fk Raven Nest Br
#Bourbon	Bagby, John	3	287	1– 6–1787	6,800½	Big Sandy
@	Bagby, John	4	273	2–15–1786	6,800	Sandy
‡Johnson	Bailey, Andrew	121	143	2– 6–1904	10	Laurel Fk Blain Cr
‡Johnson	Bailey, Daniel	66	373	6–20–1865	22	Upper Laurel Fk
‡Johnson	Bailey, Joseph	32	301	7–25–1848	150	Big Lick Br Laurel Fk
‡Johnson	Bailey, Joseph	37	54	1–30–1850	50	Big Lick Br
‡Johnson	Bailey, Mahaler	68	386	2–13–1866	200	Horges Cr
‡Floyd	Bailey, Wallace	10	35	4– 4–1842	100	Burning Sp Fk
‡Floyd	Bailey, Wallace	10	36	3– 2–1842	100	Gun Cr
‡Floyd	Bailey, Wallace	10	49	3– 3–1842	100	Burning Sp Fk

APPENDIX

County	Grantee	Book	Page	Date Survey	Acres	Watercourse
§Floyd	Baker, Bolin	(Cert. 58)		11-8-1803	400	Levisa Fk above Greasy Shoal
‡Johnson	Baker, Nath	18	34	10- 4-1845	100	Rockcastle
‡Floyd	Baldridge, John	31	335	8-25-1843	50	Patton Br
‡Floyd	Baldwin, Solomon	11	42	8-27-1843	50	Mud Cr
†Johnson	Baldwin, Thomas	5	433	11-30- 74	50	
‡Johnson	Baley, Daniel	46	37	11- 5-1854	230	Br Blain Cr
†Johnson	Baley, Daniel	3	195	4- 1- 61	65	
‡Johnson	Baley, Daniel	62	184	11- 7-1860	110	Upper Laurel Fk
†Johnson	Baley, W. W.	5	581	7-21- 77	50	
‡Johnson	Banister, Pleasant	49	299	12-13-1856	100	Rockcastle R
‡Johnson	Bannister, Pleasant	44	261	8-27-1852	100	Rockcastle Cr
‡Johnson	Bannister, Pleasant	27	97	6- 7-1847	50	Rockcastle Cr
†Floyd	Barnett, Gilbert	2	177	7-22-1816		
⊙———	Barnett, James Jr	2	185	2-13-1783	12,000	Sandy
⊙———	Barnett, James Jr	2	185	2-13-1783	500	Sandy
†Floyd	Barnett, Jesse	2	131	12-25-1815	100	
§Floyd	Barnett, Jesse	(Cert.136)		8-17-1805	400	Big Paint
‡Floyd	Barnett, Notley	4	64	10-23-1838	50	Long Cr
‡Floyd	Barnett, Wilson	6	210	7-29-1839	50	Caning Fk of M Cr
*Res. Baltimore	Barry, James	D	244	6- 1-1797	8,000	N Fk Sand R
‡Johnson	Bays, Rachel	75	127	5-11-1868	64	Pickle Fk
‡Johnson	Bays, Rachel	75	128	5-11-1868	50	Pickle Fk
‡Johnson	Bays, Samuel E	70	55	8-25-1866	5	Bridge Br Hood Fk
‡Johnson	Bays, Samuel E & Joshua	68	123	1-10-1866	6	Hoods Fk
‡Floyd	Bays, William	10	47	8- 9-1842	100	Abbott Cr
†Johnson	Bayse, Rachel E	4	331	5- 4-1868	100	
*Res. Obington	Beaty, Charles C	2	94	2- 1-1831	10,000	S Fk Sandy R
▲Floyd	Beavers, Abraham	19	282	12-23-1818	45	Sandy R
¶Floyd	Belcher, George	H	39	1-13-1820	50	Louisa Fk Sandy R
▲Mason	Bell, James	15	121	9-13-1798	504	Big Sandy
▲Mason	Bell, Thomas	17	500	8-31-1798	1,900	Big Sandy
▲Mason	Bell, Thomas	17	499	8-28-1798	1,900	Big Sandy
#Fayette	Bell, William	7	298	4-15-1784	2,000	Big Sandy
#Fayette	Bell, William	7	295	4-15-1784	7,987½	Big Sandy
———	Bell, William	3	220	3-11-1784	12,000	Sandy
	(Bell had many others)					
†Johnson	Belvin, James	2	444	4- 1- 58	96	
†Floyd	Bently, Daniel	2	199	10-29-1816		
‡Johnson	Bevins, Hiram K	27	98	11-18-1847	150	Coldwater Fk
‡Johnson	Black, James A	99	260	5- 8-1879	200	M Fk Greasy Cr
‡Johnson	Black, H. L	99	262	5- 8-1879	200	Greasy Cr
‡Johnson	Black, T. L	99	261	5- 8-1879	200	Greasy Cr
‡Johnson	Blain, Amos B	90	79	3-13-1872	35	Upper Twin Br
‡Johnson	Blain, William	53	171	4- 5-1854	200	Genneys Cr
†Johnson	Blair, Asa J	2	168	3- 6-1854	25	
†Johnson	Blair, George W	2	104	6- 6-1853	70	
†Floyd	Blair, Jesse	2	197	10-29-1816		
†Johnson	Blair, John	2	176	4- 3-1854	200	
†Johnson	Blair, John & Conley, John		197	5- 7-1867	100	
†Johnson	Blair, Noble	2	168	3- 6-1854	100	
†Johnson	Blair, Wallace B	5	202	3-18-1872	50	
†Johnson	Blair, Wallace B	5	345	12-15-1873	100	
†Johnson	Blair, William	2	355	12- 1-1856	150	
†Johnson	Blair, William	2	355	12- 1-1856	150	
†Johnson	Blair, William	2	156	2- 6-1854	50	
†Johnson	Blair, William	2	189	7- 3-1854	50	
#Bourbon	Blankenbecker, Samuel	14	166	8-17-1787	517	Sandy
‡Floyd	Blankenship, Henry	10	51	5-12-1842	50	Ivey Cr
‡Floyd	Blankenship, William	10	34	7-21-1842	50	Fraiseur Cr
‡Johnson	Blanton, Elias	97	71	2-23-1877	217	Mud Lick Cr
‡Johnson	Blanton, Emily & Jas. P	68	371	3-11-1866	120	Stuffy Br Oil Fk
¶Floyd	Blanton, George	1-2	341	12-28-1835	100	Lower Peter Cave Br
†Johnson	Blanton, James	5	595	12- 3-1877	50	
‡Johnson	Blanton, James Sr	98	9	12-14-1877	105	Gap Br
‡Johnson	Blanton, James H	66	69	4-21-1865	56	Big Paint Cr
‡Johnson	Blanton, James H	66	70	1-10-1865	3	Big Paint Cr
¶Floyd	Blanton, James H	L-2	335	3-25-1836	50	Paint Cr
‡Johnson	Blanton, Henry	109	397	6-25-1887	35	Pigeon Cr
⊙———	Bledsoe, Aaron	2	37	1-11-1783	1,083	Sandy
#Bourbon	Bledsoe, Aaron	12	333	1- 4-1787	1,083	Big Sandy
‡Johnson	Blevins, Daniel	32	302	8-29-1849	100	Mud Lick Cr
‡Johnson	Blevins, James	37	52	3- 1-1850	200	House Br
‡Johnson	Blevins, James	22	237	10- 9-1846	100	Rockhouse Fk
‡Johnson	Blevins, James	65	342	2-16-1865	720	Rockcastle
‡Johnson	Blevins, James	53	4	12- 2-1855	96	Rockcastle Cr
†Johnson	Blevins, James & Williams, Stephen	3	344	2-21-1865	150	

518 HISTORY OF JOHNSON COUNTY

County	Grantee	Book	Page	Date Survey	Acres	Watercourse
¶Floyd	Blevins, James	G-2	79	10-16-1835	100	Road Fk
‡Johnson	Blevins, Levi	37	51	3- 1-1850	125	Rockhouse Fk
‡Johnson	Blevins, Thomas A.	37	53	2-27-1850	50	Panther Cr
†Johnson	Blevins, Wiley	2	130	11- 7-1853	50	
*Res. Franklin	Blithe, Samuel	O	470	4-29-1807	183,388¼	Big Sandy R
*Res. Fayette	Bodley, Thomas	G	106	12-11-1802	15,000	N Fk Sandy R
#Fayette	Bonchman, Benedict	16	61	11-19-1785	1,200	S Fk Sandy
‡Johnson	Bond, Henry H	66	34	4-10-1865	350	Old Rk Fk, Coldwater Fk
‡Johnson	Borders, Arch	35	492	2-10-1851	300	Price Br
¶Floyd	Borders, Archibald	H	156	3-15-1821	50	Fk Sandy R
‡Johnson	Borders, David	62	181	3-28-1861	375	Tom's Cr
†Johnson	Borders, David	3	207	6- 3-1861	75	
¶Floyd	Borders, Hezekiah	H	164	3-23-1821	75	Big Sandy R
‡Johnson	Borders, John	35	493	3-12-1850	300	Georges Cr
‡Johnson	Borders, John	66	72	6- 5-1865	21	Borders Br Georges Cr
¶Floyd	Borders, John	H	138	5-16-1819	50	Sandy R
‡Johnson	Borders, Joseph	65	141	8-28-1858	45	Stafford Fk
¶Floyd	Borders, Michael	H	154	3-24-1821	50	Georges Cr
¶Floyd	Borders, Michael	F	350	9-14-1818	50	Georges Cr
¶Floyd	Borders & Price	1-2	275	6-16-1836	100	Tom's Cr
¶Floyd	Borders & Price	1-2	305	6- 2-1836	100	Tom's Cr
‡Johnson	Botner, Oliver D	28	432	11-30-1848	13½	Hoods Fk
‡Johnson	Bowen, Adam	20	457	6-18-1846	200	Bakers Br
‡Johnson	Bowen, Daniel	66	71	2-14-1865	20	L H Fk Greasy Cr
‡Johnson	Bowen, David	11	47	9-20-1843	50	Greasy Cr
‡Johnson	Bowen, Henry	18	32	2-19-1845	50	Tom's Cr
‡Johnson	Bowlin, Wm. A	105	72	10-23-1882	100	Laurel Fk
‡Johnson	Bowman, Elizabeth	46	36	3-13-1854	90	Laurel Cr
†Johnson	Bowman, Elizabeth	2	179	4- 3-1854	90	
†Johnson	Boyd, Daniel	3	119	3- 4-1861	50	
¶Floyd	Boyd, David	1-2	290	6- 6-1836	150	Lick Br
¶Floyd	Bradford, Sam'l	T	78	9-21-1824	50	Sycamore Fk Tom's Cr
‡Johnson	Bradley, Carnelius	51	273	10- 6-1857	125	Chestnut Cr
†Johnson	Bradley, Carnelius	2	411	11- 2-1857	25-200	
‡Johnson	Bradley, Carnelius	3	339	8- 8-1865	50	
‡Johnson	Bradley, Carnelius	66	374	8-10-1865	89	Chestnut Cr
¶Floyd	Bradley, Elias	6	197	6- 4-1839	100	Open Fk Middle Cr
¶Floyd	Bradley, Wm	8	319	4- 2-1840	50	Alum Lick
¶Floyd	Branham, Benj. F	6	198	2-29-1839	50	Long Fk Towels Cr
▲Floyd	Branham, John	19	354	6-13-1820	50	Louisa Fk
▲Mason	Breckenridge, John	6	316	1- 4-1796	1,000	Sandy R
‡Johnson	Briant, Wm. O	63	227	4-23-1856	30	Lt. H. Fk Meadow Br
©Fayette	Brooks, Ebenezer	4	270	2- 7-1786	1,000	Sandy
#Bourbon	Brooks, Geo	5	337	8-16-1787	7,000	Sandy R
▲Mason	Brough, Peter	14	25	4- 3-1798	2,650	Sandy R
†Johnson	Brown, A	36	19	——1858	13	
¶Floyd	Brown, Anderson G	E-2	214	9- 7-1834	50	Mud Lick
‡Johnson	Brown, Andrew	53	6	3-12-1857	190	Tom's Cr
‡Johnson	Brown, Arch	53	159	5- 7-1857	135	George Cr
†Johnson	Brown, Archibald	2	378	4- 6-1857	100	
†Johnson	Brown, Archibald	2	440	3- 1-1858	100	
‡Johnson	Brown, Daniel G	32	252	9-14-1848	200	Sandy R
‡Johnson	Brown, D. K	53	173	4-10-1856	20	None
‡Johnson	Brown, D. K	53	172	4- 7-1856	80	Wiley Br
‡Johnson	Brown, David K	32	303	5- 2-1848	425	Wiley Br
†Johnson	Brown, David K	2	217	10-14-1854	50	
†Johnson	Brown, David K	2	328	5- 5-1856	150	
‡Johnson	Brown, David K	47	110	3- 1-1855	139	Br Chestnut Cr
‡Johnson	Brown, David K	66	370	7- 5-1865	20	Wiley Br
‡Johnson	Brown, David K	66	369	7- 5-1865	27	Wiley Br
©Fayette	Brown, Elijah	3	115	12-27-1783	10,000	N Fk Big Sandy R
#Fayette	Brown, Elijah	13	534	3-12-1785	10,000	N Br Sandy R
¶Floyd	Brown, Francis A	1-2	259	12-15-1835	50	Tom's Cr
‡Johnson	Brown, Gabriel	69	295	5- 4-1866	42	White House Cr
†Johnson	Brown, George W	5	433	11-30- 74	50	
†Johnson	Brown, James	3	344	12-22-1865	200	
¶Floyd	Brown, James Y	D-2	397	5-23-1835	100	Sandy R
‡Johnson	Brown, John & David	18	33	8-13-1845	250	Wiley Br
§Floyd	Brown, John	(Cert. 119)		11- 4-1804	400	Paint Cr
¶Floyd	Brown, John	T	86	2-15-1825	100	Jenny's Cr
‡Johnson	Brown, John	31	334	6-26-1833	100	Bush Br
‡Johnson	Brown, John	14	274	4-13-1844	50	Georges Cr
‡Johnson	Brown, John	22	82	4- 7-1847	300	George Cr
‡Johnson	Brown, John	32	253	5- 2-1848	200	Greasy Cr
‡Johnson	Brown, John	32	300	3-12-1850	257	Green Fk Georges Cr
‡Johnson	Brown, John	51	275	5-13-1857	200	Georges Cr
†Johnson	Brown, John	2	398	8- 3-1857	100	
‡Johnson	Brown, John	66	371	7- 5-1865	75	Georges Cr & Tom's Cr
‡Johnson	Brown, John Sr	54	206	7-24-1858	200	Gregars Cr

APPENDIX

County	Grantee	Book	Page	Date Survey	Acres	Watercourse
‡Johnson	Brown, John J.	68	121	10–18–1865	14	Sycamore Fk
‡Johnson	Brown, John J.	68	372	3–20–1866	40	Georges Cr
†Johnson	Brown, John W.	5	433	11–30– 74	50	
†Johnson	Brown, Lelle C.	5	546	3–13– 76	200	
‡Floyd	Brown, Lewis	14	245	3–14–1844	100	Martins Br
¶Floyd	Brown, Lewis H.	33	362	4– 4–1843	100	Mill Br
§Floyd	Brown, Robert	(Cert. 27)		6– 6–1807	100	Levisa Fk
¶Floyd	Brown, Robert	C	193	7– 9–1817	50	Big Sandy R
°Fayette	Brown, Thomas	4	250	12–27–1785	5,000	S Fk Sandy
§Floyd	Brown, Thomas C.	(Cert. 9)		9——1802	400	
§Floyd	Brown, Thomas C.	(Cert. 35)		6– 6–1803	400	Levisa Fk Sandy
¶Floyd	Brown, Thomas C.	F	52	5–30–1818	50	Tom's Cr
†Johnson	Brown, Thomas S.	5	415	9– 8– 74	50	
†Johnson	Brown, Thomas S.	5	433	11–30– 74	50	
†Johnson	Brown, Turner	5	432	11– 2– 74	50	
¶Floyd	Brown, William	L-2	386	10–30–1837	50	Sandy R
‡Johnson	Brown, Wm. W. & Daniel K.	66	372	7– 5–1865	43	Sally Daniel Br
‡Johnson	Brown, William W. & David K.	56	457	2–16–1859	50	Tom's Cr
‡Johnson	Brown, Wm. W. & David K.	66	111	5–26–1865	11	Zackary Fk Sycamore Fk
†Johnson	Brown, W. W.	3	361	5–28–1865	30	
¶Morgan	Brown, William	P-2	25	11– 1–1832	100	Open Fk Paint Cr
¶Morgan	Brown, William	Q-2	503	12–10–1838	150	Laurel
‡Johnson	Brown, William W.	51	276	3–19–1857	200	Georges Cr
‡Johnson	Brown, William W.	2	381	5– 4–1857	200	
‡Johnson	Brown, William W.	64	30	2–17–1863	300	Burnt Cabbin Br Tom's Cr
‡Johnson	Brown, William W.	66	110	5–26–1865	19	Wolf Pen Cr
‡Johnson	Brown & Castle	22	338	12– 2–1846	300	Georges Cr
¶Floyd	Burchett, Benjamin	Y	196	9–19–1827	50	Johns Cr
¶Floyd	Burchett, Drury	8	314	12– 2–1840	50	Buffalo Cr
¶Floyd	Burchett, Drury	8	315	12– 5–1840	100	Cow Cr
¶Floyd	Burchett, Thomas	T	77	1–20–1825	50	Johns Cr
¶Floyd	Burchett, William	8	318	12– 4–1840	50	Buffalo
¶Floyd	Burgess, Garland	T	131	6– 9–1824	50	Big Greasy Cr
†Johnson	Burgess, James E	3	338	1–25–1865	200	
‡Johnson	Burk, John W	43	175	4–12–1849	50	Barnetts Cr
¶Floyd	Burk, Richard	P-2	162	3–11–1843	50	Barnetts Cr
‡Johnson	Burks, Richard	43	162	4– 9–1851	100	Barnetts Cr
‡Johnson	Butcher, James	65	343	2–20–1865	1,147	Pigeon Roost Fk
‡Johnson	Butcher, William	35	501	2– 3–1851	100	Road Fk Br
‡Johnson	Butcher, William	2	340	9– 1–1856	50	
‡Johnson	Butcher, William	68	122	4–27–1865	85	Brushy Fk
‡Johnson	Butcher, William	49	301	10– 1–1856	50	None
‡Johnson	Butcher, William	100	262	11–17–1880	4	Butcher Br
*Res.Dinwiddie	Byrne, James	D	299	7– 8–1799	10,000	Big Sandy R
°Fayette	Caldwell, David	3	111	12–27–1783	5,000	Main N-Fk Sandy
†Johnson	Cameron, James	2	119	11–22–1815	150	
¶Floyd	Cantrill, Elijah	O	450	9– 7–1823	50	Barnetts Cr
‡Johnson	Cantrel, John	37	57	3–18–1851	50	Petercave Br
#Bourbon	Carter, John	11	457	4–26–1787	11,400	Big Sandy R
‡Johnson	Carty, John	43	177	4– 8–1851	100	Colvin Br
‡Johnson	Casseday, Alex	47	108	12– 9–1854	175	Bakers Br
‡Johnson	Cassady, Alex	2	241	2– 6–1855	175	
‡Johnson	Cassady, Alex	47	112	4–14–1855	100	Lick Log Fk
‡Johnson	Cassady, Alex	58	356	1–26–1858	90	Bakers Br
‡Johnson	Cassada, Alex	66	443	8–31–1865	30	M Fk Rockcastle
†Johnson	Cassady, Alexander	2	369	3– 2–1857	70	
†Johnson	Cassady, Alexander	2	369	3– 2–1857	70	
†Johnson	Cassady, Alexander	2	370	3– 2–1857	30	
†Johnson	Cassady, Alexander	2	370	3– 2–1857	12	
‡Johnson	Cassady, Alexander	58	383	1–26–1858	85	Bakers Br
‡Johnson	Cassady, Alexander	58	388	1–26–1858	10	Rockcastle Cr
†Johnson	Cassady, Alexander	3	341	2– 6–1865	30	
†Johnson	Cassady, Benjamin	2	375	(?)	100	
‡Johnson	Cassady, Benjamin	27	93	11–16–1847	267	Coldwater Fk
‡Johnson	Cassady, Benjamin	27	92	11–19–1847	133	Hardin Br
†Johnson	Cassady, Benjamin	2	242	2– 6–1855	100	
‡Johnson	Cassady, Benjamin	53	176	12–18–1855	200	Casaday Br
‡Johnson	Cassady, Benjamin	53	177	6– 9–1857	30	Blacklog Cr
†Johnson	Cassady, Benjamin	2	433	2– 1–1858	3	
‡Johnson	Cassady, Benjamin	53	175	3–22–1858	55	Hardin Br
‡Johnson	Cassady, Benjamin	66	28	4–18–1865	108	Appleton Br
‡Johnson	Cassady, Benjamin	66	444	8–31–1865	4	Coldwater Fk Rockcastle
‡Johnson	Cassady, Benjamin	67	129	9–25–1865	250	John Hardin Br
†Johnson	Cassady, Benjamin	3	398	9–(?)–1865	200	
‡Johnson	Cassady, Jacob	27	96	11–19–1847	50	Orchard Br

520   HISTORY OF JOHNSON COUNTY

County	Grantee	Book	Page	Date Survey	Acres	Watercourse
‡Johnson	Cassady, Philip	58	372	12– 8–1855	200	Coldwater Fk Rockcastle
‡Johnson	Cassady, Philip	53	178	6– 6–1857	40	Coldwater Cr
‡Johnson	Cassady, Philip	66	29	4– 8–1865	360	Messer Br
†Johnson	Cassady, Wm				100	
‡Johnson	Cassady, Wm	53	5	6– 6–1857	400	Hardins Br
‡Johnson	Cassady, Wm	67	128	4–12–1865	190	Hurricane Fk
†Johnson	Cassueby, Philip	3	344	2– 9–1865	200	
¶Floyd	Castle, Bazle	E-2	221	9–14–1834	50	Tom's Cr
¶Floyd	Castle, Benjamin	T	79	9–22–1824	50	Sycamore Fk Tom's Cr
¶Floyd	Castle, Benjamin	1–2	251	5–22–1836	200	Sycamore Fk
‡Johnson	Castle, Benjamin	32	257	5– 1–1848	100	Sycamore Fk Tom's Cr
‡Johnson	Castle, Benjamin	58	353	11–22–1855	100	Sycamore Fk
†Johnson	Castle, Charles	73	374	4–11–1868	4½	Tom's Cr
†Johnson	Castle, Drury P	2	257	4– 2–1855	100	
†Johnson	Castle, Drury P	5	215	6– 3–1872	18	
‡Johnson	Castle, Drury P	105	319	4– 4–1883	18	Sycamore Fk
‡Johnson	Castle, Durry P	105	543	4– 4–1883	20	Sycamore Fk
‡Johnson	Castle, Elizabeth	66	27	5–12–1865	24	Sycamore Fk Tom's Cr
‡Johnson	Castle, Epperson	66	74	6– 1–1865	5½	Sycamore Fk Tom's Cr
‡Johnson	Castle, Henderson	18	37	8–13–1845	100	Georges Cr
‡Johnson	Castle, Henderson	37	58	4–21–1851	1,000	Fk Georges Cr
‡Johnson	Castle, Henderson	2	371	3– 2–1857	200	
†Johnson	Castle, Henderson	2	371	3– 2–1857	200	
‡Johnson	Castle, Henderson	49	308	3–13–1857	200	None
†Johnson	Castle, Henderson	66	112	6– 7–1865	55	Bradford Fk Georges Cr
‡Johnson	Castle, Henderson	66	445	7– 6–1865	95	Lick Br Tom's Cr
†Johnson	Castle, Henderson S	64	169	5–18–1863	75	Lick Br Georges Cr
†Johnson	Castle, Henderson S	3	282	9– 6–1863	75	
†Johnson	Castle, Henderson S. & E	66	376	6–14–1865	77	Sycamore Fk Tom's Cr
†Johnson	Castle, Ira	2	336	8– 4–1856	45	
†Johnson	Castle, Ira	49	307	4– 3–1856	50	None
‡Johnson	Castle, Ira	66	379	6– 6–1865	12	R H Fk Sycamore Fk
‡Johnson	Castle, Ira	66	73	4–14–1865	100	R H Fk Sycamore Fk
‡Johnson	Castle, Ira	66	378	6– 6–1865	35	Wollpen Br
‡Johnson	Castle, Israel	5	99	4– 3–1871	50	
‡Johnson	Castle, Israel & Wm	42	321	1– 8–1854	40	Tom's Cr
†Johnson	Castle, Israel, Wm. & Oliver	2	248	3– 5–1855	25	
†Johnson	Castle, Jacob	3	—	—–1860	40	
‡Johnson	Castle, Jacob	58	570	1–20–1860	25	R H Fk Upper War Br
†Johnson	Castle, Jacob	3	109	2– 6–1860	40	
¶Floyd	Castle, James	W	348	4–11–1828	50	Br Tom's Cr
†Johnson	Castle, James & Curtle, Hezekiah	4	506	1–12–1875	25	
‡Johnson	Castle, Jeff & Hezekiah	96	355	4–12–1876	25	Upper Road Br
†Johnson	Castle, Lucy	4	396	10–15–1868	100	
‡Johnson	Castle, Marcum	60	82	1–30–1860	200	Tom's Cr
†Johnson	Castle, Marcum	3	133	6– 4–1860	200	
†Johnson	Castle, Marcum	3	361	5–19–1865	30	
‡Johnson	Castle, Marcum & Johial	66	375	5–12–1865	37	Sycamore Fk Tom's Cr
‡Johnson	Castle, Math	53	174	3–24–1855	125	(Tom's Cr?)
‡Johnson	Castle, Miles A	65	180	11–22–1855	200	Sycamore Fk
‡Johnson	Castle, Miles H	66	113	6– 1–1865	17	Sycamore Fk
‡Johnson	Castle, Miles H	66	114	6– 1–1865	40	Sycamore Fk
¶Floyd	Castle, Nathan	T	93	8–12–1824	50	Fk Tom's Cr
¶Floyd	Castle, Nathan	D-2	393	6–26–1834	50	Tom's Cr
¶Floyd	Castle, Nathan	1–2	272	5–25–1836	100	Tom's Cr
‡Johnson	Castle, Nathan	14	276	12–16–1843	100	Tom's Cr
‡Johnson	Castle, Nathan	18	38	8–30–1844	50	Tom's Cr
‡Johnson	Castle, Nathan	32	255	4– 8–1847	50	Tom's Cr
‡Johnson	Castle, Nathan	32	256	10–27–1847	50	Upper Rd Br Tom's Cr
‡Johnson	Castle, Nathan	43	165	3– 8–1848	50	Tom's Cr
‡Johnson	Castle, Wm	102	484	5–16–1882	115	Mud Lick Fk
‡Johnson	Castle, Willis	69	296	6– 1–1865	23	Sycamore Fk
‡Johnson	Castle, Willis	99	419	10– 8–1880	150	Sycamore Fk
‡Johnson	Castle, Zach	22	239	12– 2–1846	50	Cave Br
‡Johnson	Castle, Zachariah	66	377	5–12–1865	49	Sycamore Fk
‡Johnson	Castle, Zachariah	69	297	6– 6–1865	3	Sycamore Fk
‡Johnson	Castle & Brown	22	238	12– 2–1846	300	Georges Cr
†Johnson	Caudill, Abner	27	94	9– 3–1847	50	Isaiah Br
¶Floyd	Caudle, Abner	20	383	3–14–1842	100	Caudles Br
†Johnson	Caudill, Andrew J	2	383	5– 4–1857	100	
‡Johnson	Caudill, Isaac	53	181	2– 4–1858	25	Paint Cr
†Johnson	Caudill, Isaac	2	441	3– 1–1858	25	
†Johnson	Caudill, James	7	107	11–16–1885	30	
‡Johnson	Caudill, John	43	155	4–19–1851	60	Hood Fk

APPENDIX 521

County	Grantee	Book	Page	Date Survey	Acres	Watercourse
†Johnson	Caudill, Martha	2	173	3– 6–1854	200	
‡Johnson	Caudill, Mathew	27	87	9– 3–1847	100	Bailey Fk
‡Johnson	Caudill, Mathew	44	244	2–14–1854	200	Barnett Cr
†Floyd	Caudill, Mathew	2	199	10–29–1816		
‡Johnson	Caudill, Mathew & Jackson	43	538	4–10–1849	100	Barnetts Cr
‡Johnson	Caudill, Reuben	53	555	4–11–1851	250	Lick Fk Barnetts Cr
‡Johnson	Caudill, Thomas	53	158	3–21–1851	100	Isaiah
¶Floyd	Caudill, Wm	T	201	9–18–1824	50	Barnetts Cr
‡Johnson	Caudill, Wm	53	10	2–18–1845	235	Little Paint Cr
‡Johnson	Caudill, Wm	27	95	9– 4–1847	100	Barnetts Cr
‡Johnson	Caudill, Wm	47	115	2–11–1854	200	R H Fk Barnetts Cr
‡Johnson	Caudill, Wm	58	385	5– 6–1858	15	Pickle Fk
‡Johnson	Caudill, Wm. I	53	180	2– 5–1858	100	Bailey Br
†Johnson	Caudill, Wm. J	2	388	6– 1–1857	100	
‡Johnson	Caudill, Wm. J	2	440	3– 1–1858	50	
†Johnson	Caudill, Wm. J	2	444	4– 1–1858	100	Orchard Br
‡Johnson	Caudill, Wm. J	68	373	3– 8–1866	484	Orchard Br
‡Johnson	Cecil, K. B	35	496	2– 4–1851	100	Rockcastle Cr
⊕Fayette	Cellers, James	4	427	12–27–1783	5,000	Sandy R
*Res. Windsore	Chaffer, H. Jr. & Jno. G	265	1–20–1797		40,000	Br Big Sandy R
‡Johnson	Chamber, Abram	49	302	11– 7–1855	3	Blain Cr
‡Johnson	Chandler, Abraham & Isaac	38	327	2–18–1852	125	Br Tom's Cr
‡Johnson	Chandler, Abram	25	331	12– 5–1846	50	Meadow Br
‡Johnson	Chandler, Henry	14	275	12–15–1843	150	Meadows Br
‡Johnson	Chandler, Henry	25	329	12– 5–1846	50	Burnt Cabin Br
‡Johnson	Chandler, Henry	32	259	7– 5–1848	225	Rock House Fk
†Johnson	Chandler, Henry	2	318	3– 3–1856	6	
†Johnson	Chandler, Henry	3	209	6– 3–1861	100	
‡Johnson	Chandler, Henry	62	210	6–14–1861	235	Meadow Br
‡Johnson	Chandler, Henry	62	211	6–22–1861	4½	Meadow Br
†Johnson	Chandler, Henry	5	296	6– 7–1873	50	
‡Johnson	Chandler, Isaac	38	329	4–12–1851	220	Brushy Fk
‡Johnson	Chandler, Isaac	38	328	4–17–1851	16	Hoods Br
‡Johnson	Chandler, Isaac	53	8	11– 7–1855	10	Hoods Cr
‡Johnson	Chandler, Isaac	62	218	4–23–1856	14	——— Br
†Johnson	Chandler, Isaac	2	444	4– 1–1858	10	
‡Johnson	Chandler, Isaac	62	216	6–21–1861	22	Rock House Fk
‡Johnson	Chandler, Isaac	66	447	6–21–1861	225	Bushy Fk
‡Johnson	Chandler, Isaac	97	480	9–27–1877	170	Road Br
†Johnson	Chandler, Isaac	99	209	6– 7–1880	165	Rock House Fk
†Johnson	Chandler, Isaac & Thomas	3	212	6–24–1861	200	
‡Johnson	Chandler, James	76	208	12– 4–1869	20	Greens Br
‡Johnson	Chandler, James L	20	460	10– 1–1846	50	Hoods Fk
‡Johnson	Chandler, Martin	93	44	1– 9–1873	40	Wiley Br
‡Johnson	Chandler, Thomas	25	328	12– 5–1846	50	Road Br
‡Johnson	Chandler, Thomas	62	215	6–27–1861	117	Meadow Br
‡Johnson	Chandler, Thomas	62	217	6–27–1861	100	Meadow Br
‡Johnson	Chandler, William	38	327	2–18–1852	125	Br Tom's Cr
⊕Fayette	Christian, Israel	3	188	2–25–1784	1,000	Sandy R
‡Johnson	Clarke, Alexander	4	71	10–29–1838	50	Prater Cr
⊕Fayette	Clark, James	2	359	8–25–1783	2,000	Sandy Cr
▲Mason	Clark, James	11	107	11– 8–1797	2,000	Big Sandy R
‡Floyd	Clarke, John H	6	179	1–11–1839	50	L H Fk Prater Cr
†Johnson	Clark, L. D	5	562	3– 4– 76	165	
†Johnson	Clark, L. D	5	562	3– 4– 76	175	
†Johnson	Clark, L. D	5	582	7–21– 77	84	
‡Floyd	Clark, Lorenzo D	4	242	7–28–1838	2,050	Little Mud Cr
†Johnson	Clark, Marie	3	—	——1860	25	
†Johnson	Clark, Marion & John, Baldridge	3	118	2–11–1860	25	
‡Johnson	Clark, Morgan	44	491	2– 8–1853	200	Greasy Cr
‡Johnson	Clark, Morgan	44	492	2– 8–1853	200	Greasy Cr
‡Johnson	Clark, Morgan	49	303	1– 2–1854	50	None
†Johnson	Clark, Morgan	2	229	12–16–1854	200	
†Johnson	Clark, Morgan	2	229	12–16–1854	200	
†Johnson	Clark, Morgan	2	229	12–16–1854	200	
†Johnson	Clark, Morgan	2	229	12–16–1854	100	
‡Johnson	Clark, Morgan	43	444	12–27–1854	200	bet M & L H Fk Greasy
‡Johnson	Clark, Morgan	43	441	12–28–1854	35	Wolf Pen Br
‡Johnson	Clark, Morgan	43	443	12–28–1854	480	bet M & L H Fk Greasy
‡Johnson	Clark, Morgan	43	440	12–27–1854	200	M & L H Fk Greasy Cr
†Johnson	Clark, Morgan	2	234	1– 1–1855	200	
†Johnson	Clark, Morgan	2	234	1– 1–1855	33	
‡Johnson	Clark, Morgan	46	225	1–14–1855	200	Wolf Pen Cr
†Johnson	Clark, Morgan	2	236	1–1"–1855	200	
‡Johnson	Clark, Morgan	43	429	12–28–1855	350	R H Fk M Fk Greasy
‡Johnson	Clark, Peter	44	254	9–27–1852	50	Black Log Br

County	Grantee	Book	Page	Date Survey	Acres	Watercourse
¶Floyd	Clark, Samuel	1–2	98	12–24–1835	100	Johns Cr
⊙Fayette	Clinkenberg, Wm	3	68	12– 1–1783	500	Sandy
†Johnson	Coalman, Peter	2	220	9– 5–1854	50	
⊙Fayette	Cogran, Robert	4	14	8–14–1784	1,000	Sandy Cr
‡Johnson	Coldiron, James H	58	391	2– 6–1858	60	Painters Lick
‡Johnson	Cole, W. D	99	159	10–30–1876	240	Alum Dirt Br
‡Johnson	Coleman	69	298	6–13–1866	68	Br Lick Br Jennies Cr
‡Johnson	Collier, John	2	144	12– 5–1853	150	
‡Johnson	Collins, Christopher	35	495	1–15–1851	100	Double Lick Br
‡Johnson	Collins, Christopher	46	38	2–22–1854	250	None
†Johnson	Collins, Christopher	2	242	2– 6–1855	100	
†Johnson	Collins, Elijah	2	400	8– 3–1857	50	
‡Johnson	Collins, Elijah	53	160	10– 1–1857	280	Paint Cr
†Johnson	Collins, Elijah	2	408	10– 5–1857	80	
‡Johnson	Collins, James M	122	24	3–12–1904	7	Oak Log Fk
¶Floyd	Collins, Joshua	L–2	373	11–17–1831	50	Jennys Cr
‡Johnson	Collins, William	58	70	9– 1–1857	35	Barnetts Cr
‡Johnson	Collins, W. N	118	71	12–29–1894	40	Double Lick Fk
‡Johnson	Collinsworth, Reuben	22	118	11– 9–1846	100	Coldwater Fk
‡Johnson	Collinsworth, Reuben	46	213	5– 8–1855	100	Orchard Br
‡Johnson	Collinsworth, Thos	44	245	2–27–1854	100	None
‡Johnson	Colvin, Johise	84	250	11– 9–1871	200	Big Fk Pigeon Fk
‡Johnson	Colvin, Johise	84	251	11– 9–1871	50	Barn Br
¶Floyd	Colvin, John	T	37	2–14–1825	50	Paint Lick Cr
¶Floyd	Colvin, John	A–2	129	6–13–1829	50	Paint Lick Cr
⊙Fayette	Colwell, James	3	121	12–29–1783	2,000	S Fk Sandy
†Floyd	Combs, Jeremiah	2	119	11–22–1815	150	
‡Johnson	Conley, C	35	497	10–22–1850	32½	Jennys Cr
¶Floyd	Conley, Constantine	D–2	384	9–26–1834	100	Main Jennings Cr
‡Johnson	Conley, Constantine	18	35	3– 1–1845	50	Jennys Cr
‡Johnson	Conley, Constantine	32	296	9–18–1848	50	Jenkins Fk Jennys Cr
†Johnson	Conley, Constantine	2	303	12– 3–1855	200	
†Johnson	Conley, Constantine Jr. & Elijah B. Arms	5	200	3– 4–1872	100	
¶Floyd	Conley, David	P	177	1– 4–1823	50	Barnetts Cr
¶Morgan	Conley, David	F–2	457	12–13–1830	50	Open Fk
‡Floyd	Conley, David	14	235	11– 3–1843	100	Salt Lick Br
¶Floyd	Conley, Edmond	R	25	9–18–1824	50	Fk Paint Cr
¶Floyd	Conley, Edmond	L–2	367	2– 5–1834	50	Oil Springs Fk
‡Johnson	Conley, Edmond	98	10	1–18–1878	28½	Barnetts Cr
‡Johnson	Conley, Freeman	61	421	9–28–1859	29	Lick Br
¶Floyd	Conley, Henry	G	408	5– 1–1820	50	Fk Paint Lick Cr
¶Floyd	Conley, Henry	L–2	377	1– 8–1834	50	Holly Br
¶Floyd	Conley, Henry	L–2	371	2– 5–1834	50	Barnetts Cr
‡Floyd	Conley, Henry	10	56	2– 5–1842	100	Jennys Cr
‡Floyd	Conley, Henry	11	10	3– 8–1843	100	None
‡Johnson	Conley, Henry	49	304	5–12–1854	200	Jenes Cr
‡Johnson	Conley, Henry	49	305	5–12–1854	50	Jennys Cr
‡Johnson	Conley, Henry	49	306	5–12–1854	200	Jennys Cr
†Johnson	Conley, Henry	2	223	12– 4–1854	200	
¶Floyd	Conley, Henry Jr	T	20	11–25–1825	100	Paint Lick Cr
¶Floyd	Conley, Henry Sr	D–2	384	2– 6–1834	100	Oil Springs Fk
†Johnson	Conley, H. E	5	367	3– 2–1874	47	
†Johnson	Conley, Hiram E	2	411	11– 2–1857	50	
‡Johnson	Conley, Hiram E	65	185	7– 5–1858	50	Jennys Cr
‡Johnson	Conley, Hiram E. & James H	96	480	2–18–1874	56	Little Lick Fk
‡Johnson	Conley, Isaiah	32	258	4–13–1849	150	Road Fk
‡Johnson	Conley, Isaiah	54	207	8–31–1858	160	Barnetts Cr
¶Floyd	Conley, John	H	528	2–25–1821	50	Jennys Cr
¶Morgan	Conley, John	B–2	451	5–25–1833	50	Open Fk
‡Floyd	Conley, John	10	54	1–31–1842	100	Lick Fk Jennys Cr
‡Floyd	Conley, John	11	45	3– 7–1843	100	None
†Johnson	Conley, John	2	184	6– 5–1854	100	
‡Johnson	Conley, John	68	209	9–22–1854	100	Little Lick Fk Jennys Cr
‡Johnson	Conley, John	73	373	2–21–1868	88	Lick Fk
‡Johnson	Conley, John	96	481	2–18–1874	6	Orchard Br Little Lick Fk
‡Johnson	Conley, John	113	37	9–28–1889	13	Pigeon Cr
‡Johnson	Conley, Jno. & Isaac	84	248	11–11–1871	500	Pigeon Fk
†Johnson	Conley, N. E. & J. W.	5	312	9–24–1873	25	
¶Floyd	Conley, Thomas	10	55	9– 2–1842	100	Abbot Cr
†Johnson	Conley, Thomas	5	139	9–27–1871	200	
†Johnson	Conley, Thomas	5	139	9–27–1871	200	
†Johnson	Conley, Thomas	5	139	9–27–1871	200	
†Johnson	Conley, Thomas B	2	198	9– 5–1854	25	
†Johnson	Conley, Thomas B	2	302	12– 3–1855	50	
‡Johnson	Conley, Thomas B	58	375	11–31–1856	433	Laurel Fk
¶Floyd	Conley, Thomas Sr	W	261	11–30–1824	50	Br Jennys Cr
¶Morgan	Conley, William	E–2	43	4– 3–1833	50	Fk Paint Cr

APPENDIX 523

County	Grantee	Book	Page	Date Survey	Acres	Watercourse
¶Floyd	Connelly, David	T	38	10–22–1824	100	Fk Paint Lick Cr
¶Floyd	Connelly, Henry	R	22	3–23–1823	50	Fk Paint Lick Cr
¶Floyd	Connelly, Henry	T	56	4–15–1825	50	Fk Paint Lick Cr
¶Floyd	Connelly, Henry	W	363	1–12–1827	100	M Fk Paint Lick Cr
¶Floyd	Connelly, Henry Sr	W	262	12– 1–1824	50	Fk Paint Lick Cr
¶Floyd	Connelly, John	T	46	9–18–1824	50	Fk Paint Cr
¶Floyd	Connelly, Thomas Jr	W	361	5–16–1827	50	Br Jennys Cr
‡Johnson	Cooper, Catherine	68	386	2–13–1866	200	Harges Cr
⊘Fayette	Copage, Isaac	4	259	1–16–1786	500	Sandy
†Johnson	Copley, Benjamin	2	414	4– 1–1858	200	
‡Johnson	Cornett, Lilburn	3	340	2– 1–1865	100	
‡Johnson	Cornett, Wilbourn	87	482	2– 8–1868	500	Lynn Bark Fk
‡Johnson	Cornett, William	66	30	4– 7–1865	143	Fk Cold Water
#Bourbon	Couch, Samuel	15	362	10–27–1788	11,000	Big Sandy
⊘Fayette	Coughman, Benedict	3	67	12– 1–1783	1,200	Sandy
†Johnson	Grace, Campbell C	3	125	4– 2–1860	50	
‡Johnson	Grace, Campbell C	60	202	4– 3–1860	88	Fk Mine Fk
†Johnson	Grace, Campbell C	3	139	7– 2–1860	38	
‡Johnson	Grace, Peter	68	374	3– 7–1866	26	Barnetts Cr
‡Johnson	Crafts & Sparks	20	458	10– 1–1846	50	Hoods Fk
‡Johnson	Craft, Tilman	32	254	7– 5–1848	50	Hood Fk
⊘Fayette	Craig, Alexander	4	259	1–16–1786	1,300	Br S Fk Sandy
⊘Fayette	Craig, John	4	155	4–20–1785	20,000	Sandy (6,873 acres withdrawn)
#Bourbon	Craig, John	12	353	4–18–1787	4,000	Big Sandy R
#Bourbon	Craig, John	13	348	4–18–1787	5,940	Big Sandy R
#Bourbon	Craig, John	12	351	4–19–1787	20,000	Big Sandy R
#Bourbon	Craig, John	12	351	4–22–1787	5,000	Big Sandy R
#Bourbon	Craig, John	12	350	4–23–1787	5,000	Big Sandy R
#Bourbon	Craig, John	15	211	4–24–1787	20,000	Big Sandy
#Bourbon	Craig, John H	14	384	8–13–1787	9,750	Little & Big Sandy
⊘Fayette	Craig, Lewis	1	126	12–13–1782	500	Sandy R
▲Mason	Craig, Lewis	10	95	11–18–1797	485	Big Sandy R
▲Mason	Craig Lewis	10	94	11–20–1797	500	Big Sandy R
‡Johnson	Crain, William	49	309	2–12–1857	70	None
¶Floyd	Crank, Nathaniel	L-2	395	9–27–1837	50	Little Paint & Sandy R
‡Floyd	Crider, John	8	361	6–11–1841	200	Johns Cr
#Bourbon	Criglor, Christopher	7	136	4–26–1787	18,520	Big Sandy R
‡Johnson	Crislop, H. R	7	412	2———1890	20	
‡Floyd	Crisp, William Jr	42	243	12– 1–1843	200	Harves Br
‡Floyd	Criss, David	11	17	8–25–1843	100	Bollen Br
‡Johnson	Crum, Adam	58	71	8–20–1858	25	None
†Johnson	Crum, Eli	3	337	1– 2–1865	200	
†Johnson	Crum, Eli	3	337	1– 2–1865	200	
‡Johnson	Crum, Eli	65	353	2–25–1865	827	Rockcastle Fk
‡Johnson	Crum, Eli	65	354	2–27–1865	436	Rockcastle Fk
‡Johnson	Crum, Pleasant	2	332	7– 7–1856	130	
†Johnson	Crum, Pleasant	2	433	2– 1–1858	100	
‡Johnson	Crum, Pleasant	58	383	6– 1–1858	50	Lick Br Rockcastle
†Johnson	Crum, Pleasant	3	635	———1858	50	
‡Johnson	Crum, Pleasant	53	179	——26–1858	100	Black Log Cr
‡Johnson	Crum, Reuben	18	36	10– 4–1845	50	Peters Cave Cr
‡Johnson	Crum, Reuben	44	258	8–25–1852	200	Rockcastle Cr
‡Johnson	Crum, Reuben	44	260	8–25–1852	150	Peters Cave Br
‡Johnson	Crum, Reuben	49	310	12–13–1856	200	Peters Cave Br
‡Johnson	Crum, Reuben	49	311	12–13–1856	200	Peters Cave Br
‡Johnson	Crum, Reuben	63	228	6– 1–1858	275	M Fk Rockcastle Cr
‡Johnson	Crum, Reuben	68	208	1–26–1858	165	Rockcastle Cr
⊘Fayette	Crutcher, Henry	4	275	2–18–1786	4,000	S Fk Sandy
†Johnson	Cully, Delora & James Williams	3	332	1– 2–1865	200	
*Res. Shelby	Curd, Edmond	E	6	9–30–1799	321	Sandy Cr
†Johnson	Curm, Ruben	2	332	7– 7–1856	200	
†Johnson	Curm, Ruben	2	332	7– 7–1856	200	
¶Floyd	Curtis, James	G-2	77	10–17–1835	200	Main Mud Lick Fk
¶Floyd	Curtis, James	G-2	123	11–17–1835	100	Main Fk Mud Lick
‡Johnson	Dale, Reuben	37	49	4–14–1849	100	Calvin Fk Cr
▲Floyd	Dameron, Richard	19	288	12–24–1818	96	Louisa Fk
¶Floyd	Daniel, Andrew	1-2	260	6–16–1836	50	Bazell Castle Road
‡Johnson	Daniel, Andrew	14	282	8–20–1844	50	Tom's Cr
‡Johnson	Daniel, Andrew	32	249	4–10–1847	50	Tom's Cr
#Fayette	Daniel, Darby	10	389	5– 5–1785	21,000	Br Sandy R
‡Johnson	Daniel, David	32	243	5– 3–1848	290	Borders Br
†Johnson	Daniel, Edward	7	25	1– 5–1785	20	
¶Floyd	Daniel, George	C	190	6–30–1817	50	Tom's Cr & Sandy R
¶Floyd	Daniel, George	T119	120	8–12–1824	100	Tom's Cr
‡Johnson	Daniel, George	32	247	4– 9–1847	50	Tony Cr (Tom's Cr?)
‡Johnson	Daniel, George	37	46	2–28–1850	50	Wild Cat Br
‡Johnson	Daniel, George	37	47	2–28–1850	150	Rockcastle Cr
‡Johnson	Daniel, George	65	179	10–10–1857	200	Staffords Fk
‡Johnson	Daniel, George	65	178	10–12–1857	200	Wild Cat Br

HISTORY OF JOHNSON COUNTY

County	Grantee	Book	Page	Date Survey	Acres	Watercourse
†Johnson	Daniel, George	3	195	4– 1–1861	60	
‡Johnson	Daniel, Geo. & Jas.	70	466	10–10–1852	50	Road Br Tom's Cr
‡Johnson	Daniel, George M	66	115	2–22–1865	112	Stafford Fk
†Johnson	Daniel, George W	3	346	2– 1–1865	200	
†Johnson	Daniel, George W	3	346	2– 1–1865	100	
‡Johnson	Daniel, George W	67	301	7–18–1865	70	Upper Road Br
‡Johnson	Daniel, George W	66	116	8–13–1865	200	Wooten Fk
¶Floyd	Daniel, Isham	M	108	8–30–1820	50	Big Sandy R
¶Floyd	Daniel, Isham	P-2	220	7– 7–1836	350	Sandy R
¶Johnson	Daniel, Isham	Q-2	298	12–23–1843	100	Hoods Fk
‡Johnson	Daniel, Isham	14	280	12– 4–1844	200	Borders Br
‡Johnson	Daniel, Isham	32	244	7– 6–1848	75	Still House Br
‡Johnson	Daniel, Isham	49	312	11–27–1855	20	Hoods Fk Cr
†Johnson	Daniel, Isham	2	303	12– 3–1855	20	
‡Johnson	Daniel, Isham Jr	22	195	4–12–1844	50	Hoods Fk
‡Johnson	Daniel, Isom	66	448	8–22–1865	46	Still House Br
†Johnson	Daniel, Isom	3	398	9——1865	46	
¶Floyd	Daniel, James	D-2	408	10– 4–1834	50	None
¶Lawrence	Daniel, James	H-2	266	2–27–1835	100	Lower Laurel Fk
‡Johnson	Daniel, James	22	319	4–12–1844	100	Hoods Fk
‡Johnson	Daniel, James	32	246	4– 8–1847	50	Road Br Tom's Cr
‡Johnson	Daniel, James	55	296	10– 9–1858	9	Hoods Fk
‡Johnson	Daniel, James B	93	43	3–29–1872	26	Br Tom's Cr
‡Johnson	Daniel, Jasper	99	419	10– 8–1880	150	Sycamore Fk
‡Johnson	Daniel, Jasper	66	74	6– 1–1865	5½	Sycamore Fk
‡Johnson	Daniel, John E	46	212	8–28–1855	40	Beech Cr
‡Johnson	Daniel, John O	47	114	8–29–1855	35	R H Fk Rich Br
‡Johnson	Daniel, Joseph	121	218	4– 4–1904	28	Sycamore Fk
‡Johnson	Daniels, Joseph	121	219	4– 4–1904	2	Sycamore Fk
†Johnson	Daniels, Peter	3	—	——1860	10	
†Johnson	Daniel, Peter	3	109	2– 6–1860	10	
†Johnson	Daniel, Peter	3	123	2–11–1860	190	
‡Johnson	Daniel, Peter	59	257	3–23–1860	275	Lick Cr
†Johnson	Daniel, Peter	3	124	4– 2–1860	70	
†Johnson	Daniel, Peter & Wyatt A	3	124	4– 2–1860	125	
†Johnson	Daniel, Peter & Wyatt A	3	124	4– 2–1860	125	
‡Johnson	Daniel, Peter & Writ A	59	255	3–29–1859	290	Borders
‡Johnson	Daniel, Peter & W. A.	71	7	5– 5–1866	1,000	Sandy R
‡Johnson	Daniel, Polly	32	248	5– 2–1848	200	Wiley Br
¶Floyd	Daniel, Thomas	H	153	3– 9–1821	50	Greasy Cr
¶Floyd	Daniel, Thomas	D-2	407	6–26–1834	100	Tom's Cr
‡Johnson	Daniel, Thomas	35	84	7–18–1851	100	Sandy R
‡Johnson	Davis, B. L.	97	149	10– 7–1873	80	Buffalo Cr
†Johnson	Davis, B. L.	5	510	2– 8–1876	40	
‡Johnson	Davis, B. S.	97	148	10– 6–1876	35	Sandy R
¶Floyd	Davis, Elias	T	111	10–21–1824	50	Colvins Br
‡Johnson	Davis, Henry	59	228	10– 4–1859	102	Barnetts Br
†Johnson	Davis, Henry	3	—	——1860	32	
†Johnson	Davis, Henry	3	110	2– 6–1860	32	
‡Johnson	Davis, Henry J	43	548	4– 9–1851	50	Dog Fk Barnetts Cr
‡Johnson	Davis, Hezekiah	43	562	5– 7–1852	40	Fk Blain Cr
‡Johnson	Davis, Hezekiah	42	322	7– 9–1853	100	Conley Br
†Johnson	Davis, Hezekiah	2	145	12– 5–1853	100	
¶Floyd	Davis, James	T	68	9–21–1824	50	Tom's Cr
¶Floyd	Davis, James	A-2	256	8– 5–1831	75	Jennys Cr
¶Floyd	Davis, James	E-2	112	4–30–1833	100	Bee Fk Abbotts Cr
†Johnson	Davis, James	5	508	2– 7–1876	50	
‡Johnson	Davis, John	33	576	——	200	None
¶Floyd	Davis, John	A-2	297	3– 8–1825	50	Abbotts Cr
¶Lawrence	Davis, John	H-2	176	8–25–1834	50	Georges Cr
‡Johnson	Davis, John	14	281	12– 6–1844	550	Chestnut Cr
‡Johnson	Davis, John	14	303	12– 6–1844	400	Chestnut Shoal Cr
‡Johnson	Davis, John	16	92	5– 2–1845	600	Big Sandy R
‡Johnson	Davis, John	32	250	3– 8–1848	50	Road Br
†Johnson	Davis, John	2	194	8– 7–1854	100	
†Johnson	Davis, John	2	391	6– 1–1857	200	
†Johnson	Davis, John	2	391	6– 1–1857	200	
†Johnson	Davis, John	2	391	6– 1–1857	200	
†Johnson	Davis, John	2	391	6– 1–1857	200	
‡Johnson	Davis, John	61	423	1– 8–1861	37	Chestnut Cr
‡Johnson	Davis, John	61	424	1– 8–1861	63	Gnats Cr
†Johnson	Davis, John	3	389	8– 8–1865	100	
‡Johnson	Davis, John	66	380	8– 9–1865	100	Chestnut Cr
‡Johnson	Davis, Richard	98	159	8– 7–1873	50	Still House Br
¶Floyd	Davis, Thomas	8	355	12– 3–1840	50	Buffalo Cr
‡Floyd	Davis, Thomas	8	373	12– 3–1840	50	Buffalo Cr
‡Floyd	Davis, Thomas	11	44	3–15–1843	300	Thorns Cr

APPENDIX 525

County	Grantee	Book	Page	Date Survey	Acres	Watercourse
‡Johnson	Davis, Thomas	32	245	4-10-1847	150	Old Road Br
‡Johnson	Davis, Thurza B	110	359	3-15-1888	42	Rockhouse Cr
§Floyd	Davis, William	133	——	6-17-1805	400	Levisa Fk
¶Lawrence	Davis, William	U	106	12-28-1824	100	Georges Cr
‡Johnson	Davis, William	37	48	12-28-1848	50	Sandy R
†Johnson	Davis, William	3	365	——1858	150	
‡Johnson	Davis, William	76	209	12-24-1869	24	Rockhouse Fk
‡Floyd	Dawson, William	8	356	5-20-1840	50	Orchard Br
†Floyd	Day, Francis	2	210	12-23-1816		
†Johnson	Dean, Joshua P	2	148	1-2-1854	20	
†Johnson	Dean, Joshua P	2	148	1-2-1854	25	
†Johnson	Dean, Joshua P	2	431	2-1-1858	25	
‡Johnson	Delong, David	3	343	2-9-1865	110	
‡Johnson	Delong, George	18	40	10-3-1845	150	Rockcastle Cr
†Johnson	Delong, George	2	242	2-6-1855	200	
†Johnson	Delong, George	2	242	2-6-1855	100	
‡Johnson	Delong, George	66	449	4-4-1855	38	M Fk Rockcastle
†Johnson	Delong, George	2	303	12-3-1855	100	
†Johnson	Delong, George	2	305	12-3-1855	100	
‡Johnson	Delong, George	58	348	12-15-1856	150	Rockcastle Cr
†Johnson	Delong, George	2	385	5-4-1857	75	
†Johnson	Delong, George	3	3	——1858	200	
‡Johnson	Delong, George	58	354	7-10-1858	1,150	M Fk Rockcastle Cr
†Johnson	Delong, George	3	174	12-3-1860	200	
†Johnson	Delong, George	3	174	12-3-1860	100	
†Johnson	Delong, George	3	174	12-3-1860	200	
‡Johnson	Delong, George	65	143	3-11-1861	1,000	Laurel Fk
†Johnson	Delong, George	3	207	6-3-1861	200	
‡Johnson	Delong, George	66	452	4-7-1865	330	Lynn Bark Fk
†Johnson	Delong, George	——	——	——	200	
†Johnson	Delong, George W	3	343	2-9-1865	200	
‡Johnson	Delong, George W	66	450	4-5-1865	170	Fk Rockcastle
†Johnson	Delong, Harry	2	450	5-3-1858	200	
†Johnson	Delong, Harry	2	450	5-3-1858	150	
‡Johnson	Delong, Harvey	58	362	8-24-1852	100	M Fk Rockcastle
‡Johnson	Delong, Harvey	58	351	8-12-1857	100	Rockcastle R
†Johnson	Delong, Harvey	3	344	2-22-1865	200	
‡Johnson	Delong, Harvey	66	24	4-4-1865	216	M Fk Rockcastle Cr
‡Johnson	Delong, Hiram J	66	451	4-5-1865	60	Lick Br
‡Johnson	Delong, James	27	99	1-8-1846	100	Scofield Lick Fk
†Johnson	Delong, James	2	95	3-3-1853	200	
†Johnson	Delong, James	2	156	2-6-1854	100	
‡Johnson	Delong, James	61	113	2-25-1854	500	M Fk Rockcastle
†Johnson	Delong, James	2	226	12-5-1854	200	
†Johnson	Delong, James	2	441	3-1-1858	100	
†Johnson	Delong, James	2	441	3-1-1858	200	
†Johnson	Delong, James	2	441	3-1-1858	100	
‡Johnson	Delong, James	61	112	3-8-1858	100	Georges Cr
‡Johnson	Delong, James	58	394	3-26-1858	700	Laurel
†Johnson	Delong, James	3	175	12-3-1860	200	
†Johnson	Delong, James	3	175	12-3-1860	200	
†Johnson	Delong, James	3	175	12-3-1860	200	
‡Johnson	Delong, James	66	453	4-28-1865	500	M Fk Rockcastle
‡Johnson	Delong, James	66	454	4-28-1865	112	Scaffold Lick Fk
‡Johnson	Delong, James	117	12	4-4-1892	30	Johns Cr
‡Johnson	Delong, John	3	343	2-9-1865	200	
‡Johnson	Delong, Joseph	14	277	11-26-1844	100	Rockcastle Cr
‡Johnson	Delong, Joseph	14	278	11-26-1844	50	Laurel Fk
‡Johnson	Delong, Nancy	58	352	6-2-1858	175	M Fk Rockcastle
‡Johnson	Delong, Nancy	66	25	4-29-1865	254	M Fk Rockcastle Cr
‡Johnson	Delong, Samuel	65	358	2-14-1857	300	S Big Br
‡Johnson	Delong, Samuel	58	346	3-27-1858	50	Rockcastle Cr
‡Johnson	Delong, Samuel	3	343	2-9-1865	200	
‡Johnson	Delong, Samuel	66	23	4-29-1865	130	M Fk Rockcastle Cr
†Johnson	Delong, Wm	3	341	2-9-1865	200	
‡Johnson	Delong, Wm	65	326	2-27-1865	300	Porter Camp
¶Floyd	Dier, Francis	1	412	4-18-1821	50	Fk Big Paint Cr
‡Johnson	Diles, Alexander	55	288	11-2-1858	12½	R H Fk Lower Laurel
†Johnson	Diles, Alexander	3	106	1-2-1860	50	
†Johnson	Diles, Alexander	——	——	——1860	50	
†Johnson	Dills, Alexander	2	427	1-1-1858	20	
‡Johnson	Dills, Alexander	58	569	1-16-1860	50	Puncheon Camp
‡Johnson	Dills, James Jr	112	279	10-22-1906	5¾	Muddy Br
‡Johnson	Dills, James M	125	302	8-12-1920	2	Keaton Fk
‡Johnson	Dixon, Isaac B	43	173	10-11-1850	57	Tom's Cr
¶Floyd	Dixon, William	N-2	222	8-30-1838	200	L Fk Tom's Cr
‡Johnson	Dixon, William	14	279	12-14-1843	50	Tom's Cr
‡Johnson	Dixon, William	29	254	8-12-1847	250	Tom's Cr
†Johnson	Dixon, William	2	230	12-16-1854	50	
‡Johnson	Dixon, William H	47	116	3-24-1855	140	Br Tom's Cr

HISTORY OF JOHNSON COUNTY

County	Grantee	Book	Page	Date Survey	Acres	Watercourse
‡Johnson	Dollarhide, Winfield	96	61	9-17-1875	50	Bobs Br
°Fayette	Donnell, John	4	281	3-23-1786	2,644	S Fk Sandy
#Fayette	Donnell, John	12	15	4-16-1786	2,644	S Fk Sandy
#Fayette	Donnell, John	10	572	4-19-1786	2,160	S Fk Sandy
¶Floyd	Dorton, Edward	D	298	6-13-1817	50	Tom's Cr
¶Floyd	Dorton, Edward	1-2	258	6- 2-1836	100	Tom's Cr
‡Johnson	Dorton, Elizabeth & Joel	32	236	3- 7-1846	50	Tom's Cr
‡Johnson	Dorton, Joel	35	500	7-26-1849	100	Pigeon Roost Br
*Res. Franklin	Drake, Samuel Sr	S	519	5-24-1819	90,793½	Ky Red & Sandy R
‡Johnson	Duncan, John M	125	383	11- 1-1921	12	Daniels Cr
‡Johnson	Dutton, James	25	330	2-23-1847	325	Greasy Cr
‡Johnson	Ealy, William	90	82	11-14-1871	20	Asa Fk Barnetts Cr
#Bourbon	Early, Joel	7	136	4-26-1787	18,520	Big Sandy R
¶Floyd	Ephram, Elliot	H	162	1-17-1821	50	None
†Johnson	Estep, Joseph	3	332	1- 2-1865	100	
‡Johnson	Estep, Joseph	65	325	12-21-1865	305	Peters Cave Br
‡Johnson	Estep, William H	119	508	5-12-1902	31	Mud Lick Cr
¶Floyd	Evans, David	M	115	4-22-1822	100	Fk Big Blain Cr
¶Floyd	Evans, David	T	114	9-23-1824	50	Tom's Cr
¶Floyd	Evans, Harrison	1-2	327	7-23-1836	100	Wiley Br
‡Johnson	Evans, James H	125	382	11- 5-1921	2	Upper Laurel Fk
§Floyd	Evans, John	(Cert. 145)		8-17— 05	200	
§Floyd	Evans, John	(Cert. 146)		9-10— 05	300	Jennys Cr
‡Johnson	Evans, Thomas	68	375	2-28-1866	22	Sugar Tree Br
‡Johnson	Evans, Warrington B	56	466	5- 5-1859	6	Spring Br Blain Cr
‡Johnson	Evans, William	105	459	5- 2-1873	11	Coppers Hollow
‡Johnson	Evans, William	105	458	5- 5-1873	27	Line Br Jennys Cr
‡Johnson	Evans, William	5	281	5- 5-1873	66	
‡Johnson	Evans, William	98	235	8- 2-1873	21	Flat Hollow Lower Twinn
‡Johnson	Fairchild, Aaron	20	461	8- 8-1846	50	Little Pincheon Camp Br
‡Johnson	Fairchild, Aaron	32	200	8- 1-1848	50	Br Mud Lick Cr
‡Johnson	Fairchild, Aaron	32	201	8- 1-1848	50	Br Hoods Fk
‡Johnson	Fairchild, Aaron	53	182	10-30-1857	28	Mud Lick Cr
‡Johnson	Fairchild, Aaron	53	183	10-30-1857	10	Mud Lick Cr
‡Johnson	Fairchild, Aaron	2	440	3- 1-1858	11	
†Johnson	Fairchild, Aaron	2	440	3- 1-1858	15	
‡Johnson	Fairchild, Aaron	—	—	—1859	20	
‡Johnson	Fairchild, Aaron	57	484	7-28-1859	20	Big Paint Cr
‡Johnson	Fairchild, Asa I	42	323	4- 1-1854	125	Jennys Cr
¶Floyd	Fairchild, Asa J	M	77	2- 8-1822	50	Jennys Cr
¶Floyd	Fairchild, Asa J	8	353	8-31-1841	100	Jennies Cr
‡Johnson	Fairchild, Asa L	37	73	4-14-1849	50	Maple Tree Br
‡Johnson	Fairchild, E	49	313	4-17-1856	200	None
‡Johnson	Fairchild, E	49	314	4-17-1856	200	None
‡Johnson	Fairchild, E	49	316	4-17-1856	200	Fairchilds Br
‡Johnson	Fairchild, E	49	317	4- 7-1856	100	Fairchild Br
‡Johnson	Fairchild, E	49	318	4- 7-1856	200	Paint Cr
‡Johnson	Fairchild, E	49	315	8-17-1856	200	None
‡Johnson	Fairchild, Ebenezer	35	498	2- 8-1850	200	Sans Br
‡Johnson	Fairchild, Ebenezer	2	328	5- 5-1856	200	
†Johnson	Fairchild, Ebenezer	2	328	5- 5-1856	200	
†Johnson	Fairchild, Ebenezer	2	328	5- 5-1856	200	
†Johnson	Fairchild, Ebenezer	2	328	5- 5-1856	200	
†Johnson	Fairchild, Ebenezer	2	328	5- 5-1856	100	
‡Johnson	Fairchild, Ebenezer	2	388	6- 1-1857	200	
†Johnson	Fairchild, Ebenezer	2	388	6- 1-1857	200	
‡Johnson	Fairchild, Ebenezer	53	184	10-26-1857	370	Jennies Cr
‡Johnson	Fairchild, Enoch	18	31	3- 1-1845	50	Jennies Cr
†Johnson	Fairchild, Enoch	2	411	11- 2-1857	50	
‡Johnson	Fairchild, Enoch	58	384	7- 5-1858	50	Jennies Cr
‡Johnson	Fairchild, George	58	49	4-15-1850	50	None
‡Johnson	Fairchild, George M	59	354	4- 1-1857	50	Jennies Cr
‡Johnson	Fairchild, Hezekiah	68	124	11-22-1865	140	Upper Peter Cave Br
‡Johnson	Fairchild, Isaac	20	462	8- 7-1846	50	Glade Br
‡Johnson	Fairchild, Isaiah	—	—	—1858	25	
‡Johnson	Fairchild, Isaiah	68	125	8-22-1865	327	Lower Laurel Fk
‡Johnson	Fairchild, Joseph	27	91	8- 6-1846	50	L H Fk Lower Laurel Fk
‡Johnson	Fairchild, Joseph	32	207	7-29-1848	100	L H Fk Mud Lick Cr
‡Johnson	Fairchild, Joseph	43	163	3-18-1851	50	Peter Cave
‡Johnson	Fairchild, Moses	46	307	11-25-1854	94	None
†Johnson	Fairchild, Moses	2	243	2- 6-1855	30	
‡Johnson	Fairchild, Shadrick	43	176	3-16-1853	30	Sugar Camp Br Jennys Cr
‡Johnson	Fairchild, Thomas E	65	357	3- 9-1867	60	Oil Br
‡Johnson	Fairchild, William	68	376	3-29-1866	163	Colvin Br
*Res. ——	Fenwick, William	B	229	6-23-1797	60,000	Big Sandy R
‡Johnson	Fields, Louisa J	105	504	3- 9-1883	25	Greasy Cr

APPENDIX 527

County	Grantee	Book	Page	Date Survey	Acres	Watercourse
†Johnson	Fields, Louisa J.	7	127	2– 2–1886	4	
‡Johnson	Fields, Louisa J.	113	132	4–13–1886	4	Big Sandy R
†Johnson	Fields, Louisa J. & Elizabeth, Ward	7	49	3– 2– 85	4	
‡Johnson	Fips, Martin	65	182	2– 4–1858	100	Mine Fk
‡Johnson	Fitzpatrick, Charles	108	286	4–13–1885	78	Jennies Cr
†Johnson	Fitzpatrick, Civilian	2	441	3– 1–1858	25	
†Johnson	Fitzpatrick, Civilian	7	42	2–14–1885	20	
‡Johnson	Fitzpatrick, Fanny	51	277	5–30–1857	20	Lick Br
§Floyd	Fitzpatrick, Ia	(Cert. 105)		9– 3–1804	400	Jennys Cr
‡Floyd	Fitzpatrick, Jas	10	41	2– 3–1842	50	Heley Br
‡Johnson	Fitzpatrick, Jas	27	90	9– 2–1847	100	Little Paint Cr
‡Johnson	Fitzpatrick, Jas	66	31	3–25–1865	13	Upper Camp Br
‡Johnson	Fitzpatrick, Jas. & John	116	34	2–12–1885	20	Holly Bush Br
†Johnson	Fitzpatrick, Jas. & John	7	42	2–14–1885	28	
‡Floyd	Fitzpatrick, Jeremiah	11	18	3– 9–1843	150	None
‡Johnson	Fitzpatrick, Jeremiah	58	363	7–14–1858	12	Rockhouse Fk
‡Johnson	Fitzpatrick, Jeremiah	106	237	9–11–1883	17	Jennys Cr
¶Floyd	Fitzpatrick, John	1	201	5–23–1821	50	Jennys Cr
¶Floyd	Fitzpatrick, John	R	26	9– 8–1824	100	Jennys Cr
¶Floyd	Fitzpatrick, John	E-2	219	9–11–1834	50	None
‡Johnson	Fitzpatrick, John	10	33	2– 4–1842	150	Jaynes Cr
‡Johnson	Fitzpatrick, John	27	89	5– 3–1847	100	Jennies Cr
‡Johnson	Fitzpatrick, John	43	531	10–27–1849	100	Jennys Cr
‡Johnson	Fitzpatrick, John	71	314	5–21–1867	50	Bobs Br
‡Johnson	Fitzpatrick, Surville	52	473	2–17–1858	25	Jennys Cr
‡Floyd	Flanery, Singleton	4	65	8–20–1838	100	Johns Cr
¶Floyd	Fleetwood, Isaac	T	49	2–15–1825	50	Jennys Cr
⊙Fayette	Fleming, Charles	4	155	4–20–1785	20,000	Sandy
⊙Fayette	Fleming, John	3	64	12– 1–1783	10,687	S Fk Big Sandy
#Boubon	Fleming, William R	5	338	8–17–1787	7,000	Sandy R
▲Floyd	Floyd, Seminary	18	279	3– 4–1814	884	Open Fk
¶Floyd	Foster, John	G-2	3	10– 8–1835	100	State Road Fk
#Military	Foster, John H	3	440	3– 2–1785	666	Sandy Cr
⊙Fayette	Foster, Thos. & David	3	79	12–10–1783	2,884	Sandy
#Bourbon	Fowler, John	3	287	1– 6–1787	6,800½	Big Sandy
#Bourbon	Fowler, John	7	291	1– 4–1787	1,162	Big Sandy R
⊙Fayette	Fowler, John	4	273	2–15–1786	6,800	Sandy
#Bourbon	Fowler, John	16	182	6–20–1787	19,756	Big Sandy
‡Floyd	Fraisiur, Robert	10	32	9–10–1842	100	Mud Cr
¶Floyd	Fraley, Benjamin	D-2	375	3– 6–1835	50	Sandy R
‡Floyd	Fraley, John	8	354	3–25–1841	100	Johns Cr
‡Floyd	Fraley, John	20	407	8–22–1843	50	Johns Cr
⊙Fayette	Franklin, Edward	2	35	1–11–1783	4,319	Sandy Cr
#Bourbon	Franklin, Edward	13	536	1– 1–1787	4,319	Big Sandy Cr
¶Floyd	Franklin, James	E-2	237	12– 3–1833	50	Tom's Cr
‡Johnson	Franklin, James	107	558	5– 1–1885	50	Laurel Fk
†Johnson	Franklin, James L	7	57	4– 6–1885	50	
‡Johnson	Franklin, Joseph	27	88	1– 1–1847	50	Millers Cr
†Floyd	Franklin, Sally	6	136	1–21–1833	100	
#Bourbon	Frazier, James	11	398	11–25–1787	4,091	Sandy
‡Johnson	Frazier, James	119	501	1–16–1902	18	Cantrills Cr
‡Johnson	Freeman, James	121	178	5– 4–1904	2½	Long Br
‡Floyd	Friend, Agnes	5	213	11–27–1827	100	
‡Floyd	Friend, Isaac B	12	425	2–15–1840	50	Hos Cr
‡Floyd	Friend, Isaac B	11	9	3– 6–1843	50	Jennys Cr
¶Floyd	Friend, John	V	427	11– 2–1827	50	Fk Paint Lick Cr
⊙Fayette	Fuller, Benjamin	9	413	3–28–1785	5,217	N Fk Sandy R
‡Johnson	Gambill, Martin	65	356	1–31–1865	80	Lost Lick Br
†Johnson	Gambill, W. H	5	581	7–21–1877	50	
¶Floyd	Gardner, Benjamin	K-2	307	10–26–1836	50	Fk Paint Cr
‡Johnson	Gardner, Benjamin F	15	382	7–10–1845	600	Litteral Fk Paint Cr
‡Johnson	Gardner, Benjamin F	52	475	2– 4–1858	25	Main Fk Paint Cr
†Johnson	Gardner, Benjamin F	2	440	3– 1–1858	25	
#Bourbon	Garrard, James	12	339	9–15–1788	23,250	Big Sandy
#Bourbon	Garrard, William	15	169	12– 7–1787	425	Big Sandy R
#Bourbon	Garrard, William	11	577	4–27–1789	2,958¾	Big Sandy R
¶Floyd	Garret, Emilick	E	326	7– 9–1818	50	Big Sandy R
‡Floyd	Gearheart, Adam	9	387	8–11–1842	150	Big Sandy R
‡Floyd	Gearheart, Crisley	10	43	7–16–1842	100	Fraisures Cr
‡Floyd	Gearheart, G. A	2	119	2– 2–1837	600	Watson Cr
‡Floyd	Gearheart, John Jr	11	14	8–24–1843	50	Shop Br
‡Floyd	Gearheart, Joseph	10	31	2–18–1842	50	Salt Lick of Beaver Cr
‡Floyd	Gearheart, Joseph Sr	2	124	5–10–1837	50	Beaver Cr
¶Floyd	George, Alexander	A-2	140	9–24–1830	50	Fk Little Paint Cr
‡Floyd	George, A. G	2	122	5–13–1837	50	Little Paint Cr
‡Johnson	George, James A	70	56	8–22–1866	60	R H Fk Lower Road Br
¶Floyd	George, John	D-2	381	5–21–1834	100	Little Paint Cr
‡Floyd	George & Gray	2	120	4– 4–1837	200	Lick Br

HISTORY OF JOHNSON COUNTY

County	Grantee	Book	Page	Date Survey	Acres	Watercourse
#Fayette	Gibbons, James	13	189	5-29-1785	10,000	N Br Sandy R
‡Floyd	Gibson, Tyrey	11	28	1-26-1843	100	None
‡Johnson	Gillett, Wiley	53	161	2- 3-1858	200	Paint Cr
‡Johnson	Gillum, John C	125	301	8-12-1920	2	Keaton Fk
‡Johnson	Ginkins, Robert	49	319	3-11-1856	50	Paint Cr
‡Floyd	Gipson, Burwell	11	35	1-26-1843	50	Jones Br
‡Johnson	Gobble, Abraham	44	451	7- 2-1853	50	None
†Johnson	Goble, Abraham	2	104	6- 6-1853	40	
‡Johnson	Gobble, David	61	420	12-13-1860	573	M Fk Rockcastle
‡Johnson	Gobble, David	64	441	3- 8-1864	100	M Fk Rockcastle Cr
‡Johnson	Gobble, John	64	440	3-11-1861	230	Laurel Fk Rockcastle Cr
†Johnson	Gobble, John	3	290	12- 7-1863	150	
‡Johnson	Goble, John	2	444	4- 1-1858	50	
‡Johnson	Gobble, Samuel	61	191	12-13-1860	233	M Fk Rockcastle
†Johnson	Goble, Samuel	3	178	1- 7-1861	200	
‡Johnson	Gobble, William	2	156	2- 6-1854	200	
‡Johnson	Gobble, William	53	11	2-25-1856	50	Lick Br
‡Johnson	Gobble, William	53	184	2-26-1856	50	Rock Cr
‡Johnson	Gobble, William	59	43	7-12-1858	40	Rockcastle Cr
‡Johnson	Gobble, William	59	46	7-12-1858	35	Rockcastle Cr
‡Johnson	Gobble, William	53	186	12- 6-1856	50	Laurel Cr
‡Johnson	Goble, William	44	493	4- 2-1853	200	Rockcastle Cr
‡Johnson	Goble, William	44	494	4- 2-1853	200	Rockcastle Cr
‡Johnson	Goble, William	44	490	2-25-1854	200	Rockcastle Cr
†Johnson	Goble, William	2	441	3- 1-1858	50	
†Johnson	Goble, William	2	441	3- 1-1858	50	
†Johnson	Goble, William	3		1860	50	
‡Johnson	Goble, William	3	114	2- 6-1860	50	
‡Johnson	Godsey, James H	34	339	1-30-1850	200	Upper Laurel Fk Blain Cr
▲Mason	Graham, John	18	89	6-27-1797	2,000	Sandy R
▲Floyd	Graham, John	17	511	2-28-1808	1,254	Little Paint Lick Cr
†Floyd	Graham, John	1	135	5-27-1811	2,000	
▲Floyd	Graham, John	18	303	2-20-1812	132	Daniels Cr
▲Floyd	Graham, John	18	285	3- 6-1814	100	Open Fk Paint Lick
¶Floyd	Graham, John	H	165	12-29-1820	125	Open Fk Big Paint
▲Mason	Graham, Richard	14	103	10-25-1797	1,174	Big Sandy R
¶Floyd	Graham, Thomas W	T	122	10-20-1824	50	Lick Fk Paint Cr
¶Floyd	Graham, Thomas W	T	30	2-14-1825	50	Paint Lick Cr
¶Floyd	Graham, Thomas W	E-2	116	1-11-1832	50	Daniels Cr
#Fayette	Gratz, Michael	9	456	5- 6-1785	28,000	Big Sandy R
*Res. Philadel	Gratz, Michael	A-2	515	2-14-1795	10,000	Sandy
#Bourbon	Graves, Richard	14	377	5- 5-1787	1,450	Big Sandy R
‡Johnson	Gray, A. S	56	465	4- 8-1859	14	Big Paint Cr
‡Floyd	Gray & George	2	120	4- 4-1837	200	Lick Br
‡Johnson	Green, Enoch	35	499	12- 1-1848	50	Briar Fk
‡Johnson	Green, Giles	32	202	7- 5-1848	200	Rockhouse Fk
‡Johnson	Green, Giles	32	203	10- 9-1849	40	Rockhouse Fk
‡Johnson	Green, Giles	57	33	2-28-1859	50	Br Rockhouse Fk
†Johnson	Green, Giles	3	651	1859	40	
‡Johnson	Green, Giles	84	249	4-12-1871	6	Green Br
‡Johnson	Green, Gyles	14	284	4-11-1844	400	None
⊙Fayette	Green, John	1	225	12-21-1782	2,311	Sandy (withdrawn)
‡Johnson	Greer, William W	114	235	7- 5-1890	12	Long Br
#Bourbon	Griffin, John	11	436	8-17-1787	684	Sandy
‡Johnson	Grim, Charles	32	204	4- 8-1847	150	None
¶Floyd	Grimes, Charles J	1-2	271	5-23-1836	200	Tom's Cr
*Res. Richm'd	Groves, Jno. & Co	B-2	166	6-16-1790	6,000	Big Sandy R
‡Johnson	Guin & Preston	53	191	4- 9-1856	36	Tom's Cr
†Johnson	Gullett, Asa	2	440	3- 1-1858	125	
‡Johnson	Gullett, Asey	66	52	8-30-1858	100	Sayer Br R H Br Little Paint
‡Johnson	Gullett, Ira	37	63	3-19-1851	300	Laurel Br
‡Johnson	Gullett, Wiley	27	86	10-31-1846	100	Fk Paint Cr
†Johnson	Gullett, Wiley	2	432	2- 1-1858	200	
†Johnson	Gullett, Wiley	2	457	6- 7-1858	100	
‡Johnson	Gullett, Wiley	60	81	12-12-1859	200	Mine Fk Paint Cr
†Johnson	Gullett, Wiley	3	124	4- 2-1860	200	
†Johnson	Gullett, Wiley	3	124	4- 2-1860	25	
†Johnson	Gullett, Wiley	3	124	4- 2-1860	200	
‡Johnson	Gullett, Wiley	59	256	4- 3-1860	688	Mine Fk Paint Cr
¶Floyd	Hager, D	1-2	308	3-16-1836	300	Big Sandy R
¶Floyd	Hager, Daniel	N-2	211	9-24-1838	150	Greasy Cr
¶Floyd	Hager, Daniel	O-2	164	7-25-1839	50	Greasy Cr
†Johnson	Hager, Daniel	2	246	2- 6-1855	50	
‡Johnson	Hager, Daniel	49	320	3- 1-1856	50	None
‡Johnson	Hager, Daniel	98	515	3-11-1856	50	Mine Fk Paint Cr
‡Johnson	Hager, Daniel	49	321	3-11-1856	50	Paint Cr
‡Johnson	Hager, Daniel	101	221	3-11-1856	50	Mine Fk

APPENDIX 529

County	Grantee	Book	Page	Date Survey	Acres	Watercourse
†Johnson	Hager, Daniel	5	478	7– 3–1875	100	
aJohnson	Hager, Daniel	603	624	3–11–1858	50	
‡Johnson	Hager, D. Mart	97	107	3–11–1876	20	None
†Johnson	Hager, D. Mart	5	512	3–15–1876	40	
‡Johnson	Hager, D. Mart	99	208	6– 8–1880	24	Jennies Cr
¶Floyd	Hager, James	1–2	123	3–30–1834	100	Sandy R
†Johnson	Hager, John J	44	724	1–16–1856	80	None
‡Johnson	Hager, William T	100	433	8– 2–1881	5	Little Paint Cr
‡Floyd	Hale, Brice	8	349	12–10–1839	100	Licking R
‡Floyd	Hale, Brice	14	253	6–17–1843	100	Mollys Br
‡Floyd	Hale, John	14	252	6–17–1843	100	Licking R
‡Floyd	Hall, Elijah	11	39	8–28–1843	100	Beaver Cr
‡Floyd	Hall, Jesse	10	59	1–22–1842	100	None
†Johnson	Hall, Jesse	7	350	4–––1889	25	
‡Johnson	Hall, Jesse	112	504	12– 2–1889	23	Lick Fk Jennies Cr
§Floyd	Hall, John	(Cert. 84)		3– 6–1804	160	Levisa Fk
‡Floyd	Hall, John	11	11	11– 2–1842	50	Apple Tree Br
‡Floyd	Hall, John	11	38	11– 2–1842	100	Beaver Cr
‡Johnson	Hall, John	59	45	7–14–1856	125	M Fk Rockcastle
†Johnson	Hall, John	3	313	2– 6–1860	60	
†Johnson	Hall, John	3	—	—–1860	60	
‡Johnson	Hall, John M	64	61	3– 2–1861	185	M Fk Rockcastle Cr
†Johnson	Hall, John M	3	270	6– 1–1863	125	
‡Floyd	Hall, Owen	11	40	8–26–1843	100	Robt. Frazier Br
‡Floyd	Hall, Riley	11	20	8–29–1843	50	Stormbough Br
‡Floyd	Hall, Roden	10	30	1–22–1842	50	——— Cr
‡Floyd	Hall, Squire	10	24	1–20–1842	150	None
‡Floyd	Hall, Squire	10	25	1–21–1842	50	Branham Cr
§Floyd	Hall, William	(Cert. 50)		9– 5–1803	200	Levisa Fk
‡Floyd	Hall, Wm., Isaac & Elenor	20	399	3–15–1844	100	Johnson Br
†Johnson	Hall, W. M	8	61	3– 6– 92	43	
‡Johnson	Hamilton, Benj	49	320	4–28–1855	46	Laurel Br
‡Johnson	Hamilton, Benj. R	5	508	2– 7–1876	5	
‡Johnson	Hamilton, Benj. R	97	304	8– 2–1877	2	None
¶Morgan	Hamilton, John	O-2	82	——3––1833	50	Paint Cr
¶Morgan	Hamilton, John	Q-2	148	3–27–1840	100	Lost Br Paint Cr
¶Morgan	Hamilton, John	R-2	187–8	1–29–1842	200	Oil Springs Fk
¶Morgan	Hamilton, John	R-2	187–8	2–27–1842	200	Open Fk
¶Morgan	Hamilton, John	Q-2	363	5–14–1845	50	Main Paint Cr
‡Floyd	Hamilton, Stephen	14	254	6–19–1843	50	Lick Fk
‡Floyd	Hamilton, Stephen	14	255	6–19–1843	50	Rough & Tough Fk
‡Johnson	Hamilton, Thomas	18	28	11–27–1845	50	Laurel Fk
‡Johnson	Hamilton, Thomas	43	168	4–16–1851	118	Br Big Laurel Fk
‡Johnson	Hamilton, Thomas	43	169	4–16–1851	8	Laurel Fk
‡Johnson	Hamilton, Thomas	49	321	4–28–1855	85	Road Br
†Johnson	Hamilton, Thomas	2	323	4– 7–1856	85	
‡Johnson	Hamilton, Thomas	64	170	1– 6–1860	125	Big Laurel Big Blain
†Johnson	Hamilton, Thomas	3	282	9– 6–1863	125	
‡Floyd	Hamilton, William	10	29	9– 9–1842	100	None
‡Floyd	Hamilton, William	10	58	9–10–1842	50	Mud Cr
°Fayette	Hampton, Richard	4	169	4–30–1785	1,000	S Fk Big Sandy R
†Johnson	Hanna, Andrew D	5	516	3–15–1876	50	
‡Johnson	Hanna, Ebenezer	11	54	8–30–1843	100	Millers Cr
¶Morgan	Hanna, Joseph	W	204	4–25–1825	50	Fk Paint Lick Cr
¶Morgan	Hanna, Joseph	B-2	440	11– 3–1832	100	Paint Cr
¶Morgan	Hanna, Joseph	E-2	38	10– 3–1833	50	Cow Fk Paint
¶Floyd	Hanna, Samuel	T	127	11– 5–1825	50	Millers Cr
¶Morgan	Hanna, Samuel	P-2	305	1–29–1841	150	Open Fk
‡Johnson	Hanna, Samuel	35	503	2–15–1851	304	Flat Woods Br
‡Johnson	Hanna, Samuel	44	452	1– 8–1852	25	None
†Johnson	Hanna, Samuel	2	441	3– 1–1858	30	
†Johnson	Hanna, Samuel	2	444	4– 1–1858	40	
†Johnson	Hanna, Samuel	2	444	4– 1–1858	100	
†Johnson	Hanna, Samuel	2	445	4– 1–1858	100	
†Johnson	Hanna, Samuel	2	445	4– 1–1858	90	
†Johnson	Hanna, Samuel	2	445	4– 1–1858	200	
†Johnson	Hanna, Samuel	2	445	4– 1–1858	25	
†Johnson	Hanna, Samuel	2	445	4– 1–1858	200	
†Johnson	Hanna, Samuel	2	445	4– 1–1858	125	
†Johnson	Hanna, Samuel	2	445	4– 1–1858	13	
†Johnson	Hanna, Samuel	2	445	4– 1–1858	150	
†Johnson	Hanna, Samuel	2	445	4– 1–1858	200	
†Johnson	Hanna, Samuel	2	446	4– 1–1858	46	
†Johnson	Hanna, Samuel	2	446	4– 1–1858	200	
†Johnson	Hanna, Samuel	2	446	4– 1–1858	200	
†Johnson	Hanna, Samuel	2	446	4– 1–1858	40	
†Johnson	Hanna, Samuel	2	446	4– 1–1858	100	

aBy Act of the Ky. Legislature 3–27–1880, Chap. 603, Page 624.

530　　HISTORY OF JOHNSON COUNTY

County	Grantee	Book	Page	Date Survey	Acres	Watercourse
†Johnson	Hanna, Samuel	2	446	4- 1-1858	200	
†Johnson	Hanna, Samuel	2	446	4- 1-1858	50	
†Johnson	Hanna, Samuel	2	446	4- 1-1858	20	
†Johnson	Hanna, Samuel	2	446	4- 1-1858	100	
†Johnson	Hanna, Samuel	2	446	4- 1-1858	150	
†Johnson	Hanna, Samuel	2	446	4- 1-1858	50	
†Johnson	Hanna, Samuel	2	446	4- 1-1858	50	
†Johnson	Hanna, Samuel	2	446	4- 1-1858	140	
†Johnson	Hanna, Samuel	2	447	4- 1-1858	100	
†Johnson	Hanna, Samuel	2	447	4- 1858	100	
†Johnson	Hanna, Samuel	2	447	4- 1-1858	123	
†Johnson	Hanna, Samuel	2	447	4- 1-1858	87	
†Johnson	Hanna, Samuel	3	113	2- 6-1860	100	
†Johnson	Hanna, Samuel	3	113	2- 6-1860	200	
†Johnson	Hanna, Samuel	3	113	2- 6-1860	200	
† Johnson	Hanna, Samuel	3	113	2- 6-1860	200	
†Johnson	Hanna, Samuel	3	113	2- 6-1860	200	
†Johnson	Hanna, Samuel	3	113	2- 6-1860	200	
†Johnson	Hanna, Samuel	3	113	2- 6-1860	200	
†Johnson	Hanna, Samuel	3	114	2- 6-1860	200	
†Johnson	Hanna, Samuel	3		——1860	800	
†Johnson	Hanna, Samuel	3		——1860	200	
†Johnson	Hanna, Samuel	3		——1860	200	
†Johnson	Hanna, Samuel	3		——1860	200	
†Johnson	Hanna, Samuel B	3	247	7- 2-1862	175	
†Johnson	Hanna, Samuel B	3	248	7- 2-1862	30	
†Johnson	Hanna, Samuel B	3	248	7- 2-1862	100	
‡Johnson	Hanna, Samuel B	65	142	5-12-1857	1,250	Hargens Cr
‡Johnson	Hanna, Samuel B	64	54	9-15-1854	19	Burnt Cabin Br Big Sandy
‡Johnson	Hanna, Samuel B	53	162	10-28-1857	45	Barnetts Cr
‡Johnson	Hanna, Samuel B	64	53	5- 8-1858	30	Twin Br Mud Lick
‡Johnson	Hanna, Samuel B	3	343	2- 9-1865	45	
‡Johnson	Hanna, Samuel B	3	343	2- 9-1865	80	
Johnson	Harkins, Hugh	43	559	10-19-1852	100	Tom's Cr
†Floyd	Harmon, Joseph	2	119	11-22-1815	150	
¶Floyd	Harris, David K	M	269	1-13-1823	50	Little Paint Cr
‡Floyd	Harris, D. K	11	36	3- 8-1843	100	None
‡Floyd	Harris, Erastus G	10	60	4- 5-1842	100	Big Meadows Br
‡Floyd	Harris, James	31	338	2- 7-1843	100	Lick Fk
‡Floyd	Harris, James	31	337	3- 7-1843	150	Lick Fk
‡Floyd	Harris, James P	15	31	3-30-1843	449	Daniels Cr
‡Floyd	Harris, James P	31	330	6-26-1843	50	None
‡Floyd	Harris, James P	31	331	6-26-1843	50	Bull Cr
¶Floyd	Harris, John	Q	218	12-15-1824	200	Sandy R
¶Floyd	Harris, John B	L-2	82	10- 3-1836	500	Sandy R
‡Floyd	Harris, John B	8	322	12-13-1840	2,475	Big Sandy
¶Floyd	Harris, William	1-2	262	2-18-1836	100	Burnt Cabin Br
‡Floyd	Harris, William	4	67	8-10-1839	100	Jennies Cr
‡Floyd	Harris, William	8	367	3- 2-1841	100	Jones Cr
‡Floyd	Harris, William	8	352	9- 3-1841	50	Bear Hollow
‡Johnson	Harris, William	43	166	10-20-1847	50	Long Br
‡Johnson	Harris, William	32	206	9-15-1849	50	Burnt Cabin Br
‡Floyd	Haskins, Moses	6	212	1-16-1839	50	Licking R
‡Floyd	Hatcher, John	4	436	1-21-1839	180	Sandy R
‡Floyd	Hatcher, John G	4	66	12- 6-1838	350	Buffalo Cr
¶Floyd	Haws, Elijah	F-2	222	9-28-1834	100	Tom's Cr
¶Floyd	Haws, Elijah	1-2	263	11-14-1835	50	Tom's Cr
‡Johnson	Haws, James H	32	205	7- 4-1848	150	Tom's Cr
¶Floyd	Haws, John	G	299	6-25-1819	65	Georges Cr
¶Floyd	Haws, Samuel	D	390	6-19-1818	50	Tom's Cr
#Fayette	Hays, William Thos	10	394	9-12-1784	2,000	Sandy Cr
#Fayette	Hays, William Thos	10	395	9-12-1784	500	Sandy Cr
▲Morgan	Hazelrigg, Thos. F	D-2	12	5-22-1833	50	Paint Cr
⊚Fayette	Hedgman, John	4	78	12-16-1784	2,000	Big Sandy R
¶Floyd	Helton, Benjamin	T	129	9- 9-1824	50	Big Sandy R
‡Johnson	Helton, Nathan	53	5	4- 2-1855	19	None
6——	Henry, Daniel	4	169	4-30-1785	2,328½	Sandy R
‡Johnson	Henry, N. H	1	222	10- 7-1861	170	
⊚Fayette	Henry, Patrick	1	272	12-25-1782	1,000	N Fk Sandy
†Johnson	Heylton, Eliphas	——		——1860	25	
†Johnson	Heylton, Nathan P	2	445	4- 1-1858	19	
‡Floyd	Hicks, George	11	41	11- 9-1842	100	Bare Cr
‡Floyd	Hicks, Hiram	14	260	6-19-1843	700	Spurlock Fk
‡Johnson	Hicks, Isaac	44	263	1-20-1854	50	None
‡Johnson	Hicks, Isaac	2	253	3- 5-1855	50	
‡Johnson	Hicks, Isaac	65	341	2- 7-1865	530	L Fk Greasy Cr
‡Johnson	Hicks, Isaac	3	343	2- 9-1865	200	
¶Floyd	Hill, Edward	1	396	1-13-1821	50	Big Paint Lick Cr
‡Johnson	Hill, E. P	20	485	10- 2-1846	400	Big Laurel Fk

APPENDIX 531

County	Grantee	Book	Page	Date Survey	Acres	Watercourse
¶Floyd	Hill, Spencer	T	66	9-23-1824	50	Fk Paint Cr
¶Floyd	Hill, Spencer	1-2	346	11- 5-1836	150	Big Paint Cr
‡Johnson	Hill, Spencer	18	29	11-27-1845	100	Laurel Fk
†Johnson	Hilton, Eliphas P	3	108	4- 6-1860	25	
¶Floyd	Hilton, Robertson	L-2	407	3- 7-1837	100	Tom's Cr
†Johnson	Hitchcock, Fanny	2	378	4- 6-1857	20	
¶Floyd	Hitchcock, John	P	176	1- 6-1823	50	Big Paint Lick Cr
‡Johnson	Hitchcock, John	27	85	9- 4-1847	50	Barretts Cr
‡Johnson	Hitchcock, John	R-2	392	4-12-1849	100	Asa Fk
‡Johnson	Hitchcock, John	43	536	4-10-1851	250	Br Barnetts Cr
‡Johnson	Hitchcock, John	43	541	4-10-1851	225	Barnetts Cr
‡Johnson	Hitchcock, John	51	278	2-25-1857	100	None
†Johnson	Hitchcock, John	2	385	5- 4-1857	75	
‡Johnson	Hitchcock, Rowland G.	71	315	4- 8-1867	22	Fk Barnetts Cr
#Bourbon	Hite, Isaac	16	196	8-13-1787	11,580	Big Sandy
#Bourbon	Hoard, Thomas	11	551	8-14-1787	3,000	Big Sandy
†Johnson	Hoge, Daniel	2	197	9- 5-1854	50	
‡Johnson	Holbrook, James	43	532	4-17-1851	175	Mill Br
†Johnson	Holbrook, James	3	635	——1858	77	
‡Johnson	Holbrook, James	55	290	12- 7-1358	53	Upper Laurel Fk
‡Johnson	Holbrook, James	55	291	12- 7-1858	27	Upper Laurel Fk
‡Johnson	Holbrook, James	65	350	1-30-1365	554	Upper Laurel Fk
‡Johnson	Holbrook, James	81	247	10-18-1870	88	Spicer Br
‡Johnson	Holbrook, John S	125	395	2- 7-1922	18	Mill Br
†Johnson	Holbrook, L. D.	7	55	4-14-1885	125	
‡Johnson	Holbrook, L. D.	107	560	5- 1-1885	125	Laurel Fk
‡Johnson	Holbrook, Pleasant	43	537	4-17-1851	150	Spicy Br
†Johnson	Holbrook, Pleasant	3	635	——1858	77	
‡Johnson	Holbrook, Pleasant	55	292	12- 8-1858	77	Keatons Fk Big Blain
†Johnson	Holbrook, Pleasant	3	643	——1859	74	
‡Johnson	Holbrook, Pleasant	57	32	2-12-1859	60	Keatons Fk
‡Floyd	Holbrook, Randolph	6	211	11-29-1838	100	Lost Fk
‡Floyd	Holbrook, William	59	227	5-26-1859	105	Keatons Fk Blain Cr
†Johnson	Holbrook, William P	3		——1860	55	
‡Johnson	Holbrook, William P	3	118	2-11-1860	50	
‡Johnson	Holbrook, Wm. & Randolph	18	30	7- 3-1845	100	Keatons Br
◦Fayette	Holder, John	3	64	12- 1-1783	10,687	S Fk Big Sandy
◦Fayette	Hollingsworth, Levi	3	426	8-14-1784	4,000	Sandy
#Military	Hollingsworth, Levi	11	460	12-16-1785	300	Beaver Cr
§Floyd	Holt, William	(Cert. 134)		6-17-1805	400	Jennys Cr
§Floyd	Holt, William	(Cert. 149)		11-18-1805	300	Jennys Cr
‡Johnson	Honeycut, William	97	147	12-15-1875	20	2-Mile Br
†Johnson	Honeycut, William	5	498	12-17-1875	25	
*Res. Windsor	Hooke, Horace	G	265	1-20-1797	40,000	Br Big Sandy R
†Johnson	Horn, John W	5	220	6- 3-1872	100	
‡Floyd	Hoskins, Moses	4	70	11- 4-1837	50	Licking R
¶Morgan	Howard, Moses	R-2	190	4-20-1842	100	Mine Fk
‡Floyd	Howard, Samuel	14	259	6-17-1843	100	Howards Br
¶Floyd	Howard, William	A-2	142	10- 1-1830	100	Puncheon Camp Br
*Res. Green	Howe, John W	T	104	10- 4-1819	250	Sandy R
§Floyd	Howe, Samuel	(Cert. 8)		9——1802	400	Beaver Cr
‡Floyd	Howel, Thomas	6	192	2-29-1839	500	Big Muddy Cr
‡Floyd	Howell, Thomas	10	26	1-19-1842	50	Bells Br
‡Floyd	Howell, Thomas	10	27	1-19-1842	50	Branches Cr
‡Johnson	Hows, Claybourn	43	182	4- 8-1851	200	L H Fk Rockhouse Fk
‡Floyd	Huff, John	8	351	3-10-1840	50	Caney Cr
‡Floyd	Huff, Harrison J	8	368	3-31-1840	100	Caney Cr
*Res. ——	Hughes, James	K	363	7-24-1806	213,866	Br Sandy R
*Res. Albermarle	Hunton, Chas B	E	376	11-21-1800	6,250	Big Sandy R
‡Johnson	Hyden, William	35	502	12- 7-1848	400	Miller Cr
‡Johnson	Hylton, Eliphas P. S	62	207	11- 7-1855	24	Br Hoods Fk
‡Johnson	Hylton, N. P. & E. L.	14	283	2-23-1844	150	Hannahs Br (Jennys Cr?)
‡Johnson	Hylton & Preston	42	331	5-28-1853	25	Bakers Fk
‡Johnson	Ingram, Justice	55	297	10-13-1858	13	Hoods Fk
‡Johnson	Ingram, Sylanus	20	468	1-28-1846	50	None
*Res. Allegheny	Irish, William B	F	148	12- 8-1801	20,200	Sandy R
†Floyd	Isaacs, William	2	199	10-29-1816	——	
*Res. Phila	Jackson, Samuel	A-2	366	3-11-1796	70,000	Big Sandy
‡Johnson	James, Abner	73	375	5-17-1867	150	Rockcastle Cr
	James, Abner	4	197	5- 7-1867	150	
†Johnson	James, Ephriam	3	148	8- 7-1860	40	
‡Johnson	James, Epram	44	255	9-27-1852	50	Coldwater Cr
†Johnson	James, John R	3	240	6- 2-1862	60	
◦Fayette	James, Julian	3	324	5- 4-1784	10,000	Br S Fk Sandy
#Fayette	James, Julian	3	2	11-22-1785	10,000	S Fk Sandy
§Floyd	Jane, Stephen	(Cert. 122)		1- 7-1805	100	Levisa Fk
‡Johnson	Janes, Daniel	42	324	11-28-1853	25	Little Laurel Cr

532 HISTORY OF JOHNSON COUNTY

County	Grantee	Book	Page	Date Survey	Acres	Watercourse
†Johnson	Jayne, Daniel	2	143	12– 5–1853	25	
‡Johnson	Jayne, David	20	469	8– 6–1846	100	None
§Floyd	Jayne, William	(Cert. 144)		8–17–1805	170	Paint Lick Cr
¶Floyd	Jenkins, Gilbert	1–2	339	8–25–1836	100	Jennys Cr
†Johnson	Jenkins, Hobert	2	336	9– 1–1856	50	
⊚Fayette	Jenkins, William	3	288	4–14–1784	500	S Fk Big Sandy
▲Mason	Jenkins, William	15	578	11–24–1797	500	S Fk Big Sandy
*Res. Paris, France	Jerome, Wm. J	U	90	11–22–1819	910,954	Ky & Big Sandy
⊚Fayette	Johns, John	2	36	1–11–1783	2,000	Sandy
¶Floyd	Johns, Thomas	P	514	7–16–1824	50	Buffalo Cr
‡Johnson	Johnson, Andrew	37	60	2–27–1850	75	Stafford Fk
‡Floyd	Johnson, Edward	11	19	8–26–1843	50	Mud Cr
‡Johnson	Johnson, George	37	59	2–27–1850	125	Stafford Fk
‡Johnson	Johnson, George	53	163	10–12–1857	200	Stafford Br
‡Johnson	Johnson, George	2	440	3– 1–1858	200	
‡Johnson	Johnson, G. M.	123	331	11– 8–1909	84	Big Paint Cr
‡Johnson	Johnson, George M	125	66	4–21–1917	81	Bear Br
‡Johnson	Johnson, James C. L	76	210	6–18–1869	12	Lower Fk Blain
§Floyd	Johnson, John	(Cert. 151)		1–20–1806	100	Jennys Cr
¶Floyd	Johnson, John	2	210	12–23–1816	—	
‡Johnson	Johnson, John	53	187	10–10–1857	150	Nats Cr
‡Johnson	Johnson, Martin	44	458	11– 6–1853	80	Blaine Cr
†Johnson	Johnson, Martin	2	130	11– 7–1853	50	
§Floyd	Johnson, Patrick	(Cert. 150)		1–20–1806	50	Rockhouse Fk
⊚Fayette	Johnson, Robert	2	36	1–11–1783	2,100	Sandy
#Bourbon	Johnson, Robert	15	191	1– 3–1787	2,428	Big Sandy Cr
#Bourbon	Johnson, Robert	12	311	1– 4–1787	2,000	Big Sandy Cr
#Bourbon	Johnson, Robert	12	337	1– 4–1787	1,046	Big Sandy
#Bourbon	Johnson, Robert	12	354	4–17–1787	7,537	Big Sandy
‡Johnson	Johnson, William	98	187	5– 2–1873	7	Line Br Jennies Cr
‡Johnson	Jones, John R	63	315	4–25–1862	40	Stone Cole Br
‡Johnson	Joseph, John	65	421	2– 6–1858	210	Bailey Br
‡Johnson	Joseph, Woodson	125	389	12–19–1921	25	Greasy Cr
‡Johnson	Justice, Abirum	28	431	11–30–1848	185	Hoods Fk
‡Johnson	Justice, Israel	8	370	8–29–1838	100	L H Fk Toles Cr
‡Johnson	Kazee, Reuben	90	83	3– 4–1872	9	Shanty Br
¶Lawrence	Kazee, Richard	E-2	266–7	6–13–1831	100	Hoods Fk
¶Lawrence	Kazee, Richard	E-2	266–7	8–31–1832	100	Hoods Fk
¶Morgan	Keaton, David	W	201	4–25–1825	50	Fk Paint Lick Cr
¶Morgan	Keaton, Elijah	R-2	184	9– 4–1842	150	Paint
¶Morgan	Keaton, Hudson	A-2	198	12–11–1830	50	Fk Paint
¶Floyd	Keaton, Nelson	1	395	4–25–1821	50	Paint Lick Cr
¶Morgan	Keaton, Nelson	A-2	415	12–15–1827	50	Paint Cr
⊚Fayette	Keith, Thomas	4	279	3– 3–1786	13,042	Br S Fk Sandy
‡Johnson	Kelly, George	55	293	12–27–1858	125	Keetons Fk
†Johnson	Kelly, George	3	638	1858	50	
†Johnson	Kelly, George	3	639	1859	75	
§Floyd	Kelly, Jesse R	(Cert. 33)		6– 6–1803	400	Mouth Johns Cr
†Johnson	Kelly, Peter	7	43	2–16–1885	15	
‡Johnson	Kelly, Peter	107	553	5– 4–1885	9¼	Keatons Fk
⊚Fayette	Kembrough, Robt	4	273	2–15–1786	6,800	Sandy
‡Morgan	Kendall, Allen	5	461	12–21–1838	250	Enochs & Open Fk
‡Morgan	Kendall, James P	4	293	5– 7–1839	500	Mine Fk Big Sandy
¶Floyd	Kendrick, William	1–2	91–2	5– 6–1836	200	Daniels Cr
▲Mason	Kenton, Simon	15	246	8–25–1798	1,200	Big Sandy
‡Johnson	Kestner, Jacob	66	75	4–28–1865	8	M Fk Rockcastle Cr
‡Johnson	Kimbler, A. B.	20	475	1–28–1846	50	None
‡Johnson	Kimbler, William	20	475	1–29–1846	50	Stone Coal Br
#Bourbon	Kimbrough, Robert	3	287	1– 6–1787	6,800½	Big Sandy
§Floyd	King, Oliver	(Cert. 135)		6–17–1805	50	Big Paint
‡Johnson	King, William	119	453	2–28–1902	30½	Big Laurel Fk
§Floyd	Kirk, James	(Cert. 130)		3– 4–1805	50	Levisa Fk
¶Floyd	Kistner, Jacob M	O	233	9–24–1823	50	Daniels Cr
▲Floyd	Lackey, Alexander	19	209	1– 9–1818	255	Sandy R
¶Floyd	Lamaster, Eleazer	R	15	9–27–1824	150	Mud Lick Fk Paint
¶Floyd	Lamaster, James	T	43	2–14–1825	50	Paint Lick Cr
¶Floyd	Lamasters, John	T	154	8–20–1821	50	Big Paint Lick Cr
¶Floyd	Lamasters, Lewis	T	106	10–20–1824	100	Fk Paint Cr
¶Floyd	Lancaster, Lancaster	T	121	9–17–1824	50	Paint Cr
▲Floyd	Lane, James S	19	209	1–16–1819	69	Louisa Fk
⊚Fayette	Langham, Elias	3	69	12– 4–1783	1,400	S Fk Sandy
⊚Fayette	Langham, Elias	3	358	6–12–1784	1,166	Big Sandy
‡Johnson	Large, William	18	14	8–14–1845	100	Brushy Fk
⊚Fayette	Lay, Benjamin	10	390	3–29–1785	15,000	Br Sandy R
‡Floyd	Layne, Andrew	6	178	1–20–1839	100	L H Fk Daniels Cr
‡Floyd	Layne, James S	6	189	1–24–1839	500	Coldwater Br
‡Floyd	Layne, Tandy M	6	186	1–26–1839	200	Sandy R
⊚Fayette	Lee, Thomas	4	270	2– 7–1786	2,296	Sandy
‡Johnson	Lemaster, Daniel	65	347	4–24–1865	125	Hoods Fk Blain

County	Grantee	Book	Page	Date Survey	Acres	Watercourse
‡Johnson	Lemaster, Daniel P	66	76	4–21–1865	77	Lick Br
‡Johnson	Lemaster, David B	65	348	1–20–1865	30	Laurel Br
‡Johnson	Lemaster, David B	65	349	1–20–1865	3	Laurel Br
†Johnson	Lemasters, Eleazor	2	184	6– 5–1854	15	
‡Johnson	Lemaster, Eleazor	49	324	11–28–1854	15	Blair Cr
‡Johnson	Lemaster, Francis	32	213	7– 1–1848	140	L H Fk Lower Laurel Fk
†Johnson	Lemaster, James	7	52	4– 6–1885	5	
‡Johnson	Lemaster, James	108	285	4– 8–1885	4	Barnetts Cr
‡Johnson	Lemaster, John B	43	554	3–16–1851	75	Big Paint Cr
‡Johnson	Lemaster, John V	66	78	4–19–1865	212	Low Gap Br
‡Johnson	Lemaster, Joseph	35	506	————	400	Puncheon Camp Br
‡Johnson	Lemaster, Joseph	20	463	1–20–1846	50	Big Paint Cr
‡Johnson	Lemaster, Joseph	42	325	1– 1–1854	29	Low Gap Br
‡Johnson	Lemaster, Joseph	54	208	4–29–1857	326	Cane Br Big Paint
†Johnson	Lemaster, Joseph & Stephen	2	378	4– 6–1857	200	
¶Floyd	Lemaster, Lewis	E-2	221	9– 1–1834	100	Mud Lick Fk
‡Johnson	Lemaster, Lancaster	20	467	1–15–1846	250	None
‡Johnson	Lemaster, Lancaster	32	294	7–28–1848	100	Br Big Paint Cr
‡Johnson	Lemaster, Lancaster	43	148	3–14–1851	125	Wile Cabbin Br
‡Johnson	Lemaster, Lancaster	43	150	3–17–1851	150	Paint Cr
‡Johnson	Lemaster, Thomas	68	126	1– 3–1866	40	bet Paint & Mud Lick
‡Johnson	Lemaster, William	22	236	12– 4–1846	175	Laurel Fk Cr
‡Johnson	Lemaster, William	32	214	7– 6–1848	500	L H Fk Lower Laurel Cr
‡Johnson	Lemaster, William	46	214	11–24–1855	125	Mud Lick Cr
†Johnson	Lester, Wm. Jeff	7	514	4– 2–1891	14	
‡Johnson	Lester, Wm. Jefferson	116	197	4– 7–1891	14	Falls Br
#Bourbon	Lewis, George	11	475	4–10–1788	4,434	Big Sandy R
#Bourbon	Lewis, George	11	489	1– 8–1789	500	None
#Bourbon	Lewis, George	15	278	4– 2–1789	15,000	Big Sandy
#Bourbon	Lewis, George	15	277	4– 3–1789	6,091¼	Big Sandy
#Bourbon	Lewis, George	11	508	4–15–1789	1,076	Big Sandy
#Bourbon	Lewis, George	5	214	4–24–1789	12,058¾	Big Sandy
#Bourbon	Lewis, George	11	476	4–27–1789	2,958¼	Big Sandy
#Bourbon	Lewis, George	11	477	4–28–1789	6,250	Big Sandy
#Bourbon	Lewis, George	15	265	4–28–1789	10,141¼	Big Sandy R
#Bourbon	Lewis, George	15	275	4–30–1789	10,000	None
#Bourbon	Lewis, Isaac	15	293	4–25–1789	2,500	Big Sandy
¶Floyd	Lewis, John	D-2	401	9– 9–1834	50	Daniels Cr
†Johnson	Lewis, John C	7	552	9–28– 91	25	
*Res. London	Lewis, Joseph Jr	N	300	1–30–1804	41,185¾	Rolling Fk & Wilsons Cr Big Sandy R
©Fayette	Lewis, Lewis	1	347	1– 2–1783	1,000	Br Sandy
#Bourbon	Lewis, Lunceford	12	376	4–25–1788	3,725	Sandy
‡Floyd	Lewis, Squire	8	345	12– 4–1840	150	Daniels Cr
‡Floyd	Lewis, Squire	8	347	12– 4–1840	100	Daniels Cr
©Fayette	Lewis, William	1	348	1– 2–1783	1,000	Br Sandy
‡Johnson	Lilly, Wm. & Henry	37	74	9–19–1849	375	Buffalo Cr
¶Floyd	Lilliards, John	W	357	3–12–1828	100	Buffalo Cr
‡Johnson	Linch, Robert	96	44	9–11–1875	30	Bobs Br
‡Johnson	Linch, Robert	96	61	9–17–1875	50	Bobs Br
¶Floyd	Litteral, George	L-2	385	1–19–1837	200	Bobs Br
‡Johnson	Litteral, George	35	505	2–17–1850	190	Bobs Br
‡Johnson	Litteral, George M	63	147	8–14–1862	50	Bobs Br
†Johnson	Litteral, George W	3	192	3– 4–1861	50	
‡Johnson	Litteral, John	20	466	6–16–1846	200	Pigeon Cr
‡Johnson	Litteral, John	20	464	6–17–1846	50	Hargus Cr
‡Johnson	Litteral, John	20	465	6–17–1846	50	Rolling Rockhouse Br
‡Johnson	Litteral, John	51	263	4– 1–1857	35	Paint Cr
†Johnson	Litteral, John	2	389	6– 1–1857	25	
‡Johnson	Litteral, J. F	99	253	6–12–1880	74	Oil Springs Fk
‡Johnson	Litteral, J. W	100	20	9– 6–1880	13	Oil Springs Fk
‡Johnson	Litteral, Hanston	59	353	4– 3–1857	600	Dry Br
‡Johnson	Litteral, Harston	68	377	3– 6–1866	1,100	Oil Fk Paint Cr
‡Johnson	Litteral, Harston	66	79	1–19–1864	457	Hargas Cr
¶Floyd	Litteral, Horiston	1–2	100	3–30–1836	100	Barnetts Cr
¶Floyd	Litteral, Houston	D-2	389	7–18–1834	50	Oil Springs Fk
†Johnson	Litteral, Houston	3	124	4– 2–1860	200	
†Johnson	Litteral, Houston	3	124	4– 2–1860	100	
‡Johnson	Litteral, Houston	35	504	7–25–1849	400	Hargis Cr
†Johnson	Litteral, Lindsey	3	389	8– 3–1865	150	
‡Johnson	Litteral, Lindsey	68	378	2–14–1866	125	Dry Br Oil Fk
‡Johnson	Litteral, Wiley	66	53	4– 1–1857	300	Paint Cr
†Johnson	Litteral, W. E.	5	406	8–22–1874	100	
*Res. Philadel.	Loinheart, Harmon Jos.	A-2	7	7– 9–1791	368,000	Sandy & Green R
©Fayette	Lunsden, George	4	273	2–15–1786	6,800¾	Sandy
‡Johnson	Luster, Harvey	46	215	3–12–1854	100	Lettyhole Br
‡Johnson	Luster, William	18	13	7– 3–1845	100	Lick Br
‡Johnson	Lyon, James	90	84	3– 5–1872	70	Big Laurel Fk Blain Cr

534 HISTORY OF JOHNSON COUNTY

County	Grantee	Book	Page	Date Survey	Acres	Watercourse
‡Johnson	Lyons, Jesse	18	15	11–28–1845	100	Keetons Fk
‡Johnson	Lyon, John	65	355	1–30–1865	323	Upper Laurel Fk
‡Johnson	Lyons, Lafayette	125	378	10– 3–1921	½	Keetons Fk
⁰Fayette	Lyon, Philip	3	118	12–29–1783	5,217½	N Fk Sandy
⁰Fayette	Lyon, Thomas	3	119	12–29–1783	15,000	Big Sandy R
‡Johnson	Lyons, William	18	16	7– 2–1845	100	Keetons Fk
†Johnson	Lyons, William	3	635	——1858	53	
‡Johnson	Lyons, William	55	287	12– 9–1858	53	Keetons Fk
‡Johnson	Lyons, William	81	248	2–16–1871	86	Keeton Fk Blain Cr
†Floyd	Maddox, George	2	202	10–30–1816	—	
⁰Fayette	Madison, Ambrose	3	37	11–12–1783	6,029½	Sandy Cr
‡Johnson	Mahon, John T	65	329	1–12–1860	160	Pleasant Run
⁰Fayette	Major, Wm. & Lewis	4	257	1–16–1786	1,000	S Fk Sandy
†Johnson	Manard, Marcus	3	344	2–22–1865	200	
‡Johnson	Manard, Marcus	66	77	5– 3–1865	200	White House Cr
‡Johnson	Maner, Dorcus	53	189	6– 9–1857	125	Coldwater Cr
⁰Fayette	Marshall, Charles	4	155	4–20–1785	20,000	Sandy
#Bourbon	Marshall, Charles	11	616	8–14–1787	1,000	Sandy
#Bourbon	Marshall, Charles	12	317	4–17–1787	20,000	Big ——
⁰Fayette	Marshall, Humphrey	1	207	12–20–1782	1,000	Big Sandy R
*Res. Woodford	Marshall, Humphrey	C	326	1–20–1798	145,937½	Rough Cr Ohio, Big Sandy & Licking
#Bourbon	Marshall, James	11	538	4– 1–1788	1,108	Big Sandy
#Bourbon	Marshall, John	11	635	8–17–1787	1,000	Sandy
⁰Fayette	Marshall, John Jr	4	242	12–14–1785	1,000	Sandy (withdrawn)
‡Floyd	Marshall, Johnston	6	269	11–22–1839	100	R H Fk Puncheon Cr
‡Johnson	Marshall, Reuben	35	511	4–11–1849	100	Fk Paint Cr
‡Johnson	Marshall, Reuben	52	471	10–27–1857	400	Paint Cr
†Johnson	Marshall, Reuben	2	409	11– 2–1857	100	
†Johnson	Marshall, Reuben	2	409	11– 2–1857	100	
‡Floyd	Marshall, Reuben Jr	11	37	3– 9–1843	100	Big Paint Cr
⁰Fayette	Marshall, Thomas	13	453	2–12–1786	8,000	S Fk Sandy
#Bourbon	Marshall, Thomas Jr	15	359	4– 3–1788	10,000	Big Sandy
#Bourbon	Marshall, William	11	553	8–17–1787	1,000	Sandy
⁰Fayette	Marshall, William Sr	4	268	2– 6–1786	5,000	Sandy
⁰Fayette	Mason, Richard	3	111	12–27–1783	27,000	S Fk Big Sandy R
⁰Fayette	Mason, Stephen T	4	25	8–31–1784	10,000	Sandy Cr
⁰Fayette	Massie, Nathaniel	3	70	12– 4–1783	2,000	S Fk Sandy
▲Floyd	Maukins, Walter	18	422	12–22–1814	32	Millers Cr
#Fayette	Maury, Abraham	12	267	3–31–1785	20,000	S Fk Sandy R
*Res. ——	Maxwell, William M	W	473	7– 9–1824	500	S Fk Sandy R
‡Johnson	May, Caleb	35	507	7–28–1848	50	Oil Sp Br
‡Johnson	May, Caleb	43	160	3–14–1851	300	Oil Sp
⁰Fayette	May, George	1	2	11–28–1782	40	Sandy Cr
#Bourbon	May, George	5	402	4– 3–1789	31,040½	Big Sandy
#Bourbon	May, George	5	401	4–29–1789	12,176¾	Big Sandy
#Bourbon	May, John	3	515	4–20–1788	25,000	Big Sandy
*Res. Suffolk	May, Joseph	D	84	6–28–1796	7,813	Sandy R
‡Floyd	May, Sam	9	240	12–27–1841	280	Sandy R
†Johnson	Mayes, Henry C	5	620	5–18–1878	25	
▲Floyd	Mayo, Henry B	19	173	4–10–1817	58	Sandy R
¶Floyd	Mayo, Wilson	H-2	406	9–24–1835	90	Wileys Br
⁰Fayette	McCann, Joseph	2	183	2–12–1783	1,338½	Br Big Sandy
‡Johnson	McCarty, John	43	164	8–23–1850	150	Panther Lick Fk
‡Johnson	McCarty, John	68	381	2–12–1866	10	Oil Fk Paint Cr
‡Johnson	McCarty, John	98	422	6–26–1879	18	Oil Sp Fk
‡Johnson	McCloud, Joseph	90	85	11–13–1871	50	Alum Cave Br
⁰Fayette	McCulley, George	3	109	12–27–1783	10,000	Big Sandy R
⁰Fayette	McCulley, George	4	171	5– 3–1785	28,000	Sandy R (surveyed)
‡Johnson	McDole, William R	42	327	3–17–1854	70	Laurel Cr
#Bourbon	McDonald, Eneas	11	481	4–29–1789	250	Big Sandy
‡Johnson	McDowell, James	37	61	2–30–1850	150	Wolf Pen Br
‡Johnson	McDowell, William	32	211	7–25–1848	50	Laurel Fk
†Johnson	McDowell, William	2	168	3– 6–1854	70	
#Bourbon	McGee, Mary & Wm	14	379	5– 1–1787	15,246	Big Sandy
#Bourbon	McGee, Thomas	14	379	5– 1–1787	15,246	Big Sandy
‡Johnson	McGinnis, Hiram	53	13	8–23–1852	200	Sand Lick Br
‡Johnson	McGinnis, Hiram	59	49	7–10–1858	1,618	M Fk Rockcastle Cr
†Johnson	McHenry, Fleming	3	393	8–10–1865	6,000	
‡Johnson	McHenry, Flemon	66	425	4–27–1865	24,600	Br Lick Cr
†Johnson	McKenzie, David	2	143	12– 5–1853	25	
‡Johnson	McKenzie, David	44	450	1– 4–1854	25	Mud Lick Cr
‡Johnson	McKenzie, David	60	530	2–20–1860	583	Peter Cave Paint Cr
†Johnson	McKenzie, David	3	156	10– 1–1860	163	
‡Johnson	McKenzie, Hugh	60	529	6–14–1860	76	Big Paint Cr
‡Johnson	McKinzie, Jackson	58	392	12–16–1857	30	Br Mud Lick
‡Johnson	McKenzie, James H	103	558	8–12–1882	8	Mud Lick
‡Johnson	McKenzie, John	42	326	11– 8–1852	200	Blain Cr
‡Johnson	McKenzie, John	42	328	11– 8–1853	200	Laurel Blain
†Johnson	McKenzie, John	2	143	12– 5–1853	200	
‡Johnson	McKenzie, Joseph	93	47	11–13–1872	118	State Br Mud Lick Cr

APPENDIX 535

County	Grantee	Book	Page	Date Survey	Acres	Watercourse
¶Floyd	McKenzie, Mark	B	43	8– 7–1816	50	Buffalo Cr
†Floyd	McKenzie, Mark	2	179	9–23–1816	—	
‡Johnson	McKenzie, Mary Magdaline	43	520	7–26–1848	50	Laurel Fk
‡Johnson	McKenzie, Newton	32	208	8– 2–1849	100	Mud Lick Cr
‡Johnson	McKenzie, O	53	14	5–21–1856	200	Laurel Br
‡Johnson	McKenzie, Stephen	61	187	12–20–1860	2	Jones Fk
†Johnson	McKenzie, Thomas J.	7	549	9–10– –91	10	
‡Johnson	McKenzie, Thomas J.	2	144	12– 5–1853	200	
‡Johnson	McKenzie, Thomas J.	50	531	3–27–1860	16	Laurel Fk Big Blain
†Johnson	McKenzie, Thomas J.	3	160	10– 1–1860	16	
‡Johnson	McKenzie, William	54	212	1– 3–1853	100	Colston Br
‡Johnson	McKinney, John	61	422	10–23–1860	124	Hog Br
‡Johnson	McKinney, Newton	20	470	1–29–1846	50	None
‡Johnson	Mead, Leash	84	250	11–9–1871	200	Big Fk Pigeon Fk
‡Johnson	Mead, Leash	84	251	11–9–1871	50	Barn Br
‡Johnson	Mead, Mary	68	386	2–13–1866	200	Hargis Cr
‡Johnson	Mead, Noah	105	72	10–25–1882	100	Laurel Fk
†Johnson	Mead, Rhoads	2	183	6–5–1854	60	
‡Johnson	Mead, Rhodes	42	329	5–10–1854	160	Mud Lick
‡Johnson	Meade, Leach	5	138	4– —1871	200	
†Johnson	Meade, Leach Williams, Alex Colvin, Johise Spradlin, James	5	157	10–5–1871	200	
‡Johnson	Meade, Robert	27	2	11–17–1847	100	Color Water Fk
‡Johnson	Meadows, Elisha	106	615	10–5–1883	20	Road Fk
‡Johnson	Meadows, Rebecca	66	32	4–7–1865	185	Lynn Fk Coldwater Cr
‡Johnson	Meek, Elias	97	279	5–8–1875	60	None
‡Johnson	Meek, Elias	3	344	2–22–1865		
‡Johnson	Meek, G. M	5	467	4–26–1875	60	
‡Johnson	Meek, Isaac	11	433	9–16–1843	50	Two-Mile Fk Greasy Cr
¶Floyd	Meek, James	P	174	4–15–1821	50	Big Sandy R
†Johnson	Meek, James	5	467	4–26–1875	60	
‡Johnson	Meek, James	105	505	6–21–1875	25	Bee Br
†Johnson	Meek, N	5	465	4–5–1875	40	
‡Johnson	Meek, Nathaniel	97	136	4–21–1875	46	None
‡Johnson	Meek, William	14	287	12–11–1844	200	Greasy Cr
‡Johnson	Meek, William	20	472	6–20–1846	50	Hurricane
‡Johnson	Meek, William	32	209	4–6–1848	100	Bee Br Greasy Cr
‡Johnson	Meek, William	32	210	4–6–1848	40	Greasy Cr
‡Johnson	Meek, William	35	512	1–29–1851	175	Hurricane Cr
‡Johnson	Meek, William	65	346	3–3–1865	336	Lick Cr
‡Johnson	Meek, Zepheniah	119	103	3–6–1900	96	Dicks Gap
‡Johnson	Miles, John R	44	249	2–6–1854	75	None
¶Floyd	Miller, Edward B	M	123	10–8–1821	100	Georges Cr
#Bourbon	Miller, Jno. & Thos.	19	67	4–2–1788	10,752	Big——
‡Johnson	Miller, Sylvester B	69	299	5–4–1866	12	Whitehouse Cr
#Bourbon	Miller, William	19	69	4–2–1788	1,000	Big Sandy
‡Johnson	Mills, Elias	65	345	3–3–1865	400	Lick Cr
‡Johnson	Mills, John	3	341	2–6–1865	100	
‡Johnson	Mills, John S. H	65	328	3–1–1865	184	Rockhouse Fk
#Bourbon	Mitchell, Robert	1	89	8–20–1787	5,128	Big Sandy
¶Floyd Lawrence	Mobley, Samuel	D-2	335	6–1–1835	200	Hoods Fk
†Johnson	Mollett, Elias	3	10	–1858	50	
†Johnson	Mollett, Hiram	35	508	2–5–1851	125	Coldwater Cr
†Johnson	Mollett, James S	2	232	1–1–1855	200	
†Johnson	Mollett, James S	2	241	2–6–1855	200	
†Johnson	Mollett, James S	2	241	2–6–1855	100	
†Johnson	Mollett, John	2	252	3–5–1855	100	
†Johnson	Mollett, John	2	425	12–7–1857	200	
†Johnson	Mollett, John	2	425	12–7–1857	200	
‡Johnson	Mollett, William E	117	335	9–22–1893	70	L Fk Greasy Cr
⊙Fayette	Montague, Thomas	3	159	1–21–1784	5,000	Fk Sandy R
‡Johnson	Moore, John	53	190	8–12–1857	150	Rockcastle Cr
‡Johnson	Moore, John	2	450	5–3–1858	150	
‡Johnson	Moore, John	65	181	7–14–1858	150	Rockhouse Fk
‡Johnson	Moore, William	53	188	6–5–1857	100	Rockhouse Cr
⊙Fayette	Mordico, Joseph	4	271	2–13–1786	200	Big Sandy
¶Floyd	Morgan, Annie & David	E	229	3–35–1819	50	Wileys Br
■Floyd	Morgan, David	P	313	2–16–1808	—	(Contract)
▲Floyd	Morgan, David	18	131–9	2–21–1810	990	Sandy
*	Morgan, Ephriam	E	233	3–5–1796	27,018	Sandy R
⊙Fayette	Morgan, Ralph	3	68	12–1–1783	903¾	Br S Fk Sandy
▲Morgan	Morgan Co. Seminary.	20	47	8–16–1824	125	Laurel Cr
‡Johnson	Morris, L. H	46	217	11–10–1853	25	None
⊙Fayette	Morton, Benjamin	2	193	2–14–1783	2,975½	Big Sandy
⊙Fayette	Mosby, John	1	140	12–14–1782	1,000	Big Sandy

536 HISTORY OF JOHNSON COUNTY

County	Grantee	Book	Page	Date Survey	Acres	Watercourse
‡Bourbon	Mountjoy, Edmund	12	394	1-1-1787	1,000	Big Sandy
‡Bourbon	Mountjoy, John	11	521	4-28-1789	6,250	Big Sandy
‡Johnson	Mullett, David	37	77	2-27-1850	150	Wooten Br
‡Johnson	Mullett, David	53	165	10-14-1857	80	Stone Coal Br
‡Johnson	Mullett, David	65	340	2-2-1865	380	Staffords Fk
‡Johnson	Mullett, Elias	20	471	8-21-1846	50	Greasy Cr
‡Johnson	Mullett, Elias	43	521	3-31-1853	100	L H Fk Greasy Cr
‡Johnson	Mullett, Elias	58	367	8-20-1858	40	L H Fk Greasy Cr
‡Johnson	Mullett, Elias & Susannah	43	522	8-21-1846	50	L H Fk Greasy Cr
‡Johnson	Mullett, Hiram	22	234	10-7-1846	100	Walnut Fk
‡Johnson	Mullett, J. S.	22	235	10-9-1846	100	Rockhouse Fk
‡Johnson	Mullett, James S.	37	78	3-2-1850	50	Rockhouse Br
‡Johnson	Mullett, James S.	37	79	3-2-1850	50	Rockhouse Br
‡Johnson	Mullett, James S.	44	148	1-15-1855	200	None
‡Johnson	Mullett, James S.	46	39	1-15-1855	300	Rockhouse Fk
‡Johnson	Mullett, James S.	44	147	1-18-1855	200	None
‡Johnson	Mullett, James S.	54	214	12-15-1856	200	Wild Cat Br
‡Johnson	Mullett, John	37	75	3-1-1850	200	Prices Br
‡Johnson	Mullett, John	37	76	3-1-1850	125	Rockhouse Fk
‡Johnson	Mullett, John	49	325	11-2-1855	100	Rockhouse Cr
‡Johnson	Mullett, John	53	166	10-10-1857	400	Staffords Fk
‡Johnson	Mullett, John	65	344	2-21-1865	617	Staffords Fk
‡Johnson	Murry, George W.	35	509	2-10-1851	75	Cold Water Cr
‡Johnson	Murry, George W.	53	164	10-12-1857	125	Coldwater Cr
‡Johnson	Murry, George W.	2	441	3-1-1858	125	
‡Johnson	Murry, Jane	72	216	4-19-1867	84	Hoods Cr
‡Johnson	Murry, Jesse	58	381	1-15-1858	130	Home Br Chestnut Cr
‡Johnson	Murry, R. H.	35	510	3-13-1850	350	Georges Cr
‡Johnson	Murry, Roderick H.	63	266	4-22-1861	180	Georges Cr
§Floyd	Murry, Thomas	(Cert. 59)		11-8-1803	400	Levisa Fk
†Johnson	Music, Andrew	2	444	4-1-1858	100	
‡Johnson	Music, Andrew	58	380	7-14-1858	20	Rockcastle Cr
‡Johnson	Music, Andrew	59	45	7-14-1858	125	M Fk Rockcastle Cr
‡Johnson	Music, Andrew	3	—	1860	60	
‡Johnson	Music, Andrew	3	313	2-6-1860	60	
‡Johnson	Musick, Andy	53	12	4-15-1854	130	Sand Lick Br
‡Johnson	Musick, James	2	104	6-6-1853	100	
‡Johnson	Musick, James	46	216	7-3-1854	170	None
‡Johnson	Musick, James	97	544	7-20-1854	96	Mullens Cr (Millers Cr?)
‡Johnson	Music, John	98	352	3-16-1876	50	Millers Cr
⊕Fayette	Myers, Jacob	4	36	9-18-1784	5,000	Sandy Cr
#Bourbon	Myers, Phillip	11	398	11-25-1787	4,091	Sandy
*	Myers, Samuel	D	222	2-15-1799	5,700	Sandy R
‡Johnson	Nelson, W. P.	56	465	4-8-1859	14	Big Paint Cr
⊕Fayette	Neth, Lewis	4	155	4-20-1785	20,000	Sandy
¶Floyd	Newcome, John	T	100	9-22-1824	50	Tom's Cr
‡Johnson	Nibert, James	43	528	2-26-1850	12	Sandy R
‡Johnson	Nibert, James	70	467	11-21-1853	525	Big Sandy
‡Johnson	Nickell, A. A.	53	15	3-25-1855	3	Blain Cr
‡Johnson	Nickell, Albert	109	101	2-28-1887	2¾	Franks Cr
‡Johnson	Nickell, Alexander	32	227	8-2-1848	350	Fk Lower Laurel Fk
†Johnson	Nickell, Alexander	2	144	12-5-1853	75	
†Johnson	Nickell, Alexander W.	2	364	2-2-1857	50	
‡Johnson	Nickels, A. W.	42	330	11-23-1853	75	None
‡Johnson	Nickell, Alex. W.	2	445	4-1-1858	3	
*Res. Philadel.	Nicholson, John	D	199	11-21-1794	47,056¾	Big Sandy R
¶Floyd	Nix, Elisha	D-2	405	2-9-1835	300	Tom's Cr
‡Floyd	Nott, Arbeth A	8	340	7-31-1840	75	Tom's Cr
¶Floyd	O'Bryant, James	T	110	9-16-1824	50	Br Big Paint Lick Cr
⁎Lawrence	O'Brian, James	H-2	222	9-3-1835	100	Lower Laurel Fk
¶Floyd	Ogle, James	Q	71	9-16-1824	50	Paint Lick Cr
#Bourbon	O'Mealy, Michael	14	392	3-19-1788	30,000	Louvisa Fk Sandy
#Bourbon	O'Mealy, Michael	14	393	3-19-1788	5,000	Fks Main Sandy R
#Bourbon	O'Mealy, Michael	14	394	3-19-1788	5,000	Fks Main Sandy
#Bourbon	O'Mealy, Michael	14	395	3-19-1788	5,000	Fks Main Sandy
#Bourbon	O'Mealy, Michael	14	396	3-19-1788	30,000	Louvisa Fk Sandy
#Bourbon	O'Mealy, Michael	14	584	3-20-1788	5,000	M Fks Main Sandy
#Bourbon	O'Mealy, Michael	14	586	3-19-1788	5,000	M Fks Main Sandy
#Bourbon	O'Mealy, Michael	14	587	3-19-1788	5,000	M Fk Sandy & Louvisa
#Bourbon	O'Mealy, Michael	14	588	3-19-1788	5,000	M Fk Sandy & Louvisa
#Bourbon	O'Mealy, Michael	14	589	3-19-1788	5,000	M Fk Sandy & Louvisa
*Res. Philadel.	Orr, Benjamin G.	B	149	8-20-1796	82,235	Big Sandy R
‡Johnson	Osborn, Andrew	18	21	7-4-1845	75	Mud Lick
‡Johnson	Osborne, Calvin	35	486	1-17-1851	50	Buffalo Cr
¶Floyd	Osborne, Edmond	G-2	80	10-16-1835	100	Stone Coal Fk
‡Johnson	Osborne, Edward	52	472	12-17-1857	180	Mill Lick Fk
†Johnson	Osborne, Edwin	2	432	2-1-1858	100	

APPENDIX 537

County	Grantee	Book	Page	Date Survey	Acres	Watercourse
¶Floyd	Osborne, Jesse	A	478	9–7–1816	50	Mud Lick Fk
¶Floyd	Osborne, Jesse	V	302	5–8–1827	50	Fks Paint Cr
¶Floyd	Osborne, Jesse	V	302	6–20–1827	50	Fk Paint Lick Cr
¶Floyd	Osborne, Jesse	D-2	388	9–3–1834	100	Mud Lick Cr
¶Floyd	Osborne, Jesse	G-2	78	10–16–1835	200	Mud Lick Fk
‡Johnson	Osborne, Jesse	18	20	7–4–1845	50	Mud Lick Cr
¶Floyd	Osborne, Jonathan	G-2	79	10–16–1835	100	R Fk Mud Lcik Fk
⊙Fayette	Overton, Joseph Sr	4	272	2–15–1786	3,000	Big Sandy
⊙Fayette	Owings, John C	2	307	6–6–1783	1,000	W Fk Sandy
†Johnson	Pack, Bartley	2	313	2–4–1856	50	
‡Johnson	Pack, Bartley	5	453	2–12–1875	20	
‡Johnson	Pack, Bartley	97	135	2–19–1875	638	Greasy Cr
†Johnson	Pack, Bartley	5	466	4–20–1875	77	
‡Johnson	Pack, Berry	35	484	———	100	Hurricane Cr
‡Johnson	Pack, Berry	65	327	3–4–1865	224	Hurricane
‡Johnson	Pack, Charles	62	210	6–14–1861	235	Meadow Br
‡Johnson	Pack, Charles	76	208	12–4–1868	20	Greens Br
¶Floyd	Pack, William	Q-2	493	3–4–1835	100	Bakers Br
¶Floyd	Pack, William	L-2	398	5–31–1837	800	Tom's Cr
⊙Fayette	Page, William	2	37	1–11–1783	1,046	Sandy
♯Bourbon	Pallard, John	5	191	1–5–1787	2,499¾	Big Sandy
⊙Fayette	Parks, Ezekiel	4	243	12–17–1785	400	S Fk Sandy
‡Johnson	Patrick, Abby	68	386	2–13–1866	200	Hargis Cr
‡Johnson	Patrick, Alexander	84	252	11–8–1871	150	Oil Sp Fk
‡Johnson	Patrick, Gilson P	43	534	3–25–1851	150	Jennys Cr
†Johnson	Patrick, J. F	—	—	———	50	
‡Johnson	Patrick, J. F	53	28	4–14–1855	325	None
¶Floyd	Patrick, Jacob F	8	339	6–22–1839	50	N Lick Fk Jennys Cr
‡Johnson	Patrick, J. P	53	29	4–14–1856	214	Jennies Cr
†Johnson	Patrick, J. P	—	402	9–——1865	50	
†Johnson	Patrick, Jilson P	2	411	11–2–1857	150	
‡Johnson	Patrick, Jilson P	54	210	4–14–1858	150	Jennies Cr
‡Johnson	Patrick, Jilson P	54	209	4–15–1858	16	Ginnis Cr
‡Johnson	Patrick, Jilson P	67	131	9–12–1865	100	Green Rock Fk
‡Johnson	Patterson & Step	53	202	3–22–1856	160	Alums Br
⊙Fayette	Patterson, Thomas	4	261	1–18–1786	1,000	S Fk Sandy
⊙Fayette	Paulin, Henry T	4	241	12–13–1785	681	S Fk Sandy
¶Floyd	Pelfrey, Alexander	V	304	8–12–1827	50	Big Paint Lick Cr
†Johnson	Pelfrey, Daniel	2	388	6–1–1857	20	
‡Johnson	Pelfrey, Daniel	53	192	5–5–1857	25	Barnetts Cr
‡Johnson	Pelfrey, Daniel	53	193	5–18–1857	10	Barnetts Cr
†Johnson	Pelfrey, Daniel	2	450	5–3–1858	25	
‡Johnson	Pelfrey, Daniel	72	217	10–17–1867	118	Asa Fk
‡Johnson	Pelfrey, Daniel	90	86	11–14–1871	32	Alum Cave Br
‡Johnson	Pelfrey, Daniel	5	202	3–14–1872	62	
‡Johnson	Pelfrey, Isaac	68	129	11–23–1865	20	Oil Sp Br
‡Johnson	Pelfrey, James	18	4	2–21–1845	100	Big Paint Cr
‡Johnson	Pelfrey, James	32	228	8–9–1848	289	Big Paint Cr
‡Johnson	Pelfrey, James	68	128	1–3–1866	3½	Mill Br
‡Johnson	Pelfrey, James M	90	87	11–14–1871	16	Alum Cave Br
‡Johnson	Pelfrey, Stephen	20	473	1–19–1846	225	Big Paint Cr
‡Johnson	Pelfrey, Stephen	43	556	3–13–1851	25	Bear Br
‡Johnson	Pelfrey, Stephen	58	357	5–19–1856	50	Big Paint
‡Johnson	Pelfrey, Stephen	60	534	8–31–1860	2	S s Big Paint Cr
‡Johnson	Pelfrey, Stephen	60	532	9–27–1860	20	Big Paint Cr
‡Johnson	Pelfrey, William	46	42	5–2–1854	100	Mud Lick Cr
‡Johnson	Pelfrey, William A	68	127	1–3–1866	4½	Mill Br
¶Floyd	Penix, Henry	1–2	321	3–25–1836	50	None
†Johnson	Penix, William Mrs	2	302	12–3–1855	65	
‡Johnson	Pennington, Levi	61	186	8–31–1860	28	Low Gap Br
‡Johnson	Pennington, Levi	68	380	2–12–1866	15	Oil Fk Paint Cr
‡Johnson	Pennington, Levi	68	381	2–12–1866	10	Oil Fk Paint Cr
‡Johnson	Pennington, Levi, Wm. & Clabourn	66	80	4–19–1865	27	Oil Fk Paint Cr
⊙Fayette	Penticost, Dorsey	3	426	8–14–1784	4,000	Sandy
*Res. Garrard	Perkins, Benjamin	D	506	9–12–1799	563	Sandy Cr
‡Johnson	Perry, G. W	97	450	9–9–1875	40	Hurricane Cr
†Johnson	Perry, G. W	5	590	10–16–1877	40	
⊙Fayette	Phillips, John	4	169	4–30–1785	30,000	S Fk Sandy R
*Res. Phila	Phillips, John	H	125	11–19–1796	31,520	Big Sandy R
¶Floyd	Phillips, William	V	305	9–8–1824	100	M Fk Jennys Cr
†Johnson	Picklesimer, David	5	618	5–8–1878	90	
‡Johnson	Pinner, Sarah	48	328	3–3–1855	110	Tom's Cr
*Res. Island St. Domingo	Plique, G	H	382	8–8–1787	10,000	S Fk Sandy R
♯Bourbon	Poge, William	12	337	1–4–1787	1,046	Big Sandy
*———	Pogue, Robert	K	363	7–24–1806	213,866	Br Sandy R
¶Floyd	Polfrey, Daniel	M	79	1–8–1823	50	Paint Lick Cr
*Res. Va	Polland, Robert	X	312	10–22–1827	50,050	Cumb & Sandy R & Tygarts Cr

HISTORY OF JOHNSON COUNTY

County	Grantee	Book	Page	Date Survey	Acres	Watercourse
‡Johnson	Porter, Benjamin	22	245	10-9-1846	50	Rockhouse Fk
‡Johnson	Porter, Benjamin	37	62	3-2-1850	200	Rockhouse Fk
‡Johnson	Porter, Benjamin	43	174	2-11-1851	100	Rockcastle Cr
‡Johnson	Porter, Benjamin	46	41	4-10-1855	200	None
‡Johnson	Porter, Benjamin	49	326	2-13-1857	200	Coldwater Br
‡Johnson	Porter, Benjamin	49	327	2-13-1857	200	Lynn Bark Br
†Johnson	Porter, Benjamin	2	371	3-2-1857	200	
†Johnson	Porter, Benjamin	2	371	3-2-1857	200	
†Johnson	Porter, Benjamin	2	371	3-2-1857	25	
‡Johnson	Porter, Benjamin Jr	58	347	8-13-1857	25	M Fk Rockcastle
‡Johnson	Porter, Benj. P	43	523	4-1-1853	250	Rockhouse Fk
†Johnson	Porter, Benj. P	2	231	1-1-1855	200	
†Johnson	Porter, Benj. P	2	247	2-17-1855	200	
†Johnson	Porter, Benj. P	2	247	2-17-1855	125	
†Johnson	Porter, Benj. P	3	57	10-1-1860	100	
†Johnson	Porter, Benj. P	3	168	10-17-1860	200	
‡Johnson	Porter, Benj. P	63	267	2-7-1861	725	Trade Fk Rockhouse Fk
‡Johnson	Porter, Benj. P	63	268	2-28-1861	150	Trace Br
†Johnson	Porter, Benj. P	3	220	9-2-1861	200	
†Johnson	Porter, Benj. P	3	220	9-2-1861	121	
‡Johnson	Porter, Benj. P	65	353	2-25-1865	827	Rockhouse Fk
‡Johnson	Porter, B. T	44	149	1-17-1855	200	Rockhouse Fk
‡Johnson	Porter, B. T	44	150	1-17-1855	100	None
‡Johnson	Porter, C. H	35	480	9-5-1851	100	Daniels Cr
‡Johnson	Porter, John	27	83	9-14-1847	100	Johns Cr
‡Johnson	Porter, John	68	244	2-23-1856	60	L H Fk Daniels Cr
‡Johnson	Porter, Joseph	46	44	12-14-1855	180	None
‡Johnson	Porter, Joseph	58	370	3-27-1858	275	Rockcastle
†Johnson	Porter, Joseph	2	268	5-13-1855	200	
†Johnson	Porter, Joseph	2	268	5-13-1855	200	
‡Johnson	Porter, Joseph	46	40	12-14-1855	200	None
‡Johnson	Porter, Joseph	46	43	12-14-1855	175	None
‡Johnson	Porter, Kennedy	58	376	1-17-1855	150	Rockhouse Fk
Floyd	Porter, Samuel	1-2	121	12-7-1833	50	Millers Cr
¶Floyd	Porter, Samuel	1-2	118	4-23-1834	100	Millers Cr
‡Johnson	Porter, Samuel	33	136	11-2-1850	25½	Big Sandy R
‡Johnson	Porter, Samuel	58	364	1-11-1855	125	R H Fk Wind Br
†Johnson	Porter, Samuel	2	259	4-2-1855	50	
‡Johnson	Porter, Samuel	58	350	3-26-1858	50	Rockcastle
‡Johnson	Porter, Samuel Jr	47	107	4-24-1855	50	R H Fk Wind Cr
¶Floyd	Porter, William	V	428	6-5-1828	50	Daniels Cr
‡Floyd	Porter, William G	8	360	8-26-1840	200	Millers Cr
‡Johnson	Porter, William G	11	52	8-30-1843	50	Daniels Cr
‡Floyd	Power, Holloway	8	273	8-25-1840	50	Licking R
‡Johnson	Pratt, B. F	7	44	8-19-1884	49	Jennies Cr
†Johnson	Pratt, B. F	7	44	2-21-1885	24	
‡Johnson	Pratt, Benjamin F	107	446	3-6-1885	25	Jennies Cr
‡Johnson	Preece, Alex	22	444	10-7-1846	100	Coldwater Cr
‡Johnson	Preece, Alex	22	246	10-7-1846	50	Cold Water Fk
‡Johnson	Preece, Alex B	53	16	— —	100	Coldwater Cr
‡Johnson	Preece, Alex.	53	17	6-4-1854	350	Coldwater Cr
‡Johnson	Preece, Alex. B	53	18	6-8-1857	140	Coldwater Cr
‡Johnson	Preece, Cornelius	43	516	2-5-1851	100	Walnut Fk
†Johnson	Preece, Cornelius W	2	441	3-1-1858	40	
‡Johnson	Preece, Cornelius W	66	33	4-10-1865	235	Walnut Fk Rockcastle
‡Johnson	Preece, Cornelius W	66	34	4-10-1865	350	Old Road Fk Coldwater Fk
‡Johnson	Preece, C. W	53	20	6-4-1857	100	Road Br
‡Johnson	Preece, C. W	53	21	6-10-1857	250	Coldwater Cr
‡Johnson	Preece, C. W	53	167	10-19-1857	25	Coldwater Cr
‡Johnson	Preece, Henry H	66	455	5-1-1865	975	Coldwater Fk
‡Johnson	Preece, William	35	482	2-5-1851	50	Mollett Br
‡Johnson	Preece, William B	53	19	6-8-1857	150	Coldwater Cr
‡Johnson	Preece, William B	59	42	10-13-1857	140	Lynn Br
¶Lawrence	Preston, Arthur	P-2	94	5-14-1840	50	Big Sandy R
†Johnson	Preston, Atchison	7	116	12-12-1885	10	
†Johnson	Preston, Atchison	7	140	4-2-1886	40	
‡Johnson	Preston, Atchison	109	105	4-3-1886	50	None
¶Lawrence	Preston, E	O-2	480	4-16-1840	200	Hoods Fk
¶Lawrence	Preston, E	O-2	481	4-16-1840	200	Hoods Fk
†Johnson	Preston, E. E	4	395	10-14-1868	—	
‡Johnson	Preston, Eliphas	18	8	4-5-1845	150	Big Laurel Cr
‡Johnson	Preston, Eliphas	5	459	3-1-1875	20	
‡Johnson	Preston, Eliphas Jr	32	229	10-27-1847	50	Lower Rd Br
‡Johnson	Preston, Eliphas Sr	32	309	11-10-1848	50	Bakers Br
‡Johnson	Preston, Frank	106	319	10-31-1883	7	Roberts Br & L H Fk Muddy Br
‡Johnson	Preston, James	14	289	4-13-1844	150	Two-Mile Br
‡Johnson	Preston, James	20	474	8-20-1846	50	Greasy Cr
†Johnson	Preston, James C	7	66	5-26-1885	125	

APPENDIX

County	Grantee	Book	Page	Date Survey	Acres	Watercourse
‡Johnson	Preston, James C	108	1	5–26–1885	100	Buffalo Cr
‡Johnson	Preston, James M	105	320	4– 5–1883	4	Tom's Cr
†Johnson	Preston, James W	4	158	11– 7–1866	26	
‡Johnson	Preston, J. W. & A	35	481	10– 6–1849	75	Two-Mile Cr
¶Floyd	Preston, Moses	G	295	6–25–1819	50	Sandy R
‡Floyd	Preston, Moses	66	126	1– 7–1835	50	Bobs Br
¶Floyd	Preston, Moses	1-2	328	1–13–1836	50	Br Greasy Cr
¶Floyd	Preston, Moses	O-2	163	10–18–1838	100	R Fk Calen
¶Floyd	Preston, Moses	O-2	431	9– 6–1841	100	Sandy R
†Johnson	Preston, Moses	2	392	6– 1–1857	200	
†Johnson	Preston, Moses	2	392	6– 1–1857	100	
‡Johnson	Preston, Moses	51	266	6–17–1857	300	Big Sandy R
‡Johnson	Preston, Moses	51	265	8–14–1857	25	Muddy Br
†Johnson	Preston, Moses	2	440	3– 1–1858	50	
¶Lawrence	Preston, Moses Jr	S	19	3–20–1825	50	Louisa Fk Sandy
†Johnson	Preston, Moses Sr	2	253	3– 5–1855	25	
§Floyd	Preston, Nathan	(Cert.No.110)		9– 3–1804	400	Levisa Fk
‡Johnson	Preston, Nathan	3	176	1– 7–1861	200	
‡Johnson	Preston, Nathen	61	425	1–21–1865	331	L H Fk Tom's Cr
‡Johnson	Preston, Nathan	107	470	4– 9–1885	3	None
¶Floyd	Preston, Shadrach	H-2	411	6– 1–1832	100	Pilot Knob
‡Johnson	Preston, Shadrach	32	230	11–28–1848	50	Hannah Br
¶Floyd	Preston, Stephen	M	116	2– 9–1822	50	None
†Johnson	Preston, Wallace W	5	508	2– 7–1876	50	
‡Johnson	Preston, W. W.	97	70	2– 9–1877	71	Buzzard Rest Br
‡Johnson	Preston, William	67	130	9–18–1865	86	Bobs Br Sandy R
†Johnson	Preston, William	4	450	3– 1–1869	50	
‡Johnson	Preston, William	90	88	3– 8–1869	50	Shoal Br Sandy R
‡Johnson	Preston, William	96	42	9–17–1875	40	Shoal Br
‡Johnson	Preston, William	96	43	9–15–1875	57	R H Fk Bobs Br
‡Johnson	Preston & Castle	35	485	11–28–1848	200	Road Br
†Johnson	Preston, & Grim	53	191	4– 9–1856	36	Tom's Cr
‡Johnson	Preston & Hylton	42	331	5–28–1853	25	Bakers Br
‡Johnson	Price, A. J.	35	483	1–17–1851	200	Buffalo Cr
†Johnson	Price, Andrew J	2	241	2– 5–1855	25	
‡Johnson	Price, Andrew J	47	106	2–23–1856	25	Stone Coal Fk Buffalo Cr
‡Johnson	Price, Andrew J	64	62	4–13–1863	40	Buffalo Cr
†Johnson	Price, Andrew J	3	270	6– 1–1863	40	
*Floyd	Price, Buel	18	411	11–23–1814	122	Johns Cr
¶Lawrence	Price, Edmon	N	214	9–12–1822	50	Sandy R
‡Johnson	Price, Hamilton	66	81	4–20–1865	145	Pigeon Cr
†Johnson	Price, Hamilton	5	139	9–29–1871	150	
†Johnson	Price, Hamilton	5	139	9–29–1871	200	
†Johnson	Price, Hamilton	5	158	10– 5–1871	125	
‡Johnson	Price, Hamilton	84	254	11– 7–1871	280	Oil Sp Fk
‡Johnson	Price, Hamilton	84	253	11– 8–1871	90	Oil Sp Fk Paint Cr
‡Johnson	Price, James	107	555	4–22–1885	4	Jennies Cr
‡Johnson	Price, James	107	556	4–22–1885	3	Jennies Cr
‡Johnson	Price, James M	7	56	4–21–1885	7	
¶Floyd	Price, Jesse	G	301	6– 4–1819	50	Prices Lick Br
¶Lawrence	Price, Jesse	J	459	8–26–1822	50	Fk Big Sandy R
¶Lawrence	Price, Jesse	L	485	9– 7–1822	50	Nats Cr
¶Lawrence	Price, Jesse	R	484	10– 2–1824	100	Br Nats Cr
¶Lawrence	Price, Jesse	D-2	329	11–13–1830	50	Lick Br
¶Lawrence	Price, Jesse	A-2	459	7– 2–1831	100	Louisa Fk Big Sandy
¶Lawrence	Price, Jesse	A-2	178	7–13–1831	50	Nats Cr
‡Johnson	Price, Jesse	18	6	1–30–1845	250	Buffalo Cr
‡Johnson	Price, Jesse	18	7	1–30–1845	100	Buffalo
‡Johnson	Price, Jesse	27	84	7– 1–1847	100	Buffalo Cr
‡Johnson	Price, Jessen	18	5	2–18–1845	50	Big Sandy R
⊙Fayette	Price, John	3	422	8– 5–1784	8,000	Large S Fk Sandy
†Johnson	Price, Kingston	4	395	10–14–1868	100	
¶Lawrence	Price, Richard	D-2	324	1– 2–1830	50	Louisa Fk
¶Lawrence	Price, Richard	A-2	469	7–18–1831	50	Nats Cr
¶Lawrence	Price, Richard	D-2	325	8–15–1832	50	Nats Cr
¶Lawrence	Price, Richard	D-2	323	2–17–1833	50	Nats Cr
‡Johnson	Price, Thomas J	97	305	2–12–1875	54	Sandy R
¶Floyd	Price and Borders	1-2	275	6–16–1836	100	Tom's Cr
¶Floyd	Price and Borders	1-2	305	6– 2–1836	100	Tom's Cr
†Johnson	Priest, William	3	—	— –1860	50	
†Johnson	Priest, William	3	313	2– 6–1860	100	
‡Johnson	Prince, Eveline	68	386	2–13–1866	200	Harges Cr
‡Johnson	Prince, Susanah	64	442	12– 2–1863	37	Upper Laurel Fk Big Blain Cr
†Johnson	P'Simer John	2	144	12– 5–1853	50	
†Johnson	P'Simer, N. P.	4	145	11– 7–1866	50	
#Bourbon	Quarrier, Alex	15	284	4– 6–1788	9,000	Big Sandy
¶Floyd	Ramey, Charles	1-2	256	12–29–1835	300	Big Paint Cr
¶Floyd	Ramey, Daniel	P	178	3–11–1822	50	Fk Big Paint Lick Cr
¶Floyd	Ramey, Daniel	1-2	270	11–16–1836	100	Mud Lick Fk

County	Grantee	Book	Page	Date Survey	Acres	Watercourse
†Johnson	Ramey, Daniel	2	176	4–3–1854	50	
‡Johnson	Ramey, Daniel	46	218	12–13–1854	50	Mud Lick Cr
§Floyd	Ramey, John	(Cert. 78)		2–6–1804	100	Louvisa Fk
¶Floyd	Ramey, John	1–2	346	11–5–1836	150	Big Paint Cr
†Johnson	Ramey, Thomas	—	—	7–21–1877	50	
‡Johnson	Ramey, Thomas	103	116	5–25–1882	50	Tom Ramey Br
§Floyd	Ramey, William	(Cert. 140)		8–17–1805	225	Big Paint
‡Johnson	Ramsey, James	53	195	11–27–1854	100	Laurel Cr
†Johnson	Ratliff, Henry	2	165	2–6–1854	50	
▲Floyd	Ratliff, Richard	19	353	4–14–1820	50	Sandy R
¶Floyd	Ratliff, Richard	8	338	11–18–1839	50	Osbourns Fk
‡Johnson	Ratliff, Silas	70	468	3–28–1854	150	Lower Twin Br
‡Johnson	Ratliff, William	90	89	3–14–1872	14	Rockhouse Fk
≠Bourbon	Redish, Joel	15	247	12–30–1787	930	Sandy R
‡Johnson	Reed, A. J.	11	56	10–5–1843	50	Big Paint Cr
‡Johnson	Reed, A. J.	35	478	3–20–1851	525	Paint Cr
¶Floyd	Reed, Asa J.	L-2	344	8–22–1837	100	Lower Salt Peter Cave
‡Johnson	Reed, Daniel W.	66	35	3–27–1865	74	Oil Fk Paint Cr
‡Johnson	Reed, Jason M.	66	35	3–27–1865	74	Oil Fk Paint Cr
≠Fayette	Reed, John	8	576	9–28–1784	6,000	Sandy Cr
‡Johnson	Reed, Thomas	44	250	11–4–1853	48	Big Blain
‡Johnson	Reed, Thomas	2	242	2–6–1855	30	
‡Johnson	Reed, Thomas	66	381	8–2–1865	16	Oil Fk Paint Cr
‡Johnson	Reed, William	32	216	8–11–1848	90	Big Paint Cr
‡Johnson	Reed, William	43	171	3–13–1851	100	Lower Peter Case Br
‡Johnson	Remy, David	20	453	1–20–1846	100	Br Mud Lick Cr
‡Johnson	Remy, John	20	455	1–27–1846	50	Big Br Mud Lick Cr
¶Floyd	Remy, Thomas	V	196	12–1–1824	50	Paint & Barnetts Cr
‡Johnson	Remy, Thomas	20	454	1–28–1846	100	None
¶Floyd	Renney, Charles	T	61	10–20–1824	50	Paint Cr
‡Johnson	Renney, Daniel	55	289	1–5–1859	7½	Mud Lick Fk
¶Floyd	Renney, John	T	69	9–16–1824	100	Big Paint Lick Cr
¶Floyd	Renney, William, Jr.	T	60	10–20–1824	50	Paint Lick Cr
‡Floyd	Reynolds, Hamilton	8	371	3–27–1840	50	Clear Cr
†Johnson	Rice, A. J.	53	23	4–15–1856	100	Jennys Cr
†Johnson	Rice, A. J.	—	—	9–...–1865	166	
–Johnson	Rice, A. J.	3	398	9–...–1865	—	
†Johnson	Rice, Andrew J.	2	409	11–2–1857	200	
†Johnson	Rice, Andrew J.	2	409	11–2–1857	200	
†Johnson	Rice, Andrew J.	2	409	11–2–1857	100	
‡Johnson	Rice, Andrew J.	67	132	9–12–1865	246	Green Rock Fk
‡Johnson	Rice, Andrew J.	67	133	9–11–1865	100	L Fk Jennies Cr
‡Johnson	Rice, B. F. & H.	120	121	10–23–1902	150	Narrow Fk Jennies Cr
‡Johnson	Rice, B. F. & H.	120	122	10–23–1902	4	Sunrise Br
‡Johnson	Rice, B. F. & H.	120	123	10–23–1902	12	Narrow Fk Jennies Cr
†Johnson	Rice, C. C.	7	9	11–1–1884	6	
‡Johnson	Rice, Charles C.	107	447	4–18–1885	6	None
‡Johnson	Rice, Harrison	7	56	4–17–1885	90	
‡Johnson	Rice, Harrison	107	550	4–18–1885	72	Jennies Cr
‡Johnson	Rice, Harrison	107	551	4–18–1885	18	Jennies Cr
¶Floyd	Rice, Isaac	P-2	163	3–7–1843	50	Lick Fk
¶Floyd	Rice, Jackson	18	9	7–8–1845	100	Jennies Cr
‡Johnson	Rice, Jackson	22	243	10–23–1846	100	None
‡Johnson	Rice, Jackson	43	546	3–25–1851	50	Upper Narrows Br
¶Floyd	Rice, John	G	297	2–5–1820	100	Jennies Cr
¶Floyd	Rice, John	D-2	374	5–11–1831	50	Jennings Cr
¶Floyd	Rice, John	E-2	214	9–27–1834	50	Licking R
¶Floyd	Rice, John	L-2	362	12–15–1836	100	R Fk Jennies Cr
¶Floyd	Rice, John	10	18	2–5–1842	100	Long Fk Jaynes Cr
†Johnson	Rice, John	32	212	7–6–1848	50	Hoods Fk
†Johnson	Rice, John	2	224	12–4–1854	100	
‡Johnson	Rice, John	55	337	11–4–1858	9	Hoods Fk Big Blain Cr
‡Johnson	Rice, John	55	338	11–4–1858	5	Hoods Fk
†Johnson	Rice, John J.	7	52	4–6–1885	67	
‡Johnson	Rice, John J.	107	417	4–10–1885	67	Barnetts Cr
¶Floyd	Rice, Martin	A-2	255	8–5–1831	125	Jennies Cr
¶Floyd	Rice, Martin	L-2	366	12–5–1836	50	Jennies Cr
‡Johnson	Rice, Martin	10	52	2–6–1842	100	Jines Cr
¶Floyd	Rice, Martin	10	17	2–7–1842	500	Jaynes Cr
‡Johnson	Rice, Martin	18	12	2–12–1845	50	Jennys Cr
‡Johnson	Rice, Martin	43	533	3–25–1851	200	Green Rock Fk
‡Johnson	Rice, Martin	53	26	4–4–1855	150	Jennys Cr
†Johnson	Rice, Martin	2	444	4–1–1858	100	
‡Johnson	Rice, Martin B.	43	157	3–26–1851	300	Jennies Cr
¶Floyd	Rice, Martin M.	1–2	285	3–25–1836	100	Holts Br
†Johnson	Rice, Martin M.	2	222	12–4–1854	200	
‡Johnson	Rice, M. M.	44	453	3–27–1851	250	Halt Br
‡Johnson	Rice, M. M.	44	454	3–27–1851	200	Halt Br
‡Johnson	Rice, Martin R.	48	101	3–26–1851	30	Old Orchard Br
‡Johnson	Rice, Martin R.	53	196	4–18–1856	200	Jennies Cr
†Johnson	Rice, Martin R.	2	394	7–6–1857	200	

APPENDIX 541

County	Grantee	Book	Page	Date Survey	Acres	Watercourse
†Johnson	Rice, Martin R	2	394	7– 6–1857	100	
†Johnson	Rice, Martin R	2	409	11– 2–1857	200	
‡Johnson	Rice, Martin R	58	368	8–15–1858	25	Br Big Sandy
‡Johnson	Rice, Martin R	53	197	10–28–1858	100	Jennies Cr
‡Johnson	Rice, Martin R	69	301	4–17–1866	70	R H Fk Jennies Cr
‡Johnson	Rice, Martin R	71	8	2–20–1867	70	Green Rock Br
‡Johnson	Rice, Martin R	81	252	3– 9–1871	30	Jennies Cr
¶Johnson	Rice, Nancy	Q-2	120	2–27–1845	150	Jennies Cr
‡Johnson	Rice, Nancy	53	24	4–16–1856	133	None
‡Johnson	Rice, Patrick G	112	505	12– 2–1889	200	M Fk Jennies Cr
¶Floyd	Rice, Samuel	1	397	11–22–1820	50	Jennies Cr
¶Floyd	Rice, Samuel	W	348	4– 1–1828	50	Jennys Cr
¶Floyd	Rice, Samuel	L-2	365	12– 2–1836	100	Rockhouse Fk
¶Floyd	Rice, Samuel	L-2	347	11–16–1837	100	Jennies Cr
¶Floyd	Rice, Samuel	O-2	280	11–28–1837	200	Rockhouse Fk
‡Johnson	Rice, Samuel	68	379	3– 2–1866	87	Little Mud Lick
‡Johnson	Rice, Samuel Jr	43	527	3–28–1851	300	Upper Twin Br
‡Johnson	Rice, Samuel Sr	37	80	2– 7–1850	150	Jennys Cr
‡Johnson	Rice, Samuel Sr	37	81	2– 7–1850	150	Jennys Cr
‡Johnson	Rice, Samuel K	58	72	4–24–1855	100	Barnetts Cr
†Johnson	Rice, Wiley	4	186	4–29–1867	200	
†Johnson	Rice, Wiley	4	186	4–29–1867	48	
‡Floyd	Rice, William	4	69	4–11–1837	50	Jennies Cr
‡Floyd	Rice, William	8	376	3– 1–1841	100	Jennies Cr
‡Floyd	Rice, William	8	377	3– 1–1841	100	Jennies Cr
‡Johnson	Rice, William	35	479	8–25–1849	16	Jennies Cr
‡Johnson	Rice, William	46	219	8–25–1854	22	Orchard Br
‡Johnson	Rice, William	53	25	11–10–1854	13	Gunnis Cr
‡Johnson	Richmond, James	43	170	1–26–1853	200	Rockhouse Fk
†Johnson	Richmond, James	2	193	8– 7–1854	200	
†Johnson	Richmond, John	3	338	1–25–1865	200	
‡Johnson	Richmond, John	65	307	3–11–1865	830	Rolling Fk
‡Johnson	Richmond, W. R	121	535	8–12–1905	40	Main Daniel & Left Fk
‡Johnson	Richmond, W. R	122	197	5–26–1906	36¼	Oak Log Fk
⊙Fayette	Riggely, Richard	4	258	1–16–1786	8,000	S Fk Sandy
‡Johnson	Right, Balis	49	329	4–28–1855	23	Blain Cr
‡Johnson	Right, Balus	18	10	11–26–1845	50	Laurel Fk Cr
‡Johnson	Rigsby, John H	81	251	10–17–1870	76	Upper Laurel Fk Blain Cr
‡Johnson	Rigsby, Travis	58	355	10–31–1854	150	Br Blain Cr
‡Johnson	Rigsby, William T	118	351	6–11–1897	36	Big Lick Br
†Johnson	Rigsby, Willis C. and Jeremiah Scaggs	3	145	8– 7–1860	—	
‡Floyd	Risner, Eli	6	201	1–16–1839	200	Licking R
†Floyd	Risner, James	6	193	6–12–1839	100	Big Lick
‡Johnson	Rittenhouse, J. S	121	180	3–24–1904	14¼	Road and Wells Fk
†Johnson	Roberson, James H	2	391	6– 1–1857	25	
¶Floyd	Roberson, John	T	96	9–25–1824	50	Jennys Cr
¶Floyd	Roberson, John	E-2	215	9–27–1834	50	Main Lick Fk
†Johnson	Roberson, Nathaniel	2	398	8– 3–1857	75	
†Johnson	Roberson, Samuel	2	383	5– 4–1857	26	
‡Johnson	Roberson, Thomas J	75	130	11–19–1868	164	Lick Fk Jennies Cr
¶Floyd	Roberson, William	L-2	372	11–27–1833	50	Little Lick Fk
¶Floyd	Robertson, John Jr	L-2	348	5–25–1837	50	Lick Fk Jennies Cr
⊙Fayette	Robertson, William	4	228	10–23–1785	618	Big Sandy
#Bourbon	Robinson, Betsy and Henry	14	379	5– 1–1787	15,246	Big Sandy
#Bourbon	Robinson, James	14	379	5– 1–1787	15,246	Big Sandy R
#Bourbon	Robinson, Benj. and John	14	376	4–13–1787	14,280	Big Sandy R
#Bourbon	Robinson, Benj. and John	14	379	5– 1–1787	15,246	Big Sandy
‡Johnson	Robinson, J. H	51	267	3–28–1857	135	Lick Fk
#Bourbon	Robinson, Michael	14	377	5– 5–1787	1,450	Big Sandy R
‡Johnson	Robinson, Nath	51	268	5– 2–1857	65	Lick Br
†Johnson	Robinson, R. E	7	345	3– –1889	10	
‡Johnson	Robinson, Samuel	43	543	9– 9–1851	50	Br Lick Fk Jennies Cr
‡Johnson	Robinson, Samuel	51	269	3–27–1857	160	Lick Fk
‡Johnson	Robinson, Thomas J	99	114	11– 5–1879	384	Lick Fk Jennies Cr
#Bourbon	Robinson, Wm. and Michael	14	379	5– 1–1787	15,246	Big Sandy
⊙Fayette	Rogers, John	3	329	5–12–1784	9,500	Sandy
†Floyd	Rogers, William	2	197	10–29–1816	—	
‡Johnson	Rose, Thomas	18	11	7– 2–1842	100	Kellons Fk
‡Johnson	Rose, Thomas	43	530	4–16–1851	50	Kenton Fk
‡Johnson	Rose, Thomas	43	558	4–17–1851	350	Keetons Fk
#Bourbon	Ross, David	3	515	4–20–1788	25,000	Big Sandy
‡Johnson	Ross, Joseph	46	45	11–11–1853	100	Laurel Br
†Johnson	Ross, Joseph	2	144	12– 5–1853	100	
‡Johnson	Ross, Joseph	60	80	5–26–1860	22	Lower Laurel Fk
‡Johnson	Ross, Robert	32	215	6–29–1848	50	Middle Laurel Fk

County	Grantee	Book	Page	Date Survey	Acres	Watercourse
‡Johnson	Ross, Stephen and Joseph	32	218	6-28-1848	50	Laurel Fk
‡Johnson	Rowland, John	43	181	4- 7-1851	75	Line Br
¶Floyd	Rowland, Samuel	W	354	8-10-1827	50	Jennys Cr
⊙Fayette	Ruddle, Cornelius	2	35	1-11-1783	1,697	Sandy
#Bourbon	Ruddle, Cornelius	13	524	1- 2-1787	1,697	Big Sandy Cr
‡Johnson	Rule, Andrew J	60	533	10-25-1860	18	Muddy Cr
†Johnson	Rule, A. W	3	168	10-17-1860	20	
‡Johnson	Rule, Wallace	53	27	2-10-1857	90	Muddy Br
‡Johnson	Rule and Ward	42	339	2-27-1854	100	Orchard Br
‡Johnson	Russell, Flemon M	68	380	2-12-1866	15	Oil Fk Paint Cr
⊙Fayette	Russell, William	1	270	12-25-1782	1,000	S Fk Sandy
‡Johnson	Sagraves, Edmon	76	211	6-18-1869	4	Lower Laurel
‡Johnson	Sagraves, Gorden	72	218	6- 1-1867	13	Chestnut Hollow Fk
‡Johnson	Sagraves, Samuel	60	76	5-26-1860	20	Laurel Fk
‡Johnson	Sagraves, Samuel	3	133	6- 4-1860	120	
‡Johnson	Sagraves, Samuel	68	382	2-26-1866	143	Low Gap Br
‡Johnson	Sagraves, Thomas	2	143	12- 5-1853	64	
‡Johnson	Sagraves, Thomas	60	83	5-28-1860	40	Lower Laurel Fk
‡Johnson	Sagraves, Wilburn	72	516	1-24-1868	20	Fk Mud Lick Cr
‡Johnson	Sagraves, William	32	223	6-28-1848	100	Little Laurel Fk
‡Johnson	Sagraves, William	43	154	4-18-1851	50	Little Laurel Fk
‡Johnson	Salmon, Carter	24	446	7- 3-1847	50	Daniels Cr
‡Johnson	Salyer, Andrew J	60	536	2-17-1860	75	Mud Lick Fk Big Paint
†Johnson	Salyer, Andrew J	3	156	10- 1-1860	36	
¶Floyd	Salyer, Benjamin	A-2	298	5- 3-1831	200	Mud Lick Fk
¶Floyd	Salyer, Benjamin	1-2	342	12-16-1835	100	Br Mud Lick Fk
¶Floyd	Salyer, Benjamin	1-2	343	12-16-1835	100	Peter Cave Br
¶Floyd	Salyer, Benjamin	1-2	340	12-17-1836	300	Mud Lick Fk
‡Johnson	Salyer, Benjamin	35	473	8- 3-1849	100	Sugar Camp Br
‡Johnson	Salyer, Benjamin	42	334	3-14-1854	100	Mud Lick
†Johnson	Salyer, Benjamin	2	175	4- 3-1854	100	
†Johnson	Salyer, Benjamin	2	436	3- 1-1858	50	
‡Johnson	Salyer, Benjamin	53	204	5- 5-1858	50	Martins Br
‡Johnson	Salyer, Benjamin F	51	272	5- 5-1857	5	Blain Cr
†Johnson	Salyer, Benjamin F	2	387	6- 1-1857	50	
‡Johnson	Salyer, Benjamin F	68	386	2-13-1866	200	Harges Cr
‡Johnson	Salyer, Benjamin F	68	383	3-13-1866	160	Sand Lick Br
†Johnson	Salyer, Benjamin F	—	—	10- 5-1871	180	
‡Johnson	Salyer, David J	32	298	4-13-1849	350	Barnetts Cr
‡Johnson	Salyer, David J	43	540	4-11-1851	300	Lick Fk Barnetts Cr
‡Johnson	Salyer, David J	43	547	4-11-1854	100	Barnetts Cr
‡Johnson	Salyer, David J	103	111	8- 1-1882	30	Barnetts Cr
‡Johnson	Salyers, David L	20	451	6-16-1846	130	Barnetts Cr
‡Johnson	Salyer, Heirs	32	299	8- 8-1849	100	Mud Lick Fk Paint Cr
†Johnson	Salyer, Henderson	2	305	12- 3-1855	200	
‡Johnson	Salyer, Henderson	68	388	2-27-1866	200	Joe Salyers Cr
¶Floyd	Salyer, Henry	10	16	6-30-1842	50	Paint Lick Cr
‡Johnson	Salyer, Henry	44	246	2-12-1854	200	Stefly Br
†Johnson	Salyer, Henry	2	173	3- 6-1854	200	
‡Johnson	Salyer, Henry	46	221	11-30-1854	200	Mud R
‡Johnson	Salyer, Henry	53	168	10-28-1857	200	Fk Paint Cr
†Johnson	Salyer, Henry	2	432	2- 1-1858	200	
¶Floyd	Salyer, Isaiah	27	45	12- 5-1843	100	Fk Bucks Cr
¶Floyd	Salyer, Jacob	F-2	201	2- 5-1834	100	Oil Springs Fk
‡Floyd	Salyer, Jacob	6	202	11-16-1839	100	Mud Lick Fk
‡Johnson	Salyer, Jacob	27	79	9- 2-1847	100	Springs Br
‡Johnson	Salyer, Jacob	35	471	7-26-1849	100	Little Paint Cr
‡Johnson	Salyer, Jacob	35	472	7-26-1849	400	Tick Lick Br
‡Johnson	Salyer, Jacob	53	22	2-12-1855	300	None
‡Johnson	Salyer, Jacob	58	382	1-12-1858	250	Oil Springs Br
†Johnson	Salyer, Jacob	2	432	2- 1-1858	200	
‡Johnson	Salyer, Jacob	53	169	2-14-1858	400	Paint Cr
†Johnson	Salyer, Jacob	2	440	3- 1-1858	200	
†Johnson	Salyer, Jacob	2	444	4- 1-1858	100	
‡Johnson	Salyer, James	32	222	6-30-1848	290	Lower Laurel
¶Floyd	Salyer, John	6	187	12-20-1839	100	Half Mt Cr
‡Johnson	Salyer, John	53	204	11-24-1854	245	Laurel Br
†Johnson	Salyer, John	2	242	2- 6-1855	20	
‡Johnson	Salyer, John	51	271	5- 8-1857	60	Blain Cr
‡Johnson	Salyer, John	58	568	2- 4-1860	4	Hoods Fk
‡Johnson	Salyer, John	68	386	2-13-1866	200	Harges Cr
¶Floyd	Salyer, Joseph	1-2	338	12-19-1835	100	Br Mud Lick Fk
‡Johnson	Salyer, Joseph	46	220	3-18-1854	130	Mud Lick Cr
†Johnson	Salyer, Joseph	2	444	4- 1-1858	180	
‡Johnson	Salyer, Joseph	68	384	2-27-1866	97	Sugar Camp Br
‡Johnson	Salyer, Joseph	68	385	3- 3-1866	200	Joe Salyers Cr
‡Johnson	Salyer, Joseph, Sr	53	30	11-28-1855	180	None
†Johnson	Salyer, Joseph A	2	176	4- 3-1854	130	
¶Floyd	Salyer, Samuel	6	199	6-24-1839	200	Buck Cr
‡Johnson	Salyer, S. B	37	65	4-18-1851	50	Puncheon Camp Br
†Johnson	Salyer, Thomas	5	426	10-21-1874	32	

APPENDIX 543

County	Grantee	Book	Page	Date Survey	Acres	Watercourse
†Johnson	Salyer, Wiley	2	176	4- 3-1854	50	
‡Johnson	Salyer, William E.	68	387	3- 9-1866	490	Stufly Br
¶Floyd	Salyers, Wm. J. M.	8	327	12-13-1839	300	Trace Fk
†Johnson	Samonds, Wm., G.	7	117	12-25-1885	18	
¶Floyd	Saulsberry, Hiram	11	29	8-24-1843	50	Patton Br
‡Floyd	Saulsberry, Hiram	11	32	8-25-1843	50	Patton Br
‡Johnson	Scaggs, Emily, Jane and Peter F.	95	550	10-10-1873	47	Fall Br
†Johnson	Scaggs, James	—	—	— -1858	95	
‡Johnson	Scaggs, James	55	295	12- 8-1858	95	Keetons Fk
‡Johnson	Scaggs, Jeremiah	60	339	7-30-1860	60	Upper Laurel Fk Blain
‡Johnson	Scaggs, Jeremiah L.	114	195	6- 7-1890	16	Big Laurel Fk
‡Johnson	Scaggs, John	35	477	7-25-1848	100	Blain Cr
‡Johnson	Scaggs, John	66	37	4- 1-1865	12	Upper Laurel Fk
‡Johnson	Scaggs, John A.	69	302	5-24-1866	76	Upper Laurel
¶Lawrence	Scaggs, Lewis	R	495	5-24-1825	50	Hoods Fk Blain
‡Johnson	Scaggs, Lewis F., and John E.	95	550	10-10-1873	47	Fall Br
‡Johnson	Scaggs, Peter	66	36	4- 1-1865	32	Upper Laurel Fk
†Johnson	Scaggs, Peter J.	7	65	5-16-1885	10	
‡Johnson	Scaggs, Walter	81	247	10-18-1870	88	Spicer Br
⊕Fayette	Scott, Charles Genl.	4	256	1-14-1786	1,100	S Fk Sandy
¶Floyd	Sellard, John	D	382	11-20-1818	50	Buffalo Cr
¶Floyd	Sellard, John	T	34	1-28-1825	50	Sandy R
¶Floyd	Sellard, John	1-2	145	6- 9-1836	100	Sellard Br
¶Floyd	Sellards, John W.	8	334	12- 4-1840	50	Buffalo Cr
¶Floyd	Sellards, Susan	8	332	12- 3-1840	100	Buffalo Cr
¶Floyd	Sellards, Thomas	8	329	12-14-1840	50	Buffalo Cr
‡Johnson	Selsor, George	32	55	10-27-1849	120	Jennys Cr
†Johnson	Selsor, George	2	192	8- 7-1854	100	
⊕Fayette	Shepherd, William	3	289	4-14-1784	714¼	S Fk Big Sandy
†Johnson	Sherman, B. G.	5	508	2- 8-1876	40	
†Johnson	Sherman, H. R.	107	317	9-27-1884	1	Muddy Br
†Johnson	Short, Silas J.	7	52	4- 6-1885	2	
†Johnson	Short, Thomas	2	199	9- 5-1854	25	
†Johnson,	Short, Thomas	49	331	11- —1857	25	Buffalo Cr
¶Floyd	Simer, Abraham	1	403	9- 5-1821	50	Fk Big Paint Lick Cr
¶Floyd	Simer, John P.	8	374	10-28-1840	500	Barretts Cr
‡Johnson	Simer, John P.	42	332	12-10-1854	50	None
‡Johnson	Simer, Nath	53	194	5- 5-1858	200	Coal Br
¶Floyd	Simer, Nathaniel P.	T	67	10-19-1824	50	Paint Cr
¶Floyd	Simer, Nathaniel P.	W	452	5- 9-1827	100	Paint Cr
¶Floyd	Simer, Nathaniel P.	1-2	310	7-16-1836	200	Mud Lick Fk
‡Johnson	Simer, N. P.	32	224	8- 1-1849	150	Mud Lick Cr
‡Johnson	Simer, N. P. Jr.	71	9	2-21-1867	137	Pickle Fk
‡Johnson	Simer, Samuel P.	71	10	2-22-1867	22	Long Br
‡Johnson	Simer, William P.	100	432	4-12-1878	50	Slick Road Br
†Johnson	Simpkins, John	7	637	7-12-1892	15	
†Johnson	Simpkins, John	8	1	7-23-1892	5	
‡Johnson	Simpkins, John	82	250	7-28-1892	17	Fk Daniels Cr
*Res.Richmond	Singleton, Anthony	A-2	548	6-20-1795	10,000	N Fk Sandy R
⊕Fayette	Skinner, Cornelius	4	238	12-13-1785	2,466	Br Fk Sandy
†Johnson	Smith, David	7	41	2- 3-1885	3	
†Johnson	Smith, David	7	344	3- —1889	3	
¶Floyd	Smith, Elijah	P	175	4-25-1821	50	Fks Paint Lick Cr
‡Johnson	Smith, James	61	185	9- 1-1860	84	Lick Paint Cr
†Johnson	Smith, James	3	157	10- 1-1860	112	
¶Floyd	Smith, William M.	D-2	380	12-12-1834	250	Sandy R
¶Floyd	Smith, William M.	M-2	307	8-24-1837	100	Jennys Cr
¶Floyd	Smith, William M.	11	30	3- 7-1843	100	Lick Fk
¶Floyd	Smith, William M.	11	31	3- 8-1843	100	Stillhouse Cr
*Res. Frankfort	Sneed, Achillis	P	122	5- 7-1813	1,525	Sandy R
‡Johnson	Sparks, Allen	14	291	4-24-1844	50	Laurel Fk
‡Johnson	Sparks, Allen	32	221	6-27-1848	100	Little Laurel Fk
‡Johnson	Sparks, Elijah	32	220	8- 2-1848	100	Puncheon Camp
‡Johnson	Sparks, Henry	61	187	12-20-1860	2	Jones Fk
†Johnson	Sparks, Mathew	2	143	12- 5-1853	100	
‡Johnson	Sparks, Nathan	42	335	11- 5-1853	100	None
‡Johnson	Sparks, Nathan	69	303	5-16-1866	2	Hood Fk
†Johnson	Sparks, Nicholas	2	147	12- 6-1854	25	
‡Johnson	Sparks, Nicholas	60	338	6- 5-1860	17	Lower Laurel Fk Blain
¶Lawrence	Sparks, Thomas	D-2	310	6-22-1832	50	Lower Laurel Fk
‡Johnson	Sparks, Thomas	20	452	8- 6-1846	100	Lower Laurel Fk
‡Johnson	Sparks & Crafts	20	458	10- 1-1846	50	Hoods Fk
‡Johnson	Spears, Harvey	44	130	1-17-1854	200	Daniels Cr
†Johnson	Spears, Harvey	2	226	12- 5-1854	200	
†Johnson	Spears, Harvey	2	242	2- 6-1855	200	
‡Johnson	Spears, Henry	18	23	11-18-1845	50	Sycamore Cr
‡Johnson	Spears, John W.	120	302	8-28-1902	38	Daniels Cr
‡Johnson	Spears, Rosey	54	211	3-20-1854	400	Fk Daniels Cr
†Johnson	Spears, Samuel	3	114	2- 6-1860	40	

County	Grantee	Book	Page	Date Survey	Acres	Watercourse
†Johnson	Spears, Samuel	3	—	— —1860	40	
‡Johnson	Spears, Samuel	97	308	2–11–1875	430	None
‡Johnson	Spears, Thomas M	35	470	2– 3–1851	50	Daniels Cr
‡Johnson	Spears, Thomas W	66	382	4– 2–1865	369	Double Lick Fk
‡Johnson	Spears, Wiley	35	469	12–20–1850	50	Buck Lick Fk
‡Johnson	Spears, William R	107	554	2–28–1885	8	None
‡Johnson	Spence, Jordon	49	332	2–11–1854	50	Big Paint Cr
‡Johnson	Spencer, Armen	22	240	11–30–1846	50	Greasy Cr
‡Johnson	Spencer, Job	22	241	11–30–1846	75	Greasy Cr
‡Johnson	Spencer, Job	32	226	4– 6–1848	250	Greasy Cr
¶Floyd	Spencer, Spears	O-2	242	6–11–1840	100	r Fk Daniels Cr
¶Floyd	Spencer, Thomas	M	268	10–10–1821	100	Georges Cr
‡Johnson	Spradlin, B. F	60	535	10– 5–1859	16	Tiny Br Barnetts Cr
†Johnson	Spradlin, B. F	3	159	10– 1–1860	16	
‡Johnson	Spradlin, Daniel	112	263	9– 4–1889	39	Jennies Cr
†Johnson	Spradlin, Daniel M	4	185	4–24–1867	200	
‡Johnson	Spradlin, Daniel M	73	377	2–22–1868	200	Jennies Cr
†Johnson	Spradlin, Daniel M	7	375	8–22–1889	50	
‡Johnson	Spradlin, D. M	84	256	5– 2–1871	16	Twin Br
‡Johnson	Spradlin, D. M	98	342	12–18–1878	155	Upper Line Br
‡Johnson	Spradlin, D. M	99	161	4– 8–1880	70	Upper Twin Br
¶Floyd	Spradlin, James	T	132	9–18–1824	50	Jennies Cr
¶Floyd	Spradlin, James	E-2	211	9– 7–1834	100	Jennies Cr
¶Floyd	Spradlin, James	L-2	408	3– 3–1837	50	Jennies Cr
‡Floyd	Spradlin, James	8	335	8–30–1841	50	Jennys Cr
‡Floyd	Spradlin, James	8	336	8–30–1841	100	Jennys Cr
‡Johnson	Spradlin, James	18	22	2–28–1845	50	Barretts Cr
‡Johnson	Spradlin, James	43	179	3–28–1851	50	Jennys Cr
‡Johnson	Spradlin, James	43	180	3–27–1851	500	Twin Br
†Johnson	Spradlin, James	2	108	6– 7–1853	25	
‡Johnson	Spradlin, James	84	250	11– 9–1871	200	Big Fk Pigeon Fk
‡Johnson	Spradlin, James	84	251	11– 9–1871	50	Barn Br
‡Johnson	Spradlin, James Jr	49	334	7–10–1854	39	Jennys Cr
†Johnson	Spradlin, James Sr	2	167	3– 6–1854	50	
¶Floyd	Spradlin, John	T	130	9– 8–1824	50	M Fk Jennies Cr
¶Floyd	Spradlin, Jonah	1–2	284	1–12–1836	50	Upper Twin Br
¶Floyd	Spradlin, Robert	1–2	313	8– 8–1836	100	Line Br Jennies Cr
‡Johnson	Spradlin, William	58	365	5–21–1858	15	Holly Br
†Johnson	Spradlin, William	3	612	— —1858	15	
¶Floyd	Stafford, John	D	386	5–13–1818	100	None
¶Floyd	Stafford, John	H-2	402	5–13–1831	200	None
¶Floyd	Stafford, John	L	484	9–13–1822	50	Sandy R
¶Lawrence	Stafford, John	R	478	11–29–1824	50	Rockhouse Fk Blain
¶Lawrence	Stafford, John	R	479	11–30–1824	50	Hoods Fk Blains Cr
¶Lawrence	Stafford, John	R	480	12–21–1824	50	Louisa Fk Sandy R
¶Lawrence	Stafford, John	V	460	12– 3–1827	490	Fk Big Sandy R
‡Floyd	Stafford, John	8	331	10–27–1840	500	bet Blackberry Br and Jenny Cr
‡Johnson	Stafford, John	12	26	12–13–1843	100	Meadows Br
‡Johnson	Stafford, John	12	22	12–14–1843	100	Hoods Fk
‡Johnson	Stafford, John	12	23	12–14–1843	50	Hoods Fk
‡Johnson	Stafford, John	12	24	4–26–1844	150	Hoods Fk
‡Johnson	Stafford, John	12	25	4–26–1844	150	nr Hoods Fk
‡Johnson	Stafford, John	14	292	12– 4–1844	145	Lick Cr
‡Johnson	Stafford, John	14	293	12– 5–1844	355	Whitehouse Cr
‡Johnson	Stafford, John	14	294	12– 7–1844	50	Rockcastle Cr
‡Johnson	Stafford, John	17	522	5–30–1845	800	Big Sandy R
‡Johnson	Stafford, John	76	79	9–15–1845	141	Big Sandy R
‡Johnson	Stafford, John	16	116	9–17–1845	25	None
‡Johnson	Stafford, John	35	475	11–27–1849	500	Whitehouse Cr
‡Johnson	Stafford, John	32	297	11–28–1849	480	Big Borders Br
†Johnson	Stafford, John	33	574	—	23½	None
†Johnson	Stafford, John	33	575	—	7½	None
†Johnson	Stafford, John	2	196	8– 7–1854	200	
‡Johnson	Stafford, John	46	222	8– 8–1856	200	None
‡Johnson	Stafford, John Jr	49	333	8– 8–1854	100	Burnt Cabin Br
‡Johnson	Stafford, John Sr	20	450	4–20–1846	450	None
¶Lawrence	Stafford, William	A-2	126	9–10–1824	50	Sandy R
†Johnson	Stafford, William	2	196	8– 7–1854	200	
‡Johnson	Stafford, William	65	351	3– 4–1865	425	Br Sandy R
‡Johnson	Stafford, William	65	352	3– 4–1865	100	Sandy R
†Johnson	Stafford, William	3	389	8– 8–1865	200	
†Johnson	Stambaugh, Benjamin and Brown, William	3	266	3– 2–1863	100	
†Johnson	Stambaugh, John	2	220	12– 4–1854	100	
†Johnson	Stambaugh, John	3	270	6– 1–1863	100	
‡Johnson	Stambaugh, Samuel	68	210	12– 8–1854	80	Tom's Cr
†Johnson	Stambaugh, Samuel	2	395	7– 6–1857	16	
†Johnson	Stambaugh, Samuel and Jonathan	3	260	12– 2–1862	200	
‡Johnson	Stapleton, Allen	68	390	2–22–1866	60	Tar Kiln Br

APPENDIX 545

County	Grantee	Book	Page	Date Survey	Acres	Watercourse
‡Johnson	Stapleton, Charles	68	391	2-28-1866	114	Fk Mud Lick Cr
†Johnson	Stapleton, Edward	2	410	11- 2-1857	50	
‡Johnson	Stapleton, Edward	53	205	12-16-1857	100	Peter Cave Br
‡Johnson	Stapleton, Eli	68	130	12-30-1865	31	Bakers Br
‡Johnson	Stapleton, Elizabeth	68	389	2-22-1866	248	Joe Salyers Cr
‡Johnson	Stapleton, Isaac	73	376	4-14-1868	5	Tom's Cr
‡Johnson	Stapleton, James H	113	148	1-10-1890	26	Sugar Camp Br
‡Johnson	Stapleton, John A	122	115	4-11-1904	30¾	Andy Br
†Johnson	Stapleton, J. H.	7	376	8-22-89	20	
‡Johnson	Stapleton, Polly	58	73	11-19-1854	40	Bakers Br
‡Johnson	Stapleton, William	97	108	4-- 7-1877	41	Tom's Cr
‡Johnson	Stansbaugh, Fred	35	474	10-10-1850	540	Chestnut Cr
¶Floyd	Steel, Alexander	N-2	230	4-30-1838	50	Burnt Cabin Br
‡Johnson	Step, James	43	152	2- 8-1851	100	Big Black Log Fk
†Johnson	Step, James	2	145	12- 5-1853	100	
‡Johnson	Step, James	46	46	1- 8-1855	200	Bakers Br
‡Johnson	Step, James	47	105	9-25-1855	100	Big Black Log Br
†Johnson	Step, James	2	377	3-30-1857	200	
†Johnson	Step, James	2	377	3-30-1857	200	
†Johnson	Step, James	2	377	3-30-1857	200	
†)ohnson	Step, James	2	377	3-30-1857	200	
†Johnson	Step, James	2	377	3-30-1857	200	
†Johnson	Step, James	2	434	2- 1-1858	200	
†Johnson	Step, James	2	434	2- 1-1858	30	
†Johnson	Step, James	2	374		35	
†Johnson	Step, James	2	374		100	
†Johnson	Step, James Sr	2	241	2- 6-1855	200	
†Johnson	Step, James Sr	2	241	2- 6-1855	100	
†Johnson	Step, James and Wm	3	337	1- 2-1865	200	
†Johnson	Step, James and Wm	3	337	1- 2-1865	100	
‡Johnson	Step, Joseph	11	46	7-26-1843	50	Coldwater Fk Cr
‡Johnson	Step, Joseph	22	115	11- 9-1846	100	Coldwater Fk
‡Johnson	Step, Joseph	22	116	11-10-1846	200	Black Log Cr
†Johnson	Step, Moses	2	406	9-21-1857	200	
†Johnson	Step, Moses	4	363	8-25-1868	144	
‡Johnson	Step, Robert	43	549	2- 6-1851	227	Coldwater Fk
†Johnson	Step, William	27	78	11-19-1847	200	Collins Br
†Johnson	Step, William	3	113	2- 6-1860	100	
†Johnson	Step, William	3	---	----1860	100	
†Johnson	Step, William		---	----1860	100	
‡Johnson	Step, William	4	363	8-25-1868	14	
‡Johnson	Step and Patterson	53	203	3-22-1856	160	Alums Br
‡Johnson	Stephens, James B	125	310	9-22-1920	3	Upper Laurel Cr
‡Johnson	Stephens, John C. M	114	194	5-24-1890	11	Big Laurel
¶Floyd	Stevens, Andrew	W	362	9-10-1827	50	Paint Lick Cr
#Bourbon	Stewart, John	14	378	5- 6-1787	3,121	Sandy R
¶Floyd	Stone, Ezekiel	T	87	2-15-1825	120	Jennys Cr
¶Floyd	Stone, Thomas	T	123	2-15-1825	50	Fk Jennys Cr
¶Floyd	Stone, Thomas	E-2	236	8-28-1830	100	M Fk Jennies Cr
‡Floyd	Stone, William	6	215	10-17-1839	200	bet Lick Fk & Middle Cr
¶Floyd	Stratton, James	G	481	7- 3-1820	100	Buffalo Cr
▲Floyd	Stratton, Harry	18	126	12- 4-1809	451	Sandy R
¶Floyd	Stratton, Harry	1-2	96	4-16-1836	100	Ivy and Tom's Cr
¶Floyd	Stratton, Harry	L-2	331	2- 7-1837	200	Sandy R
¶Floyd	Stratton, Henry	T	124	1-27-1825	50	Tom's Cr
¶Floyd	Stratton, Polly	D-2	376	9-30-1834	58	Sandy R
¶Floyd	Stratton, Polly	1-2	72	4- 7-1836	100	Sandy R
▲Floyd	Stratton, Richard	19	289	1- 4-1819	48	Sandy R
#Bourbon	Strother, Joseph	14	471	4- 1-1788	7,221	Big Sandy
‡Johnson	Stumbaugh, Benjamin	58	374	12- 6-1854	35	None
‡Johnson	Stumbaugh, Benjamin	58	377	12- 6-1854	100	Tom's Cr
‡Johnson	Stumbaugh, Benjamin	64	30	2-17-1863	300	Burnt Cabin Br Tom's Cr
‡Johnson	Stumbaugh, John	32	219	4- 6-1849	100	Road Br Fk Tom's Cr
‡Johnson	Stumbaugh, John	97	546	2-17-1852	25	Road Br
‡Johnson	Stumbaugh, John	58	371	3-12-1857	100	Road Br
¶Floyd	Stumbaugh, Jonathan	1-2	273	5-25-1826	100	Tom's Cr
¶Floyd	Stumbaugh, Jonathan	1-2	274	5-24-1836	200	Big Lick Fk Tom's Cr
¶Floyd	Stumbaugh, Jonathan	L-2	397	1-14-1837	200	Tom's Cr
¶Floyd	Stumbaugh, Samuel	1-2	78-9	11-20-1835	100	Tom's Cr
‡Johnson	Stumbaugh, Samuel	58	378	11-22-1855	200	Sycamore Fk
‡Johnson	Stumbaugh, Samuel	51	270	5- 2-1857	15	Blain Cr
‡Johnson	Stumbaugh, Samuel and Jonathan	53	438	3-30-1861	200	Tom's Cr
‡Johnson	Sturgeon, Elijah	14	290	12-14-1844	100	Pigeon Roost Fk
‡Johnson	Sturgill, Elijah	32	225	4- 6-1848	100	Pigeon Roost Fk
‡Johnson	Sturgill, Elijah	2	176	4- 3-1854	200	
‡Johnson	Sturgill, Elijah	44	252	6-17-1854	300	Pigeon Roost Fk
‡Johnson	Sturgill, Elijah	44	253	6-17-1864	200	Pigeon Roost Fk
‡Johnson	Sturgill, Joseph	53	206	5-- 5-1828	10	Local Br
‡Johnson	Sturgill, Joseph	44	248	8-22-1853	25	Lick Cr

HISTORY OF JOHNSON COUNTY

County	Grantee	Book	Page	Date Survey	Acres	Watercourse
†Floyd	Sullivan, Peter	2	199	10–29–1816	—	
†Floyd	Summer, John	2	119	11–22–1815	150	
⊚Fayette	Swearingin, Thomas	3	64	12– 1–1783	10,687	S Fk Big Sandy
¶Floyd	Tackett, John	P	180	3–10–1822	100	bet Big Paint Lick and Barnetts Cr
¶Floyd	Tackett, John	Q	71	9–17–1824	100	Paint Lick Cr
¶Floyd	Tackett, John	W	353	5–15–1827	50	None
¶Floyd	Tackett, Lewis	T	128	9–17–1824	50	Paint Cr
¶Floyd	Tackett, William	E-2	122	6– 3–1834	100	Barnetts Cr
†Johnson	Tackett, William	2	92	3– 7–1853	100	
‡Johnson	Tackett, William	47	111	11–10–1854	100	Barretts Cr
⊚Fayette	Tarrison, Bartholomew	3	110	12–27–1783	20,000	S Fk Big Sandy R
*Res. Franklin	Taylor, James	Z	93	1– 1–1831	10,000	S Fk Sandy R
‡Johnson	Teass, John W	121	554	9–28–1905	207	Rule Br
†Johnson	Thomas, Henry J. and Chas. A. Ward	2	433	2– 1–1858	50	
‡Johnson	Thompson, Russell	32	231	4– 5–1849	29	Hoods Fk
#Fayette	Thompson, Stephen	13	269	9–18–1785	12,000	Sandy Cr
‡Johnson	Todd, Lewis	34	546	4– 9–1851	45	Colvin Fk
‡Johnson	Todd, Lewis	34	547	4– 8–1851	30	Colvin Br
#Fayette	Tompkins, Humphrey	9	604	1–26–1786	7,991	S Fk Sandy
⊚Fayette	Tompkins, Humphrey	3	79	12–10–1783	3,441	S Fk Sandy
⊚Fayette	Tompkins, John	3	66	12– 1–1783	7,991¾	S Fk Sandy
¶Floyd	Trimble, Edwin	B-2	277	10– 5–1832	100	Sandy R
‡Johnson	Trimble, James	66	83	4–21–1865	8	Lick Br Barnetts Cr
‡Johnson	Trimble, William	90	555	11–14–1871	28	Cantrill Fk
†Johnson	Trimble, William	5	202	3–14–1872	28	
#Bourbon	Trotter, James	16	182	6–20–1787	19,756	Big Sandy
‡Johnson	Turner, Eleazor, Heirs	37	66	2– 1–1850	100	Mud Lick Cr
‡Johnson	Turner, Ezra	93	47	11–13–1872	118	State Br Mud Lick Cr
†Johnson	Turner, I. R.	7	64	5–13–1885	100	
¶Floyd	Turner, James W	A-2	304	6– 5–1831	50	Johns Cr
¶Floyd	Turner, John	F-2	223	9–27–1834	100	Tom's Cr
¶Floyd	Turner, Suddith	D-2	397	4– 2–1835	200	Tom's Cr
#Bourbon	Twyman, Reuben	12	354	4– 7–1787	7,537	Big Sandy
*Res. Hanover	Underwood, George	K	78	10–20–1799	1,000	Sandy
⊚Fayette	Underwood, Thomas	4	296	4–29–1786	5,000	Sandy
‡Johnson	Vanhoose, Bracken	32	295	11–28–1848	50	Bear Br Fk Muddy Br
‡Johnson	Vanhoose, Bracken	35	513	10–28–1847	100	Road Br
‡Johnson	Vanhoose, Bracken	43	526	4– 2–1850	40	Muddy Br
†Johnson	Vanhoose, Bracken R.	2	217	10–14–1854	25	
‡Johnson	Vanhoose, Bracken R and James	57	489	7– 5–1859	100	Lower Rd Br Tom's Cr
†Johnson	Vanhoose, Bracken R, Vanhoose, Jesse and Robt. Meade	3	160	10– 1–1860	50	
‡Johnson	Vanhoose, Felty	58	369	7–15–1858	20	Big Sandy R
¶Floyd	Vanhoose, James	R	25	9–18–1824	50	Fk Paint Cr
¶Floyd	Vanhoose, James	W	352	6–29–1825	50	Br Sandy R
‡Johnson	Vanhoose, James	18	24	3– 6–1845	50	Buffalo Cr
†Johnson	Vanhoose, James	2	148	12– 6–1853	50	
‡Johnson	Vanhoose, James	42	336	12–15–1853	50	Tom's Cr
‡Johsnon	Vanhoose, James	47	109	3– 1–1855	15	Tom's Cr
‡Johnson	Vanhoose, James	98	197	3–10–1873	24	Long Br and Tom's Cr
‡Johnson	Vanhoose, James	98	198	3–10–1873	21	Tom's Cr
‡Johnson	Vanhoose, James Sr	20	476	8–20–1846	50	Two-Mile Cr
†Johnson	Vanhoose, James and Beecher	—	—	1859	20	
‡Johnson	Vanhoose, Jesse	61	189	10– 3–1860	26	Lower Road Br
¶Floyd	Vanhoose, John	M	129	5–23–1822	100	Jennys Cr
¶Floyd	Vanhoose, John	R	29	8–11–1824	50	Fk Jennys Cr
‡Johnson	Vanhoose, John	35	514	9–18–1849	294	Two-Mile Cr
‡Johnson	Vanhoose, John	7	55	4–14–1885	40	
‡Johnson	Vanhoose, John	107	548	5–30–1885	38½	Big Sandy R
‡Johnson	Vanhoose, John	107	549	5–30–1885	1½	Lick Cr
†Johnson	Vanhoose, Henry J	4	23	11– 3–1865	6	
‡Johnson	Vanhoose, Henry J	68	132	12–19–1865	6	Tom's Cr
†Johnson	Vanhoose, Levi	—	—	1859	100	
†Johnson	Vanhoose, Robert	4	206	7–13–1867	50	
¶Floyd	Vanhoose, Valentine	1-2	329	1–13–1836	200	Buffalo Cr
‡Johnson	Vanhoose, Valentine	32	232	5– 4–1848	50	None
*Res. Philadel.	Vanuxem, James	A-2	7	7– 9–1791	36,000	Sandy R and Green
¶Floyd	Vaughan, Ayers	E-2	225	9–17–1834	50	Johns Cr
‡Johnson	Vaughan, Isabel	60	79	5–12–1860	20	Mud Lick
¶Floyd	Vaughan, Jacob	38	382	2– 4–1842	1,306	Johns Cr
¶Floyd	Vaughan, John P	1-2	102	3–17–1836	75	Little Paint Cr
¶Floyd	Vaughan, Patrick	W	210	7–30–1827	50	Sandy R
¶Floyd	Vaughan, Patrick	1-2	301	1–19–1836	400	Sandy R
¶Floyd	Vaughan, Patrick	L-2	405	4– 4–1837	200	Young Br
*Res. Goochland	Vaughan, Shadrack	D	417	11– 5–1799	2,500	Sandy R
#Bourbon	Voss, Edward	11	491	4– 7–1788	9,000	Big Sandy

APPENDIX 547

County	Grantee	Book	Page	Date Survey	Acres	Watercourse
#Bourbon	Walker, John	12	354	4-17-1787	7,537	Big Sandy
*Res. Henrico	Walker, John	A-2	513	5-23-1790	10,000	Sandy R
⊙Fayette	Walker, Mathew	4	260	1-13-1786	1,000	S Fk Sandy
⊙Fayette	Walker, Merry	3	141	1-12-1784	103,518	Sandy R
‡Johnson	Walters, Shadrach W	63	147	8-14-1862	50	Bobs Br
‡Johnson	Walters, Winfrey H	84	257	3-13-1871	30	Buffalo Cr
†Johnson	Walters, W. H.	7	47	3- 2-1885	10	
#Bourbon	Walton, Mathew	15	325	4- 3-1789	6,091¼	Big Sandy
‡Johnson	Ward, Belinda	11	53	9- 6-1843	50	Lick Br
‡Johnson	Ward, Bleuford	27	74	2-24-1847	300	Lick Br Greasy Cr
‡Johnson	Ward, Davis	65	184	8-15-1858	125	Staffords Fk
†Johnson	Ward, George W	2	332	7- 7-1856	100	
‡Johnson	Ward, George & Jonathan	69	304	5-11-1866	55	Greasy Cr
‡Johnson	Ward, Hiram	37	68	12- 3-1849	100	None
§Floyd	Ward, Ia Sr	(Cert.44)		8- 2-1803	100	Levisa Fk
‡Johnson	Ward, Jackson	35	520	10- 6-1849	100	Two-Mile Cr
§Floyd	Ward, James	(Cert.10)		9- —1802	200	
‡Johnson	Ward, James	11	48	9-16-1843	50	Greasy Cr
‡Johnson	Ward, James	20	481	9- 5-1846	50	Rockcastle Cr
§Floyd	Ward, James Jr	(Cert. 44)		8- 2-1803	400	Tom's Cr
‡Johnson	Ward, James Jr	66	54	1- 8-1855	300	M Fk Rockcastle
‡Johnson	Ward, James A	65	341	2- 7-1865	530	L Fk Greasy Cr
‡Johnson	Ward, James A	3	343	2- 9-1865	150	
‡Johnson	Ward, Jas. and Jesse	14	299	9-15-1843	150	Two-Mile Cr
†Johnson	Ward, Jane	7	127	2- 2-1886	8	
‡Johnson	Ward, Jane	108	288	3-29-1886	8	Buffalo Cr
‡Johnson	Ward, Jesse	20	484	8-20-1846	50	None
‡Johnson	Ward, Jesse	32	237	4- 5-1848	100	Greasy Cr
‡Johnson	Ward, Jesse	32	304	4- 5-1848	304	Greasy Cr
‡Johnson	Ward, Jesse	36	157	7-13-1850	50	Sandy R
‡Johnson	Ward, John	14	296	11-29-1844	100	Greasy Cr
‡Johnson	Ward, John	14	297	12-10-1844	100	Greasy Cr
‡Johnson	Ward, John H	32	240	4- 5-1848	100	Greasy Cr
‡Johnson	Ward, John K	35	515	1-28-1851	100	Two-Mile Cr
‡Johnson	Ward, John K	58	386	8-19-1858	35	Two-Mile Br
¶Floyd	Ward, Jonathan	T	113	9-20-1825	50	Greasy Cr
‡Johnson	Ward, Jonathan	37	72	12- 3-1849	300	Greasy Cr
‡Johnson	Ward, Joseph	14	298	11-30-1844	100	Greasy Cr
‡Johnson	Ward, King S	104	420	1-15-1883	64	Big Br
†Johnson	Ward, Minta	3	398	8- —1865	90	
‡Johnson	Ward, Minta	66	456	8-30-1865	490	M Fk Rockcastle
‡Johnson	Ward, Nathan	43	149	2-20-1851	175	Little Field Br
‡Johnson	Ward, Nathan	62	183	2-25-1861	70	Lick Br
†Johnson	Ward, Nathan	3	195	4- 2-1861	70	
‡Johnson	Ward, N and W	20	480	9- 5-1846	100	Rockcastle Cr
‡Johnson	Ward, Ramson	107	316	4-25-1884	10	Licks Cr
‡Johnson	Ward, Ransom	97	310	2-13-1875	151	————R
¶Floyd	Ward, Shadrach	F	53	6-23-1819	50	————R
¶Floyd	Ward, Shadrach	T	80	9-10-1825	100	Sandy R
‡Johnson	Ward, Shadrach	20	482	6-19-1846	25	Sandy R
‡Johnson	Ward, Shadrach	20	483	6-20-1846	75	Greasy Cr
‡Johnson	Ward, Shadrach	43	525	2-12-1851	150	M Fk Greasy Cr
†Johnson	Ward, Shadrach	2	176	4- 3-1854	100	
†Johnson	Ward, Shadrach	3	340	2- 1-1865	200	
‡Johnson	Ward, Shadrach	70	442	2-24-1865	1,055	Br Rockhouse Fk
¶Floyd	Ward, Solomon	R	16	9-14-1824	50	Tom's Cr
¶Floyd	Ward, Solomon	1-2	86	3-25-1836	50	Tom's Cr
‡Johnson	Ward, Solomon	27	75	8-21-1846	150	Greasy Cr
‡Johnson	Ward, Solomon	27	76	2-24-1847	50	Greasy Cr
†Johnson	Ward, Solomon	2	217	10-14-1854	200	
‡Johnson	Ward, Solomon	46	48	1-15-1855	150	Rockcastle Cr
‡Johnson	Ward, Thompson	58	359	8-25-1858	25	Two-Mile Cr
‡Johnson	Ward, Washington	66	55	1-12-1855	283	Nr M Fk Rockcastle
‡Johnson	Ward, Wells	20	479	9- 5-1846	50	Big Br
‡Johnson	Ward, Wells	43	557	2-10-1851	100	Potato Hollow
‡Johnson	Ward, Wells	44	257	8-23-1852	60	Rockcastle Cr
¶Floyd	Ward, William	Q	68	9- 9-1824	50	Greasy Cr
¶Floyd	Ward, William	L-2	384	2- 3-1837	50	Sandy R
†Johnson	Ward, William	2	253	3- 5-1855	100	
†Johnson	Ward, William	4	230	8- 5-1867	60	
‡Johnson	Ward, William	74	128	8- 7-1867	60	Otter Br
‡Johnson	Ward, William Jr	14	300	8-22-1844	50	Big Sandy R
‡Johnson	Ward, William Jr	14	310	12- 1-1844	50	Wiley Br
‡Johnson	Ward, William Jr	32	239	4- 9-1847	50	Road Br
‡Johnson	Ward, William Jr	32	233	10-11-1847	50	Upper Road Br
‡Johnson	Ward, William Jr	46	224	1-17-1855	55	Wileys Br
‡Johnson	Ward, William Jr	14	302	12- 3-1844	50	Big Sandy R
†Johnson	Ward, William A	7	66	5-26-1885	10	
†Johnson	Ward, William A	7	127	2- 2-1886	8	
‡Johnson	Ward, William A	108	287	3-29-1886	18	Garden Br

548 HISTORY OF JOHNSON COUNTY

County	Grantee	Book	Page	Date Survey	Acres	Watercourse
‡Johnson	Ward, William J	35	518	3-30-1850	180	Sandy R
‡Johnson	Ward, William J	105	125	6- 9-1881	10	Two-Mile Hollow
‡Johnson	Ward, William S	5	453	2-12-1875	20	
‡Johnson	Ward, William S	96	30	3- 6-1875	10	Little Buzzard
‡Johnson	Ward, William S	96	31	4- 6-1875	47	Two-Mile Br
¶Floyd	Ward, Wm & Shadrack	E-2	224	9- 5-1834	100	Greasy Cr
‡Johnson	Ward and Rule	42	339	2-27-1854	100	Orchard Br
○Fayette	Ware, Markham	4	271	2- 9-1786	500	Sandy
○Fayette	Watkins, James	4	1	8-14-1784	5,000	Sandy Cr
#Bourbon	Weaglesworth, John	14	515	5- 3-1787	16,000	Big Sandy R
‡Johnson	Webb, Alexander	68	135	4-27-1865	494	Daniels Cr
‡Johnson	Webb, Alexander	110	269	2- 2-1888	15	Brushy Fk
†Johnson	Webb, Edmond	2	246	2- 6-1855	50	
‡Johnson	Webb, E. R	46	47	2-22-1855	150	Daniels Cr
‡Johnson	Webb, George	65	361	1-12-1865	18	Big Paint Cr
‡Johnson	Webb, George J	2	148	1- 2-1854	50	
‡Johnson	Webb, George J	71	11	2- 7-1867	32	Mud Lick Cr
‡Johnson	Webb, G. T	20	478	2-29-1846	100	None
‡Johnson	Webb, George W	43	542	3-14-1851	250	Little Paint Cr
‡Johnson	Webb, George W	43	153	3-17-1851	50	Big Paint Cr
‡Johnson	Webb, George W	2	130	11- 7-1853	25	
‡Johnson	Webb, George W	65	362	12-26-1864	56	N Paint Cr
‡Johnson	Webb, George W	3	332	1- 2-1865	100	
‡Johnson	Webb, George W and Jonathan	32	234	8-12-1848	250	Mud Lick Cr
‡Johnson	Webb, Jackson	42	338	12- 7-1853	50	Laurel Br
‡Johnson	Webb, Jackson	2	242	2- 6-1855	60	
‡Johnson	Webb, John	46	49	2-22-1855	192	Daniels Cr
¶Floyd	Webb, Jonathan	A-2	300	10- 1-1829	100	Daniels Cr
¶Floyd	Webb, Jonathan	1-2	117	4- 9-1834	50	1st Lt Fk Daniels Cr
¶Floyd	Webb, Jonathan	6	195	8-21-1839	250	Sandy R
‡Johnson	Webb, Jonathan	22	359	1-26-1847	100	Daniels Cr
†Johnson	Webb, Juda	7	77	7-11-1885	4	
‡Johnson	Webb, Thomas	43	529	10- 6-1850	100	L H Fk Daniels Cr
‡Johnson	Webb, Thomas	2	444	4- 1-1858	25	
‡Johnson	Webb, Thomas	95	19	3-10-1874	45	Brushy Ridge Millers C
‡Johnson	Webb, Thomas	99	204	4- 5-1876	100	Millers Cr
‡Johnson	Webb, Thomas	5	522	4-10-1876	100	
¶Floyd	Webb, William	T	133-4	8- 5-1824	100	Johns Cr
¶Floyd	Webb, William	N-2	212	9-14-1838	100	L Fk Daniels Cr
#Bourbon	Webb, William C	13	557	1- 2-1787	1,876	Big Sandy
¶Floyd	Weddington, Henry	H	146	1-19-1821	100	Sandy R
‡Johnson	Welch, Thomas	107	448	3- 3-1885	34	Buffalo Cr
†Johnson	Welch, Thomas	7	46	3- 2-1885	14	
†Johnson	Wells, Aaron & Moses	3	345	2-28-1865	—	
‡Johnson	Wells, Albert	100	431	9- 1-1881	120	S Daniels Cr
‡Johnson	Wells, Albert G	99	402	8-20-1880	370	Daniels Cr
‡Johnson	Wells, Allen C	7	562	11-27-1891	20	
‡Johnson	Wells, Allen C	116	398	12-12-1891	20	Buck Lick Fk
‡Johnson	Wells, Charles M	118	35	5-24-1894	15	Raven Nest Br
¶Floyd	Wells, George	L-2	390	12-25-1835	100	R Fk Daniels Cr
¶Floyd	Wells, George	O-2	169	1-16-1839	100	Daniels Cr
‡Johnson	Wells, George	2	155	2- 6-1854	50	
‡Johnson	Wells, George W	2	178	4- 3-1854	100	
‡Johnson	Wells, George W	81	253	2- 8-1871	150	Daniels Cr
‡Johnson	Wells, G. W	106	614	8-21-1883	8	None
‡Johnson	Wells, G. W	118	13	8-30-1894	24	Daniels Cr
‡Johnson	Wells, James	43	515	1-26-1853	200	Lick Br
‡Johnson	Wells, James	44	251	1-13-1854	100	Daniels Cr
‡Johnson	Wells, James	2	155	2- 6-1854	100	
‡Johnson	Wells, James	121	113	8- 8-1903	30	Road Fk
‡Johnson	Wells, James W	68	135	4-27-1865	494	Daniels Cr
‡Johnson	Wells, James W	120	167	8-18-1902	56	Road Br
¶Floyd	Wells, John	1-2	89	5- 4-1836	100	Oak Log Fk Daniels Cr
‡Johnson	Wells, John	44	457	1-18-1854	107	Daniels Cr
‡Johnson	Wells, John	2	240	2- 5-1855	73	
‡Johnson	Wells, John	51	274	4-14-1857	25	Daniels Cr
†Johnson	Wells, John	2	380	4-21-1857	25	
‡Johnson	Wells, Marion & David	2	193	8- 7-1854	200	
‡Johnson	Wells, Marion & Hiram	43	167	1-26-1853	200	Rockhouse Fk
‡Johnson	Wells, Moses	11	50	8-27-1843	50	Greasy Cr
‡Johnson	Wells, Moses	35	516	10-14-1847	50	Oakley Cr
‡Johnson	Wells, Moses	44	256	2-18-1854	100	None
‡Johnson	Wells, Moses	2	227	12- 5-1854	50	
‡Johnson	Wells, M. L. K	119	454	1-10-1902	40	Lick House Br Greasy Cr
¶Floyd	Wells, Richard	1-2	287	9- 4-1836	50	Dry Fk Daniels Cr
‡Johnson	Wells, Richard M	3	343	2- 9-1865	200	
‡Johnson	Wells, Richard & Wm	66	457	3-20-1855	516	Lick & Whitehouse Crs
‡Johnson	Wells, Ward	2	130	11- 7-1853	60	
‡Johnson	Wells, Washington	44	265	1-18-1854	175	None
‡Johnson	Wells, Werd	59	48	5-27-1857	870	Orchard Br M Fk

APPENDIX 549

County	Grantee	Book	Page	Date Survey	Acres	Watercourse
†Johnson	Wells, William	3	10	— —1858	50	
‡Johnson	Wells, William Jr	32	238	10–14–1847	50	Oak Log Fk
†Johnson	Wells, William A	3	343	2– 9–1865	200	
‡Johnson	Wells, William G	2	95	3– 8–1852	200	
‡Johnson	Wells, William G	44	455	1–26–1853	400	Rockcastle R
‡Johnson	Wells, William G	44	456	1–26–1853	200	Buck Fk
‡Johnson	Wells, William G	2	229	12–16–1854	200	
†Johnson	Wells, William G	2	229	12–16–1854	200	
†Johnson	Wells, William G	2	229	12–16–1854	200	
†Johnson	Wells, William G	2	229	12–16–1854	100	
‡Johnson	Wells, William G	43	430	12–27–1854	200	Rockhouse Fk
‡Johnson	Wells, William G	43	431	12–27–1854	200	Rockhouse Fk
‡Johnson	Wells, William G	43	432	12–26–1854	100	Rockhouse Fk
‡Johnson	Wells, William G	43	433	12–28–1854	200	Rockhouse Fk
‡Johnson	Wells, William G	43	434	12–27–1854	200	Br Rockhouse Fk
‡Johnson	Wells, William G	43	435	12–28–1854	200	bet Rockcastle and Greasy Crs
‡Johnson	Wells, William G	43	436	12–27–1854	200	Rockhouse Fk
‡Johnson	Wells, William G	43	437	12–28–1854	200	Rockhouse Fk
‡Johnson	Wells, William G	43	439	12–27–1854	200	Rockhouse Fk
‡Johnson	Wells, William G	43	672	1–20–1854	300	Daniels Cr
‡Johnson	Wells, William G	43	673	1–13–1854	229	Oak Log Fk
‡Johnson	Wells, William G	43	674	12–17–1854	450	Rockhouse Fk
‡Johnson	Wells, William G	43	675	12–27–1854	350	Greasy Cr
‡Johnson	Wells, William G	2	234	1– 1–1855	200	
‡Johnson	Wells, William G	2	234	1– 1–1855	200	
†Johnson	Wells, William G	2	234	1– 1–1855	200	
†Johnson	Wells, William G	2	234	1– 1–1855	200	
†Johnson	Wells, William G	2	234	1– 1–1855	200	
†Johnson	Wells, William G	2	234	1– 1–1855	200	
†Johnson	Wells, William G	2	242	2– 6–1855	70	
‡Johnson	Wells, William G	58	373	8–24–1858	50	Long Br Greasy Cr
†Johnson	Wells, William G	3	341	2– 6–1865	200	
†Johnson	Wells, William G	3	341	2– 6–1865	200	
‡Johnson	Wells, William G	66	458	2–13–1865	200	Lick Br
‡Johnson	Wells, William G	66	459	2–13–1865	690	L H Fk Greasy
‡Johnson	Wells, William G	65	345	3– 3–1865	400	Lick Cr
†Johnson	Wells, William G	5	438	12– 7–1874	100	
‡Johnson	Wells, William J	97	341	12–14–1875	100	Oak Log Fk
*Res. Fayette	Wenzel, John C	X	177	10–22–1825	20,000	Sandy R
‡Johnson	Werd, J. M	53	208	2–28–1855	133	Werds Br
*Res. Philadel	Wescott, Henry	E	171	10– 3–1800	23,250	Big Sandy R
ºFayette	West, Edward	2	36	1–11–1783	2,100	Sandy
#Bourbon	West, Edward	14	133	1– 4–1787	2,100	Big Sandy
‡Lawrence	Wheeler, Amos H	9	369	4–12–1839	100	Hood Fk
†Johnson	Wheeler, Dan	3	338	1–26–1860	200	
†Johnson	Wheeler, Dan	3	338	1–26–1860	200	
†Johnson	Wheeler, Dan	3	338	1–26–1860	200	
†Johnson	Wheeler, Dan	3	338	1–26–1860	200	
†Johnson	Wheeler, Dan	3	338	1–26–1860	200	
†Johnson	Wheeler, Dan	3	338	1–26–1860	200	
†Johnson	Wheeler, Dan	3	339	1–26–1860	200	
†Johnson	Wheeler, Dan	3	339	1–26–1860	200	
†Johnson	Wheeler, Dan	3	339	1–26–1860	200	
†Johnson	Wheeler, Dan	3	339	1–26–1860	200	
†Johnson	Wheeler, Daniel	58	571	1– 9–1860	15	Lower Laurel Fk
†Johnson	Wheeler, Daniel	3	154	9– 3–1860	200	
†Johnson	Wheeler, Daniel	3	155	9– 3–1860	100	
†Johnson	Wheeler, Daniel	3	168	10–17–1860	200	
‡Johnson	Wheeler, Daniel	62	180	10–10–1860	245	Lick Br
‡Johnson	Wheeler, Daniel	62	179	2–25–1861	170	Lick Br
‡Johnson	Wheeler, Daniel	62	178	4– 2–1861	65	Buffalo Cr
‡Johnson	Wheeler, Daniel	75	129	10–10–1868	35	Lower Laurel Fk
‡Johnson	Wheeler, Daniel	95	20	3– 9–1874	8	Panther Cr
†Johnson	Wheeler, David	5	89	3–15–1871	50	
‡Johnson	Wheeler, Elizabeth	63	316	1–30–1861	20	Upper Laurel
†Johnson	Wheeler, Jesse	3	168	10–17–1860	20 0	
†Johnson	Wheeler, John B	3	620	— — 1858	10	
‡Johnson	Wheeler, John B	55	294	11–13–1858	10	L H Fk Little Laurel
‡Johnson	Wheeler, John P	37	69	1–30–1850	25	Laurel Cr
†Johnson	Wheeler, John R	2	156	2– 6–1854	25	
‡Johnson	Wheeler, Joshua M	110	492	5– 1–1888	8	Keetons Fk Big Blain
‡Johnson	Wheeler, Samuel G	3	332	1– 2–1865	200	
†Johnson	Wheeler, Samuel G	4	45	11– 7–1866	200	
†Johnson	Wheeler, Samuel G	4	45	11– 7–1866	50	
‡Johnson	Wheeler, Samuel G	74	129	2– 6–1868	200	Fk Bakers Br
†Johnson	Wheeler, S. G	5	581	7–21–1877	200	
‡Johnson	Wheeler, Samuel J	66	38	4–13–1865	116	Stafford Fk Rockcastle
§Floyd	Wheeler, Stephen	(Cert. 143)		8–17——05	400	Levisa Fk
‡Lawrence	Wheeler, William	10	428	3–27–1843	100	Laurel Cr

550 HISTORY OF JOHNSON COUNTY

County	Grantee	Book	Page	Date Survey	Acres	Watercourse
†Johnson	Wheeler, William	3	—	— — 1859	74	
‡Lawrence	Wheeler, William H	14	423	4–29–1839	200	None
‡Johnson	Wheeler, William R	32	235	6–29–1848	500	Lower Laurel Fk
‡Johnson	Wheeler, William R	60	78	7–29–1859	10	Laurel Br
‡Johnson	Wheeler, William R	60	337	7–30–1860	8	Laurel Fk Blain
‡Johnson	Wheeler, William R	3	290	12– 7–1863	125	
†Johnson	Wheeler, William R	3	389	8– 8–1865	200	
‡Johnson	Wheeler, William R	66	283	7–25–1865	20	Upper Laurel Fk
‡Johnson	Wheeler, William R	68	380	2–12–1866	15	Oil Fk Paint Cr
‡Johnson	Wheeler, William R	72	219	5–23–1867	117	Lynn Bark Fk
‡Johnson	Wheeler, William R	5	83	3– 6–1871	94	
†Johnson	Wheeler, William R	5	98	4– 3–1871	30	
†Johnson	Wheeler, William R and Cornelius, Price	3	398	9— —1865	104	
†Johnson	Wheeler, William R and Cornelius, Price	3	398	9— -1865	200	
‡Johnson	Wilcox, Thomas	122	404	6–24–1907	5⁷⁄₁₀	Levi Br
‡Johnson	Wiley, Adam B. V	18	17	8–21–1844	50	Wiley Br
‡Johnson	Wiley, Andrew J	68	134	1–30–1866	7	Bakers Br
¶Floyd	Wiley, James	D	297	7– 1–1817	130	Sandy R
§Floyd	Wiley, Thomas	(Cert. 114)		11– 6–1804	400	Levisa Fk
¶Floyd	Wiley, William	A-2	124	9–10–1824	50	Sandy R
¶Floyd	Wiley, William	A-2	302	5– 4–1831	200	Sandy R
¶Floyd	Wiley, William	E-2	222	9–13–1834	100	Sandy R
¶Floyd	Wiley, William	1–2	254	3–25–1836	50	Wileys Br
¶Floyd	Wiley, William	1–2	297	3–25–1836	50	Wileys Br
¶Floyd	Wiley, William	10	97	5–25–1842	100	Big Sandy R
‡Johnson	Wiley, William	14	295	8–21–1844	50	Wiley Br
‡Johnson	Wiley, William	32	236	3– 7–1848	50	Tom's Cr
‡Johnson	Wiley, William	32	241	3– 7–1848	100	Tom's Cr
‡Johnson	Wiley, William	43	539	3– 8–1848	35	Tom's Cr
‡Johnson	Wiley, William	47	113	3– 2–1855	118	Tom's Cr
†Johnson	Wiley William	2	261	4– 2–1855	100	
‡Johnson	Wiley, William	68	133	1–30–1866	63	Bakers Br
‡Johnson	Williams, Alexander	84	250	11– 9–1871	200	Big Fk Pigeon Fk
†Johnson	Williams, Campbell	5	218	6– 3–1872	50	
‡Johnson	Williams, C. H	103	112	2–23–1880	10	Mud Lick Fk
‡Johnson	Williams, C. H	103	115	2–23–1880	5	Mud Lick Fk
‡Johnson	Williams, C. H	7	62	5– 7–1885	30	
‡Johnson	Williams, Cornelius H	70	57	8–29–1866	29	Caboos Br
‡Johnson	Williams, David	65	359	1– 9–1865	35	S Big Paint Cr
‡Johnson	Williams, David F	97	139	4– 9–1875	67	None
‡Johnson	Williams, E	11	51	8–25–1843	100	None
‡Johnson	Williams, Elijah	11	49	7–25–1843	50	None
‡Johnson	Williams, Ellison E	72	514	2– 1–1868	20	Fk Mud Lick Cr
‡Johnson	Williams, Ellison E	81	254	2– 4–1870	42	Wolf Pen Br
‡Johnson	Williams, Harden H	42	340	11– 9–1852	50	Upper Laurel
†Johnson	Williams, Harden H	5	465	4– 5–1875	14	
‡Johnson	Williams, H. H	37	70	1–28–1850	50	Briar Fk
‡Johnson	Williams, H. H	37	71	1–28–1850	50	Briar Fk
‡Johnson	Williams, H. H	46	50	10–30–1854	275	Br Blain Cr
†Johnson	Williams, H. H	7	51	4– 6–1885	100	
‡Johnson	Williams, H. H	107	559	5– 1–1885	100	Laurel Fk
‡Johnson	Williams, Henderson	107	557	5– 4–1885	50	Keetons Fk
‡Johnson	Williams, Henderson A	7	49	3– 2–1885	50	
†Johnson	Williams, James	2	449	5– 3–1858	145	
‡Johnson	Williams, James	66	85	1–10–1865	23	Big Paint Cr
‡Johnson	Williams, James	66	86	4–20–1865	9	Pigeon Cr
‡Johnson	Williams, James	53	207	6–14–1866	198	Mud Lick Fk
‡Johnson	Williams, James	95	21	8– 6–1873	150	Pigeon Fk
†Johnson	Williams, James	5	387	5–16–1874	150	
‡Johnson	Williams, John	37	67	1–29–1850	100	Flat Gap Br
‡Johnson	Williams, John	107	552	5– 1–1885	100	Laurel Fk
‡Johnson	Williams, John B	97	451	8–29–1877	63	Wolf Pen Fk
†Johnson	Williams, J. B	—	—	7–21–1877	100	
†Johnson	Williams, John H	7	51	4– 6–1885	100	
‡Johnson	Williams, John L	56	464	5–14–1856	30	Little Paint Cr
‡Johnson	Williams, John L	65	360	1–11–1865	125	Paint Cr
‡Johnson	Williams, John L	99	158	7– 4–1879	83	Mine Fk Paint Cr
‡Johnson	Williams, John M	18	18	7– 1–1845	100	Wolf Pen Br
‡Johnson	Williams, John M	43	535	4–30–1851	600	Mud Lick Fk
‡Johnson	Williams, J. M	7	378	8–28–1889	15	
‡Johnson	Williams, J. M	113	38	1– 9–1890	15	Lancaster Br
⊕Fayette	Williams, Joseph	4	155	4–20–1785	20,000	Sandy
¶Floyd	Williams, Joseph	L-2	329	8–22–1837	100	Big Paint Cr
‡Johnson	Williams, Joseph	11	55	10– 5–1843	100	Paint Cr
‡Johnson	Williams, Joseph	20	477	1–16–1847	150	None
‡Johnson	Williams, Joseph	32	306	7–25–1848	100	Tar Kiln Br
‡Johnson	Williams, Joseph	32	307	7–28–1848	50	Cows Gap Br
‡Johnson	Williams, Joseph	32	308	8–10–1848	250	Big Paint Cr
‡Johnson	Williams, Joseph	43	556	3–13–1851	25	Bear Br

APPENDIX 551

County	Grantee	Book	Page	Date Survey	Acres	Watercourse
‡Johnson	Williams, Joseph	58	379	5–19–1856	480	None
†Johnson	Williams, Joseph	2	388	6– 1–1857	124	
‡Johnson	Williams, Joseph	60	537	6–13–1860	15	Big Paint Cr
‡Johnson	Williams, Joseph	60	538	8–31–1860	20	Little Paint
†Johnson	Williams, Joseph	3	159	10– 1–1860	30	
‡Johnson	Williams, Joseph	66	84	5–23–1865	3	Paint Cr
‡Johnson	Williams, Julia F	70	57	8–29–1866	29	Caboos Br
†Johnson	Williams, King	3	195	4– 1–1861	10	
‡Johnson	Williams, Lewis	43	561	3–18–1851	60	Lick Br
‡Johnson	Williams, Lewis	60	539	4– 4–1860	8½	Low Gap Br Paint
†Johnson	Williams, Lewis	3	133	6– 4–1860	60	
‡Johnson	Williams, L. P.	18	19	7– 1–1845	100	Stone Coal Br
‡Johnson	Williams, Lucas P.	70	57	8–29–1866	29	Caboos Br
‡Johnson	Williams, Martin M	2	110	7– 4–1853	50	
‡Johnson	Williams, Moses	56	463	5–13–1859	24	Big Paint Cr
‡Johnson	Williams, Nine	2	143	12– 5–1853	25	
‡Johnson	Williams, Ning	42	377	11– 9–1853	25	None
‡Johnson	Williams, Ning	62	177	4–30–1861	20	Lower Laurel Fk
‡Johnson	Williams, Noah H	7	62	5– 7–1885	10	
‡Johnson	Williams, Noah K	70	57	8–29–1866	29	Caboos Br
‡Johnson	Williams, N. M	103	114	5–25–1882	25	Laurel Fk
‡Johnson	Williams, Parmelia J	70	57	8–29–1866	29	Caboos Br
‡Johnson	Williams, Preston C	93	48	11–14–1872	50	Tom's Cr
‡Johnson	Williams, Robert	60	77	5–26–1860	3	Laurel Fk
‡Johnson	Williams, Robert R	43	545	9– 9–1848	1,000	Mud Lick Cr
‡Johnson	Williams, Robert R	43	517	4–15–1851	50	Wolf Pen Fk
‡Johnson	Williams, Robert R	42	341	11–19–1852	50	Upper Laurel
‡Johnson	Williams, Robert R	2	144	12– 5–1853	50	
†Johnson	Williams, Robert R	2	445	4– 1–1858	24	
‡Johnson	Williams, R. R	35	519	8–16–1848	120	Laurel Fk
‡Johnson	Williams, R. R	53	2	4– 1–1856	24	Blain Cr
‡Johnson	Williams, Samuel	70	57	8–29–1866	29	Caboos Br
‡Johnson	Williams, Sanford J	70	57	8–29–1866	29	Caboos Br
‡Johnson	Williams, Sanford	120	82	6–16–1902	24	Mud Lick Br
‡Johnson	Williams, Sarah A	70	57	8–29–1866	29	Caboos Br
†Johnson	Williams, Stephenson	3	195	4– 1–1861	100	
†Johnson	Williams, Stephenson	3	195	4– 1–1861	180	
‡Johnson	Williams, Thomas	58	358	11–10–1853	25	None
†Johnson	Williams, Thomas	42	342	11–27–1853	37	Little Laurel
‡Johnson	Williams, Thomas A. and Arminta M	70	57	8–29–1866	29	Caboos Br
†Johnson	Williams, Thomas F	2	105	6– 6–1853	50	
‡Johnson	Williams, Thomas F. and Lucas P	66	384	7–13–1865	14	Fk Lower Laurel Fk
†Floyd	Williams, William	2	230	2–24–1817		
‡Johnson	Williams, William	35	517	2–28–1850	300	Rockcastle Cr
‡Johnson	Williams, William	49	330	11– 2–1855	40	Rockhouse Fk
‡Johnson	Williams, William K	93	49	2–20–1873	160	Br Big Blain
†Johnson	Williams, W. R. and N. M	5	268	2– 3–1873	160	
‡Johnson	Williamson, Elijah	22	232	4– 6–1846	50	Lynn Bark Fk
‡Johnson	Williamson, James	58	567	9–28–1859	31	Lick Br
‡Johnson	Williamson, Samuel	64	428	2– 4–1858	100	Mine Fk Paint Cr
‡Johnson	Williamson, Stephen	62	185	2–26–1861	280	Br Rockcastle Cr
⁰Fayette	Willing, Charles	3	426	8–14–1784	4,000	Sandy
¶Floyd	Wills, George	Z	452	11– 3–1830	50	Daniels Cr
⁰Fayette	Wilson, James	3	426	8–14–1784	4,000	Sandy
⁰Fayette	Wilson, James & Co	4	6	8–14–1784	6,000	Sandy Cr
⁰Fayette	Winecup, Cornelius	3	67	12– 1–1783	1,000	Sandy
‡Johnson	Witten, George H	68	131	1–31–1866	100	L H Fk Tom's Cr
‡Johnson	Witten, John	32	242	8–28–1849	100	Tom's Cr
¶Floyd	Witten, Thomas	A-2	254	10–20–1831	50	Sandy R
¶Floyd	Witten, Thomas	E-2	117	3– 5–1830	50	Buffalo Cr
¶Floyd	Witten, William	F	57	4–20–1819	50	Sandy R
*Res	Woodsworth, John	E	233	3– 5–1796	27,018	Sandy R
■Floyd	Wooten, Silas P	(Cert.115)		11– 6–1804	400	Levisa Fk
†Johnson	Wright, Balis	2	323	4– 7–1856	23	
‡Johnson	Wright, C. C	125	392	1– 5–1921	1	Mill Br
‡Johnson	Wright, David	103	113	5–16–1882	45	Laurel Fk
‡Johnson	Wright, Henry	43	159	11–26–1845	50	Laurel Fk
‡Johnson	Wright, James	43	161	11–26–1845	50	Laurel Fk
⁰Fayette	Wright, Patrick Capt.	4	283	3–23–1786	4,000	Sandy Cr
¶Floyd	Wright, Rebecca	5	191	2–26–1827	100	
‡Johnson	Wright, Wayne	125	147	11–29–1920	2	Keeton Fk
*Res. Philadel.	Wynkoop, Benjamin	A-2	15	8– 7–1788	5,000	Sandy R
⁰Fayette	Yancy, Charles	2	36	1–11–1783	2,828	Sandy
#Bourbon	Yancy, Charles	15	191	1– 3–1787	2,428	Big Sandy Cr
▲Floyd	Young, Alexander	19	351	2–23–1820	40	Sandy R
‡Johnson	Young, Charles	54	216	8–29–1855	30	Fk Buck Br
¶Floyd	Young, Charles W	Z	205	8– 1–1827	50	Johns Cr
‡Johnson	Young, Charles W	29	255	4– 9–1847	50	Tom's Cr

County	Grantee	Book	Page	Date Survey	Acres	Watercourse
†Johnson	Young, Charles W	2	253	3– 5–1855	25	
▲Floyd	Young, James	19	355	6–13–1820	150	Louisa Fk
¶Floyd	Young, John	E	164	6–13–1817	50	Tom's Cr
¶Floyd	Young, John	T	94	9–22–1824	50	Tom's Cr
‡Johnson	Young, Rhoderac	96	31	4– 6–1875	47	Two-Mile Br
†Johnson	Young, Rhoderac	5	461	4– 5–1875	25	
#Bourbon	Young, Richard	14	376	4–13–1787	14,280	Big Sandy R
#Bourbon	Young, Richard	3	34	5– 5–1787	5,000	Big Sandy
#Bourbon	Young, Richard	14	378	5– 6–1787	3,121	Sandy R
#Bourbon	Young, Richard	14	515	5– 3–1787	16,000	Big Sandy R
#Bourbon	Young, Richard	14	516	5– 6–1787	1,546	Big Sandy R
¶Floyd	Young, William	1	401	9– 6–1821	50	Br Big Sandy R
‡Johnson	Young, William	18	25	8–14–1845	100	M Fk Buckeye Cr
⊕Fayette	Young and Carr	4	228	10–23–1785	1,387¾	Sandy
⊕Fayette	Young & Robinson	3	177	2–10–1784	16,000	Sandy

www.ingramcontent.com/pod-product-compliance
Lightning Source LLC
Chambersburg PA
CBHW060347080526
44583CB00012B/207